Widor

Eastman Studies in Music

Ralph P. Locke, Senior Editor
Eastman School of Music

Additional Titles of Interest

A complete list of titles in the Eastman Studies in Music series may be found
on the University of Rochester Press website, www.urpress.com.

Phot. P. Borger-Paris

Adolf Eckstein's Verlag Berlin-Charlottenburg

10582

Charles-Marie Widor. Photo by P. Borger, Paris, 1909. One of four poses taken during the same sitting. The first known publication of one from the set appeared in *Le Courrier Musical*, December 1, 1909. Author's collection, through the kindness of M.-A. Guibaud.

Widor

A Life beyond the Toccata

John R. Near

UNIVERSITY OF ROCHESTER PRESS

First published 2011

University of Rochester Press
668 Mt. Hope Avenue, Rochester, NY 14620, USA
www.urpress.com
and Boydell & Brewer Limited
PO Box 9, Woodbridge, Suffolk IP12 3DF, UK
www.boydellandbrewer.com

ISBN-13: 978-1-58046-369-0
ISSN: 1071-9989

Library of Congress Cataloging-in-Publication Data

Near, John Richard.
   Widor: a life beyond the Toccata / John R. Near.
      p. cm. — (Eastman studies in music, 1071-9989 ; v. 83)
   Includes bibliographical references and index.
   ISBN 978-1-58046-369-0 (hardcover: alk. paper)
   1. Widor, Charles-Marie, 1844–1937. 2. Composers—France—Biography. I. Title.
ML410.W648N44 2011
780.92—dc22
[B]

                                                           2010038177

A catalogue record for this title is available from the British Library.

This publication is printed on acid-free paper.
Printed in the United States of America.

In memory of my dear friend
Aran Vartanian

Contents

Illustrations

Foreword

Gradually over the decades and with the advent of massive potential for publication and unlimited conveying of material over the internet, access to the remotest corners of artistic endeavor from the past has become ever readier. However, it seems that appreciation of the riches thus opened up is not correspondingly disseminated across a broad spectrum of receivers: increased supply does not automatically enhance demand, while curiosity and discovery, to the extent they require initiative and discernment, have not necessarily benefited in effective proportion to the wonders of the new technologies and channels of communication.

Charles-Marie Widor provides, within the confines of the Belle Époque in France, a stellar example of a figure of truly grand stature who has for decades fallen through the cracks of daily musical awareness and practice. Whether a victim of monoculture saturation, with his ubiquitous, prototypal *Toccata* ensconced in its double-edged-sword popularity, or simply a creator of all too subtle distinction for our nuance-averse epoch, he epitomizes the nineteenth-century *maître secondaire*, "unfairly neglected" at present as much as he was feted in his own day.

Paradoxically, it is precisely as an organist that Widor could be seen as an ultimately one-sided or, more accurately, monolithic figure. His teaching is remembered for its laudable, indeed crucial, professional rigor and seminal reinstatement of healthy principles of repertory, technique, phrasing, and esthetic approach, although the strength of the French school he contributed to so lastingly comes largely from the playing out of his input against that of complementary, highly contrasting personalities, particularly Guilmant and Gigout; this fecund and biodiverse seed could not have fallen upon more fertile terrain than that of the Tournemire/Vierne and later the Dupré/Bonnet generations. It is well enough recognized that Widor improvised inspiringly, but he seldom did so in formal concert settings, leaving this calling card to the likes of Lefébure-Wély, Franck, Guilmant, and Gigout. (This is an interesting aspect of his particular affinity with Lemmens.) Finally, his legitimately lofty view of his chosen instrument, but all the more the demands of his multifaceted activity overall, led him as a performer to restrict himself to (or fall back on?) a most narrow, peak-of-the-pyramid repertory consisting, fundamentally, of Bach and himself. In this, of course, he was largely in step with most composer-performers of his era, implicitly aspiring to transcendental achievement on the level of Paganini and Liszt. He nonetheless may fall short of the conception we harbor today of the "complete" organist, but he is an all the more potent advocate for the instrument outside of the organ microcosm.

How important it is, then, to do everything necessary to flesh out our feeling for and familiarity with this flourishing era, through the discovery of such figures as Widor, who, partaking of an immense humus of musical tradition, succeeded in forging a personal style and corpus, without which no truly full picture of that era may emerge. Having spent his active youth and young adulthood entirely in the Second Empire ambience of festivity and expansion in one of France's largest and most elegant and vibrant provincial cities, he was subsequently able to move freely in the Parisian *salon* culture that would continue for decades hence; yet his true character was better revealed in the context of the Third Republic and its dialectic of positivism and pregnant artistic renewal, indeed iconoclasm, that suited his intellectual bent and ambitions as a composer/virtuoso and virtuosic composer. The chances of finding considerable riches in the work of this prestigious figure are great indeed.

Studies on Widor focusing on his organ works have not been lacking in the past decades, but it remained to cast an overarching regard onto his career and personality in the broadest context. With a groundbreaking but heretofore largely out-of-reach 1980s dissertation on the musician, painstaking editions of the organ symphonies, and long endeavors researching the primary and secondary sources, John Near has now proven the wait to have been worthwhile. While any such author must obviously make a choice of aspects and events to emphasize, we are here sure to be guided securely and deftly through Widor's career, the various events providing so many springboards to insight into his life and views on musical and other matters. His image, whether visual (the invariably commanding, austere, indeed dour demeanor) or anecdotal (the aristocratically oriented master endowed with life-of-the-party wit), surely tends to color our perception of his music as being in its own way aristocratic and austere, albeit witty too on occasion. But we make acquaintance here with another Widor as well, the warmhearted benefactor of promising artists and worthy causes, the advocate of fairness in artistic and human discord, the open-minded, indeed eager promoter of healthy novelty in musical language. His stature as a writer is brought out and his intellectualism subjected to critical appraisal. His role in shaping significant institutions such as the Casa Velásquez and the American Conservatory in Fontainebleau remains an exemplary contribution to the building of mid-twentieth-century musical culture through high-level training and transnational exchange. A portrayal of the activities of the Concordia choir under Widor's direction epitomizes the gray areas of the musician's life work that are made vivid here; similarly, his place in the critical response to the Solesmes reforms needed summarizing—*c'est chose faite*. And of course the essential evaluation of an unusual matrimonial situation receives its due in a dispassionate account.

Widor's prime claim to fame may be to have defined over the span of ten crucial works the symphony for organ, and the *Romane* is arguably one of the historically most significant individual creations within a half millennium of viable repertory. That he didn't come up with a *Carmen*, a *Pelléas*, or a *Sacre* certainly does not diminish the value of the music he did write or the historical import of such concrete contributions as the orchestration treatise, so revelatory of his own philosophical tack and artistic convictions. Widor's oeuvre in its broad diversity forms indeed a poignant counterpoint to that of the more universally recognized masters of the periods he lived through. He asserts in a thought-provoking aphorism quoted by the author that "the nature of a masterpiece is to remain eternally new; time glides by without leaving its mark on it," and a convincing case may be made for regarding the very life of this artist as a masterwork in its own right. Some of his musical works may, to be sure, bear more heavily than others the stamp of their time and wear only moderately well, but certainly his strong personality and his impact on French culture are highly out of proportion with the scant exposure he enjoys in our musical context today. Well beyond the organ works, much remains to be revived and evaluated. With John Near's study there is no longer any reasonable excuse not to do so; it is not merely a matter of tapping artistic resources needlessly lying fallow but one of sheer intellectual honesty vis-à-vis a brilliant period in the artistic history of France.

Kurt Lueders
Docteur en Musicologie, Université de Paris–Sorbonne
Vice President of the Association Aristide Cavaillé-Coll
Organiste titulaire de l'Église Réformée du Saint-Esprit, Paris

Preface

Widor could only be flattered to know that his F-Major Toccata and the D-Minor Toccata commonly attributed to "père Bach" are arguably the two most recognized pieces of organ music in the world today. If anyone has ever heard of Charles-Marie Widor, it is certainly because of the ubiquitous Toccata from his Fifth Symphony for Organ. My introduction to Widor's music came when, as a young teenager, I felt the exhilaration that emanates from that piece when I heard my organ teacher play it. Though beyond my technical grasp at the time, I soon discovered another piece that I could play, and I have never forgotten the satisfaction of having learned the beautiful Andante Cantabile from his Fourth Symphony. Years later, when I auditioned at the New England Conservatory of Music, for my "romantic" piece I innocently played the Adagio from the Sixth Symphony, which I had found ravishing. My tastes, however, were not in accord with those of the head of the organ department who, although years later had a change of opinion, informed me: "We don't play Widor here; you know, he really didn't write good music." In spite of the prevailing attitudes, I continued to investigate Widor's organ music on my own, and my wonderful teacher Mireille Lagacé taught me the *Symphonie gothique*.

When in 1982 I needed to find a topic for my DMA dissertation at Boston University, my desire was to write about a composer who had not been given much attention, but whose life and music would be engaging enough not to consign my work to oblivion when I finished. I began to think my goal was hopeless, as it seemed every significant organ composer had been well covered. At that point, my advisor, Dr. Max Miller, suggested that Widor was in real need of scholarly study. I had already noted a dissertation from the mid 1960s and discounted him as a subject, but Dr. Miller insisted that I should look deeper. I went over to Harvard to read the dissertation and discovered that its author had written a modest work about the organ symphonies and concluded almost apologetically with a quote to the effect that Widor's works had lost their glimmer and been eclipsed.[1] My next appointment was with Dr. Murray Lefkowitz, chairman of the musicology department at Boston University, to propose the topic to him. The *New Grove Dictionary of Music and Musicians* had recently been published, and I recall that we discovered the entry on Widor to be cursory—scarcely a page in length. I was immediately given the green light to proceed. My intention was to write a dissertation about Widor's life as an organist and organ composer, as that was basically what I knew about him. Then I began the research. I was soon overwhelmed to discover that Widor was not at all just an organist and organ composer, but rather a mainstream musician who composed in nearly every genre, and who had been a sort of cultural ambassador for France. It became clear to me that it would do Widor a grave injustice if I considered him only from the single aspect of his career as an organist; I had to write a biography—a "life and works."

What began as an academic project soon became a labor of love. I did little else for nearly three years, and I owe an enormous debt of gratitude to my dissertation advisor, Dr. Joel Sheveloff, who continually encouraged me and indeed allowed me to leave no stone unturned. In hindsight, I clearly arrived at the right moment to research Widor, as it seemed no one was yet much interested in him. We were still very much in the time that had begun around the death of Widor's close friend Camille Saint-Saëns, when composer-critic Reynaldo Hahn, a Saint-Saëns student, expressed with regret an attitude commonly held about many nineteenth-century composers who had lived well into the twentieth century: "Today it takes courage to admire Saint-Saëns."[2] And a French critic exclaimed that he "would be delighted to exchange the whole of Saint-Saëns' work for a single page from Bach's Matthew Passion."[3] Those were certainly the attitudes toward Widor that I had confronted as an early graduate student. After decades devoted to the revival of early music and with the blossoming of progressive twentieth-century styles, the bulk of nineteenth-century organ music had yet to enjoy renewed attention and scholarly investigation beyond the works of César Franck, which never slipped from popularity. My dissertation, completed in July 1984, became the first full-scale posthumous biography of Widor in any language. Although it encompassed his entire work, it naturally highlighted his career as an organist and organ composer, and I felt certain that if there were to be a resurgence of interest in Widor's music, it would be through the organ works. Marcel Dupré said Widor often repeated: "You have the duty to do a thing if you are sure it is necessary to the general interest!"[4] I kept that phrase on my desk, and the study of Widor became a kind of mission.

As I continued my research, I found important original source material and a cache of original photographs that I put into an article, "Charles-Marie Widor: The Organ Works and Saint-Sulpice," for an impending collection of articles that Daniel Roth, the titular organist of Saint-Sulpice, was compiling on the church and its organists. So vital was this new information to current scholarship—and so delayed was the projected book—that I published the article in the *American Organist* in February 1993.

During my dissertation years, I had become aware that the composition and publication history of Widor's organ works was knotty at best, and that a critical edition of the organ symphonies was sorely needed. As an organist, I put that as a priority, but I had no idea how complex the puzzle would be. It required ten years, 1987–97, to research and to publish my edition with A-R Editions. And just when I thought I might start this biography in earnest, it was proposed that the Philadelphia Orchestra would perform Widor's Symphony in

G Minor for Organ and Orchestra at the July 2002 national convention of the American Guild of Organists, with the stipulation that it had to be published. They had last performed the work from manuscript copies in 1919!

On the heels of my critical edition of the Symphony for Organ and Orchestra, I was given a year's sabbatical as the first recipient of the Dorothy D. Moller Research Fellowship for Advanced Study from Principia College to begin work on this biography. Although I had my doctoral research to build on, I had collected a great deal of additional material in the intervening years that I had not yet fully digested. I have always thought it surprising that there were only a couple of fairly extended biographical studies of Widor during his lifetime: Reynaud (1900) and Rupp (1912). Perhaps Widor's own attitude on the subject had something to do with it: "Concerning the proposition of a biography," wrote Widor in a letter of December 4, 1914, "it is best to wait. A last chapter not ending at Père Lachaise [one of the main Paris cemeteries] leaves some irritation in the spirit of the reader. Such, at least, is my impression when reading through the studies of x, y, and z of our contemporaries."[5]

I found Widor's grandniece, Marie-Ange Guibaud, in 1988. While reading dozens of Widor's letters, both at the Bibliothèque nationale and the Institut de France, I saw that many were addressed from l'Arbresle, a town not far from Lyon. I wondered if there might be any family members there who still held rights to Widor's works. I phoned the Paris office of SACEM to inquire; after a few moments of checking, a clerk informed me that there were indeed descendants still holding rights. When I asked if they lived at the letterhead address, the answer was again affirmative, but I was told the information was confidential. As I continued to explain the nature of my research, the SACEM clerk hesitantly yielded a last name. I immediately went to the central post office in Paris where every phone directory in France could be consulted. I found four or five people in the l'Arbresle directory with the same last name I had been given. I dialed the first number and explained to the lady who answered that I was researching the life of Charles-Marie Widor. Her voice took on an edge of enthusiasm as she exclaimed, "Mon oncle!" She invited me to come for a visit the next day.

I took the TGV to Lyon and a commuter train to l'Arbresle. This kind woman met me at the train station in an old Citroën 2CV. We soon turned off the main highway and rambled out into a wooded countryside on a narrow winding road as she honked her horn without any decrease in speed at every blind curve. We eventually veered off the "paved" road and passed onto a little dirt road that wound between barns, past some chickens and grazing cows. We arrived at a very sharp turn that required a couple of maneuvers before she could thread the deux chevaux through an old iron gate that opened onto an estate with an ancient stone country house, generous grounds, and a tranquil pond. Everything about it spoke of the nineteenth century and earlier. I learned that Madame Guibaud lived there with two of her brothers and their families. It had been the family homestead of Widor's sister, Marie Pierron. My first visit was one of several that followed over the years, the last in August 2001.

On that first visit, after a time of pleasantries Madame Guibaud asked if I wanted to see anything. I'm sure my heart began to race. The first thing she plucked from a large antique armoire was an envelope in which I discovered the 103-page manuscript of Widor's "Souvenirs autobiographiques."[6] It turned out to be only the tip of the iceberg. In future visits, sometimes staying three days at a time, I plumbed the depths of that armoire as well as the memories of the family members who as youngsters had known "Oncle Charles." One of the great joys of my work was getting to know these wonderful people, especially Madame Guibaud, who cooked meals and talked endlessly about everything. At one large dinner gathering in which she had invited family members to meet this American studying her uncle's life, she announced that she had seated me in Widor's place at the table. I learned that one eats well in that part of France, and we lived by her favorite phrase: "Au travail, on fait ce qu'on veut, mais à la table, on se force" (At work you do what you please, but at the table you push yourself).

During one visit when I finally reached the bottom of the armoire—its contents spread over every available table—there was a cardboard roll in which I found the original hand-drawn and colored console plan of the Saint-Sulpice organ. When I unrolled it, I could hardly believe my eyes. I explained to Madame that they would undoubtedly like to have that document at Saint-Sulpice. With her typical graciousness she simply replied, "Well, all they need to do is ask for it." I immediately phoned Daniel Roth to explain what I had found and told him to write to her. I think his letter arrived the very next day, so I took the plan back to Paris where it is now beautifully framed in the "Salon de Widor" behind the organ at Saint-Sulpice. These are just two of the amazing number of precious documents I consulted and photocopied or photographed.

One of the most difficult decisions I have had to make for this book concerns which of the dozens upon dozens of photographs I could include. Many formal portraits of Widor have been published over the years, and while some are included—even the most well known—I have also included a few less formal snapshots—those that offer a more everyday face. I regret I could not have included even more of them; a particular favorite that did not make the cut shows Widor—decked out in his usual formal attire, flowing polka-dotted lavallière, and a huge Panama hat—wheeling his little great-grand nephew Eugène in front of the Persanges family home.

In this biography I have wanted as much as possible to let Widor tell his own life's story, either through his prolific writings or the recollections of friends and students. In addition, critical reviews, primarily from two leading French music journals (*Le Ménestrel* and *La Revue et Gazette Musicale de Paris*), have been drawn upon liberally, as they were an invaluable resource for piecing together the composite picture of Widor's lengthy professional career and the critical reception of his works. Most of this material appears in English translation for the first time. Although it might have been valuable to some readers to have the original French texts included, the length of the book would have become untenable. The translations are my own, although I sought occasional help from the French faculty at Principia College. I did not want to turn the work of translation over to anyone else, as I had grown accustomed to Widor's handwriting and turns of phrase. Most important, I understood the contexts in which he was writing. While remaining as close as possible to the original texts, in making the translations I have regularized sentence structure, punctuation, and verb tenses to achieve fairly idiomatic English. I remembered that in my dissertation, Thomas Dunn, a member of my committee, felt my translations had retained "a bit too much French perfume."

The "Souvenirs autobiographiques" occasionally presented thorny verbiage. The ninety-one-year-old composer had dictated it in a highly conversational manner, often wandering from one topic to another with little or no connection and peppering it with a plethora of personages whom he had known. It is apparent throughout the "Souvenirs" that he was well connected in various social and professional circles; as can be determined, the personages mentioned in quoted passages are identified within the text or a corresponding note. That the work was broken off with no effort to refine it is all too apparent. The entire "Souvenirs" have not been included in the present biography because the recollections occasionally veer into tangential information that does not elucidate Widor's life story.

I have often been asked, as the Pope queried Michelangelo of his work in the Sistine Chapel, "When will it be finished?" For years I have contented myself with Widor's oft-repeated recommendation: "Patience and perseverance accomplish great things. Everything comes to him who only cares to wait."[7] And when Albert Schweitzer complained to Widor that his book on Bach was growing in length and detail, Widor retorted, "So much the better, your work will only be more interesting; write as many chapters as are necessary, nothing is pressing."[8] While I have followed these bits of advice, the time has come to draw the curtain on this book. After examining hundreds of reviews, articles, essays, prefaces, letters, and the like, I have concluded that there will always be more sources to be found, facts to be verified, and rumors to trace. I had originally intended to include a chapter titled "Widor's Maxims on Organ Performance Practice and Technique," but as completed to date it has grown to nearly seventy pages, I have decided to publish it later since it is nonbiographical and more specifically of value to organists. I have also purposely excluded any in-depth analyses of Widor's works; only occasionally has some broad structural plan of a work been given.

Since Widor once referred to three creative periods in his life, I have organized the book into five parts: the first acts as a prelude to three central parts reflecting the three creative periods, and the last acts as a capstone that details

Widor's remarkable years as a member of the French Institute, after he had more or less stopped composing. The years encompassed by each part can be prescribed as follows: part 1: 1844–63; part 2: 1864–79; part 3: 1880–94; part 4: 1895–1909; part 5: 1910–37. Headings within each part serve to separate various topic areas. Since Widor was a great organist and seminal organ composer, these aspects of his life naturally take on some prominence.

Over the years, I have observed how quickly the research trail grows cold. I heard Widor's pupil and successor Marcel Dupré at Saint-Sulpice on a few occasions, and sat with him on the organ bench two Sundays in November 1969. In fact, I heard him play the Widor Toccata, though rather poorly on account of the severe deformation of his fingers at that point in his life. I have often thought that had I known then what I know now, we might have had some fascinating conversations! I also endeavored to meet Georges Favre, who was among Widor's last composition students. But because he happened to be taking his bath at the time I called one day, I missed the opportunity. One Sunday in the 1990s I was introduced to an elderly woman who had been a member of the Saint-Sulpice parish all her life. With a shrug, she thought nothing of saying, "Oh, I heard Widor all the time!" Widor's family members knew him only as "Oncle Charles"; they knew he was very famous, but not being musicians they could only relate his always proper but kindly and good-humored nature, his passion for boating, his doing finger exercises while reading, his love of playing the popular French game of "boules," and his sometimes risqué teasing of the children.[9]

Although I have handled countless numbers of Widor's letters and manuscripts over the years, while researching his personally owned scores now at the Biblithèque nationale I occasionally came across evidence that brought on some emotion. As Widor revised his music, his fingers would become stained either with ink or colored pencil and he inevitably left a few fingerprints on the pages. I felt particularly close to him at those moments. There will certainly be others in the years to come who will add new discoveries, insights, and analyses to the Widor arena, but none will have more respect, enjoyment, and love for the subject.

John R. Near
June 1, 2009

Acknowledgments

There are many people who could be mentioned here, but I especially want to thank those whose support and help have been indispensable at key moments in the preparation of this book. First, although mentioned in the Preface, I owe Madame Marie-Ange Guibaud, Widor's grandniece, an enormous debt of gratitude for her unstinting generosity over a period of many years and numerous visits to her home in Persanges. Without access to the family's collection of documents, photographs, letters, news clippings, and artifacts, this biography would have been greatly diminished in scope and completeness, and my life would have been poorer for not knowing her. When I wrote to her to report the completion of this book, which I thought had about 212,000 words, she replied on April 13, 2010: "Dear friend, Bravo! And hearty congratulations for this marvelous work! I thank you 212,000 times for having devoted so much time to my dear Uncle Charles. He will bless you for it, and I do too. . . . I am very happy to hear your news and do not forget you. I often look at the photos you took. I have aged a lot and it's not pleasant—that explains the delay in thanking you for your charming letter. With kindest regards, MAG."

My dear friend Paula Bradley, Professor Emerita of French, has been ever ready to untangle a particularly gnarly French phrase, and occasionally Drs. Hélène Brown and Diana Swift of the Principia College French Department have come to my rescue. Dr. George D. Moffett, former President of Principia College, encouraged me consistently over several years and never failed to enthuse over every note of the Widor Toccata. Kenneth R. Johnson, Associate Professor of Computer Science, performed magic digitizing every illustration in this book from my vast collection of prints and negatives. Gregory Kuhn made child's play out of the complicated computer formatting process needed to ready the manuscript for the University of Rochester Press. Professor Yves Gérard kindly transcribed all of Widor's letters to Saint-Saëns at the Saint-Saëns Archives in Dieppe. Daniel and Odile Roth have enthusiastically followed my progress, sending me tidbits of valuable information every now and then, and Odile helped with translations of a few Latin phrases. I am eternally grateful to my friend Kurt Lueders for writing the Foreword; in addition, his fresh eye, keen insights, and generous suggestions have been invaluable in the final stage of work on the manuscript. Thank you to Mary

Petrusewicz for her masterful work as copy editor and to Dave Prout for creating the excellent index. I must also express deep appreciation to my dear friend and colleague in the Principia College Music Department, Dr. Marie Jureit-Beamish, who has supportively followed every step in the unfoldment of this biography.

Finally, I am very grateful to the special projects committee of the San Francisco chapter of the American Guild of Organists for their unanimous and enthusiastic approval of subvention funding for this biography.

Introduction

"Sunday Morning in a Paris Organ Loft"

Trinity Sunday, June, 1907

Like a king's box at the royal opera: private, desirable, magnetic. Our king plays both the host and the organ—equally skillfully; for, since admirers come (on invitation only), it is essential to possess both social and digital technic.

In short, we come to the Mass and go from a reception. This reception is punctuated not by drinks, but by music, very largely Gregorian responses to the phrases sung by the choir at the opposite end of the church; also Bach, followed by original pyrotechnics.

Widor—it is his reception at St. Sulpice to which I refer—chats in the best French to some. To those who have no best French he speaks, in a discreet adagio, the language whose past participles are always behind time [German]. The new operas are discussed prestissimo (when in Gallic), after which he vigorously pulls the signals for the "wind" and the Leipsic Cantor's C major Prelude begins.

These lulls in the conversation, which exist only when musical masterpieces hold sway, form the only silent devotions of the "second story guests" (for we are high above the heads of the worshippers and almost function on the astral plane!).

When Bach is laid aside we hear the chancel organist, a hundred and fifty feet away, working hard at his task of accompanying. He is the soldier who works overtime; "ours" is the general who appears on the field only at significant moments . . .

Last, the postlude, woven most originally and beautifully from the rythmic [*sic*] essence of the plain song for Trinity Sunday.

That is what Sunday mornings in Paris were made for: conversation and marvelous improvisations.

A last brief summing up reception and one passes down by the spiral staircase so often trod by the genius of organ builders, Cavaillé-Coll.

A morning in the organ loft is uplifting—although we may neither see nor hear what is taking place below.

This is the modern salon!

—T. Carl Whitmer
The Way of My Heart and Mind, 166–68.

Part One

Widor's Ancestry, Musical Education, and Heritage (1844–63)

[Cavaillé-Coll] disait toujours de moi que j'avais "de la technique et une bonne tête."

[Cavaillé-Coll] always said about me that I had "technique and a good mind."

—Ch.-M. Widor
Chr. Leray, "Souvenirs d'un maître"

—1—

Ancestral parentage: "I was born in an organ pipe"

At the ripe age of ninety, Charles-Marie Widor was asked how he had chosen the profession in which he had become one of the most honored musicians in the world. "My vocation? It's quite simple. I was born in an organ pipe."[1] Truly, vocational atavism stood out in the Widor family, as at least two generations had been involved in the organ-building trade.

While the exact roots of the Widor ancestry remain uncertain, it is thought that "Vietor" may have been the original spelling of their surname. Legend has it that Widor's great-grandfather, Jean Widor (d. 1777), a stonecutter, emigrated from Hungary to Laufen, Switzerland; there, he married Claudine Werner. Their son Jean-Baptiste Widor (September 5, 1775–April 30, 1854) was born in Laufen, and toward the turn of the nineteenth century he moved to Rouffach (Alsace), France. When on June 23, 1806, he married a local Rouffach girl, Marie-Anne-Eve Frey (October 27, 1789–March 25, 1851), the marriage notice referred to him as an organ builder. Likewise, his *Certificat de Service* of December 1815 states that he entered the service of the Republic in 1793 as Sergeant Major and listed his profession as "facteur d'orgues" (organ builder).[2] He eventually joined the employ of the celebrated Alsatian organ builder Joseph Callinet (1795–1857) and became one of the pillars of the Callinet firm, remaining there until his death.[3]

Charles-Marie Widor's knowledge of his lineage was little more than an oral history handed down through his family:

> My grandfather, who pursued the profession of organ builder, lived in Rouffach, near Colmar. His father, consequently my great-grandfather, was part of, as commander, the famous half-brigade of Sambre-et-Meuse. Unfortunately, we do not have any family papers proving our Hungarian origins. Wouldn't it interesting to know where one comes from, other than by tradition? Being in Budapest a few years ago, I applauded a namesake—a talented artist, author, director, and actor in one of the most frequented theatres of the capital. Count Zichy introduced us and we got along together very pleasantly for several days.[4]

A plausible account reports that Grandfather Jean-Baptiste Widor assisted with the 1834 and 1839 Callinet reconstructions of the great organ of Saint-Sulpice in Paris, where his future grandson would one day hold the coveted post of organist.[5] Apart from their business association, Jean Widor and Joseph Callinet enjoyed a close personal relationship. Each of them had large families—Jean Widor had eleven children[6]—and a testament to their friendship is that Widor named his children after those of Callinet.[7] Jean's third child, François-Charles, was born on May 28, 1811, in Rouffach (d. April 7, 1899, 4 rue Sala, Lyon).[8]

Following in his father's footsteps, François-Charles learned the organ-building trade in the Callinet workshop, and at the same time he devoted himself to musical studies, including both piano and organ.[9] Traveling regularly to the nearby town of Guebwiller (Haut-Rhin), he studied with Charles Kienzl, organist of Notre-Dame de Guebwiller from 1825 until his death in 1874;[10] and, perhaps more important, François-Charles became a student of one of the renowned Herz brothers, both of whom studied and later taught at the Paris Conservatory.[11] Before long, the enterprising young man secured a position as professor of music at Lachapelle, not far from Rouffach, and took the position of organist at Gray (Haute-Saône) from 1833 to 1838.[12]

Both Jean and François-Charles went to Lyon in 1838 to assist in the installation of an impressive new four-manual, forty-eight-stop Callinet organ for the church of Saint-François-de-Sales.[13] After inaugurating the organ in November, François-Charles was offered the position of organist, which he eagerly accepted. Finding lodgment just around the corner from the church, at 19 rue Sala, he remained the *titulaire* until December 1884.[14] He also became professor of piano at the Jesuit Collège de la Trinité.[15] When François-Charles visited Paris to play the new Daublaine-Callinet organ at Saint-Eustache in the fall of 1844, the celebrity he had already attained in Lyon was duly noted in the press:

> Mr. Charles Widor, distinguished composer, pianist, and organist, who has performed in Paris with much success before an audience composed of artists and connoisseurs, just set out again for Lyon where a large clientele

awaits him. This excellent artist has won the lively approbation of those who have had the opportunity to hear his charming works, some of which will soon be published.[16]

Le Ménestrel even compared François-Charles to the astounding German organist Adolph Hesse (1808–63) in his mastery of the pedal clavier.[17]

Widor appeared in Paris again in 1852 to play the new organ at Saint-Vincent-de-Paul. One critic opined, "His melody is in good taste, even distinguished, and his harmony is pure and severe, though a little cold."[18] In the Lyon region his notoriety as composer, pianist, and organist continued to increase; *France Musicale* approved of his manner: "The pious young man understood well what religious music of the church was supposed to be."[19] He and the renowned Louis-James-Alfred Lefébure-Wély (1817–69) shared the inaugural program for the Cavaillé-Coll organ in the Belley Cathedral on April 15, 1860, an event his eager sixteen-year-old son Charles-Marie would certainly have attended.[20]

During the 1850s and early 1860s, press reports that refer to Charles Widor must be taken as references to François-Charles and not Charles-Marie.[21] Not until 1863 do reviews begin to refer to "a young organist, Mr. Ch. Widor, from Lyon."[22] Reports concerning François-Charles certainly continued to appear, though unless the reviewer referred specifically to father or son, such references are ambiguous. For example, the 1864 inauguration of the Cavaillé-Coll organ in the church of Sainte-Perpétue de Nîmes was reported in *Ménestrel* as being given by "Mr. Ch. Widor from Lyon."[23] The *Revue et Gazette* was more specific in identifying "Mr. Ch. Widor from Lyon, a student of Fétis and Lemmens."[24]

In June 1861, Édouard Batiste (1820–76), organist of Saint-Eustache in Paris, joined François-Charles to inaugurate the organ rebuilt by Merklin-Schütze for Saint-Bonaventure in Lyon.[25] One review reported that Widor was "strongly esteemed in Paris where he is considered as a modern notability in the art of Sebastian Bach, Froberger, and Lemmens. . . . Next to the Parisian organist [Batiste], Mr. Widor made himself listened to with sustained attention in his last improvisation on the individual stops."[26] The Lyon *Salut Public* raved over Batiste's performance and said Widor's "brilliant improvisation seemed to reduce the great difficulties to nothing, and the boldness of his playing and fecundity of his verve produced a cascade of new feelings."[27]

On April 13, 1842, François-Charles Widor married Françoise-Elisabeth "Fanny" Peiron (December 22, 1817–April 10, 1883) from Annonay (Ardèche).[28] Descendant in an esteemed lineage of inventors, her granduncle Joseph-Michel Montgolfier (1740–1810) invented the hot-air balloon and pioneered in air navigation.[29] Another relative, Marc Seguin (1786–1875), had numerous inventions to his credit—the suspension bridge and steam boiler chief among them.[30]

Charles-Marie-Jean-Albert was the first of their three children (see fig. 1). Among sources, a long-standing inconsistency has existed as to the correct date of his birth. As early as 1880, Arthur Pougin's supplement to Fétis's *Biographie universelle des musiciens et bibliographie générale de la musique* gave an incorrect date of February 22, 1845.[31] Often in articles by Widor's closest friends and pupils, as well as in books for which he had written the preface, incorrect dates of his birth abound. As late as 1931, the *Encyclopédie de la musique et dictionnaire du conservatoire* offered two possible dates—both incorrect: "22 or 24 February 1845 (his biographers give the two dates)."[32] Two pieces of evidence testify that Widor himself thought he was born in 1845: first, on his mother's death certificate (carrying his signature) of April 10, 1883, he is described as "composer of music in Paris, Rue Garancière 8, aged thirty-eight years";[33] second, upon his nomination to the Institute of France in 1910, he completed the official registry form by inscribing the day of his birth very clearly as "22 févr." and the year a bit ambiguously as "45."[34] Although he wrote the "4" very distinctly, the mark for "5" is nothing more than a vertical line with a tiny loop at the top (see fig. 18). Still, Gustave Bret (1875–1969) attested that Widor "affirmed to me many times" that he was born in 1844; Bret gave the day as February 24, however.[35] Dates may have seemed unimportant to Widor. When Jean Bouvard (1905–96), founder of l'Association des amis de l'orgue in Lyon, once sought Widor's signature, the *maître* signed his name and then wrote "31 juin 29." Upon being reminded timidly by Bouvard that June has only thirty days, Widor retorted, "All the better, this will make us immortals!"[36]

In the 1844 birth records of the Lyon Municipal Archives, entry number 700 confirms the correct date as February 21, and the precise time as two o'clock in the afternoon:[37]

> The twenty-second of February, one thousand, eight hundred, forty-four, at nine o'clock in the morning, before you, Mayor of Lyon, has appeared Mr. François-Charles *Widor*, aged thirty-three years, organist at the church of Saint-François—residing rue Sala, no. 19; who has presented an infant male, born yesterday, at two o'clock in the afternoon, in his said residence, being born to him and to damsel Françoise-Elisabeth Peiron, his wife; to which infant is given the first names Charles-Marie-Jean-Albert. Messrs. present: Benoît-Joseph Simon, aged twenty-eight years, druggist, residing rue St. Joseph, no. 3, and Jean-Meichel Bildstein, of the same age, stockholder, place de la Charité, who, as well as the father, have signed with you the present document, after being read.

Ironically, during a lifetime of more than ninety-three years this simple fact was never definitively clarified. Above Widor's solitary tomb in the narrow crypt of Saint-Sulpice is chiseled:

CHARLES MARIE WIDOR
1845–1937

—2—

"My earliest childhood memories" and siblings

In his "Souvenirs autobiographiques," Widor reminisced:

> My earliest childhood memories take me back to Lyon, to a house at 17 rue de Bourbon [now rue Victor Hugo]. I was born there on the second floor. I still see perfectly the garden over which our windows opened, and through which every day I could see Mr. de Castellane [1788–1862; Governor of Lyon] walking after dinner in his full uniform as a French field marshal, a form of dress that he never abandoned even in the least formal circumstances. The sight of this display excited my child's imagination to the highest degree, and, brandishing my wooden saber, I shouted to him: "Marshal, Marshal, I have a saber as handsome as yours." The great man smiled and moments later sent his secretary to me with a barley candy. Every morning Mr. de Castellane went to the nine o'clock mass at the neighboring church of Saint-François. On coming out, his uniform attracted the kids in the neighborhood. In a broad gesture, the Marshal freed himself of their tumultuous admiration by throwing a few handfuls of small coins. This neighborliness and fine example might have been able to kindle a military career in me. But atavism and parental authority, as much as my own personal tastes, were bound to decide otherwise.[38]

Widor belonged to the *garde nationale* in the early 1870s, and perhaps his memory of the old marshal had something to do with the military bearing that, in the eyes of many, he always maintained.

After Charles-Marie, two more children were born to Charles and Fanny Widor: a son, Marie-Joseph-Albert-Paul (February 5, 1847–June 4, 1930; married Thérèse Verzier) and a daughter, Jeanne-Marie-Françoise (April 10, 1848–May 18, 1917; married Eugène Pierron).[39] Each child's name included Marie, apparently taken from their paternal grandmother, Marie-Anne-Eve Frey. While nothing is known about the musical proclivities of daughter Marie, the second son, Paul, "possessed a talent as pianist and organist quite exceptional for an amateur."[40] Also gifted with a "splendid bass voice,"[41] in the late 1860s Paul sang in the choir of Saint-Sulpice in Paris. Although in 1877 he settled on a career as chief clerk at the Lyon Court of Justice and "administrateur du Dispensaire,"[42] music remained a focal point in his life. When his brother Charles inaugurated the splendid new Cavaillé-Coll organ at Saint-François-de-Sales in 1880, Paul sang an aria—with religious words adapted—from Beethoven's *Die Ruinen von Athen* (The Ruins of Athens).[43] He succeeded his father as titular organist of Saint-François in December 1884, remaining in that position until September 1889.[44]

Both sons received their first musical studies under the tutelage of their father, but the gifts of the first-born proved to be exceptional: "As to the musical talent of the eldest, it manifested itself very early and classified him from the first among child prodigies."[45] By age eleven, Charles-Marie had already received an appointment as organist of the Collège des Jésuites,[46] and he sometimes filled in for his father at Saint-François.[47]

> I was scarcely four years old when my father put me at the keyboards of the organ for the first time, thus beginning my musical education. Later, I went every evening to practice on the instrument at Saint-François, tackling arduously the formidable technique of the organ and, under the vaults of the church, filling myself with the incomparable grandeur of my art.
>
> At the age of eleven, my parents pushed me into secondary school [lysée Ampère de Lyon].[48] In that period, the State had not yet divorced itself from the Church, and it granted two free scholarships: one was awarded to the drummer, and the other to the organist of the institution. I easily obtained the second. I paid for my studies during some years by playing the organ at mass and vespers in this former Jesuit Chapel—remarkable in its simplicity, arrangement, the beauty of its marbles, and, moreover, its history, for it saw the République Cisalpine offer its presidency to Bonaparte.[49]

—3—

"Charles-Marie will need to go study in Brussels"

Since at least 1844, François-Charles Widor had been a good friend of Aristide Cavaillé-Coll (1811–99),[50] the most illustrious French organ builder of the nineteenth century (see figs. 2 and 3). Whenever visiting Lyon, Cavaillé-Coll, who was the same age as François-Charles, was a welcomed guest in the Widor home.[51] When Cavaillé-Coll needed to recommend someone as an organ authority to the treasurer of Sainte-Madeleine in Tarare, he did not hesitate naming his friend: "We know Mr. Widor, organist of Saint-François, who is both extremely talented as a musician and possesses extensive knowledge of the theory and practice of organ building: his judgment would be that of a well-informed expert, and would be sufficient guarantee for the Council."[52] Cavaillé-Coll's visits to Lyon left vivid impressions on Charles-Marie: "The famous organ builder interested himself right away in the early development of the young musician who conserved Cavaillé-Coll's least words in his memory and held them as from an oracle."[53]

> We lived opposite from the church [Saint-François] . . . and it was a festivity when Mr. Cavaillé-Coll, in coming to Lyon, was the guest of my parents. I was fourteen years old when, at the family table, he proclaimed the

following words to us one day: "When Charles-Marie finishes his studies, he will need to go study in Brussels with the great organist [Jacques] Lemmens [1823–81] to whom I will introduce him. I have already sent to him the young [Alexandre] Guilmant [1837–1911], from Boulogne-sur-Mer, who is gifted to the point of being able to play at sight a work of Bach with his hands and feet simultaneously.[54]

Charles-Marie completed his secondary schooling in Lyon with emphasis on the humanities.[55] He was accorded his *Diplôme de Bachelier ès Lettres* "in the name of the Emperor [Napoléon III]" on August 12, 1862, and was eager to follow Cavaillé-Coll's advice.[56] Widor explained the pivotal decision that sent him to Brussels for study:

> When my studies were completed, my father, who was very close to Aristide Cavaillé-Coll, decided, on the counsel of the latter, to send me to perfect my musical studies in Brussels with two illustrious masters who were his [Cavaillé-Coll's] friends: one, a professor of organ, was Lemmens; the other, a professor of composition and Director of the Conservatory, was [François-Joseph] Fétis [1784–1871]. I was supposed to stay a year in Brussels, from 1862 to 1863.
>
> This year of study determined my career.[57]

Cavaillé-Coll had formulated the plan to send Charles-Marie to Brussels, and the time had now come to inform Lemmens of his intentions for the boy. Sensitive to the politics of the situation, however, Cavaillé-Coll felt it would be better if a formal recommendation, especially to Fétis, came from the offices of the Belgian organ builder Joseph Merklin (1819–1905). Accordingly, the Widors petitioned Merklin on behalf of their son. Upon receiving the good news of his acceptance, euphoria swept over the Widor household. Overflowing with gratitude, a letter from Elisabeth Widor, dated January 29, 1863, addressed to the Merklin Company, 49 Boulevard Montparnasse, Paris, amply conveys the family's emotions and confirms that Merklin and the manager of the Paris branch of his company, Louis-Grégoire Brassine, were responsible for Charles-Marie's acceptance by Lemmens and Fétis as their private pupil; the "Sir" of Madame Widor's letter was Brassine:

> Sir:
>
> Permit me to be the secretary for Mr. Widor and with him to offer you my sincere thanks. I cannot express to you, Sir, the joy among us that your kind letter has brought; my son is happy beyond all expression, and his father, overwhelmed with work, cannot bear seeing the mail go out without expressing to you all his gratitude. He has thus charged me, Sir, while waiting until

he himself will have this pleasure, to tell you how much we are touched by what Mr. Merklin and you, Sir, have obtained for my Charles. Lessons with Mr. Fétis and Mr. Lemmens were the continual dream of my dear child, and it was the ambition of his father. Thank you a thousand times, Sir, for the immense favor of working with these masters of the masters! The first day of Lent we will be on the train for Brussels . . .

Kindly accept, Sir, the expression of my highest regards.

E. Widor

Not knowing where to address a letter of thanks to Mr. Merklin, I ask you to be so kind, Sir, to express to him our utmost gratitude. We hear that he is expected here; therefore, I hope we will be able to see him soon, but we would all be very desirous that he receive as early as possible, with our warmest thanks, the assurance of our sincere gratitude.[58]

Meanwhile, in Paris, Cavaillé-Coll did not know that the arrangements had already been made for Charles-Marie to study in Brussels, as the following day he wrote to Lemmens:

Paris, January 30, 1863

Dear Mr. Lemmens,

I just now wrote to you so quickly [this was his second letter to Lemmens on that date] that I believe I forgot one of the principal requests I had to make of you. One of our good friends—Mr. Widor, an organist of the good sort in Lyon, and to whom I have given the advice of sending his son to you, an intelligent lad and already well hewn—this worthy friend asks my advice in order to know definitely where he is supposed to apply, either to Brussels, or to Paris if there is someone in our capital who would be able to substitute for you.

I replied to him that if I was certain you were staying in Brussels, there wouldn't be any need to hesitate [addressing you there], but that I would ask your advice.[59]

The nameless personage [*facteur anonyme*: Joseph Merklin] is supposed to recommend him to you. I told our friend that he could also convey my recommendation to you, but that it would be good to accept the other recommendation [Merklin's] for the Director of the Conservatory.

The young man is very well brought up, and I believe that he has a good aptitude. The parents are good people and merit every consideration. When you write to me, tell me a word about what Papa Widor will have to do for his son.[60]

After Merklin's successful entreaty on behalf of Charles-Marie, and with Cavaillé-Coll's enthusiastic endorsement, the boy and his mother set off for Brussels for what would be the completion of his formal education. It did not commence before late February 1863, as Madame Widor wrote that she and her son would be on the train for Brussels the first day of Lent, which was February 18 that year. On March 7, Cavaillé-Coll again wrote to Lemmens expressing his hope that the boy would be a worthy charge:

> Madame Widor has only just now passed through Paris on her return [from Brussels]; she saw my wife and made the highest praise of your hearty welcome and kindness. I hope that you will make of her son a good pupil and that he will not be ungrateful.[61]

When Widor reported—more than seventy years after his term of study—that he stayed in Brussels from 1862 to 1863, he had forgotten the exact length of time spent there. It had been just about two weeks shy of five months, as it concluded on July 9.

—4—

Off to learn "the main principles, the pure Bach tradition"

Harmony, counterpoint, fugue, composition, and instrumentation studies would be under the watchful eye of elder statesman of music François-Joseph Fétis (see fig. 4), a man of vast culture, a prolific composer, publisher of many theoretical and musicological writings, director of the Brussels Conservatory, founder of the *Revue Musicale,* and in the process of issuing his monumental *Biographie universelle des musiciens et bibliographie générale de la musique.*[62] Widor later wrote that "Fétis was one of the most erudite and judicious men of the time; his critique made law."[63]

As important, Cavaillé-Coll wanted young Charles to receive intensive organ training from reputed Bach interpreter Jacques Lemmens (see fig. 5), whom Cavaillé-Coll and Fétis both felt held the key to the future of correct organ playing. Having obtained first prizes from the Brussels Conservatory in piano, counterpoint, and fugue in 1844, and in composition and organ in 1845, Lemmens went on to study with Adolph Hesse in Breslau in 1846. Widor held the conviction that Hesse was the "heir of the pure classical tradition,"[64] and that Lemmens had learned from Hesse "the main principles, the pure Bach tradition" as handed down from the great Cantor himself through several generations of master/pupil successions.[65]

But was that "tradition" really what it was touted to be? Curiously, Guilmant and Widor traced this musical lineage differently:

Guilmant:[66]	Widor:[67]
Johann Sebastian Bach (1685–1750)	J. S. Bach
Johann Christian Leberecht Kittel (1732–1809)	Bach's sons (W. F.; C. P. E.; J. C.)
Johann Christian Heinrich Rinck (1770–1846)	Johann Nikolaus Forkel (1749–1818)
Adolph Friedrich Hesse (1808–63)	Hesse
Jacques-Nicolas Lemmens (1823–81)	Lemmens

Widor's version is obviously flawed: Hesse had not yet attained the age of ten when Forkel died, and it is unreasonable that such a grand tradition could have been handed over meaningfully to a child. On the other hand, Guilmant's version holds up: Rinck studied with Kittel, one of Bach's last students, and Hesse studied with Rinck from early October 1828 until early March of the following year.[68] Marcel Dupré (1886–1971), a student of both Widor and Guilmant, traced his pedigree even differently from those of his masters, giving further rise to the question of authority:

Dupré:[69]
Wilhelm Friedemann (1710–84) and Carl Philipp Emanuel Bach (1714–88)
Johann Ludwig Krebs (1713–80)
Johann Philipp Kirnberger (1721–83)
J. C. Kittel (1732–1809)
then:
Friedrich Wilhelm Berner (1780–1827)
J. C. Rinck (1770–1846)
A. F. Hesse, intimate friend of Mendelssohn, professor of:
J. Lemmens, professor of:
A. Guilmant and Ch.-M. Widor

Historian Orpha Ochse does not find written evidence that Lemmens himself ever laid claim to any of these arguments: "This notion was publicized originally by Fétis and later by students of Lemmens—most vehemently and persistently by Widor."[70] Indeed, Widor believed in this line of tradition beyond the shadow of a doubt, reiterating often: "A Belgian artist, Lemmens, came back from Germany where he had gone to acquire from Hesse in Breslau the pure interpretation of Bach";[71] "Lemmens was my master, as well as Guilmant's, and he left us these traditions to transmit in our turn."[72] When in 1928 Jean Huré (1877–1930) dared to dispute the tradition from Bach to Lemmens and fingered Lemmens's disciples for having promulgated such a fanciful idea, Widor did not hesitate to brand Huré "an ass, understudy for a fool!"[73]

—5—

A spurious tradition: "Mr. Hesse has taught me very little"

After Lemmens's period of study in Breslau, Hesse purportedly wrote to Fétis, "I have nothing more to teach Mr. Lemmens; he plays the most difficult music of Bach as well as I am able to do it."[74] Fétis used this alleged endorsement to praise Lemmens and thereby reap benefits for his conservatory. The initial presumption of truth in this statement highlights the importance of Cavaillé-Coll's plan to send the young French organists Guilmant and Widor to study with Lemmens. However, that Hesse later denied publicly in the *Neue Zeitschrift für Musik* of April 2, 1852[75] having ever written such a letter was little, if at all, known in France or Belgium. His alleged approval of Lemmens was thus completely specious, a political stratagem on the part of Fétis in order to justify a grant from the Belgian Minister of Interior for Lemmens to study in Breslau and to facilitate his nomination to the Brussels Conservatory.[76] Hesse further refuted Fétis's statement, writing: "The talent of Mr. Lemmens at that time turned out to be extremely mediocre, and if he later became the great man that Mr. Fétis thinks he is, I am in no way responsible for it."[77] What Hesse could not have known is that Lemmens had already put his own opinion of Hesse's teaching in a letter to his parents on November 9, 1846, during his stay in Breslau; with a healthy dose of youthful self-esteem, Lemmens exclaimed:

> Here is the news from Breslau. Mr. Hesse has taught me very little, so little that it is a trip which I made for nothing, but I am not a man not to profit from it. I play every day three or four hours of organ. Mr. Hesse comes approximately once a week in order to be able to say that he comes, because he has nothing to tell me. In the beginning he told me that I played too fast. That is the only remark that he has been able to make to me.[78]

Even were it possible that the "Bach tradition" could have been handed down unsullied from the great cantor of Leipzig to Hesse, the comments by both Hesse and Lemmens, as well as their less than warm teacher/pupil relationship, indicate a major breakdown in the line of transmission between them. From this, Ewald Kooiman deduced, "The German tradition underlies Lemmens and his followers. However, it is not the tradition of Johann Sebastian Bach, but that of later generations of organists."[79]

Lemmens returned to Brussels and became organ professor at the conservatory in 1849. Widor later assayed, "Then began for us the new era of our art."[80] Clearly, whatever Widor had learned from Lemmens did not originate with Hesse, and it appears quite likely that many of the ideas promulgated by Lemmens were a combination of what he had learned while in Germany and ideas that came directly from Fétis.[81] Kooiman posited:

> I can only conclude that it is Fétis who gave birth to the whole story of the continuing Bach tradition. It was undoubtedly very important to him to build up the international reputation of his conservatory, preferably at the expense of her sister institution in Paris. He was miraculously successful at it. . . .
>
> When Lemmens had returned from Breslau, Fétis began a vigorous campaign in France on behalf of the man who had become organ professor at his conservatory in 1849. He also got the organ builder Cavaillé-Coll, whose star was rapidly rising, involved in the plan. . . . So Lemmens was proclaimed Bach interpreter *par excellence* and inheritor of traditions going back to Bach. . . . On top of that, Lemmens had the good luck to have several gifted French students come to Brussels on the recommendation of Cavaillé-Coll. They soon spread the new doctrines, with their accompanying myths, throughout their own country.[82]

As for Hesse's true role in the awakening of French organists to a new tradition, Jean Ferrard seems to have most correctly identified it as that of the "detonator": "His visit to Paris in 1844 remains a unique occurrence, while the Belgian Jacques-Nicolas Lemmens will play, some years later in part under the impetus of Cavaillé-Coll, a much more determinant role."[83] If Guilmant and Widor inherited any tradition then, it was only that of Lemmens.

—6—

Widor's musical heritage:
"It seemed the sap had ceased to flow"

The place of Charles-Marie Widor in the history of French organ music is best understood in the context of the immediate generations to which he was heir. In addition, his perception of his forebears is critical to understanding his attitude toward them and his excitement over the dawning age in which he was such a significant participant. In his later years, he had much to say about what had come before him and the new era of enlightenment for the organ.

Widor greatly admired many French Renaissance and Baroque composers, but he noted periods of decline when "it seemed the sap had ceased to flow."[84] Citing first the Italian-born Jean-Baptiste Lully (1632–87) as coming to France "to shake off our lethargy and exert on his contemporaries a beneficial tyranny," Widor noted many composers who carried on a healthy tradition "informed by the past, respectful of the Palestrinian doctrine, and inspired by antique vocal polyphony—something quite natural when you are dealing with a clavier having sounds of unlimited duration."[85] He specifically pointed out the merits of organ works by several seventeenth- and early eighteenth-century composers, notable because of "their intelligence and their profound understanding of the character of the organ, its special resources, power and intended purpose."[86] For Widor, the organ had one intended purpose, and he stated it repeatedly throughout his writings over many decades: "*It is by the idea of the infinite that the organ evokes in us the religious idea.*"[87]

On the other hand, he found much of the organ music in the latter half of the eighteenth century severely wanting, and for good cause. He explained, "At the same time that the orchestra and theater took vigorous flight, and from Lully soared to the period of Gluck [1714–87], the organ drooped, losing its character and forgetting its mission. Is it the fault of the artists alone, or isn't it also necessary to blame the instruments? It's the fault of both."[88] "From Lully to Gluck we had great musicians who did not make use of the organ because the organ did not allow them to express their thought."[89] As for the organists, Widor observed that "little by little [they] distanced themselves from the [earlier] School in search of novel impressions—purely sensual effects drawn from the variety of timbres and the progressive growth of the number of registers."[90] As for the instruments, with but a few exceptions the decline leading up to and including the Revolution was dramatic, as pointed out by Fenner Douglass:

> The Revolution left French organs in ruins. Had the Reign of Terror (1792–94) continued to the end of the 18th century, it is likely that the art of organ building would have vanished from France altogether. The great builders were dead . . . and the rest had dispersed to seek a livelihood in joinery. There was virtually no work for organ builders for more than a quarter-century. Countless organs were vandalized, or their pipes melted down for bullets; confiscated churches were transformed into "Temples of Reason." Those instruments surviving the pillage were neglected and often unplayable. By the time of the Second Restoration (1815), only two experienced organ builders remained in Paris. . . . No one else in the capital was capable of reviving a tradition that had only recently (1790) produced Cliquot's [*sic*] masterpiece at the Cathedral of Poitiers, but since then had all but disappeared.[91]

With the prevailing decadent character of organ playing and the atrocious condition of French organs at the beginning of the nineteenth century, the importance of Cavaillé-Coll and Lemmens to the later nineteenth-century French organ school cannot be overstated. "Two names are indispensable," wrote Widor in 1899: "Cavaillé-Coll and Lemmens; an inspired builder, a peerless virtuoso. Both of them have succeeded in setting in motion the great long-inert pendulum and determining the movement that is going to accelerate without cease in our country."[92]

—7—

The Saint-Sulpice organ:
"A full chorus of old women's voices"

In view of Widor's eventual life-long service at Saint-Sulpice, tracing a few incidents in the history of that church and its famous organ provides an important backdrop to the present topic, and it serves as a good example of the signs of the revolutionary and postrevolutionary times. Compared to many other organs, however, the one at Saint-Sulpice fared quite well during that turbulent era.[93]

Although slated to be destroyed, the instrument was spared by an astute and brave bellows pumper who placed false seals on the door leading to the organ gallery. Nonetheless, the instrument remained silent for a number of years and suffered from extreme neglect and abuse. Between 1793 and 1795 its bellows were removed to the Luxembourg gardens where they were used to blow furnaces for the manufacture of arms.[94] The church itself became the site of a variety of secular activities: military enlistments, public welfare meetings, a market place, idolatrous worship, and finally a "Temple de la Victoire," replete with decorative tapestries, flags, and an impressive statue of Victory.[95] Organ music had practically no place during that period. One of the few times the organ was used was for entertainment at a grand banquet (15 Brumaire VIII [November 6, 1799]) for Generals Bonaparte and Moreau upon their return from the Egyptian campaign: "During the meal, recalled Louis Bonaparte, some excellent music was played, and the organs which had remained in the Temple were played by [Gervais-François] Couperin [1759–1826]."[96] Because the instrument had fallen into such disrepair, however, it first had to be cleaned and "somehow or other 'made to sound again.'"[97]

Appreciation of the elegant craftsmanship represented by such a noble national treasure and any subsequent interest in the historic preservation of organs in general was practically nil. A governmental effort in the 1820s to restore some cathedral organs failed and "contributed more to the destruction of French organs than to their preservation."[98] There can be little wonder that when Felix Mendelssohn (1809–47) visited Saint-Sulpice in 1832, he expressed dismay at the disgraceful condition of the instrument: "I have just come from St.-Sulpice, where the organist showed off his organ to me; it sounded like a full chorus of old women's voices; but they maintain that it is the finest organ in Europe if it were only put into proper order."[99]

—8—

1838: "The art of organ playing is in utter decadence today"

The decline in the art of French organ building and haphazard attempts at organ restoration closely paralleled the increasingly limited technical means of organists and secular musical tastes of audiences. In the first year of its publication, the *Revue et Gazette Musicale de Paris* noted, "Everywhere, in the organist you will discover more or less a pianist who misuses the instrument, not knowing at all how to draw out its immense resources."[100] As Cavaillé-Coll was making innovative strides in organ construction, by the 1840s his instruments' new expressive potential and orchestrally imitative voices provided organ players with the means of satisfying prevailing popular tastes. The fine art of the liturgical organist from a century or more earlier had decayed to its lowest ebb, and the once inspired tradition of sacred organ music seemed lost. Church music had become hopelessly secularized. An oft-quoted review of the 1838 inaugural concert for the new Cavaillé-Coll organ at Notre-Dame-de-Lorette indicates the prevailing tastes and standards of performance:

> The acceptance of the organ in Notre-Dame-de-Lorette took place last Monday, before a large and distinguished audience; to see the fashionable people in that church, decorated with quite worldly luxury, one was able to imagine that he was in attendance at a concert in rue Vivienne; and the pieces that were performed on the organ were not of a nature to destroy the illusion. Some waltzes and coquettish worldly melodies, reminiscent of the Opéra and Salle Musard, that's what the *pianists* who had come to try the new instrument played. It is a sad fact, but it is necessary to say it: the art of organ playing is in utter decadence today.[101]

Extracts from popular operas were considered appropriate as accompaniments to the Mass.[102] Among French organists of the period, it seems that only Alexandre-Pierre-François Boëly (1785–1858) maintained a traditional approach to organ music in the church.[103] Boëly modeled his music on the works of J. S. Bach, C. P. E. Bach, Rameau, and Couperin.[104] For him, the ability to play Bach was the benchmark of a good musician.[105] However, Boëly's conservative conscience eventually put him out of his job at Saint-Germain-l'Auxerrois, to be replaced by a younger artist "with the taste of the day."[106]

In a lengthy review of the inauguration of the organ of Saint-Eustache on June 18, 1844, critic Stephen Morelot wrote, "The German School, so little known among us . . . seems to have attained a perfection that will be difficult to surpass."[107] Its most renowned exponent, Adolph Hesse, participated in the inaugural concert and left the French audience of some seven thousand awed by his technical abilities, but little moved emotionally. Acclaimed for his meticulously refined interpretations of Bach and admired for his athletic ability on the pedal clavier "that we have for so long considered an accessory without importance in France,"[108] Hesse's lack of complete success was that he relied on the inherent interest in the music itself, and that simply was not enough to satisfy the taste of a public whose attention he lost. A critic for *France Musicale* wrote, "He is passionate for power and noise; his playing astonishes but it does not go to the soul. He always seems to be the minister of an angry God who wants to punish."[109] French fashion demanded music of a worldly character and an interpretation marked by the novel contrasts of registration that recent developments in organ building had made possible.[110]

—9—

Lefébure-Wély:
"Thunderstorms, bells, bird songs, tambourines, bagpipes"

Completely unlike Hesse, the showy Lefébure-Wély, catering to public tastes with colorful and tuneful improvisations, made a phenomenal success and dominated the arena of French organ music. As Cavaillé-Coll's favorite organist at the time, Lefébure-Wély invariably received the appointment as organist of the church with the newest and most impressive of the influential builder's instruments; he succeeded from Saint-Roch to La Madeleine, and finally to Saint-Sulpice.[111] "Because of Cavaillé-Coll's success in endearing himself to the cream of musical society and particularly to the clergy, he frequently found himself in a position to influence appointments."[112]

In spite of Lefébure-Wély's great popularity with the public, however, conservative critics disapproved of his style. The erudite historian, organist, organ builder, writer, and publisher Jean-Louis-Félix Danjou (1812–66) abhorred Lefébure-Wély's flamboyance and described his technique as pertaining more to the piano than the organ; his pedal execution was "similar to those of the French organists who scarcely employ but the left foot and do not practice the German style."[113] No less a master than Alexandre Guilmant, on the other hand, remembered Lefébure-Wély as "the finest extemporaneous player on the organ that France has produced."[114] Still, Abbé Joseph Régnier's review of Lefébure-Wély's 1845 inaugural concert for the organ of Saint-Sernin in Toulouse aptly described the generally perceived shallowness of his style, and it can be inferred that with a couple of notable exceptions this model represented the best of the norm throughout France at the time:

> Our old cathedrals become indignant when one is deafening them with these um-pah-pahs and their echoes, grasping these tunes, excerpts, strains and trite notions, repeating them, mixing them up, shortening them, making them ridiculous, and scrambling them for the listener. Now when will French organists understand that their instrument demands only majestic ideas, a broad style, grandiose effects, exalted melodies, rich harmony, and solemn execution? Mr. Lefébure-Wély is very young; he can still acquire what is lacking in his talent; we urge him to study, to imitate the two fine models that he has before him, Messrs. Boëly, organist of Saint-Germain-l'Auxerrois, and [François] Benoist [1794–1878], professor at the Conservatory; these are the two great artists who know how to respect their art, and who do not prostitute our organs with the barcarole, contra-dance, gallop, waltz, and polka.[115]

Even after such harsh criticism, Lefébure-Wély showed no intention of reforming. He knew his audience, and the following year for the inaugural concert of the new Cavaillé-Coll organ at La Madeleine he proved himself to be in top form when he improvised a descriptive piece in memory of recent flood victims in the Loire Valley. Various episodes of the disaster served as his inspiration; rampaging waters and the wails of the victims were all too vividly portrayed: "The entire assembly shuddered; one saw tears of pity flowing on the most impassive faces."[116] In a letter to Cavaillé-Coll, Lefébure-Wély summed up his resourcefulness: "When a smart performer wants to fill the house, he shows off his skill at the door: trumpets, bass drums, etc. As for us [organists], we have to attempt imitating our worthy colleagues. Let's pack them in, using thunderstorms, bells, bird songs, tambourines, bagpipes, and 'human voices' [*voix humaines*]."[117]

Lefébure-Wély's obituary in *Revue et Gazette* pointed out that he had purposefully assumed a secular attitude, even during the course of church services:

> People reproached him principally for the not very religious character and irrepressibleness of his ideas; however, it was to a large extent there that the secret of his success laid in a church . . . where the offices were supposed to maintain a grand character of austerity. He couldn't bring himself not to shine, not to please, not "to create a diversion," and he sacrificed the serious to it.[118]

In an 1856 article entitled "L'orgue mondaine et la musique érotique à l'église" ["The Worldly Organ and Erotic Music in the Church"], Fétis summarized what he saw as the essential problems in contemporary French organ style. He began by quoting from a review of an inaugural concert given by Lefébure-Wély:

"The style of the Parisian organist differs essentially from the German style: he has less religious austerity, less classical solemnity, less musical symmetry than the virtuosos nourished from the traditions and principles of the German school; but, on the other hand, he has more verve and coloring, more popular eloquence, if we can say it. It is he, as a matter of fact, *after Simon*,[119] who has done the most to popularize the organ in France. It is not to say that he lacks knowledge or that he is unaware of the secrets of harmony—No! But leaving the fugal style to the great German masters, *he conforms deliberately to the sensualistic instincts and urges of his public.* In a word, he aims to please and he succeeds. We have had proof of it *in the hearty applause and prolonged bravos* that greeted his offertory . . . *and especially his storm effect.* The organizers of the concert deserve mention here *for the ingenious idea that they had of dimming the gaslights in the middle of the storm. THIS STAGING DETAIL only added to the illusion!*" What do you say about that? . . .

The complete inferiority of French organists has precisely for its prime cause the fad that they call *improvisation*. Not one of them has what can be called *an organist's education.* . . . Not one of them would be capable of masterfully playing the great pieces of Bach; not one of them knows what style is, nor would be able to distinguish one school from another. All their attention is turned toward the effects from the instrument, the oppositions of sonority, the combinations of the stops and keyboards, and the means of exciting and gratifying the sensual instincts. . . . It is in the eighteenth century that the trouble began, and the effects, gratifying or astonishing, became the end of every effort. *The storm* is tradition since that time. In my youth, there was a *monsieur Miroir*[120] who was greatly renowned for playing this sort of phantasmagoria. Everyone rushed to Saint-Roch when Mr. Miroir was supposed to perform a storm piece. People were stricken with terror; but Mr. Miroir had the good taste to calm the excitement of his listeners with some little solos on the musette, piccolo, vox humana with tremulant, and *tenor chromorne.*[121]

Fétis minced no words in his appraisal, and, although severe, Cavaillé-Coll agreed, conceding to Lemmens that it was just what French organists needed to hear: "The lesson given by Mr. Fétis to our friend Lefébure and to French organists in general is a bit strong, but it is good. Our friend Lefébure was not pleased with it."[122]

—10—

Lemmens: "Crystalline, prodigious interpretations . . . of the great masters"

At the height of Lefébure-Wély's popularity, the tide in France began to shift. Lemmens made his debut in Paris, and from his earliest appearance in 1850,

it apparently began to dawn on Cavaillé-Coll that the serious art of organ playing and the future of that style belonged to this Belgian organist; his playing
brought a totally new and enlightened understanding of organ music to the
builder, and it must have been a revelation to many others as well.[123] On May
21, 1850, shortly after Lemmens's visit to Paris, Cavaillé-Coll wrote to Fétis:

> Although Mr. Lemmens spent only a short time in Paris, he did not go unno-
> ticed. Our most skillful organists . . . all hastened to place their instruments
> at the disposal of this professor from your Conservatory, and they acknowl-
> edge the eminently distinguished talents that he possesses as a composer and
> organist.
>
> I should have liked to arrange a public recital by Mr. Lemmens, but the
> same obstacle that prevents this sort of performance in Belgium is encoun-
> tered in Paris as well. However, I must add that thanks to the kindness of Mr.
> Lefébure-Wély, we were able to hear him four times at the organ of la Mad-
> eleine: at three weddings and at high mass on Whitsunday; also in several
> other recitals arranged for him by Mr. Neumann at the church of Panthé-
> mont, and finally at a small party given by Mr. Lefébure-Wély at his home.
> On this occasion, Messrs. Ambroise Thomas, Adolphe Adam [1803–56], . . .
> plus Mr. Danjou, who happened to be in Paris, heard this learned musician
> and were no less delighted than we were to compliment Mr. Lemmens on the
> crystalline, prodigious interpretations he gives of the great masters, as well as
> on the scientific originality of his splendid compositions.
>
> I reiterate my sincerest thanks for the opportunity of meeting Mr. Lem-
> mens and admiring his great talent.[124]

Lemmens returned to Paris in 1852 and played three private recitals,
apparently including one all-Bach program at Saint-Vincent-de-Paul for a
select group of musicians; noted among them were Boëly, Charles-Valentin
Alkan (1813–88), César Franck (1822–90), and Charles Gounod (1818–93).
Composer and critic Joseph d'Ortigue (1802–66) described how the small
audiences of musicians crowded around Lemmens at the console "eager to
watch him manage the colossal instrument."[125] In a letter of March 12, 1852,
Cavaillé-Coll again wrote to Fétis of the wonderful impressions left by Lemmens's extraordinary talent:

> Your worthy student, Mr. Lemmens, returns to you laden with laurels won
> in the artistic world of our capital. His technical skills as well as his talented
> interpretations were deeply appreciated by the leading musical figures dur-
> ing the three recitals he gave on the organ in St.-Vincent-de-Paul. Several
> clergymen and discerning music-lovers, in attendance among the artists
> invited, told Mr. Lemmens how pleased they were not only with the merit
> of his compositions and the perfection with which he played them, but also
> with the deeply religious quality of his musical works.

Many regretted not being able to hear Mr. Lemmens. The reputation he established in a few days has spread throughout the music world. Several recitals would not have sufficed to satisfy the distinguished public, eager to share in the admiration he elicited from the artists.

You may be proud of having guided the musical development of Mr. Lemmens and of having added such a professor to your Conservatory. I merely express the opinions of numerous admirers of his talent. In my capacity as an organ-builder, my only desire would be to provide him soon with one of our instruments so that he might display his talent to the utmost.[126]

After hearing Lemmens, Paris Conservatory organ professor Benoist wrote to Cavaillé-Coll on March 18, 1852: "What has struck me above all is this calm, religious grandeur, this purity of style which is so fitting to the majesty of the temple of God."[127] Three-quarters of a century later, Widor pinpointed those recitals at Saint-Vincent-de-Paul as the turning point in Cavaillé-Coll's thought: "For Cavaillé, this was the light. He found in the style of the master virtuoso the general rules he had missed until then, the principles which are essential."[128]

For the inauguration of the Ducroquet organ in Saint-Eustache on May 26, 1854, Lemmens returned to Paris again to join organists Auguste-Ernest Bazille (1828–91), Piétro Cavallo (1819–92), and Franck in a performance of some of his own music as well as that of Bach and Mendelssohn. His playing elicited from one critic some of the qualities that set him apart from his colleagues: "It's especially by the strength and correctness of style that he distinguishes himself among his rivals. He wants above all to be classical; he descends from Bach in a straight line, and would deem himself failing the dignity of the instrument if he allowed himself to make the slightest concession to worldly and modern tastes."[129]

César Franck showed keen interest in Lemmens's new style of finger substitution, still unknown in France; and his fellow countryman's virtuosic pedal technique so impressed Franck that he procured a dummy pedalboard on which to practice his own pedaling.[130]

Many years later, in 1877, Lemmens affirmed to Cavaillé-Coll the impact of his organ playing in France:

> I believe that it's my visits to Paris in 1850, 51, 52, etc., that started the regeneration of the art of organ playing in France. The adoption of my organ school by the Paris Conservatory, and later the successive placement of four of my pupils in as many important Paris positions, are the proof of the solidity of my school.[131]

Lemmens's influence on Cavaillé-Coll was also far-reaching, effecting important changes in the builder's tonal designs. "In Paris," Widor later explained, "Cavaillé-Coll was building these remarkable instruments, perfecting the mechanism, refining the sonority, searching and inventing, but working without direction, a little at random, after an ideal more scientific than practical. The advice of Lemmens came in the nick of time to enlighten him."[132] From his thorough understanding of the organ and its literature, Lemmens demonstrated to Cavaillé-Coll the consistent need for mixture stops in a well-balanced ensemble, and he confirmed traditional keyboard compasses, including the consistent application of the German-style pedalboard. Widor observed aptly: "Like his predecessors, [Cavaillé-Coll] found himself engulfed in the indifference and ignorance of contemporary organists, for the most part musicians without brains and performers without fingers."[133] He continued:

> Lemmens went to inform Cavaillé-Coll (about something which no one had ever made known to him) that the organ of Johann Sebastian required a right proportioning of Foundations and Mixtures, at least two manual keyboards, each of fifty-four notes [fifty-six notes became the norm in France], and a pedalboard of thirty notes beginning from the low C of 8', or 16', or 32', according to the case.
>
> The pedalboard of Saint-Denis began at F, that of Saint-Roch at A, that of Notre-Dame-de-Lorette at A for the Foundations and C for the Reeds. As to that of La Madeleine, it numbered only twenty-five keys, dangerously close together. There was no rule and no principle. Bach was not playable on our style of organ.[134]

Lemmens soon became the favored organist of Cavaillé-Coll, who increasingly requested that he inaugurate his latest instruments. Cavaillé-Coll found in Lemmens an organist educated in the polyphonic tradition, one whose "fame did not rest on pleasing the crowd with portrayals of storms, or the woeful cries of victims of flood and shipwreck."[135] Cavaillé-Coll knew that Lefébure-Wély's style would simply perpetuate decadent trends, and it became the builder's conviction that only Lemmens could set a new course and establish a reputable standard for French organ performance for the generations to come. Cavaillé-Coll wrote to Lemmens in 1862 confiding this hope: "We must not try to reform the old. They have acquired their bad habits and their rectification would be impossible. But the young school will be able to profit from your excellent precepts."[136]

Those precepts would have to be instilled through Lemmens's pupils, however, as Cavaillé-Coll was unable to entice the Belgian to accept a position in Paris. As Widor understood it:

> Aristide Cavaillé-Coll would have liked to attract Lemmens to Paris, either to have him named *titulaire* of one of his instruments or to have him named to the directorship of a notable school. But it was England that attracted the master, for he had married Madame [Helen] Sherrington [1834–1906], who

joined to her talent the qualities of charming wife and mother of an excellent family that included two daughters.[137]

From this brief perspective, the historic importance of Cavaillé-Coll's determination that Guilmant and Widor study with Lemmens becomes clear. Not only were the greatest organs of the period credited to his industrious genius, but also he indirectly merits credit for establishing the preeminent school of organists who played them.

—11—

Lessons with Lemmens and Fétis:
"I rapidly became a virtuoso"

By his own account, Widor submitted to an extremely rigorous plan of study, and he completed his term in Brussels by July 9, 1863.[138] Some four and a half months of intense work sufficed:

> Subjected to the severe discipline of Fétis and Lemmens, every bit of my time was devoted to work. Every morning, Fétis handed me a fugue subject that I was to treat during the day and hand back the next morning. Since I was practicing the organ from morning to evening, I devoted two or three hours every evening to writing my daily fugue in four parts. I didn't search for any original formula, but, on the other hand, my work had to be of an impeccable correctness. The next morning, at seven o'clock, I went to knock at the door of Fétis, who corrected my work; when the Conservatory students arrived for their turn at eight o'clock, the master read it to them, commenting on it. As for me, I was a private student of Fétis, along with two other young men.[139]

Those few months in Brussels instilled in Widor the discipline of daily "mental gymnastics"—mental exercises that he indulged in every morning before setting about his work of the day. He would later tell his own students, "Be sure and go through a line or two of counterpoint every morning, and also interpret several measures of given bass. Do it as a routine, just as you comb your hair and brush your teeth."[140]

Not only through Lemmens, but also through Fétis, Widor proudly traced his musical ancestry back to Bach: "Very often Dr. Fétis, while initiating me in the principles of counterpoint and fugue in Brussels, spoke to me of Rinck whom he had frequented, of Kittel his musical father, and of their great ancestor Sebastian Bach."[141] Of his work with Lemmens, Widor would later recall (though not quite accurately regarding the length of study), "For one year, I worked with Lemmens. The park was all that I knew of Brussels. It's that I was obliged to cross it every day. I rapidly became a virtuoso."[142] In his pupil, Lemmens found a "born organist."[143] And in Lemmens, Widor found the perfect model to be emulated:

Tall, vigorous, and well built, Lemmens, more than anyone else, knew how to command the attention of an audience. His hand, like that of Liszt, molded the sonorous paste; moreover, the master organist had remained the master pianist, the marvelous interpreter of Beethoven and Weber. Watching him at the organ, you thought of the trainer handling the wildcat. [It was] magnificent playing made of greatness, clarity, and suppleness.[144]

One of several slightly differing accounts of Widor's daily activity at the organ describes the rigors under which he "rapidly became a virtuoso":

Each day, from eight o'clock in the morning, he sat before the organ keyboards, and left the grand instrument only toward the end of the afternoon. Also, every day before the dinner hour he would play in front of Lemmens the important composition that he just studied and learned by heart—either a large fugue of Sebastian Bach or some old master, or a prelude, or a vast organ chorale by the great Leipzig *cantor*.[145]

Although almost totally consumed by work, Widor did eek out a little social life at the behest of his friend Alphonse Mailly (1833–1918), a piano and organ virtuoso who taught at the Brussels Conservatory:

Scarcely any time remained for me to relax. Only on Sundays, I joined up with a little club of musicians in a town brasserie. Mailly, a student of Lemmens, had introduced me to them. I met there the nursery of remarkable violinists who counted then in Brussels, notably Vieuxtemps, Léonard, Thomson, and the young Ysaÿe.[146]
  In Brussels I also knew de Bériot, who had married [García-]Malibran, whose sister, Mme Viardot[-García], inspired Camille Saint-Saëns [1835–1921]; also Peter Benoît, director of the Antwerp Conservatory (and who later came to perform his oratorio with organ and orchestra at the Trocadéro), a legendary individual who provoked the famous little quatrain that the students whispered when they saw him:

Peter Benoît a du genie   [Peter Benoît has genius,
À son chapeau cela se voit.   You can tell from his hat.
Et l'on respire l'harmonie   And you're breathing harmony
Quand on entend Peter Benoît.[147]   When you hear Peter Benoît.]

Widor's organ study with Lemmens culminated in a special recital:

On July 9, 1863, after a term of relentless study, before I left Brussels, Lemmens wanted me to give an organ recital at the Ducal Palace. He brought together about fifty musician friends and students that day "to prove to them what he had been able to obtain from a good student to whom his lessons had profited."

I was not at all nervous for this recital. I was perfectly familiar with the palace organ—a very beautiful instrument of Merklin[-Schütze]—on which, during the year, I had practiced several hours a day, a special favor accorded to me by the organ builder upon the intervention of Lemmens. Alexandre Guilmant had also obtained this honor two years before [Guilmant studied in Brussels three years earlier]. There still weren't any electric motors at that time, and I gave a little tip to the pumpers who instructed me not to indulge too much in the *tutti organi.*

I played with assurance that day, yet fully aware of the severity of my teacher.[148]

Widor left Brussels bursting with newborn confidence and ready to demonstrate the fruits of his concentrated months of study and practice (see fig. 6). Before returning to Lyon, where he would continue to share the duties of organist at Saint-François with his father,[149] he stopped in Paris to pay a visit to the man who had so rightly guided him—the man whom he would often refer to as "Père Cavaillé." The builder received him enthusiastically and, eager to show off what the gifted young musician had gained by study with Lemmens, arranged what likely was Widor's debut in the French capital. It had been only fifteen months since the inauguration of Cavaillé-Coll's masterpiece, the one-hundred-stop organ at the Church of Saint-Sulpice. What better place could he offer the young organist to demonstrate all he had learned from Lemmens! Quite prophetically, Cavaillé-Coll put Widor before the five keyboards of the *grand orgue* where he would spend his life's career.

Part Two

The First Creative Period (1864–79)

On pourait [*sic*] dire qu'il se conformait, sans y songer peut-être, à l'immortel principe du vieil Horace: *lucidus ordo.* Par une intuition lui révélant que les lois de l'art correspondent aux lois de l'esprit humain, il estimait que l'ordre, c'est-à-dire l'harmonieuse réalisation que nécessite une idée organisatrice, est véritablement une source de lumière.

It could be said that [Widor] conformed, perhaps without thinking of it, to the immortal principle of the aged Horace: *lucid order.* By an intuition revealing to him that the laws of art correspond to the laws of the human spirit, he assessed that order, that is to say the harmonious realization that an organizing idea necessitates, is truly a source of light.

—Adolphe Boschot
Notice sur la vie et les œuvres de M. Charles-Marie Widor

—12—

"The young artist made a good show of it"

The organ of Saint-Sulpice, completed in 1862, was the largest instrument ever built by Aristide Cavaillé-Coll; it had to have the sonic resources to command a space capable of holding ten thousand people—a space second in size only to the Cathedral of Notre-Dame. Having five manuals, one hundred speaking stops distributed over seven levels, and requiring several strong men to pump the bellows, it was a technical and tonal marvel.[1] The builder had expended over three times the amount of the contract to produce his magnum opus.[2]

Cavaillé-Coll was always deeply concerned—perhaps never more so than at Saint-Sulpice—that the most able and deserving organists play his instruments and gain appointments to important posts. Eager to hear Widor, fresh from instruction with Lemmens, Cavaillé-Coll offered his young friend an occasion to try out his newest and grandest instrument:

A gathering of artists took place Tuesday [July 28, 1863] at Saint-Sulpice to hear, on the *grand orgue* of Messrs. Cavaillé-Coll, a young organist, Mr. Ch. Widor of Lyon. This program consisted of seven pieces by different masters: Handel, Hesse, [J.] S. Bach, Lemmens. One especially took note of an Allegro by Handel, a Fanfare, a *Prière*, and a *Grand-chœur* Finale by Lemmens, perfectly adapted to the character of a large organ in a large church. Moreover, the young organist interpreted the works very well, and particularly those by Mr. Lemmens, of whom he is one of the best students.[3]

Widor honored his *maître* by his excellent playing and musicianship, and he gave Cavaillé-Coll ample reason to be proud of him. In a letter to Lemmens on August 3, 1863, the eminent builder expressed his sheer delight over the program:

> Your excellent pupil Ch. Widor spent a few days with me and reminded me of the fine days that we spent together at the time of your first trip to Paris. He spoke a lot about all the interest that you have shown in him and of the fine lessons that he has received from you. I had him perform for several artists in a small group at my place on an excellent small organ on which one distinguishes all the parts of the grand music well, and in a performance at Saint-Sulpice, the program of which I am sending to you.
>
> Performance of organ music given by Mr. Charles Widor of Lyon
> on the *Grand orgue* of Saint-Sulpice, Tuesday, July 28, 1863, at 2 o'clock.
> (The listeners were invited by "Messrs. A. Cavaillé, Coll and Co.")
>
> Order of performance:
>
> 1. Allegro (Handel).
> 2. Variations (Hesse).
> 3. Sonate (Andante) (Widor).
> 4. Fanfare (Lemmens).
> 5. Prière (Lemmens).
> 6. Concerto (Bach).
> 3.[*sic*] Final (Lemmens).

> Your *Fanfare* and your *Marche*, which I believed impossible at Saint-Sulpice because of the movement, are the clearest pieces and have produced the most effect. The young artist made a good show of it. I had invited the organists of Paris to Saint-Sulpice and, although a little jealous of your fame, they were obliged to confess that your music is well suited to the *grand orgue* and that your pupils would be able to give them some lessons.[4]

At the end of the eventful year, Charles-Marie wrote from Lyon to Joseph Merklin on December 29, 1863, to express abundant appreciation for the many kindnesses the Belgian organ builder had extended to him. Widor was fully cognizant that Merklin had made possible the life-changing opportunity of studying in Brussels with Lemmens and Fétis:

> I am writing to wish you, as well as all your good family, a happy new year, and at the same time to present to you my thanks for all that you have done for me during the year just passed. I was hoping that we would soon have the pleasure of seeing you in Lyon, and to express to you better than by letter how highly I regard you.
>
> I am taking advantage of this moment to remind you that you had promised me the address of an amateur to whom I am supposed to send a sonata manuscript.
>
> If you would be so good as to make it known to me, I will be very pleased. I also have an account to settle with Mr. Dubois, an account that I have still not been able to take care of, and that I would be very desirous to pay.
>
> I am certainly taking advantage of you, dear Sir, in [*illegible*: troubling?] you with all this, but if there is anything that emboldens me to ask it of you, it is my conviction that you will be good enough to use me in any way you need.[5]

In his last paragraph, saying "it is my conviction that you will be good enough to use me in any way you need," Widor seems to be inviting Merklin, indirectly at least, to think of him for organ inaugurations—really the only significant way Widor might have been of service to him. In truth, however, it was Cavaillé-Coll who was thinking of using Widor for that purpose. He was a charismatic, handsome young man with musical talent and technique to spare. "Although there was never any agreement between us," Widor later affirmed, "père Cavaillé-Coll, to whom I was more and more the thing [*la chose*], thought of me—as of Guilmant—for every inauguration of his instruments, but the latter less and less because of his age. So I inaugurated most of his organs."[6] This did not escape Merklin's attention, and his offended feelings simmered for a quarter century until they exploded in a letter of April 29, 1889, addressed to the parish council of the church of Notre-Dame du Saint Cordon in Valenciennes. In it, Merklin brought up the letters of Madame Widor (January 19, 1863) and Charles-Marie (December 29, 1863), substantiating all he had done for the young man twenty-six years earlier, and then concluded: "The day when Mr. Widor had finished his studies with Messrs. Lemmens and Fétis, the Cavaillé-Coll firm stole him over and knew how to turn him against us."[7]

But in 1863, with the youthful naiveté of a nineteen-year-old, Charles-Marie could hardly have been thinking of the virulent emotions that could erupt between different philosophical camps, competing organ builders, or of any other contentious affairs far into the future. For now, he had his whole life ahead of him and he was tooled up to make his mark. It did not matter from which direction the prospects came.

—13—

"This accomplished virtuoso is a very young man"

Unable to coax Lemmens to take a position in France, for the inaugurations of his instruments Cavaillé-Coll now turned to the two bright young talents whom he had encouraged—Lemmens's prize pupils, Guilmant and Widor. For Widor this meant increasing opportunity and public exposure; one such opportunity came his way at the beginning of the fresh new year:

> The new church of Sainte-Perpétue [Nîmes] just received a new organ from the establishment of A. Cavaillé-Coll, the inauguration of which took place last Saturday [January 9, 1864]. . . . One very much noticed the fine talent of . . . and Mr. Ch. Widor, from Lyon, a pupil of Fétis and Lemmens, who does the greatest honor to his *maîtres*. Mr. Widor first of all performed a Prelude and Fugue in E by [J.] S. Bach, then an improvisation on the foundation stops, and he finished with a superb Finale by Handel. This artist, this accomplished virtuoso is a very young man, almost a child.[8]

On March 8, 1865, Cavaillé-Coll wrote to Lemmens of Widor's continuing progress: "I spent eight days in Lyon with your pupil Widor who is working wonders at his organ and his piano. He will come to spend the month of April with us in Paris."[9] During the next few years, Widor traveled frequently to inaugurate new organs, and often found himself in the French capital. At the time of one such visit, he related:

> Lemmens was making himself heard from time to time in Paris. It was in the workshop of Cavaillé-Coll where Lemmens had come to play for him that I made the acquaintance of Meyerbeer. The latter took a lively interest in the dramatic effects that one could draw from the organ, as well as the technical details of the construction of the instrument. With Lemmens, I met Meyerbeer again in a hôtel du Rond-Point des Champs-Elysées, when there was a matter of engaging Mme Sherrington [Lemmens's wife] in *l'Africaine*.[10]

Widor rapidly made the acquaintance and attracted the encouragement of many prominent musicians in Paris. Camille Saint-Saëns, César Franck, Ambroise Thomas, and Gioacchino Rossini (1792–1868) all became attached to him.[11] In a charming reminiscence, Widor later related one remarkable evening he spent at Rossini's, along with the great French pianist Francis Planté (1839–1934) and the Russian superstar Anton Rubinstein (1829–94):

> I still see him [Planté], across my very youthful memories, dining with Rubinstein at Rossini's, in this great and beautiful house situated at the angle of

the boulevard and the Chausée-d'Antin. It was towards the end of May and the weather was superb; we were looking through the window to see if Rubinstein was arriving, for the half-hour just sounded, and the illustrious author of *Guillaume Tell*, who dined ordinarily at seven o'clock, didn't like to wait. At last, we saw him coming tranquilly on foot, inhaling deep breaths of the mild early summer air, and apparently not the least bit thinking he was late. We sat down at the table, and he drank and ate like a horse. The conversation was very animated. Rossini had infinite wit and no less good sense; Rubinstein knew many things beyond his art, and spoke very judiciously about what he knew. We discussed and even squabbled a bit—courteously and humorously, that goes without saying. I remember that an argument had begun about rhythm and Wagner [1813–83], who at the time was discussed and almost rejected. Rhythm "*saves all,*" said the *maître* of the house. A satiric newspaper had recently attributed to Rossini a ridiculous remark: upon listening to the piano score of *Lohengrin* he had exclaimed, addressing the accompanist, "You are mistaken, my friend, you are reading upside down; turn your score right side up, perhaps we will arrive at understanding what the author has meant!"

"Yes! Rhythm saves all," repeated Rossini; "Wagner is rhythmical; rhythm— it's the light!"

And a whole group of people revolted against the exaggerated benevolence of the *maître*, reproaching him for his exaggerated generosity with regard to a German who was insulting him every day or who was inciting others to do it.

In short, the dinner was very spirited, almost noisy.

Rubinstein, being very warm, was red. Planté didn't open his mouth; he tranquilly observed this brilliant exchange of arguments, scarcely eating, and drinking from time to time mouthfuls of pure water.

He knew that, after dinner, Rubinstein and he were supposed to play alternately before a handpicked audience curious about the encounter, and he was on his guard.

Rubinstein went to smoke some cigars, while consuming a half decanter of brandy. Planté remained in the salon, beside Madame Rossini, who talked to him about her abhorrence of people and the annoyance it caused her to have dinner guests once a week; she explained to him the gradual rise in the price of butter, and the difficulty of procuring unadulterated wine, a subject apparently not at all bothersome to the soul of a pianist.

The salon filled up little by little, and soon the crowd became compact— people were packed up to the stairway.

The concert commenced.

Rubinstein and Planté performed at two pianos the Preludes of Liszt, quite poorly—one has to admit—in ensemble and in steadiness, each seeming to doubt his partner, one in a hurry to arrive, one inclined to slow down.

Then, in the middle of a deep silence, the great, the colossal, the incomparable Rubinstein remained alone before the ivories.

It was stupefying!

Not one accurate note, a dreadful sonority, not a successful run, no more scales, no more octaves! After an Allegro of Beethoven, he attempted an

Andante of Mendelssohn, a Scherzo of Chopin, a Romance of his own composition. Nothing came out right!

He shrugged his shoulders, saying, "Let's go to bed!"

And arriving unexpectedly, Planté, smiling and calm, unstrung the pearls
of his jewel case before a charmed audience until long after midnight. He
didn't miss a note.[12]

Although at this point in time Widor placed a higher priority on organ
performance than composition, his versatility as both pianist and organist
afforded him many opportunities to perform and to present his own recent
compositions to the public:

We attended [May 1, 1865] at the Salle Pleyel [in Paris], an interesting performance of pedal-piano music, given by Mr. Charles-Marie Widor, organist
from Lyon. Independent of the classical works of [J.] S. Bach and Lemmens
that he played authoritatively, this young organist, scarcely twenty years old,
performed some of his own compositions, which were greatly appreciated.
Mr. Ch.-M. Widor possesses a marvelous execution as pedal-pianist and
augurs well as a future composer. This same artist has performed on a *grand
orgue* at Cavaillé-Coll's, where he was much applauded.[13]

As already mentioned, Widor later boasted that "Cavaillé-Coll made the habit
of taking me with him each time he had an organ to inaugurate, and I became,
as it were, his 'official inaugurator.'"[14] Although Guilmant might more deserv-
edly have claimed this title, Cavaillé-Coll favored Widor highly, and frequently
called upon him for inaugurations and also to test his instruments either before
they left his shop or when they were ready to be accepted by the church.[15] Out of
devotion to Cavaillé-Coll and the conviction that his instruments were superior,
Widor limited himself almost solely to performing on them.

He and others often performed in the large exhibition hall of Cavaillé-Coll's
shop. As pictured in *L'Illustration* in 1870, a large and distinguished-looking audience is about to hear the three-manual, forty-one stop organ destined for the residence of the London music publisher Mr. John Turner Hopwood in Bracewell,
England.[16] In the background of the illustration is another large instrument with
positif de dos, and partially visible at the left appears to be an *orgue de chœur*. Widor
and Saint-Saëns put the Hopwood instrument through its paces in a program in
March 1870, and Guilmant presented a program shortly thereafter.[17]

Widor understood Cavaillé-Coll's instruments perfectly and knew how to
draw from them the maximum effect. Through the years, those who heard
him felt they had been invited to a "king's feast."[18] After the inauguration
of the organ in the Hôtel-Dieu de Vitry-le-François—an instrument with
two expressive divisions—a priest was rapturous over the "ideal perfection"
Widor had attained:

When in an improvisation on a delightful theme he introduced all the stops one after the other, wonderfully shaded by the judicious use of the double expression—Oh! We felt ourselves in the presence of a musical manifestation of high understanding: the science and inspiration of the eminent builder calling to his aid the science and inspiration of the genius organist in order to pass into the soul of the audience a heavenly echo by a masterly performance of supreme distinction.[19]

—14—

"Mr. Widor and his English ladies"

Cavaillé-Coll's guidance bordered on being paternal from the beginning of Widor's career and continued over many years. The twenty-one-year-old virtuoso's appearance in Portugal for the first International Exposition of Porto afforded him many prospects—both artistic and social (see fig. 7).[20] Widor recounted:

In [September] 1865, the city of Porto opened an exposition for which a great concert hall was provided. An English builder [J. W. Walker] had been solicited for the construction of its organ. They asked Cavaillé-Coll if he had an organist available to stay four or five months in Porto to play the organ publicly in daily performances from noon to one o'clock and on Sundays and holidays in open performances. Cavaillé advised me to give way to the temptation offered by this opportunity, and I accepted, delighted to see some of the country and to live under such a sky. So, I played every day; soon I was happy to notice that a small group of enthusiasts, including a certain number of English ladies, came daily to listen to me with such assiduousness that I next felt a certain annoyance. I was obliged to vary my programs, so I invented some works, attributing them to such and such an author. I improvised, but confess here my embarrassment when by chance one of these works, having pleased one of my female listeners, was requested again by her a week later. Was my fraud ever discovered? I don't think so, but today I still feel sincere remorse for it.

My sojourn in Porto brought me another artistic benefit—that of hearing my music performed by an orchestra for the first time. For the end of the exposition, they asked me to compose a grand overture for orchestra and organ. I wrote a very plain work, according to my ability. Even though it was well received, I did justice to it some years later by destroying it. At the same time, I found in Porto, summoned by the exposition, an excellent flutist, Dupuis, an excellent Brazilian pianist, Arthur Napoléon [Napoleão dos Santos, 1843–1925] (former pupil of the Paris Conservatory, who has since died in Rio), and an accomplished cellist, Casella. I wrote for them a little Sérénade [later Op. 10?] that they premiered and that has been played right and left ever since.

My sojourn in Porto gave me a certain notoriety. Before my departure, the king paid me the honor of giving me the Portuguese decoration in the Order of Christ.[21]

The decoration proclaims Widor "Chevalier de l'Ordre du Christ" and was accorded on May 22, 1866, by Napoléon III in the name of Portuguese King Luís I (1838–89).[22] Concerning the Overture for Organ and Orchestra, one reviewer reported:

An orchestra of one hundred thirty musicians, directed by a distinguished artist, Mr. Arthur Napoléon, and reinforced by the magnificent organ built by Walker of London, has worthily opened this great national festival. We have heard on the organ a piece composed for the occasion and admirably performed by Mr. Vidor [*sic*], pupil of the celebrated Fétis.[23]

News of Widor's success in Porto traveled quickly; upon learning of his former pupil's activities, Lemmens proudly wrote to Cavaillé-Coll, "I see with pleasure that Widor has some success in Porto."[24] Almost simultaneously, Cavaillé-Coll sent a letter to Lemmens, alluding to more than Widor's musical popularity: "I received, a few days ago, a letter from your pupil Widor, who is the delight of the English society in Porto. He doesn't appear content with the Portuguese, although they pay him well. But he is mad about the English, especially the English ladies. As they say, in the country, *Mr. Widor and his English ladies.*"[25] To the end of his life, Lemmens enthusiastically followed the musical doings of his former pupil, sometimes inserting little queries about him in his letters to Cavaillé-Coll.[26]

In the company of Cavaillé-Coll and Guilmant, Widor made what was likely his first trip to England in early July 1866 for the inauguration of a new instrument, and he never forgot the occasion:[27] "Cavaillé-Coll took me to England to inaugurate the organ for the Carmelite Church in Kensington; [it's] a heartbreaking memory, for while I played, the Battle of Sadowa was lost."[28]

—15—

"I thought very favorably of Rossini"

As Widor's reputation expanded, he became increasingly visible in the circles of the musically elite. A longtime supporter of Cavaillé-Coll, the revered Gioacchino Rossini paid more than passing attention to his friend's instruments, and the press always noted Rossini's presence at an inaugural program. One such occasion took place on February 1, 1866, when Widor performed in the music salon of the influential banker, Frédéric Émile Baron d'Erlanger (1832–1911).[29] Some seventy years later, Widor recalled his relationship with the d'Erlangers and his growing acquaintance with Rossini:

The baron d'Erlanger and his brother-in-law, the count of Saint-Roman, resided during the summer in Gouvieux, near Chantilly. The musical gatherings of the rue Taitbout [d'Erlanger's Paris townhouse] found themselves transported to Gouvieux in the summer. I went every week and it is there that I had the occasion to compose some Italian songs [*Trois mélodies italiennes*, Op. 35] for a charming Greek, Marie Caradja, whose father had been the Greek ambassador to Paris. She had an admirable mezzo-soprano voice. The first reading (for she was a very good musician) took place outdoors after dinner.

Convalescing recently [1935] in Chantilly, I passed one day in front of the property of the d'Erlangers, and was sad to see on the gate a notice announcing its sale.

It was through Cavaillé-Coll that I made the acquaintance of the baron Émile d'Erlanger when I was still quite a young student. Cavaillé had constructed an organ in 1861 for the music salon of the banker/music lover, whose townhouse was located at 20 rue Taitbout, where the boulevard Haussmann cuts through today. Well, some twenty-five or thirty years later, the music salon and its organ were removed from the townhouse and installed at 76 avenue Kléber.

One day, Cavaillé-Coll took me off to rue Taitbout to play an organ piece for Rossini that he [Rossini] had just written, but for which he had not determined the registration, considering his inexperience as an organist. The assignment fulfilled, Cavaillé asked him to give me a lesson, really *to rebuke me*, for an "attempt" [*essai*], the spirit of which he judged very alarming for the future. After having listened to it, Rossini said, "It's not bad, the piece has rhythm and purpose, that's a lot." I thought very favorably of Rossini.[30]

Another great musician with whom Widor had early contact was the legendary pianist, conductor, and composer Franz Liszt (1811–86), who traveled to Paris when his mother died there in 1866. Lefébure-Wély demonstrated the Saint-Sulpice organ for him,[31] and César Franck gave a special concert in his honor at Sainte-Clotilde on April 13. The press especially noted that Widor, Alexis Chauvet (1837–71), and Théodore Dubois (1837–1924) were among the select gathering of auditors.[32] Widor later recalled, "[Liszt] admired the good César Franck. I still see Liszt at Sainte-Clotilde, listening to the *Six grandes pièces d'orgue* by the future author of the *Béatitudes*, *Rédemption*, Symphony in D Minor, and Sonata for Piano and Violin, congratulating and thanking him."[33]

—16—

First works: "Those Duos never brought me two cents"

In addition to his expanding career as a performer, this period witnessed the first real fruits of Widor's budding compositional talent. The compilation of Widor's complete opus listing is somewhat problematic; nonetheless, Opuses 1 through 9 can be determined to date from the middle and late 1860s. With the exception of the Op. 3 Six Duos for Piano and Harmonium, the Op. 7 Piano Quintet, and the enigmatic Opus 8, the other pieces from this half-decade are for solo piano.[34]

Marcel Dupré related that Widor also composed a piano concerto at the tender age of thirteen; but this may be a chronological mistake.[35] It seems more reasonable that this concerto was the one premiered in Lyon in May 1867. If so, Widor likely composed it closer to that time—at about age twenty-three:

> This Concerto is truly a marvelous thing—the best unquestionably that Lyon has produced in a number of years. The style of this piece indicates a study and profound knowledge of the German masters, and its development recalls sometimes the manner of Mendelssohn, sometimes that of Schumann. We hasten to declare, moreover, that it discloses above all a characteristic individuality, particularly in its orchestration.[36]

As a whole, this early concerto did not survive. Dupré reported that Widor tore up all but the middle movement a few years later:[37] "Do people know that the delightful Andante from his Fourth Symphony for Organ . . . is nothing but a transcription of the slow movement from a Concerto for Piano and Orchestra that Ch.-M. Widor composed as quite a child for a charity concert and performed himself at the piano?"[38]

An advertisement for Widor's first published works appeared in *Le Ménestrel* in May 1867. Two works for piano—*Variations de concert sur un thème original*, and a Suite of "six pensées musicales" titled *Pages intimes*—were initially issued without opus numbers, though Widor's publisher J. Hamelle eventually assigned to them Opus 1 and Opus 2, respectively. Many years later, under Opus 29, Hamelle published *Variations sur un thème original*, which is a revised version of Opus 1. Assigning a new opus number to a revised work was highly unusual for Widor, as he normally reissued revised versions—sometimes several of them over a period of many years—under the original opus number; the organ symphonies are the most dramatic example of this practice.[39] Hugues Imbert (1842–1905) pointed out a failing that Widor often acknowledged: "As a composer, he conceives rapidly, distrusting, however, his facility and, as a rule, regretting having delivered to the publisher some pages which would have gained by being matured."[40] A *Pages intimes* also appeared much later, as Opus 48, but in this case it is a completely different work from the Opus 2 composition of the same title.

Reports concerning the musical events of the 1867 Universal Exposition in Paris filled the pages of weekly music journals; and it was often noted regretfully that the French capital lacked a grand concert-hall organ.[41] As early as 1850, Cavaillé-Coll had written to Fétis expressing the desire to see such an instrument in Paris:

What you seek for music in Belgium would be no less useful in France; a cathedral organ for use on public occasions, on which organists of all nations could play the works of the great masters that are not appropriate in church. This is done in Germany and England, and it would be a great asset to music in general, as well as a powerful stimulus for our young organists.[42]

Nonetheless, organists were provided with some opportunity during the exposition to perform on the popular harmonium, also called "orgue expressif," developed by Alexandre-François Debain (1809–77). Widor was among those chosen to play for the daily concerts, and for the occasion he composed a Suite of six Duos for piano and harmonium—likely inspired by Saint-Saëns's six Duos of 1858 for the same instruments.[43] Also, Cavaillé-Coll had recently completed an organ that remained in his workshop during the exposition. Often doubling as a concert hall, the "organ show room" was described by Widor:

> Cavaillé himself had constructed this firm at 15 avenue de Maine. . . . His home was next door. He lived there with his family—Madame Cavaillé and his children. Adjoining his home was a great hall, a model of good sonority—that is to say, a rectangular hall of perfect proportions. Cavaillé-Coll had placed his instruments everywhere and that permitted him to test the best acoustical conditions. He himself had made some experiments of which the principle is as follows: "Sound must be produced in rectilinear surfaces; curved surfaces generate echoes."[44]

Cavaillé-Coll entrusted the official presentations in his show room to Widor. It was perhaps there that a competition of some sort, in which several prominent organists participated, discerned Widor as "undisputed winner" [*unbestrittener Sieger*].[45]

> In 1867, my faithful protector (Cavaillé), who just set up a small organ of 18 stops—a real jewel—and next to which was situated an Érard piano, asked me to come on two different occasions to spend a month in Paris to give a daily concert. Little by little these programs became a real vogue. It's at this time that I wrote my first six Duos, and that I became a bit Parisian, acquiring, thanks to Cavaillé, a certain notoriety. In fact, at the same time, he had me play at the Louvre on Mondays, at the home of Mr. de Nieuwerkerke, superintendent of the Beaux-Arts, who lived above the passage Marengo. All the artists in Paris came there. I played my Duos with the pianist [Alexis-Henry] Fissot [1843–96]. The work made a great success and was much applauded. Unfortunately, those Duos never brought me two cents. I had them published by Prévot, who was the choirmaster of Saint-Sulpice; now, Prévot had no faith in me and I made a dupe's transaction. Several years later, I was quite astonished when, in the sale of a music business, the publisher Heugel told

me that he had just paid 17,000 francs for the ownership of these Duos. I was certainly flattered, but a little vexed not to have had a single penny from it.[46]

In addition to concert appearances in 1868, Widor saw the publication of his newest piano compositions. A reviewer especially recommended the two Italian Suites for Piano, *La barque* and *Le cabriolet*, Op. 6, "to the devotees of good music."[47] The most substantial composition Widor produced was the Quintet in D Minor, Op. 7, for Piano, Two Violins, Viola, and Cello: "In Lyon, between my engagement in Portugal and my nomination to Saint-Sulpice, I embarked on a work in classic style—a quintet for piano and string quartet—that I was so bold as to dedicate to Gounod, who was kind enough to accept the dedication."[48] For the Quintet's publication, Widor entered into an arrangement with Jacques Maho (1817–89), who became his publisher until Julien Hamelle (1836–1917) took over Maho's business as successor in 1877.[49] In all, works representing the first nine opus numbers were completed by the end of 1868.[50]

—17—

Organ inaugurations: Notre-Dame de Paris and La Trinité

Every inauguration of a new Cavaillé-Coll organ was a well-publicized event, attended not only by the most noteworthy musicians but also by the elite of French society. After some three decades in the organ-building profession, which included the construction of numerous uncontested masterpieces, Cavaillé-Coll was awarded the contract to build a monumental organ of eighty-six stops for perhaps the most famous cathedral in Europe—Notre-Dame de Paris. Upon completion of the instrument in 1868, the impending inauguration roused considerable excitement. Widor returned to Paris to participate. Officially, the prefect of the Rhône recommended that he be named one of the eight organists to play,[51] but Cavaillé-Coll surely influenced the decision. On the evening of March 6, 1868, Widor joined the august company of organists Clément Loret, Auguste Durand (1830–1909), Alexis Chauvet, Camille Saint-Saëns, César Franck, Alexandre Guilmant, and Eugène Sergent (1829–1900), *titulaire* at Notre-Dame, for the greatly anticipated event. Only Widor, the youngest of the group, presented an improvisation "on different stops of the organ."

Of the program, one critic concluded: "Among this avalanche of modern pieces, it is necessary to cite two of genuine merit that have obtained all the praises: the *Noël*, of Mr. Chauvet, and the *Marche* from the Exposition cantata, of Mr. Saint-Saëns."[52] It may seem surprising that Franck won no critical accolades, but the nascent version of his *Fantaisie* in C Major failed to satisfy the popular tastes of the audience. Perhaps Widor's youthful improvisation helped evoke the phrase "avalanche of modern pieces" from the critic's pen. Still, that

this young organist from Lyon, just turned twenty-four, was brought to participate in such a significant musical event indicates the reputation that he already
enjoyed, especially in the eyes of Cavaillé-Coll. Widor described the quality of
his performance in honestly blunt terms:

> In 1868, the solemn inauguration of the *grand orgue* of Notre-Dame in Paris
> took place. I confess that I was awful. I had wanted to compose a sensational
> piece for this occasion. At the last moment, I found it so devoid of interest
> that I naively yielded to an improvisation that seemed to me quite ordinary.
> This didn't discourage the builder, and the following Sunday, having asked
> me to come play the instrument again, he took me to Gounod, who encour-
> aged me, and from that time did not stop encouraging me.[53]

Charles Gounod was not the only person who encouraged the young organist. Shortly after the Notre-Dame inauguration, Franck assisted Widor in a joint
program of organ and piano music at Cavaillé-Coll's shop.[54] Saint-Saëns, too,
befriended Widor and performed some of his early piano music in concert.[55]

Still a resident of Lyon, Widor shuttled often to Paris and various other
engagements to inaugurate Cavaillé-Coll's latest instruments. He garnered
favorable press reports, such as the following, everywhere he went:

> The consecration and inauguration of the choir organ that the government just
> gave to the cathedral drew, last Thursday [May 26], the elite of Toulouse soci-
> ety. . . . Mr. Ch.-M. Widor, from Lyon, organist of the greatest talent, has played
> this magnificent instrument from the workshops of Mr. A. Cavaillé-Coll.[56]

In Paris for the impending inauguration of Cavaillé-Coll's splendid new
organ for the church of La Trinité, Widor attended the funeral Mass of Hector
Berlioz there on March 11, 1869. Five days later he joined organists Chauvet,
Fissot, Saint-Saëns, Durand, and Franck for the inauguration: "Mr. Ch.-M.
Widor, from Lyon, [performed] an Andante and a Scherzo where he displayed
a very great technical ability."[57] Lest there be the impression that this press
review simply glossed over the inauguration in a complimentary manner, the
same reviewer's comments on Saint-Saëns's solo dispels it: "a *Bénédiction nup-
tiale*, piece of little effect and few ideas."[58] Widor's account of the inauguration was less inclusive by not mentioning all the organists who performed, and
he did not recall that Franck had been *titulaire* at Sainte-Clotilde for nearly a
decade, but he distinctly remembered Franck's performance that day:

> The organ of La Trinité is one of the excellent instruments of père Cavaillé.
> It was inaugurated March 6 [*sic*], 1869 by César Franck and me. Franck was
> at that time choirmaster at Sainte-Clotilde, where he was later to become *titu-
> laire* of the *grand orgue*, passing the baton to Théodore Dubois. The day of the

inauguration, [Franck] improvised an exposition of an admirable bearing, style, and proportions, and which made a great impression on the public. When I came down from the organ, the baron d'Erlanger was won over: "It was charming, charming, the improvisation of Mr. Franck," he told me.[59]

A week after the Trinité inauguration, at the concert salons of Pleyel, Wolff, and Company, Widor presented a concert of his new works, featuring his Quintet, Op. 7, and an *Allegro de concert pour deux pianos*, with Saint-Saëns playing the second piano.[60]

—18—

Saint-Sulpice: "It's a great organ without an organist"

The early organists of Saint-Sulpice included some fine musicians: Guillaume-Gabriel Nivers (1632–1714); Louis-Nicolas Clérambault; and Nicolas Séjan (1745–1819), who garnered the praise of Fétis as "the only organist of talent in Paris" in the second half of the eighteenth-century.[61] Some of their successors, however, were not viewed as having such sterling reputations. Louis-Nicolas Séjan (1786–1849), son of Nicolas, succeeded his father at Saint-Sulpice, but was assessed only as "among the best of second-rank organists in the historic gallery of French organists."[62]

Upon the death of Louis-Nicolas Séjan, German immigrant Georges-Gérard Schmitt (1821–1900) won the position at Saint-Sulpice, and held it until 1863, the year following the completion of Cavaillé-Coll's major rebuilding of the original Clicquot organ. In a letter to Lemmens of October 1, 1862, Cavaillé-Coll bemoaned the prevailing unhappy situation: "We have had, these holidays, the visit of a great number of French and foreign organists to Saint-Sulpice. Unfortunately, as you had foreseen it, it's a great organ without an organist; the *titulaire* shows himself little worthy of such an instrument."[63] And writing to Fétis of the perfection and completeness of the instrument, Cavaillé-Coll complained once again: "but the organist does not yet exist, it is a mechanic who holds the post of a musician."[64] At a time when Bach's organ works were beginning to be admired in France—especially as performed by Lemmens—a few lines written by Schmitt himself are telling:

We believe it impossible to find in the work of J. S. Bach more than some twenty pieces capable of being heard with pleasure by today's worshippers: the form is obscure and incomprehensible, except to the musicians who are able to follow its development. There are only a few fanatics who could persist in seeing the final word of art in some compositions that, in spite of their scientific value, are condemned to the dust of libraries.[65]

Cavaillé-Coll loved each of his instruments like one of his children; he often surpassed parish budgets, making personal financial sacrifices if he felt it necessary to make an instrument more perfect and complete. Church councils consulted with him on the choice of an organist and, naturally, he wanted the organist to be one "whose technique and musical temperament was best adapted, according to him, to the character of each instrument."[66] Without Cavaillé-Coll's support, the mediocre Georges Schmitt was destined not to preside very long over the magnificent new instrument at Saint-Sulpice. Watching his masterpiece underutilized, Cavaillé-Coll sought to entice Lemmens to take the position. Even Adolph Hesse had not impressed Cavaillé-Coll as an organist up to the task of playing such an instrument. After Hesse's visit to Paris, Cavaillé-Coll expressed his opinion of the German master in his letter to Lemmens of October 1, 1862, and at the same time pointedly reminded Lemmens that he had promised to try out the new Saint-Sulpice organ:

> The famous Hesse from Breslau came to see our organ; I believe he found it too large and preferred to be heard at Sainte-Clotilde. There is still not a real modern organist there. And you, when are you coming to try out our organ? You told me that you would come to play your new works on our new organ and I am waiting for the fulfillment of your promise.[67]

Writing again to Lemmens on January 30, 1863, Cavaillé-Coll complained, "the titular organist of Saint-Sulpice [Schmitt] is becoming more and more impossible," and he effusively flattered Lemmens by telling him he had even suggested to Fétis, "that his worthy pupil, Mr. Lemmens, would be in his place before the five manuals, that he's the hyphen between the old art and the new art, and that it's regrettable we do not have an equal organist in France."[68] Even with such wholehearted approval and obvious encouragement from Cavaillé-Coll, Lemmens turned away from the possibility of becoming the *titulaire*, as he had other commitments to fulfill. Cavaillé-Coll was devastated; in a lengthy letter to Lemmens on April 5, 1863, he expressed his supreme disappointment, writing in part: "I will not hide from you that I had for one moment dreamed of the possibility of seeing you in that position. . . . This dream is upset for the moment, but I do not give up hope to see you one day at one of our great instruments."[69]

While Cavaillé-Coll ranked Lemmens as "the most learned and skillful organist of our time," Lefébure-Wély had won his praise as "the organist best acquainted with the resources of our instruments."[70] Unable to lure Lemmens to Saint-Sulpice, Cavaillé-Coll immediately cast his eye toward Lefébure-Wély. He saw no other choice. Something had to be done about Schmitt, and soon. With the support of the organ builder, the curé, and other influential members of the church's clergy, Lefébure-Wély was suddenly appointed to replace Schmitt, to begin on May 1, 1863.[71] Cavaillé-Coll and Lefébure-Wély had been longtime friends, and after this new appointment, the builder "didn't miss a Sunday to climb to the tribune in order to better enjoy the playing of this incomparable improviser. Lefébure became aware, nonetheless, that the ideas of his friend on organ music had evolved; he joked with him about it, [but] not without a little bitterness."[72]

Lefébure-Wély's reputation classed him as the most popular French organist of the period—a reputation bequeathed to him by a public emotionally swayed by a clever improviser. Saint-Saëns had succeeded Lefébure-Wély at La Madeleine, but refused to continue in the popular style of his predecessor.[73] When one of the parish vicars cautioned Saint-Saëns that "the parishioners of the Madeleine are for the most part persons of wealth, who frequently go to the theater of the Opéra-Comique, where they have become accustomed to a style of music to which you are expected to conform," the independent Saint-Saëns retorted, "Monsieur l'abbé, whenever I shall hear the dialogue of the Opéra-Comique spoken in the pulpit, I will play music appropriate to it; until then I shall continue as hitherto."[74]

Official attitudes at Saint-Sulpice differed quite a lot from those of La Madeleine, and Lefébure-Wély soon found himself under fire for the lack of religious character in his music. Though his ebullient style did not usually knit well to conservative contrapuntal forms, on a page in his notebook dated May 1865, he wrote: "I have improvised an interminable Fugue for them today; I hope very much that they will no longer say that I only know how to play some polkas!"[75] The promise of his artistic contribution to Saint-Sulpice slowly turned sour. It seemed only a matter of time before his tenure would come to an end, but no one could have predicted how unexpected it would be.

—19—

"Mr. Cavaillé seems wonderfully disposed toward Charles"

During the late 1860s, it must have become evident to Widor that residency in the French capital was necessary to his career. The date of his move from Lyon remains uncertain, though some sources have suggested that in order to become Saint-Saëns's assistant at La Madeleine it was as early as 1867.[76] That Widor ever held such a title is not confirmed by primary sources, and every press review, inclusive of the inaugural concert at La Trinité in March 1869, repeatedly referred to Widor as "from Lyon" or "organist in Lyon." Although he certainly spent increasingly more time in Paris, it appears that he did not move there until mid-1869. As to his possible appointment as Saint-Saëns's assistant, the following evidence must be weighed: La Madeleine ranked as the most fashionable and socially elite of Paris churches;[77] changes in its music staff were immediately newsworthy and no reports have surfaced that Widor had the title of "suppléant"; Widor never advertised himself as Saint-Saëns's assistant—a title any young organist would have coveted. If any such arrangement existed, it must have been an informal one. What is not in question, however, is that Widor did substitute for Saint-Saëns from time to time.

Widor's younger brother, Paul, had joined the mounted guard and his company was stationed in Paris. Letters from Paul to his sister, Marie, suggest that Charles was frequently in and out of the city. The following excerpts carry fascinating news pertaining to Lefébure-Wély, Cavaillé-Coll, Saint-Sulpice, and Charles:[78]

> June 29, 1868: Lefébure, whom I saw . . . was delightful and eagerly asked news of Charles and of father.
> May 19, 1869: I just learned some news that should interest Charles. Lefébure-Wély is very ill. He has a lung disorder and is considered a dying man. He no longer has the strength to play the organ, is continually asking for a substitute, and when he plays, as on Sunday, for example, it's pitiful. People are already in a flurry to ask for his job; I believe it's good to keep an eye on it. Moreover, Mr. Cavaillé seems wonderfully disposed toward Charles at this time, especially since receiving a letter from Lemmens, who, speaking of Charles's most recent compositions, says that he's the best French musician today.
> June 20, 1869: Last Sunday, I made my debut in the choir of Saint-Sulpice; I sang throughout the service, sight-reading; it went very well. This morning I sang a very beautiful Motet of Mozart, and played the organ during part of the Mass. I am now very well acquainted with Abbé de la Fouillouse, whom I have seen several times at his home. I have spoken to him highly of Charles; from this side all goes very well.
> Sunday evening I had dinner at Mr. Cavaillé's home with the Guilmants, father and son, and Abbé Lamazou.[79] We spoke a great deal about Charles. Guilmant played for us all that he remembered of his [Charles's] works. In this regard, he asks me to thank Charles for having promised to have copied for him his Chasse or Fanfare that begins like, or nearly like, this: [Paul then wrote out the first sixteen notes of what became the Scherzo of the Second Symphony]. Guilmant has a very great desire for it and says to send it to him in exchange for a volume of his organ works. . . .
> Don't tell this to anyone—Mr. Cavaillé has a plan in his head that, if it succeeds, would open almost at once a wonderful organist position that he is reserving for Charles. You can imagine if I'm pushing him to carry out his plan. I'll speak to you about it again in a few days. Everything is still too much in uncertainty. . . . P. W.

Unfortunately, if Paul wrote again in a few days, the letter does not survive. Nonetheless, it is not difficult to understand what Cavaillé-Coll was planning for Charles. The unfolding of events came to a head on New Year's Eve, 1869, when just before the stroke of midnight Lefébure-Wély died. Having recently returned to Paris after inaugurating a new Cavaillé-Coll organ with Alexis

Chauvet,[80] Widor was filling in at La Madeleine in Saint-Saëns's absence.[81] One particular service remained permanently ingrained in his memory:

> Liszt asked Saint-Saëns to come and direct the rehearsals of *Samson et Dalila* in Weimar, where he was the grand master of music; consequently, Saint-Saëns asked me to substitute for him at La Madeleine. It was during the week of Christmas 1869. Naturally, I was quite young and previously happy to fill in for my illustrious friend at the console of his beautiful instrument. One evening, as they were singing *Adeste fideles*, one of the singers whispered to me, "Lefébure, organist of Saint-Sulpice, just died; the post is vacant." A great emotion came over me, considering Cavaillé desired me at Saint-Sulpice. I was soon to feel the hostility of numerous Paris organists—a hostility directed against a newcomer whom some wanted to appoint to one of the finest posts, to make *titulaire* of the most beautiful and largest organ in France and in Europe at that time. The celebrated German organist Hesse, who had had the occasion to play it, said that it was the most complete and most perfect in the world. A real cabal was thus directed against me—a cabal in which Cavaillé-Coll, Saint-Saëns, and Gounod refused to take part.
>
> I will never know how to voice sufficiently my gratitude for the devotedness of the one whom I called "père Cavaillé." From morning to evening, he tirelessly took me on visits, from some politician's place to some clergyman's, from some scholar's place to some artist's: Foucault, le baron Thénard, Lissajous—who was then teaching physics at the Collège de France—etc., etc.; weren't they surprised to see us drop in like that![82]

In relating this story, Widor incorrectly identified the circumstances that called Saint-Saëns away from Paris; *Samson et Dalila* was not produced until 1877. In actuality, Saint-Saëns was in Weimar on New Year's Day 1870 "playing Liszt's *Hungarian Fantasy* to the composer's great satisfaction."[83]

Dupré related the incident as he heard it from Widor:

> "One day," Widor recounted to me, "Mr. Cavaillé-Coll being seated near me [in the organ gallery of La Madeleine], the chanter said to us upon arriving: 'I have some sad news to tell you: the organist of Saint-Sulpice, Mr. Lefébure-Wély, is dead.'"
>
> "The first moment of stupor passed; Mr. Cavaillé-Coll looked at me and uttered these simple words: 'I'm just thinking.'"[84]

—20—

"Mr. Charles Widor is provisionally charged"

Even after he had created the brilliant tonal palette of the Notre-Dame organ, Cavaillé-Coll always held a special love for his Saint-Sulpice "enfant."[85] Unable to tolerate the unimaginative improvisations and dull handling of the Notre-Dame organ by its *titulaire*, Eugène Sergent, Cavaillé-Coll was determined to place an organist at Saint-Sulpice who could utilize his magnificent instrument to its best advantage. Upon the death of Lefébure-Wély, it was time to act decisively. The builder saw enormous potential in the twenty-five-year-old Widor, whom he had been shepherding since childhood for an illustrious career (see fig. 8). And now the perfect position was available.

Tucked away on the left bank of Paris, the Church of Saint-Sulpice has little of the prominence of Notre-Dame Cathedral and is scarcely noticed by the casual visitor; nonetheless, it has an impressive history: "One may say that Paris has two cathedrals equaling each other in dimensions and spiritual influence but opposing each other in the conception of their styles and in the fashion in which they touch the artistic sensitivity and sense of fervor of the faithful."[86] As organist at Saint-Sulpice, Widor would be in a position to set the new standard of organ playing in France that Cavaillé-Coll found so needful.

Paul Widor's letters to Marie once again evidence the excitement and anxiety generated by the pending appointment of a new organist:

Paris, January 3, 1870

Very dear sister,

You have learned by telegraph the news of the death of Lefébure. His funeral was held this morning at Saint-Sulpice. Mr. Cavaillé, Charles, myself, and all our friends are not losing a minute, and everything seems well on the way to a happy resolution. Naturally, it is improbable that Charles will come back to Lyon this week; nevertheless, I don't believe that the position will be vacant very long. I will keep you up to date during our negotiations. Try to receive my little notes directly in order to prepare father and mother for whatever resolution is attained.

Up to now, our situation is the best; what I fear most and what Mr. Cavaillé wants to avoid is a competition and a reduction in the salary. We hope to avoid both.

Abbé de la Fouilouse just told me to be at his house this evening at six o'clock. He told me that it's important.

In sum, don't worry too much; I'll keep you up to date on all that is happening.

Poor Lefébure died almost immediately upon coming back from a walk. We learned of his death at La Madeleine, at the moment when Charles was beginning his New Year's Day Mass; he played wonderfully. That evening we met and he came to my place, where we chatted more than two hours about our little matter. After that, we had dinner at Mr. Cavaillé's house and, during dinner, a letter from you to Miss Cécile [Cavaillé-Coll's daughter and Marie Widor were good friends] was brought in, which seemed to bring her the greatest joy. Charles prevented her from reading it to everyone.

I just received a box of bonbons. It is welcome, all the more since at five o'clock this evening there is a meeting in my room [with] . . . Charles and perhaps Mr. Cavaillé. . . .

Goodbye, best to everybody, perhaps I'll write to you tomorrow if there is any news. P. W.

Paris, (Tuesday), January 12, 1870 [Tuesday was actually the 11th]

My dear sister,

Would you believe that the official nomination is still not signed, and after what the curé sent word of through Mr. de Monclar? Yesterday, seeing Charles in anxiety, I went to Saint-Sulpice and there I found the curé. He told me that a recalcitrant church warden, who had stopped being opposed [to the appointment of Charles] after the letter from Gounod, had begun to hesitate again and to ask for a competition and, at the same time, to ask that the appointee be [Antoine-Louis] Dessane, one of the candidates and the choir organist who is playing the organ next Sunday, for the Feast of the Patron of Saint-Sulpice.

It's absurd. The curé has put the decision off until Thursday at two o'clock, and it is probable that, annoyed by these delays, he will make a definitive decision then. As for the curé, he is completely in our favor. And I hope that in spite of this lateness, Charles will be able to make his debut Sunday.

Goodbye, I wanted to inform you of this delay. . . . P. W.

[P. S.] In any case, there is no need to have any fears.[87]

In the midst of the flurry of negotiations that were certainly taking place, an unforeseen hitch in Cavaillé-Coll's plan suddenly arose: César Franck posed his name for the position. "Bound to Franck by a friendship of twenty years, a profound admirer and defender of his genius—then so unrecognized—Cavaillé opted, nonetheless, for Widor."[88] Widor's musical and technical prowess had already been well proven to his unflagging mentor. Franck's skill as a performer, on the other hand, was largely confined to that of a most gifted improviser:[89] "Those who heard him say that his virtuosity was limited. It doesn't matter, since he knew it himself, saying, when he played his own music: 'I play it badly, but you will understand me all the same.'"[90] In Cavaillé-Coll's mind, Widor was the closest he could come to Lemmens.

At the earliest opportunity, the builder presented Widor directly to Abbé Hamon, the curé of Saint-Sulpice, who would make the appointment.[91] Both Gounod and Saint-Saëns were summoned by the churchwardens to arbitrate in the decision,[92] and after a meeting of the Vestry Council of Saint-Sulpice on Thursday, January 13, 1870, the question was quickly settled in favor of the young organist from Lyon. The minutes of the council's meeting indicate very clearly the careful thought that was given to the appointment. In a letter to the council, one of the vestrymen argued strongly on behalf of Widor without ever mentioning his name:

> Mr. Eugène Cauchy [a member of the vestry] gives a reading to the committee, as he has been willing to prepare on the subject of the organist's functions at Saint-Sulpice, the position having become vacant upon the death of Mr. Lefébure-Wély [deceased December 31, 1869].

Sirs:

The recent premature death of the eminent artist to whom the vestry had entrusted in 1863 the care of making the most of all the resources of the *grand orgue* of Saint-Sulpice, an instrument which by its restoration became one of the finest instruments in the world, leaves you faced with a great sorrow and a difficult choice to make.

The nomination of Mr. Lefébure-Wély to this post, so worthy of exciting the ambition of the most distinguished talents, had won the complete concurrence of the musical world; the superiority that seemed attached to this name, either as organist or as composer, was not, it appears, contested by anyone.

Therefore, the replacement with which you are concerned merits the most serious attention, by reason of both the status that this *grand orgue* holds in the opinion of experts and the justly renowned reputation that the playing of the great artist [Lefébure-Wély] just added to this magnificent instrument.

And one must not be astonished if in the number of candidates who are presenting themselves is found several artists having, in their favor, titles of such importance that they can keep your settlement in suspense.

To enter here into a comparative discussion of the titles, considered from the point of view of the record of each candidate and from the honorable testimonies that each puts forth, it would be necessary to deal in depth with questions of personality—questions as delicate to handle as perplexing to resolve—and with the merits of diverse natures, several of which can counterbalance each other in the minds of the most competent judges.

But above all consideration of personalities is a higher ground that seems able to serve as the basis for your decision: and that is the interest of musical art considered by itself and in its application to the parish worship services.

In order to show the best possible side of an instrument as powerful in its effect as it is varied in its resources, it seems to me that this "interest" will lead you to choose a talent who would join a rich imagination with profound knowledge, a mind as accustomed to the theory of composition as to the difficulties of its practice, a hand as young and strictly trained as it is early inclined to the solemn paces of the religious music in our churches. If there was still something lacking in this generous nature—in order to fulfill all that it promised—if it was needing to mature its precocious experience and to perfect its brilliant qualities by study, why wouldn't a trial period be given to him that would allow him to prove himself in the most vast theater before being judged worthy, if need be, to take a place among the masters of the science and to sit with them in the first row.

After this statement, the recorder places in front of the vestry members the demands addressed to the curé by the various competitors for the position of organist of the *grand orgue*, and reviews the pieces *brought forth* in support of each one of them.

The vestry, after having deliberated about it, decreed the following:

Article 1: It is deferred until the month of January 1871 to rule on the definitive replacement of Mr. Lefébure-Wély as organist of the *grand orgue* of Saint-Sulpice.
Article 2: Mr. Charles Widor is provisionally charged to take over this organ during the course of the year 1870.
Article 3: The matter of the salary to be paid for this temporary function will be submitted to the vestry council.[93]

—21—

"The organists of Paris were not pleased"

Not only did the decision deliver a blow to Franck, who had participated in the organ's inauguration in 1862, it caused a small flurry of protest among Parisian organists who were already upset that Widor substituted for Saint-Saëns at La Madeleine.[94] Widor later recounted, "père Cavaillé 'pushed' me. The organists of Paris were not pleased."[95] A letter of disapproval with several signatures was delivered to Abbé Hamon, who quickly called Cavaillé-Coll: "Looking over the signatures, the latter remarked that not one single name was that of an important organist. 'I noticed that myself,' said the pastor, and he sent for Widor."[96] Upon arriving, the good abbé welcomed him with these words: "I am taking you on trial for one year and will let you know next January 1 if I can make you *titulaire*."[97] Widor described the situation:

The curé of Saint-Sulpice, Abbé Hamon, was a man of great distinction. Unfortunately, he knew nothing about music. In the presence of his organ builder, he was naturally very impressed; not enough, however, to completely commit himself. Thence my *provisional* nomination on January 13, 1870, which was never made official—and I make note of it today [ca. 1935].

However, a few days later, on [Sunday] January 16, I took over the organ on the occasion of the patronal feast.

At that time, Père Cavaillé made it a point of honor to show me under my different aspects: as pianist, as composer, and as organist.

I was an excellent pianist, having been well trained under the direction of the conductor of the Grand Théâtre of Lyon, [Giuseppe] Luigini [1820–98], who gave a concert every year for his own benefit. He paid me the great honor of putting on the program the piano concerto that I had just composed; it achieved a great success. [The concert took place in late April 1867.]

All these events were to cooperate in establishing me at Saint-Sulpice, where I would have had free scope without a vicar who persisted in wanting me to play little frills.[98]

At its next meeting, on January 24, the Vestry Council again took up the subject of Widor's appointment, reconfirming its decision and then fixing his salary at twenty-five hundred francs for the year 1870.[99] It is noteworthy that Lefébure-Wély's salary had been set at three thousand francs per year beginning January 1, 1864.[100] The salary reduction given Widor, which Cavaillé-Coll had hoped to see avoided, would not be the last in the coming few years.[101]

Newspaper notices, usually profuse in their announcements of such important appointments, were brief:

Abbé Hamon, the venerable curé of St.-Sulpice, has just called Mr. Ch.-M. Widor to occupy the post of organist of the *grand orgue*, left vacant by the death of Mr. Lefébure-Wély. The new organist takes possession of this great instrument today, Sunday [January 16, 1870], feast day of the parish patron.[102]

La Revue et Gazette Musicale de Paris made an even shorter announcement.[103] No biographical sketches of the newcomer's accomplishments figure in the notices. By the summer, however, Widor was able to write to his mother: "At Saint-Sulpice, I think they will give me some vacation, for *everyone* is very much for me now."[104]

The following New Year's Day, Widor went to Abbé Hamon to offer his best wishes for the New Year; but he did not dare pose any questions as to his temporary status. Apparently, the Abbé was pleased with Widor's services and had either completely forgotten or chosen to ignore the conditional nomination, as he made no allusion to it.[105] In the young organist, Cavaillé-Coll's monumental instrument finally found a worthy master. Widor became the ninth organist of Saint-Sulpice, and when he retired on the last Sunday (December 31) of 1933, he delighted in having been "provisional organist for sixty-four years!"[106] Though his appointment certainly fulfilled the tradition that most organ positions were held for life if all the requirements by the church administration were met successfully, he had never been made the official *titulaire*.

Through two truly providential initiatives (sending Widor to Brussels in 1863 and nominating him for the post of organist at Saint-Sulpice in 1870), Cavaillé-Coll proved to be an affectionate, faithful, and even clairvoyant guide, decisively fashioning Widor's career.[107] Widor spoke often of their close relationship and how important it was to his early days in Paris:

> Although there was never any agreement between us, père Cavaillé-Coll, to whom I was more and more the thing, thought of me—as of Guilmant—for every inauguration of his instruments, but the latter less and less because of his age.[108] So I inaugurated most of his organs; in that period I inaugurated the organs at Calais, Trouville, and Bon-Secours [Rouen]. Between times, in order to make an impression on the Parisian musical public, his organ showroom on the Avenue du Maine became for me a concert hall nearly every two weeks. All the Parisian music enthusiasts and intellectuals interested in the arts frequented there. Not only the organ was played; Érard had sent over one of his most beautiful instruments. There was at that time a remarkable violinist, White, and a cellist no less excellent by the name of [Jules] Lasserre [1838–1906]. It's there that I made the acquaintance of most of the great Parisian artists: [Élie Miriam] Delaborde [1839–1913], who was head of the [piano] school at the Conservatory; [Claude-Paul] Taffanel [1844–1908], the eminent flutist who became the conductor at the Opéra; [Ernesto Camillo] Sivori [1815–94], who was the pupil of Paganini. Naturally, all the churchwardens of Saint-Sulpice were invited with their families.
>
> I specially composed several little pieces with organ, of which I have saved some, but carefully destroyed some others.
>
> In short, I made a kind of name for myself before the public that counted in Paris, thanks to these evening programs.[109]

—22—

8 rue Garancière: "One lives as two hundred years ago"

In the early months of 1870 Widor took up residency at 8 rue Garancière, a stone's throw from Saint-Sulpice, and he would remain there until October 1892. The old Hôtel de Sourdéac had been built in 1646 by the Marquis de Sourdéac, and it had witnessed the comings and goings of generations of high society that passed through its portico, perhaps to attend a performance in the small theatre the Marquis had installed within its walls. The exterior retained its original appearance; pilasters topped by capitals in the form of rams' heads seemed "to watch over the street and guard the house."[110] Telltale remnants of past times were the stone blocks on either side of the portico that permitted the elegant ladies of an earlier period to mount their horses without the help of a valet. Upon entering the large courtyard, plantings and centuries old trees gave the illusion of a small park. Widor loved the serenity of this old quarter: "One can read and philosophize comfortably while strolling down the tranquil streets between these old walls that tell you the stories of former times; no danger, no surprise to avoid, neither tramway nor omnibus; one lives as two hundred years ago, before the natural *andante* of humanity became an *agitato con moto.*"[111]

Widor's apartment occupied two floors: his study—which he called his "cellar" [*cave*]—on the ground level, and modest living quarters on the second floor.[112] The long rectangular-shaped study with a grand piano, Érard *pédalier*, work table, and three chairs immediately gave evidence of the cultured taste of its occupant; mementos and numerous art works that Widor had collected over the years greeted the eye: portraits of his literary and artistic friends; photographs of Charles Gounod, Paul Bourget (1852–1935), Guy de Maupassant (1850–93); engravings by Rembrandt; a portrait by Van Dyck; a sketch titled *Jésus sur la barque* by Eugène Delacroix (1798–1863); a charming etching by James Tissot (1836–1902) dedicated to Widor: "In remembrance of Sunday lunches and music before Vespers—June 1891"; a delightful watercolor by Henri-Joseph Harpignies (1819–1916); a pencil drawing of some horses by Henri-Alexandre Regnault (1843–71); a grouping of pretty heads in red chalk by François Boucher (1703–70); and perhaps most notable, the vibrant oil painting of Widor himself, painted in 1890 by Carolus Duran (1838–1917), the "French Velásquez."[113] On the grand piano proudly stood a plaster statue of Joan of Arc that sculptor Emmanuel Frémiet (1824–1910) offered to Widor after the performances of his grand pantomime *Jeanne d'Arc.* Widor was particularly fond of the painting of "a young miss, student of Carolus Duran, painted by herself" showing the subject wearing a gracious smile and pretty beret jauntily perched on her head.[114]

Hugues Imbert, music critic and founder of *L'Indépendance Musicale et Dramatique,* characterized the once-a-week gathering of friends that Widor hosted at his home: "A charming communion of ideas between all these artists, enamored by the divine muse! One listens in the silence to the entrancing utterance of the masters of the past and present; one lives in their intimacy. Chamber music, you lay bare the soul of those whom we love!"[115]

—23—

Franck: "The man who ran in order to save time"

As for Franck, he remained the *titulaire* at Sainte-Clotilde. Cécile and Emmanuel Cavaillé-Coll claimed that their father wanted him to have a professorship at the Paris Conservatory, and that through their father's discreet influence

Franck became organ professor there in 1872, upon Benoist's retirement.[116] In his memoirs, Théodore Dubois took credit for seeing Franck named organ professor,[117] a claim Widor confirmed: "It's Ambroise Thomas who, on the advice of Théodore Dubois in 1872, had the organ class of the Conservatory entrusted to César Franck."[118]

If Franck held any bitterness about being passed over for the Saint-Sulpice post, it did not last: "At first, Franck felt deeply distressed about it," wrote Cécile and Emmanuel Cavaillé-Coll, "but this great man did not stoop to holding grudges; he forgot his competitor and remained the friend of Cavaillé, whose frankness had affected him a bit harshly."[119] This good, kindhearted man was unable to harbor ill feelings toward Widor, who related that Franck often came to Saint-Sulpice to hear the organ:

> The Mass at Sainte-Clotilde was at 9:00 on Sunday mornings, and the Mass at Saint-Sulpice was at 10:30. Franck was known in the neighborhood, from the Institute to the Boulevard Saint-Michel, as the man who ran in order to save time. At the moment of the service, he crossed through Saint-Sulpice to shorten his route; he looked at the tribune and often noticed the velvet cap of père Cavaillé in the balcony of the organ. Sometimes he climbed the sixty-seven steps, other times he listened from below and then took off running again.[120]

Sometimes he waited to greet Widor after the service at the foot of the stairway.[121] Although Franck was a little more than twenty-one years Widor's senior, mutual respect was always maintained between the two musicians. Franck recognized Widor's innate abilities and superb training, and Widor admired Franck as "a very fine musician . . . a very good man, and very goodhearted."[122]

Imbued with classical principles of counterpoint and harmony, as well as an impeccable organ technique, Widor took over the reins of his new post with confidence and definite resolve:

> He aspires to nothing less than renewing the long-time broken chain of sound traditions; he wants to put in honor again the genius and work of J. S. Bach, a meritorious enterprise, since he has openly had to take issue with the perverted tastes of the public and the routine of too great a number of organists addicted to a genre unworthy of our sacred ceremonies.[123]

The judgment of Cavaillé-Coll, Gounod, and Saint-Saëns would prove to be sound. In just a few short years, Widor would justifiably render the post of organist of Saint-Sulpice as one of the most honored and prestigious in the world.

—24—

"We have the right to be proud of our musicians"

Continuing to appear as both organist and pianist, Widor took advantage of every opportunity to present his music to the public, which was not always an easy task. Works by German composers held such a monopoly on instrumental and vocal programs that French composers found it difficult to win the attention of conductors and other performers, especially within France. Saint-Saëns explained the only solution to the dilemma: "[Before 1871], a French composer, who had the audacity to risk himself on the terrain of instrumental music, had no other means of having his works performed than to give a concert himself, and to invite his friends and the critics to it."[124] This point was not wasted on Widor, who noted in one of his columns for *Estafette*:

> Isn't it sad today to see Mr. Delibes's work for the theater in Vienna and Mr. Saint-Saëns giving the premiere of his [*Samson et*] *Dalila* in Weimar? Regarding this, a foreign newspaper said: "A French premiere in Weimar, such is the curious phenomenon of which we were just witness. Very hospitable to foreign artists, the capital of the grand duchy of Saxony already took pleasure, and more than once, in making a formal reception to such a master, and to such a work that the Parisian public was hesitating to sanction."[125]

In several of his critical reviews, Widor showed himself to be an ardent nationalist when arguing for an "essentially national theater,"[126] and when writing such phrases as: "the glory of our modern French art";[127] "our beautiful country of France";[128] "the flag of our national art is . . . proudly carried [by Saint-Saëns]";[129] "it is necessary that French contemporary art have a serious outlet."[130] And he was equally proud of France's illustrious past; when writing an article about old French music, he evoked such names as de Vitry, de Muris, Dufay, Machaut, Binchois, Ockeghem, Jannequin, Gombert, and Josquin: "In reading their works, one is conscious that there existed at that time a strong and powerful school in our country."[131] "Since the Middle Ages we've had a French school; we still have it today and we have the right to be proud of our musicians, just as we are of our painters, sculptors, and architects."[132]

On the eve of World War II, Widor spoke movingly of his homeland: "Certainly, the hour is difficult, but haven't we gone through difficult hours, and haven't we learned never to despair? France counts on her sons. In the dark days of her history, leaders of men—statesmen and warriors—always came forward to sustain her in her traditions of order, discipline, devotion, and sacrifice that respond to her genius and that have made her greatness."[133]

Widor was among the early members of the Société Nationale de Musique, founded by Saint-Saëns in 1871 to promote the composition and performance of symphonic and chamber music by living French composers.[134] Even waving the *Ars gallica* flag, they had a difficult time getting others to perform their music. Saint-Saëns himself appeared several times on programs with Widor to assist in performances of his friend's music:[135]

> The performance of organ music, given last Sunday at Mr. Cavaillé-Coll's by Messrs. Camille Saint-Saëns and Ch.-M. Widor, was altogether remarkable. The two virtuosos worked wonders in turn on the *grand orgue* and on the piano. Perhaps never has the association of the two instruments been tried with more unity and good fortune, either in the interpretation of established works or in those of original composition.[136]

Twenty years after the founding of the Société Nationale, concert programs still lacked the diversity some had hoped for. *Le Ménestrel's* H. Barbedette observed:

> For many years we have followed the concerts called *popular* instituted by Pasdeloup, and continued by Lamoureux and Colonne. In the beginning, the variety of these concerts was very great. . . . Afterwards, the programs have been less varied; for three or four years, except for a few novelties, we have lived on nearly the same works. . . . Seeing the infatuation of a certain public with Wagnerian sauerkraut and its substitutes, a taste of conviction for some and of pose for others, [Lamoureux] has opened a large demand for this foodstuff from beyond the Rhine. We have the firm hope that people will grow weary of this nourishment, which is a bit heavy for our French stomachs, and turn back to new programs. It's not the material that will be lacking. . . . Let's not forget that the serious artists Saint-Saëns, [Benjamin] Godard [1849–95], [Édouard] Lalo [1823–92], and Widor have composed some remarkable symphonic works that are performed for us only every now and then, without granting them the attention they merit.[137]

—25—

"Yes, an exquisite pianist of the most limpid purity"

Publishing a work in a variety of arrangements afforded a composer increased opportunities for performance, and that added possibility was not lost on Widor. For example, although two of his early works had gained popularity in their original instrumentation—Six Duos for Piano and Harmonium, Op. 3; Sérénade in B-flat Major for Piano, Flute, Violin, Cello, and Harmonium, Op. 10—they soon appeared in multiple arrangements, some made by the composer and some by others.[138] As described earlier, Widor had taken an interest in the harmonium, and his Sérénade won a spot on the third concert of the Société Nationale's programs in 1871.[139] This work held a prominent position on his chamber music programs for some time. It eventually appeared in nine different arrangements, perhaps partially because some critics found its unusual quintet of instruments to be a strange marriage of sonorities,[140] but also because it allowed broader exposure for the work and its composer.

It was always important to Widor that he be part of the performing ensemble as either pianist or conductor. In his chamber works he usually performed the keyboard part himself, but for his piano concertos and orchestral works he preferred to be on the conductor's podium where he could best realize his intentions. Consequently, the inclusion of piano and organ (or harmonium) in Widor's music is hardly surprising, as he could then include himself as one of the performers. Examining his total oeuvre, with only a few exceptions, either the piano or organ is part of an ensemble, or the accompanying or solo instrument.

With a technical mastery and an artistic sensitivity quite at home on the piano, Widor often became his own best interpreter. "I recall the exquisite manner with which Widor played the piano," wrote Paul Landormy. "It was an enchantment: suppleness, lightness, easiness, and what sweet and penetrating sonority when it was necessary, and on occasion supremely brilliant!"[141] In a letter, French virtuoso pianist Francis Planté described Widor, "whom I like as much as I admire," as an organist, composer, conductor, and pianist: "yes, an exquisite pianist of the most limpid purity."[142]

Planté often performed Widor's piano works, and on one occasion the two men delighted an audience by playing together "with what mastery!" Bach's Concerto in C Minor, Franck's *Variations symphoniques*, and a work by Saint-Saëns—Widor taking the orchestral parts on a second piano.[143] Widor was a highly accomplished accompanist and enjoyed performing the works of his contemporaries in the spirit of helping them get their works heard.[144] He also joined other pianists in performances of works such as Schumann's Variations for Two Pianos (Op. 46?), one of Bach's Concertos for Three Pianos (BWV 1063 or 1064), Mozart's Concerto for Three Pianos (K. 242), and so forth.[145]

Widor had a thorough knowledge of the repertoire, and upon becoming organ professor of the Paris Conservatory he insisted that his students have more than a perfunctory acquaintance with masterworks in various genres. Vierne reported:

[Widor] initiated us into the different symphonic forms, beginning with Philipp Emanuel Bach, Haydn, Mozart, and Beethoven (on whom he laid much stress), Schubert, Mendelssohn, and Schumann, down to the modern symphonists. He sent to the library for scores, and two magnificent sight-readers, [Jules] Bouval [1867–1914] and [Henri] Libert [1869–1937], played through them on the piano. Then he would analyze them, comment on them, and urge us to make an effort to practice these forms. We were completely ignorant of it all. One day the maître exclaimed, "What! You've played the

Beethoven sonatas and never had the curiosity to wonder how they were constructed? Why, that's the mentality of a parrot, not of an artist. It must stop."[146]

As an organist who also counted as a pianist of the first order, Widor possessed a rare technical and intellectual grasp of the idiomatic characteristics of both instruments: "Mr. Widor . . . gave last week, in Rouen, a concert where he appeared, with well-founded success, as pianist and as composer. He has also given proof of a very great talent at the inauguration of the beautiful organ of the chapel of Bon-Secours."[147] However, standing nearly alone amidst hosts of made-over pianists-turned-organists, Widor was emphatic in demonstrating the clear distinction between the two instrumental techniques and aesthetics:

By his example, he showed that an organist is something other than a pianist gone astray, and that playing the organ is acquired only by a special and persistent labor, guided by some controlling principles of which the essential ones consist of: absolute *legato*, suppleness of touch, broad phrasing, and impeccable playing of the pedals.[148]

The following descriptions indicate the physical bearing and mental authority that Widor exhibited at the organ:

His supple and extensible hands, svelte and slender stature, made it easy for him to move his arms about the five manuals, and his feet about the pedal clavier and the combination pedals: Widor possessed in the highest degree the physical gifts of the organist.[149] He knew how to develop these gifts in all their fullness. He applied himself to overcome, as performer, all material obstacles—obstacles of which many, before him, did not even suspect the existence. He had ambition, he knew the intoxication of virtuosity, but instead put it to the service of art.[150]

   Motionless in the center of the bench, his body leaning slightly forward, he drew and withdrew stops with mathematically precise gestures keeping to a minimum the loss of time. It was at once wonderful and discouraging to watch. He had sculptured, admirably groomed hands, and extreme suppleness in all his bodily motions. No ungraceful contortion, no vain gesture marred the visual harmony always in accord with the sonorous harmony born of his contact with the organ. A lion's claw![151]

   Ch.-M. Widor, to cite the lovely expression of one of his friends who listened to him in the tribune of the Saint-Sulpice organ, seemed "to pour light on the head of his listeners." Hands that, without appearing large, could reach astonishing spans served his prodigious mind in this. The strictest legato thus became easy for him. His pedal technique was of an absolute sureness and precision, and the dosing of articulations communicated a surprising accentuation to his playing.[152]

[His] playing especially possessed an extraordinary rhythmic palette; admirably considered, without heaviness, clear and brilliant in virtuosity, always exact and scrupulous, he did not aim for effect, but nonetheless held the listener under a kind of beneficial influence. The improvisation was of a perfection of form, color, and movement difficult to equal.[153]

These descriptions of Widor at the organ mirror almost exactly how he described Bach at the organ; Widor had purposefully emulated the master of all organists:

[Bach] played with his body inclined slightly forward and motionless, with an admirable sense of rhythm, an absolutely perfect polyphonic ensemble, an extraordinary clearness, and not fast; he was master of himself, and, so to speak, of the beat, producing the effect of incomparable grandeur.

His contemporaries speak enthusiastically of his exquisite art of combining the stops and of his manner of treating them, at once so unexpected and original.

Nothing could escape him that was related to his art, adds Forkel. He observed with the greatest attention the acoustical properties of the church where he was to play.[154]

—26—

The Franco-Prussian War and the
Paris Commune: Letters home

With the outbreak of the Franco-Prussian War in July 1870, the German siege of Paris, and the ensuing Commune, life in the French capital was in an upheaval from September 1870 until the following June. France began a rapid mobilization of her forces, and faced with ill-prepared and insufficient numbers, all potential soldiers were pressed into service.[155] On September 6, 1870, Paul Widor wrote to his sister, Marie: "Charles might enlist in the mounted guard and join my company."[156] While still continuing to fulfill his duties at Saint-Sulpice, Charles soon joined the mobilized artillery garrisoned at Saint-Denis. Although Saint-Sulpice continued its usual functions, the edifice took some direct hits during the German bombardment and services had to be moved to underground rooms.[157] Widor sustained his only war injury during this time, though not on the battlefield: "I recall once in 1870 when I came to play the organ at Saint-Sulpice—I was then an artilleryman—I hadn't taken off my spurs, and I hurt myself very badly in the leg trying to maneuver this pachyderm of an organ. I didn't have a musical ear in my feet."[158]

While negotiating an armistice with the Germans, the new French National Assembly moved to Versailles, leaving Paris vulnerable to the Communards— political extremists who took over the unprotected city from March through May 1871. During this period they took Archbishop Darboy (1813–71) hostage, eventually executing him, and commandeered many city churches, including Saint-Sulpice, for their political clubs. Before government troops were able to return to Paris and squelch the uprising, mayhem gripped the capital, though its citizens tried to find moments of reprieve. Charles related one such moment in a letter to his mother:

> It's particularly for moral influence that this uprising is being carried out. Everyone here wants to leave; there are barely two or three thousand hooligans who are making a little disturbance; apart from that people are very calm. Sunday evening I witnessed with the Pérouse family a charge of the armored soldiers that was made against the hooligans in the Place Vendôme, in the rue de la Paix and on the boulevard. We were at the Café de la Paix, which is on the corner at the new Opéra. There were a good five hundred people having beers, syrups, and ice cream; there was such a panic upon seeing the armored soldiers on the sidewalk that in a second everything at the café was broken, the little Pérouse was coated from head to toe with redcurrant syrup and vanilla ice cream.[159]

The turmoil of the time was sufficient to halt publication of Parisian music journals for about a year (roughly October 1870 to October 1871), and a void exists in the musical happenings in and around Paris during that period. From December 1870 through May 1871, however, Widor sent numerous letters— often greatly delayed in the mail—to his family in Lyon.[160] Many envelopes are marked "par ballon monté" [balloon], which was often the only way to get mail in or out of the city over enemy lines. His surviving letters carry vivid descriptions of the prevailing horrible conditions in Paris and the frightful toll of the war and the Commune. Following are some poignant excerpts:

December 30, 1870; to his mother

> Try to send me a word! I am homesick remaining without news from you all. This situation is very hard; finally, everything will end within a month, and I think then people will be able to write to each other. I am doing very well; I have very little to do in my service to G[ener]al R., and I work as in ordinary times; I have almost no interruption in my service at S[aint] S[ulpice]. Sundays I am always free. Adieu, I love you very much and want to wish you a better year than the one we are leaving. I embrace you most affectionately.

January 11, 1871; to his mother

I have a dreadful homesickness from not receiving anything from you! When will all this end? I'm so weary of it. For two days I'm living on rue Montmartre because during the nights that I had [off duty] to sleep in my bed, there was such a whistling of shells around me that I couldn't close an eye. I moved my things to the cellar and no longer return home [8 rue Garancière] in the evenings. There is nothing more enervating than this shell music; moreover, one fell on my roof, penetrating to the second floor, but without coming into my place. At rue Montmartre, we don't hear anything and are far from all strikes. Send me a word; I'm greatly in need of it. All my love. Ch.

January 16, 1871; to his mother

Finally I received your letter dated November 22. I knew the battalion where Paul was had been very mistreated; it's the best thing that can happen to him to be made prisoner, for he will escape all the hazards now;[161] . . . I'm beginning to be greatly bored because for a month I'm no longer able to work on account of the cold, the *time* that I'm lacking, and the din from the bombardment; however, I don't regret the [earlier] time of the siege because I wrote a lot of successful things, and I practiced the organ more than ever. Yesterday (Sunday), the patronal feast of Saint-Sulpice, the church was closed because three shells burst through the vault, though without taking any victims and without doing serious physical damage. Every day I go to see if anything has happened to the organ; fortunately, it is protected by the very solid façade of the church and by the towers. Those [shells] that did come in on that side have not penetrated.[162]

All the left bank of the Seine has become uninhabitable. Moreover, since I'm on duty from midnight to noon every other day, each time that I have a night to spend in my bed, I'm very happy to sleep, something the whistling of the shells in my street made impossible. Thus I'm at rue faubourg Montmartre; but if you address a letter to me, always write to rue Garancière, since I go by there every day. . . . Everyone here is in the National Guard and leads a very beastly and hard life, bedding down on the ground outside the fortifications. Yesterday, I relieved poor Saint-Saëns, who for a week was in the fields, his knapsack on his back! Our battery, on the other hand, is very much "as it's needed"; there is nothing but former school students, and everyone is on equal footing, each being considered as artillery lieutenant; . . . it's a warfare of amateurs.

Yesterday I had lunch with the *battalion commander* Parseval! We ate a very well-prepared roast *rat* and an excellent dog cutlet.[163] I believe that in a month it will be finished here on one side or the other, for the bread will begin to be barely sufficient for everyone; moreover, I've had enough of it and have no other desire than to eat a piece of beef at 4 rue Sala [the family home in Lyon]. I would have been willing to send my photograph as artillery lieutenant but cards are not received by balloon.

Goodbye, I embrace you all. Write to Paul for me; in a month we will see each other again. Thank you for your note, it cured me a bit of my homesickness and cheered me up, for I couldn't be more anxious. Goodbye, Ch.

Saturday, January 28, 1871; to his mother

Finally, it's over! I don't know what you are thinking of it in Lyon, but here all the sensible people and especially the military are thrilled about it. For one month, one couldn't know if one would be killed at home or outside; this began to be very irritating. . . . The day before yesterday we were walking quietly on the rampart when a shell came and decapitated a poor worker beside us; at every instant one is exposed to gather up one's neighbor's brain when he isn't gathering up yours. I find this life sickening, and I cannot get used to it. I came back to my place today, and tomorrow I take up my service at Saint-Sulpice again, which is very enjoyable to me; if the armistice permits me to cross the lines, I will go to see you, as my vacation for Lent has begun. I have a great need to see you and I hope that the days will pass quickly until that moment. . . . Mr. Cavaillé was quite happy not to have any shells [fall] on his house; it's amazing because his whole quarter has been heavily damaged. As for Saint-Sulpice, there are three shells that fell on the vault above the organ, but without breaking through it; two others burst through the transept and the dome of the Chapelle de la Sainte Vierge. When communications are reestablished, I would be grateful to you for sending me a little money, as I didn't pay my rent to Plon on January 19 by prudence and necessity; and with the absence of marriages taking its toll for six months, I've scarcely moved ahead [Widor earned extra money from weddings and funerals]. . . . Life has been very expensive, especially in these recent times; a pound of butter costs 30 francs minimum, a pound of ham 45 francs and even 50, and all in unison, so that money ran out fast; dog or cat were prohibitive. . . . Be well and don't worry; all is well that ends well and if the war ended badly, we must console ourselves in thinking that it might have ended still worse; adieu, I love you with all my heart, and until soon I hope. Ch.

February 7, 1871; to his mother

How is it that I have received the letters from all cardinal points, one this morning from Paul in Leipzig, one from Switzerland, and nothing at all from you? Is it that the post isn't working in Lyon? I am very worried about you. Paul tells me that he received a letter from Marie from January 20, but since this time what are you doing and why haven't you written? . . . In a word, write to me quickly, for I'm beginning to be homesick. . . . [P. S.] I just received a letter from Marie dated October 28 . . . and nothing at all from you!

February 10, 1871, to his brother, taken a prisoner of war and sent to Leipzig

It is very fortunate for you to have been taken so quickly and put in a shelter, away from shelling, cold, and hunger. The poor devils who took to the fields in December and January have paid dearly for it; and I really believed two or three times that I myself was frozen during the cursed siege. Finally, all that is over. Saint-Sulpice has not been demolished, [and] the organ is intact. . . . I hope to go to Lyon toward the 20th of this month, and I think that, the peace being made, you will become French again. I think that we won't have to fight between ourselves, for this foul and idiot republic will serve as its own grave digger, burying itself with the honors due its majority, and it will save us the trouble of making its funeral oration with gun salutes—that would be wasted powder. You have to see up close the heroes that it has lost to have an idea about it; how sad to have fallen so low!

April 25, 1871; to his sister

I would like very much to be with you especially these days; I am beginning to be homesick, as during the siege, it is so disgusting to endure the machinations of this crapulence.

May 4, 1871; to his sister

This instant I received your letter of April 24, which gives me great pleasure.

Here, it's always the same menagerie, and I believe that it can still go on quite some time, perhaps all month. Don't worry, I'm doing very well, and have worked more since I am here than from the beginning of this year. In reading the papers and posters of the Commune, I don't lack any diversion. Thus, one is not bored in Paris, and with a bit of nerve, you don't run great risk. I do regret, however, not having swapped my revolver for yours because all my pockets are beyond repair; I'm going to have them made double in hide!

There was another visit of the National Guard to Saint-Sulpice on Sunday, during the day, but between the masses; they inspected everything—even the organ—under the pretext of looking for arms, but they didn't ruin anything and the services weren't disturbed.

You will be able to please my father in admitting that Rochefort [a journalist and political leader] is a scoundrel; he . . . has become a sort of public prosecutor. It's quite nasty.

Paris is fantastic—you stay for hours on the boulevards without meeting a carriage, no one! Everything is closed, shops and houses! Along with this, every night the sky is reddened by the fires started by bombs, bombardment, and fusillades; it's an incessant uproar. From my house I hear without cease two or three cannon shots a second; I don't know where one can go without this thunder; neither day nor night, there is no interruption! Never will one see a time so strange, and I don't regret being here; the Prussian siege was nothing by comparison.

Thursday, May 21, 1871; a short note to his mother

I am doing very well and haven't the courage to write before breakfast, I have been so hungry, having lived since Monday on 2 pounds of bread. I think the trumpet of Jericho and the Last Judgment will leave me cold after the phantasmagoria that just ended.

Tuesday, May 26, 1871; to his mother

You must have been very anxious, but I think that you will have received my note of yesterday.

Almost all the Paris monuments are destroyed! A number of streets and private houses no longer exist! What a war! My quarter has fortunately been mostly preserved except for the windows broken by the explosions from the powder-magazine and the bullets fired from the rooftops; my drawing room is open to all breezes, and window-glass makers are rare; at the moment of the explosion I had my little black cap on my head, and I don't know what became of it.

The rue de Vaugirard is heartbreaking; at Mr. Cavaillé-Coll's place on the avenue du Maine there are only a few little chips on the interior walls. Saint-Sulpice has been spared except for several windows.

One has no idea of a horror like this! The Tuileries, the Palais Royal, the quai d'Orsay, the ministries, the rue du Bac, the rue de Lille, the Hôtel de Ville, the rue Royale, etc., no longer exist. There is a suffocating cloud of smoke over Paris. Fortunately, it's pouring rain since this morning and the insurrection is almost checked except on the Buttes Chaumont where the communards are armed and from where they're putting their last hours to profit by bombarding the quarters around the boulevards, the Bourse, and Notre-Dame. It's unbelievable![164]

In addition to these extraordinary letters to his family in Lyon, many pages in the "Souvenirs autobiographiques" carry similar remarkable recollections of the period; the following excerpt illustrates its narrative character:

When the bombardment of Paris occurred, père Cavaillé padded the exterior of his villa, covering the walls with beams. On the door waved the American flag, as Gabriel Reinburg [1834–91, one of Cavaillé-Coll's voicers] who lived there was Alsatian and, like all the Alsatians who had not opted for the French regime, remained under American protection.

During the Commune, I went often in the evening to catch up on their news. From the rooftop we had a view that extended over all Paris. In all the newspapers, they were talking about the Commune and the pulling down of the Vendôme column. From our observatory, we kept an eye on it for a certain number of nights, but all of a sudden one night we no longer saw it; it was knocked down.

Toward the end of the Commune, at the moment of the taking of Paris by the army of Versailles, I lived in the old mansion of [Sourdéac] 8 rue Garancière. Early every Monday, the cook of a friend from Lyon came to ring at my door to ask for his week's pay. One Monday morning, he jangled sharply at my door and said: "The troops of Versailles are in Paris. From my window, I could see the Trocadéro black with troops. Don't go out, people say that they are going to fight in Paris! I won't be back for a week." A quarter hour later, I heard a ringing of bells such as I have never heard since: all the bells of the capital sounding the alarm. The battle raged, as we all know, for a week. From my rooftop, in the evening, all you could see was fires. One night, I was filled with amazement: I noticed the fleche of Sainte-Chapelle surrounded by flames. I thought that the next day I would no longer see it. Fortunately, it was only an optical illusion, and Sainte-Chapelle escaped destruction.[165]

Sometime after, all the windows in the quarter were broken by the explosion of a powder-magazine that had been placed in the Luxembourg garden.[166] It was General de Cissey [1810–82] who came to occupy the Luxembourg with his corps on Thursday. It's only that day that I was able to leave my house. On the corner of the rue de Vaugirard, bullets whizzed by, prohibiting any strolling on the street.

Upon leaving the Luxembourg and my call on General de Cissey, I hurried to the house of the curé of Saint-Sulpice, the Abbé Hamon, whom I found working calmly at his table. "They have made a lot of noise in the neighborhood," he said to me, "but I believe it's over!"

On the other hand, coming down the rue Garancière, I noticed leaving the church, the Abbé Fouillouse, throwing himself into the arms of the sergeant who was commanding a squad that was arriving in the square [Place Saint-Sulpice].

It was only on Sunday that I was able to go get some news from my friend Cavaillé-Coll, at the end of the rue de Vaugirard, the sidewalks of which were still littered with bodies.

One morning, I was on the balcony of my house at 8 rue Garancière, where I had opened all the doors, having remained its only inhabitant. All of a sudden an amazing spectacle appeared: I saw in the street a non-commissioned officer by himself leading sixteen Communards who had been captured with weapons in hand, and this officer was making them kneel as they were coming out of the barracks without one of them putting up the least resistance. Seeing me at my window, his revolver in his fist, he said in a slow voice devoid of all emotion, "Did you ever have the notion, in the middle of Paris—a civilized city, light of the world—to see in 1871 anything like this! Killing people who have behaved like brutes!" Saying this, he was firing his pistol around their ears.

The nephew of the Bishop of Langres, a young seminarian, had escaped from the Communards, the guards of the Roquette [Prison] having taken pity on him. One of them, coming up to him the day of the execution of Monseigneur Darboy, pushed him abruptly into the street through a little door and, slamming it in his face, shouted, "Beat it! I don't want to see you here anymore!" He found himself in the rue de la Grande Roquette, completely bewildered. The Communards held the barricade at the end of the street. At the other end, the troops from Versailles were arriving. The fusillade began. And there, [he stood] alone, hungry and dazed. A window opened slightly and a voice [called], "Come quick! Get in, get in!" He crossed the street and, the door shut again, found himself under cover. He was taken in by some kind of strange boarding school. [There were] nothing but women [inside], who said to him, "What are you doing out there?" —"I don't know anything about it myself. I was designated to be shot with the Archbishop of Paris, and it was my guards who put me through the door." —"Have you had breakfast? No? Eat with us!" They made him sit down at the table and explained the situation to him. The fusillade broke out. Finally, after the meal, the troops of Versailles having cleared the street and relieved the situation, the young abbé asked, "How can I acknowledge your assistance? You have saved my life." They surrounded him, kneeling and responding, "Give us your blessing!"

Meanwhile, Saint-Sulpice had become a political club [Club de la Victoire]. Anyone could take charge; packs of playing cards were all over; the Sunday services were suppressed; people came in with hats on. One day, one of the Communards came to ask me to play the *Marseillaise*. I explained to them, that being appointed by the parish, it was impossible for me to accommodate this whim.

In 1793, the Saint-Sulpice organ had been threatened. Its bellows had been dismantled and taken away in order to feed the forge of an arms factory. Then, they discovered that the church could serve as the setting of great political meetings and they had them put back. When Bonaparte presided over the famous banquet, the organ, which had its bellows reinstalled, was heard. It was threatened a second time, but was saved thanks to the intelligence of the organ pumpers who put false seals on the little entry door to the tribune, on the second floor in front of the Chapelle des Saint-Anges.

It was in the Chapelle du Sacré-Cœur of Saint-Sulpice that the voluntary enlistees signed up, and not in the square, as has been written, for it rained torrents. . . .[167]

During the Commune, three shells struck Saint-Sulpice: two on the central nave and one on the charming cupola over the Chapelle de la Vierge, enclosing the fresco of Lemoine. The organ was exposed to an unparalleled trial; the temperature was frightful, the holy water froze in the basins. Nonetheless, nothing faltered in the instrument. The same forty-three years later, during the war of 1914: the organ of Notre-Dame escaped destruction by a miracle, whereas all the lead ornaments outlining the fleche were contaminated by the cold. At the Trocadéro, on the other hand, the leaden feet of the pipes were corroded by the humidity, and the organ was put out of use. Lead is of an extraordinary fragility. At the Louvre, every object, all the rare pieces that contain lead are the object of special conservation.[168]

—27—

Four Symphonies for Organ: "Soar Above"

At the end of the siege and the bloody Commune, Widor's service in the military ended. Despite the inconvenience of the war, the period from his appointment to Saint-Sulpice through 1872 evinced a highly fruitful burst of compositional activity. He completed a few new piano pieces (Opuses 11 and 12) and his first set of art songs: *Six mélodies*, Op. 14, for Voice and Piano. Most important, he focused on his first formal organ works. Suddenly having the greatest organ in France before him, Widor explored the new possibilities provided by such an instrument, and he experienced a creative exhilaration. Could he have imagined that his organ works were, in the words of Henri Libert, destined "to regenerate the style of the organ by bringing to it new rhythmic and melodic accents, furthered magisterially by the power and warmth of a symphonic virtuosity absolutely unknown to the organ before that"?[169]

The publication of four multimovement organ works, modestly comprising the single Opus 13, laid the foundations for what would be called the greatest contribution to organ literature since the works of Johann Sebastian Bach.[170] Widor described the creative impulse:

> It's when I felt the 6,000 pipes of the Saint-Sulpice organ vibrating under my hands and feet that I took to writing my first four organ symphonies (published together by Maho). I didn't seek any particular style or form. I wrote feeling them deeply, asking myself if they were inspired by Bach or Mendelssohn. No! I was listening to the sonorousness of Saint-Sulpice, and naturally I sought to extract from it a musical fabric—trying to make pieces that, while being free, featured some contrapuntal procedures. . . . My first four organ symphonies appeared original although being of classic style.[171]

Indeed, others have observed that "the symphonies of Widor seem to have been written not only for the 'modern organ,' but also for his own organ and for the surroundings of his church. The work, the instrument, and the edifice are quasi-inseparable."[172] In view of their originality and scope, it is astounding to find that publisher J. Maho at one time actually marketed the new symphonies as "pour grand orgue ou piano avec claviers de pédales" (for grand organ or piano with pedal clavier).[173]

The manuscript for the first four organ symphonies must have been sent to the engraver, C. G. Röder of Leipzig, by the fall of 1871, as the first prints appeared early in 1872.[174] Out of profound devotion to his great friend and mentor, Widor respectfully dedicated these new organ works to Aristide Cavaillé-Coll.[175] Never short on gratitude, Widor frequently acknowledged the inspiration he derived from Cavaillé-Coll's magnificent instruments, especially that of Saint-Sulpice; for him, the bottom line was quite simple: "If I had not felt the seduction of these timbres, the mystic spell of this wave of sound, I would not have written any organ music."[176] And he pointed out a remarkable fact: "It's a curious thing, contrary to the logic of facts and the teaching of history: here it's the instrument that has created the instrumentalist; it's the body that made the soul!"[177] "It's the instruments that gave rise to the works. . . . These works will bear witness to the nobility and the science of Cavaillé-Coll, this inspired poet-architect of sounds."[178]

Widor's first symphonies resulted directly from the work he accomplished during his first year and a half at Saint-Sulpice, though evidence suggests that some individual movements predated that period. Opus 13 included twenty movements in the original version. Some may date back to his fugue-writing student days with Fétis—the first edition of Opus 13 contains three formal fugues, as well as other contrapuntally oriented movements. Certainly, some of the pieces composed for his concerts during the 1860s could have found their way into Opus 13.[179] Various reviews of Widor's participation in organ inaugurals during the late 1860s report that he played specific written works of his own composition, not just improvisations. By his own admission, he later destroyed some of these early efforts. Yet, as already stated, Widor was generally inclined to revise works rather than to discard them completely.

The predominantly vapid style of French organ music during the previous one hundred years was something of an embarrassment to Widor. Practically none of his contemporaries, with the notable exception of César Franck—whose *Six pièces* were published in 1868—had produced any serious organ music of quality. Even then, there were those who qualified the work of the two men:

Until the arrival of Widor, organ music had not ceased to decline in France. Our great "cantor" of Saint-Sulpice amplified the traditions and principles and made them flourish anew. He will hold the place as the most active artisan in the renaissance of our organ music. I am not unaware that César Franck, who as far back as 1862 [*sic*] had published his *Six grandes pièces pour orgue*, had preceded him in the noble task. In this crusade, it must be said that Widor knew how to occupy himself with an energy better immersed and directed, a more effective ability, than that of the Liége master.[180]

Seriously devoted to Bach's music, Widor aspired to reidentify the organ with the nearly forgotten but solid traditions of the distant past. He was no mere imitator, however; he sought to restore greatness to the instrument in the new language of the Cavaillé-Coll organ. He explained that his ideal literally grew out of the sounds he heard: "The very essence of organ sound explains the psychology of its literature, the character of its themes and their developments, their mysticism, their serenity, *even* in minor as in major there is never agitation or nervousness."[181] Prominently displayed on the title page of the new symphonies, the fashionable English motto "Soar Above" proclaimed that these were organ works of a new and elevated style—so much so that Abbé Hector Reynaud warned him not to go too far: "Mr. Widor, you have a fine slogan: *Soar Above*; but be careful not to discourage the momentum of your audience—I would even say your admirers. Or, if you will allow me another comparison, don't introduce us into the labyrinth of harmonic combinations without a thread from Ariadne that lays out the path or at least guides our way step by step."[182]

Inspired by the profession of his maternal ancestors—the Montgolfiers, inventors of the hot-air balloon and pioneers in balloon navigation—the slogan held a special significance to Widor as he forged ahead in his own field with the same pathbreaking spirit. The Op. 13 Symphonies were absolutely original in concept; at the same time, they presented a virtual compendium of modern organ technique:

> Well beyond the possibilities that the method of Lemmens had shown or suggested in the ingenuity of its musical language, the *Symphonies* of his pupil, as long ago as the first period, open to the performer anxious to acquire full command of his instrument a field of training that is new and of an infinite variety. One can say that they are the basis, like the *Sonatas* of Bach, of the modern virtuoso's technique.[183]

—28—

"Without Cavaillé-Coll, French organ literature would not exist"

There can be no doubt that Widor's concept of the definitive organ, capable of realizing a composer's every intention, was in complete unison with the "modern organ" developed by Cavaillé-Coll: "By 'modern organ,'" wrote Widor, "I mean an instrument endowed with a wind system and a mechanism entirely foolproof, at the same time one with a proper equilibrium of timbres and beauty of sound."[184] Throughout his writings, he extolled the instruments of his beloved builder, and he proclaimed numerous times that without them French organ music and playing could never have progressed to attain the status of one of the most important organ schools in music history.

Widor's boundless admiration for Cavaillé-Coll's instruments and what he perceived to be a previous lack of progress in organ building strongly colored his views of the past:

> What we reproach in the old instruments is, owing to their weak pressure, their monochromatic sonority. All the varieties within a particular family of

tone resemble one another to the point of becoming identical, and as we have at command only three families—foundations, reeds, and mixtures—their palette is reduced to three colors.[185]

It would be very unjust to be severe on our [organist] ancestors without studying their means of functioning—I mean *their instruments*. The poverty of the one explains the discretion from the other. Defective wind supply, impractical coupling of the manuals, rudimentary pedal clavier, no expressive means—such was the seventeenth-century organ. It's an extraordinary thing: the successors of the organists of the time exercised no influence over the organ building of their time, asking for no reform, inciting no research, satisfied with what little they had. And this state of the instrument remained the same, without any progress in the sonority or the mechanism—with the exception of the rich pipe work of Clicquot—without perfecting the timbres until the first half of the nineteenth century, until what Lemmens came to teach Cavaillé-Coll.[186]

After the innovations and refinements that Cavaillé-Coll brought to organ building came the renaissance of the French organ school, and Widor trumpeted the progress at every opportunity:

What a difference between the organ of former times and the one of today! It's the same as between the harpsichord and our concert grand piano. Never would Beethoven have written Opus 111 if he had had only the metallic clinking of the harpsichord of our fathers to interpret it.[187]

In reality, since Archimedes and Ctesibius, the organ has served as a testing ground to all the mechanics and acousticians on earth. Its continual transformations have found their definitive state only within this last century thanks to the genius of Aristide Cavaillé-Coll. . . .

. . . If the advice of master organists has had a successful influence on his works, in their turn his works have exercised a decisive influence upon musical production. Often he had Saint-Saëns and Franck join us.

Without him, French organ literature [since the mid-nineteenth century] would not exist.[188]

As for Cavaillé-Coll, it's owing to him that the honor of our organ school returns and attracts to us students of all nationalities. In front of his instruments, of distinctive timbres, instant speech, and a mechanism of absolute obedience, French composers become as enthusiastic as in front of a beautiful orchestra.[189]

We owe the great progress accomplished in the French art of organ building in our days to Cavaillé-Coll and his masterpieces, which lend themselves to all the manifestations of thought be they in the past or the present.[190]

Indeed, as pointed out in the last quotation, Widor saw Cavaillé-Coll's instruments as the perfect vehicle for interpreting organ music of *every* period: "Nothing is more just than to honor the memory of our distant predecessors by putting the richness of our instruments to the service of their thought."[191]

In spite of what he perceived as failings in old instruments, Widor did value many of their qualities, and once complained: "Several contemporary French organ builders have made the great error of deliberately scorning the registrations of olden days, and almost no longer take any account of them. What a shame!"[192] When he served as president of the commission to oversee the conservation and restoration of the Couperin organ at Saint-Gervais, very strict and exacting standards were set for the instrument's careful preservation:

> The *grand orgue* of Saint-Gervais offers considerable historic interest. Restored, it will not have intense modern sonorities. It is by other qualities that it will be distinguished. Its restoration must not in any case be a remaking, not even partially. The instrument of Couperin must be conserved as it is, with its voicing and its pitch. . . . No modification must be made to its mechanism. It will therefore be an interpreter of preference for the performance of old organ music when French artists excelled, and which constitutes such an abundant and rich literature.[193]

Cavaillé-Coll nurtured nuance of color and multifarious shadings within each family of tone to an extent previously unknown in France, and he endowed his instruments with new expressive power. For Widor, the instrument had attained a mystic quality that he could not concede to earlier organs: "The religious idea, meditation, and prayer are poorly accommodated to the rigidity of the organ pipe. When, a century later [the nineteenth], the sound of this pipe will be able to vanish under the deep vaults of our cathedrals, carrying our souls toward the infinite, then the organ alone will be the *mystical instrument.*"[194]

> Of a shimmering variety of tones is the rich modern palette of his flutes, his gambes, his montres (foundation stops); his trompettes, hautbois, cromornes and bassoons (reed stops); his mixtures terracing the harmonic series that, alone of all instruments, the organ realizes and from which it draws all its brilliance.[195]

At the base of all Cavaillé-Coll's tonal advances and refinements, which so seduced Widor's aural sense, were sweeping mechanical innovations that rendered the expanded tonal resources manageable and allowed organ music to achieve its newfound character and dimensions. The mechanical action of even the more modest plans of some seventeenth- and eighteenth-century organs bordered on the impractical. Widor's travels brought him in contact with many old instruments, and he experienced both their strengths and weaknesses. Citing the large seventeenth-century Arp Schnitger organ of the Saint-Jacobi Church in Hamburg, he noted: "Noble impression for the listener, but great fatigue for the organist, considering, for the hands, the depth, the heaviness of the touch"; and he continued, "Thanks to the invention of the pneumatic lever, attributable to the English engineer Barker, the finger has an effect on the mechanism only by the intermediary of a small bellows, which, expanded by the air pressure, overcomes the resistances. The sound is instantaneous and the heaviness of the key does not exceed that of the piano."[196] Cavaillé-Coll's application of the "Barker machine" was a triumphant success. In his largest instruments with a machine for each keyboard, the touch was equalized regardless of the physical location of the respective pipe-work, and the coupling of the total resources was made possible without changing the weight of the key touch.[197]

Manual and pedal compasses, accompanied by the alteration in the dimensions of the pedal clavier, were standardized as at Saint-Sulpice in the early 1860s. The pedal keys of many old organs had been too short to allow efficient use of the heel; Widor observed that the mandatory legato of his style was impossible when only the toe of the foot could be used:[198] "it is necessary to hop from key to key, like a sparrow on the branch."[199]

Two of Cavaillé-Coll's most important mechanical developments, essential to the romantic aesthetic, were the application of the "boîte expressive" (swell or expression box)[200] and the unique system of "pédales de combinaison" (combination pedals). With these two developments the French organ received its first genuinely expressive means. By skillful manipulation of the expression box—the dynamic range of which Cavaillé-Coll improved enormously—in conjunction with the combination pedals, smooth grand-crescendos and decrescendos were made possible for the first time on French organs. Widor found these simplest of means completely adequate to his expressive needs:

> An expression box and, per clavier, two combination pedals, one for coupling, the other to put the reeds on, such is the very simple disposition that leaves to the organist full and complete freedom. . . . A light pressure of the toe, the scene changes.[201]

With its one hundred stops, the seemingly unlimited resources of the Saint-Sulpice organ opened Widor's creative thought. The expanded palette of aural color and innovative expressive means motivated him to find a new kind of organ music befitting the instrument. To him, the organ became an orchestra with innumerable timbres and a prodigious range of effects, just as it had for César Franck, who declared that his organ was an orchestra.[202] The concept of a multimovement work of symphonic scope for solo organ began to dawn in Widor's mind. Marcel Dupré affirmed, "He thought too much in terms of the orchestra not to see in the one-hundred stops of his organ groups corresponding to those of the orchestra."[203] Widor put it simply: "The organ is, in reality, an orchestra of wind instruments. An organ of thirty, forty, fifty stops is an orchestra of thirty, forty, fifty musicians."[204] And his way of handling the instrument did not escape the notice of those who observed him; Henry Eymieu

(1860–1931) remarked, "[Widor] made a veritable orchestra of his instrument and drew from it extremely varied effects."[205]

Franck had already introduced the first truly symphonic concept to organ music with his largest organ composition—the cyclical *Grande pièce symphonique*, Op. 17, which unpretentiously appeared as one of his *Six pièces* written between 1860 and 1863.[206] In terms of expressivity and registration color, Franck's treatment of the organ remained essentially the same in his other organ works, but he never returned to develop the symphonic genre of organ music. It is impossible to know what influence the *Grande pièce symphonique* had on Widor, though he had certainly heard it—probably under Franck's fingers. In any case, Franck's timidity became Widor's resolve. Boldly and uncompromisingly, Widor's Opus 13 carried the title *Symphonies pour orgue.*

The title of "symphony" for an organ composition has been misunderstood since the beginning: "When they appeared, these symphonies . . . stirred up some impassioned discussions. Why such a title, people said; and why treat the organ as an orchestra?"[207] "People were astonished that he had chosen this title ordinarily reserved for orchestral compositions."[208] In 1941, noted music historian Paul Henry Lang (1901–91) ignored the entire corpus of Widor's non-organ music in his gigantic *Music in Western Civilization* to reference only the organ symphonies, which he damned as "contrapuntally belabored products of a flat and scant musical imagination, the bastard nature of which is evident from the title alone."[209] And in 1965 Georges Robert (1928–2001), organist at Notre-Dame de Versailles and organ professor at the Institut National des Jeunes Aveugles in Paris, wrote: "I practice with interest the music of all periods: . . . Widor? Certainly, he introduced innovations on the plane of instrumental technique, but his work marks too much his time period and he was wrong to make the organ a veritable symphonic instrument; the imitation of the orchestra on the organ does not interest me."[210]

Once, when responding to a critic, Widor offered a formula for evaluating an artistic production: "It is impossible to judge the work of an artist without first carefully inquiring what was the ideal, what were the tendencies, and what was the spiritual condition of the generation immediately preceding that of the artist in question?"[211] It is requisite to consider these questions with regard to Widor's own artistic production, especially if one is to understand properly the title and worth of his *Symphonies pour orgue* and the prominent position they won for him in the history of organ music—a position that has called forth some astounding appraisals:

[Widor] holds a unique place in the history of contemporary organ music. The novelty and importance of his compositions for this instrument give him the rank of creator. . . . It is he who has best understood what the nineteenth-century organ with its new symphonic resources is supposed to express.
—Alexandre Cellier and Henri Bachelin[212]

They are, since J.-S. Bach, the greatest monument raised to the glory of the organ. —Louis Vierne[213]

The organ works of Ch.-M. Widor—the most considerable that have appeared since J.-S. Bach, have opened a new way to the organ. —Marcel Dupré[214]

In the history of French organ music, [Widor's work] occupies a place of prime importance by its newness, originality, and architectural and thematic richness. It's by this work, it seems, that the name of Widor will live in posterity. —Georges Favre[215]

How could a symphony be written for only one instrument? As a result of the controversy raised by this question, Widor wrote a substantial preface explaining his ideal in the 1887 edition of *Symphonies pour orgue*.

The modern organ is essentially symphonic. The new instrument requires a new language, an ideal other than scholastic polyphony. It is no longer the Bach of the Fugue whom we invoke but the heartrending melodist, the preeminently expressive master of the Prelude, the Magnificat, the B-Minor Mass, the Cantatas, and the St. Matthew Passion.[216]

In giving the organ the power of dynamic expression and the means of manipulating the tonal resources with relative ease, Cavaillé-Coll created a sort of rival to the orchestra; but there is an important distinction to be made. Even though certain stops were orchestrally inspired, the organ of Cavaillé-Coll was not intended strictly to imitate the orchestra;[217] rather, the organ was endowed for the first time with an expressive capacity comparable in some ways to that of the orchestra. Nonetheless, it still continued to maintain its own idiomatic integrity and aesthetic. Adolphe Boschot (1871–1955) observed:

Each Sunday at Saint-Sulpice, the composer [Widor], in improvising, began to explore, to experiment with the innumerable resources that an enormous instrument furnished him; and he had discovered another sonorous world, which was not that of the orchestra, but which likewise had unlimited riches.[218]

In his preface, Widor discerningly declared that the organ was not intended to be treated as an orchestral surrogate in his new works:

No promiscuity is to be feared. One will never write indifferently for the orchestra or for the organ, but henceforth will have to exercise the same care with the combination of timbres in an organ composition as in an orchestral work.[219]

And he later explained to his organ class:

> Grandeur is the organ's essential characteristic. This is because, of all musical instruments, the organ alone can sustain sound indefinitely and with the same intensity. The organ can be picturesque only rarely, and, even then, care must be taken not to expect it to imitate orchestral and pianistic effects. That would be an inartistic parody.[220]

Several decades before Widor's measured delineation of the organ's essential character, Jean-Louis-Félix Danjou had weighed in with his own concerns, pointing the finger at Cavaillé-Coll for diverging too far from the organ's historical character and inviting a style inappropriate to the instrument's role as an exponent of sacred music. In a rebuttal, Cavaillé-Coll agreed perfectly with Danjou's appraisal that he had indeed perfected the organ in mechanism, tonal quality, power, and stops that were more akin to their orchestral counterparts; initially, he had purposefully reduced or excluded "those forests of *nazard*, *quarte*, *tierce*, and *cornet* stops with which old organs were infested."[221]

In Widor's creative imagination, the augmentation of the medium invited an expansion of the message. The style of the hundreds of composed interludes, Kyrie responses, Psalms, Canticles, Offertories, and the like, created to serve the structure of the Roman Rite by composers such as Boëly, Lefébure-Wély, Batiste, Benoist, Lemmens, Guilmant, and Gigout, did not meet the artistic sensitivities and compositional necessities of Widor. He never produced one work in these styles that he considered worthy only of improvisation. Consequently, searching for a new mode of expression that fully conformed to the potential of the Cavaillé-Coll organ, he seized the grand multimovement plan of the orchestral symphony, and from it he derived a new genre, effectively adapting it to the expansive sonorities of the organ:

> [He] aimed to produce, in the symphonic form, a music in which the disposition, writing, and architecture was perfectly adapted to all the means that the Romantic organ, conceived by Cavaillé-Coll, put at the disposal of composers.[222]
>
> Ch.-M. Widor had understood the organ of Cavaillé-Coll, divined its artistic possibilities and, being able to test them at Saint-Sulpice every Sunday, felt appointed to create the new form capable of making the most of the multiple resources.[223]

—29—

"The time of 'cataclysms' on the organ . . . has passed"

With Widor's ideals and objectives defined, the last criterion in his formula for judging an artistic production remains: the spiritual climate of the preceding generations. As already posited, since the great flowering of the French Baroque era, organ music and playing had fallen into a state of decadence; during the twilight of that rich era, popular Noëls, vapid imitations of nature, and all sorts of secular program music had already begun to displace music of sincere religious import. For nearly a hundred years nothing would evolve in France to improve the situation. Sensuous effects, often combined with pyrotechnical display, became the order of the day.

How did Widor appraise the generations of which he was the immediate beneficiary? In several writings, he traced the prevailing trends of his predecessors and demonstrated that he was not at all unaware of his inheritance:

> Read the writings of the times; letters, reviews, memoirs. If they're talking about an organist, it's to speak of his virtuosity, of his interludes in the *Gloria, Magnificat,* and *Te Deum,* of his fantasias that entertained the congregation . . . and sometimes scandalized it by his *hunting songs, minuets,* and *rigaudons.*[224]

Widor had researched this subject and found some original critical sources to cite as examples of the decadent trends. From the Paris tableau *Mercier:*

> The almost general abuse of having only some formulated figurations under the fingers, and this by lack of genius and diligence, this abuse has become so shocking that nonsense has prevailed on the organ, so that it has nothing more of the majesty suitable to a temple. . . .
>
> At the Midnight Mass, [Louis-Claude] Daquin [1694–1772] imitated the song of the nightingale on the organ so perfectly . . . that the utmost amazement was unanimous. The treasurer of the parish sent the head usher and the vergers to explore in the vaults and on the ridge of the church: not at all a nightingale, it was Daquin.[225]
>
> . . . It was that day that Daquin, more sublime than ever, thundered in the *Judex crederis,* which made such vivid and profound impressions on the minds that everyone blanched and shuddered. . . .
>
> The archbishop of Paris has forbidden the evening *Te Deum* and the *Midnight Masses* in music at Saint-Roch [where Claude-Louis Balbastre (1729–99) was organist] and at the abbey of Saint-Germain [where a Mr. Miroir was organist], because of the multitude that came to hear the organist and did not preserve the respect owed to the sanctity of the place.[226]

Evidence of what needed correction in French organ music existed in abundance. In the preface that he authored for Eugène de Bricqueville's *Notes historiques et critiques sur l'orgue,* Widor narrated the discovery he made of an organ method from this infamous period:

I admit to having been very much intrigued the other day, while on the quai Malaquais, to read in the shop window of a secondhand bookseller this flamboyant title in gold letters on the green binding of a respectable folio: *Organ School*, by Martini. What? Father [Giovanni Battista] Martini [1706–84], the religious scholar from Bologna, the author of the *Unfinished History of Music*, of the *Treatise on Fugue and Counterpoint*, would have written a work on the art of organ playing and we would not know about it?

I feverishly opened the volume, and this dedication popped out at me: *To Her Majesty the Empress Josephine*. (Paris, 1804). I was transfixed. It was not at all a question here of the Reverend Father Martini, but indeed of the [Jean-Paul-Égide] Martini [1741–1816], choirmaster of Louis XVI and Napoleon, a composer who would be absolutely forgotten today in spite of the great number of his productions if he had not had the luck of signing two pages that became popular: *Plaisir d'amour*.

He speaks of everything in his method, the excellent Paul-Égide Martini (Schwartzendorf, by his real name): of the mechanism of the instrument, its history, its sonorous riches, its *typical* stops, its *extraordinary* stops, and the manner of using them. He speaks to us seriously of the *carillon*, the *echo*, the *bird song* produced by some pipes coming into play under wind pressure with water contained in a tank [the ends of the pipes were mitered in such manner that their ends were dunked in the water, which caused them to warble when blown]; the *star* [*Zimbelstern*], composed of a series of metal plates turning on their spindle, always by the action of the wind, and ringing a little like some cymbals; the *cuckoo*, the *tremulant*, a stop which, "when it does not go too fast, inspires sadness," he assures, "and when it goes precipitately, recalls the beating of a mill-wheel."

Here is the little program placed at the head of a composition that he gives as a model of organ style: "Picturesque piece on the resurrection of Our Lord: The gloomy silence of the sepulcher (A Minor in triple meter). The disappearance of the morning haze (*tremolo* from low to high). The earthquake (one tramples on the pedals). The descent from heaven of a cherub who takes away the stone from the tomb (chromatic scale *prestissimo* from the [high] F of the piccolo to the low C of the contre-bass). The coming out from the tomb of Our Lord (*allegro giocoso, ma risoluto*). The terror and flight of the Roman soldiers (little fugue on flat keys [many organs of this period were undoubtedly still tuned in some kind of unequal temperament, and a piece played on the black keys would have been terrifying indeed!]). The triumphal song of the angels (trumpets and timpani, fifes and clarinets)."[227]

And thus presented, the whole drama fits on a few pages having no rapport with the program—pages so destitute of feeling, intelligence, and character . . .

A film director would refuse them.[228]

When Widor wrote this account in 1899, he undoubtedly looked upon Martini's programmatic description with a good deal of amusement, and probably a sigh of relief that it represented a past chapter in the history of French organ music: "We must admit that we have made some progress since Martini."[229] Widor had happily reported in 1895, "The time of 'cataclysms' on the organ, thunder, tremolos, goat choruses called *voix humaines*, and all these 'nurses' toys has passed."[230] And again in 1919: "Of these playthings of old, there remained evidence of them until recent years: our instruments still had *storm pedals, hail, nightingale*, and *voix humaine* stops, this last more imitative of a goat chorus than of a human throat. But all this tends to disappear."[231]

Ironically, Widor was once severely reproached for perpetuating the same vapid qualities that he disdained in organ music. The spiritually confused Belgian Symbolist Joris-Karl Huysmans (1848–1907) wrote so disparagingly of Widor in *En route* (1895),[232] a book about his longing for monastic life, that Alexandre Cellier (1883–1968) and Henri Bachelin (1879–1941) felt impelled to come to Widor's defense:

> People know with what beautiful architectural order, with what special feeling of expression appropriate to the organ Mr. Widor improvises at Saint-Sulpice. In this regard, it was a total error of Huysmans to write in *En route*: "Mr. Widor, seated before his organ-case, poured out some faded remnants, gurgled from up there—imitating the human voice and flute, the Breton bagpipes and fipple-flute, the musette and bassoon—rasped some gibberish that he accompanied on the bagpipe, or else weary of simpering he blew the whistle furiously and finished by simulating the rumbling of locomotives over cast-iron bridges in unleashing all his bombards." This is humorous, nothing more. I will not point out the technical errors that are rampant in these few lines. There are, on the other hand, certain essential truths that apply to the playing of poor organists, but the "tirade" totally misses the mark concerning Mr. Widor, for one might begrudge him a certain severity rather than simpering or the use of the *voix humaine* that he condemns and calls a "herd of nanny-goats"—as Mendelssohn said, a "choir of old women." Nanny goat? Huysmans was wrong to make Mr. Widor the scapegoat.[233]

One visitor who came to Saint-Sulpice for a Christmas Eve Mass recalled quite a different scene from that conjured up by Huysmans:

> I will always remember those astonishing Christmas Eves. . . . Widor performed—and as he knew how to do it!—a fantasy of his composition on a series of popular noels—a fantasy that was a masterpiece of musical imagination and registration, a perpetual surprise, an enchantment. And he finished the ceremony with his famous stunning *Toccata*.[234]

Widor eventually commented on Huysmans's unjust attack in a footnote in his preface to Charles Bouvet's *Les Couperin*: "The occasion presents itself to declare that in one of his books, having reproached me for the use of these playthings that I have always protested against, Huysmans later apologized for it: 'someone had badly misinformed him,' he said."[235]

When Widor first entered the musical pastiche of Paris in the mid-1860s, Franck and Saint-Saëns were only then making fledgling efforts toward improving the scene in their organ galleries. The accounts cited above represented the not-too-distant past; Lefébure-Wély was still alive and very popular. After his meticulous training with Lemmens and Fétis, however, Widor felt quite at odds with the preceding couple of generations. In terse stricture of two of the leading French organists of that time, which included his predecessor at Saint-Sulpice, he wrote:

At the inaugural program of the organ at La Madeleine [1846]: three "Improvisations" by Mr. [Alexandre-Charles] Fessy [1804–56], organist of the parish, and three "Improvisations" by Mr. Lefébure-Wély, organist of Saint-Roch. Two hours of twaddle. The imitation of the sound effects of nature was then in style: "Mr. X . . . ," says one critic, "made us hear a storm that he was wrong in not announcing by a few flashes of genius."

With the sole exception of Boëly, whom people reproached for his improvisation "in the German style," but who left us some very creditable pieces, nothing remains of the contemporaries.[236]

As Widor had pointed out, organs of the time were replete with storm pedals, hailstorm stops, nightingales, and so on, and organists conjured up numerous other special programmatic effects to evoke a desired mood. Orpha Ochse discovered a manuscript dated January 22, 1829, in which "the organ is used to create a doleful atmosphere for a Requiem Mass. Among the techniques for special effects illustrated or described are clusters of keys in the low register of the pedal; both arms on the manual keys, moving them to produce an undulating sound; sudden outbursts; dramatic silences; and plaintive phrases on the voix humaine alone."[237] Of course, the Saint-Sulpice organ was no exception, with its nightingale, rain machine, and thunder pedal.[238] While it is unclear whether or not Cavaillé-Coll retained the nightingale and rain machine devices in his 1862 rebuilding of the organ, the storm pedal did survive and was presumably frequently employed by Lefébure-Wély. During Widor's tenure, however, "a conspicuous hole in the toe-board where the pedal operating it once had been, mutely testified to the esteem in which the contrivance was held by the incumbent of that particular post."[239]

—30—

"His work comes like a clap of thunder out of a clear sky"

Emerging from these generations, Franck's *Six pièces* of 1860–63 announced a renaissance of French organ music; musicologist Norbert Dufourcq (1904–90) proclaimed: "It's a moral revolution that the organ works of César Franck preach."[240] Curiously, Franck offered nothing further to the literature of his instrument until 1878. From that perspective, Albert Riemenschneider (1878–1950) declared: "Certainly there is no preparation in the scheme of things for the appearance of a Widor. His work comes like a clap of thunder out of a clear sky, and not even the work of Franck can explain it. It is due entirely to the outstanding personality of the man."[241]

The Paris publisher J. Maho published Widor's new *Symphonies pour orgue*, Op. 13, in 1872. Gustave Bret and others gave incorrect dates of publication early on: First Symphony in 1876; Second, Third, Fourth Symphonies in 1879.[242] However, notice of the publication of the whole set appeared in music journals in 1872,[243] and *Le Ménestrel* lists the symphonies among other important compositions of the year:

> By a ministerial decree that again bears witness to all the interest that musicians and their works inspire, the Director of Fine Arts has just been authorized to subscribe to a certain number of musical publications able to interest our conservatories, our cathedral music schools, and our public libraries. . . . Here are the modern and classical works that have been posed on the official subscription:

1. *Djamileh*, opéra-comique de M. G. Bizet.
2. *Le passant*, opéra-comique de M. Paladilhe.
3. *La princesse jaune*, opéra-comique de M. C. Saint-Saëns.
4. *Fiesque*, opéra de M. Lalo.
5. *Ruth*, églogue biblique, de M. C. A. Franck.
6. *Stabat Mater*, de Mme de Grandval.
7. *Symphonies pour orgue*, par M. C. M. Widor.
8. Collection complète, texte, dessins et musique, des *Clavecinistes*, par M. Amédée Méreaux.[244]

J. Maho did not include Widor's *Symphonies* in its advertisements until 1876, but reviews report Widor performing from them early in 1873.[245]

In March 1870, "a beautiful *fantaisie pastorale*" appeared on one of Widor's organ programs.[246] Could this have been the Pastorale that appeared two years later in the Second Symphony? It does not appear likely that the exact genesis of the composition of the Op. 13 Symphonies can be determined, as the whereabouts of the autograph manuscripts, if they are extant, remains a mystery. Even should they be discovered, it is questionable that the autographs would reveal the likely complicated evolution of Opus 13.

Widor's lifelong practice of revision affected these early organ works most noticeably, undoubtedly because many of them were either born of his Sunday improvisations at Saint-Sulpice or of an earlier conception. Only in his later organ works does the process of revision become less substantive. In the different editions of Opus 13, pieces often reappeared in a drastically different guise, but rarely were they entirely discarded. Even when Widor eventually excised the Scherzo from the Second Symphony and the Fugue from the Third Symphony, he republished them as *Deux pièces pour grand orgue.*[247] He lived by his maxim that "it is necessary to be very severe on oneself and to criticize oneself more rigorously than you would someone else."[248]

Speaking primarily of Opus 13, Harvey Grace (1874–1944) observed:

> The title "symphonies" is perhaps hardly suitable for the works which are really collections of pieces. As some of the movements . . . are of slender proportions, and as we now associate the term with music on a big scale, the works might be more fairly called suites.[249]

This assessment is especially true of the first edition of Opus 13. In many respects, these symphonies were experimental works on which Widor continued to reflect the rest of his life. Undergoing many stages of revision, whole movements were added, omitted, or altered—several were fleshed out considerably. When compared to the later Symphonies (Opp. 42, 70, and 73), those of Opus 13 show that Widor was finding his way, seeking to define what an organ symphony could be. Although in their final version the Op. 13 Symphonies include movements composed or revised at the end of his life, these works never quite attained the sense of integrality found in the later ones. The cohesive scope and broad gestures are simply not as inherent in these earlier works. It can also be argued—be it good or bad—that the revisions are sometimes so sweeping that the stylistic integrity of the original conception is left far behind. As Grace noted, they give the impression of being suites of pieces, not unlike the numerous organ suites that appeared throughout the French Baroque period; and Widor's own definition of the orchestral suite would appear to confirm this notion: "a collection of fantasy pieces, most often without ties between them."[250]

Still, the movements of the Op. 13 Symphonies—there are either six or seven movements in each symphony—constitute an artistic meld of traditional forms of organ music and symphonic music, although the classical sonata form is not represented. Some forms are revived from the Baroque—toccata, prelude, fugue—and others resemble nineteenth-century character pieces—pastorale, intermezzo, minuet, scherzo, march. Movements are juxtaposed for variety of form, compositional procedure, key relationship, coloration, rhythm, dynamic level, and mood.

In this period, Widor earned his living primarily by playing the organ and publishing his music.[251] The Op. 13 Symphonies fulfilled the varied musical requirements of church services, organ inaugurations, and salon concerts. In addition, Widor's *Symphonies* comprised the first real body of French organ repertoire that seemed destined for the concert hall; by the twentieth century,

Norbert Dufourcq would declare, "Widor can be considered, if not the creator, at least the renovator of the concert organ,"[252] and "With Widor, the concert organ is king."[253] Yet, at the time of their publication, no concert hall organs existed in France. Critics of his new-styled organ works voiced their complaints: "Hasn't the author written for his instrument more than for the Church or in view of the liturgical ceremonies? 'The organ speaks as a philosopher,' says Mr. Widor; I would like better if it spoke as a Christian."[254] To this detractor, movements with such secular titles as "Intermezzo," "Scherzo," "Minuetto," "Cantabile," and so forth seemed inappropriate to accompany ecclesiastical functions.[255] The issue was more one of semantics than musical style, however; if Widor had applied liturgical titles like "Communion," "Élévation," and "Offertoire" to the various movements, he would likely have avoided the misunderstanding that brought on disapproval. The argument simmered for decades, and in 1900 Abbé Reynaud wrote in defense of Widor:

> I know many an offertory that is only a sort of scherzo, a piece such as an elevation that is only a sort of romance. In fact, the question is less complicated than it seems, and these objections have quite the air of a quarrel over words. Do we dare pose the question: Is there a religious music? One can doubt it. To put it better, there are no more religious strains than there are religious colors and religious tints, nor even, with a few exceptions, religious words. But there is a religious sentiment in music, just like in painting, or poetry, or oratory. And this sentiment, both mild and austere, I recognize in most of the pieces [of Widor's *Symphonies*].[256]

Whatever his critics had to say, Widor undeniably devoted all his ability as an organist and his inspiration as a composer to the service of his art. Organ music represented his supreme offering to the Church. If his new symphonies were not sacred music per se, they expressed a spiritual quality that was of the Church. He wrote time and time again of the religious nature of the organ: "These sound waves that can be prolonged at will evoke the Infinite, Eternity, and the religious idea";[257] "Of all instruments, the organ is the only one whose sound, if it has a beginning, can have no ending. And it's by the idea of the *Infinite* that it evokes the religious idea."[258]

Some complained that he turned the services at Saint-Sulpice into concerts, and it cannot be denied that when not playing the works of previous masters— especially Bach—or improvising, Widor's usual practice was to play movements from his organ symphonies to serve various liturgical functions.[259] If some of the movements from these works seemed more appropriate to the concert hall, then Widor must be credited with initiating a new style of church music while at the same time establishing a concert repertoire for the organ. One of his pupils described the fine musical fare at one Sunday Mass:

[Widor was] improvising on the Gregorian tones of the Mass being sung at the other end of the church, playing a Bach fugue at the offertory, and finally at the close of the service turning the full power of the organ loose in a brilliant toccata improvised on the phrases that we had just heard from the choir. . . . Widor's feats, even now, still seem incredible, not because they were spectacular, but because they were such profoundly good music.[260]

—31—

First Symphony for orchestra:
"One is not an artist if one lacks courage"

While Widor had established himself as a pianist and an organ virtuoso, his debut in the field of composition with only a handful of light piano pieces, a couple of chamber works, a set of six songs, and his newly published Organ Symphonies was a long way from fulfilling the true test of a nineteenth-century instrumental composer: to write a full-fledged orchestral symphony. With the exception of Berlioz's remarkable symphonic contributions and a couple of youthful works by Bizet, French composers neglected that art form until the last quarter of the nineteenth century. In 1877, Widor noted, "The study and art of the symphony has taken quite a notable development in our country these recent years; this musical movement grows stronger and is concentrated so much around us each day that we cannot pay too much attention to it or spare too much encouragement for it."[261] Widor felt that serious symphonic composition was the mark of being an artist:

We must rejoice in seeing the public listen to and favorably greet scores of such long duration, of such colossal proportions; we must encourage with all our wishes and promote by all our means . . . inclinations to return to the symphony, which is the correct and complete form—the form prescribed by good sense and logic. The "Orchestral Suite" came one moment to knock it off its legs and try to supplant it in the mind of the crowds; in the suite, one has no other guide than one's fancy, one is not at all held to develop one's ideas, one goes where one can, one stops where one wants—it's the domain of do-what-you-like: but it is not at all great art. The duty of artists is to guide opinion and to train it; courage is needed, I confess, but one is not an artist if one lacks courage or fears not being understood and followed. If you do not dare to clear the path, if you wait until the crowd has passed by in order to fall into step, you have a thousand chances to remain eternally in line without ever being able to judge what this crowd is looking for, for you will see it only from the back.[262]

As a consequence of this deeply-seated conviction, concurrent with the publication of the Symphonies for Organ, Widor composed his First Symphony, Op. 16, for Orchestra. On October 4, 1872, he addressed a letter to the Concert Society of the Paris Conservatory in his most beautiful handwriting and with a servile tone reminiscent to that of Bach requesting a court title from Frederick Augustus II:

> I dare to come and solicit of your Illustrious Society the permission to submit to it a symphony; I will be most pleased if you deem to accord me such a favor.
>   Please believe, Sirs, in the high regard of your very respectful and very obedient servant.[263]

In November 1872, the Concert Society of the Paris Conservatory began hearing new works as candidates for inclusion in their upcoming season. The music press announced, "several unpublished works have been assayed and we believe we can affirm that Mr. Ch. Widor is from the very small number of those chosen."[264] With this venture into symphonic writing, Widor endeavored to come of age as a serious creator. Of the two movements that appeared on the program, the reviews were mixed, though they generally expressed optimism for the future:

> The young and skillful organist has made there [at the Conservatory concert] a very honorable debut in a career that Haydn, Mozart, Beethoven, and Mendelssohn have rendered quite difficult. The personality in his works is not yet today fully determined: his Andante lacks a little character and variety; but the workmanship, style, and musical sentiment are excellent, and by certain indications, by certain brilliant strokes, we believe we can predict that these qualities will complete themselves sooner or later by those more valuable, which emanate from the creative faculty. The Scherzo is charming; its Trio has the allure of a pretty opéra-comique intermezzo. We cannot explain very well why Mr. Widor finishes with this Trio instead of going back to the Scherzo; the piece turns short, and the effect of this finds itself certainly diminished.[265]

Perhaps the work was cut short only for this first hearing, as in the published version the Scherzo does return *da capo*, with coda, after the Trio. In one of his articles for *Estafette*, Widor articulated the essential need for young composers to hear their works performed:

> You learn a lot in school, but you know something only after having passed through the frightful trials of listening to an orchestral performance. You can only judge your work well across the footlights when you are separated

from this work by the thick barrier of a completely indifferent audience that you are supposed to interest and, if you can, to move. It's then that each detail appears in its true value, in its true microscopic proportions, whereas it had kept you busy for entire days in the studio; it's only then that your whole concept, your broad outlines come to you, that you see them in their quasi-nudity, brutally; everything else disappears in distant shadows.

Too bad for you if your concept is uncertain, if your grand themes lack strength and boldness; no detail can save your composition, it will perish. What master can teach such things? Where are the magnifying glasses that can make you see in the night? There is only experience.[266]

From the vantage point of a seasoned composer, Widor later offered his assessment of his First Symphony: "My First Symphony in F for Orchestra, which was partially performed at the Conservatory during a concert on November 6, 1872—when the Andante and Scherzo were given—I judge today completely unskilled and naïve from the orchestral point of view."[267] Despite this later denunciation, the symphony represents an admirable testing of the waters at a time when few Frenchmen had embarked into the symphonic domain. Widor's study of classical and early-romantic-era symphonic masters is clearly evident in his more than competent handling of orchestration, form, and melodic and rhythmic contrast.

—32—

Gatherings at Cavaillé-Coll's showroom

Widor continued to perform numerous organ inaugurals and to make appearances at Cavaillé-Coll's showroom, giving an interested Parisian public a chance to experience his artistry outside the parameters of the church service.[268] On one series of recitals, shared with Saint-Saëns, he displayed the glories of the new organ built for the Town Hall of Sheffield, England.[269] And on another occasion, Widor assisted Lemmens during one of his former teacher's visits to Paris. From Le Ménestrel's report, Cavaillé-Coll must not have had an organ set up in his showroom at the time, though the report may be inaccurate; performing these substantial organ works on the piano would hardly have been very satisfying or worthy of bringing together a group of "devotees":

> Mr. Lemmens, the famous organist, recently brought together some devotees at Cavaillé-Coll's, in order to submit to them his new compositions, which will form a collection titled: *The Catholic Organist*. The scholarly professor, assisted by his former pupil, Mr. Widor, performed on the piano three grand sonatas for organ, of the best character; then a *Pontifical March* and a fanfare in fugal style, all very much applauded.[270]

Widor knew his *maître*'s style thoroughly, and it is easily discernable in his early organ works.

Another small gathering at Cavaillé-Coll's, perhaps on the large instrument destined for the Amsterdam Palace of Industry, brought together four of the most respected Parisian organist-composers. Marcel Dupré related:

> One evening, Franck played his *Six pièces* at the Cavaillé-Coll factory for Saint-Saëns, Widor and Guilmant who were gathered there. This was related to me, first by Guilmant, then later on by Widor, and lastly by Saint-Saëns. . . . All three agreed about the year of their meeting, which took place in 1875.[271]

Widor remembered a similar occasion when he heard Franck perform some of his works at Cavaillé-Coll's. Or could it have been the same occasion, but inaccurately recalled by either Dupré or Widor? Widor's recollection would have to date back to about 1878 when Franck premiered his *Trois pièces*, of which the *Pièce héroïque* is part; it is also known that Liszt visited Paris that year:

> He was a very worthy man, very noble in heart. He played almost all of his organ compositions for us at Cavaillé-Coll's one evening after a dinner that Saint-Saëns also attended. I recall among others the *Pièce héroïque* that he himself played poorly, not having the time to practice, for he gave many lessons. He had a very long hand, from whence the difficulty of his pieces for others. He made less pure organ music than musical thought that expressed itself by means of an organ. It was this *Pièce héroïque*, moreover, that he played one day for Liszt at Sainte-Clotilde.[272]

—33—

"I cannot understand an ignorant musician"

Although Widor has been remembered chiefly as an organ composer, his realm was confined neither to the tribune of Saint-Sulpice nor to Cavaillé-Coll's shop; he fast became a respected participant in the larger musical life of Paris and beyond. He had an insatiable thirst for knowledge in all fields of music. When in Vienna to supervise the rehearsals of his ballet *La Korrigane*, he still found time to attend ten programs:

> Out of eight days spent in Vienna, Mr. Ch.-M. Widor was able to hear *Lohengrin*, *Meistersinger*, and *Rheingold* of Wagner, *Fidelio* of Beethoven, and what else? The two German ballets *Rococo*, *Flik and Flok* [*Flick und Flocks Abenteurer* by Johann Wilhelm Hertel (1727–89)], and finally two Italian operas [Donizetti's] *Lucia* and [Verdi's] *Simon Boccanegra*. . . . But this is not all, the Viennese are not content with seven operas and two ballets in eight days, Mr.

Widor heard in addition: (1) at the Conservatory, the *Seasons* of Haydn . . . ,
(2) the Mass in E Flat of Schubert . . .[273]

From his own experience, Widor would constantly admonish his students:
"Go to concerts. Listen to a Weber overture, an allegro from a Mendelssohn
symphony, or the slow movement from one by Mozart. Then, take the piano
arrangements, and from them make an orchestration of your own. You can
compare your versions with the authors [*sic*]. There is no better lesson."[274]

Studying great music, art, and literature represented more than idle
pleasure to Widor; it was his passion. He often spent part of his vacations
visiting museums—whether in Italy, Germany or wherever he happened to
be.[275] He had a vast knowledge in all areas, and reportedly: "he amused
himself by writing Latin verses and had not forgotten his Greek."[276] When
counseling the young Louis Vierne on the merits of a complete education,
extending well beyond musical studies, Widor stated his philosophy on
such matters. Vierne related:

When the material of the lesson was exhausted, Widor read to me from
works on music history, biographies, analytical studies, chronologies, evolution since antiquity. . . . Then, Widor urged me to read in order to perfect
and complete my classical studies; he pushed me to study Greek and Latin,
to read the authors of these languages, to study French literature and the history of art in general. "I cannot understand an ignorant musician," he said to
me, "all that relates to the intellectual domain is intimately bound together
by obvious connections: music has certain rapport with painting, sculpture,
architecture, design, literature, and even with the exact sciences; look at
acoustics; read, read hard and retain; your memory is a tool of the first order,
let it be your library."[277]

As an inveterate worker and learner, Widor's erudition was renowned, and
those who knew him greatly admired it:

Widor was a man of exceptional culture, his knowledge on historical and art
matters, especially, being encyclopaedic. This background of cultural knowledge he drew upon richly during the lesson hour.[278]

Widor, in order to make his necessarily complex instruction more intelligible, frequently used comparisons with painting, architecture, and even
literature, to make concrete in our minds the forms that we should know.[279]

Well-read, a man of taste, open to beauty in all its forms, he lived an intellectual life of infinitely varied facets; a charming conversationalist, a memory
always alert and full of anecdotes to be relished . . .[280]

Let an engraver, or a painter, or a sculptor ask for some information or make
a slip, Widor will answer or correct the error. What a mine of information![281]

Throughout his life, Widor cultivated friendships with leading musicians, artists, sculptors, and literary figures. In his view, "The musician who does not know how 'to see' will never be great; I scarcely know a painter worthy of the name who hasn't learned how 'to listen.'"[282] Even here, Widor spoke from his own experience, as he had dabbled at painting in his formative years.[283]

—34—

Les salons musicaux: "The hostesses of that day had their salon"

The music salons of aristocrats and the otherwise well-heeled Parisians provided composers a venue in which to mingle and perform their music to an adoring audience. In his "Souvenirs autobiographiques," Widor titled one section "Les salons musicaux"; there, he provided a small window into that demimonde in which he figured regularly. He sometimes reels off names of other habitués at these gatherings that read like a *Who's Who* in the artistic, political, and literary realms of the time:

The hostesses of that day had their salon. One was thus sure to encounter them. In my quarter, for example, were the salons of the Trélats (Dr. Trélat) [on rue Jacob and later rue de Seine] and that of the Marquise de Blocqueville, daughter of Davout. They naturally had quite different [political] leanings; that of the Trélats was Republican—Father Trélat having been minister in 1848, and his son having remained the friend of the political complements of his father and, being endowed with a great talent as orator, campaigned against the Empire at its end. He was, for example, very close with the two brothers, Jules and Charles Ferry, friend of Émile de Girardin, Renan, Gambetta, and Bardoux (father of the senator). His wife [Marie Trélat] was a consummate musician, playing the piano perfectly, and singing with much talent, although possessing only a small voice. Her salon was one of the most curious; every Monday evening there was a dinner and gathering. Vaucorbeil, director of the Opéra, Bardoux, minister of the Beaux-Arts, Émile de Girardin, Bizet [1838–75], and Saint-Saëns met there regularly. As for myself, I had known the Trélats unceremoniously when I came to be named organist of Saint-Sulpice. Madame Trélat had come to see me there, announcing herself with simplicity, and she presented the two Ferry brothers to me. In order to thank me for my welcome, she graciously invited me to come to her Monday evenings.

On one of those Mondays, I recall very well Bizet playing some fragments from *Carmen*, which he had not yet completed.[284]

There, I made the acquaintance of one of the most curious figures that I ever met in my life: Dr. Marey, who was the first inventor of the *fusil-photographique* capable of taking ninety prints per minute, an invention that was later to lead to the development of cinematography. Marey had given some evening lectures at the Sorbonne in order to study there all the movements the eye was incapable of seeing pass by.

He had developed a girdle adorned with a recorder that, placed around the chest of a singer, allowed a more or less straight line to be produced on a mural surface or a projection screen. If the singer did not prolong the sound in an exact fashion, the line would indulge in all sorts of fantasies instead of being horizontal. Without flourishes or waves, the line was absolutely straight; it could even record all the reactions of the organs of a horse dashing in a race. . . .

Dr. Marey was a little Bourguignon, quite ugly with little eyes, always admirably dressed in frock-coat that seemed to have just come from the maker.

Some twenty years later, I was having lunch one morning at Foyot's when I saw Maurice Emmanuel [1862–1938] arrive: "You used to know Dr. Marey," he said to me. "He is in Paris at this moment and he is going to die shortly. He has begged me to come and look for you in order to ask you to play the sonatas of Beethoven for him, as before."

Very moved, I responded to Emmanuel: "When do I need to go?" —"Very quickly, as soon as possible, for he is going to die very soon." —"I will go see him this evening."

The savant had long ago settled in Naples, where he had set up his laboratory to indulge in the study of a rare species of little fish that one finds only in the Gulf of Naples or at the mouth of the Timiş River.

I arrived at the precise hour at Marey's house and was surprised to find him looking very well, admirably dressed in frock-coat, boots polished, etc.

"What, is this joke?" I said to him.

"I am at the end of my heart disease. . . . I have at maximum about a week. I have asked you to come. If by chance I was dying, people would have deterred you from coming." He did not laugh, but had conserved a sense of irony.

"You still play the piano well," he said to me, after having heard me play some famous sonatas for him, "but with less equality in the trills than in previous times!" He died seven days later.

It's also at the Trélats that I met for the first time Vaucorbeil and Bardoux. . . . I put myself at the disposal of Bardoux, a charming man, for several charity festivals. Vaucorbeil had composed several pieces for piano, and one or two cantatas that I had put under my fingers.[285]

Widor dedicated his *Six mélodies*, Op. 14, to Marie Trélat, and he often appeared at the Trélat's *Salon Orfila*. At one particular soirée, the press noted that Mlle Ella Lemmens-Sherrington, the talented daughter of Widor's former organ professor, sang one of Widor's *Mélodies italiennes* that she had sight-read only the day before. The reviewer commented, "Ch.-M. Widor played the piano the whole evening, and so very well, that in order to thank him on behalf of everyone present, Rosita Mauri (1856–1923) who was simply attending . . . danced the charming Sabotière from [Widor's] *La Korrigane*."[286]

Scores of letters over nearly two decades from Widor to Marie Trélat exude a certain warmth that raises questions as to whether their relationship remained completely platonic even before Dr. Trélat died in 1890. From his family's country home outside l'Arbresle (near Lyon) Widor wrote to her in Paris on September 3, 1884: "Your [recent] letter was so favorable that I have been living without anxiety, although very far from you. . . . Don't forget the hermit in the mountain—the hermit whose thought wanders constantly towards the north."[287] On July 14, 1891: "I send you all the affection there is in my heart, the unchangeable!"[288] Again, from l'Arbresle on September 15, 1892: "It seems to me that thinking of you constantly, it isn't necessary to write. . . . I send you all that there is of the most affectionate in the brain of a musician!"[289] On March 5, 1898: "Good day! Arrived this morning; are you expecting me this evening? . . . Delighted to be back after an ideal trip and to return to the loved home."[290]

In the fall of 1898, however, something had gone strangely awry in their relationship that required some urgent apologies from Widor. In an undated letter, though arguably from October 1898, Widor endeavored to reassure Marie of his enduring devotion:

Please believe that nothing has broken down in me, that no one has changed me, that the people to whom you allude are only an amusement or an artistic interest. I have never been able to speak frankly with you about it, for I have always seen that you would not believe it. I have no other *deep* affection but you, which has been and is beyond all testing. These last days you have caused me a great affliction by seeing an offensive intention so far from anything imaginable. If I had changed, I wouldn't have suffered so long, and unfortunately I am suffering from it *more* each day. How would you like me to act on Friday? Tell me the evening when you will be alone, and I will come to try to make you believe me; otherwise is it possible? I will do anything you want, in any case.[291]

On October 14, 1898:

I saw Madame [Anita] Kinen [a socialite singer]. It is unbearable to think that I have caused you pain and I don't know how to beg your pardon for it. But after the change of reception these recent months, I believed it was best for me to withdraw. What great surprise from your very affectionate letter from Villerville; then a second letter between Dieppe and Paris explaining your wavering. . . . I felt great pain from it, but that is secondary; what can't be and what I don't want is that you bear a grudge against me.[292]

A follow-up letter, dated October 1898, continued:

I'm sorry about all this. I never wanted "to punish you." Nothing in my letter can mean such a thing! Nothing like that came into my thought, *never*!

You cannot imagine how much you have changed for me these past months; you cannot imagine what this handshake was the day before your departure! Every day I said to myself that I was deluding myself, that I was mistaken, but no, no, I still felt the sensation of this arm pushing me back!

[Only] *one single* letter [from you] is certainly without an answer—the one that expressed doubts about your travel plans.

No one told me that you had come—my brother and my sister-in-law dragged me hither and yon that week outside Paris. Not a word added to this letter, the sight of which produced the effect on me that you can imagine and left me standing aghast! I remained in this nice state during my whole vacation!

Anita [Kinen] came without any intention, I know it well—only to tell me that I had caused you pain. Well, I *don't want* that, I *can't allow* that! I will never change, any more than I have changed in more than a quarter of a century. I've been terribly saddened, that's certain, but if I've been so, it's precisely *because*!

I am and remain *your* Ch.[293]

Marie and Charles apparently patched up their relationship, as letters after December 1898 resume the same warm tone of earlier ones. On August 26, 1899, for instance, Charles closed his letter to Marie: "a thousand very affectionate feelings from your ordinary musician!"[294]

In another portion of his "Souvenirs autobiographiques," Widor described the salon of Marquise Adelaide-Louise de Blocqueville, where he was "house accompanist." He also related his relationship with the widow of Édouard Bertin (1797–1871). Bertin's father Louis "l'Aîné" (1766–1841) ran the *Journal des Débats* and hired Berlioz as music critic; Édouard was a painter, a student of Eugène Delacroix, and later assumed the directorship of *Débats*. Widor was not customarily a name-dropper—he did not need to be—but the following excerpt again indicates the milieu in which he comfortably mingled, and it also demonstrates his penchant for storytelling. The informal, rambling style of the narrative is typical of the "Souvenirs autobiographiques":[295]

On the Left Bank, at the corner of the rue Bonaparte and the quai Malaquais, lived the daughter of Marshal Davout, the Marquise de Blocqueville—a widow without children, a very distinguished woman of refined spirit, having known almost the whole century, never leaving her home, having every evening some friends coming to court her, and on Mondays a dinner reception. She was connected with everyone. There, I met Liszt, and I will never forget him playing Beethoven's Sonata in C-sharp Minor for us one evening.

The Countess d'Haussonville, . . . , Claude Bernard, [Louis] Diémer, the sculptor Eugène Guillaume, etc. [were frequent guests].[296] The house is historic . . . [and] became a club. Some girls came there in the evenings. It was there that the Abbé Prévost [1697–1763] wrote his *Manon*. He had written a number of novels, twelve, I think, but he had submitted only eleven to his publisher, who tormented him to obtain the twelfth in order to be able to publish the work. It's thus that, pressed by time, he wrote the twelfth novel—that of the girl Manon with whom he had lived. He simply wrote his own love affair with Manon in this bawdy house. It was the very subject of Massenet's *Manon*, and the subject that also tempted Puccini, whose *Manon* [*Lescaut*] includes a gripping fourth [*sic*] act in which people help with the embarkment of these women for America—a scene that gives rise to some admirably treated choral developments.[297]

Madame de Blocqueville was haunted by the fear of being evicted from this house by the Beaux-Arts, whose school had already taken over the neighboring buildings. She had lived there about forty years, and in fact did not have to suffer this distress: she died, and the house still exists.

There were some beautiful portraits there, some interesting marble statuary from the Empire period and, on her mantle, in a frame like those that hold our little photographs, a wonderful pencil sketch by Ingres—the head from the *Apothéose d'Homère* that the master had dedicated to her.

I had become, so to speak, the accompanist of the house, frequently dining there on Mondays. I never entered this salon without my attention being drawn, in spite of myself, to this sketch by Ingres.

We all know the beautiful portrait of Édouard Bertin by Ingres.[298] Madame Édouard Bertin lived on the quai, 22 quai Malaquais, on the second floor, and if she did not have daily receptions, at least she received many friends. . . .

[Édouard] Bertin . . . had a very musical salon. Every Thursday, Berlioz, Saint-Saëns, Bizet, etc. passed by there. He was also very close with Ingres and Delacroix. People have long spoken of the quarrel between Ingres and Delacroix. Well, when Delacroix was received at the Academy, he began by leaving his card at Ingres's house; then he paid him a courtesy visit in the course of which the two great artists almost reconciled. A dinner at the Bertins' reconciled them completely, and Madame Bertin recounted to me several times how Delacroix apologized to Ingres: "You accuse me, my dear *maître*, of not knowing how to draw; I assure you that I knew how, only I let myself be swept away by the effect of color."

And, after that evening, Ingres and Delacroix dined every Thursday at the Bertins'.

I had the great misfortune not to know either Ingres or Delacroix. . . .

We have all read the *Mémoires* of Delacroix, which relate that he despaired over not being able to work on Sundays on his frescos in the chapel of the Saint-Anges at Saint-Sulpice. The curé had forbidden him, saying, "It is necessary to respect the rest of the Lord!" Before the separation of the Church and State, when the city of Paris had ordered from Delacroix the frescos in this chapel, the curé Hamon did not know Delacroix at all, but rather had connections with Ingres.

—"Dear Mr. Ingres," he said to him one day, "who is this Mr. Delacroix to whom they have entrusted the decoration of my chapel?"

—Grumbling of Ingres.

—"Would you like to see his work? He has been working for some time. I would like to have your opinion."

—"At what time does he go away?"

—"At 11:00, when he goes to lunch."

—"At what time does he come back?"

—"At 2:00. Never before."

—"I will come at 11:30 next Thursday."

He arrived; the work was already well along. He looked: *Héliodore Chased from the Temple; Saint Michel Crushing the Demon*. Suddenly, he took the curé by the throat and exclaimed, "Are you sure there's just one hell!" and thereupon he departed, leaving the poor man disconcerted.[299]

Unlike Ingres, Widor loved the Delacroix murals that greeted him at the foot of the stairway leading to the Saint-Sulpice organ gallery: "Before leaving the church he would pause with his friends before the magnificent murals . . . making his guests admire them. 'Isn't it beautiful, isn't it splendid,' he would cry, 'isn't this worthy of Rubens?'"[300]

—35—

Restaurant Foyot: "Its charm is difficult to describe"

Widor had the custom of dining daily at the famous rendezvous of intellectual Paris, the Restaurant Foyot, located opposite the Palais de Luxembourg at 33 rue de Tournon (today Place Francis Poulenc).[301] It was no corner bistro. The ambiance, cuisine, and service followed the best French traditions. In his restaurant guide of 1929, Julian Street classed it one of "six restaurants beyond compare" in Paris:[302]

The Left Bank of the Seine has fewer restaurants de luxe than the Right Bank, but it is rich in restaurants and cafés having associations with the distant past, and among those none is more charming, or more expensive, than Foyot's.

. . . Its charm is difficult to describe. It is quiet, dignified, restrained; the lighting is low and agreeable, the carpets seem softer than in other places, one does not hear the waiters move about, and there is never a clatter of silverware and dishes. It is not an ostentatious place, and puts on no airs, yet to me it is the very embodiment of refinement and distinction, and I never feel in better humour with my surroundings or with myself than when I dine at one of Foyot's tables.

Naturally, the cuisine and service are perfection, and the cellars are of the best.[303]

The entry in Robert-Robert's *Paris Restaurants* (1924) agreed:

> What a delicious place this is, so calm, so perfect in its restraint! . . . The service is admirable. The waiters, quiet and attentive, perform their duties with dignified efficiency, as they dispense the most succulent dishes.
>
> The cellar yields nothing in excellence to the *cuisine*. As Montesquieu would say: "This is one of the most venerable places on earth."
>
> The hall mark [*sic*] of both the establishment and its *clientèle* is a restrained excellence. Nothing jars. Moreover it is impossible even to imagine anything like pretentiousness in this environment of the old régime, so close to the Senate, to the Odéon with all its traditions, to the Sorbonne. Foyot is the haunt of the old French aristocracy and gentlemen of the older generation whose style is unequalled and unapproachable.
>
> The most famous dishes of this house are: Lobster, Suprême de soles, côte de veau, bécasse à l'Armagnac, cœurs d'artichauts, crêpes Suzette soufflées. Among the wines should be noted Croton 1895, Vougeot 1889, Chambertin 1878, Margaux 1877, Laffitte 1875.[304]

For many years, Widor found no better place to satisfy his gourmet palette and to join company with his friends and colleagues. Dupré was impressed that "Widor knew everyone at Foyot's: senators, writers, painters, the entire Parisian artistic élite."[305] To name but a few, at sundry times one could see gathered around Widor's table litterateurs: Alexandre Dumas *fils* (1824–95), Guy de Maupassant; philosopher Henri-Louis Bergson (1859–1941); painters: Léon Bonnat (1833–1922)—who painted two portraits of Widor (1887 and 1922), Jean-Louis Forain (1852–1931), Carolus Duran—who painted a portrait of Widor (1890), painter and playwright Henri Cain (1857–1937); singers: Emma Calvé (1858–1942)—famous as Carmen, Jean de Reszké (1850–1935); composers: Charles Gounod, Camille Saint-Saëns, Jules Massenet, Léo Delibes (1836–91), André Gedalge (1856–1926); and when they were in Paris: conductor Vassily Safonoff (1852–1918), composer and pianist Leopold Godowsky (1870–1938), pianist Alexander Glazunov (1865–1936), conductor Arthur Nikisch (1855–1922), conductor Sir Henry Wood (1870–1944), composer and pianist Ferruccio Busoni (1866–1924)—whom Widor particularly enjoyed; and of course many of his own pupils[306] (see fig. 9).

Widor enjoyed entertaining his friends at Foyot's in little get-togethers that he liked to refer to as "Foyotières";[307] he even turned Foyot into a verb, writing, "we Foyoted" [*on a Foyotté*].[308] In this richly diverse coterie, Widor was known to be a brilliant conversationalist and raconteur: "Whoever has enjoyed the charm of Mr. Widor's conversation understands the irresistible seduction of his music; when he speaks, one might think he is improvising, and it's always delightful";[309] "What thrilling conversations I had with him! His intelligence, his vast culture, his spirit held you under a spell";[310] "There were moments when the outside world disappeared for us, when we immersed ourselves into the ideal atmosphere where the fairies of dreams dance to the sound of celestial music, when my good *maître* dwelt with curious insight on painting, sculpture, engraving (he was a remarkable critic of art), also on history (Widor knew the *Mémorial de Sainte-Hélène* by heart), and finally on all that makes beauty in the world";[311] "Conversations were interesting, often fascinating, sometimes turning into impassioned artistic debates."[312] After he became a member of the Institut de France, Widor also became a regular at the Café de Paris and the Restaurant Lapeyrouse, which were nearer the Institute.

Widor thrived on the kind of artistic intercourse provided by his daily Foyotières, and these contacts were an important stimulus to his own creative process, as he described it:

> The brain of a composer is a sort of sponge that absorbs every day the multiple impressions of life, preserves them a longer or shorter period, and then, one day, reproduces them either spontaneously or under the influence of the will, with a relish, an intensity, a colouring, more or less powerfully, or more or less personally.
>
> Such is the phenomenon which is called "creation."
>
> Indeed, spontaneous generation does not exist in this order of things; the idea which seems to us newest always proceeds from another idea. "On est toujours le fils de quelqu'un" [One is always the son of someone], affirmed Beaumarchais a hundred years ago, and nothing since then has proved the contrary.[313]

The truth of this statement is clearly seen in Widor's works. In terms of performance style, instrumental technique, and idiomatic writing, Widor accomplished for the organ much of what Mendelssohn, Chopin, Schumann, and Liszt did for the piano, and he drew inspiration directly from these composers. Certain apparent borrowings can be seen, for example, in the similarity between the opening measures of Widor's Fifth Symphony and the twelfth etude of Schumann's Symphonic Etudes, Op. 13, for Piano; or in the opening four-measure phrase of the Andante Cantabile from the Fourth Symphony that is closely akin to a four-measure phrase in the fourth piece of Mendelssohn's *Lieder ohne Worte*, Op. 19, for Piano.

In addition to knowing Liszt personally, Widor had other personal links to the first half of the nineteenth century that certainly influenced him: "I knew two contemporaries of Chopin, the pianist Georges Mathias (1826–1910), his student who became a professor at the Conservatory, and Ambroise Thomas, the director of the Conservatory. . . . For six years, sitting at his [Thomas's] side [during the piano class examinations], I had the chance to take in some very precious memories."[314] Still, Widor knew that the creative process involves much more than precious memories. Questioning Bach's offhanded remark, "I have worked hard; whoever will work as hard will attain the same result,"

Widor asked: "Is this really true? I doubt it a little."[315] And then he defined the unique qualities that feed the creative process:

> Certainly, the necessity of constant work has been absolutely demonstrated to me, but still it's necessary that the terrain on which one works has been properly prepared. Atavism, primary education, the milieu in which one lives, the means of existence, the weather, the country—many are the sources, more or less favorable, to artistic blooming. . . .
>
> There are, then, causes other than work, causes completely independent of the necessary daily effort. . . . I would write "inspiration" or even "genius."[316]

—36—

Wagner and *Der Ring des Nibelungen*

The zealous pursuit of "the multiple impressions of life" led Widor into one of the most fortuitous experiences of his long career. In August 1876, he journeyed with Baron Émile d'Erlanger—a banker, amateur violinist, serious music enthusiast and ardent Wagnerian—to Bayreuth for the premiere of Wagner's epic tetralogy, *Der Ring des Nibelungen*.[317] "One noticed only a very few Frenchmen at this premiere," Widor would later recall.[318] Although he related only a few impressions of his time in Bayreuth, he later devoted entire articles to Wagner—articles in which he praised the wonders of Wagnerian opera.[319] From the few impressions that he did relate, it would seem that those in attendance—and what they wore—captured his attention as much as the music:

> Peculiar memories! In the park in front of the theater, there was an audience as variegated as cosmopolitan: an emperor, princes, financiers, poets, musicians, and the tall stature of Wilhelm the Great [1797–1888]—with top hat, impeccable frock coat, alone among men in soft hats and flannel shirts; no retinue, no police. In the hall, in front of us was the Countess de Schleinitz [1842–1912], in a very elegant evening gown; Liszt and his daughter Madame Cosima Wagner [1837–1920] were next to her. The Countess de Schleinitz— later Countess Wolkenstein—was ambassadress from Austria to Paris.[320]

In another recollection, he elaborated a bit further:

> I had before me Madame Wolkenstein, seated between her husband, Prussian minister at Saint-Petersburg, and Liszt, then at the height of his glory. Whatever might have been the impression produced on me by the music of Wagner, I couldn't take my eyes off of the sumptuous bare shoulders of Madame Wolkenstein, in this house where few women were décolleté.[321]

Widor struck up enough of a friendship with the Countess and Cosima Wagner that he could later boast: "It was at the Embassy, the Galliera mansion, that Madame Cosima Wagner stayed during the performances of *Siegfried* at the Paris Opéra. The Countess and Madame Wagner sometimes came to 7 rue des Saints-Pères [Widor's residence] to listen to a chorale prelude of Bach on my organ."[322]

Although Widor's background disposed him as a romantic-classicist, his work occasionally bears Wagnerian characteristics, but always instilled with his own French sensibilities: "The [French] eclectics . . . borrow from Wagner certain processes without openly breaking with the French tradition. It is among this group that it would be necessary to classify Mr. Widor."[323] Albert Schweitzer (1875–1965) rightly noted that in Widor's Sixth Symphony for Organ, the "*Adagio* was created under the influence of Richard Wagner. . . . The deep impression he received shows in this movement, which was written two years later."[324] It is consequently totally incorrect to classify Widor as a "notorious anti-Wagnerian,"[325] as has sometimes been alleged:

> Charles-Marie Widor is a Classicist. He has a fluent phrase, often mild, sometimes saccharine. But, he does not fear, above all in his theater works, certain violences, sometimes even a din, almost like Wagner, even though he has nothing otherwise of a Wagnerian.[326]

Reviewing countless performances of Wagner's operas in Paris and throughout Europe, Widor had only commendation for the "genius" of the "most daring innovator of our time."[327]

At the same time, servile imitation was anathema to Widor, and speaking of those French composition students who failed to express independent creative thinking, he wrote caustically: "We have here quite a host of apprentice musicians who scarcely trouble themselves except to assimilate the procedures of the lord of Bayreuth, and who do not fear to put on his boots—seven-league boots . . . goodbye personality, progressive thinking, and new direction; it's always the same tramp by the same boots."[328] Despite this comment, a few Wagnerian identifiers can be discerned upon occasion in Widor's music. One of the most revealing—and surprising—of these is the presence of the "Tristan" chord and the "Isolde" motive in one of his works having the strongest religious content, the *Symphonie romane* of 1899.[329]

Stage design and mechanical innovations were more than of little interest to Widor, and he was not particularly enamored of the orchestral placement at Bayreuth, where the pit is sunken quite deeply under the apron of the stage and partially covered by a shell. Extolling a performance of *Die Walküre* at the Paris Opéra, he explained his preference for the disposition there:

Die Walküre makes the maximum [effect] at the Opéra. It's completely legitimate: the work is superb and the execution very remarkable. . . .
   The dimensions of the auditorium of our Opéra are exceptionally favorable to the Wagnerian orchestra. People have spoken recently of lowering
the musicians' floor in such a fashion as to obtain a more distant and softer
ensemble, in imitation of Bayreuth.
   I believe that this would be a mistake.
   The delicacies of the Wagnerian symphony are exquisite at the Opéra, and
its power is in no way exaggerated. . . .
   I remember the impression produced in Bayreuth the day of the premiere performance of *Die Walküre*: we all had the sensation of cotton in our
ears, the mass of brass instruments in the "Ride of the Valkyries" producing
scarcely more impact than the four horns of Delibes in the picturesque prelude to *Sylvia*. . . .
   If the gentle effects have so much charm in Bayreuth where they come to
us as through a sort of vapor, poeticized by the distance, in contrast, the powerful effects absolutely lack energy and brilliance.[330]

In one recollection, Widor wondered why Wagner had not conducted the
tetralogy in Bayreuth:

[Wagner], who made such an uncontested reputation by directing the works
of Beethoven which he knew and directed by heart, had he doubted himself and been afraid of his nerves . . . when it was a matter of commencing
the great battle of Bayreuth? It was the greatest German conductor, maestro
[Hans] Richter [1843–1916], who conducted the famous tetralogy—an irreproachable performance that the audience at this musical feast will never
forget.[331]

In another recollection, Widor described an amusing incident he witnessed:

I still see poor [Albert] Niemann [1831–1917, in the role of Siegmund] complaining to Wagner about the smoke emitted by the smokestack to the right
of the stage in the first act [of *Die Walküre*], and begging that the intensity
of it be diminished. "Nothing will be diminished," responded Wagner; "this
smoke is my music—my music is this smoke; everything must be that way and
will remain that way." —"But it gets in my throat, this damned smoke, and I
can no longer sing!" —"You will sing." —"I can't!" —"I don't care, you will
sing!" [Very calmly, Niemann stepped aside and drew a cigarette from his
pocket. "Well?" said Wagner.] "Well!" replied Niemann, "make your smokestack sing; as for me, I will smoke during that time!" Everyone began to
laugh; Wagner himself went to temper his volcano, and Niemann sang the
wonderful duet with "fire."[332]

Liszt wanted Widor to meet Wagner during one of the intermissions of *Göt-terdämmerung*, but when they went to find him, he was vehemently rebuking the singer in the role of Hagen over some blunder he had made. They quickly withdrew, Liszt expressing the hope that there would be a more appropriate time.[333] Neither did Widor's friendship with Baron d'Erlanger gain him the opportunity to meet Wagner: "D'Erlanger had been Wagner's banker, and Wagner did not take much account of his presence, which reminded him of the fact. During the performances, we saw Wagner at the entrance of the orchestra seats, but we did not go to Wahnfried."[334] Widor also remembered seeing "Wagner crowned with laurels, circulating about the tables in the large room of the restaurant where people dined during intermission, and clinking his glass against those of the guests,"[335] but he never found the opportunity to be introduced to the man whose music he held in such high esteem. "I left the day after the last performance and returned to France via Switzerland, to see my family in the environs of Lyon."[336]

—37—

"I have the honor to live in the century of Liszt"

Widor's friendship with Liszt, whom he described as "politeness itself,"[337] soon had an eventful turn that he guarded as "the most extraordinary recollection of my artistic career."[338]

For the 1878 Universal Exposition in Paris, Cavaillé-Coll obtained on very short notice the important commission to build a monumental concert organ. To complete the project on time, he modified the organ he was in the process of building for the church of Notre-Dame d'Auteuil and installed it in the cavernous forty-seven-hundred-seat Moorish-styled Trocadéro Exhibition Building.[339] On March 31, 1878, Cavaillé-Coll summoned Widor to his workshop to be the first to test the new instrument;[340] he improvised for more than an hour as he explored all of its resources "in a series of pieces of diverse styles," and concluded with "a triumphal *sortie* in which [he] displayed an imposing masterly skill."[341] In his regular *Estafette* column, Widor reported:

> Recently in the workshops of Mr. A. Cavaillé-Coll, in the presence of the minister of public works, was the first hearing of the *grand orgue* built for the festival hall of the Trocadéro. The organ is superb: its basses have a power and a precision of attack altogether admirable; the mechanism is perfect. The general voicing of the instrument, entrusted to one of the most remarkable specialists in the field, Mr. Félix Reinburg, couldn't be more successful.[342]

After the organ's installation, however, Widor expressed regret over its placement: "It is encased in a sort of niche at the back of the orchestral shell—encased and imprisoned in such a way that the general sonority is reduced and, in a way, veiled. The real power is enormous, but the force that is manifested to the listener seems less considerable. This harms a bit the ensemble effects, but, on the contrary, becomes extremely favorable to the delicacies."[343] The acoustical problems in the hall were later subjected to attempts at rectification, but as Widor described them, they were not at all successful: "The shell where the orchestra is placed produces some false resonances. To attenuate them, they have padded this backdrop with thick shag; it's an unfortunate idea, for the instruments and choristers in closest proximity, that is to say all the basses of the orchestra, no longer have sound. They're killing the patient to spare him from suffering."[344]

Liszt happened to be in Paris just as the organ's installation was completed; of course, he wanted to see the new instrument. Widor was awakened with the urgent news:

I was living on rue Garancière at the time. One fine morning at 7:00 père Cavaillé came to ring at my door and said, "Get up quickly. Liszt expects us at 9:00 at the Trocadéro, where I just completed my organ. He is asking to hear it."

Naturally, I was eager and the two of us arrived at the Trocadéro, where we found Liszt chatting as ordinarily as possible with the voicers in the interior of the instrument, where he looked at all the details with the greatest care. Our friendship was to commence there and continue at Madame de Blocqueville's, where we met again frequently.

Liszt was extremely friendly and had absolutely no kind of arrogance; he even sometimes seemed to be thanking you for whatever you could ask of him. He spoke and wrote wonderful French. He read all that was published in our language, all the philosophy and poets. A close friend of [Victor] Hugo [1802–85], he went donkey riding on country outings with him and his entourage. (Write a little note about Liszt's kindness.)[345] He was greatly admired in all the salons—political or philosophical—where the Parisian clique reigned. . . .

I played for him the Bach that he asked of me. Having had the kindness to ask me to play my latest work for him, I performed my Third Symphony.

He was still keenly interested in the mechanism of the organ, the studies of the pressure and the harmonic schemes of père Cavaillé, and toward noon he invited the two of us to lunch in one of the exposition restaurants that was already open. He said to me, "How can I thank you for the time that I have made you lose this morning?" At the word "lose," I blushed and responded, "I have the honor to live in the century of Liszt and I have never heard Liszt!" —"Well fine, I have a little free time at this moment. Madame Érard has given to me [her place at] rue du Mail; I have established my residence there. Do you want to come tomorrow at 2:00? I will play anything that you wish."

Nearly all week, he played for me all the works of the time as well as his own.

On Sunday, I dined at Madame Érard's—at the chateau de la Muette.[346]

Widor was bowled over. He had described Liszt in one of his recent *Estafette* columns as "an artist of genius . . . the most marvelous instrumentalist who ever sat before a piano keyboard . . . one of the glories of the century,"[347] and now he experienced Liszt's artistry firsthand. That special Sunday evening at Madame Érard's left another indelible impression on him, and he wrote about it a few years later in one of his *Piano Soleil* articles:

Like Rubinstein, Liszt at the piano gave the impression of the "extraordinary." One conjured up the vision of a Michelangelo grinding the material and molding the marble in order to make the design burst forth from it.

I still see him during his next to last sojourn among us, at a time when he was vigorously carrying his sixty-seven years (in 1878), in the grand salon of La Muette, during the Exposition. . . . Madame Érard had invited only five or six close friends, from fear of disappointing a more numerous audience if the *maître* was not disposed to perform. Émile Ollivier [1825–1913, prime minister under Napoléon III and Liszt's son-in-law by his first marriage], Gounod, Madame [Marie-Gabrielle] Krauss [1842–1906, soprano], and two or three gentlemen of lesser importance were there.[348]

After dinner, Liszt asked Madame Érard if it was agreeable to her that he play a little music; Madame Krauss and some among us had never heard him. You can imagine the response.

He began to prelude, improvising in four parts a sort of soft and tranquil singsong; from time to time, when it seemed to him that the attention could grow tired of the uniformity of the rhythm, a light accent, a fleeting glimmer immediately came to break the monochrome of this autumn sky. He played, holding the wrist very low, the base of the hand resting on the key slip, and his long fingers making angular gestures on the ivories like crabs' legs.

The improvisation did not seem at all long, and yet it had lasted nearly half an hour. It had remained in perfect harmony with the character of this immense salon in which a semi-obscurity prevailed, and with the frame of mind of the little audience silently grouped around the piano.

Liszt got up and addressed Madame Krauss: "Do you want to sing the *Erlking*? I know that you interpret it like no one else; I will accompany you." And he began the first measures of it, quite tranquilly, in a moderate tempo allowing him to give the octave passages all their character and value; at the entry of the voice, the sonority grew softer without, however, ceasing to remain rich and deep; then as the drama unfolded, the intensity grew: it was no longer the simple text of Schubert that we heard, but a sort of admirable piano reduction of a wonderful and fantastic orchestration. Madame Krauss was pale; she felt herself carried off, she too, in the vertiginous race that she related, and her singing was bloodcurdling.

We listened, breathless.

At the supreme crescendo, the lid of the piano gave us the effect of the mouth of an enchanted cavern, as in *One Thousand and One Nights*, which would open suddenly to let the furious accents escape from an orchestra of angry demons.

It was terrifying.

And, when all was finished, no one had the idea to applaud.

One didn't even dare to speak any more.

Never will we forget that evening on a beautiful June Sunday in 1878.[349]

Liszt had exhibited his characteristic collegial generosity, and the memory of his humanity, musicianship, and technical prowess never ceased to inspire Widor. Even in such a short time, he assimilated much from the Lisztian aura, and it became an enduring part of his own life's aesthetic.

—38—

"Art is made of will, affirmation, logic"

Of the approximately thirty works dating from the middle and late 1870s, several stand out as mileposts in Widor's creative development: the Mass (whose date of composition remains uncertain), three concertos, and two additional organ symphonies. If the critics did not unanimously applaud some of these works, they usually conceded the conscientious and skillful craftsmanship that Widor lavished on all of his compositions. Common were appraisals such as this review for his *Trois pièces* for Cello and Piano, Op. 21, which lauded "the very distinguished workmanship that one knows of this young composer."[350] Throughout his life, Widor was known for his intellectual mien, and his works were often branded as too erudite and not emotive enough:

> Mr. Widor is an intelligence more than a heart (from the point of view of artistic production, of course); he thinks, he ponders more than he feels. Also, all that is the most difficult in the art of harmony is for him only a game. What's more, he now goes beyond what can be known and taught in school. His spirit, always outstretched, always in quest of new combinations, does not stop before the most grating clashes of sounds, if they have for him the appearance of reason. When one listens to him, one is less charmed than interested; one follows him with a lively interest without being swept away with enthusiasm, and one admires him more than one enjoys him.[351]

Without question, Widor's style represents an aesthetic in which the overt emotionalism associated with some music of the period bows under the dominion of intellect. Perhaps a parallel can be drawn in this regard with Johannes

Brahms (1833–97), whom Widor admired as one of the most remarkable representatives of contemporary German music:[352]

> Brahms has a style of his own, forms of his own, a very personal and very sincere turn of phrase, a manner of developing an idea—absolutely born from the idea itself, and by this absolutely necessary to the comprehension of this idea. He is, in a word, a great artist, owing nothing to anyone, being concerned about those around him only to judge and compare, and not to borrow anything, disdaining effect, shunning convention, and having a holy horror of banality.[353]

Classical purity, restrained control, structural balance, an emotional domain characterized by elegance—such are the intrinsic qualities of Widor's aesthetic. Generally speaking, his was a more conservative romantic culture, but the lack of instant outward appeal does not signify banality, a fault with which his work has sometimes been equated. Those who studied and performed his music thought otherwise, however. Though speaking of the Symphonies for Organ, the objection raised by Albert Riemenschneider could well serve a wider sphere of Widor's music:

> How often have we heard the expressions "the bunk in Widor" and "the dry and weary wastes" and similar statements! How little did these supercilious dogmatists know how much they were expressing their own ignorance. . . . Verily it takes some much longer to comprehend than it does others, especially when something really worth while [sic] is under consideration.[354]
>
> While I do not wish to maintain that [these works] are all of equal worth or interest, I involuntarily feel that such remarks . . . come from minds either not attuned for various reasons to receive the import of these compositions or from the plain lack of study of the same.[355]

Many beauties lie behind the sometimes austere façade: "[Widor] has stood first and always for the nobility, the seriousness, one might almost say the severity of thought."[356] For Widor, the emotional domain of musical expression could not supersede formal considerations—logical structure.[357] Everything had to express proportions as perfect as a Michelangelo's *Moses*. Widor explained his primary concern for the structural element in music this way: "Music, like architecture . . . lives from symmetry and from recurrences. Art is made of will, affirmation, logic";[358] "in a musical work, proportions as calculated as those in a Greek temple are necessary."[359] Both Fétis and Lemmens had indoctrinated Widor with the principles of clarity, order, care—with all the etceteras those words include—and they were a law to him in every aspect of his affairs. One of his students noted, "Widor had many of the qualities of the engineer (and, perhaps, even of the efficient engine) throughout his life."[360]

Most of those who spoke or wrote of him seemed to employ the word "clarity" as the epitome of the Widorian aura:

> This clarity, if we think of his compositions and of the judgments that came back like avowals in his conversations on music, resulted from a rigorous and logical construction. Indeed, in the retouches that he made to his works, even a long time after their publication, he sought above all to balance them better and to render their order more precise, more easily apparent, in some needful manner. It could be said that he conformed, perhaps without thinking of it, to the immortal principle of the aged Horace: *lucid order.* By an intuition revealing to him that the laws of art correspond to the laws of the human spirit, he assessed that order, that is to say the harmonious realization that an organizing idea necessitates, is truly a source of light. The clarity of a work can result from the sincerity and strength of the idea that animates it; but to be complete, it also requires an exact placing of the essential elements, the expressive details, and their mutual subordination.[361]

—39—

Trio in B-flat Major: "Full of qualities of the first order"

For completely reliable assessments of a musical composition, leaning too heavily on evaluations of music critics—who in Widor's time were anonymous for the most part—carries considerable risk. As with any review, the evaluation of the writer is always subjective and does not necessarily validate or invalidate a work simply because it either exceeds or falls short of the critic's preconceived notions. Still, critical reviews do serve as historical chronicles of a kind, and when enough of them are taken into consideration a fairly accurate impression can be gained. In addition, they indicate the critical reception of a work within its historical context. Musicians of today and tomorrow—at a distance of well over a century in the case of most of Widor's works—are in a better position than his contemporaries to evaluate his work for posterity and judge its potential for reentry into the repertoire. However, since many of Widor's scores are difficult to locate and available recordings represent only a small portion of his output, period reviews form an essential evaluative resource.

Reviews of Widor's major compositions from this evolutionary period often indicate that he had not yet arrived at a completely personal idiom. For example, reviews of the Trio in B-flat Major, Op. 19, for Piano, Violin, and Cello clearly recognized his stylistic leanings:

> This work is remarkable for the life and the warmth that the author has lavished on it, sometimes even to excess. It is very worked, very involved, and draws close, in style, to some chamber music compositions of Schumann

and Rubinstein. In order to be rightly appraised, the first Allegro and the Finale would need a second hearing; as for the Scherzo, it is bright, lively, and charming, and the Andante is striking at first sight by the nobility and the breadth of its melodies no less than by the interest of its craftsmanship. The role of each instrument, taken separately, is full without being brilliant; and that is perhaps the principal reason why this Trio, conscientiously made, strongly conceived, and full of qualities of the first order, will not truly make all the effect on which the author would be justified to count.[362]

There are some very earnest qualities in the Trio . . . but the style of it is chopped up.[363]

The first critic's appraisal, that a second hearing would be required before he could comment on two of the movements, affirms a quality already pointed out and that some saw as intrinsic to Widor's work: it sometimes did not offer the kind of facile listening experience that appealed immediately to the galleries; the combination of intellect and emotion escaped the understanding and did not always satisfy the listener on a single hearing. Nonetheless, Liszt was attracted to the Trio and played the piano part in a performance in Weimar, and he recommended it to Hans von Bülow (1830–94).[364] Later, however, Liszt assessed: "Widor's Trio, while distinguished, does not seem to me to be on the same level as those by Saint-Saëns and Bronsart."[365]

In performances of his chamber music, Widor generally played the piano part "with a real talent, where correctness and refinement dominate,"[366] and he engaged his friends—performers of the first rank—to take the other parts or perform the solo role in his concertos:

The premiere of the Trio in B Flat dates from the month of March 1874; I played it all over the place with Marsick and Delsart. In 1875, I wrote several cello pieces [*Trois pièces*, Op. 21] for Delsart. My first serious work, following the time-honored formula, was the Concerto in F for Piano and Orchestra [Op. 39], which made a big impression at the Châtelet (directed by Colonne [founder of the Concerts du Châtelet]) under the fingers of Diémer on November 19, 1876. Diémer, who was then professor at the Conservatory, was endowed with an incomparable technique. It was a great success. Diémer, who had had the kindness to take a chance with it, was recalled three times.[367]

The eminent violinist Martin-Joseph Marsick (1848–1924), cellists Jules Delsart and Jules Lœb (1852–1933), flutist Claude-Paul Taffanel, and pianists Francis Planté, Louis Diémer, and Isidor Philipp appeared regularly in performances of Widor's music. All were extraordinary musicians. Marsick was violin professor at the Paris Conservatory and Widor considered him "one of the two or three most remarkable virtuosos of this time."[368] Of Diémer, Widor wrote in the most glowing terms: "His fairylike fingers run over the keys with unparalleled sureness and elegance; never dryness in the sound, never brutality nor irritability in the attack of the note. The instrument becomes a melodious and suave voice that leaves us unaware if any difficulties exist, and that transmits pure and sound musical impressions to us."[369] Quality of performance seems never to have been an issue, and Widor never complained of ill-prepared performers or poor performances.

—40—

"This service, the most beautifully religious it is possible to imagine"

As in the majority of French Catholic churches, the *grand orgue* of Saint-Sulpice speaks from its commanding position in the rear gallery over the front entrance of the church, and a smaller accompanimental *orgue de chœur* is situated in the apse at the opposite end of the church, some 390 feet from the *grand orgue*. The choir fills the spacious chancel area between the choir organ and the altar, which at Saint-Sulpice is placed just on the chancel side of the transept.

In the preface to his *Messe*, Op. 36, Widor described the luxurious resources that Saint-Sulpice afforded him: "This Mass was written for the choir of the Church of Saint-Sulpice, in Paris; that is to say for a double choir: one, of approximately two hundred voices from the seminary, the other of approximately forty performers of the choir."[370] About fifty boys were included in these choral resources, and a group of string basses regularly joined the large chorus of men and boys, for additional support.[371] For the great feast days, the addition of a small string orchestra of about ten musicians reinforced the accompaniment of the choir.[372]

The prelude, offertory, and postlude were played on the *grand orgue*, and it joined in antiphonally for the Kyrie, Psalm, and canticle versets.[373] The interludes and organ responses provided many opportunities for the organist to exhibit improvisational skill in developing the liturgical theme of the moment, sometimes to the considerable length of a fully developed fugue, complete with grand crescendos.[374]

The Saint-Sulpice services were as beautiful to watch as to listen to. There was a great sense of religious ceremony, especially on high feast days. One such colorful occasion was described by American music professor Frederic Benjamin Stiven:

> When the curé had finished the sermon, we all went back into the organ loft, and Widor, taking his place again at the great organ, began to improvise brilliantly in a march rhythm. The procession of the Feast of the Assumption

had started. Leaning over the stone balustrade of the loft, we saw approaching far down the great center aisle, altar boys in their red cassocks and white cottas, bearing lighted candles. These were followed by young men swinging burning censers in rhythm with the march. Then the young girls . . . some 20 or 30 were marching together, two by two, the center ones of the group bearing a large banner from which wide ribbons were strung and carried by the first and last girls of the group. There were several of these groups . . . in their white dresses and flowing veils. Then came more candles, more censers, and finally the priests . . . all garbed in the vestments of their office. But the culminating interest of the procession centered in the passing of the archbishop. . . . He walked beneath a brilliant red and gold canopy, supported by four gold standards, fastened together some three feet from the floor by elaborate brass railings. These standards were on wheels, and the canopy was rolled by four acolytes carrying candles.[375]

Such scenes easily explain the two dramatic marches in Widor's Op. 13 *Symphonies.* The way in which organ music was interwoven into the service, and Widor's manner at the organ, fascinated and inspired those who witnessed it:

This service, the most beautifully religious it is possible to imagine, is an incessant occupation of and interchange between grand and chancel organs, choir and priest. . . .

When not actually playing [Widor] chats constantly in subdued vivacious tones and gracefully demonstrative manner. . . .

Fond of his organ, he is like a boy showing off his toy engine to companions. . . .

. . . Many times while finishing a sentence, without seeing either book or instrument, his hands unconsciously seek the chords connecting with the closing tones of the choir, but he never pulls a stop without examining it carefully. He frequently traces the notes being sung with his finger, indicating curious or interesting features of the composition, sometimes humming the air, more than once bringing out an unusually beautiful strain in full baritone voice. . . . Easy with everything, negligent with none! Every accent, turn, change of the chancel music is reflected in face or hand, conversation going on all the time. He is never one instant still or settled. Indeed Widor never "settles."

He plays a strain; it is taken up, as if continued, by the chancel. Again, this time the grand organ echoes; again, the other responds, the great sweep of the vocal ensemble merging absolutely, now uniting, again separating, imploring, majestic, tender, praying! . . .

Then came the vocal "sortie." "Mediocre!" If ever a composition was damned by one word it was this. I expected to see the poor, pale sheet of Gregorian chant burn up and blow away. But the most was made of the mediocrity, and the best was to come. . . .

. . . Widor shut his eyes for a moment, not as an artist, but as a business man might who had many things in his mind and sought to bring one to the surface. Then the music began. And here I must stop, for a Widor improvisation inspired by genius and warmed by a sincere desire to please, is not to be described by pen.[376]

For a time, between October 1871 and January 1874, Widor enjoyed a sort of musical sparring relationship with Gabriel Fauré who took the position of choir organist of Saint-Sulpice for a meager eighty francs per month.[377] "We were both young," Widor recalled. "Fauré, still unknown by the public and himself unaware of his capabilities, had accepted the modest functions of accompanist to the choir of Saint-Sulpice."[378] Each musician, improvising on the themes of the other, played a game of one-upmanship, "doing his best to engineer some daring modulation at the moment of the 'takeover.'"[379] Those exchanges became renowned for their quick-witted displays of improvisational skill, "Widor inspiring himself from the themes of Fauré . . . and Fauré returning to him the same."[380] In 1892, Widor could reminisce fondly about those Sundays when their interchanges traversed the length of the great nave of the church, sometimes in fiery dialogue:

> It's [at Saint-Sulpice] that I knew him; we were nearly contemporaries, new in our respective functions, recently transplanted from the provinces to Paris, having common ideas on almost everything, very sympathizing in character, understanding each other wonderfully.
> It often came to me to take a theme from his songs as an improvisation subject. A few moments later, Fauré's organ returned to me the same courtesy, and I heard myself commented on with infinite ingenuity and charm by the most agreeable of colleagues.
> I remember an office on Christmas Eve when our two organs returned to each other subjects and responses, episodes and countersubjects, a song of Fauré serving as countertheme to a noël of the good old days, and the same noël immediately being returned to me with many allusions to my first symphonies, and with the most artistic developments.[381]
> . . . Thus every Sunday, it was a competition or rather a contest between the two organs—a courteous contest, that goes without saying.[382]

Courteous perhaps, but not without an edge of competition; it may have been the first vestiges of the bad blood that would develop between the two men. But that would be some forty years later; during Fauré's short tenure at Saint-Sulpice, Widor at least had a partner at the *orgue de chœur* equal to his own artistic prowess.

In 1893 Fannie Edgar Thomas (b. 1870) opined, "The choirmaster and chancel organist of St. Sulpice evidently do not figure in M. Widor's mind as musical entities."[383] Actually, this was not the case; Widor was blessed with some fine musicians at the front end of the nave. André Messager (1853–1929), a disciple of Fauré and a fresh graduate of the École Niedermeyer—a school founded by Louis Niedermeyer (1802–61) that specialized in the education of church musicians—became choir organist in 1874 when Fauré replaced Théodore Dubois as choirmaster at La Madeleine. Widor recalled their harmonious musical exchanges to be much as they had been with Fauré: "The *grand orgue* and the *orgue de chœur* responded to each other tit for tat, sacredly, liturgically, in perfect harmony. Often one proposed a theme that the other developed. Quite often, I questioned my choir colleague, imploring his critique on the interpretation of a work, its effect at a distance and in light of the amplitude of a one-hundred meter long nave."[384]

Philippe Bellenot, another former Niedermeyer student, succeeded Messager in 1879. In five years' time, however, Bellenot became choirmaster, succeeding Charles Bleuzé (choirmaster, 1867–84), and he held that position for the next forty-four years, until 1928. Another former student of the École Niedermeyer, Jérôme Gross succeeded Bellenot as choir organist and held that position until 1924;[385] both Widor and Vierne considered Gross to be a fine musician and an accomplished organist.[386] Marie-Joseph Erb (1858–1944) confirmed, "It was a marvel to hear the blending of the work of these three artists."[387] Widor, Bellenot, and Gross worked together to provide the fine palette of music at Saint-Sulpice for several decades.[388]

Nearly twenty years after Widor and Fauré engaged in their improvisational duels, Widor found himself in a similar situation with the redoubtable Charles Gounod, whom he held in the highest esteem; Widor related:

The Gounod town house is separated from the Poirson town house by the rue Montchanin, a sort of blind alley, very elegantly constructed. . . . The windows of the two music salons face each other; from the first evenings of June, they open them wide, and if you wander in these solitary corners, you have the chance to hear a curious concert: from the right and from the left shoot torrents of harmony; two organs responding to each other—a combat between the two façades, a melodious combat assuredly.

One evening last July [1891], at the Poirson town house, Gounod read to us after dinner his very literary translation in verse of the charming legend by Mistral, *La communion des saints;* then he sat down at the piano to accompany Mlle Laudi, who sang the reserved music of the *maître,* composed for his poetry. I was at the organ, sustaining quietly the harmonic thread of his composition. When the piece was finished he said, "Stay at the keyboard, I'm going to my house; we will improvise on two organs!"

He left, and soon we heard in the silence of the night the first chords of the Bach chorale, *O Christ, tu es la pureté du jour;* it was the text to develop.

And I did my best to respond to him, rendering phrase for phrase, and modulation for modulation.

Gounod was wonderful, and I was shamefully beaten.

He was delighted. . . .

He remained at the keyboard, drawing his inspiration from a new theme that he treated no less magisterially; we listened enraptured to him, forgetting the hour.[389]

—41—

Mass: "A godsend"

The potential of the large and varied—one might almost say theatrical—resources available at Saint-Sulpice, including the special acoustical and spatial properties of the church itself, served as the impetus for the sacred choral works that Widor composed. The unique situation influenced the novel design of each work: *Motets*, Opp. 18 and 23; *Messe*, Op. 36. Hector Reynaud, Widor's early biographer, wrote:

This ensemble, formed from elements so varied, and moreover unique, lent itself to vast combinations, but the discovery and realization of them did not fail to be difficult; an artistic imagination and a thorough knowledge of counterpoint was necessary, as well as a special study of the instruments and voices; Mr. Widor has lacked nothing. I have for proof of it the very success of this Mass, which has not taken long to win every commendation, gaining respect by virtue of [its] power and originality. It is, in fact, the characteristic of truly great works to provoke from the outset some astonishment, after which they win many commendations and finally raise, from all their strength, the esteem and admiration of all. . . .

This Mass for two organs and two choirs is a novelty, if it were only studied from a technical point of view. I see in it a very skillful carrying out of the elements, but only those that the choir of Saint-Sulpice furnishes; successive or simultaneous employment of the voices of the choir and the seminary; the role of the two organs, at times separated, at times reunited, all contribute to the variety. Notice, besides, the relative brevity of the score and how the composer has known how to avoid the stumbling block, against which many famous masters have hit, namely, of constant repetition, without being tedious, of a group of words, and of the oversubordination of the sacred text to the pure fantasies of the musical phrase. Mr. Widor . . . makes use of the word . . . only for the thought; he speaks . . . only in order to say something—something new or unexpected. In his style, the idea is clear, the phrase is quite rhythmical, developed very learnedly, without the harmonic progressions, even the most daring, ever causing the principal motive to be forgotten. Charm, emotion, power, these are the qualities of this music; there is some Handel and some Bach in Mr. Widor, and I mean by this that one finds in his style the strength of these masters; there is also, and in a large measure, a penetrating grace that recalls Mendelssohn, all of it animated by catholic sentiment.[390]

All agreed that the Agnus Dei is a jewel that transcends the ordinary:

> The [Agnus Dei], if it may be compared to an antique cameo, is chiseled with an infinite art, but the workmanship does not diminish the breath of it, does not hold back the ardor, and thwarts nothing of the powerful flight of inspiration.[391]
>
> The Agnus Dei, this exquisite page, [is] one of the most delicate and inspired of the work of Mr. Widor. A godsend like that is sufficient to make a composer a master.[392]

The Mass's date of composition is uncertain. Although its opus number places it in the second half of the 1870s, the publisher's plate number indicates the date of publication as 1885. In any case, by 1890 the press reported that the Mass was performed every year at Saint-Sulpice on the third Sunday in January—the feast day of Saint-Sulpice.[393]

Although Widor had yet to venture into the domain of the theater, his religious works exhibited a tinge of that sphere, and he was not unaware of the proximity of the two styles:

> It would seem perhaps a paradox to affirm that the greatest musicians of the theater, commencing with Mozart,[394] are also the greatest musicians of the church, and yet isn't the Mass a drama? To have fathomed the human passions, to have learned how to put in place—in an unbroken progressing thread—the elements of action and emotion all together, isn't this yet a natural preparation to sacred dramaturgy? Certainly, there is contrast, but also affinity, transposition of the human onto the divine plan, where the agitations of the earth go to lose themselves in the serenity of heaven. And no one, more than the man of the theater, can know how naturally to adapt his means of expression to those two classes—at the same time so distant and so close.[395]

—42—

Three Concertos: Piano, Violin, Cello

Of the three concertos composed during the second half of the 1870s, the Op. 39 Piano Concerto appeared first. As mentioned earlier, Widor preferred to conduct his piano concertos and rarely, if ever, performed the solo part. He dedicated the work to his friend Louis Diémer, a champion of new music. At the outset, the *Revue et Gazette* had little praise for the work:

> This concerto . . . is a respectable work, but nothing more; well written and conducted rather skillfully, it completely lacks character. In the first place,

notably, one scarcely finds anything other than some passagework, which could pertain to a collection of etudes. Mr. Widor has made and will make better works than this concerto, which we can only consider as a pause in his career as composer.[396]

Musica Sacra tellingly described the concerto as "highly metaphysical music that the Parisian public, too spoiled by the theater, has not yet been able to appreciate fully, but which is a great work in the judgment of connoisseurs."[397] Just a little over a year later, the *Revue et Gazette* reported quite a different impression from its initial one:

The Piano Concerto of Mr. Widor . . . is a composition in three movements where fantasy plays quite a large role, if not in the character of the motives, at least in their succession and arrangement. There are pages of excellent effect in all the movements, above all in the first.[398]

Le Ménestrel expressed a similar change of mood in its reviews. In 1876, it had criticized Widor for having "yielded a little to this urge that inclines the new music school to be more concerned about form than substance,"[399] and a year later, the journal reproached Widor only for recalling Schumann too often.[400] In time, the concerto became the object of considerable popular enthusiasm.[401] Isidor Philipp first heard the concerto in 1886 and used the occasion to seek out its composer; their close friendship endured to the end of Widor's life:

The work pleased me tremendously—it was musical and brilliant, and I set myself to studying it with the idea of suggesting its performance to one of the orchestra conductors in Paris or in the provinces. I was most anxious to consult the composer, whom I knew to be very busy with his various duties . . . and of whom rumor said that only handsome and aristocratic ladies could arouse his interest, that he was something of a snob, and that on Sundays the console of his organ was surrounded by a bevy of countesses and *marquises*. I confided in Saint-Saëns, my mentor, who immediately said to me: "That is just talk, Widor is charming; a little distant, it is true, but I am sure that he will receive you with pleasure."[402]

A Violin Concerto (without opus number, though perhaps planned to be Op. 38), of 1877 appeared exactly one year after the Piano Concerto, but unlike the latter work, which only gained in favor, the Violin Concerto failed dismally in spite of a fine performance under the sure baton of Édouard Colonne:

The public of the Châtelet concerts had, last Sunday [November 18], the first fruits of a Concerto for Violin by Mr. Widor, interpreted by Mr. Marsick. We found in this new work more life and sentiment than in the preceding compositions of Mr. Widor, which one has reproached, and not without reason, for a certain dryness, imperfectly compensated for by an always very artistic workmanship. The progress, nonetheless, is not complete; there is still more than one part denuded of interest in this Concerto (or rather *concert piece*, for it consists of one piece in which different movements follow one another). What is necessary to praise is the beautiful character, the nobility of the slow movement by which the work begins, and which one finds again in fragments, alternating with the diverse phases of the Allegro; this is the style of the entire composition, this is the art with which the orchestra is employed, which is treated symphonically and plays an important role. But almost all the Allegro episodes are of an unsuccessful invention; one does not at all feel a sure and frank inspiration there. The ending also lacks breadth and turns short. The composer could not have desired, in order to make the most of his work, a more precise, more solid, more colored performance than that of Mr. Marsick, who knew how to draw some excellent effects from a violin part where the virtuoso is not given much chance. Neither in this violin part nor in the ensemble of the composition has the public found cause to let itself, as one crudely says, be grabbed. And, indeed, there was no chance for resounding success, this genre of composition being more particularly addressed to the discerning. But we hardly understand the marks of disapproval that followed the applause of which the virtuoso was the object; these things are usually reserved for the composers who "break the windows," or who are absolutely incompetent; and Mr. Widor is neither.[403]

Shortly after the concert, Édouard Lalo wrote a brief evaluation to violinist Pablo de Sarasate (1844–1908) that concurred with that of the press: "a concerto of Widor, or rather one formless piece without design that lasted more than half an hour, very well played by Marsick, made a colossal failure at the Châtelet."[404]

The Violin Concerto seems never to have been performed again, and Widor's own assessment of it confirmed that he knew it needed further work: "I wrote a Violin Concerto for Marsick, a work more mechanical than melodic. This Concerto was not published, and since then I have always had the intention of one day putting it again at the mercy of my fantasy. I had immediately, like the public, ascertained the defects in it."[405] In a letter dated September 6, 1886,[406] Widor wrote that he planned to revise the Violin Concerto, but he never did.

A reception like the foregoing would have destroyed the self-confidence of many a composer, but less than four months after the debacle that greeted the Violin Concerto, Widor premiered his new Op. 41 Cello Concerto at the Salle Érard. Like the Op. 39 Piano Concerto, it did not immediately win the full approbation of critics, but it ultimately enjoyed the admiration of many. For the premiere, Widor enlisted the superb talent of the foremost cellist of the day, Jules Delsart, who performed as soloist in the work several times in the coming years:

The first movement, strange in form, wrongly gives the instrument a role scarcely compatible with its nature. It is very difficult, it is true, to write a concerto for this instrument, the sonority of which loses itself in the orchestral mass; but it is to take away from the character of the instrument only to write for it endlessly in the high register, and to entrust to it some rapid passages and repeated notes.

The second movement, a simple Romance in G, is exquisite in poetic grace and mysterious charm; the entrance of the phrase, with its arpeggio leaving the low strings, to climb on the E string [*sic*], is dazzling. . . . This admirable piece was encored. The Finale of the Concerto came out perfectly. It is as elegant as possible. There is above all a delightful phrase, a sort of ritornello, which comes back after each solo.[407]

Regardless of other initially unenthusiastic reviews,[408] by 1900 the Cello Concerto had gained a respectable place in the repertory: "the Cello Concerto [is] an exquisite work, too long neglected, but in full favor today, judging by the frequency of the performances."[409]

Many sets of art songs (*mélodies*) are interspersed throughout Widor's oeuvre, and a substantial number of them date from the second half of the 1870s. Aside from operatic and religious vocal works, more than eighty *mélodies*, including six in Italian and six duets, make up Widor's song production. Various among them appeared regularly on his programs, and they never failed to win high acclaim: "As to the vocal part of the program, we will praise it without reserve."[410]

The *Six mélodies* [Op. 37] that he just published are recommended by diverse merits, but always, and above everything else, by a profound skill in the art of writing. His accompaniments are always studied and quite difficult. In order to perform these pages well, a consummate singer and a pianist who is not a simple accompanist are necessary.[411]

Regardless of the vocal form—*mélodie*, chorus, or motet—Widor sought perfect union between text and music; he wrote: "The literary text [is] above all: if it is permissible to 'compose,' that is to say to divide the poem according to a plan—in the form of a triptych, for example—the work will only be more solid for it."[412]

As in other genres cited previously, the influence of earlier romantic composers is manifested in Widor's *mélodies* from this period: "The songs of Mr. Widor arouse the memory of the *Lieder* of Mendelssohn, Schubert, and Schumann."[413] Widor felt very much at home in song composition, and that assurance lent a personal character to this genre of his compositional output:

We experience very great charm when happy fortune permits us to hear a page of Mr. Widor, harmoniously vying with Victor Hugo, Sully Prudhomme, or Paul Bourget.

In this arduous task, he is on an equal par with some masters of high inspiration or of incontestable skill, César Franck, Édouard Lalo, Ernest Reyer [1823–1909], and Gabriel Fauré. Indeed, what is his originality here? It is first of all the intimate fusion of melody and harmony, to such an extent that one would not know how, save with very few exceptions, to imagine them as separate, one from the other. This character [is] already clearly indicated in the first collection of Mr. Widor.[414]

—43—

Fifth and Sixth Symphonies for Organ

Not to be neglected during this period is Widor's continuing activity as an organist and an organ composer. Among numerous inaugural recitals, one was especially important. As mentioned earlier, Cavaillé-Coll completed his large new instrument for the Trocadéro Exhibition Building just in time for the 1878 Universal Exposition. Of great significance as the first concert hall organ in Paris, this organ would play a highly visible role in the musical scene of the capital for many years to come. Shortly after its installation, Widor was engaged to present one of the inaugural concerts:[415]

The 5th organ performance at the Trocadéro Palace will take place Saturday, August 24 at 3 o'clock, and will be given by Mr. Ch. Widor, organist of Saint-Sulpice. The program follows:

1. 5me Symphonie (1re audition)	Widor
Choral et Allegro	
Andante	
Intermezzo	
Cantabile	
Finale	
2. Andante	Mendelssohn
3. Fanfare	Lemmens
4. Pastorale	Widor
5. Fugue en ré	J.-S. Bach
6. Allegretto (transcription)	Widor
Finale de la 3e Symphonie	

Mr. Ch.-M. Widor gave the organ performance of August 24. The performing talent of this artist, as one has been convinced of it many times at Saint-Sulpice, is of the most brilliant sort. Mr. Widor is skilled in execution, and there is scarcely a difficulty that stops him. He happens sometimes, however, to press the tempo of the movements too much; for example, in the Fugue in D [Major, BWV 532] of Bach. We would have also desired the use of more subdued stops in the piece that the program called as briefly as inexactly "Andante of Mendelssohn," and which is the Adagio from the First Sonata of the master. Mr. Widor has shown himself as composer, in this performance, with his Fifth Symphony for Organ, which is rather a suite than a symphony, and in which we will point out the successful debut of the first piece, the Andante, which is very gracious and recalls, by its descending semitones, the manner of Wagner; lastly the Intermezzo, brilliant, but written rather for the piano than for the organ, as are the other fast parts of this work and more than one piece of which we have had to speak in these preceding performances. The Pastorale [Second Symphony] of Mr. Widor is a charming piece and filled with harmonic subtleties. The Allegretto (transcription of a Duo for piano and harmonium) was honored with an encore, and quite justly, for this piece is elegant and of a delightful inspiration. We find some passing modulations quite brusque in the Finale of the Third Symphony that closed the concert. Why, with the virtuosity and the compositional talent that he possesses, hasn't Mr. Widor followed the example of his French colleagues, who have all reserved a place on their programs for improvisations?[416]

Assuming the press reports to be accurate in describing Widor's new work as the "5me Symphonie," this program yields two very important pieces of information:[417] first, from the above description of the new symphony, there can be no doubt that the work in question is known today as the Sixth Symphony; second, the date of this work is proven to be earlier than had been assigned to it. The movements of the Sixth Symphony are entitled respectively: Allegro (actually a Choral and Allegro), Adagio (as it was correctly identified in *Estafette* of August 24, 1878), Intermezzo, Cantabile, and Finale. This order of movements matches those on the above program, and the reviewer described these movements in his review. The question of chronology for the Fifth and Sixth Symphonies, both included in Opus 42, is immediately posed.

As discussed earlier, the genesis of the four Op. 13 Symphonies will probably never be determined, but Widor at least ordered them by ascending key: C Minor, D Major, E Minor, F Minor. And he continued to order the Symphonies of Opp. 42, 70, and 73 by ascending key: Op. 42: F Minor, G Minor, A Minor, B Major; Op. 70: C Minor; Op. 73: D Major. If Widor originally intended to continue the Opus 13 scheme for his Op. 42 Symphonies, the next work would naturally be a Fifth Symphony in G Major or Minor, and indeed a Fifth Symphony in G Minor appeared on the Trocadéro program. The fact remains, however, that what is now known as the Fifth Symphony is a completely different work in F Minor. If that work had already been composed in 1878, it certainly would have preceded the Symphony in G Minor by reason of both its chronology and its key order. The evidence clearly indicates that the Symphony in G Minor antedates the second Symphony in F Minor.

One might wonder if even a partial score for the second Symphony in F Minor existed in August 1878. The evidence suggests that it did not, as if it were being composed or even contemplated, and presuming that Widor planned to follow the key sequence ordering of Opus 13, he certainly would have made a place for it—before the Symphony in G Minor—in his ordering of Opus 42. To reason further and suppose that the key sequence ordering of Opus 13 was not originally to have been a factor with the Op. 42 Symphonies, it would appear logical that the new works would be ordered chronologically instead. The same conclusion is still reached: the Symphony in G Minor antedates the second Symphony in F Minor.

From this, it becomes evident that the Op. 42 Symphony in F Minor must have been in the process of being composed only a few short months after the Symphony in G Minor (between mid-1878 and early 1879), as Widor performed the first movement in February 1879, and both works were published together the following June. The earlier plan of ordering the symphonies by ascending key took precedence over chronological ordering at that time; the Symphony in G Minor became the Sixth Symphony and the second Symphony in F Minor became the Fifth Symphony—which placed it sequentially after the Op. 13 Fourth Symphony in F Minor, and ignored its chronological order. *Le Ménestrel* announced the publication in June 1879:

> We are quite naturally led, when we speak of the organ, to draw attention to the publication by Maho of two new symphonies for organ of Mr. C. M. Widor. We heard some fragments from them this winter performed by the author. We have been fascinated by them; also, we will return to these beautiful and interesting compositions when we have studied them as they deserve to be studied.[418]

The date of 1878 for the Symphony in G Minor is significant: it places this astounding work as exactly contemporaneous with Franck's *Trois pièces* (*Fantaisie* in A Major, Cantabile, *Pièce héroïque*), which were also composed especially for the 1878 Exposition, and performed by Franck at the Trocadéro on October 1, 1878.[419] The Symphony in G Minor shows Widor to be a truly innovative figure in organ composition; its advanced conception in terms of scope and technical audacity is sufficient to place him at the forefront of the French organ movement. Even his former organ teacher was mightily impressed. Lemmens was in Paris in the last week of February 1878:[420] "It's when I completed my Sixth Symphony in G Minor for organ that I played for Lemmens, who was passing through Paris, and demonstrated an organ for him that he didn't know. Lemmens approved of my Symphony, as did [F. A.] Gevaert [1828–1908], who accompanied him. At the end, he leaned toward Cavaillé-Coll and told him, 'Widor is in the process of becoming a serious artist!'"[421] (see fig. 10).

The inauguration of the Fermis & Persil organ of Saint-François-Xavier, on February 27, 1879, brought together Franck, Gigout, Albert Renaud (1855–1924)—organist of the church—and Widor in a mixed program of solo organ music and choral music with orchestra.[422] Among the works on the program, Franck performed his recent Cantabile in B Major, Gigout an Andantino Cantabile, and Widor the first movement of his Fifth Symphony and the fourth movement of his Sixth Symphony; Renaud concluded with the Finale from Widor's Fourth Symphony.

This appears to have been the premiere of the first movement of the Fifth Symphony in F Minor. While one critic enthused, "This work, of remarkable construction, was brilliantly performed,"[423] another critic who would have preferred offertories and communions wrote that the work was "learnedly written; it was very correctly performed, but who has understood it?"[424]

Among the numerous choral works performed was an elaborate new psalm setting by Widor: *Psaume 112: Laudate, pueri Dominum* (without opus number) for two organs, two choirs, and orchestra.[425] The work made a stunning effect with a total of 220 performers under the direction of the renowned conductor Édouard Colonne: "One imagines the difficulty of performing such a piece with its diverse elements disseminated in an immense church. It has been interpreted with a marvelous unity."[426]

> The psalm "Laudate, pueri" of Widor, written for the occasion with choirs, orchestra, and two organs, has produced a gripping effect. The trombones and trumpets, which take up the same melodic fragment alternatively with the *grand orgue* and the choir, increasingly tightly, have contributed to giving this piece a dazzling vigor.[427]

The work greatly impressed the critic of the London *Times*, and Widor received an important commission from the London Philharmonic as a result:

> I had just produced my *Psaume 112* for the inauguration of the organ of Saint-François-Xavier, a psalm for organ, orchestra, and choruses; chance had it that the music critic of the *Times* attended. He said many good things about it in his review, so much so that the London Philharmonic asked me to write a work for its concerts, proposing three parts to me: a fierce piece—a sort of horse ride; a piece a little bit lunar—melancholic; a bacchanal.
> I wrote *La nuit de Walpurgis*, which I conducted in person in London.[428]

Although the critics and public received Psaume 112 enthusiastically, Widor decided differently: "I have not judged it useful to publish."[429] Still, it spawned the two works that open Widor's second style period: *La nuit de Walpurgis* and his greatest hit, the ballet *La Korrigane*:

> Bardoux [minister of Fine Arts], wanting in his turn to be nice to me, and having learned of my success, kindly proposed to me either the red ribbon

[of the Legion of Honor] or the commission of a ballet for the Opéra. Naturally, I chose the ballet. Vaucorbeil [director of the Opéra] applied to [François] Coppée [1842–1908], who proposed a first-rate subject. But it did not seem to satisfy the traditions of the Opéra and, a few days later, he [Vaucorbeil] made us take the scenario of *La Korrigane*.[430]

It is still unclear when the Op. 42 Symphony in F Minor received its first complete performance, but it may have been in July 1879 during a private concert at the Trocadéro:

> Last Wednesday, the minister of Fine Arts, accompanied by several officials, attended an intimate audition of the *grand orgue* in the festival hall of the Trocadéro. Mr. Ch.-M. Widor, the masterly organist of Saint-Sulpice, performed his new symphonies for organ.[431]

Once more at the Trocadéro, on October 19, 1879, Widor performed movements from a work designated as "*Cinquième symphonie* (Widor) première audition," and the movements were identified as "a. Allegro avec variation[s]; b. Cantabile; c. Final."[432] Although he performed only three of the movements, this would appear to be the Symphony in F Minor—since it was published four months earlier as the Fifth Symphony:

> The concert of last Sunday at the Trocadéro was already one of the most brilliant of the season. Mr. Widor, for quite a long time, has not appeared in public and dilettantes protested against his absence. As a performer, Mr. Widor has qualities of his own; the organ under his fingers assumes quite another character and a new expression. That is due to the perfection of his technique, which makes everything clear and pure; he also has a profound knowledge of the innumerable resources of the instruments of Mr. Cavaillé-Coll. Mr. Widor has played his Fifth Symphony for Organ, for which the *Ménestrel* could not have more praise.[433]

The Fifth Symphony became Widor's signature work and he performed it often. On December 16, 1880, the symphony served as the centerpiece for the inauguration of the new Cavaillé-Coll organ in Saint-François-de-Sales in Lyon, where his father was *titulaire*.[434] Widor reportedly composed the work especially for that momentous inauguration[435]—yet another reason that suggests its composition came after that of the Symphony in G Minor (composed especially for the 1878 Exposition). It is also evident that Widor composed the Fifth Symphony with an instrument other than Saint-Sulpice in mind; several passages require an expressive Positif division—something that the Saint-Sulpice organ did not have, but which Saint-François-Xavier, Saint-François-de-Sales and the Trocadéro instruments included.

Describing the Trocadéro concerts in 1878, *Le Ménestrel* reported that serious organ music still had not entirely captured the hearts of the Parisian public, but that their growing enthusiasm was at least partially attributable to Widor's new symphonies and his impeccable performances:

> Always a full house. The public is little by little getting used to classical organ works. It still hastens to dislike the place a bit as soon as a serious name appears on the program; but this does not prevent an important majority from listening to even the compositions of [J.] S. Bach. Haven't you in fact seen Mr. Widor raise a tempest of bravos with the Fugue in D? It is true that the virtuosity of Mr. Widor has now passed into legend.[436]

A little over a year later Eugène Gigout wrote an article in which Widor's organ symphonies were praised as models of excellence:[437]

> If it is difficult to deny that mediocre organ music still meets with some approval, it is impossible not to recognize that works of real value are gaining acceptance everywhere today. No doubt after the two remarkable new Symphonies (Fifth and Sixth) of Mr. Ch.-M. Widor, . . . organists will need to strive to make everyone appreciate polished compositions.[438]

The Fifth and Sixth Symphonies show the composer in full control of his craft, and thus provide a pivotal point to mark the transition to Widor's second creative period.[439] In his first period, 1864–79, he composed a substantial quantity of music—nearly forty-five opus numbers.[440] Inclusive of a wide variety of genres, it was necessarily an experimental time—a time in which the young composer sought a musical language of his own, a time that had its disappointments, and a time that had some remarkable achievements and successes. Still in his mid-thirties, Widor had emerged a mature and successful composer, working in large forms and leaving his own distinct musical personality within their framework.

As Widor repeatedly put pen to paper in the attempt to try something new or to improve something old, he continually honed his skills. The immediate years ahead would witness a flurry of still more outstanding successes and his rise to almost universal renown. Throughout his long career Widor continued to evolve stylistically; to compare a composition from the middle of his career with an early work, or a late composition with a middle-period work is to find quite a different composer. Even at ninety, he would be able to say, "I think I am finding something new about organ playing. And possibly also about writing for the organ."[441] Stylistic discovery and artistic development were hallmarks of his career.

—44—

"Tibicen" and "Aulètes"

In January 1877, Widor succeeded Saint-Saëns as music critic for the Paris daily newspaper *Estafette*, which had commenced publication only eight months earlier. His contributions under the heading "Revue musicale" were signed using one of two pen names. The first seven reviews appeared under the name "Tibicen." However, the discovery that another anonymous writer was already using the pseudonym led Widor to adopt the new name of "Aulètes." The editors of the paper explained the change to their readership:

> Our musical chronicler, desiring to maintain anonymity, had taken as a pseudonym the Latin name *Tibicen*, which means, as one knows, *flute player*.
> It appears that he [*Tibicen*] already existed in a little newspaper, the existence of which we did not surmise; a *flute player* took offence. Our chronicler, who desires to avoid all ambiguity, leaves *Tibicen* to his unfortunate fate and, since it pleases him to remain *flute player*, he changes language, and from now on will sign with the Greek name *Aulètes*.[442]

By June 5, 1882, apparently his last entry, Widor had contributed some seventy-seven "articles of musical criticism, very elegantly written and marked with a moderation that, however, does not at all cloud the decisiveness of his judgments on our musicians and their works."[443] Perhaps Aulètes no longer offered Widor a haven of anonymity, for he signed the final seven articles Charles Widor or Ch.-M. Widor.

The yen for writing music criticism did not lie fallow for very many seasons. In August 1891, Widor would accept the artistic directorship of *Piano Soleil*, a "grand journal musical," as it proclaimed itself, and therein he would write even more prolifically.[444] But he never used his position at the journal to promote himself. When an article about him and André Messager appeared in *Piano Soleil*, the editors explained: "As misfortune would have it, Mr. Widor, our eminent artistic director, is so excessively modest that he would not forgive us the slightest indiscreet remark about his doings; therefore, we will speak only of his works."[445] Although retaining the title of artistic director at least into 1906 (when the run of the periodical ends at the Bibliothèque nationale de France), his last articles appeared in 1898, there having been over one hundred fifty by then.

Widor was as gifted a writer as he was a musician. Throughout his life he penned hundreds of critical reviews, authored books, articles, monographs, necrologies, prefaces, and wrote thousands of personal letters. All provide a wellspring of information and insight that make Widor one of the most fascinating of musicians. And his keen wit was legendary. His lengthy and carefully reasoned review of a performance of Meyerbeer's opera, *Le pardon de Ploërmel*, concluded: "One sole role was played poorly: that of the goat. It missed its exit in the second act."[446]

Figure 1. Young Charles-Marie with his parents, François-Charles and Françoise-Elisabeth. Daguerreotype, ca. 1850. Reproduced by the author, courtesy of M.-A. Guibaud.

Figure 2. Aristide Cavaillé-Coll. Reproduced by George Cooke, courtesy of M.-A. Guibaud.

Figure 3. The inscription on the back of the figure 2 photo is to François-Charles Widor: "Au bon Papa Widor / Souvenir affectueux / du vieux facteur / A. Cavaillé-Coll / Paris le 29 juillet 1879" [To good Papa Widor / Fond remembrance / from the old builder / A. Cavaillé-Coll / Paris July 29, 1879]. Reproduced by George Cooke, courtesy of M.-A. Guibaud.

Figure 4. François-Joseph Fétis, engraving by C. Deblois, 1867. Author's collection.

Figure 5. Jacques-Nicolas Lemmens. Reproduced by the author from Lemmens's *Du chant Grégorien*, 1886, courtesy of Agnes Armstrong.

Figure 6. Charles-Marie, ca. 1865, fresh from studies in Brussels. Reproduced by
the author, courtesy of M.-A. Guibaud.

PORTRAITS BREVETÉS S.G.D.G.
Phot. N.º 9. Avenue de Ségur.

Figure 7. Charles-Marie at the studio of Mechanostares Brevetés, Paris. The back of the photo identifies it for use at the "Exposition de Lisbonne [Porto], 1865." Reproduced by the author, courtesy of M.-A. Guibaud.

Figure 8. Widor, about the time of his appointment as "provisional organist" at Saint-Sulpice. He was always partial to ties with polka-dots, and he is showing the beginnings of the moustache he would retain throughout his life. Reproduced by the author, courtesy of M.-A. Guibaud.

Figure 9. Widor, Ferruccio Benvenuto Busoni, and Isidor Philipp at the Restaurant Foyot, 1914. Reproduced by the author, courtesy of M.-A. Guibaud.

Figure 10. Charles-Marie Widor, oil portrait on canvas by Léon Bonnat (1833–1922), signed "L. Bonnat/Bayonne/1887 [or 1889]." In his eulogy of Bonnat on November 24, 1923 before the Academy of Fine Arts, Widor spoke of the painter's skill in rendering his subjects with precision. "This painter . . . wanted his portraits to resemble his models. Even among the less good of them, there are none that are not proclaiming truthfulness." Widor, *Fondations, portraits,* 171. Author's collection, through the kindness of Richard J. Hutto. Reproduced by George Cooke.

Figure 11. *La Korrigane* poster by E. Buval, 1880. 23×30 in. The scene depicts the moonlit heath and marsh of Act II. The inset shows Spanish ballerina Rosita Mauri, who danced the role of Yvonnette. Printed on pale green, the lettering is orange and the illustrations are black. Author's collection.

COLLECTION FÉLIX POTIN

WIDOR

Figure 12. This photo captures well Widor's features as described by Octavia Hensel, Fannie Edgar Thomas, and even the passport agency. Félix Potin owned a chain of grocery stores; inside boxes of tobacco, coffee, and chocolate products, he gave customers collectible photographs of famous people as a promotional gimmick. He produced over 510 portraits between 1900 and 1907; many photos date from much earlier, however, as some of his celebrities were long deceased. Author's collection.

Figure 13. Widor's commodious music room at 3 rue de l'Abbaye shows his new *orgue de salon* and a grand piano. Another photo (not pictured here) shows the opposite aspect of the room with the portrait of Widor by Carolus-Duran; these photographs match exactly the description given by Fannie Edgar Thomas in *Organ Loft Whisperings.* Reproduced by the author, courtesy of M.-A. Guibaud.

Figure 14. Widor, Guilmant, and Gigout photographed in Widor's apartment at 7 rue des Saints Pères. It appeared in *Monde Musical*, December 15, 1903, under the heading "Le jury d'orgue." As Conservatory organ professors, Guilmant succeeded Widor in 1896, and Gigout succeeded Guilmant in 1911. Reproduced by the author.

Figure 15. "The King of French Organists" at the five-manual, one-hundred stop Saint-Sulpice organ, 1901. This most famous of all photos taken of Widor is inscribed to Albert Riemenschneider, Paris 1914. Courtesy of Riemenschneider Bach Institute at Baldwin-Wallace College, Berea, Ohio.

Figure 16. Louis Vierne at the Notre-Dame organ. The photograph is signed to G. Huntington Byles, "en toute sympathie" [with all best wishes]; Byles studied in Paris with Widor and Vierne during the summer and fall of 1933. Author's collection, through the kindness of Dr. Janet Knapp Byles.

Figure 17. *Les Pêcheurs de Saint-Jean* poster by Fernand-Louis Gottlob, 1906. 33×24½ in. Tinted in pale greens, yellows, and browns, Gottlob has captured the beginning of Act IV when a tumultuous storm threatens to engulf the fishing boat of Jean-Pierre; his daughter Anne-Marie prays for his deliverance. Author's collection.

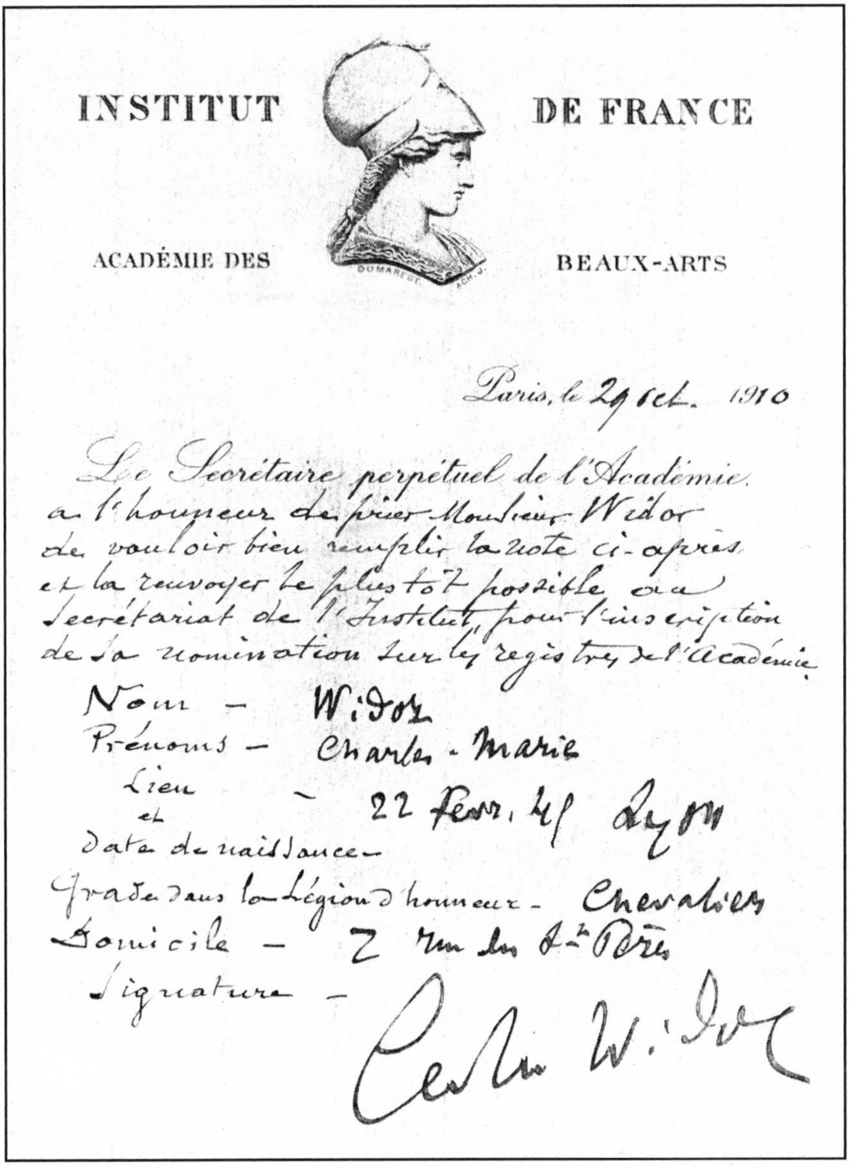

INSTITUT DE FRANCE

ACADÉMIE DES BEAUX-ARTS

Paris, le 29 oct. 1910

Le Secrétaire perpétuel de l'Académie a l'honneur de prier Monsieur Widor de vouloir bien remplir la note ci-après et la renvoyer le plus tôt possible au Secrétariat de l'Institut, pour l'inscription de sa nomination sur les registres de l'Académie.

Nom — Widor

Prénoms — Charles-Marie

Lieu et date de naissance — 22 Févr. 44 Lyon

Grade dans la Légion d'honneur — Chevalier

Domicile — 7 rue des Sts Pères

Signature — Charles Widor

Figure 18. Widor's letter of nomination to the Institute of France, October 29, 1910. The text reads: "The Perpetual Secretary of the Academy has the honor of asking Mr. Widor to please fill in the note below and to send it back as soon as possible to the Secretariat of the Institute, for the inscription of his nomination on the register of the Academy." It then asks for his family name, given name, place and date of birth, rank in the Legion of Honor, address, and signature. Reproduced by the Institut de France for the author.

Figure 19. Albert Schweitzer "to his dear *maître* Widor, 1/3/02." Schweitzer had gone to study with Widor in 1893. Reproduced by the author, courtesy of M.-A. Guibaud.

47 Rue Dumont d'Urville   G.L.Manuel frères

Figure 20. Widor at his *orgue de salon* in the Salle de Caen, Institut de France, where Widor initiated a monthly concert series. Reproduced by the author, courtesy of M.-A. Guibaud.

Figure 21. French President Alexandre Millerand and Queen Marie of Romania are escorted by Widor and Camille Saint-Saëns at the time of their visit to the Institute of France, ca. early 1921. Reproduced by the author, courtesy of M.-A. Guibaud.

Figure 22. Widor married Mathilde-Marie-Anne-Elisabeth de Montesquiou-Fezensac on April 26, 1920, at the Château de Hauteville in Charchigné (Mayenne). Although she went by her first given name, Mathilde, she signed her letters Montesquiou Widor. Reproduced by the author, courtesy of M.-A. Guibaud.

Figure 23. Widor at the piano; he was described as "an exquisite pianist of the most limpid purity." Reproduced by the author, courtesy of M.-A. Guibaud.

Figure 24. Widor in 1929, while director of the American Conservatory, Fontainebleau. The photo is inscribed "to his friend Walter Damrosch," the multitalented
former conductor of the New York Symphony and music director of the National
Broadcasting Co. Author's collection, through the kindness of Gerald Russell.

Figure 25. Jean Cardinal Verdier, archbishop of Paris (1929–40), congratulates Widor after the inauguration of the organ of Saint-Ferdinand des Ternes, Paris, November 5, 1931. Reproduced by the author, courtesy of M.-A. Guibaud.

Figure 26. In front of the Salzburg Cathedral after Widor's last foreign organ recital (left to right: Comte Clauzel—French ambassador to Austria, Widor, Kappelmeister Joseph Messner), July 31, 1932. Reproduced by the author, courtesy of M.-A. Guibaud.

Figure 27. Widor and Marcel Dupré, ca. 1923, at the time of a visit by Samuel Casavant to Paris. Courtesy of Casavant Frères, Saint-Hyacinthe (Québec), Canada.

Figure 28. Aunt Hélène Standish, Mathilde, and Charles-Marie on vacation in Switzerland, ca. 1930. Reproduced by the author, courtesy of M.-A. Guibaud.

Figure 29. Madame Widor took a number of snapshots when she and Charles-Marie vacationed on Lake Geneva during the 1920s. Author's collection, through the kindness of M.-A. Guibaud.

Figure 30. One of Mathilde's candid photos of her husband. Author's collection, through the kindness of M.-A. Guibaud.

Figure 31. One of Widor's favorite pastimes: boating on Lake Geneva, 1929. Author's collection, through the kindness of M.-A. Guibaud.

Figure 32. At his Farewell Concert, April 19, 1934, Widor is at the conductor's podium on the orchestral dais constructed beneath the organ tribune at Saint-Sulpice. Reproduced by the author, courtesy of M.-A. Guibaud.

Figure 33. Widor awards the Legion of Honor's "rosette d'officier" to Dupré (between them is Mr. Huisman, director of the Beaux-Arts, who presided at the banquet), Majestic Hotel, Paris, March 16, 1935. Reproduced by the author, courtesy of M.-A. Guibaud.

Figure 34. Taken on the patio of the Madrid Casa Velásquez; Widor attended the
formal inauguration on May 15, 1935. Reproduced by the author, courtesy of M.-A.
Guibaud.

Figure 35. Farewell at Nyon, Switzerland. Reproduced by the author, courtesy of M.-A. Guibaud.

Part Three

The Years of Mastery (1880–94)

Ch.-M. Widor fait de l'art pour l'art, sans concessions coupables au public: il ne se rattache à aucune école ni à aucun groupe: il est lui-même, et c'est le meilleur éloge qu'on puisse faire d'un artiste.

Ch.-M. Widor does art for the sake of art, without guilty concessions to the public; he is not attached to any school or group; he is himself, and that is the highest praise that one can make for an artist.

—H. Eymieu
L'Art Musical 33 (February 1, 1894): 33–34.

—45—

La nuit de Walpurgis:
"Can one render the grotesque in music?"

The two principal works of 1880 hurled Widor into the limelight of almost universal musical renown—the first work by dint of the arrant reaction that it drew from both critics and concert-going public alike, and the second work, in total contrast, by the manner in which it utterly captured their imaginations.

Hector Berlioz (1803–69) cut the way for programmatic revelry with his revolutionary *Symphonie fantastique* of 1830. Departing from his classical leanings, Widor continued down the same path when in 1880 he took part of Goethe's *Faust* epic as the literary basis for his vividly programmatic symphonic poem *La nuit de Walpurgis* (*Nuit de Sabbat*).

The first movement (Ouverture) depicts a raging, tempestuous storm, the wild reveling of Walpurgis Night—the witches' Sabbath in full bent; in complete contrast, the calm second movement (Adagio) is a musical illustration of the meeting of Helen of Troy and Paris, and has no direct connection with the theme of the first and last movements; the final movement (Bacchanale) returns to the revelry of the Brocken—the drunken dance of the boisterous guests in the devil's lair.

There was certainly nothing new in recruiting the Faust theme or the Walpurgis Night scene for musical portrayal. As far back as 1833, Mendelssohn had taken the same poetic basis for his famous secular Cantata *Die erste Walpurgisnacht*, Op. 60. Interestingly, Widor's work has more than the title and literary text in common with Mendelssohn's work; Widor's *Nuit de Walpurgis* is also his Opus 60. The resemblance stops there, however: after an overture, Mendelssohn actually set some of Goethe's text, employing soloists and chorus; Widor's work is a strictly orchestral "poematic" symphony. He even applied suggestive titles to some of the thematic material—descriptions such as "idée philosophique générale" (general philosophical idea), "la phrase morale" (the moral phrase), "une sorte de chasse fantastique" (a type of fantastic chase), and so forth.

In the chapter "Composition" from his primer *Initiation musicale*, Widor explained the radically different compositional approaches between works of "pure classical form" and the "literary and descriptive" symphonic poems of Liszt, Berlioz, and Saint-Saëns:

> It's Liszt who popularized the *Symphonic poem*. . . .
> Here, no more classical form, no more traditional architecture; as in the theater, one must follow as closely as possible and translate as accurately as possible the episodes of the drama. Whether the drama is with or without words, opera, cinema, or lyric poem, the musician collaborates with the librettist and keeps pace with him. Sometimes, in this union of *poetry and music*, the balance breaks to our own prejudices.[1]

Reporting in 1877 on a performance of the *Symphonie fantastique*, Widor revealed his inner feelings about Berlioz's success in this work:

> People have written a lot on the *Symphonie fantastique*. The composer himself has taken care to relate to the public, at the head of his score, the very personal story of a very agitated heart. This story *is* the fantastic symphony; if you haven't read the preface, you will not be able to understand the book.
> Here, I say some dreadful things parenthetically: Berlioz seems to me much more a great artist than a great musician; I am not even absolutely convinced that he is not mistaken occasionally about what language will translate the strange reveries of his brain—reveries sometimes less from the domain of music than from literature or painting. The language that he uses is not always sufficient to him; the costume is too tight, he is uncomfortable in it.
> But when the subject treated reenters the true limits of our art, when the development of his artistic thought can go on a par with that of the musical idea, the work that results from it attains the greatest height and the most powerful effects.
> The "Songe d'une nuit de sabbat" . . . includes some beautiful pages and remarkable developments. At the peroration of a fugue boldly carried out, the *Dies Irae* bursts forth. It's frightful as regards destiny. On the other hand, I remain completely indifferent to the attempts of grotesque horror searched for by the composer. Can one render the grotesque in music?[2]

Eventually, he must have come to believe it was possible. If once unmoved by Berlioz's dazzling effects of grotesquery, Widor brought his own efforts in that direction to new heights in *La nuit de Walpurgis*. French critics and audiences found the tone poem absolutely scandalous; it struck them as programmatic music gone berserk. Audiences had come to expect something along the more conservative line of Widor's classical aesthetic, and perhaps Mendelssohn's *Erste Walpurgisnacht* loomed too highly in their thought. In any case, a veritable raft of critical invective followed the Paris premiere on February 8, 1880.

> *La nuit de Walpurgis*, by Ch.-M. Widor, the first performance of which took place Sunday at the Châtelet concert, has only the title in common with the great scene of Mendelssohn. It is a symphonic score in three movements, pushing the descriptive style as far as abuse, particularly in the Overture, which is certainly one of the most astonishing things we have heard. Under pretext of portraying the horror of the abyss, the din of the tempest, the ride of the sorceresses, Mr. Widor unfolds to us a series of sonorous incoherencies that are of cold dementia. Never has a man of talent more completely gone astray; never has one better shown up to what point program music can be deranged, in going beyond certain limits. The two other movements don't go as far in the same way, but the Overture has strange repercussions on them, and its memory is not extraneous to the not very favorable effect that they produce. It is, in sum, a distressing stage in the composing career of Mr. Widor; but he is one to make it be forgotten soon by some sane work, strong and virile, which does not set up as a principle that "horrible is beautiful." . . . The beautiful Concerto for Three Pianos of Bach . . . came after the symphonic poem of Mr. Widor, and produced the effect of a wide and calm clearing after a race in the darkness.[3]

Another reviewer admitted that although the public was more than a little surprised at the music, its composer had "a perfect knowledge of the orchestral resources."[4] And at least one critic found the Overture praiseworthy: "This whole ravishing piece, which one could say now and then escaped from the pen of Berlioz, is filled with feeling, delicacy, and grace."[5]

Widor sought further performances of the work in 1883 and 1884 from the Société des Nouveaux Concerts, writing on two occasions to its director, Charles Lamoureux: "Will you be able to reserve a place for *La nuit de Sabbat* this year? You were willing to give me hope last year! I would be very happy for a place. Please be persuaded that the work will not dishonor your program, and pardon the request."[6] After the 1880 premiere, however, Widor's tone poem apparently did not receive another performance until the London Philharmonic Society invited him to guest conduct during its 1888 season as one of three foreign composers, each of whom was to conduct a work of his own: Peter Ilyich Tchaikovsky (1840–93) for Russia, Edvard Grieg (1843–1907) for

Norway, and Widor for France.[7] Widor left his recollection of the work's genesis in his "Souvenirs autobiographiques":

> The music critic of the *Times* [London] having heard at Saint-François-Xavier, at the inauguration of the organ [February 27, 1879], a *Psaume* [112] that I had written for choir and orchestra for this inauguration wrote a very enthusiastic report . . . and in the same article asked the Philharmonic of London to commission a work from me. A bit later, the London [Philharmonic] Society asked me to write an orchestral piece treating, in a maximum of three parts, a subject a little fantastic drawn from *Faust* by Goethe. This work interested me, naturally, but at that moment my cousin Paul Bourget just published in the *Revue des Jeunes Poètes* two hundred extremely poetic verses on the apparition of Hélène in *Faust*. Instead of choosing the German subject, I preferred the antique subject treated by a Frenchman.
> I took the following verses from part two as a theme:
>
>> Il était à ses pieds, couché sans plus rien dire;
>> Elle aussi se taisait. Ils écoutaient bruire
>> Tous les soupirs d'amour lointains et palpitants
>> Qui flottent dans la paix d'une nuit de printemps.
>> [He was at her feet, reclining, saying nothing;
>> She too was silent. They listened to
>> All the distant throbbing sighs of love
>> That float in the breathless peace of a spring night.]
>
> Consequently, I went to London to direct the performances and I can say that the work was very well received. (The premiere took place in Queen's Hall [April 19, 1888].)[8]

Although the Philharmonic commission was for a new symphony and the dedication claimed the work was "composed expressly for the Philharmonic Society," it appears that only the last movement, dated February 1888, fell under Widor's pen for revision. Until the different versions can be compared, just how much of the original composition remained unchanged is not known. The London critics voiced feelings similar to the Paris reports of 1880, although conceding, "Mr. Widor conducted with clearness and force, and was applauded with considerable heartiness":

> There is much wild and rough power in the music, but a great deal of it is incoherent, or at least seems so on first hearing, while still more of it is noisy. . . . He has an abundance of ideas and great technical skill, but he lets his imagination run riot at times, and incoherence results.[9]
> The novelty of the evening was M. Widor's "Walpurgis Night." . . . In the first movement M. Widor attempts a musical description of certain lines from Goethe's drama: night black with mist—grinding and cracking forests—an

infuriate glamouring song; such is the poetic basis. To represent all this, the composer employs a very large orchestra, including cornets, trombones, tuba and many instruments of percussion. There was a great deal of noise, and, indeed, clever noise, but very little music in the true sense of the term. . . . In his attempt to be realistic, the composer again appears to forget the true province of music.[10]

Although the first and third movements appeared disturbing, at least the middle movement pleased: "We have no hesitation in counting [the Adagio] among the finest specimens of its class produced in recent years. Here genuine melody is poured forth in never-ceasing currents till a perfect climax of passion is attained. . . . [It] is a perfect *chant d'amour*—a song without words, and needing no words to be fully understood."[11]

Nearly twenty years would intervene before the work received another performance. It would then be the Paris of 1907, which was seeing almost coincidentally the premiere of *Salome* by Richard Strauss (1864–1949).[12] Early twentieth-century ears more readily accepted what those of 1880 and 1888 had rejected; *Le Ménestrel*'s Arthur Pougin (1834–1931) wrote favorably:

We heard next, for the first time at the Conservatory, a very beautiful, very interesting and very curious symphonic work of Mr. Widor, *La nuit de Walpurgis*, which made a great impression. This work comprises three movements: Overture, Adagio, and Bacchanal, each of very distinct color. The Overture, very difficult to perform, full of color and character, is uncommonly powerful in its use of the orchestra: one is a little surprised, after its very logical developments, to see it end all of a sudden and brusquely, without preparation, and in a way that astonishes the ear. I do not make this remark in a critical manner; it is simply the statement of the impression received at a first hearing, and which does not at all take away from the worth of this warm and stirring page. After the Adagio of caressing contours and of a design full of grace and languor, comes, as contrast, the Bacchanal, with its gleaming, powerful, colored orchestra, with its rapid and serried rhythms, with its fantastic and sometimes bizarre character, which is not sounded without evoking the memory of Weber. The fine composition was, in its entirety, well received by the public of the Conservatory, which does not always enjoy works presented to it for the first time.[13]

Still, not everyone was convinced; Paul Locard (1871–1952) felt some chagrin for Widor: "I don't think—and I'm not alone—that *Nuit de Walpurgis* gives a just idea of the very remarkable personality of Mr. Widor to those who know it less well, and that's a shame."[14]

Widor's assessment regarding the need to hear a work several times before being able to make an intelligent assessment seems apt to recall here: "Is it possible to judge in an instant a work on which a composer meditated some weeks, even entire months? Several performances will certainly be necessary . . . in order to arrive at understanding a page filled with profoundness and mysterious power. To hear is not at all to know."[15] The *Times* critic agreed, pointing out some inner strengths that repeated hearings of *Nuit de Walpurgis* would bring to light: "Let it not be thought that M. Widor's music is confined to . . . external things. It goes deeper than this, to the very root of the matter; even amid the revels of the Brocken, scholarship and counterpoint are never lost sight of, and what is more poetic, unity is preserved by means of a striking 'leitmotive,' or representative theme, which pervades as it were the whole work."[16] Widor apparently valued the work enough to put it under his critical pen for corrections as late as January 23, 1935, and August 16, 1936.[17]

—46—

La Korrigane: "The music is . . . one of the glories of French art."

La nuit de Walpurgis represents Widor's only venture in pure program music unrelated to any dramatic action. Henceforth, he would direct his efforts toward the theater, an area in which he was not yet noted.[18] Widor had, however, completed his first opera in 1878:

> Messrs. Louis Gallet [1835–98] and Édouard Noël [1846–1926] for the words, Mr. Ch.-M. Widor for the music, are finishing at this moment an opéra-comique in three acts, *Le capitaine Loys*, the subject of which is borrowed from the adventures of the famous Lyon poetess of the sixteenth century, Loyse Labé, nicknamed "la belle Cordière." This work is destined for the Opéra-Comique.[19]

For unknown reasons *Le capitaine Loys* seems not to have been produced at the time. It may have been concerning this work that Widor beseeched the aid of Charles Lamoureux, for a short time conductor of the Opéra-Comique: "If on occasion there was talk about an act from me for the Opéra-Comique . . . dare I ask you to help me a little and to speak favorably of me to the management! I have a great desire not to remain eternally at the door, but to enter into the sanctuary!"[20] Not until 1900 did the work come to fruition as incidental music to accompany a "comédie héroïque" in five acts with verse by Noël and Lucien d'Hève for the Théâtre des Célestins in Lyon.[21]

With his second important work of 1880, Widor did indeed "enter into the sanctuary"; he scored one of the most impressive successes of his career—a success far removed from the organ gallery, though begun there: "I was invaded at the organ by a band of fools who came to tear me away from sensible plans and drag me off to dinner in St. Cloud."[22] The ultimate outcome of that first meeting was *La Korrigane*, Op. 45, a two-act "ballet fantastique" based on a scenario by François Coppée with choreography by Louis Mérante (1828–87)—who danced the principal male role, Lilèz (see fig. 11).

Expectations ran high as music journals announced the new ballet in advance of the premiere, whereupon poet Charles Grandmougin (1850–1930) addressed a letter to *Le Journal de Musique* crying foul. Grandmougin claimed that he and another poet had written a similar scenario two years earlier for collaboration with composer Benjamin Godard, and that it had been widely announced in the journals at that time. Coppée squelched the dispute by responding that the Korrigane and Brittany belonged to everyone, that no one could have a monopoly on the story, and that he had no recollection of any previous announcements by Grandmougin.[23]

La Korrigane's premiere on December 1 at the Paris Opéra launched Widor's career in the theater. Accolades were showered upon the composer and the poet from every direction; the ballet immediately earned Widor a place among the ranks of French master composers. Just a few years earlier, he had written in a review: "When there is perfect equilibrium between the force of thought and its expression, between substance and form, art becomes great and touches perfection. Of what importance is it whether the plan is more or less vast?"[24] *La Korrigane* attained that perfect equilibrium, and the press immediately classed its composer "*di primo cartello.*"[25]

The composition of *La Korrigane* had been hard work, though enjoyable. Widor recalled, "to rehearse twice a day—and two or three hours in a row each time, to orchestrate the modifications made during the rehearsal in the meantime, to reduce the whole orchestra to the piano and finally to prepare my work for the next day, this is quite enervating."[26] Nonetheless, it all seemed effortless to Coppée, who observed that "on twenty occasions, between one day and the next, often on the vaguest suggestion from the choreographer, [Widor] would bring a page of exquisite melody. If that did not suit, he would immediately write another without a trace of weariness or a sign of ill-humour."[27] Widor's improvisational gifts permitted him to compose some of the most masterful moments of the ballet on the spot. Coppée continued, "I saw him—if I might say—improvise in that way the *Sabotière* [Act I], the voluptuous Waltz of Act II, and the main parts of his work."[28]

Spanish ballerina Rosita Mauri danced Yvonnette, the leading female role in the ballet. She had premiered at the Opéra in 1878 in the divertissement of Gounod's *Polyeucte*, and had shown herself to be a dancer of extraordinary abilities. Widor could not have been more pleased: "I was lucky to have for the principal interpreter a young Milanese student from the Milan School, Mademoiselle Mauri, who was precisely the person of one's dream for Coppée's ballet. She was filled with talent, vigor, elegance, and spirit, all at the same time."[29] Coppée was equally enthralled with her:

La Mauri is divine. . . . Indeed, I regard it as one of the greatest events in my life as a dramatist to have seen that extraordinary artist, that ethereal being who . . . after soaring in the air, returned to the stage, so lightly, so delicately, that you could not hear a sound, no more than when a bird descends and alights on a twig.

La Mauri is dancing personified. . . . She whinnied and darted like a young foal; she soared and glided in space like a wild bird.[30]

After the initial rehearsals, the press voiced enthusiastic expectancy:

La Korrigane will be not only quite a choreographic event, to the greatest triumph of Miss Mauri, but also a "musical premiere"; for we will be invited to hear a realistic score from the pen of a young composer already classed among the best. Mr. Ch.-M. Widor wanted to write a symphonic work, without, however, disavowing the genre of music appropriate to the ballet, and the two orchestral readings of his score that were just made at the Opéra testify that he has completely succeeded in attaining the double end proposed. Well-rhythmed melodies abound in his essentially symphonic work. It is of exquisite orchestral workmanship.[31]

Optimism over the impending premiere filled the air, and Widor began to sense a triumph: "They are all telling me here that we will have a great success. The music is much favored by the ballerinas and consequently by their armchair admirers; it's very encouraging, but despite everything I'm beginning to feel the first symptoms of author's stage fright."[32]

The synopsis of *La Korrigane* (The Goblin Maiden) reveals an enchanting retelling of the Cinderella tale picturesquely set in seventeenth-century Brittany—an exotic setting that offered the public the novelty of a strong folkloric atmosphere, traditional peasant dances, ethnic costumes, and show-stopping numbers, such as the "Sabotière" and "Gigue bretonne":

Act I opens on the festival of a religious feast day, which has brought a great pilgrimage to a small Breton village. The townspeople have also gathered, arrayed in all their finery. The poor Yvonnette, servant of Loïk the innkeeper, enviously gazes at the beautiful wives of the village notables. Contemplating her own tattered clothing, she ruminates sadly that she cannot participate in the celebrations, nor win the attention of the handsome piper, Lilèz, with whom she is secretly in love. If only she had a beautiful gown, she would be able to turn his head! Just then, an old beggar woman, bent over under a heavy bundle of wood, passes by the inn and slips and falls. Having a charitable heart, Yvonnette goes to the old woman to help her put down the burdensome load so she can rest. The old beggar declares that Yvonnette will be rewarded for this kindness; and right there the old woman transforms into a dazzling fairy—she is the Queen of the Korriganes (the malevolent spirits of

Brittany). "To you, Yvonnette, rich apparel and beautiful jewels, under one condition, however: before the bell announcing the time for the Angelus, you must win Lilèz to you; if not, you will belong to me and serve as a Korrigane yourself." How can she resist such beautiful clothes? How can she renounce the chance to win the love of her entire soul? And isn't a victory certain? The pact is sealed! Vespers has finished and everyone returns to the great square to begin the festival. Yvonnette is admired by all the people, and the young men flirt with her—especially Lilèz. He declares his love; everything goes as Yvonnette had hoped. But, unfortunately, the mean hunchbacked parish bell ringer, Paskou—ridiculously enamored with Yvonnette and extremely jealous—has overheard the pact with the Queen of the Korriganes. He has advanced the hands of the great clock. The Angelus sounds prematurely, before Yvonnette and Lilèz have made their vows! The Korriganes rush in from everywhere and, in spite of the protests of Yvonnette and Lilèz, seize her as their prey.[33]

Act II is set in a heath in the moonlight; the sad Yvonnette, wailing under her terrible plight, is a captive in the Korrigane's fantastic kingdom. She gains only a little satisfaction in seeing Paskou, who has lost his way in the evil region, ensnared, intoxicated, and thrown into a marsh by the Korriganes. Meanwhile, the hapless Lilèz has been looking for his dear Yvonnette. He finds his way to the Korriganes and entreats the Queen to restore his sweetheart. She tells him, "Yvonnette is yours if you can recognize her among all the Korriganes." All the fantastic beings start to file by him, each trying to captivate him; but he disdainfully repulses their advances. It is Yvonnette's turn; but under the Queen's magic powers and despite all of Yvonnette's seductions, Lilèz does not recognize her. Suddenly, Yvonnette gets an idea: she will dance a very difficult step that she alone knows—the sort of Breton *gigue* with which she had originally conquered Lilèz in Act I. Now Lilèz no longer has any doubt; he has found his Yvonnette. In spite of the Korrigane's furor, they are reunited. He flashes a precious rosary at the Korriganes, and they flee in fright. Meanwhile, a troop of peasants happens along, homeward bound from their pilgrimage to the festival; a magnificent Breton procession ensues to crown the scenario.

The resounding success of the premiere was everything a composer could wish for, and the reviews put Widor squarely in the headlines:

The music of the new ballet of the Opéra is of a symphonic importance so considerable that we do not hesitate to refer to it first in this review of *La Korrigane*. We have, moreover, a newcomer to the theater in the person of Mr. Ch.-M. Widor, and it is only proper to wish him welcome right from the start. . . .

The situations and contrasts throughout the music score have served the muse of Mr. Widor, who has poured out a perfume of Breton music amply sufficient to give his work a true mark of originality. This music absolutely stands out from what one usually hears at the Opéra. Had it only that merit it would still be noteworthy. But there is here, and we relish repeating it, a work of art that reveals to us a young master with whom our lyric theaters are going to have to take account.

In sum, Mr. Ch.-M. Widor just affirmed himself a musician of inspiration and knowledge. This is a lyric symphonist whose place is henceforth close to Léo Delibes, the author of *Sylvia* and *Coppélia*. —H. Moreno.[34]

The musician, Mr. Widor, is a "youth," and his debut at the theater is a masterstroke. He ranks among the leading organists of Paris, and has made himself known among musicians, if not the general public, by some excellent symphonic compositions and chamber music applauded at the Châtelet concerts and elsewhere. His score has achieved a complete success; its great qualities are originality, sensitivity, clarity, and rhythm. The instrumental style is treated with great lightness, due in large part to the frequent use of the brass and woodwinds, and offers a variety of colors and effects that marvelously suits the diverse scenes that Mr. Widor wanted to portray. This orchestral system, in which the sonorous mass of strings seems relegated to the second level, sometimes makes the instrumentation appear a little thin, but it also has the advantage of giving to the scene a variety of the most agreeable colors and tints. Mr. Widor has reproduced and developed some Breton melodies in his score, . . . but above all, he has drawn on his imagination, and he has done well, for it has richly and valiantly served him. . . .

We will not follow the musician in all the caprices of his fantasy. Here, it's an expressive melody, there, a successful combination that is quite a scene; farther on, a witty episode laughs in the score. The first act is, in our opinion, the best. The scene of Yvonnette and the hunchback Paskou is full of spirit and grace; while the bell ringer expresses his grotesque love, the young girl taunts him, and the two melodic ideas are interlaced with infinite bliss. The joyous entry of the piper Lilèz is full of show and gaiety, and the first meeting of Lilèz and Yvonnette is treated with infinite finesse and grace. The dance of the Korriganes that follows this scene . . . is one of the best pages of the score; the vigorous and colorful orchestra courses a well-developed theme: it is a remarkable composition. The ballet comes next, one of the great successes of the evening. In this brilliant segment, long and varied, the composer portrayed a series of scenes that are all extremely successful. The stick contest is of a solid rhythm and well cadenced; the Breton *gigue* is alert and lively, and here the quartet is all the more striking as it is more rare in the score; but the great music and dance success was the *sabotière* (wooden-shoe maker). It is a sort of rapid mazurka, in the coquettish rhythm, and nicely set off by some syncopation on the first beat; the toc-toc of the wooden shoes gaily beats the time to the charming piece. . . .

From the musical point of view, the principal scene of the second act is the duo in which the little beggar Janick intoxicates Paskou. There is much spirit and finesse in this piece, and especially in the scherzo of the nightmare of Paskou. . . . At the beginning of this act, it is necessary to take note of a curious association of timbres between a humming chorus and the typophone-Mustel, a type of metallic harmonica. In the dance of the moths, people loudly applauded a gracious violin solo in G. . . .

Such is the ballet of Mr. Widor, a work of real talent that has had great success. —H. Lavoix *fils*.[35]

The ballet of Mr. Widor is the work of a composer endowed with all the qualities that make masters. We accept this gift of joyous advent as the sign of the most splendid promises.[36]

The ovations of an enraptured public only increased during the whole evening. . . . There's a composer definitively classed.[37]

For the first time, Widor tasted real celebrity, and he later remembered a bit of motherly advice offered to him:

On December 1, 1880, the premiere of *La Korrigane* took place at the Opéra. The rehearsals had been delightful, without a hitch—no accidents or incidents. The premiere ballerina, Mademoiselle Mauri, by her spirit, her good grace, and her talent, captured all our hearts. The countess d'Haussonville, mother of the count d'Haussonville, having heard some social gossip about what was going on at the Opéra (to which she was a subscriber) told me: "She is charming, but above all don't marry her!"

The premiere was very well received. A select audience including both Gambetta and the Prince of Wales [1841–1910; reigned 1901–10] was unexpected. The little Korriganes, in the wings, cried out: "Vive Mr. Widor! Vive Mr. Widor!" when I passed by. I walked out on the stage at all the intermissions with the future Edward VII.[38]

Widor's ballet was such an immediate and superlative triumph that he was henceforth often referred to simply as "the composer of *La Korrigane*." Even Franck sought Widor's advice on some ballet music that he was writing for a scene in his opera *Hulda*. Widor recalled:

When I wrote *La Korrigane*, Franck said to me: "I just wrote an opera, *Hulda*; there is a ballet in this opera."

"Are there some choreographic necessities—necessities of form, background, movement, and opposition—that are essential?" he asked me.

"I don't understand; I was guided by Mérante, the choreographer, who indicated a bit of the way to me. In any case, either at your place or mine, I am at your disposal to tell you in detail the things that were imposed on me."

Three weeks passed without my meeting with Franck; I wrote to him, "I am still waiting for you." To this letter, the following response arrived: "I don't need your advice, I don't want to bother you." I said to him further, "Have you met with Delibes?" —"No, but I don't need your advice. My ballet is very danceable. The other day, I had my piano moved into my bedroom, and there, in night-shirt, I danced my ballet following my music that Madame Franck played on the piano!"[39]

To such a serious-minded composer as Franck, Widor thought it best to remind him of one important point: "You know, *cher ami*, the girls of the Opéra ballet are not very highly evolved musically!"[40] Still, Franck could likely do better than Widor when it came to trying out his dance steps. In an article titled "Inept at Dance," a journalist wrote, "Would people believe that Charles-Marie Widor was never able to learn how to dance? He often had the desire, however. We were astonished: 'To dance, it suffices to have a sense of rhythm,' we said to him; 'you have to have it.' He nodded his head, laughing: 'I have it—obviously I have it. But not where it would be necessary; my feet don't have a musical ear!'"[41]

La Korrigane remained very popular and continued to draw critical acclaim for decades to come. Eduard Hanslick (1825–1904), the influential critic of Vienna's *Neue freie Presse* who so loved Brahms and so hated Wagner and Bruckner (1824–96), praised Widor's ballet in the most flattering terms when he heard it in Carlsbaden.[42] In 1896, *Korrigane* received its one hundredth presentation at the Paris Opéra; and a unique fact in the choreographic annals of the Opéra is that the same principal, Rosita Mauri—who was also famous for her role in Delibes's *Sylvia*—danced all one hundred performances:[43]

> It's truly a delightful score, this *Korrigane*, and it can take its place right alongside of the ballets of Delibes. . . .
> This *Korrigane* is as young as in the first days, and yet it already dates back to the year 1880, which is an age for a ballet, as it would be for a rose or a butterfly. But here everything remains animated as if breathed by Weber or Mendelssohn. It dances, but in the aerial manner of sylphs and moths; it is a music that brushes the tips of reeds or the surfaces of lakes, but rarely allows the foot to rest on ground, and it is this that gives to it the enchantment of the dream and the illusion.[44]

By 1910, there would be still thirty-eight more presentations at the Opéra,[45] and historian Henri de Curzon (1861–1942) wrote in 1933 of a revival, "Never will one have as much pleasure celebrating his hale and hearty old age as in listening anew to the score of *La Korrigane*, admiring its freshness and its always so youthful grace. . . . Let's hope now that the work will regain its place next to *Coppélia* and *Sylvia*."[46] And the *Guide Chorégraphique* proclaimed in its analysis of *La Korrigane*, "The music is . . . one of the glories of French art."[47]

—47—

Symphony in G Minor:
"The union of . . . 'the Emperor and the Pope'"

On the heels of the brilliant premiere of *La Korrigane* came the inauguration of Cavaillé-Coll's newest organ, at Saint-François-de-Sales in Lyon. This important occasion brought Widor back to perform in the very church—a stone's throw from the house of his birth—where his father had taught him to play and still remained *titulaire*, and where his brother Paul sang and filled in occasionally for their father. The Widors had collaborated closely with Cavaillé-Coll to design an instrument that would represent the latest developments of the builder.[48] Remarkably, the instrument remains today in its original condition—one of the few large Cavaillé-Coll organs that have not been altered over the years. On December 16, 1880, "all of Lyon" crowded into the modest-sized church and were soon awash with the sounds of Widor's latest organ symphony—the Fifth (though perhaps only the first, second, and fifth movements were played): "On the admirable instrument of Cavaillé, the maestro launched the feverish sonorities of his opening work with abandon"; the second movement offered a "very gracious foretaste of concerts in the heavenly city. Then came the finale with its persistent arabesques running on all the timbres of the keyboard, receding in their harmonious course to imperceptible thinness, and coming back little by little to make the deepest bourdons of the instrument resonate; . . . The symphony was over—too early."[49] Paul Widor sang an aria, fitted with a religious text, from Beethoven's *The Ruins of Athens*, and the choir sang an *Ave Maria* and *Tantum ergo*.[50] The program concluded with an improvisation by Charles-Marie.

As mentioned, the Prince of Wales graced the rehearsals of *La Korrigane*, and his enthusiasm for Widor's work resulted in the offer of an irresistible commission—one that prompted the composer to create a symphony for organ and orchestra.[51]

At that time, the future Edward VII, Prince of Wales, was spending the autumn in Paris and coming every evening to the Opéra. I [still] see myself, daily chatting cordially with the future majesty on the stage of the Opéra during rehearsals. He was filled with intelligence and was interested in everything. Before leaving Paris, he asked me if I would agree to come and play the organ in Royal Albert Hall for a fundraising festival that he was organizing for his hospital in London. I accepted, and it's in memory of my trip to London that he gave me the curious portrait of Handel that currently adorns the mirror above the fireplace of the little organ salon of Saint-Sulpice.[52]

For the Albert Hall concert, I orchestrated my Symphony in G Minor, with which I played two pieces of Bach.[53]

Rooted in three movements from the composer's solo organ symphonies, the work may properly be considered an arrangement for organ and orchestra, as it realizes the combined orchestral and solo potential of the music. The first and third movements were drawn from the Sixth Symphony in G Minor (first and fifth movements, respectively), and the second movement came from the Second Symphony in D major (third movement). Widor premiered the new

work in a concert at the Trocadéro on April 13, 1882,[54] almost four years after
he had premiered the solo version of the G Minor Symphony:

> The last festival of the Trocadéro . . . drew an enormous audience. [It was]
> a great success for everyone. . . . One of the principal interests of the per-
> formance was the premiere of a symphony for organ and orchestra of Mr.
> Widor. The young master himself interpreted his work.
>
>   The first movement of this symphony, a highly developed Chorale, first
> exposed by the full organ, is of an imposing effect. Nothing is lost from the
> numerous episodes of this piece, thanks to the wonderful virtuosity of the com-
> poser. The Andante that follows left a lovely impression; the flute stops of Mr.
> Cavaillé-Coll found there an excellent opportunity to display their charm. The
> third movement, a very brilliant *Tempo di marcia* would have gained, it seems to
> us, from having been taken less fast. In sum, this new symphony of Mr. Widor
> is a magisterial composition that highlights perfectly the resources of the mod-
> ern organ united with the powerful orchestra of our day.
>
>   We would have to be grateful . . . if . . . only that one work [had been per-
> formed].[55]

A few weeks later, on May 20, 1882, Widor, hailed as "le roi des organistes
français"[56] (the king of French organists), performed the Symphony in the
presence of the royal court in London's Royal Albert Hall, with the Royal
Amateur Orchestral Society, George Mount, conductor:[57] "I stayed a week
or so for the rehearsals and dined two or three times at the duke of Edinburgh's."[58] Widor recounted a surprising incident that happened during the
concert:

> In the same concert, the duke of Edinburgh, brother of the future Edward
> VII, played on the violin the prelude of Gounod's *Ave Maria*, which was sung
> by Marie Rose, a singer much loved by the public. In the middle of the pre-
> lude, the prince was taken with stage fright and his hand began to tremble.
> The ten thousand people that filled the vast hall were left in dismay by a
> stupendous burst of laughter from the royal box, where the wife of the unfor-
> tunate duke was seated and roared with laughter.[59]

After his return to Paris, Widor reported in his *Estafette* column on the
music in three London theaters: Covent-Garden, Drury Lane, and Her Majesty.
It appears that he had had time to attend Verdi's *Il trovatore* at Covent-Garden,
part of the *Ring* at Her Majesty, and other Wagner operas at Drury Lane. In
addition, Saint Paul's choir, led by Sir John Stainer (1840–1901), enchanted
him: "I heard . . . some children sustain the high B flat with the most perfect tranquility, the most absolute accuracy, and an astonishing fullness in the
immense nave. In London, that doesn't astonish anyone."[60]

A review of the Albert Hall performance was reported in the French press as much for Widor's being connected with the royal family as for the success of his music:

Great success for the Symphony for Organ and Orchestra of Mr. Ch.-M. Widor at the festival given at Albert Hall for the hospital sponsored by the Prince of Wales. The composer, who interpreted the organ part, was acclaimed and recalled at the end of the work. Then, after making a brilliant improvisation on the organ, Mr. Widor had the honor of attending the last part of the program in the box of the Princess of Wales, who had had herself introduced to our compatriot by the duke of Edinburgh.[61]

Widor had clearly demonstrated the brilliant possibilities of putting the organ and orchestra on equal footing in an extended composition—albeit only an arrangement. In 1904, when commissioned to revise Hector Berlioz's orchestration treatise, Widor took strong exception to the older composer's view that "a secret antipathy seems to exist between these two powers. The Organ and the Orchestra are both kings, or rather, one is Emperor, the other Pope; their mission is not the same; their interests are too vast and too diverse to allow of amalgamation."[62] Widor countered: "If Berlioz were still alive he would forswear his views of yore, or rather the views that were so unfairly instilled into his mind. Admirable new effects may yet be drawn from the union of the two former rivals, 'the Emperor and the Pope,' who, converted into fast allies, manifest ever growing mutual sympathy."[63] It was not at the feet of Berlioz that Widor laid the blame:

If Berlioz spoke of "hubbub, disorder, entanglements of sonorities, hideous lampoons excellent for depicting an orgy of savages or a dance of demons," it is because the miserable organist who set him on the wrong track must have served him up some Bach with a copious supply of bombardes and trumpets, an effect comparable to that of a string quartet in which one would double the parts with trumpets and trombones.[64]

The Symphony seems not to have been performed by Widor very often. One such occasion occurred on October 11, 1888, during the Universal Exposition in Barcelona. In a "brilliantly successful" concert devoted to his works at the Palace of Fine Arts, he performed his "superb Symphony for organ and orchestra" as soloist and was "recalled several times with enthusiasm."[65] The Symphony was also "greatly applauded" when he performed it for the inauguration of the Schyven organ at the Liège Conservatory on March 2, 1890.[66] In its new garb, the Sixth Organ Symphony took on an identity of its own.[67]

Although in 1894 Widor went on to compose his magnificent and completely original Third Symphony for Organ and Orchestra, Op. 69,[68] the Op. 42[a] *arrangement* continued to be admired, especially in the hands of the Belgian virtuoso organist Charles-Marie Courboin (1886-1973). He first performed the work on April 11, 1904, with Antwerp's Société Royale d'Harmonie,[69] but it was on March 27, 1919, that Courboin and the one hundred members of the Philadelphia Orchestra under the baton of its famous music director, Leopold Stokowski (1882-1977), gave the auspicious American premiere at John Wanamaker's Philadelphia store. From every description, the concert remains the high point in the history of the Wanamaker organ and the Philadelphia Orchestra. The reported size of the crowd in attendance at the Wanamaker premiere varies considerably from source to source, though it was likely about twelve thousand.[70]

—48—

Concordia: "Most honorable and conscientious"

Following the nineteenth-century trend to bring amateur performance into the public arena, in 1880 Widor assumed the directorship of Concordia, a new volunteer amateur choral society founded by mining engineer Edmond Fuchs (1837-89) and his singer wife Henriette, both of whom deplored the generally poor quality of male choirs.[71] In imitation of German, English, and Swiss choral societies,[72] the Concordia Society officially proclaimed as its credo: "To lend . . . aid to modern composers and above all to bring to light again the masterpieces of the old masters, of which the execution necessitates the cooperation of constituents that individual initiative can bring together [only] with difficulty."[73] Widor signed on enthusiastically, seeing it as an opportunity "for the study of the polyphonic masters of the Renaissance and their successors: Bach, Handel, Mendelssohn, Schumann . . . the old and the modern":

> Gounod was the president of it, and I the conductor. Thus, we gave, in the hall of the Conservatory, the *Saint Matthew Passion*, the *Mass in B Minor, Saint Paul, Paradis et la péri*, etc. The rehearsals took place Saturdays, [at the] Oratoire du Louvre. The most brilliant composition students—Claude Debussy [1862-1918], among others—succeeded one another as accompanists when, having obtained the Prix de Rome, they left us for the Villa Médicis. The publisher Fischbacher was our librarian.[74]

Widor had progressive ideas; in one of his *Estafette* columns three years earlier, he had vented his frustration at the lack of choral works represented on concert programs in the French capital:

I will permit myself to ask . . . why the vocal repertoire or rather the choral repertoire of the Concert Society [of the Conservatory] seems to be reduced to five or six works—to some fragments of [Weber's] *Euryanthe, Oberon,* of Mendelssohn or Handel. Is our art thus so poor? But no, a thousand times no! There are some treasures to exploit, masterpieces to make known, popular names abroad to inscribe on our programs. German societies possess rich libraries, a considerable repertoire. Why [do we] live in a range so limited when, on the other hand, in welcoming the formerly dreaded names of Schumann and Berlioz [on our programs], we seem to forsake a more liberal and progressive current?[75]

Through the programs of Concordia, Widor aimed to bring "liberal and progressive" works as well as staples of the choral literature to the Parisian public. He quickly made a formidable success with the new group, and by 1887 the active membership of the society numbered 138.[76]

The highly respected work of the Concordia chorale spawned an instrumental version about a year later:

Amateur instrumentalists will learn with pleasure of the birth of the *Concordia instrumentale.* Like its older sister, the *Concordia chorale*—the importance of which affirms itself each day—this Society, exclusively composed of devotees, is founded and directed by a committee of fashionable society with Mr. Charles Gounod as honorary president, and Mr. Ch.-M. Widor as conductor.[77]

Widor was excited about extending the venture in this new direction, although he still had limited experience as a conductor:

On several occasions, some Alsatians—strays from sacred choral societies in Strasbourg, refugees in Paris—had asked me to direct a concert for the sake of their works. I had practiced conducting choirs and the orchestra on account of this request, when one day they had the idea to send their directors to me. Mr. and Mrs. Fuchs, both Alsatians—the husband a very distinguished engineer, and his wife, a musician of the first order—came to tell me, "We want to reconstitute permanently our former society from Strasbourg in Paris. We are Protestants for the most part. The Reformed Consistory occupies a house, rue du Louvre, in which there is a large meeting room. Do you want us to form a society that will be called, as formerly, the Concordia, of which you will be the orchestra conductor under the patronage of Gounod?" I accepted with all the more eagerness as these performances, in which we had taken up some cantatas of Bach and some interesting pieces of Schumann, had taught me a little about the primary elements of my profession as an orchestral conductor, and because the suggestions of Gounod, who came to hear a rehearsal the Saturday of the Institute's centennial, had taught me one thing of which I was absolutely ignorant: the art of singing

Palestrina—that is to say [the art] of voices articulating with a certain vigor and not slurring the sounds, the art of making the sound carry in a large room, and rendering clarity to the vocal text, whereas it was lost with tied and slurred sounds. We had a series of very beautiful performances that for the most part took place in the hall of the Conservatory (or of the Consistory?) [Widor's recollection was uncertain]. We sang the Mass in B Minor, the [*St. Matthew*] *Passion* and quite a number of cantatas with my *confrère* Alexandre Guilmant at the organ. The Society lasted close to twenty years and came to an end only because Mrs. Fuchs, who was the prima donna of it, suffered the impairment of age and no longer had all the former freshness in her voice; also, the death of her husband [1889] caused her profound grief.[78]

For the bicentennial of Bach's birth in 1885, Concordia presented the French premiere of the *Magnificat* [BWV 243].[79] The wide variety of classical and contemporary repertoire performed by the Concordia Society included many major works: Bach's *Saint Matthew Passion* (BWV 244), Mozart's Requiem (K. 626), Haydn's *Seasons* (H. XXI:3), fragments from Gluck's *Alceste* and from several of Rameau's operas. Works by Bach, Handel, Lully, Mozart, Beethoven, Berlioz, Schumann, Liszt, Wagner, Brahms, Massenet, Pierné, Fauré, Paul Vidal, Saint-Saëns, Gounod, Emmanuel Chabrier (1841–94), Rubinstein, and others appeared on Concordia programs.[80]

The Concordia's most important concert, from a historical perspective, was its performance of Bach's *Saint Matthew Passion* on May 16, 1888; it represented "a decisive point in the public recognition of Bach."[81] Widor later recalled, "When I directed Concordia, I will never forget the hours devoted to the study and performance of this admirable series of lyric works that we crowned with the *Saint-Matthew Passion*, at the Conservatory."[82] Seeking words of wisdom on interpretive matters, Widor wrote to Joseph Joachim (1831–1907), the great violinist and director of the Hochschule für Ausübende Tonkunst in Berlin. Joachim graciously declined to offer any advice about "'St.' Jean Sébastien," as he referred to him, since he was preparing exams at his school and felt uneasy about expressing himself in detail in French. Nonetheless, he extended his encouragement to Widor, assuring him of his confidence: "You will know how to make your performers understand the work."[83] *Le Ménestrel*'s reviewer Julien Tiersot hailed the program, even if he found it a bit dry:

We can't overpraise the eminently artistic initiative to which we owed this hearing of a reputedly inaccessible masterpiece. The performance of the *Passion* by Concordia was, if not faultless, at least most honorable and conscientious. . . . Mr. Widor, nonetheless, directed the performance, if not with sufficiently communicative warmth, at least with a perfect precision and a thorough knowledge of the music of Bach.[84]

Widor believed his role as a conductor went beyond simply directing the performers: "[the conductor's] duty consists of forming the taste of the public and not of following it, to see beyond the present hour, above the little passions and coteries. And so their memory will remain: they will have served the great artistic cause."[85] He felt especially duty-bound to bring Bach's works to the public: "We have to educate a public still closed to the esthetic of the Master."[86] Throughout his life, he devoted himself to the music of "Père Bach,"[87] and he used the Concordia Society to promulgate his mission: "The society that I directed close to ten years, the Concordia, produced a good number of cantatas, the *Magnificat*, the *Matthew Passion*, etc. . . . Several other choral societies have been formed since, for the same end."[88]

In May 1881, Widor premiered his own *Chant séculaire*, Op. 49, for Soprano, Chorus, and Orchestra, which he composed especially for the Concordia concerts:

An unpublished work of Widor: *Chant séculaire*, from a poem by Mr. A. Grimault, in imitation of the ode of Horace. It's a sort of processional march, during which the voices of the warriors, women, children, young men, and old people are raised successively, and which is only interrupted in order to allow the "inspired priestess" to prophesy the brightest future to the Gallic sons. The work is strong and powerful and the effect of it was grand. . . . The orchestra and choruses worked wonders under the direction of the composer.[89]

Reviewers consistently praised the high quality of both branches of Concordia:

The Concordia . . . performed . . . with great success. The choruses, under the skillful direction of Mr. Ch. Widor, are almost irreproachable: it would be difficult to find elsewhere more freshness in the voices and more nuances in the style.[90]

After the *Concordia chorale*, its twin sister the *Concordia instrumentale* . . . gave a brilliant concert. . . . The young orchestra has truly worked wonders under the direction of its adroit conductor, Ch.-M. Widor.[91]

Although Widor said Concordia lasted nearly twenty years, Albert Schweitzer reported that after about a decade of activity the support of Concordia's backers flagged and the organization had to be disbanded because it had not attained enough stability to survive as an independent organization without financial backing.[92] A notice in *Le Monde Musical* in 1900 claimed that Concordia had just changed its name to La Société mondaine d'auditions under the same direction and with the same goals, but Widor's involvement had likely ended long before.[93]

—49—

"He was extremely fond of well-dressed young ladies"

Widor had quite a reputation for attracting to himself the socially elite and, as mentioned earlier, he became one of the most sought-after musicians in Paris, particularly by the older noble families whose elegant salons played host to many soirées featuring renowned Parisian composers performing their music.[94] As the borders of his fame expanded, he became acquainted with almost everyone who counted, and they all came to Saint-Sulpice, where one could rarely pay a Sunday visit to the organ gallery without encountering a bevy of important people crowding about the console—famous artists, politicians, musicians, aristocrats, royalty, and even a French president. Widor boasted that Marie-François-Sadi Carnot (1837–94), president of France from 1887 to 1894, was "one of my fervent listeners."[95]

With the splendor—some even thought theatrical brilliance—of the Saint-Sulpice service, the magnificence of the organ, and Widor's captivating personality, a large following was almost always present. "He, smiling and even joking, played to the astonishment of those who, coming to see him for the first time, received a kind of shock."[96] Widor did not submit to the kind of edict handed down to Vierne by the clergy when he assumed his duties as organist of Notre-Dame in 1900: "You should remind your guests, either verbally or by a notice posted on the organ case, that they are attending a religious service and must observe silence."[97] At a time when organists were not normally permitted to play recitals in church, Widor seemed to use the Mass to that very end:

> He was extremely fond of well-dressed young ladies and succeeded in turning the Low Mass into an organ-recital, which was attended to capacity by fashionable people. The organ-gallery was open to actresses, singers and other distinguished ladies of all nationalities.[98]

Cavaillé-Coll couldn't resist teasing Widor a bit about his distinguished following when he wrote to him, "Sunday I went to Saint-Sulpice where I found [choirmaster] Bellenot, who manages his organ quite well, but Mr. Widor's princesses are missing."[99]

In his memoirs, the great Polish pianist Ignace Paderewski (1860–1941) described, with perhaps a tinge of envy, Widor's special popularity with the Parisian socialites:

> The organ of St. Sulpice was a remarkably beautiful one and Widor's famous organ recital every Sunday morning was a rendezvous of the whole aristocratic and artistic Paris world. The church was always crowded with the most brilliant gathering of beautiful and fashionable ladies. I think there is an

interesting comment to be made here when speaking about a church, for the church, it seems to me, is almost exclusively a feminist institution. I have always felt this to be so, and in this particular instance it certainly was, for there were only the most influential, fashionable ladies present and it was always the same audience. All the beautiful ladies of Paris were present; there were even some foreign ladies of great distinction and especial brilliance always to be found there on Sunday, as near to the organ and Widor as they could possibly get. And of course, naturally, it was very agreeable to him, for it is very pleasant to anybody to look at beautiful faces and charming dresses, and so on. To hear Widor on Sunday morning at St. Sulpice became a habit and a fashion that lasted many years.[100]

The two men enjoyed a warm relationship, and Paderewski referred to Widor as "a man of remarkable ability and a wonderful character altogether":

Yes, I knew him well. I saw him here in Paris a few years ago—two years ago I think [1934 or 1935], and we talked about various things of great interest to us both. I asked him, I remember, if he knew anything concerning the interest Charles the Great took in music. "Well," he said, "I know a little—I know that he was very much interested in music and that he was surrounded by musicians of that time (eighth century) but I shall look up some documents to enlighten you." And he did. Just two days afterwards I received a little book where all the works of the composers (of plain-chant) were mentioned. Yes, he sent me that book. He had thought about it, and found it. He had taken the trouble—a man over ninety. That gives you some idea of the quality of the man—does it not?[101]

Widor had intended to "make a kind chapter on Paderewski" in his incomplete "Souvenirs autobiographiques," but he never accomplished the task.[102]

With the number of admirers who regularly crowded into the cramped quarters around the console, mishaps were inevitable. American organist Edward Shippen Barnes (1887–1958) described one such scene:

Widor loved to talk to the people—especially the fair ladies who were often there—and sometimes he'd almost lose his place in the mass. When he occasionally forgot to give the wind signal to the blowers there would arise the most awful ascending series of yowls from the organ that you could imagine while the wind came gradually up—much to his disgust. . . .

One day, when I was present, a grand duchess of Russia was up there. She was very grand—exceedingly swell in every sense of the word. Pearls and things hung off her in every direction. Widor had full organ on, all coupled, of course, to the pedal, and during the mass the grand duchess stepped on bottom C. Everybody jumped at the roar that came out and the poor lady collapsed like a balloon with a hole in it. Widor patted her hand violently and said, "C'est rien du tout, Madame" [It's nothing at all, Madame]. After enough patting she recovered, but she wasn't half as grand after that.[103]

One precocious seven-year-old perpetrated a similar incident, and related it to Widor many years later:

> Animated by a burning curiosity, I had the imprudence to step up to the pedal clavier and, in consequence to a false move, I clutched one of the pedals. Alas! The bellows were still full and under pressure, the reeds drawn and the keyboards coupled to the pedals. A stupendous sonority burst forth, suddenly interrupting the preacher, who wasn't expecting such an oratorical effect.
>
> As for you, my dear *Maître*, with a glance from your irritated eye you discovered the guilty one and quickly ejected him with the toe of your boot. . . . Such was the first and only lesson that I received from you.[104]

. For those in the organ gallery, the Mass being celebrated in the church below must have seemed almost incidental. As soon as the sermon began, Widor opened his private salon behind the organ in order for the elegant spectators who were in the tribune to visit more comfortably, or sometimes he led them up the narrow entrance stairway to the Chapelle de Notre-Dame des Étudiants to see the little chamber organ of Queen Marie-Antoinette.[105]

Purportedly, Widor was reprimanded (around 1882) for having allowed the organ gallery to become too social during the Mass:

> Some fashionable women behaved with so little propriety that the Archbishop of Paris forbade women to go up to the organ, where "la Sirène" [the notorious Paris socialite Countess Emmanuela Potocka (née Pignatelli)] turned the pages of Widor's music, seated on the same bench, while councillor [Jacques-] Clovis Bachelier [1818–98] appeared like an old dog panting around a bitch.
>
> The newspapers publish[ed] some reports that attracted more socialites to Saint-Sulpice, [and] Monseigneur replaced Widor. People forgot about him. Then absolved, he began his organ recitals again.[106]

Although official church records report the firing of a careless bell ringer, there is no record that Widor was ever the subject of a complaint.[107]

The young Ennemond Trillat, whose father Paul was a well-known organist in Lyon and eventually the organist of Saint-François-de-Sales (1904–9), recalled the routine of his visits to the tribune of Saint-Sulpice:

> I was thirteen years old [1903] when I disembarked in Paris and [Widor] was the first *maître* who welcomed me with an almost paternal tenderness. Every Sunday for the Grand Mass, my brother Joseph made me climb the little corkscrew stairway, nestled in the north [actually the south] tower. . . .

One first entered into a dark room where the scent of incense mixed with the odor of sweat from the blowers who pedaled in double strokes to inflate the enormous bellows; their cadence depended on the power of the combinations and the *ff* of the 32' stops. Waiting for the respite of a quiet registration, these nameless slaves had to struggle to maintain the millions of liters of air that gushed out into the vast nave. It was as hard as making the Galibier [Pass] on bicycle. . . .

Finally, through a narrow door in the tribune one arrived at the sonorous monster. The raised console housed the keyboards, a hundred stops and a number of imposing pedals.

The impassive *maître* reigned over the "Pope of Instruments" (F. Liszt).

I only knew my father's old organ at the Primatiale [Lyon], situated between a pillar and the thick Roman walls of the choir. It was a little niche so narrow that I had some trouble staying on the bench. . . .

The Cavaillé-Coll of Saint-Sulpice was more welcoming. On the extended bench to the left and to the right of Widor were two faithful admirers or more often lady admirers. When it was free, I took the left side and entered that sonorous world, astounded by the transcendent virtuosity of the *maître*.

But was this a religious service or was something else going on in this little coterie?

Nevertheless, in the distance a ceremony took place, of which one heard the echoes during the silences of the *grand orgue*. An unknown organist, on a modest instrument in the choir accompanied the plainchant of the choir.

These silences were sufficiently prolonged to permit us a pause in a little nearby salon behind the organ case and the forest of pipes. In this way, outside all liturgy, one could chat, listen to an anecdote of the *maître*, smoke some "Murati," and admire an adorable little organ—that of Marie-Antoinette.

An electric house-bell announced the end of this amusement and we went back to the tribune.[108]

A legendary spinner of anecdotes, Widor charmed those around him: "Mr. Widor's conversation is such that you would want to be able to remember it word for word. But it's difficult to use a pencil and scratchpad. . . . An anecdote is scarcely in your thought when he says very watchfully to you, 'keep that one to yourself.'"[109]

Cavaillé-Coll gave Widor an autograph book—unfortunately stolen in the early 1920s—in which he collected the signatures of all the illustrious visitors who had come to hear him and the Saint-Sulpice organ. When celebrated musicians appeared in the tribune at Widor's invitation or by surprise, he willingly surrendered his place at the console. Ennemond Trillat particularly remembered a visit of Saint-Saëns:

It sometimes happened during the service that Saint-Saëns, just back from Cairo or the Canary Islands, appeared unexpectedly in an "Allegro vivo" wearing his famous trousers of black and white squares and, without preparation, took the place of Widor before the five manuals: brilliant improvisation, technique almost impeccable—although a little nervous, all modernism being absent. It was his joy to find a friend again in C major, but in total unawareness of the sacred place that surrounded us.[110]

Saint-Saëns dedicated his Prelude and Fugue in E major, Op. 99, no. 1, to Widor, and the latter quickly extended an invitation to him to come hear it at Saint-Sulpice:

Have you forgotten your very kind promise to come to Sunday lunch at Foyot's? If you come by Saint-Sulpice, I shall desire your critique regarding how to register this beautiful *Prélude* that you have done the honor of dedicating to me, and that I will try to play for you.

I have asked the Countess Potocka to come to lunch and I also invited [Albert] Périlhou [1846–1936] and Vierne.

I like you very much and admire you even more. [Signed] Widor
Until next Sunday, the 17th, okay?[111]

—50—
Violin Sonata: Prix Chartier

The feverish pitch of compositional energy with which Widor had produced about forty-five opus numbers in the 1870s began to taper off during the 1880s. A significant amount of light piano, vocal, and chamber music had been composed for his regular appearances in the salons of Parisian aristocratic society—"the charm of Paris," as he referred to them: "The traditional Monday or Friday receptions at this or that noble residence, brought together handsome men and beautiful women, people of letters and science, painters, sculptors, musicians."[112]

Beginning in the 1880s, works of more substantial proportions began to appear. For his 1881 Sonata in C Minor, Op. 50, for Piano and Violin, the French Academy of Fine Arts awarded him the "Prix Chartier," a prize established to encourage the composition of chamber music; with it came the handsome sum of five hundred francs.[113] Widor dedicated Opus 50 to Princesse Bassaraba de Brancovan, the daughter of a Turkish ambassador, wife of a Rumanian prince, and a fine amateur pianist. Her exotically decorated salon mirrored her cultural background, and a fashionable audience could be expected at her musicales. She and violinist Guillaume-Antoine Rémy (1856–1932), professor of violin at the Conservatory, performed the Sonata in June 1882 along with a number of piano pieces drawn from *La Korrigane*. "The gathering of the elite who crowded into the salons of the Princess Brancovan did not stop applauding and requesting encores."[114] As indicated in the title, the piano takes the lead through the greater part of the work. Although classic in form, proportion, and key relationships, the Sonata exhibits clear romantic tendencies by its heightened drama, dynamics, texture, chromaticism, and Brahmsian rhythmic play of two-against-three. Indeed, the powerful key of C minor and resolution to C major recalls Beethoven's Fifth Symphony and Brahms's First Symphony. The noted success of the Sonata encouraged Widor to consider future works for violin and piano.[115]

A few months earlier, when describing another impressive soirée peopled with dignitaries and socialites, the press lauded Widor for his superb accompanying skills:

Mr. and Mrs. Trélat have opened the salon Orfila to us, not only for the enjoyment of music, but also in connection with the intelligent, artistic, literary, and scientific sphere that one encounters at their home, rue de l'Arcade, where the illustrious of every type take pleasure. Last Saturday, around Mr. Jules Ferry (Minister of Public Instruction and the Fine Arts) and Mr. [Louis-Adolphe] Cochery [1819–1900] (Minister of the Post and Telegraph) gathered the painters Hébert, Bonnat, Carolus Duran, the sculptor Guillaume, Renan of the Académie-française, General [Albert] Cambriels [1816–91], Colonel [François] Perrier [1835–88] of the Institute, and twenty other friends of good music whose names escape our memory. Mrs. Trélat, after having sung as she alone knows how, presented to her company the daughter of Lemmens, the great Belgian organist, and Mrs. Sherrington, the great English singer who is dedicated to the oratorios of Handel. Miss Ella Lemmens-Sherrington is already a singer of high style; she notably interpreted a *Mélodie italienne* [Op. 35] of Ch. Widor with such perfection that one would never have suspected that she had sight-read it the day before. . . . Yet one more word: Ch.-M. Widor played the piano the whole evening and so well, so very well, that to thank him in the name of all present, Rosita Mauri, a mere onlooker in long dress, danced the charming step of the Sabotière from *La Korrigane*. The composer and interpreter were acclaimed. —H. M[oreno][116]

Widor typically composed sets of *mélodies* and piano works between his larger compositions, though he lamented to Isidor Philipp, "The pianists hardly spoil me with too much attention."[117] Writing in 1967, pianist Ennemond Trillat, who had premiered Widor's little piano piece *Fugue sur Haydn* in 1911, assumed the attitude of shallow criticism taken by many: "[Widor's] excursions into the lyrical domain were flops; his *mélodies* for ladies and his piano pieces of 1900 have preserved only the attractiveness of their covers!"[118] T. Carl Whitmer concurred in similar dismissively pejorative language; after praising the ten organ symphonies, he tossed away the rest of Widor's music: "[The organ music] is in addition to an incredible pile of piano music (mostly poor), songs, organ concertos, etc., etc."[119] Whitmer's mention of "organ concertos" shows to what degree he lacked knowledge of Widor's output; the one work that might be considered an organ concerto, *Sinfonia sacra*, had not been composed at the time of this statement. That pianists of the ilk of Francis Planté, Louis Diémer, and Isidor Philipp often performed Widor's music speaks more tellingly of its appeal, and suggests that pianists should assess the repertoire anew.

—51—

Second Symphony: "A most remarkable work"

Widor's Second Symphony, Op. 54, for Orchestra was the next large work to appear. Benjamin Godard agreed to conduct the new symphony, writing to Widor, "You will be the first on the program."[120] Obtaining performances usually required a devoted effort on the part of the composer, who once groveled a bit when he sent the score to the Concert Society of the Conservatory: "I will be proud and grateful if you deem it worthy to be tried at one of your rehearsals."[121] Some critics found it to their liking:

> Of Widor, we also heard his Second Symphony, a most remarkable work, certain pages of which are worthy to be compared to the best productions of Schumann. The first part is distinguished quite particularly by the beauty of the conception: it is a modern classic.[122]

Others disagreed. Had it any power, the pithy condemnation pronounced by George Bernard Shaw would have sent the symphony straight into oblivion: "Berlioz himself, in his most uninspired moments, could not have been more elaborately and intelligently dull."[123] Another critic, however, found it regretful that the Second Symphony received only rare performances:

> The fate of the Symphony in A of Mr. Ch. Widor is not exactly encouraging for young musicians who desire to devote themselves to this genre of composition. . . . Modern art is not, however, so rich in symphonic works that entrepreneurs and concert directors can turn away from scores of such value as Mr. Widor's and entrench themselves behind the block of classical symphonies . . . alleging that the modern production does not offer sufficient interest. The Symphony in A of Mr. Widor is of an essentially French character, even though conceived in the forms of the exemplary symphonies from beyond the Rhine. It distinguishes itself by its clarity and its brio, by the conciseness of its developments and by the elegance and the finish of the workmanship; the invention, it is true, is not greatly abundant, but one is scarcely aware of it because of the copious yield from the themes used.[124]

Richard Strauss conducted a concert that included Widor's Second Symphony in its revised, second edition (1892). On the same program, Pablo de Sarasate performed Saint-Saëns's *Rondo capriccioso*, and at the conclusion of the concert he addressed a letter to "My dear Widor":

> I'm very happy to tell you of the beautiful and unequivocal success of your Symphony in A Major at the Berlin Philharmonic. It gives me great pleasure to join my applause to that of the three thousand people who were in the hall and who acclaimed the French *maître* as he so merits.[125]

—52—

Flute Suite: the *"Romance* style"

Among Widor's most enduring and popular works, the Suite for Flute and Piano, Op. 34, appears to have been composed later than its opus number would suggest. With the possible exception of the Mass, Op. 36, the Suite is surrounded by many opuses that date from the second half of the 1870s. However, the premiere took place in April 1884 when Paul Taffanel, the Suite's dedicatee, performed it in a concert of the Société des instruments à vent.[126] The leading flutist of the time, Taffanel received critical accolades for his wonderful performances of the work: "the eminent flutist is truly extraordinary and, despite the very serious style of the work, he produced a very great impression on his audience."[127] Sensitive to "anything associated with the vapid musical world of the salons," Taffanel included only the best of old and new compositions on his programs.[128] The Suite was the first substantial composition written for the famed flutist, and Widor showed that he was completely up to the task of creating a "superbly idiomatic" work that "stretches the voice of the flute to its limits and far transcends the salon."[129] Taffanel honored the work by performing it often throughout the rest of the 1880s. Publication of the Suite, or possibly a revised edition, was noted in a letter of November 1896 from Widor to Wallace Goodrich: "I will send the Suite for piano and flute to you as soon as I see my publisher."[130]

The third movement, Romance, appears to have spawned the Romance in Widor's suite of incidental music, *Conte d'avril* (1885), and is one of a few examples of his self-borrowing.[131] It is unclear which work was composed first, though the Flute Suite received its premiere before *Conte d'avril*, where the Romance is scored for solo flute, harp, strings, and sporadic wind chords. There, the accompanying text suggests the character with which the music is infused: "Night made for love, oh gentle April night." The flute tenderly expresses the imagery of the text. The movement had been titled Andante at its premiere, but when Taffanel performed it again in March 1885 it appeared under the suggestive title Romance, a likely result of its connection with the *Conte d'avril* text.

Georges Barrère (1876–1944) had requested that Widor orchestrate the other movements of the Suite, "but he was always so busy that he never fulfilled the promise he gave me to do so."[132] Since Barrère enjoyed playing the Romance and Scherzo with orchestra, and Widor had only orchestrated the Romance, Barrère orchestrated the Scherzo himself.[133] Flutist Raymond Meylan (b. 1924) saw important beginnings in the Romance: "This poetic imperative in instrumental performance seems to me to announce the launch of the modern French School."[134] Indeed, after Widor's Romance, Blakeman cites a dozen works in "*Romance* style" that poured in with dedications to Taffanel.[135]

Widor contributed to the Romance style again in 1889 with an independent *Romance* for Violin and Piano, Op. 46. Aptly titled, this idyllic piece, in song form, falls into that genre of chamber music best categorized as salon music. Pure melody dominates as the violin sings its "song without words." As noted previously, Widor can be numbered among those composers who maintained a fatherly interest in the improvement and currency of their older works. He never hesitated to revise his work, often numerous times, and he published a revision of this *Romance* in 1912.

—53—

"*Maître Ambros* leaves the door open to every hope"

More than symphonies and chamber music, theatrical productions in the form of ballet, opera, or incidental music carried the mark of real distinction for late nineteenth-century French composers, many of whom produced theatrical works annually. The importance of theatrical genres was no less important to Widor, and he had the deeply held conviction that composition of dramatic works was a necessary constituent of the complete musician.[136] After *La Korrigane*, he composed two minor scores of incidental music: *Conte d'avril* (first version, September 1885) for a play by Auguste-Léon Dorchain (1857–1930) based on Shakespeare's *Twelfth Night*; *Les Jacobites* (November 1885) for François Coppée's historical drama. In the theatrical arena, however, Widor devoted his full energies during the first half of the 1880s to an opera.

The libretto was to have been crafted entirely by Coppée, but it turned into a collaboration between Coppée and Dorchain. Widor explained:

> At that time, Coppée was working on his drama *Les Jacobites* and was not able to give me as rapidly as I wished the modifications that I was asking of him at each instant; it's he who called Dorchain to the rescue. And it's upon Dorchain that I inflicted the torture of the "monsters."

Odious torture, as you will see:
In principle, the musician makes his music on the verses of the libretto, but sometimes the melodic idea requires some development or a meter that the poet has not foreseen. Then the musician arranges and submits the words in question to a rhythm in order to indicate to the librettist the number and place of the long and short syllables that he requires; and it's to this mannequin, to this "monster," that the unlucky poet must give a presentable figure. It's bad enough when the monster is naturally formed according to the laws of anatomy, I mean of the *Gradus*! But often it has nine, eleven, or thirteen feet![137]

Maître Ambros, a "drame lyrique" in four acts, received a trial reading under the title *Nella*, the opera's heroine, in December 1882.[138] However, the public premiere had to wait until May 6, 1886, when it appeared as *Maître Ambros* at the Paris Opéra-Comique (Salle Favart). Widor and Coppée had hoped for a premiere at the Opéra, and to that end Widor had written to its director, Emmanuel Vaucorbeil,

to ask him not to forget us, Coppée and me, in the distribution of his official commissions. The best solution for our matter is in his hands; Coppée seems to me little inclined towards [Léon] Carvalho [1825–97; director of the Opéra-Comique], and in touching up my work, I feel more and more the need of a dramatic soprano [in the role of Nella] and that of a baritone [in the role of Ambros] for *real feeling*. . . . One would always find the "necessary" singer at the Opéra.[139]

The story of the opera is a combination of some historical facts—it takes place in the Dutch Republic of 1650—and characters of fantasy:

Guillaume II (William of Orange) has resolved to stage a military occupation of Amsterdam. The townspeople have closed the gates of the city, pointed their canons to the country, and are waiting for the ensuing attack; if necessary, they have decided to open the dikes and drown the enemy. Maître Ambros, a formidable former pirate, has put himself at the head of the defense movement. At his house, a meeting concerning the plans for the country is taking place. Also at Ambros's house is Nella, a frightened young orphaned girl who came to Ambros seeking refuge from the enemy. The daughter of a famous admiral killed in combat, Nella knew that Ambros, the old friend of her father, would protect her. But before long, the old seaman falls in love with her. At first, he is unaware, but when a handsome young officer, Hendrick, comes to ask for her hand, Ambros feels himself gripped by all the torments of jealousy. He wants to choke back his passion, but he can no longer contain it when he learns that Nella also loves him! At this point, Hendrick recalls a sad incident in Ambros's life as a seaman. Ambros had not always been the honored man that he is today. Once, in a drunken orgy, Ambros had lost a gamble; he had nothing but his honor to pay the debt. With pistol raised and ready to die, Ambros was saved by Hendrick, who paid the debt. Poor Ambros, not wanting to be ungrateful to Hendrick for saving him from such a humiliating death, decides to step aside and let Hendrick take Nella. But how will he heal Nella of her love toward him? Ambros realizes he must offend her. In the face of the townspeople, he feigns a drunken scene. Disgracefully wallowing on the floor, he grossly insults Nella, and she goes off with Hendrick. Meanwhile, some traitors have been conspiring to deliver the city to Guillaume that very night. Still feigning drunkenness, Ambros lies under a table and overhears their conspiracy. There is just enough time for him to thwart it. He rushes to open some dikes, and Guillaume's army flees. Nella had promised her heart to the one who would save the country—an oath accepted even by Hendrick. All the townspeople celebrate their liberation at the hand of Maître Ambros. As they leave the scene, Nella and Ambros are left alone, reunited and happy.

Of the ten reviews printed in *Le Ménestrel*, most found praiseworthy things in Widor's new opera.[140] Although *Maître Ambros* was not an unqualified success, it served as an indicator of what all hoped would certainly follow:

The evening performance last Thursday at the Opéra-Comique was one of the most interesting for French music that we have had for a long time. It has revealed to us an artistic personality of a rare power. I purposely employ the word personality, for there is a quality there that must take precedence over all the others in an artist's style. Mr. Widor is not pulled along in the tow of any other master, and, going very far in modern ideas, he knows how to safeguard his own originality. It is the mark of a superior talent. Most certainly, one can hope for much from a composer who, for his first try in the theater, writes a score like *Maître Ambros*. We don't want to exaggerate and we don't claim that this work is perfect from head to foot; we very much notice some needless complications in the orchestration that make it difficult to comprehend, some underbrush that would be necessary to prune without pity; but we also notice how the orchestration remains almost consistently vivid and charming, and how the ideas remain inspired! Like all manifestations of art somewhat new and personal, the score will not fail to astonish initially and perhaps even baffle novice ears. It is only by the intimate and thoughtful study of the work that one will succeed in understanding it, and its fate will then perhaps equal that of *Carmen*, the initially controversial work by Bizet, whose death we still mourn. *Ambros* is like it; the discussion and the passions aroused by a work are generally a certain sign of its strength. Widor already has some enthusiasts and still more detractors. The future is his. If we would have the perilous honor of being the director of the National Academy of Music [the Opéra], we would not hesitate, after this experience, to entrust a poem to Mr. Widor. His temperament seems to us to carry itself more toward this great dramatic stage than toward the Favart Hall, where his talent is a little cramped for space. He has seen in this first try his weakness, and no doubt before long he will give us a perfect and well-balanced work, without sacrificing anything of his high aspirations. . . .

Thus we have this unusual work, in which the novelty of the form vies with the loftiness of the ideas. If it doesn't succeed immediately, the hour will undoubtedly come when we will understand the originality of it, and, in any case, this work portends a future of remarkable scores by the same hand. Coming after *La Korrigane*, which was very much noticed at the Opéra, *Maître Ambros* leaves the door open to every hope. —H. Moreno.[141]

Maître Ambros received only ten or so performances;[142] but the five-movement orchestral suite that Widor extracted from the opera became quite popular on his orchestral programs, and Nella's "Ballade" remained a favorite on song recitals. Shortly after the opera's premiere, Widor went to Amsterdam to present a festival of his music; he conducted the Second Symphony and the Orchestral Suite from *Maître Ambros*, and he performed the Fifth Symphony for Organ:[143] "The journey of Mr. Widor to Amsterdam has real importance for the interests of French art in Holland. With the triple title of composer, organist, and conductor, this eminent artist has produced a profound impression here."[144]

The Second Symphony was acclaimed as carrying "the imprint of a very chastened taste. Not one oddity, not one spot of sterile affectation."[145] Of the *Maître Ambros* Orchestral Suite, the critic extolled the poignancy with which Widor had captured the semblance of Dutch life and landscape in his music. His broad knowledge of art had served him well in capturing the correct spirit: "truly, one was struck by a peculiar analogy of inspiration and color between the canvases of Rembrandt, Van Ostade, Teniers, Jan Steen, and the pages of the French master—an analogy completely from intuition, however, since before painting Holland, their author had never seen it."[146]

The artistry that Widor exhibited as an organist commanded the highest praise of all, his refined modern approach to organ playing being almost totally unknown in Holland:

As to the talent of the organist, here where the organ in general remains in a quite different state [from that of Cavaillé-Coll], he excited us as much from astonishment as from admiration. The imperturbable surety, the finesse and vigor of Mr. Widor's technique never falter; never does he deviate from the most classical correctness, but at the same time he excites you, he carries you away, he knows how, in a word, to captivate by an inexpressible charm. By the choice and blending of the sonorities in which nothing clashes, even in the contrasts, where all is linked and based in harmonious unity, he achieves effects of an almost immaterial poetry. At times, especially in the Andante of the Symphony in F [Minor], the organ disappeared, so to speak; there remained only the impression of an indefinable and penetrating suavity. But also, the artist had under his hands one of the most beautiful instruments of Cavaillé-Coll.

The triumph was complete. The fanfares from the orchestra doubled the bravos and the enthusiastic cheers of the entire hall.[147]

—54—

Two monumental organ symphonies: Seventh and Eighth

Widor once explained to family members, "I don't write my music for shepherds!"[148] As stated earlier, critics sometimes pointed to the sophisticated and introspective nature of Widor's compositional style as a barrier to an unabashed public appreciation of his work: "The music of the master needs to be heard several times in order to appreciate its beauties properly."[149] Appraisals such as the foregoing one are equally applicable to the two monumental organ symphonies produced in the mid-1880s. The Seventh and Eighth Symphonies were added to the Fifth and Sixth to comprise the single Opus 42—twenty-three movements in the original version. Unlike the universally popular Fifth and Sixth Symphonies, the Seventh and Eighth remain less known and infrequently performed. By far the weightiest in terms of length and difficulty, and the most orchestral in conception, their advanced style sets them quite apart from their predecessors:

> In these last symphonies we approach a Widor that is very little known, even among organists. Often lengthy, always complex, and never easier than moderately difficult to play, the very appearance of the score is calculated to discourage all but enthusiasts and players of high technical attainment with large modern instruments at their disposal. If however we pluck up courage and give some of the movements a fair trial, we shall find that many difficulties will straighten themselves out, and that we are making acquaintance with a lot of music which as keen lovers of the organ we shall not readily part with when once we know it.[150]

The exact genesis of the Seventh and Eighth Symphonies is as elusive as that of the earlier ones. In an undated letter, Widor wrote to his sister:

> I am so busy at the moment that I can't write; I have on my table fifty letters that demand urgent responses, since days ago! The Violin Concerto, orchestral corrections of *Maître Ambros*, and the end of the organ symphonies, which still lack the last two movements but which will be finished and forwarded to the publishers this month—all this engulfs me. Besides, we have a concert Wednesday of the Concordia when we sing the second act of *Parsifal* and Schumann's *Faust*, which occasions an enormous loss of time.[151]

It can be ascertained from the information in this letter that it was written between January 20 and 25, the Concordia concert in question having taken place on January 26, 1887.[152] On April 10, 1887, Widor wrote to Alexander Wilhelm Gottschalg (1827–1908), director of the newspaper *Urania* in Weimar:

> In a few days the last two symphonies and the new edition of the first four will appear, corrected and considerably augmented. I wanted to balance the first works and give to them the amplitude of the following. The whole is at the engravers, Röder in Leipzig. I will send them to you soon in the hope that they will interest you despite their mysticism and severity at first sight.[153]

An advertisement for these two symphonies first appeared in the January–March 1888 issue of the *Biographie Musicale Française*.[154] The press notice of Widor's Trocadéro concert during the 1889 Paris Exposition simply did not present accurate information regarding the Eighth Symphony:

> Wednesday, July 3, at exactly 2:30, in the Festival Hall of the Trocadéro, the fifth performance, given by Mr. Ch.-M. Widor. Here is the program for it: Symphony VIII, unpublished (Widor), played by the composer; Aria for cello (J. S. Bach), played by Mr. Jules Delsart; Symphony V (Widor), played by the composer; Sarabande for cello (J. S. Bach), played by Mr. J. Delsart; Toccata and Fugue (J. S. Bach), played by Widor.[155]
>
> The organ concert given at the Trocadéro by Mr. Widor was of the most interesting kind. He performed two of his beautiful organ symphonies: the 8th, still unpublished, of a severe and highly elevated style; the 5th, completely appealing, and which conquered and charmed the public.[156]

The juxtaposition of the two symphonies allowed a telling comparison; another reviewer also noted the wide stylistic hiatus between them: "There is perhaps more unity and grandeur in [the Eighth Symphony], but [the Fifth Symphony] by the grace of its abundant inspiration will remain the preferred symphony with the public."[157] Though included within the same opus number, about eight years separated the Fifth and Sixth Symphonies from the Seventh and Eighth Symphonies. Widor had matured as an organ composer to the point that one might imagine the latter two symphonies having come from the pen of a different composer. With the Mahlerian scope of the seven-movement Eighth Symphony (original version), Widor seemed to have exhausted the possibilities of his instrument, as well as his own compositional technique. The Eighth represented the ultimate achievement in the art of organ composition at the time:

> It seems scarcely possible, while studying symphonies' [*sic*] 5, 6 and 7, that any greater breadth of treatment could be secured. Yet he has accomplished it here [with the 8th].[158]

> The eighth symphony . . . forms the most stupendous work ever written for organ. It is doubtful if a more difficult work exists. The performer is constantly in a position to desire extra resources for its adequate performance.[159]

That Karl Straube (1873–1950), the great German organist and champion of the contrapuntally dense organ music of Max Reger (1873–1916), was drawn to Widor's Eighth Symphony some twenty years after its composition is an indication of the powerful and advanced aesthetic with which the work is infused.[160] Of the Seventh Symphony, little is written in original sources, though Madame Widor affirmed: "The Allegro [Finale] of the Seventh Symphony was one of the pieces that I heard Charles-Marie play the most often."[161]

Saint-Saëns composed his *Troisième fantaisie*, Op. 157, in 1919, and compared its technical demands to those of his colleague. He wrote to Widor from Strasbourg:

> Upon my return, I will have the honor of offering you a *Fantaisie* for organ that was just published. I wrote it at the request of the young King of Portugal and I strove to make it easy, which makes it very ordinary; in spite of that, I doubt that the addressee can play it! Such as it is, I think that it will be much welcomed by the great majority of organists who are not of your powers and who recoil terrified in front of your works![162]

With the completion of his cycle of eight symphonies for organ, Widor made clear his intention of not writing any more organ music: "The master declared to us [as of 1892] that henceforth, he renounced writing for the organ. He will now dedicate himself to the orchestra and to the stage."[163] However, Widor's lifelong process of revising the organ works had already begun in earnest. Coincidental with the 1887 publication of the Seventh and Eighth Symphonies, the four Op. 13 Symphonies were reissued in their first substantial revision: Widor had composed five new movements, revised several others, and added a Preface. As he saw it, "the life of an artist is but a perpetual disappointment; it's the running after an ideal that always flees, after a chimera that one never overtakes."[164] And he relished pointing out that Bach, too, loved to rework his earlier compositions:[165] "It was . . . the usual work procedure, the habit to which Bach remained faithful all his life—to take up former works to improve them. A piece no longer satisfying him, he composed another."[166]

A work fathered by the Eighth Symphony and published the same year (1887) was the *Cavatine* for Violin and Piano, Op. 57. It draws its main theme from the fifth movement (Adagio) of the Eighth Symphony composed a year earlier. Widor must have loved this theme greatly, for he clothed it in new raiment yet a third time, still retaining the key of F-sharp major, for the second movement (Adagio) of his *Symphonie antique*, Op. 83, of 1911. The title *Cavatine* suggests a short aria, and the outer sections of this song form are deeply expressive. The long-breathed melody with its characteristic three-note motive is one of Widor's most eloquent—fashioned of wide, expressive leaps, and compact chromatic turns. The melody of the central B section is more motivic, being constructed of chains of sigh motives and their permutations, as in the Adagio of the organ symphony.

Later in 1888, Widor scored a success as composer and conductor in a concert of his works in Marseille's Salle Valette. The program included his Cello Concerto, Op. 41, a work of "great effect that permitted the virtuoso to show off his essential qualities," the "Ronde de Nuit" from *Maître Ambros*, "a work to which connoisseurs attribute real value," and the Sérénade for Violin, Flute, Cello, and Orchestra, Op. 10, "exceedingly gracious and in which a charming motif passes successively from one instrument to another, finally engraving itself on the memory of everyone. The Sérénade was repeated at the unanimous demand of the audience."[167]

—55—

Fantaisie: "One of the most beautiful pianistic works"

Returning to London in March 1890, Widor conducted his new *Fantaisie*, Op. 62, for Piano and Orchestra for the opening concert of the Philharmonic Society's seventy-eighth season.[168] Dedicated to Isidor Philipp, the *Fantaisie* had been premiered by him the year before, on February 23, 1889, at the Salle Érard in Paris.[169] Recalling the event years later, Widor did not quite remember as perfectly as he had thought:

> The premiere of my *Fantaisie* in A Flat took place at the Châtelet, under the Colonne's direction, with Philipp as soloist. I remember perfectly having listened to it from the back of a loge where I found myself with the d'Erlangers.
> On April 7, the Érards, in their turn, organized a concert to have two of my works performed, one of which was the recent *Fantaisie* in A Flat for Piano and Orchestra, which Durand published.[170]

Widely heralded as "one of the most beautiful pianistic works of the contemporary period," the *Fantaisie* retained a prominent place in the repertoire for piano and orchestra until the end of Widor's life.[171] Philipp championed the work and received accolades for the fluency of his pianistic facility: "one was able to admire his velocity in the octave passages and the easiness of his trills with the weak fingers. Composer and interpreter have shared the bravos."[172]

> The work is something more than a merely brilliant and effective piece, since, like all M. Widor's compositions, it has earnestness of purpose, great

originality, and no small amount of melodic beauty. Nor is all, or even the greater part of, the musical interest given to the solo part, for the scoring, though frequently too heavy, is evidently the work of no tyro in orchestral effect, and some extremely slight details, such as the way in which momentarily use is made of the triangle and, in another place, of the stopped horn, show with what care and delicacy the accompaniments have been written.[173]

The last performance of the Concert Society of the Conservatory . . . the very great success of the performance was for the *Fantaisie* for Piano and Orchestra of Mr. Widor, the piano part of which was entrusted to Mr. I. Philipp. Here is a serious, inspired, well-conceived, masterfully written work, which leads us far from the fussy and the over-subtle. The fact is that Mr. Widor has ideas, that he knows how to make use of them and to develop them, that the tonal sense is not a superfluous thing to him, and that he is aware of a certain musical element that is called rhythm, which some people would like to make go out of fashion. In a word, the new work that Mr. Widor has performed is straightforward, constructed in a logical fashion and from an assured hand in its free and easy bearing, strict in form, with inspired impulses and an instrumental coloring that grasp the listener and draw applause out of him. . . . I repeat, the success of the composer and his interpreter was complete, remarkably pronounced, and I have seen few examples at the Conservatory of a new work welcomed with this warmth and enthusiasm by a public that is generally rather defiant and skeptical. A similar spectacle had not been offered to us since the performance of the fine [Third] Symphony in C Minor of Mr. Saint-Saëns, which had also thawed the listeners so often unmoved on the rue Bergère. —Arthur Pougin.[174]

The day following Widor's appearance with the London Philharmonic, he paid an unannounced visit to the Royal Academy of Music and gave an impromptu organ recital. Even faced with an inadequate instrument, the magic of Widor's communicative mastery held those present spellbound. Dr. Alexander Mackenzie (1847–1935), principal of the Royal Academy, thanked his French colleague in the following words:

The greatest men are those who delight in overcoming difficulties, and who rise superior to circumstances. We have here an eminent organist, whose performance seems all the greater because the instrument at his command is weak and limited in its quality and compass. I confess that I never believed in the supreme excellence of the Academy organ until now. Students of organ literature are well acquainted with M. Widor's wonderful Symphonies, which you have just heard; but it is, indeed, a matter of congratulation that we have made their better acquaintance through the instrumentality of the composer. We have just listened to an exhibition of unsurpassed technique and rare musical expression. It was recorded of Sir Joshua Reynolds that on one memorable occasion he laid aside his brushes and painted no more that day. As I do not wish to efface so delightful an impression, I propose that we shall also "paint no more to-day."[175]

London's Hampstead Conservatory also invited Widor to perform a program of his music. In addition to his Fifth and Seventh Symphonies, he and Philipp performed the harmonium Duos on organ and piano, and the Andante from an unspecified concerto.[176] To round off his London sojourn, a visit to the prominent London organ builder William Hill allowed him to see the monumental instrument being constructed for Sydney, Australia. Widor had to search his imagination to find an apt comparison: "I had the pleasure to see and study it in 1889 in the workshops of this intelligent builder. The 64' bass resembled an enormous drain pipe."[177]

—56—

Jeanne d'Arc: "Music on horseback"

It was to be only a few weeks later that Widor would come face to face with an ultimate challenge—a challenge that would truly test his ability to "rise superior to circumstances." He described how it all transpired:

It was the 3rd or 5th of May [1890] that my friend Delsart, the cellist, invited me to lunch with some of his friends, who were not completely unknown to me.

I went there good-heartedly, unsuspectingly, without suspicion of ambush; and there, before even the pear and the cheese, the little room that we occupied in Foyot's saw the perfect scene of the recruiters reproduced. Although more than twenty years old, I played the draftee, while Houcke, Thomas the costume designer, and Whittmann the conductor sought to wring a grave decision out of me.

It was quite simply a matter of writing for the Hippodrome, in four weeks, the music of a pantomime as heroic as colossal—to create a *Jeanne d'Arc*.

Ah! As all was well planned to force my hand, the ground had been carefully hoed. To each inclination of resistance, a rejoinder nailed me to the spot.

—"What is this score for you," insinuated Delsart, "but a game and more a novelty that will divert you from your usual business?"

—"The Hippodrome is almost a cathedral," insisted Houcke. "We would be able to place a *grand orgue* of your friend Cavaillé-Coll there."

—"You would have preferred the Opéra," added Thomas, "but be calm, all will not happen without words. You will have choirs, celestial voices, and even a ballet on the [Hippodrome's] ring. If only you would see my costumes!" And the tempter spread out the most seducing sketches on the end of the tablecloth.

—"Look, decide, Widor," added a fourth guest whom discretion prevents me from naming. "What more do you need? As a subject: an epic; as a character: a heroine extremely likable; as a stage: a ring more vast than the largest of our theaters; and if you would know all of the grandiosity that we have conceived in order that the piece match the setting! You must help us realize it and give to the public of the Hippodrome an incomparable spectacle." . . .

What could I say? I gave myself a shot of self-esteem, and half serious, half laughing, I accepted this equestrian collaboration. I said yes, and this became for me a wager to keep my word.

I took the scenario, detailed it bit by bit, miming the scenes approximately myself, then writing them feverishly. My worktable saw me nineteen hours a day, and I composed the whole first scene without knowing exactly where I was going. . . .

. . . When in one month I had finished *Jeanne d'Arc*, I was like a lunatic from cerebral anemia and nervous fatigue.[178]

The rehearsals were very amusing: the orchestra on one side, the choirs on the other, the trumpets of the Republican guard in the right foyer, the solo-ists in the left, the actors seeking to time their movements with the music and to make their reciprocal entries coincide, the authors forced to review the effects and to move about ceaselessly on the immense ring of nearly one hun-dred meters. A horse or a Roman chariot was proposed to me; to conduct on horseback is very hard, and the Roman chariot lacks springs—I chose the horse. The first one that I mounted was smart; he knelt as soon as the riding crop brushed his left knee; I still see the profound astonishment of the cho-rus ladies when my beast and I bowed to them like that after one of the first ensemble rehearsals where everything went correctly.[179]

The rehearsals took place in the scorching heat of June and were a challenge for everyone. The dancers, practicing in the sand and dust of the ring, were quite a sight; "their shoulders glistened, blackish and bizarrely streaked."[180] In spite of the risks of the venture, the fatiguing effort paid off and the con-cept of grand-scale pantomime set to music exceeded every expectation. The completed work, *Jeanne d'Arc*, grand pantomime in four scenes, used a text by poet Auguste Dorchain as its basis; Widor referred to it as "a great decorative fresco."[181] Although he said that he did not know exactly where he was going with the music, only one scene, set in Reims Cathedral, had to be deleted; the scene was simply impossible to mount effectively. An important organ part that might have been included in the scene never materialized.[182]

The press announced the premiere more out of curiosity, it seems, than serious consideration:

> We are going to have the musical Hippodrome! Very shortly, a grand pan-tomime of *Jeanne d'Arc* with quite an extensive score of Mr. Ch.-M. Widor, broadly written in large frescoes, as is fitting for the immense hall: music on horseback. The attempt is interesting.[183]

However, the performance turned out to have an artistic substance, the likes of which had not been seen before in the great horse arena:

> And now, on horseback, gentlemen! We are here at the Hippodrome. It is . . . pantomime, but not in the intimate genre. . . . It is the grandiose pantomime,

the epic, since it is a matter of the glorious legend of Joan of Arc. Three chapters only, the most salient, chosen in this story of chivalrousness: Domrémy, the siege of Orléans, and the stake.

If it was a matter of one of those great roaring cavalcades, like the Hippodrome usually gives us. . . . I would not bother to tell you of such rubbish. But this is a truly artistic endeavor, since a musician of Mr. Widor's worth has attached his name to it. One would truly have believed this endeavor to be an act of folly. To brush in great strokes such a score, in the space of a few weeks, for a building whose vastness and resounding echoes could, with good reason, inspire some anxiety! To dream of staging anything using other than ordinary equine music at this immense hall was a great audacity! Perhaps that is what tempted Mr. Widor. And fortune has smiled on him.

It is, in truth, from a good soul, this score, unctuous and sonorous in all its parts; not a bit of it is lost. It is a great feat just to be clearly heard in such a cavernous building. But that is not the only quality of this special and curious work; for it is inspired from one end to the other. . . .

. . . Mr. Widor has victoriously demonstrated that one could make music even in the Hippodrome. May others boldly follow his path![184]

The success of the first season of productions was followed a year later by even greater popular acclaim; curiously, the work seems never to have been performed after that—perhaps owing to the colossal nature of the production:

The revival was magnificent from every point of view. The action of this pantomime of grand character captivates and moves the audience. The music of Mr. Widor has the picturesqueness, variety, and power necessary to charm the ear in so vast a space, and then this music is orchestrated with a rare understanding of effects. The staging is superb; the orchestra . . . leaves nothing to be desired. With *Jeanne d'Arc*, the Hippodrome has guaranteed receipts until its closure.[185]

The success enjoyed at this revival still exceeded that of the first production, and the hall, packed from top to bottom, was overwhelmed in its frenzied bravos.[186]

Jeanne d'Arc contained a strange mixture of semiprogrammatic orchestral music to accompany the pantomimed dramatic action, and ballet and choral music. Previously, incidental music had occasionally been written for the popular pantomime art of the eighteenth century; and in France, a few operatic scores had contained pantomimic elements—the title role of *La muette de Portici* by Daniel-François Auber (1782–1871) being especially notable. As a genre of genuine musical significance, however, pantomime did not have a definitive identity until 1890. André Wormser (1851–1926) is generally credited with establishing musical pantomime with his *L'enfant prodigue*, but the June 14 premiere of Wormser's pantomime at the Cercle Funambulesque in Paris preceded Widor's pantomime by only eleven days. Still, between Wormser's intimately scaled work and Widor's epic type, a new genre sprang forth, and later contributions were made by Richard Strauss, Igor Stravinsky (1882–1971), and Béla Bartók (1881–1945). After seeing the first productions of *Jeanne d'Arc*, the respected critic of *Revue Bleue*, René de Recy, was so taken by the emotional impact of musical pantomime that he envisioned the dissolution of opera as it was known, in favor of the new form:

> Who would have believed it, that the Hippodrome would one day console us from the dullness of the opera, that musical drama would come there to seek a new path. . . .
> . . . The unforeseen thing of this splendid endeavor is not the fine score of Mr. Widor; we knew him perfectly capable of it. . . . The important thing is the revelation of the power of the music.
> The music asserted its independence. . . . I see more than a success there; it is almost a climactic event, and if not the preface, at least the indication of an impending artistic evolution. Increasingly, the music of the theater will do without the assistance of language: the sung word is essentially lyrical, and moreover words age; devoid of meaning, [they] no longer open the heart. Much more intense is the double emotion of a thing seen and with the sentiment suggested.
> Pantomime will be the musical drama of the future.[187]

In spite of the success and musical import of Widor's epic pantomime, no temptation could have succeeded in getting him to compose the music for another one. In his words, "there are some things that one doesn't do again."[188] His collaborators urged him to take on *Néron* as a successor to *Jeanne d'Arc*, but they found that Widor had definitively closed the book on pantomime, fearing that he might become too closely associated with the genre:[189] "So much had I been seduced by the subject of *Jeanne d'Arc*, by the curiosity of hearing myself outdoors, so to speak, by the desire of having a try at painting a grand musical scene in less than thirty days, and the coup so much succeeded that it seemed dangerous to me to try it again. That's why, having solicited Lady Luck with *Jeanne d'Arc*, I denied myself the indiscretion to solicit her again with *Néron*."[190] Widor suggested that perhaps Delibes, Ernest Guiraud (1837–92), or Édouard Lalo would be interested in such a project; the commission fell to Lalo, and it turned out to be his last work.[191] *Néron* never attained any success.

—57—

Professor of Organ:
"No intrigue was mixed with this appointment"

If Widor felt he had been "ambushed" into writing the score for *Jeanne d'Arc*, one can only imagine what his feelings would have been had he known what other propitious responsibility would fall his way before the end of that year—a responsibility in which he would shape the great school of French organists and composers that has endured to this day. On November 8, 1890, César Franck died, leaving the professorship of organ and improvisation at the Paris Conservatory vacant.

Although Franck attracted an imposing number of friends and supporters during his lifetime, some officials of the music community considered him somewhat of an insurgent because of his creative independence and lack of conformity to the Conservatory traditions.[192] Many of Franck's students maintained that there was a general boycott of the funeral by representatives of both the French Institute and the Conservatory; but Widor related something different:

> I seize the occasion and I have the duty to deny here a legend obstinately propagated; in what interest I do not know. People have said and written that the Conservatory shined by its absence at the funeral of Franck. The truth is that the director, Ambroise Thomas, retained by the examination of one hundred candidates for admission, and moreover very much suffering, had himself represented by Delibes, professor of composition and member of the Institute. I still see Delibes, next to Franck's son, responding officially to the condolences of an emotional crowd in which were found most of our colleagues, as it happens each time one of us passes away.[193]

Franck had extremely devoted students, and feelings ran strong regarding his potential replacement. In his *Souvenirs*, Louis Vierne recalled the strong sentiment of Franck's pupils: "When we returned from the funeral, we all decided to resign from the class. To see again that hall, that organ, the place formerly occupied by the dearly departed, taken by another? Never!"[194] Vierne undoubtedly reflected the feelings of his classmates: "I worshipped Franck with a combination of passionate admiration, filial affection, and profound respect. I experienced with intense joy mixed with a certain mysterious awe, the almost magnetic fascination that emanated from that man, at once so simple, so natural, and so truly good."[195] In rethinking their position, the students of the organ class decided they could better serve Franck's memory by continuing on. Jules Bouval suggested:

> Our first indignant reaction was quite natural, but I think we're on the wrong track. We have a standard to carry. To abandon our position at the Conservatoire would be desertion. . . . The battle is on! No one has a right to think of himself any more. So let's stay in class to defend the *maître*'s artistic ideas, for after all, we're his last heirs.[196]

Out of their love and respect for "père Franck," the students maintained a vitriolic attitude aimed at defying the new professor, whoever he might be:

When replacing a deceased professor, it is customary to let some time elapse before choosing the new incumbent. But before the official announcement of the appointment, predictions are made based on hearsay. In the present case three candidates were mentioned, three members of the jury with well-established reputations: Guilmant, Gigout, and Dallier. Who would it be?

It was Widor. We did not know him. We knew only that he was organist of Saint-Sulpice, composer of the ballet *La Korrigane*, and organ symphonies. . . . His nomination appeared in the *Officiel* for Monday, December 1, 1890, and we were informed that he would begin his duties on Thursday, the eleventh, at two o'clock. We looked forward to that moment not without some wary hostility. We were young.[197]

Some saw Widor's appointment as a much needed breath of fresh air. Auguste Dorchain, Widor's librettist for the opera *Maître Ambros* and author of the play *Conte d'avril*, for which Widor composed incidental music, wrote to him on October 10, 1891:

I am very pleased with your success at the Conservatory. This must change them—to have a good-natured young man instead of an old pontiff, an "unrecognized genius(?)." Oh, he must have been boring to judge from his "Béatitudes"!—your eminent predecessor![198]

During Franck's professorate, Conservatory Director Ambroise Thomas presided over the competitions, and members of the jury varied from year to year. Widor sat on the jury in 1874, 1875, and 1877–79,[199] and noted that the organ exams "require the most diverse qualities, the most artistic nature, presence of mind, invention, virtuosity, control, feet and hands."[200] Franck had always hoped to obtain an appointment as professor of composition, and some years earlier had thought Widor to be the perfect candidate to replace him as organ professor. It seems curious that Franck appealed directly to Widor to intervene with Thomas, but Franck may have believed that he would not succeed if he acted on his own behalf.[201] In any case, Widor related Franck's intention:

Permit me to evoke here a recollection from a long time ago, contemporaneous (I believe) with the death of Victor Massé [1822–84, composition professor at the Conservatory]. Franck came to see me: "There is vacant," he told me, "one of the three composition classes; you know the director [Thomas]; speak to him of my candidacy, and, if I am named, you will be able to take my organ class." I was very young then, quite unacquainted with the teaching methods of the Conservatory and afraid to assume the heavy responsibility of them. . . . Therefore, I abstained from taking any steps.[202]

Not only did the rigid structure of Conservatory procedures put him off, but Widor also felt uneasy presenting his own candidacy in such a situation:

When César Franck came to find me at the foot of the organ gallery of Saint-Sulpice, I then knew Ambroise Thomas [only] a little; I told him that I dared do nothing and that I did not know if the minister would be capable of pushing my candidature. At that time, professors were appointed upon the presentation by the director of three candidates in order of merit.[203]

When the opportunity presented itself again upon Franck's death, Vierne reported that Widor said he hesitated a long time.[204] In truth, it was only a matter of hours. Widor's appointment as organ professor did not happen without the same kind of anxiety evidenced during the days before his appointment at Saint-Sulpice. And a healthy dose of intrigue rounded off the process, although Widor denied it: "At the death of Franck, I was nominated . . . by Ambroise Thomas, but I can say that no intrigue was mixed with this appointment, that I had been organist of Saint-Sulpice since 1870, that I had given numerous concerts and already published my first eight organ symphonies, and in no way did I turn my attention to my appointment."[205]

On November 9, the day after Franck's death, Widor wrote to Thomas in the simplest terms: "The organ class becoming vacant at the Conservatory, I put myself at your disposal, in case you would judge that I can be of service to the cause of the great art."[206] Thomas had earned a reputation for being, in Vierne's words: "upright, just, and kind, hating intrigue, favoritism, and political accommodation, unmoved by anything other than artistic considerations."[207] Widor apparently knew that Thomas was well disposed toward him; still, in a letter to an unknown addressee, he asked for help that would confirm the decision in his favor:

Saturday [November 15, 1890]

Dear Friend,

Mr. Thomas is recommending me at the top of the list in the Minister's choice for the succession of Franck. I will be very grateful for a word from *you* to him on this matter, since, as I hope, this word will solidify his decision. It appears that one must fear the furious assaults of "the blind one," as you say, alias Guilmant!

From the bottom of my heart,
Ch. M. Widor

P.S. It appears this is urgent.

Across the top of the letter Widor wrote: "I'll be delighted to be of the Delibes clan at the Conservatory."[208] Mail was collected and delivered more than once a day in Paris, and a letter addressed to Widor that very evening appears to be the response:

Saturday evening

Dear friend,

I am up to date on everything, I know everything, and I will say everything!
Presently, I brought our Director [Thomas] to Heugel's in order to make him confirm a second time, and *very secretly*, all that he thinks of you.
It seems to me absolutely certain that it's *you* of whom he is speaking *first*; for me, there is no possible doubt.
The two others are *Guilmant* and *Gigout*, and above all it's necessary that you remain first on the list that will be sent *Monday* to the Minister. For me, there is no possible doubt.
So there it is, dear friend, on this I'm keeping doubts and wishes for you quiet; and I'm going to contrive to send to the Ministry a *masked* petition.
As soon as I have something from this side, I'll send it to you.
Now, dear friend, don't show this letter to *anyone*; and Believe me

Your old devoted,
Léo Delibes

P.S. Now, don't fear anything; act with confidence around the Ministry if it's in your conviction![209]

Pressures on Thomas were being applied from others as well. In addition to Delibes's covert dealings, Thomas received a letter on Widor's behalf from the esteemed French statesman and former minister of public instruction and fine arts, Jules Ferry.[210] Under the letterhead of the Office of the Director of the Conservatory, Thomas responded to Ferry on Tuesday, November 18: "I am very happy that my appraisal is in accord with yours. I share your liking for Mr. Widor, and this very day I am addressing to the Minister my presentation list on which he figures at the top."[211] Ferry apparently wasted no time forwarding Thomas's letter to Widor; at the top he scribbled a note to the effect: "Wouldn't you say we've sufficiently succeeded? J. Ferry." Thomas had already drafted his letter of recommendation to the minister on November 17:

Monsieur le Ministre,

The very regrettable and unexpected loss that the Conservatory just felt from one of its most devoted and eminent teachers, Mr. César Franck, leaves vacant the position of organ professor.

Among the candidates who have presented themselves, I believe it my duty
to indicate to you, particularly, three very distinguished organists enjoying a
merited reputation:

> Mr. Widor, organist of Saint-Sulpice
> Mr. Guilmant, organist of La Trinité
> Mr. Gigout, organist of Saint-Augustin

But the teaching given in our organ class does not consist solely of forming
skillful performers; it also includes improvisation.

It is thus essential that the professor join the authority of a composer to
a virtuoso talent. By virtue of this, I had to place on the first line Mr. Widor,
author of a great number of works whose value is highly estimated by his colleagues, and who has rightly obtained public favor.[212]

The decision came a few days later, and on Thursday, November 27, Widor
wrote to Thomas, "I have been very moved by the confidence you have been
willing to place in me. I will give all my heart and all my strength to justify it.
Tomorrow at two o'clock I will have the pleasure of thanking you."[213] Widor's
nomination was publicly announced on December 1, and his first class was to
be held on December 11. Vierne reported Widor's modest, public rationale
concerning his appointment:

> I accepted the class, urged by Cavaillé-Coll, and in order to please Ambroise
> Thomas, who wished me well. Also, I hoped to help resuscitate the tradi-
> tion of Bach, and I aimed to renew the link from organists who played their
> instrument rationally. Deep down, my intention was to establish a private
> school to that end when Franck died. I have disdain of all that is official and
> attach an inestimable price to my independence.[214]

On his last trip through Paris, Lemmens had told his former students, "It's
up to you to defend [the tradition]."[215] Widor took the charge seriously. At the
opening class meeting, he announced, "I finally decided to [accept the position that falls to me today] with the determination to restore the level of organ
playing in general, and, in particular, to revive the authentic tradition of the
interpretation of the works of Bach."[216] Widor saw himself as a direct musical
descendant of the Leipzig master:

> Here is the quick account, the history that ties us like the links of a chain to
> the one we call "our holy-father Bach":
>   The first historiographer of the cantor of Saint-Thomas, the erudite
> Forkel (1749–1818), friends with [Bach's] sons Friedemann, Philipp Eman-
> uel, and Johann Christoph, knew and penetrated the thought of the master
> through them. His book is of the highest interest.

From Forkel, Adolph Hesse received the pure tradition. . . .
From the hands of Adolph Hesse, the chain passed to those of the no less reputed master organist Lemmens. . . .
It is to Lemmens that the young Guilmant came one day to search the holy tradition. Some years later, I followed his example.[217]

When he took over the organ class, Widor was forty-six years old and of a certain bearing. Octavia Hensel described his features admiringly five years earlier:

A pale face, high forehead, from which dark brown hair is brushed back, but so thin on top of the head as to be almost bald, large grey eyes, very prominent Greek nose and a faultlessly beautiful mouth, which in speaking wears a most fascinating smile, these are the distinguishing marks of Widor's features, but no idea of his appearance can be gained from mere description. He must be seen at the organ in St. Sulpice; there, and there only, is he king in a realm all his own.[218]

And interviewing Widor in 1893, Fannie Edgar Thomas observed his "elegant manners and cultured conversation . . . with an added tinge of bold energy":

Looking about thirty-five, he is brown, boyish, forceful, easy and elegant. Above medium height, solidly slender, straight, with natural grace, with hands and feet of a well bred gentleman, in gray trousers, rough blue sack coat (the most fascinating style man ever wore) buttoned all the way up to the loose student's tie (dark blue with light blue dots), well made polished shoes, a white handkerchief with dotted blue border peeping out of a side pocket—a fascinating, gentlemanly young man; the most careless observer would find him without noting his face or knowing of his mind.

His coloring is brown. It is a long face, the features regularly divided, even with an unusually high brow, and a strong, straight nose. The head is pleasingly shaped; the hair upon it slight and fine and brown. The mouth is firm, neither stern nor smiling, and not covered by the stiff looking mustache that is without French point or turn. The eyes are large, round, brown, clear and inquiring, full of a changing expression that is very interesting to watch. The slender fingers have that slight turn upward at the point indicating the musician, and he has a very slight lisp.

In the course of a two hours' conversation on every known topic, smiling often, the only time Widor threw his head back and laughed was at the remark: "What would the old kings of France do who should peep into Paris today?" He has all of the Englishman's politeness without French effusiveness. He does not shrug his shoulders nor make slides of his hands. He listens—oh, how he listens! He talks delightfully. He thinks constantly. How I dreaded Widor five minutes before I saw him! How I liked him five minutes after![219]

A passport issued to Widor ten years later, on January 22, 1903, before a trip to Russia, described him in a mechanically accurate manner: "height: 172 centimeters [5' 6 ½"]; hair: gray; forehead: high; eyebrows: gray; eyes: dark; nose: roman; mouth: average; beard: gray; chin: round; face: oval; complexion: clear"[220] (see fig. 12).

Frederic Benjamin Stiven was greeted by Widor "with a kindly smile and a warm welcome," but found his appearance and mannerisms somewhat peculiar:

> Widor is naturally of an austere and serious nature. His eyes twitch notice-ably, he has a nervous habit of almost constantly biting his lower lip, and when he glances at you from the corner of his eye, it is most disconcerting to one who is not acquainted with him. But when you come to know Widor you forget all about these little peculiarities; you think only of the intense seri-ousness of the man, of his deep and far-reaching knowledge of music, of his great desire to impress most enduringly upon his pupils the broad founda-tions which are so necessary to the good musician. . . . He wears habitually a small-cut blue serge suit, low collar and flowing blue and white polka-dot bow tie. An old-fashioned soft hat and an overcoat at least three sizes too small for him, make him appear almost grotesque when one meets him on the street, but there is something shining from his eyes, something in his determined manner that marks him as a man distinctly out of the ordinary.[221]

—58—

The organ class: "We were all in our places right on time"

The first class meeting in which Widor was introduced to his new students remained engraved in the memories of its ten members: Runner and Ternisien were in their third year; Bouval, Burgat, Büsser, Guiraud, Libert, and Tour-nemire in their second year; Berger and Vierne in their first year.[222] Vierne sketched the first impression of their new professor:

> On the eleventh [of December], we were all in our places right on time, and [Émile] Réty [1833–1915], the general secretary, presented us to our professor. Widor was still a young man and looked younger than his actual age, rather tall, well-built, with a somewhat military bearing; navy blue suit, felt hat, polka-dot tie knotted loosely in a bow [lavallière], well-poised, dis-tinguished looking, rather cold.[223] In measured terms, in chosen words, he spoke of his predecessor, whom he described as an "improviser of genius." Then, he immediately made a declaration, a sort of statement of general principles, which may be summarized as follows:
>
>> In France we have neglected performance much too much in favor of improvisation. This is not only wrong, it is nonsense. To improvise in the

artistic sense of the word, one must have ideas, certainly; but that is not sufficient. In order not to be false to one's thoughts, in order to translate them exactly with all the variety, complexity, and flexibility required for their development, the organist must possess an instrumental technique capable of playing any figuration at any tempo. Improvisation is spontaneous composition; it can be accomplished only with profound knowledge and assiduous practice of all the resources offered by the manuals and pedalboard of the organ.

Furthermore, I do not see why organists should be the only artists exempt from having to know the entire literature of their instrument. What would be said of such a pianist or violinist? He would be compared to King Midas, and not wrongly. If, numerically speaking, organ literature is less abundant in masterpieces than that of the piano or of the voice, it comes immediately after; and what it lacks in quantity it makes up, perhaps, in quality. I shall cite only that incomparable miracle, the organ works of Bach, the greatest musician of all time.

To interpret Bach's organ works in their absolute integrity, it is necessary to have the technique of which I speak. It must be scientific and methodical, not empirical. . . .

This declaration made, he continued: "We shall proceed in order. I choose at random from my list. Monsieur Burgat, play something for me." And the poor fellow, more dead than alive, was kept on the bench for nearly an hour and a half. He played the Allegro from the Vivaldi Concerto in G Major, transcribed by Bach, a piece supposed not to be difficult, but which became extremely so when it had to pass all this teacher's requirements. Widor made him begin each measure twenty times, explaining everything with relentless logic, passing to the next one only after an absolutely perfect rendition "to the hair," as would be said nowadays. Strict legato in all parts, precise articulation of repeated notes, tieing of common notes, punctuation, breathing, phrasing, shading by degrees, all was dissected, explained, and justified with marvelous clarity. We were astounded, dumbfounded, and discouraged, clearly discovering our complete ignorance of all these technical details, relying upon luck to lead us, and our ears as our only guide. For him luck did not exist, and he considered the ears unreliable, for, being under the brain's control, they were not capable of infallible listening.

To end that first class, Widor sat down at the organ and played the piece that he had just criticized so harshly. We were overwhelmed. Our classroom's antique "bagpipe" was transformed. Seeing our astonishment, the Maître said, "To be sure, willpower can't make a poor instrument better, but it can take the maximum advantage of the few available resources and give the illusion of something artistic all the same. Isn't that true?"[224]

After what we had just heard we could only agree.

["Saturday we shall improvise," said Widor, taking leave of us.

"If he stops us at every note in improvising the way he did to-day in the study of performance," declared Büsser, "it certainly will lack spontaneity."]

"It won't be funny," Bouval nodded.

"Well, old man," Tournemire said to me, "it's clear: we don't know anything. If we have to do everything all over we'll have a weird competition. The prize is done for!"

I was of the same opinion and profoundly discouraged. I was going to have to verify, note by note, everything I had learned over the last three years, for I could not dream of relying on the "chance" of my memory. . . .

On the thirteenth of December we had our first improvisation class. Tournemire, as the first *accessit* of the preceding competition, was first to play. He improvised a very correct academic fugue and [a nice piece on] a free subject. However, our professor made minute criticisms. First, the academic fugue seemed to him too arbitrary; he found it strange that the subject should be obliged to change modes, particularly if that change made it lose its character completely. The tonal scheme also seemed questionable, and in that regard he cited the liberties taken by Bach in numerous organ or clavier fugues:

> I am forced to retain these forms in view of the competition, since it appears that they can't be changed. However, you must consider them only as conventional formulas, a framework that the jury is counting on, not as forms suited to the expression of all ideas. For five hundred years the masters have done otherwise. It is true that obtaining the first prize in organ does not confer complete mastery upon its holder, but simply stamps him as a good workman, well acquainted with the specialized craft learned in school. If there must be discipline, this is as good as any. Therefore, I shall change nothing. It will be up to you to go further, to free yourselves, and to develop your own personal style, if, later on, your nature and your will allow it.

. . . Widor wished only to assess our knowledge, reserving the note-by-note scrutiny for later meetings. It was very hard on us.[225] He seemed to be trying to make us think just as he did, and to submit us to a training, the import of which, for the moment, we could not understand. He also proved to be very exacting about construction, the art of development, transitions, contrasts, rhythmic variations of the theme, the creation of new elements with a motive taken from anywhere in the principal theme, an alternate thinning and thickening of the writing, the unexpected return of the subject instead of the servile use of the dominant to lead back into the recapitulation.

Finally, something almost paradoxical, considering the instrument we were using, he called our attention to the changes in timbre that were possible without making any shocking contrasts. For all this he would give examples of remarkable ingenuity, but when he claimed that we should be able to reproduce them to the letter we were completely disconcerted.

In contrast to Franck's method of bringing us subjects especially prepared for the class, Widor would take them from anywhere, from the classics as well as from plainsong, and transform them rhythmically into free themes or fugue subjects. Even the Romantics were included, and it was singularly difficult for us to free our memories of the development given to the proposed

themes by their composers. But *to do otherwise* was just the sport he was imposing upon our imaginations. For my part, it took quite a long time to acquire
such habits of thinking and to realize the benefits of such teaching. . . .

Since we were so far behind in preparation for the January examination,
Widor held supplementary classes two evenings a week at Cavaillé-Coll's. It
was a severe winter. In the unheated hall on the Avenue du Maine we had
to keep our coats and scarves on and played that way, with freezing hands—
an unpleasant memory! He, the professor, came without an overcoat; he was
never cold. . . .

In spite of these supplementary classes, the January examination was not
brilliant; we were confused, insecure, and scarcely knew which way to turn.
The class had taken on something of the atmosphere of a barracks—the maître precise and cold; we, always hostile, but proper.

"Chance," since there appears to be such a thing, suddenly intervened to
change this mutual attitude. Widor, astute, shrewd, and who had remained
young in spirit, one day suddenly broke the ice by saying, "Come now, gentlemen, I want you to know that I am much more your friend than your professor, and all these things I ask, as arduous as they may seem, are only for your
future benefit." That was all that was needed to win us over completely; youth
is like that. We had no desire to be outdone by the *patron* and what we had
done until then, under coercion and force, we now began to do with the idea
of pleasing him. The following month showed such obvious progress that, for
our encouragement, he could not resist telling us so.

"Well, that's coming along. It's neater, it has a little more style. If you keep
this up you'll play very well. I want to be proud of my class at the next competition."

The great reform brought by Widor to organ instruction dealt especially
with performance. That reform, which was to give birth in our country to the
most brilliant school of organists in the world, will not be the maître's least
claim to fame in the eyes of posterity.[226]

The rigor and minutiae in Widor's lessons often tired the students, and the
preparation time for the first examination was short. The new professor simply had not had enough time with his students. Aside from their being "not
brilliant" at the examination, Widor was severely criticized for not having had
them play something by Franck. But, as Vierne described the situation, "He
would no more have stood for our playing Franck only fairly well than he would
Bach, and he felt that bringing a piece by the former to perfection was a more
delicate task than the strict realization of a prelude and fugue by the latter."[227]
Generally, the students played Bach: "a Bach prelude one week, the fugue the
following week."[228] Widor himself did not play Franck's music, and how much
of it he actually taught is questionable, although he requested Vierne to play
Franck's *Prélude, fugue et variation* in the middle of his own inaugural program
on March 17, 1892, for the restored Stoltz organ of Saint-Germain-des-Prés.[229]
Also, Vierne stated that he prepared the *Pastorale*, the *Prélude, fugue et variation*,

and the lengthy *Grande pièce symphonique* for Conservatory competitions, adding: "When one of us remarked to Widor that at its proper tempo the piece lasted twenty-six minutes and that it might be advisable to cut it a little, the maître objected vigorously: 'Ah! But do those gentlemen of the jury have such a horror of music that they can't bear a quarter of an hour more than the amount they think reasonable[?] The piece will be played in its entirety; it's worth the effort, I vow!'"[230] Ennemond Trillat claimed, however, that Widor had put Franck's *Trois chorals* "on the black list."[231]

Archibald Martin Henderson (1879–1957), conductor of the Glasgow Bach Choir and organist at the University of Glasgow, studied organ with Widor during the summers of 1908, 1909, and 1912. He noted that Widor tended to teach only Bach's works and later his own symphonies: "From my conversations with other Widor students of the same time, such as Marcel Dupré and Nadia Boulanger [1887–1979], I believe this was Widor's usual practice. Widor greatly admired Guilmant as an organist, and Saint-Saëns and César Franck as composers, but I never heard him play or teach anything by any of these masters."[232] American organist Clarence Eddy (1851–1937) concurred: "He plays almost nothing but Bach and Widor."[233] In 1893, Fannie Edgar Thomas reported that if a student wanted to learn Widor's music, they had to go to his home. At the Conservatory, students were fed a steady diet of Bach: "Time enough for the lesser work," he added modestly; "it is the master they need now."[234]

It was no secret that Franck had concentrated almost totally on improvisation in the class. An 1882 article concerning the organ exams at the Conservatory matter-of-factly stated, "People know that the organ class at the Conservatory is above all an improvisation class; to follow it with success, the student must be a capable harmonist and contrapuntist."[235] Maurice Emmanuel considered Franck's organ class as "a family reunion"; Henri Büsser thought of it as a "musical sanctuary"; and d'Indy described it as a "true composition class."[236] In Widor's opinion, Franck's organ class had had little success: "As an organist, the technique of the instrument worried him little; he was content to make a free improvisation course on a plan immovable from andante."[237] Émile Réty, secretary of the Conservatory, confirmed, "We have here an organ professor who permits himself to transform his class into a composition class."[238] It is clear that Widor's foremost concern was for excellence of performance—something new to his pupils.[239]

Franck's Swiss student Édouard Bopp (b. 1866) recalled, "I don't remember having heard Franck make an observation on the manner of playing a piece of Bach or Mendelssohn; there was no counsel on the tempos, the style, the technique, or the registration. He seemed to believe us perfectly capable of feeling in what way our playing could be at fault, and he thought it in vain to tell us."[240] And Louis de Serres (1864–1942) agreed: "To tell the truth, Franck showed himself neither very particular nor very exacting for many of the technical details, yet all the same he helped us a little too much with the registration and the expression pedal; but no one more than he knew how to make his students understand what can be a strictly sober organ style . . . yet at the same time expressive and profoundly felt."[241]

Because of Widor's philosophy that an organist must be trained in matters of technique and interpretation, Franck's perceived lack of attention in that direction was quite loathsome to him. After sitting on the organ jury in 1877, Widor wrote a review on the Conservatory competitions that included a tart criticism of Franck's organ class:

> One of the most interesting competitions—which demands the most diverse qualities, the most artistic nature, the presence of spirit, invention, virtuosity, head, feet, and hands—the organ competition, in short, happened in private! And why? Could students not bear the full light of the sun? But the organ school of the faubourg Poissonière [the Conservatory] has turned out some remarkable individuals; does it not remember? But, [you might object], [the class] obtained a first prize this year. So what?
>
> Next year let's exhibit our future organists, since they cannot give us any serious reasons why not; our art will profit by it, you can be sure, for we will inspire the young students—who are, in short, so little worried by a final test between four tranquil and paternal walls—by the healthy fear of the full light of public judgment, and they will be better for it.[242]

And in his "Souvenirs autobiographiques," Widor cited one of Franck's students to drive his point home:

> As for Franck's class, here is the recollection that one of his greatest students, an eminent conductor, has preserved of it ("La classe d'orgue de César Franck, 1889" [by Henri Büsser?]):
>
>> This class, was it truly a class devoted to the study of the king of instruments? Above all, one worked on free improvisation there, the master leaving the student at the mercy of his fancy without the least rigorous plan.
>>
>> One also worked on the improvisation of the fugue, this with a more precise method. César Franck was, above all, devoted to pretty modulations; after some unexpected harmonic progressions, he would say, "I love . . . ," and his face would radiate.
>>
>> The study of the instrument was quite neglected; one employed the pedals floating along with the stream, using the left foot above all, playing pizzicato, and letting it lag behind, prolonging itself in a decrescendo when the piece finished. Bach, Mendelssohn, and the works of César Franck made up the repertoire of exam pieces that one prepared a few days before the trials.
>>
>> A surprising thing, the arpeggiated attack of chords was frequent, and it was a veritable revolution in our teaching when our new *maître*, Widor,

required the simultaneous attacks of the two hands, feet and hands, and both feet playing the pedal parts.[243]

As for improvisation, it was based on the "quasi" written form, drawing its inspiration from the sonatas and chorales of Bach that we discovered at the Conservatory in 1890.[244]

Charles Tournemire, another of Franck's devoted students, won his first prize in organ with Widor in 1891. With perfect candor he acknowledged, "Everything that I must retain from the six months spent in contact with the organist of Saint-Sulpice rests on his formidable technique. Everyone knows that Widor had been the most brilliant student of Lemmens. Having the capacity to teach, he rapidly brought about a rectification of the class from *the unique point of view* of performance."[245]

Widor placed new requirements on Franck's students:

I astounded the students very much by telling them that there was a bearing for the feet like that for the hands, that it was necessary to avoid holding one's left foot on the low C of the pedalboard, and that it was necessary to conserve the freedom of one's movements. I had in my class at that time some very brilliant students, among whom I will cite Büsser, Tournemire, Libert, and Vierne, who obtained the first prize that year [Vierne and Libert did not attain a first prize until 1894], and all of whom had worked the preceding year with Franck.[246]

Moreover, Widor insisted that the students have a broadly based musical knowledge and thorough familiarity with organ literature: "When I succeeded Franck, my first care was to form a library of the most necessary works for the organ class."[247] When Widor inherited Franck's class, he confronted a void in knowledge of Bach's organ music; Vierne related:

An event of considerable importance in our artistic development occurred at the beginning of October 189[3], when school reopened. This was the discovery of Bach's chorale preludes. When I say "discovery" the word is not an exaggeration, as you may judge for yourself. At the first performance class, Widor was astonished that since his arrival at the Conservatoire no one had brought in one of the celebrated chorale preludes. . . . My classmates did not even know the names of these pieces. On looking through the music cabinet, where there were several books of the old Richault edition, three volumes were discovered, two of preludes and fugues and one of chorale preludes, the latter completely untouched, its leaves unopened.[248] The maître spent the entire class time playing these pieces for us, and we were bowled over. The most overwhelming part of the giant's organ works was suddenly revealed to us. We all started working on them at once, and for three months nothing else was heard in class. All of us played some chorale preludes in

January for the trimester examination, and the surprise of the jury was no less than ours had been. Upon leaving the hall, I heard Ambroise Thomas say to Widor: "What music! Why didn't I know about that forty years ago? It ought to be the Gospel for all musicians, and organists in particular."[249]

Thomas's comment reflected the prevailing slim knowledge about Bach's music. Writing in 1895, Widor singled out the "conscientious Boëly"[250] as the sole organist in the earlier part of the nineteenth century who had familiarity with this repertoire, and he sketched a scenario in which Bach's music was more generally discovered:

Disgusted, one day some of the "young," who were more curious than their elders, began to page through some dusty volumes by the great Sebastian; some of it seemed a bit dry to them, but nonetheless interesting, at least so far as performance. One could learn something there! While practicing with their fingers, they were soon wonderfully surprised to feel their hearts touched. And then acquiring a taste for the adventure, they went through the book of chorales, and then they came to the Cantatas! . . . To exonerate our elders a bit, it must be said that in Germany as well, Bach has been long neglected. Let's pay homage to Mendelssohn who on March 29, 1829 directed . . . the Saint Matthew Passion.[251]

In addition to focusing his students' attention on organ literature and the correct approach to organ performance, Widor had to teach improvisation. At first he did not know just how to go about it:

In the course of my first year of professorship as titular of a performance and improvisation class, I sustained a serious mental crisis: how to teach improvisation. I asked around: "How did Franck train you in improvisation?" —"Franck told us: 'just forge ahead'; we forged, but always pretty much in the same direction."
I said to myself: Can one teach improvisation? My friends believed I had suffered some ailment in seeing my depression and didn't dare question me.[252]

Improvisation apparently came naturally to Widor, as there is no record of his having studied it with either Fétis or Lemmens. Vierne affirmed: "He improvised with splendid craftsmanship and a fertile imagination, served by a perfectly disciplined control of the elements he wished to put into it."[253] Almost by chance he found an approach to teaching the ingenious art:

One day the mystery was revealed by one of my students—a first prize in piano—whom I asked: "Improvise a sonata-allegro for me."

He turned, looked at me, and said: "Excuse me, I don't know what a sonata-allegro is."

"You must have played all the sonatas of Beethoven, Mozart, and Schumann?"

"Excuse me," the student responded, "my attention has never been drawn to the form of these works."

"It's very simple: (1) The classical work is composed of two themes—the thematic group and the singing group, one following the other. (2) The development of the first theme (thematic group), of which the objective is to prepare the re-entry of the two themes, this time in the tonic key. (3) The two themes returning in the same key."

I invited him to lunch; he just healed me of this secret malady—that of a professor charged with teaching a science of which he does not know all the ingredients.[254]

Vierne compared Widor's teaching of improvisation with that of Franck:

If I compare Franck's teaching of improvisation with Widor's, the former was interested above all in detail: melodic invention, harmonic discoveries, subtle modulations, elegant figurations—in a word, everything that touches upon purely musical expression. The latter, on the contrary, spent most of his time on the formal side: construction and logical development. Curiously enough, though, Franck was much stricter in fugue than Widor. He had studied with Reicha. He permitted liberties, to be sure, but they had to be strictly justified by the logic of the voice leading. The examples that Widor gave, often departing from strict counterpoint, surprised us. He forced nothing upon us, moreover, and his criticisms remained absolutely objective, leaving us free to take what we wanted. Widor instituted two classes a week in improvisation and one in plainsong and performance.[255]

—59—

Educational reforms and better facilities:
"Let's beg on two knees!"

Although employed as a professor at the Conservatoire national de musique et de déclamation, Widor used his pen to argue for educational reforms there, as well as facilities that lived up to the prestigious institution's name. When a new commission was charged to study modifications to the school's regulations, with the goal of creating two conservatories because the building was too small to house both schools, its organ professor devoted an article in *Piano Soleil* offering his viewpoint:

Already the gazettes have informed us of the first discussions of the Reform Commission.

It's a question, it seems, of cutting the program of studies in two and pronouncing the divorce between music and declamation. . . .

Is the idea coming exactly at the right time?

Doesn't it contradict the facts a bit?

Is it advisable, at the very moment when poets, tired of old forms and rhythms, seem to be asking a new element from music, when composers, having misgivings, no longer dare to write without relying on a literary idea?

The two arts tend to mingle further with each other every day. . . .

It's no longer the confusion as at the tower of Babel; on the contrary, it's the fusion of the two languages [music and declamation].

Fifty years ago, when we were invaded artistically by Italy and Germany, we heard hardly anything on our premier stages but detestable translations, our ear—accustomed to everything—could hear everything without revolting, and without laughing we read the verses of Scribe set by Meyerbeer thus: Ô prin/cêsse/chéri/e.

Fifty years ago, I say, music and declamation made a very pitiful married couple, and if divorce had legally existed then, it would certainly have been better to divorce than to live in perpetual dispute.

But since Meyerbeer, who very quickly made progress in the art of submitting our language to rhythm, Gounod came to show us that one could both recite well and sing well at the same time.

When Gounod reads to the candidates ready to start working for the Prix de Rome, it seems that he dictates the music to them at the same time, his declamation is so correct! If these young people were able to take note of his voice inflections and the accentuation of his speech, their job would be half done.

Instead of separating music and declamation, on the contrary, I would ask that regular attendance in courses in comedy and tragedy be imposed on future composers.[256]

Widor further suggested that the sale of the old conservatory property would allow for the purchase of new premises permitting an urgently needed expansion of the facilities and the program of study:

Space, silence, a corner of Paris made for dreaming, that's what [the musicians] would find there. One would be able to house concert halls, rehearsal halls, examination halls, libraries, instrument museums, directors, assistant directors, administrators, etc., etc.

Let's beg on two knees!

And while we are in the posture of imploring, let's ask one more thing— one very important thing.

The fortunate laureates for the Prix de Rome have never heard their music performed with an orchestra before the solemn meeting of the Institute where they perform the prizewinning cantata. They study orchestration theoretically under their masters, either by reading classic works or by consulting special treatises, but the opportunity is never given to them to work with a real orchestra producing their timid essays, they are never permitted to ascertain if they are mistaken or if they have known how to say exactly what they wanted to say.

To learn about the orchestra like that, without an orchestra, is almost as difficult as learning to play the piano without a piano.

What are we asking for? . . .

The students in singing classes are forced, under penalty of expulsion, to attend regularly the [vocal] ensemble classes; why not submit the instrumentalists to the same requirement?

We need a weekly orchestra class.[257]

Just in case members of the commission had not seen his article, Widor submitted his plan of study to them directly.[258] When the modified Conservatory rules were released, Widor was particularly pleased about point four of the "general dispositions": "The *vocal ensemble* course is required for *all* female students who have passed the age of sixteen and for *all* male students over seventeen who do not take part in the *instrumental ensemble* classes."[259]

The fourth paragraph seems excellent to me in the sense that it forces *all* the students indiscriminately to take part in an ensemble class, whether or not they have a good voice; pianists and organists must take part in the choruses, that is to say, to be familiar with the basic elements of singing, to know how *to draw out* a sound, and to sketch a vocalization, things of primary necessity for whosoever aspires to the title of musician.[260]

He must have been pleased also to see the instrumental ensemble requirement: students could enroll in either a chamber music course or an orchestra course.[261]

The organ students arrived in the fall of 1892 to face a rigorous, reorganized curriculum. To be admitted to the organ courses, they first had to demonstrate a thorough knowledge of harmony. The initial stage of organ study consisted of the following components: manual study; pedal study; dexterity on the manuals and pedals together; plainchant accompaniment according to the liturgical modes, note-against-note and in figured harmony. The superior class included: improvisation of fugue; improvisation of a piece on a given theme using diverse forms; transposition; knowledge of plainsong modes and their historic formation; thorough knowledge of written organ works and their chronology; study of registration and combinations; elementary knowledge of organbuilding.[262]

At the end of 1895, although new regulations were in place, the Conservatory's facilities were still insufficient and the buildings "of an unsightly dreariness where comfort was ignored," wrote Widor.[263] Once again, he put pen to paper and decried the situation publicly:

Do you know that we can no longer be accommodated in the Conservatory? The building is too inadequate—I am not speaking of its state of dilapidation—it is not only made up of rooms too small for the number of students in each class, but it hasn't even the number of rooms necessary for the courses established by the new regulations. . . .

The classroom where the organ is located is, to be sure, larger than the others; . . . [but] all day the room remains occupied by courses and meetings of all sorts, following one another without interruption from nine o'clock in the morning until four o'clock in the afternoon, the appointed time when the lights are put out. They close!

"Do you know, Mr. Minister," I wrote to Mr. Leygues, . . . "where my students go into training for the exam at the end of the year? —To the Jardin d'acclimatation!"

As a matter of fact, there is an organ in the Palmarium of this garden, originally intended for the raising of ducks, rabbits, monkeys, and seals, today a provisional terrestrial paradise for wandering musicians; on the mornings when Pister's orchestra is not rehearsing, a *highly recommended* organist can sometimes hope for the hospitality of a few hours.

Isn't it thus heartbreaking that in Paris, where we have the most wonderful contemporary organ school, where Americans, English, Swiss, and even Germans come to complete their studies, we don't have a little corner to ourselves with an instrument at our disposal—an instrument blown by some kind of motor as in Brussels, Liège, Vienna, and everywhere else! It's necessary to beg for charity here and there, in a convent, a chapel, a suburban church at times when the services permit it, and often they leave you at the door.[264]

Widor's desire to quit the organ class for one in composition can only have been spurred on by this untenable situation—one that must not have improved in the ensuing years. In 1903 Widor had to write to the Conservatory's general secretary to excuse himself from class, complaining: "I'm not coming today, having taken a terrible cold last Thursday in the unheated Conservatory and now suffering a cruel lumbago!"[265]

—60—

Conte d'avril: "So delicate and so fine"

In 1891, concurrent with the second season of *Jeanne d'Arc*, Widor and poet Auguste Dorchain collaborated on another dramatic production, its scenario a very free imitation of Shakespeare's *Twelfth Night*:

Sylvio and his sister Viola are twins and so closely resemble each other that people can recognize them only by the difference in their clothing. During a sea voyage, they are shipwrecked, but Viola is rescued. The governor of the

country where she finds herself is the Duke Orsino, who is seeking the love
of Olivia, whose husband is dead and whose loss so afflicted her that she has
renounced the company of men. Viola feels drawn towards Olivia and, in
order to see her, enlists as a page to Duke Orsino, who sends her, under the
name of Cesario, as missionary to the beautiful Olivia. Olivia falls in love with
this charming "young man" who has come to plead in favor of Orsino, but
this *young man* is *herself* in love with her master Orsino.

In the midst of all this, Sylvio, who was also rescued, arrives at Olivia's and
she mistakes him for Cesario. She receives his attentions with eagerness and
obtains a priest to unite them on the spot.

Then Cesario (Viola) resumes her true gender and the Duke Orsino,
seized with a new passion, consoles himself for the loss of Olivia by marrying
Viola.[266]

Premiered on March 12, 1891, at the Odéon in Paris, the play had actually first been staged there on September 22, 1885, with only a minor score by
Widor.[267] Titled *Conte d'avril*, it had initially contained some background music
that, in the style of a melodrama, served only to underline the dialogue of the
play during the more sensitive moments.[268] Widor explained, "The director
and poet asked me for a little bit of symphony 'to put the audience in a lyrical
mood,' they said."[269]

At first, I composed three pieces of stage music [to be] played behind the
scenes. Later Dorchain and the administration of the Odéon asked me to
make a score for orchestra from it. There were scarcely two serenades in the
backstage [version], following the text. *Conte d'avril*, in the orchestral form
was very well received. People have played it often since then. Dorchain's
play, the scenario of which is borrowed from Shakespeare's *Twelfth Night*, is
presented today on radio programs.[270]

Even in its nascent form, Widor found a place for it on his concert programs; in October 1888 he wrote urgently to the conductor of the Odéon
orchestra that he needed the score "as quickly as possible" for a concert
in Angers.[271] The composer took up the expansion of the score in earnest
during the summer of 1889, writing to Marie Trélat: "I have been shut in,
rue Garancière, at work on the Overture and Entr'actes of *Conte d'avril*,
which are almost finished, and have seen no one outside of our nice Friday morning concerts on the Champ de Mars, which have become lunch-
time concerts."[272] The revised score of *Conte d'avril*, Op. 64, contained an
Overture, three Entr'actes, and fourteen additional pieces from which conductor Édouard Colonne later extracted two Orchestral Suites for solo performance.[273] Widor noted in his memoirs that the entire score received a
performance at the Châtelet concerts on November 15, 1891, under the
direction of Colonne.[274]

Widor's works often appeared in multiple arrangements, made both by him and others, and those of *Conte d'avril* are notable by their sheer number. That Widor encouraged this is evidenced by his "Avis aux chefs d'orchestre," printed in the full score:

> One can draw from this orchestral score two Suites for symphonic concerts, as has been done by Mr. Édouard Colonne in Paris.
> 1re Suite: 1. Ouverture; 2. Romance; 3. Appassionato; 4. Sérénade illyrienne; 5. Marche nuptiale.
> 2e Suite: 1. Presto scherzando; 2. La rencontre des amants; 3. Guitare; 4. Aubade; 5. Marche nuptiale.
> If one performed both Suites on the same concert, as did Mr. Colonne, it would naturally be necessary to suppress no. 5 from the first Suite, in order that the Marche nuptiale not come back a second time. Conductors are free, moreover, to adopt any other combination that suits them better. They may, for example, make a Suite from which the cornets and trombones would be excluded, by simply taking the following four numbers: 1. Sérénade illyrienne; 2. La rencontre des amants; 3. Guitare; 4. Aubade.[275]

Though perhaps not of the sustained inspiration of *La Korrigane, Conte d'avril*'s success and popularity endured, and the Orchestral Suites became especially popular concert pieces:

> The delicate and fine music composed by Mr. Ch.-M. Widor for Mr. Dorchain's play, *Conte d'avril*, was presented at the Châtelet concerts in the form of two Orchestral Suites. A perfect and colorful performance enhanced their exquisite qualities: at first, the charm, the distinction of the melodic phrase, now imprinted with tenderness and sentiment as in the Nocturne with flute solo . . . , now [imprinted] with an original and spiritual buoyancy as in the Sérénade illyrienne, the Allegro giocoso, the Guitare; then the orchestration, of a bright and free style, making with charming dexterity the divers groups of instruments contrast between themselves; [in the] always clear and bright texture, air and light circulate abundantly and with a thousand reflections. The public warmly welcomed every piece of these two Suites. —Amédée Boutarel.[276]
> The music of Mr. Widor for *Conte d'avril* has made the play's reputation. The writing for the Romance for Flute, of an elegiac feeling, is so perfect that the notes, even in the rapid passages, seem to be born from themselves under the fingers of the virtuoso, and never deviate from the general feeling of which this ravishing novelette is stamped. . . . The other fragments from *Conte d'avril* . . . were also very much relished.[277]

Widor and Miss Berthe Max performed the two-piano version in London in 1892 for the benefit of a relief fund for impoverished foreign artists living in

England.[278] In his "Souvenirs autobiographiques," he recorded this sojourn to England with the intriguing entry "1892—10 June: Toccata Albert Hall."[279]

Besides *Jeanne d'Arc* and *Conte d'avril*, five other substantial works figured in Widor's output from the first half of the 1890s: *Soirs d'été*, Op. 63, a set of eight songs on verse by Paul Bourget; Quartet, Op. 66, for Piano, Violin, Viola, and Cello; *Suite pittoresque*, Op. 67(?), five pieces for orchestra; Quintet, Op. 68, for Piano, Two Violins, Viola, and Cello; Third Symphony, Op. 69, for Orchestra and Organ.

—61—

Soirs d'été: "A bleak but superior beauty"

Widor began composing French art songs early in his career; for these he drew upon the best French poets, Victor Hugo holding the majority. For the two song cycles, *Soirs d'été*, Op. 63, and *Chansons de mer* (1902), without opus number, Widor turned to the poetry of his famous cousin, the novelist, dramatist, and critic Paul Bourget. Composed in 1889, *Soirs d'été* evinces a sustained high level of inspiration, and Widor handles Bourget's verse with great sensitivity. The first complete performance apparently did not occur until 1893.[280] Recalling a tradition more commonly heard in opera is the use of spoken text (*mélodrame*) between the seventh and eighth songs. Hector Reynaud, the earliest writer to offer a substantive study of Widor's works to that date (1900), wrote:

> Indeed, one discovers there new marks by which the talent of the composer is revealed and characterized: I mean, on the one hand, the finish of the harmonic chasing, the perfection of the style and, if I so dare to speak, I don't know of a style more tightly woven or more condensed in the writing; on the other hand, the delicacy and the sovereign distinction of sentiment, the sincerity of the emotion, the intimate and profound feeling, and, to say it all, a soul in the broadest and highest sense of the word—a soul that palpitates and sometimes a heart that bleeds. . . .
>
> . . . I have therefore admired and felt more sharply than ever this unusual masterpiece, the force of the breath that animates it, the pathos that from one end to the other sustains it, the originality and the perfection of the form, and to say everything, a bleak but superior beauty.
>
> One can doubt that Mr. Widor has ever soared higher or, inversely, that he has touched more secret fibers in the human heart.[281]

Writing to Widor, "You bring to these already old verses a little of the youthfulness of your music" and "know that your beautiful talent applied to my verses brings me joy," Bourget still offered numerous suggestions regarding some textual details and the order of the songs.[282] The score may already have been in print, however, as it carries none of the poet's wishes. Pauline Viardot wrote to Widor requesting the songs in a lower key for a student, but they were published in only one range.[283]

—62—

Piano Quartet and Piano Quintet: "Two of the best compositions of Widor"

Chamber music held an important place in Widor's life. In addition to composing for a variety of combinations—there are at least sixteen opuses and numerous arrangements of chamber works—he regularly participated in performances of his and others' chamber music, and always found time to host informal gatherings of musician friends for the enjoyment of making music together—even if sometimes only as coach:

> For several years, on Tuesdays, Lefort, Balbreck, Van Waefelghem, and Delsart come to my place to play chamber music, either to call to mind old works or to read through recent publications.
> Nothing is more instructive.
> The audience scarcely bothers us; we have no listeners—or almost none—so that we remain free to reread, several times if necessary, the piece whose execution has not satisfied us.
> When the arrangement concerns an ensemble with piano, Countess X, the most wonderful devotee that we have in Paris, is willing to play the piano. She was the student of Alkan; and after his death, Rubinstein has had her work on the entire classical repertoire—a repertoire that she knows by heart and that she interprets today like her illustrious master.
> My role consists of turning the pages by following the score attentively and indicating from time to time the rhythm whenever the work being sight-read presents some troubling combinations or unexpected time changes.
> Last Tuesday, we had the charming Horn Trio and the new Clarinet Quintet of Brahms, works that I recommend to you. . . . The Quintet is wonderful.[284]

"Countess X" can most certainly be identified as Countess Emmanuela Potocka, the dedicatee of Widor's *Suite polonaise* for Piano, Op. 51, and the Piano Quartet, Op. 66. Besides her questionable reputation as "la sirène"—noted earlier—the Countess played the piano splendidly, judging by the demanding piano writing in the works mentioned by Widor.

In lieu of composing for string trio or quartet alone, Widor followed a tendency in the nineteenth-century of enriching those ensembles with piano. His superb Piano Quartet, premiered in February 1891, was soon followed by his second Piano Quintet, Op. 68. These two works were products of his interest in writing for different instrumental combinations and each exhibited his penchant for carefully crafted musical structure:

> The Quartet for piano, violin, viola and cello . . . constitutes, by the clarity of its lines and the sureness of its development, an edifice of sonorities and rhythms, the equilibrium of which is admirable. . . .
>
> Images borrowed from architecture intrude on the thought when one wants to qualify the particular nature of this art. It has been said that architecture was the sister of music. The work of Mr. Widor, secular or religious, does not at all invalidate the accuracy of this comparison. It delights in the precise design of a monumental ensemble, in the supple elegance of a springing arch; and the sometimes complex grace of its volutes never obscures the purity of its lines.
>
> —Maurice Léna.[285]

In his review, Léna aptly compared Widor's music to architecture, for in their varied manifestations the arts were a significant source of inspiration to him. Widor once exulted, "Music, painting, and architecture, in their most beautiful attire, vying in eloquence—isn't it a feast without parallel, a banquet worthy of the gods!"[286]

At the end of December 1891, Widor traveled to Antwerp to join his old friend Alphonse Mailly, professor at the Brussels Conservatory, and Joseph Callaerts (1838–1901), cathedral organist, in the inauguration of the recently installed ninety-stop Schyven organ: "I listened to them while contemplating [Rubens's] *Descente de la croix*, *Élévation de la croix*, and *Assomption*—marvels of art! . . . I will not hesitate to assert that the five or six thousand listeners who so religiously endured three hours of music, in the middle of December, in a church without heating, owe their singular stamina only to this stimulating vision. Rubens in the position of a 'cordial'! Oh, power of great art!"[287]

The Piano Quintet, dating from 1894, formed an interesting sequel to the Piano Quartet, and it enjoyed equal acclaim and numerous performances:

> From the first, this music seduces by its distinguished character, by a rare harmonic variety and delicacy. The first Allegro is extremely noteworthy. The savor of the themes, the skill of the development, and the ingenuity of the treatment are worthy of the pen of a Schumann. The Andante is of a beautiful development, the Scherzo warm, colored, scored with a master's hand. An Allegro of charming instrumental color closes the work in a luminous fashion.[288]
>
> The Quintet, of very tight form and very homogeneous style in its classic cut, is remarkable above all in its two last movements; the Scherzo is full of brilliancy, grace, and motion, and the Finale, of a very warm accent, is excellent from every aspect.[289]

In a letter to Hugues Imbert, Widor wrote of the Quintet, offering a rare analysis of one of his works:

After a few measures of introduction, the piano presents the theme in triple time (D major, of calm character) on which is built the Allegro theme that the quartet takes up next after a short episode. The second or "lyrical" group (F-sharp minor) is presented by the string quartet. This theme appears only episodically in the Allegro; it will be developed later in the Andante. All the developments in the Allegro are derived from the first theme or built on its rhythms. The movement concludes with a sort of coda in the calm character—I was about to say in the good humor—of the piece.

The Andante is composed exclusively on the F-sharp-minor theme of the preceding movement and its countersubject. Notice, however, the rhythmic transformation of this theme, now in duple time. Its minor mode and the melancholy color of the initial phrase make of it the "passionate" number of the quartet—the expressive number.

The Scherzo itself is not connected to any theme from the preceding movements. It is in six-eight, generally in vigorous notes and having the sonority of the ensemble, except, however, for the delicate dialogue between the instruments toward the middle of the piece—a dialogue between strings on the constant rhythm of the piano.

As to the Finale, we return to the calm and melodic tones of the first movement, again in triple time and in D major, *moderato assai*. Moreover, the "lyrical group" is here an evocation of the theme of the first movement. The Finale develops while remaining in these soft hues, and becomes a little fiery only in the peroration when the string instruments sing and modulate the principal theme over the thick harmonies in the piano.

The form of the first movement and that of the last remains absolutely in the pure tradition of the classics. Alone, the Andante and the Scherzo have a completely fanciful plan.[290]

Thirty-five years after their composition, both the Quartet and the Quintet showed they had lost none of their original allure:

The performance of some works of the master Widor opened with the Quartet for Piano and Strings and finished with the Quintet for the same instruments. In spite of snobbery and current passing fancies, these two works have obtained the liveliest success. The musical sap that animates them, the melodic abundance that overflows from everywhere in them, the mastery with which the ideas are presented and developed make them two of the best compositions of Widor.[291]

—63—

Gabriel Cavaillé-Coll and Albert Kastner-Boursault

In the course of an article in October 1892 for *Piano Soleil*, Widor interrupted his discourse: "I humbly ask you to forgive the incoherence of my pen. It's the fault of circumstances: for the first time in my life, I'm moving; is there nothing more troubling and distracting?"[292] For some twenty-two years 8 rue Garancière had been his home; but he needed more space—space for an organ, among other things.

In July 1892, Widor chronicled what he perceived, imagined or not, to be the financial collapse of Aristide Cavaillé-Coll's firm and its immediate rescue by Aristide's son Gabriel (1864–1916) and his financier Albert Kastner-Boursault (d. 1913). After extolling the new partnership and their retention of Aristide's talented personnel—particularly mentioning the Reinburg brothers (Gabriel and Félix), Paget, Veerkamp, Glock, Bonneau, Dussourd, Béasse, and Puig—Widor proudly boasted, "It's this unrivalled workforce that is in the process of building for me a salon organ for my impending move to the old abbatial palace of Saint-Germain-des-Prés."[293] But there is much more to the story.

Cavaillé-Coll had urgently written to Widor on March 21, 1891:

> I am again asking a little favor of you for cash, finding myself short this evening for my payroll. If it is possible for you to make me a loan of 2,000 francs by the Maison E. d'Erlanger for a fortnight's wages, that would be a great favor. Please give your response to the bearer of this letter.[294]

It is not known how many times Cavaillé-Coll may have asked Widor for monetary assistance, but the builder's financial condition continued to worsen. When Widor approached his old friend Jules Ferry to help shore up Cavaillé-Coll's business, the senator responded pessimistically:

> Musicians are charming dreamers. Where do you want me to find 50,000 francs for this good Cavaillé-Coll, whom I revere but who is clearly not worthy of it on this point? The hole must be much deeper. Never would the commerce court adjudge such an honest man bankrupt for 50,000 francs. It's not bankruptcy, but doubtless liquidation that is threatening him. . . . In short, my dear friend, I can do absolutely nothing.[295]

Although a great organ builder, Cavaillé-Coll had proven many times over to be a poor businessman.[296] In an article in *Le Novateur Musical*, dated August 30, 1892,[297] Widor announced that Cavaillé-Coll's firm had been liquidated, the premises sold and the personnel disbanded.

Théodore Puget (1849–1940), an organ builder like his father, recorded in a notebook some further facts: at a dinner Widor declared publicly that "Cavaillé-Coll was finished, that one could no longer order work from him that he could no longer do." Puget continued, "Not only did C.-M. Widor say all that and more in the course of the dinner where there were about twenty people present, but, even more, he dwelt on the situation for two-and-a-half columns in the journal *Le Novateur Musical* and in articles in the *Piano Soleil*."[298]

In 1892 Cavaillé-Coll reached the age of eighty-one; his finances were in ruin and his business on the brink of dissolution. In the *Piano Soleil* article, it seems that Widor genuinely believed his old friend's career was finished:

> Aristide Cavaillé-Coll was born in 1811. Since 1833, when he came to settle in Paris, he has worked uninterruptedly and has equipped our cathedrals with incomparable instruments. His rivals, his English, American, and German *confrères*, have imitated or copied him, but none have equaled him.
>
> You will believe perhaps that this great artist, this old gentleman of eighty-two years, is now a rich man?
>
> You are mistaken.
>
> Scrupulous has been his industrial conscience, and very expensive is the manpower. The parishes are poor, and the price of great art is prohibitive. The construction expenses of the great organs of Notre-Dame and Saint-Sulpice in Paris, and of Saint-Ouen in Rouen, to cite only these monuments . . . were settled in the strong-box of the builder with some considerable deficits. . . .
>
> It's thus that after a whole life of labor, after having built some marvels, he came to ruin.
>
> One day the firm of Aristide Cavaillé-Coll was put up for liquidation. The building was sold and the personnel laid off.
>
> French art found itself in peril.
>
> Happily for us, the story has turned out well.
>
> Aristide has a son, Gabriel Cavaillé-Coll—heir to the traditions, work, and honor that we just extolled, impassioned for the profession of his ancestors, very intelligent, knowing thoroughly the necessary sciences, having some personal ideas that have already put him on the track of very interesting discoveries leading towards some new ways.
>
> The day before the sale of the paternal business, Gabriel Cavaillé-Coll was wandering sadly about the silent workshops, thinking about the next day. Someone knocked at the door; it was a friend who entered, . . . Mr. Kastner-Boursault, a great devotee of music and a distinguished organist. "I come to make you a proposition," he said; "we are going to form a partnership and I am going to finance you. To lay off this host of marvelous workers trained by your father, this incomparable personnel that makes up the celebrated firm of Cavaillé-Coll, would be an irreparable fault. Let's engage them as a whole. The firm is going to be sold? I know a piece of land and a building at Ivry that seem made for us, and the low rent will permit serious savings; it will suffice for us to have an office in Paris and the telephone. Is this agreeable to you? Is it suitable?"
>
> And that's how the firm of G. Cavaillé-Coll & Kastner-Boursault was founded.[299]

Widor made the grave error of throwing his full support behind Gabrielle Cavaillé-Coll, who had worked with his father for eleven years, and his business partner Albert Kastner-Boursault.

Aristide Cavaillé-Coll had followed with interest and even encouraged the development of electric action, charging his son Gabriel to experiment with it.[300] At a decisive moment, however, Aristide came down on the side of the mechanical system that had proven reliable for more than half a century. In a letter printed in the *Écho de la Frontière de Valenciennes* on October 2, 1891, Cavaillé-Coll wrote:

> We do not attach extreme value to the electric system. It is a little more costly in setting up and maintaining, and a little more unreliable in the action than our pneumatic system. Also, in accord with the most famous organists, we prefer the latter only with the Barker machine that we inaugurated more than fifty years ago and that has widely proven itself in the organs of Saint-Denis, Saint-Sulpice, etc. Smoothness, equality, quickness, and delicacy of the touch, the drawing of registers and various combinations, it's up to playing everything with the best guarantees of solidity and durability.[301]

According to Puget, Gabriel Cavaillé-Coll had grown discontent with the traditional stance of his father. With the perceived demise of the firm, he and Kastner-Boursault announced their new business on May 14, 1892.[302] Within a few days they tendered a bid for a new organ that was identical to one proposed by Aristide three months earlier.[303] On June 21, Aristide issued a circular stating that his firm, founded in 1834, was still under his direction in the same location; furthermore, no one was authorized to use his name or present himself as the successor to his firm.[304] The rupture between father and son was complete.

During this time, Widor ordered a two-manual, ten-stop salon organ from Gabriel for the commodious music room of his new residence at 3 rue de l'Abbaye. The instrument had a disposition identical to several by Aristide.[305] Its façade, inspired by that of the "Orgue du Dauphin" installed in Saint-Sulpice, was executed by Emmanuel Cavaillé-Coll (1860–1922), the older brother of Gabriel: "It was finished in the French style, with a natural fine tin front of pipes in decorative sweeps and curves, the woodwork being in white enamel with oil painting decorations in the panels."[306] Although Widor received a fine new organ from Gabriel, the new firm had a short life. A little more than a year after they had opened their doors, Gabriel Cavaillé-Coll and Albert Kastner-Boursault declared bankruptcy and closed their firm. Gabriel soon disappeared with the money to Spain, where he remained until his death in 1916.[307]

Although Aristide's firm continued to struggle financially, it actively produced noteworthy instruments, and if some of Cavaillé-Coll's artisans had followed Gabriel, "they returned quickly to the fold."[308] Not until March 15, 1898, did Aristide relinquish control of his firm, to Charles Mutin.

Widor had gotten caught in a regrettable morass of speculation and a disastrous family crossfire. Worst of all, he had abandoned his old friend "to follow the fortune of his son," and that had to be rectified: "[Widor] didn't show himself for a certain time; then since there is no sin but should find mercy, he extolled the father more than ever, wanting without doubt to make his past conduct forgotten."[309] Cavaillé-Coll forgave him and their friendship regained its firm footing. Cécile (1854–1944) and Emmanuel Cavaillé-Coll related that in their father's last years, Saint-Sulpice became his parish again when he moved to the neighboring rue du Vieux-Colombier: "When the ascent of the sixty-seven steps had become too difficult for him, it was from below, in the nave, that he listened to his masterpiece and his favorite organist."[310] Just six months after the passing of François-Charles Widor on April 9, 1899, Widor experienced a second deep sadness when "père Cavaillé-Coll" died on October 13. Fittingly, the funeral Mass took place at Saint-Sulpice.[311]

—64—

3 rue de l'Abbaye: "A secret door of mysterious use"

Widor adored Paris, its timeless streets, old residences, gardens, and rich history. Until his marriage in 1920, he always chose to live on the Left Bank.[312] Isidor Philipp said Widor "knew the history of every stone; like Anatole France, he could conjure up the past as we walked along the winding streets, and tell the names of those who had lived there."[313] A passage in Widor's "Souvenirs autobiographiques" strolls through his memory as if through the very neighborhoods being described:

> Horace Vernet lived in the house that was demolished last year at 1 rue de Seine. Nearby, at 12 rue Jacob, a modest house still exists where Richard Wagner sought a haven. Now, it seems impossible that he had lived in this narrow house, and it is very likely that he lived at 14 rue Jacob: at the back is a garden in which Marshal Maurice of Saxony had had built a little temple of love dedicated to Adrienne Lecouvreur. The temple still exists.
>
> Nearby sleeps the medieval Place de Furstemberg, where the stables of the prince bishop existed; it's there that Delacroix had moved his celebrated workshop. Finally, going on further, one falls onto the rue de l'Abbaye. Eugène Guillaume, who was director of the Villa Médicis, had a workshop in the former palace of Furstemberg, at no. 2; it's there that I myself lived.
>
> When I was named professor of organ at the Conservatory [November 1890], I had to move out of rue Garancière and settle on the ground floor of rue de l'Abbaye [he moved in October 1892], where I enjoyed a vast salon that was completely favorable to the installation of a grand organ. Later, the curé of Saint-Germain-des-Prés bought back the palace and put in an asylum for old women. At his insistence, Guillaume and I had to give up the place [Widor moved out on August 14, 1900]. But we still strongly regret that this

historic building has had this fate, for its architecture has suffered for it, and since then they have even put in a dispensary, whereas it would have been interesting to make a museum of it.[314]

Through a large window in Widor's modestly sized studio lay a "landscape of green grass, trees, mutilated statuary and the walls of St. Germain."[315] Inside were all the trappings of the composer/musician who worked there:

> On [his] table lies a pile of manuscript music and supplemental notes that speak volumes for the owner's industry. Surrounding the paper lies every convenience for writing; a huge cut glass ink bottle holding a quart; a smaller one, flat and generous; a dish of pencils, blue and red and black, all nicely pointed; a dish of the ordinary little high-shouldered French pen . . . ; a few flat music books; a fine lamp and an ivory ruler. The other desk seems to be a reserve fund, similar in furnishing, with more books and paper, a larger lamp, a metronome and one or two bits of bric-à brac upon it. The order and fitness of things everywhere, a feature of French equipment—nothing omitted, nothing superfluous—is evident everywhere.[316]

The music room containing the new organ was "large, light, square, lofty, antique in effect and modern in elegance and comfort," with Directoire-style furniture; a modern contrivance in which Widor demonstrated great pride was the "first class, large sized, nickel plated base burner" that heated the room[317] (see fig. 13).

Paul Landormy (1869–1943) noted a peculiar feature of the apartment: "a secret door of mysterious use that opened into a little alley."[318] And when Fanny Thomas visited Widor, his glance drew her attention to a piece of red damask hanging over a rail; upon further investigation she discovered a hidden stairway behind it. Widor chuckled as he explained that it was his "secret": "in case of an unwelcome visitor's coming in by the front door, he can easily disappear this way. His Parisian instinct is evidently stirred by this theatric descent, and he is quite satisfied if you consent through it to drop into the cold and grey and old and narrow, quaint and historic Paris."[319]

An antiquarian bookseller lived above Widor on the second floor, and the famous violinist/violist Victor Balbreck, to whom Widor dedicated his Op. 57 *Cavatine*, resided on the third floor. As well as having his own group, Balbreck was a member of the Théodore Heymann Quartet. He possessed three marvelous violins—Stradivarius, Guarnerius, Balestrieri—and a Montegna viola. Quite naturally, a close rapport immediately developed between the ground floor and the third floor. Widor's sumptuous apartment consisted of several large rooms; the one dominated by his new Gabriel Cavaillé-Coll organ provided the perfect setting for chamber music gatherings. Paul Landormy, who sometimes played viola in Balbreck's quartet, sketched a picture of the close artistic relationship between the musicians at 3 rue de l'Abbaye: "When visitors of note came to Widor's apartment and he wanted to have them hear one of his chamber works, he beckoned the Balbreck Quartet. We went down in haste. How many times like that, with Widor at the piano, I had the occasion to play his beautiful Quintet."[320]

—65—

Opus 69: "The Symphony triumphed beyond all hope"

Two orchestral works of 1893 achieved enormous success and lasting popularity. As a whole, not much has been learned of a *Suite pittoresque,* premiered on April 11, 1893, in the new eight-thousand-seat concert hall of the Jardin d'acclimatation: "The performance opened with the premiere of a *Suite pittoresque,* comprising five pieces among which we can point out above all an 'Ouverture espagnole' and 'Mélancolie,' a very interesting part with its pretty violin solo."[321] Another source referred to the work as being for "organ and orchestra."[322] Only the *Ouverture espagnole* appears to have survived, and it took on quite a life of its own as a separate concert piece:

> And for the "Ouverture espagnole" there is only to say, after having tasted its powerful, warm, and sharply colored rhythm, that Widor has grasped the Spain of another sort, but quite as authentically as Lalo and Chabrier.[323]

It is unclear what Widor originally had in mind for the piece, though it appears to have been composed earlier as part of some incidental music. In the summer of 1892, he had been commissioned to write a score to accompany Beaumarchais's comedy *Le Mariage de Figaro* to be performed at the Grand-Théâtre (ex-Éden) during the following season.[324] Widor wrote to conductor Édouard Colonne, "I really believe in the effect of the Overture I wrote for the 'Marriage of Figaro' that is unpublished; it's necessary to give it a Spanish name; it's tinted in the [hues] from the other side of the Pyrenees [tras-los-montes]—very powerful and high-spirited."[325]

Widor's imposing Third Symphony for Orchestra and Organ, Op. 69, resulted from a special commission for the inaugural concert of the new eighteen-hundred-seat Victoria Hall in Geneva, Switzerland:

> Mr. Barton, counsel general of England, was president of the Nautical Brass Band of Geneva. Being very wealthy, he had the idea to have a hall built—Victoria Hall—for the rehearsals and the performances of the brass band. He installed an organ, and for the inauguration of the hall he requested of me a special work for organ and orchestra. We had a French scholar as an

intermediary, Massol, a resident in Geneva where he was in charge of the hygiene and public health of the city, and also represented the Institute Pasteur. An old bachelor filled with spirit, he had the most adventurous life in the world. . . . He had close ties to the Paris Conservatory, Saint-Saëns, Bizet, and all that generation. . . .

Massol had said to Barton, "Ask Widor to write this piece for you. Widor is an organist in addition to being a composer. It's he who will compose it for you!" . . . And it's thus for Barton that I went to Geneva to rehearse several times and to test the organ (by a Swiss builder—Kuhn) in the hall.

The solemn inauguration of the hall took place on December 2, 1894, [the correct date was November 28] before a wonderful audience. I played this Third Symphony.[326]

Although completed in 1893, the Symphony's premiere did not take place until the following year because of delays in the construction of Victoria Hall. The compositional process had been as rewarding as it had been arduous.[327] Fannie Thomas visited the composer as the work neared completion:

"Almost done!" It is easy to see where the tired look in the eyes has come from. His face lightens as he looks at it[;] his fingers touch the leaves lovingly as he turns them over, indicating—"Tum-tum-tum, ta-ra-ra-ra"—where the organ comes in! Every page perfect—200 of them—small, clear notes, all done with his own hands, the writing perpendicular as the notation. This is the copy. The "original" is "illustrated" freely by red and blue blotches, each one indicating the decision, rejection, double seeing and persistent effort of genius in its pathway from vague conception to detailed expression, which is—creation!

. . . He laughs at the blotches, as if seeing them from the first, but persistently points out how clear and intelligible the music may be made by putting the marks out of mind and regarding only the notes between. He seems jealous of the thought that even the first writing should be valueless on account of "a few little corrections."

"Yes," he said, "no wonder that Verdi said it was dread of note making which prevented his writing another opera. 'C'est vrai, c'est une grande travaille.' [It's true, it's a huge amount of work.] But," and the fact is reflected in the speaker's clouding features, "the weariness, the fatigue, the wear of such work is the coming in of ideas at the start; the trooping, flying, lumbering, burning sweep of mental things, all pleading, none asserting. No rule, no precedent, no law governing the choice of one more than another, and the subtle but dominating cord [sic] selection stringing together those most suitable to its purpose: the pain of rejection, the burden of holding all till some are taken, the arrival of new comers to be cared for or sent away, the looming up of form and outline, compelling attention to shape where no shape is present, the unlearned laws of sequence, symmetry, balance, the unwritten regulations governing force—the martyrdom of the creator to a perfection of no man's devising—weariness indeed the development!

"But what joy and satisfaction, also! How rich in discovery, how gay with decision, how ineffably happy at the close—yes, there is no such happiness in life as that of the creator. It is the same exactly with the writer of romance or drama, the sculptor or painter who design, all the same art—expression!

"The writing of symphony is much more difficult than that of opera, being mathematical in its restrictions and equilibrium. In the case of the later one may leave the writing and return, take on new colors, adapt new ideas. It were best in writing symphony if one could write on continuously and finish at a sitting, so concentrated is the essence."[328]

On the day of the premiere, Widor opened with a brilliant performance of Bach's Toccata and Fugue (likely the D Minor), and then yielded the organ bench of the three-manual, forty-five stop Kuhn organ to Otto Barblan (1860–1943)—organist of Geneva's Cathedral of Saint-Pierre—in order to conduct his new symphony. E. Delphin reported in *Ménestrel*, "His success has been the most enthusiastic type."[329] Widor himself wrote proudly to Hugues Imbert, "The Symphony triumphed beyond all hope in Geneva; the German party was the first to cry bravo!"[330]

Like Saint-Saëns's Third Symphony for Orchestra and Organ, Op. 78, Widor's Third Symphony is divided into two large sections: Introduction—Allegro—Andante; Scherzo—Finale.[331] Unlike Saint-Saëns's Symphony, in which the organ largely adds to the sonority of the orchestra, Widor's Symphony has a large, integral role for the organ, and once he even referred to it as a "grand organ concerto."[332] The work enthralled audiences, proving the combination of the two great instrumental forces a resounding success and disproving anew Berlioz's old argument that the Emperor and the Pope were incompatible rivals.

Over the next fifteen years, whether conducting or performing as soloist, Widor enjoyed unanimous acclaim for his great Third Symphony throughout Europe, including Paris, Stuttgart, Rome, Cologne, Berlin, Warsaw, Moscow, Mannheim, Liége, Zurich, Strasbourg, and London. "The public, who listened religiously to this beautiful work, stood, after the superb sonorities of the conclusion, to acclaim the composer, who directed it."[333] Still, like so many of Widor's works, Opus 69 faded from the repertoire as time went on. In a tribute to his *maître* upon his death, Vierne expressed his bewilderment at Widor's fall from the mainstream: "The ostracism that banishes Widor from music performances of all categories to the bare minimum seems perfectly unjust. In hearing again his Third Symphony for Orchestra and Organ, broadcast on the radio last March 31 [1937], I could not understand why such a work was discarded from the repertoire of the symphonic societies."[334]

—66—

To Budapest on the Orient-Express

By 1895, Widor had produced an impressive list of works, and he was in demand to conduct them all over Europe. Productions of *La Korrigane* and *Conte d'avril* were being mounted here and there, and garnered enormous successes for him. Widor went to Vienna, Aix-les-Bains, and twice to Budapest (December 1882[335] and January 1893[336]) to oversee rehearsals and conduct performances in those cities. He occasionally offered the readers of his *Piano Soleil* columns a glimpse of life on the road. A vivid report of his 1893 trip appeared in the article, "À Budapest":

I left Paris on January 15 to conduct at the Royal Theater of Budapest the two premier performances of *La Korrigane.*

In ordinary weather, nothing is easier than this trip of thirty hours by fast train, the Orient-Express, which runs two times a week from Paris to Constantinople. But last month, tracks covered with snow posed some hazard; all passage was interrupted as soon as light wind happened to accumulate some snow on the winding tracks of the route. The trains then experience considerable delays, or don't even arrive at all. . . .

. . . At the [Austrian] customs station, the thermometer registered minus twenty-eight [Celsius]. The wine they served us was partly solidified. In spite of the overheating of our stoves, the temperature of the car didn't attain six degrees above zero.

We arrived in Vienna four hours behind schedule, in the state of blocks of ice. And six hours were still required to reach Pest! . . .

The Opera house of Pest was inaugurated on September 27, 1884. The auditorium is vast and of a rare elegance: three tiers of boxes in very harmonious red and gold decoration; in the middle of the first gallery, opposite the stage, a vast, richly decorated bay soars upward—the royal box.

The stage is wide and deep; as at the Vienna Opera, all the movements and all the scene changes are made by hydraulic machinery.

It's thus that they can make appear instantaneously, at the end of *La Korrigane*, a set representing the palace of the Queen of the Korriganes—a fantastic palace enhanced with fountains gushing real water, under beams of electric light. . . .

The Hungarian ballet corps is justly reputed. . . .

The premier ballerina, Madame Müller, has a lot of talent; they love her a lot in Pest.

The costumes and sets merit every commendation.

As for the orchestra, the good things that my friend Delibes, whose death was such a loss, told me don't seem at all exaggerated. They seem to divine the least whims of the baton and to execute them as though they had studied them for a long time.

The Budapest Opera is directed by a great man and distinguished artist, Count [Géza] Zichy, who carries the title of *Intendant* and leads everything in royal fashion.

Did you know that under this intelligent and active administration they perform sixty different operas there each year!

During my stay, I saw rehearsed or performed *Don Giovanni* [Mozart], *Robert le Diable* [Meyerbeer], *Allenor* (by the Hungarian violinist Hubay), *Lalla-Roukh* [David], *La Reine de Saba* (by Goldmark), the *Tetralogy* (by Wagner), *Bastien et Bastienne* (by Mozart), etc., etc.! . . .

You have certainly heard of the Philharmonic Society of Pest. . . . The concerts take place in the hall of the Redoute, a vast rectangle of excessive height. It's more a ballroom than a concert hall. The sound floats there.

I confess to not having been at all satisfied with my Overture to *Conte d'avril*, which appeared to me, while conducting it, as if enveloped in a sort of fog more autumnal than spring, which had not been my plan.

The other pieces of a less symphonic style were more accommodated by this setting of exaggerated proportions. The audience was willing to ask for the last ones again. . . .

There are in Budapest some excellent quartet societies and excellent interpreters for chamber music. I had the pleasure to hear my Op. 50 Sonata and my Trios wonderfully executed. . . .

After ten exquisite days in the Hungarian capital, the day after a grand banquet organized in honor of *La Korrigane* in the foyer of the Opera, I took the train to Vienna, where I stopped only some hours, and I returned to Paris on the fast train.[337]

Programs entirely devoted to Widor's works were not uncommon.[338] Even when not conducting, he attended many Paris concerts that included his music. And he was sometimes easily persuaded into taking the podium to conduct his own work impromptu, as at the Jardin d'acclimatation one evening:

The excellent conductor of these concerts, Mr. Louis Pister, having glimpsed in the midst of the crowd (there were more than 4,000 listeners!) Mr. Ch.-M. Widor, asked him to please conduct the suite from *La Korrigane* himself. Solicited by the whole audience, Mr. Widor went up onto the platform. Whence, a great enthusiasm from every side for the composer and his charming Suite, so varied and pleasant.[339]

Widor's fame had become such that the music press followed his activities quite closely; nearly every weekly issue carried some news of his work or whereabouts. Though often cursory, reports such as the following have served invaluably, almost as well as a diary might have in piecing together his perambulatory activities:

Scarcely back from Monte-Carlo, where his success was very great, Mr. Ch.-M. Widor left that same evening for Frankfurt, where they are going to perform his new Quintet.[340]

Mr. Ch.-M. Widor left Paris last week for l'Arbresle, near Lyon, where, during his vacation, he is going to put the finishing touches to the *Pêcheurs de Saint-Jean*. . . . Mr. Widor will come back to Paris only in the first days of October in order to resume his Conservatory class.[341]

—67—

Honorary decorations, music organizations, organ inaugurations

To honor his work at the Paris Conservatory, the French Légion d'honneur bestowed the first of many decorations on Widor in 1892.[342] And a year later, the Belgian Ordre de Léopold knighted him.[343] In conjunction with the eminent conductor Charles Lamoureux, Widor and several other composers—including Emmanuel Chabrier, Gustave Charpentier (1860–1956), Ernest Chausson (1855–99), Gabriel Fauré, Benjamin Godard, Georges Hüe (1858–1948), Vincent d'Indy, and André Messager—founded the Association des concerts de l'école moderne in 1893. Formed to aid contemporary composers, both French and foreign, the programs of this artistic association were to include only premieres of new works.[344] Widor remarked: "The signers of the association's rolls belong to schools with very contrary artistic tendencies; this is a condition of lasting success: one-sided organizations do not last."[345] Two years later, a chamber music society called Société de musique nouvelle was formed under Widor's patronage for the express purpose of mounting monthly programs of contemporary music at the Salle Érard.[346]

Widor sat on juries regularly for the French Academy of Fine Arts in the discerning of its prestigious Prix de Rome, and of course for the Conservatory examinations.[347] He sometimes used his weekly journal articles to follow up with "very interesting and extremely elegant chronicle[s] on the distribution of the prizes of the Conservatory."[348]

Every facet of Widor's profession interested him profoundly. He even became involved in the design for the new theater of the Opéra-Comique in Paris, being charged with studying and reporting on the various dispositions of orchestral placement as well as the means of elevating or concealing the orchestra as required by the repertoire.[349] Later, he authored an article on new systems of theatrical electric lighting and the dramatic impact it brought to the staging. Describing a theatrical sunrise, he marveled: "Proportionately as the music became animated, the sky began to glow; the silvers and blues harmonized with the strings and flutes, the reds and yellows with the brass. . . . The theatrical picture entered into the particular domain of music, that is to say into 'time,' whereas until now it had only been able to develop in 'space.'"[350]

As much as ever, Widor continued to be in demand for organ recitals on new and restored instruments; several inaugurations during this period are noteworthy. On March 2, 1890, he and Alphonse Mailly joined to inaugurate the Pierre Schyven organ at the Liège Conservatory.[351] A few weeks later, on April 17, it was on the magnificent new Cavaillé-Coll instrument of four manuals and sixty-four stops at Saint-Ouen in Rouen that Widor "masterfully performed several classical pieces and improvised with a marvelous boldness, drawing inspiration from his remembrances and erudition. One can imagine nothing more beautiful than such an organ vibrating under such fingers."[352] Of the Saint-Ouen instrument, Widor liked to say: "There is some Michelangelo in this organ."[353] Noting the strength of the sound despite relatively low wind pressures, he classed it with the organs of Saint-Sulpice and Notre-Dame as one of "the three most beautiful instruments in the world."[354]

The inauguration of the organ in Newcastle Cathedral took Widor to England in 1891 for the May 23 event; the *Daily Journal* reported that he played Bach, Mendelssohn, Beethoven, and some of his own works.[355] The following month he performed a Toccata and Fugue of Bach, his Fifth Symphony, and some pieces with cellist Jules Delsart for the inauguration of a Cavaillé-Coll in Saint-Jean-Baptiste, Roubaix.[356] In 1892, for the inauguration of the Stoltz restoration of the organ at the Paris church of Saint-Germain-des-Prés, Widor performed Bach's C-Minor Passacaglia (BWV 582), as well as movements from his Symphonies.[357] In 1894, Cavaillé-Coll restored his instrument at Saint-Vincent-de-Paul, and Widor joined Dubois, Gigout, Guilmant, and Léon Boëlmann (1862–97)—the *titulaire* of the church—for the reinauguration.[358] Last, in 1894, Cavaillé-Coll restored the organ of Notre-Dame; twenty-six years after they had participated in the original inaugural concert, Widor, Guilmant, and Sergent—the *titulaire*—were joined by Gigout for the reinauguration on July 31, 1894.[359] Before the inaugural concert, they had been called upon to form a commission to judge the builder's work; Widor made the report and concluded: "Unanimously and without reserve, the Commission approves the work of the restoration that Cavaillé-Coll just accomplished."[360] For his part in the inauguration, Widor performed the Allegro from the Fifth Symphony, the Andante [Adagio] from the Third Symphony, and finished with his famous Toccata.[361] He would later inaugurate Notre-Dame's new *orgue d'accompagnement* on June 15, 1910, and, incredibly, he would live to participate in yet another reinauguration of the *grand orgue* on June 10, 1932.

Although Widor's programs were limited largely to works by Bach and his own compositions, it is evident that he occasionally played a group of excerpted movements in lieu of a complete symphony.[362] In this regard, it is important to note that Widor did have the strong conviction that works ought to be performed in their entirety. As a music critic, upon hearing only two movements from a symphonic work in a concert, he admonished:

> I have the firm resolution of wanting to judge a new symphonic work only when I can hear it in its entirety.
>
> Imagine a painting jury uttering something like: "Monsieur, we cannot receive your painting; it is too long and not full enough. But there, on the left, is a well-shaped nymph's leg. Please extract it from your canvas and send it to us; we will place it well framed between two masterpieces. You will be pleased."
>
> A work is good or bad; play it or don't play it. If it really has only two good parts, . . . ask the author to rework his composition until the whole is acceptable; but for pity's sake, leave the legs on the nymphs![363]

In sum, Widor's middle period (1880–94) witnessed the production of some of his finest works; the French theater hailed his first productions; he launched into a new career as professor of organ at the Paris Conservatory; and he continued to be in demand to perform and conduct his music. By age fifty, these successes had placed him squarely in the mainstream of French music.

Part Four

The Twilight of Widor's Compositional Career (1895–1909)

Vous avez le devoir de faire une chose si vous avez la certitude qu'elle est nécessaire à l'intérêt général!

You have the duty to do a thing if you are certain that it is necessary to the general interest!

—Ch.-M. Widor
"En parlant de Ch.-M. Widor avec Marcel Dupré."

—68—

"The music of the eternal"

As a result of numerous demanding engagements, the pace of Widor's compositional productivity necessarily lessened, and that trend continued ever more markedly with each passing year. He had barely passed the midpoint of his life's journey, yet in the remaining forty-two years he would compose only about two dozen more major works. 1895 marks the beginning of Widor's third and last creative period, as in that year he published his latest organ symphony, the *Symphonie gothique*, Op. 70. With this work, a new style and ideal in organ music was ushered in—one that turned to Gregorian plainsong and thereby exhaled a particularly spiritual aura. Some of the composer's most profound inspiration fills its pages.

During the plainsong restoration of the second half of the 1800s, there evolved a principle for contemporary liturgical music that eventually became codified in the *Motu proprio* of Pope Pius X (1835–1914; pope 1903–14) on November 22, 1903: "The more closely a composition for church approaches in its movement, inspiration and savor the Gregorian form, the more sacred and liturgical it becomes; and the more out of harmony it is with that supreme model, the less worthy it is of the temple."[1] Widor sensed the correctness of this direction well before it was officially articulated, and the *Symphonie gothique* was born of his desire to create a work supremely worthy of the Church.

Albert Schweitzer, a long-time pupil, friend, and collaborator of Widor, out-lined his view of the stylistic development, traced through the Op. 13 and Op. 42 Organ Symphonies, leading to the *Symphonie gothique*:

His ten symphonies reveal the development of the art of organ playing as he himself has experienced it. The first are creations perfect in form, per-meated by a lyric, melodic, sometimes even a sentimental spirit, which show however in the wonderful structure of their themes the peculiar endowment of the creator. With the fifth symphony he deserts this road; the lyric with-draws; something else strives to take form, first in the fifth and sixth sym-phonies, which are among his best known, and which are still in melodic form. The seventh and eighth are transition works; they are of the organ, and yet conceived in a boldly orchestral manner. What a marvel is the first movement of the eighth symphony! At the same time the austere appears ever more clearly—the austere that Widor brings back to sacred art in his last two symphonies. "It is noteworthy," he said to me in that period, "that except for Bach's preludes and fugues—or, rather, except for certain preludes and fugues of Bach—I can no longer think of any organ art as holy which is not consecrated to the church through its themes, whether it be from the cho-rale or from the Gregorian chant." Thus the ninth symphony (*Symphonie gothique*) on the theme "Puer natus est" is written as a Christmas symphony.[2]

Widor formed a very personal concept of organ music through long years of observation and experimentation. He had written for the organ in a way that many considered secular, perhaps even popular; now he expelled all that did not reflect the sacred and spiritually profound. Organ music became for him "a special kind of music, the music of the eternal, awakening thoughts of immortality."[3] This was the aesthetic that he instilled in his newest organ symphony. He once told Schweitzer, "the organ represents the *rapprochement* [bringing together] of the human spirit to the eternal, imperishable spirit, and it is estranged from its nature and its place as soon as it becomes the expres-sion of the subjective spirit."[4] In this statement, Widor's thought closely paral-leled that of Pope Pius X:

Pius X expressed himself with great clarity when posing the fundamental axiom of his musical aesthetic. All that awakens in the spirit of the faith-ful secular memories and turns it from prayer must be rejected from the Church. Let's seek an art that is appropriate to the Church: choral song, the organ, a musical theory inspired from Gregorian chant in its modalities and rhythmic formulas, and, to enliven this still inert material, an inspiration that believes and prays.[5]

This needful, serene character is mirrored in the quiet endings of the outer movements of the *Symphonie gothique*, as well as the later *Symphonie romane*.

Widor came to believe, "It is quite modern, the speculative idea of a *crescendo* leading to an apotheosis-peroration. It is modern and theatrical, and by this even not devoid of some banality: it's to force the applause. And it's precisely about this obligation that religious art has little concern."[6]

On July 27, 1894, Widor wrote, "I am finishing these days a 9th Symphony for organ that I was commissioned to give to Schott of Mainz."[7] Fulfilling his promise to the parish priest of Saint-Ouen in Rouen "to compose a special work in honor of his admirable church,"[8] Widor dedicated the *Symphonie gothique* to the great Gothic edifice bearing the seventh-century bishop's name: *Ad Memoriam Sancti Andoëni Rothomagensis* (To the memory of Saint Ouen of Rouen). The splendid Cavaillé-Coll organ in Saint-Ouen was one of Widor's favorite instruments; he had played the inaugural concert there on April 17, 1890, and quipped: "There is some Michelangelo in that organ."[9] The exterior and interior of the church were said to have been the inspiration for the first two movements of the symphony.[10] The first movement seems to portray the severe and angular lines of the pure Gothic exterior,[11] while the repose of the interior floats serenely through the second movement. The fugal third movement introduces the plainsong theme *Puer natus est nobis* (the Introit from the Christmas Day Mass), and the fourth movement wholly embodies the plainsong as its theme, five variations (three canonic), and free Finale. Evidence points to the possibility that this fourth movement was already being conceived at the time of the 1890 inauguration of the Saint-Ouen organ, when Widor played "'Magnificat versets,' a fragment composed for the occasion (*Symphonie gothique*)."[12]

Widor ardently believed in the importance of trio playing, and he used all six Bach trio sonatas when assigning lesson material to his organ students, who were then instructed: "As registered on the organ, the Trio-sonatas should be thought of in the spirit of chamber music; the three voices as though played by three different instruments; a flute, viola and 'cello; or oboe, flute and 'cello."[13] The fifth variation in the final movement of the *Gothique* is a masterful canonic trio and merits special mention in view of the opinion purportedly held of it by Widor. A secondary source states: "The composer later decided that this section was superfluous and instructed his pupils to omit it."[14] No primary source corroborates this statement, and in the forty years after the publication of the Symphony, that variation was never excised—something Widor never hesitated to do in other works when he disapproved of something—though he did make other revisions in the *Gothique*.[15] His own personal copy, now in the Bibliothèque nationale, shows no indication that he desired the Trio to be omitted. It is, in fact, of very special interest, being a sort of "woodwind trio" for the organ (a clarinet in the top voice, oboe in the middle voice, and a flute with oboe coupled—acting as a bassoon—in the pedal). Perhaps Widor did instruct a pupil to omit the variation; it is challenging, as is the whole Symphony, which Widor considered "highly complex and technically very difficult."[16]

Louis Vierne attained a "very great success" when he premiered the first three movements of the new work in March 1895 for the inauguration of a new instrument at the Église d'Écully in Lyon.[17] The Symphony was given its full premiere at the time of Widor's own performance at Saint-Ouen in Rouen just a few weeks later, on April 28:

> Last Sunday, Mr. Ch.-M. Widor came to our city to perform for the first time the new organ symphony—*Symphonie gothique*. . . . At the time of the inauguration of the monumental organ of Saint-Ouen, Mr. Widor had promised the parish priest, Mr. Panel, to write a special work in honor of his admirable church, and Sunday there was a full crowd in the immense nave for the announced performance. The work is composed of four movements: a Prelude (C minor, moderato) of grave and reserved character passes through the gamut of tonalities on a uniform design without episodes or strange things happening to the subject, until the striking return of the theme. The movement finishes in decrescendo. An Andante (E-flat major) on the eight-foot stops, very calm and very diatonic, is made in order to contrast with the severe chromaticism of the Prelude. A Fugue (G minor) evokes the antique sonorities of the *cornets* and the *mixtures*, during which the chorale that is going to serve as theme to the Finale appears three times. This last movement (C major), is very curious with its contrapuntal commentaries of the liturgical text *Puer natus est nobis*, its three canons, its development in five parts on the foundation stops, and its powerful conclusion sustained by the great basses of the organ. This is "new" in the classical literature of the organ. The acoustics of the immense nave of Saint-Ouen (130 meters in length), ordinarily unfavorable to works of a complex and tightly woven style, found itself marvelously transformed Sunday by the crowd that flocked to the event. It was between Vespers and solemn Benediction that this first performance of the *Symphonie gothique* took place; listened to in the most religious silence, not a detail, not a note was lost for the audience. All came forth with an absolute clarity. The impression was profound.[18]

Counterpoint is in evidence throughout Widor's organ works, even in apparently homophonic passages, but nowhere is it more consistently in the foreground than in the *Gothique*. Just as he was completing the Symphony, he defined contrapuntal art and the necessity of bringing it to light with absolute clarity of performance: "What is counterpoint, if not the art of writing luminously? It is not filling, *trompe-l'œil*, false means, possible tricks; all is displayed in broad daylight, out in the full sun; each note has its value in the whole; each detail, each modulation, each plan must assert itself in its turn, sparkling as the facets of a diamond. We need, we want, to hear *everything*."[19] Nonetheless, the very contrapuntal character of the *Gothique* not only made it "new" but also baffling. The strict "contrapuntal commentaries" seemed overly austere, beyond the popular interest, sentimental tastes, and intellectual grasp of many late nineteenth-century organists. Even in 1919, Harvey Grace referred to the *Symphonie gothique* as a "sealed book."[20] Clarence Eddy, a popular American organist, described the work as "overladen . . . with contrapuntal design. It is full of canon and fugue and all that sort of thing, exceedingly difficult and not particularly interesting."[21] And the celebrated London organist Alfred Hollins (1865–1942) called it "dry bones."[22] Widor did not compose the *Symphonie gothique* with the aim of acceding to popular fashion, however, and the Symphony exemplifies his highest ideals: "He wanted intelligent music first of all, then sentimental, knowing well that a work of art cannot be artistic if it isn't first scientific."[23] Widor knew how to write for ephemeral salon tastes; he also knew that what was immediately appealing might not endure: "It's posterity that decrees the masterpieces."[24] The *Symphonie gothique* has proven this maxim to be correct.

As to Widor's own favorite organ symphony, one observer wrote, "He loves always the last best."[25] Truly, the *Gothique* became very special to Widor; he often performed his Fifth Symphony because it had achieved almost universal fame, but the *Gothique* took a place of equal prominence on his programs for a completely different reason: its uncompromising spiritual ideal.[26] Each year at Saint-Sulpice he used the first movement for the Feast of All Saints' Day and the last movement during the Christmas Midnight Mass.[27]

—69—

"Song belongs to musicians, and particularly plainsong"

During the 1880s, Widor had taken a great interest in the plainsong restoration movement and consequently in the work of the French scholars and editors of plainchant, Dom Joseph Pothier (1835–1923), Dom André Mocquereau (1849–1930), and the Solesmes monks; he was also vitally interested in the history of Gregorian chant and how the Church of Rome had developed its poetic and musical culture. In this connection, Widor wrote a quite erudite article entitled "La musique grecque et les chants de l'église latine" (Greek music and the chants of the Latin Church) for the *Revue des Deux Mondes* of October 1, 1895. In the article, Widor sketched a short history of Greek music, with the aim of showing the foundations of the church's heritage. Although today the theory that Gregorian music has roots of Greek origin has been highly debated in favor of a variety of other sources,[28] Widor followed the path of Peter Wagner (1865–1931) and François Gevaert, whose writings had just been published, tracing Gregorian chant to the Greeks.[29]

It will be recalled that Widor wrote music criticism for *Estafette* as far back as the 1870s. Since then he had written numerous articles for several different publications, and gained a reputation for his scholarly style and integrity of judgment. His penchant for writing had always been strong and this latest article was but another omen of what during the rest of his life would become almost a second career. *Le Ménestrel* highly recommended the article to its readership:

> Well worth reading, in the *Revue des Deux Mondes*: a remarkable article of Mr. Ch.-M. Widor on "Greek music and the chants of the Latin Church." It is a substantial abstract, written in a sober and clear language, of the diverse and important works of Mr. F. A. Gevaert. . . . The work of Mr. Ch.-M. Widor is most fascinating and, curiously, given the severity of the subject, it is not for a minute boring. It has dash and color.[30]

The work of the Benedictine monks at Solesmes to restore the authentic tradition of plainsong, under the direction of Pothier and Mocquereau, received the special privilege of the Holy See soon after Cardinal Sarto became Pope Pius X in 1903. As patriarch of Venice, the Cardinal had already expressed enthusiastic support for the revival of Gregorian plainsong in its original form, which he viewed as the supreme model for sacred music. In 1904, as Pope, he sanctioned the publication of a new official Vatican edition of chant in order to reinstate its practical use.[31] He proclaimed, "I have sought only one thing, to separate the church from the theater and to put a little order in religious chant."[32] At the same time, Pius X was aware that this work would not meet with immediate universal approval:

> I know the difficulties this reform must come up against; I know the resistances with which it must clash. It takes more than a day to banish the music of dance and opera from the Church, to bring Christian musicians back to the study of Gregorian art and the polyphonic art of the sixteenth century, to restore to liturgical chant its primitive purity. It is necessary to combat the bad traditions that have become deeply rooted and to struggle against the routine of public taste.[33]

Predictably, the work of the Solesmes monks soon fell under criticism from various points of view, including considerable controversy over the rhythmic interpretation of plainsong. Even Mocquereau and Pothier did not agree on the best approach, which eventually brought an end to their association.

Widor joined the critical fray in two articles published in *Le Correspondant* (July 10, 1904; October 25, 1905) and an article in *Figaro* (February 3, 1906). In a stinging fourteen-page private letter, dated June 15, 1904, and addressed to Baron Rudolph Kanzler at the Vatican, Widor communicated substantially the same content that appeared in his first *Correspondant* article; he wrote to Kanzler: "I would be very grateful if you would transmit to the Commission du chant liturgique, of which you are a member, some observations that seem essential to me after an attentive reading of the Solesmes books. Is it possible for artists to be disinterested in a question touching them so closely?"[34] Although admitting that "the work of the Benedictines in assembling, comparing, and editing all these old texts was admirable," as a musician Widor felt impelled to enumerate his many concerns about the outcome:[35]

> I feel no hostility toward the archivists who piously research, study, compare, and collect these precious papers in order to show us the agreements and contradictions between them; what would we do without them and what services wouldn't they perform? It's the process of the past that they teach; they bring the pieces to us with conviction. It's now up to us to critique them, to point out the errors in them, the accidental blemishes and faults that crept in here and there in the shaping of the page; in a word, to judge this music with our conscience as musicians and to do our job as artists.[36]

Widor ardently believed that plainsong and its interpretation was a living tradition that had been unfolding and developing for centuries; as such, it was inappropriate to put it under museum glass. He argued, "Old or modern, since the world began, song belongs to musicians, and particularly plainsong."[37] One "restoration" that particularly offended him was the Solesmes version of the *Te Deum*—"one of the three or four most beautiful songs in the world" in Widor's estimation:[38]

> The *Te Deum* is mutilated in the Solesmes edition. . . .
> The composition of the piece is admirable as time has transmitted it to us (and it's time that makes masterpieces). . . .
> Alas! What has become of this piece at Solesmes? The statue is on the ground, an arm broken and the nose cracked. . . . Is there an artist—a being endowed with a heart and a soul—who could remain unimpassioned in front of such vandalism and not protest violently?[39]

A year later, in his article "L'édition vaticane," Widor reiterated, "we have spoken of the *Te Deum* and the version established by the ages; we have seen that, on the faith of some parchments, the paleography students put forward a weakened and lame *Te Deum, ad usum hemiplegicorum*, for lukewarm believers. There is no doubt that the version is at fault, for it cannot stand up aesthetically."[40] "How can you conceive a hymn of thanksgiving that suddenly changes to a lament, a text that sings of joy while the music weeps? Disagreement between poet and musician—what more severe and just criticism can you make of it?"[41]

Widor also disagreed with returning plainsong notation to neumes, the abundance of ornaments and markings "devoid of meaning," the "dangerous, often even faulty intervals," and a host of other issues that led him to question:

"will all this makeup [*maquillage*] tend to bring us closer to the primitive purity [of plainsong]?"[42]

The primitive purity cannot be discovered; it is only hypothetical. But, if its door remains shut to the archivists, it opens a bit to musicians. What is a beautiful theme, if not the translation of a beating heart? And who better than anyone could see through the mold and creative emotion of an old text if not those who have sometimes felt it?

Let's open the Solesmes *Antiphonaire.*

Why this complicated notation without cause, using means abandoned little by little and condemned by universal experience? More than six hundred years were needed to attain the precision of our current system, and now we are suddenly retrogressing to the epoch of neumes, in full medieval fog?

If sustained attention is needed by a very good musician to read these neo-archaic figurations, what will happen to the average musician of our parish churches? And what will become of our country churches? I see from this the poor singers closing their lectern and going to the pub to bawl out less liturgical songs to console themselves from their forced resignation.[43]

How many singers can we count in Paris who have enough authority not to fear the test and to solfege, without accompaniment, melismas of fifty or sixty notes without breathing? How many in the provinces?

Even with their accompaniment, most of the Solesmes chants remain inaccessible to the vast majority of parish singers. . . .

I am stopping [here] and permitting myself to address these words to the Benedictines:

In publishing in your *Paléographie Musicale* these very interesting studies on the old texts, in reproducing this quantity of precious manuscripts, in delivering to us secrets from your work, intelligence, and faith, you have elevated a colossal monument and won the grateful admiration of your contemporaries.

Your work is imperishable. . . .

As for the interpretation [of these manuscripts], neither Aurelian, Hucbald, Guido of Arezzo, writings nor writers give the least indication that can enlighten us. Your version is fanciful [Widor substituted the words "lacks certainty" for "fanciful" in the *Correspondant* article]. . . .

The aesthetic of Solesmes seems to me to diverge a bit [Widor crossed out "a bit" in his copy of the *Correspondant* article] from the right path and to lose the notion of beautiful lines.[44]

As a solution, Widor proffered publishing two versions:

If the archivist's conscience makes him publish his unfortunate text [of the *Te Deum*], the musician's conscience will not cease to complain until his own has been published right beside. . . . If the two texts appear side by side, paleographers and composers will be equally satisfied, the first having done their duty, the second having been able to rescue for the profit of the Gregorian treasury the immortal work—the most enthusiastic cry that, since Aeschylus, has ever come forth from a human chest.[45]

Clearly, Widor did not appreciate the unfamiliar Solesmes versions of his favorite timeworn chants, and he pressed them mercilessly at the conclusion of his article, "La révision du plain-chant":

Why hasn't the commission consulted composers? At the risk of astonishing many among you, I will dare to assert that musicians who have written dramatic music are better equipped than others to write and judge religious music. Moreover, when two or three undisputed artists[46] exist who are illustrious for their scholarship and know thoroughly the history of their art, why are they not working with you?

When your sessions are finished, if you proclaim some texts pure that we judge altered, if you classify as old some modern songs, if you declare intact some mutilated pieces, what will happen? Do you think for an instant that a decree can make beautiful what is ugly and make admired your version of the *Te Deum*, for example? How, in order to avoid comparison, would you at once make the better version disappear from all the libraries in the world?

You must produce a *practical and durable* work, and as it happens in this particular case to be a work of art, you will succeed only with the collaboration of artist friends, and enemies, if indeed you have any.[47]

The Solesmes monks certainly might have considered Widor their enemy after he blatantly condemned their work: "Their *Paléographie*, which had begun so well, finished like a watercolor course taught by the blind."[48]

Widor had gained an understanding of Bach's perfect marriage of music and text from Albert Schweitzer, and this brought him to examine more closely the same relationship in the Solesmes version of plainsong. In their edition, he questioned several instances where dichotomies of texts were set to the same music:

How do you explain that the same melismas serve to express sentiments or describe things diametrically opposed?

Here, for example, in the mass for the dead, the Gradual *Requiem aeternam*; and here, right beside, in the marriage mass, the Gradual *Uxor tua sicut vitis*: for the two texts, the same music. It certainly will not occur to anyone to find fault with the anonymous authors of these plainsongs and to attribute to them some humorous intention in assimilating the idea of eternal peace with that of marriage; the cantilena seems to say, "Your young bride is a sure investment."[49]

Henri Potiron (1882–1972), choirmaster of Sacré-Cœur and author of *Treatise on the Accompaniment of Gregorian Chant*, wrote somewhat in defense of Widor:

> Let's not be too severe on a man whose customs were suddenly overturned. Note well that it was not precisely the Solesmes principles of performance that he was not able to accept; it was the restoration itself that he would have liked musicians to collaborate on. Having read in *l'Orgue et les organistes* . . . a long article in which I tried to demonstrate the independence of rhythm and accent (at least a certain type of accent) in classical music in order to deduce from it that the Solesmes theory on this point was truly musical, he one day expressed to me his satisfaction about it. I had even hoped to have a more explicit testimony; but he was much too prudent not to see this kind of trap, and he answered me with a very kind note (that unfortunately I cannot publish) in which he more than forthrightly expressed his opinion on the work of the Vatican Commission.[50]

Widor traveled to the Holy City in November 1909 to inaugurate the new Mutin organ in Santa-Maria del Trastevere; Italian music journals praised both organ and organist and saw the occasion as a good omen for a future monumental instrument at Saint Peter's Basilica.[51] On November 15, Widor and Mutin had an audience with Pope Pius X, and the first order of business seems to have been the Saint Peter's organ project that had languished for nearly thirty-five years under the papacies of Pius IX (1792–1878; pope 1846–78) and Leo XIII (1810–1903; pope 1878–1903). Pius X rekindled interest in an organ, but now for a "mobile" instrument, as the Italian government's Commission for Historic Monuments opposed the attachment of an organ tribune over the entrance to the Basilica. A committee was formed in Paris with Widor as chairman; yet, in spite of journal articles and personal pleas for funds, little more than sixty thousand francs were raised. Discouraged, the committee eventually turned the funds over to Cardinal Rampolla (1843–1913), who asked for funding to repair the tiled floor of the choir of Saint Peter's.[52]

Widor also used the occasion of his Papal audience to bring up his displeasure with the Vatican edition, about which the Pope spoke somewhat dishearteningly: "What did I want? To separate the music of the church from the music of the theater, and to put a bit of order into ecclesiastical chant."[53] Widor related that the Pope "complained of the ideological sectarianism of ideas attributed to him and of the anarchical disorder of those congresses that multiply in direct proportion to their uselessness," and he related how Pius concluded quite sadly, "They just don't listen to me."[54]

Widor's public criticisms did not fail to draw some biting responses. An appendix in Giulio Bas's *Rythme grégorien* first tackled perceived flaws in Widor's articles at some length, and then concluded:

It is impossible to let pass without protest the undeserving manner in which the Solesmes monks are treated. Mr. Widor questions their knowledge. . . . Mr. Widor informs them that their method is faulty. . . . He questions their competence to formulate a method of performance: [he says] this is the business of musicians and not "paleography students." . . . It is hard under these circumstances to hear them treated as "amateurs" by an organist.[55]

That the Vatican edition continued to be a sore subject in Widor's mind was apparent when, in 1927, he brought it up anew and with no less acrimony in his notice on the life and work of Émile Paladilhe (1844–1926):

When in 1904 the Congress for the revision of ecclesiastical chant opened in Rome, the astonishment here [in Paris] was legitimate: neither Saint-Saëns, nor Dubois, nor Paladilhe had been sounded out. The most authoritative in the genre, the author of the *Mélopée antique dans le chant de l'église latine* . . . Gevaert himself was forgotten. This musical Congress excluded the musicians. . . .
. . . We are asking for a new study.
The doubtful pieces give themselves away: *there are some more than doubtful.* More unsettling are the alterations, the mutilations. . . .
Saint-Saëns, Théodore Dubois, Paladilhe are no longer with us. As trustee of their thought, the duty remains for me to make myself the expounder of it in the name of the art of chant, its history, and dignity.[56]

Widor's sharp rhetoric again elicited a rejoinder in kind:

The eminent perpetual secretary of the Academy of Fine Arts protests "a bit strongly" against the establishment of the official version of liturgical chant. . . . If we must pay respectful tribute to the Benedictine School of Solesmes and its immense works with the admiration that they are worthy of, sometimes we must recognize that the peaceful spread of Gregorian chant suffers particularly from the blind zeal of a host of parasites who suck the strong sap from the Benedictine oak without profiting their weak spirit that is little inclined to calmness.[57]

In an article titled "M. Widor, l'édition vaticane et le *Te Deum*," Dom Lucien David took Widor to task in a lengthy rebuttal of his most pointed criticisms of the Vatican edition. David commenced by calling into question Widor's authority: "the competence of the illustrious musician as regards Gregorian tradition or even Gregorian art is not up to the present well affirmed."[58] David then upbraided Widor for his too general, unsupported assertions and especially his criticism of "some versets of the *Te Deum,* that he—a musician—would have wanted to correct in his own way."[59] In spite of his multiple arguments against Widor's judgments, David still found the grace to praise the composer's *Symphonie antique* and its artful use of the *Te Deum* as one of its themes.[60]

—70—

Monaco, Belgium, Germany, and "Our beautiful country of France!"

Two festivals in 1895 devoted performances to Widor's works: one in March at Monte Carlo, and a second in July at Ostende, Belgium. The Monte Carlo review proclaimed the concert "a splendid victory for the composer,"[61] and in Ostende: "On the demand of the public, *all* these pieces had to be played again Thursday in a second concert at which the author was no longer present, recalled to Paris by the jury of the Conservatory."[62]

Within a few days, Conservatory director Ambroise Thomas designated Widor and pianist Louis Diémer to represent the institution as jurors at the International Rubinstein Competition being held in Berlin during the last two weeks of August.[63] Thomas wrote to the minister of fine arts, "The state of my health not permitting me, to my great regret, to go to Berlin for the Rubinstein Competition, I have the honor to propose to you my confrère and friend Mr. Widor, professor at the Conservatory, whose talent as composer and as virtuoso are known to you, and who is willing to be appointed to substitute for me."[64] In articles for both *Piano Soleil* and *Le Ménestrel*, Widor reported the event in great detail upon his return to Paris. Although his command of German was not fluent, it must have been passable: "All our deliberations being in German, our president, professor Johannsen, spoke very clearly and slowly enough that ears little accustomed to the sonorities of the German sentence could understand it without difficulty."[65] Widor amusingly described one session in which each contestant was required to perform one of the five Piano Concertos of Rubinstein:

> We were seated every day [in Bechstein Hall], in the morning from 9 until 1, and in the afternoon from 3 until 7. On the platform, the orchestra was conducted by either Professor [Karl] Klindworth [1830–1916] or the composer Busoni. . . .
> . . . The morning performance was very interesting for us, but rough for the orchestra, which played almost without stop from 9 until 1! One day we heard the Concerto in D Minor of Rubinstein seven times in succession; the orchestra finished by playing by heart, but the horns were no longer able to do it and quacked—making a shower of wrong notes! . . .
> . . . Naturally, we took a holiday on Sunday and went to spend the day in Potsdam [Sans-Souci and Babelsberg], trying to flee the pianistic obsession.[66]

After the competitions, members of the jury visited the Berlin Museum and the National Library. Widor wrote excitedly about seeing and hearing Bach's harpsichord, Weber's and Mendelssohn's grand pianos, and travel keyboards that belonged to Mozart and Meyerbeer—all demonstrated by Louis Diémer.

Awestruck before numerous autograph manuscripts at the National Library, Widor even thumbed through some of Beethoven's sketchbooks:

> If the city of Berlin has the right to be proud of its museum, it can also boast of its National Library, of which Dr. Heinrich Reimann [1850–1906] is the very distinguished conservator. What a collection of precious manuscripts! Almost all the works of Bach, Beethoven, Weber, Mendelssohn, Schumann. There, under our eyes, the autograph of the B-Minor Mass, the *Matthew Passion*, the Well-Tempered Clavier, *Der Freischütz*, *Die Zauberflöte*, *Elijah*, then the symphonies of Beethoven—the Ninth with its erasures, scratchings, over-writing, blue and red pencil strokes . . .[67]

Before departing from Berlin, Widor's fellow jurors insisted that he play an organ concert for them, which he consented to do on the large Sauer organ at the Church of St. Paul the Apostle.[68] After Berlin, Widor availed himself of the opportunity to stop over in Dresden to visit its famous museum.[69]

In Paris, an equally rich collection of manuscripts, scores, precious books, and instruments of all types were brought together under the roof of the Paris Conservatory, which had been founded by the National Convention of 1795; by decree, the Conservatory buildings included a library and a museum. Théodore Dubois, director of the Conservatory from 1896 to 1905, hoped to enlarge the library's holdings even further. As an avid bibliophile, Widor questioned the wisdom of such an undertaking:

> [Dubois] would have wanted, and we spoke together often about it, that all the musical treasures we possess, currently dispersed at the Mazarine, Sainte-Geneviève, Arsenal, and National libraries, and the Opera archives be brought together either at the Conservatory or in some other specially designated building. But wouldn't that be imprudent? Is it really wise to group so many masterworks in the same locale, and isn't it terribly sad that . . . there is no edifice that fire or war might not one day destroy? Every morning, from my window [at the Institut de France where at the time of this writing Widor had an apartment as perpetual secretary of the Academy of Fine Arts], I contemplate the well-ordered magnificence of the Louvre, and every day I fear for the Louvre. . . .
> . . . What a loss, indeed, if some stupid accident deprived the history of our art of these documents![70]

Dubois came to agree with Widor, and they devised a forward-looking plan:

> Dubois and I were of the opinion that, while leaving all these treasures in a dispersed state that might perhaps save them from total disappearance, it would be good, at least, to bring together photographic reproductions of

them, methodically catalogued in a single locale where researchers would be able to come and consult them. In that way, one would have all the advantages of concentration without the risks.

An institution of this kind always has, as a necessary complement, the founding of a society supported by financial subscriptions, initiatives, and activities. This would be, to give a name to it, the *Society of French Music Bibliophiles.* . . .

Let's not forget, we are responsible for the treasures that our predecessors have left us.[71]

In the same regard, after the destruction of World War I, Widor raised a cry of alarm that historic French organs had not been adequately inventoried. Félix Raugel (1881–1975) began a series of studies of significant French instruments in 1919, and he enlisted Widor to write the first preface:

Had one ever dreamed, for example, to take stock of and classify as historic monuments our organ cases from the fourteenth to the eighteenth century? Who could have foreseen the day when not even a simple photographic reproduction would remain of our bombed instruments in the north or in the east? . . . And if we pass from the exterior into the interior, from the case to the sounding body, although less irreparable, is the disaster less cruel? . . .

I have the facts from Mr. Raugel. Now it's Mr. Raugel whom we must thank for this book [*Les orgues de l'Abbaye de Saint-Mihiel* (1919)], which is the first attempt at a general review of our instruments, the preface to work that we are ashamed not to have undertaken and finished already many years ago. Let's hasten to do our best to collect our documents and carefully record the result of our activity in this life—such is our duty to our successors!

What riches in our beautiful country of France! What invention, fantasy, variety, harmony of proportions, architectural elegance in these organ tribunes from the Renaissance to our day, from the thirteenth to the nineteenth century![72]

—71—

The French organ school: "Manifestly loved by the gods"

At the Conservatory, Widor made substantial strides with his young organ class; in only six short years he laid the foundations of a new French organ school— one of unsurpassed quality and promise founded on the principles he had learned during his study with Lemmens:[73] "I imposed this tradition upon the Conservatory when I became titular of the organ class in 1890. Six years later, having become professor of composition, I handed the class over to Guilmant (see fig. 14), like me a student of Lemmens and consequently fully designated to impose in his turn the same 'immortal principles.'"[74] In 1937, Louis Vierne estimated that Widor's greatest legacy was to create the most brilliant school of organists in the world—a school Widor claimed to be "manifestly loved by the gods."[75] Some of France's most noted future organist/composers passed under his stewardship either privately or at the Conservatory; he pointed proudly to a number of students who represented the best of what France had to offer: "People know the reputation of our organ school and what artists have come out of it: Vierne, Marcel Dupré, J. Bonnet, Libert, Jacob, Fauchet, Cellier, Philip, Huré, Mulet, Letocart, Decaux, and how many others, celebrated in France and elsewhere."[76]

Of Widor's Conservatory organ students, several achieved distinguished careers as organists and composers, but perhaps none more than Tournemire and Vierne. Conservatory professors assessed their students twice a year, and Widor had little more than a month (December 11, 1890, to January 24, 1891) to make a first evaluation of his students.[77] Tournemire, in his second year of study, quickly made an outstanding impression; Widor wrote: "Already a mature performer; excellent individual, temperament of a musician; very intelligent, greatly in love with his art. Truly gifted." However, Widor had had very little exposure to Vierne; he wrote, "Admitted eight days ago. Good willed and has a certain knowledge; execution weak."[78]

For the June 13, 1891, evaluation, Widor graded Tournemire—who would win first prize in organ that year—"*Excellent*," and Vierne—who had gained rapidly in his professor's eyes—"Will be excellent, knowing a lot already."[79] In the following years, Widor could not sing Vierne's praises highly enough: January 20, 1892, "*Excellent* in every way"; June 13, 1892, *Exceptional individual*"; January 31, 1893, "*Excellent* in every way"; June 13, 1893, "Excellent in every respect"; January 18, 1894, "Knows *perfectly well* his craft, has nothing to learn but experience; lacks nerve"; June 12, 1894, "Knows his craft completely; a real organist; has no more to learn but experience."[80] When Fannie Thomas observed the class in 1893, she wrote: "Widor seemed to listen [to Vierne] more in pleasure and interest than criticism, dropping gentle words of praise through the piece."[81]

As Vierne's star rose, Widor offered to work with him outside the class to broaden the scope of his study:

[Widor] became angry when I spoke of fees: "Keep that for yourself to buy music," he told me; "although I am not rich, I can allow myself the whim of giving some time to whomever I please. I know what deep attachments bind you to Franck; I have respected and will continue to respect the artistic imprint that this great musician has left on you. However, there are some purely professional aspects that I will teach you, since you are taking the organ class but not the composition class. I will initiate you in chamber music—little practiced at the Conservatory, symphonic music—for which you seem to me to be born, in musical prosody, lyric declamation, and the orchestra. This is a program that will require a few years of us. Do you feel strong enough to take it and to neglect nothing to become a complete musician?"[82]

Thus developed a truly "spiritual affiliation" between *maître* and student based as much on respect as on affection.[83]

In fact, Widor cared deeply about all of his students and he wanted to see the important organ posts in Paris filled with musicians worthy of the title. When mediocre musicians attained positions out of favoritism instead of demonstrated skill and talent, he became indignant, and he once wrote an article, "Nouveaux organistes," in which he expressed disdain for such sham appointments. Invoking the towering requirements of the Conservatory examinations, Widor advocated applying those as the standard for competitions for church positions; they were ready-made to weed out all but the hardiest trained:[84]

The parish council of Saint-Vincent-de Paul, which last month lost its promising young organist Léon Boëllmann—carried off at the age of thirty-five by consumption—just named as successor Mr. [Albert] Mahaut [1867–1943], for some years *titulaire* of the church of Montrouge and, at the same time, professor of harmony at the Institution nationale des jeunes aveugles [National Institution of the Blind].

Due to a few recent appointments to vacant positions in notable Paris parishes having been made from recommendations ignorant of art, and even more due to the fear of seeing a system of favoritism set up as a principle—to the great detriment of our flourishing organ school—some of the candidates were impelled to ask that the position at Saint-Vincent-de-Paul be put to a competition. As a matter of fact, musicians have been nominated here and there who have neither training, organ technique, knowledge, nor experience in the wonderful and special literature, who have never written or published a single page of music for their admirable instrument, who are incapable of playing by heart and without preparation ten lines of Bach, and who scarcely know how to hold themselves correctly at the keyboard; whereas, we can cite five or six matchless individuals with diplomas who are waiting in vain for any position—individuals who are dedicated, recognized as masters by the masters of French art, and absolutely worthy of esteem both as men and as artists.

Hence, the very natural exasperation of these young men!

The title of first prize in organ at the Conservatory implies the idea of a very difficult competition, the most difficult of all—a competition passed before an outside jury that is sometimes more hostile than sympathetic to the class that it examines. During the six years that I conducted the organ class of our national school, this jury proved to be very severe and two times refused to award a first prize. I have had during this period only four first prizes: Messrs. Tournemire, Vierne, Libert, and Galand. It seems the same severity was applied last year; the best student of the class, Mr. Quef, from Lille, who had brilliantly undergone the tests in counterpoint, plainsong, fugue improvisation, and free improvisation, saw himself refused the supreme compensation due his talent for having committed, in executing by heart Bach's Fugue in D Major, a little slip of memory—of two or three measures only. That was enough; in the final voting, he was one vote short of obtaining the absolute majority.

Judge by this example the difficulty [of obtaining] the first prize in organ at the Conservatory.

Last year, when the matter of naming an organist to the Basilica of Saint-Denis came up, I advised the parish council about the competition system. "But it's going to last a week; we have eighty candidates signed up!" the president of the council responded to me. "Never mind; impose the program of our school upon the candidates and you will see immediately how many fall by the wayside. You are asking me to be part of the jury. Very well, I pledge to remain in my chair without drinking or eating for the duration of the exams." Thus, it was settled and done; at the announcement of a serious program, the battalion of eighty evaporated as if by magic. Only four came to confront destiny, and of the four, two asked for the favor of being excused from improvising the fugue—something that was graciously granted them; we were no longer menaced with starvation, since the competition was not supposed to last more than two hours.

Mr. Libert won based on a considerable number of points and was officially named a few days later.[85]

Of the four first prizes I mentioned above, only two have the position today that they deserve: Mr. Libert, and Mr. Tournemire—who became organist of the Chapelle des Pères Jésuites on the rue de Madrid and professor in their school.

Mr. Vierne, who has already made a justifiable reputation as a virtuoso, and who has written some very interesting pieces for organ, for piano and voice, a string quartet, suites for viola, for oboe, etc., who knows by heart his Bach, including the chorales, and even all his plainsong, Mr. Vierne is still not organist anywhere. He takes my place at Saint-Sulpice when I must be absent; furthermore, I had taken him as private tutor for my organ class at the Conservatory, and when I left that class to teach one in composition, I handed him over to my successor, Mr. Guilmant, who readily took him as assistant, and since then has been only very pleased with this collaboration.

Mr. Galand until now has also obtained no official position; but it must be said that he is the youngest of this interesting nursery, that his prize dates back only two years, and currently he is still at the Conservatory, where he is studying for the Prix de Rome.

It appears that the request from the serious applicants for the position of organist at Saint-Vincent-de-Paul to be put to a competition arrived too late to succeed; but it seems that it has not been useless. Indeed, some disquieting rumors went around; [some candidates] got themselves warmly recommended and supported by musicians who have produced a few romances and even symphonic pieces, but who are profoundly inexperienced in things concerning the organ—amateurs belonging to that special class of philosophers who go up into the organ loft without preparation, without meditation of any sort, letting their fingers run haphazardly on the spur of the moment, reeling off no matter what, no matter how, in contempt of their function and of the respect of their art, perfectly incapable of interpreting correctly from one end to the other Bach or Handel or César Franck, considering the position as a little revenue, and permitting themselves to think of everything else from Monday to Saturday.

Fortunately, these fears did not materialize.

The fortunate winner, by reason of the choice of the curé and the parish council of Saint-Vincent-de-Paul, has been Mr. Mahaut, as I said at the beginning of this article. And we can only applaud this choice, Mr. Mahaut having obtained the first prize in organ at the Conservatory in 1889.

. . . As an organist, he has a real talent as a performer, a great sense of rhythm, and real virtuosity. He improvises easily and knows how to conceive rapidly and architecturally, and how to carry through a symphonic project successfully. A distinguished wit and a good-hearted man, he is among those who honor the corps of French organists and who work ceaselessly to improve.[86]

To support his pupils and other worthy young organists in publishing their organ compositions, Widor initiated *L'Orgue Moderne*, a quarterly edition under his directorship and published by Alphonse Leduc. Begun in 1894, the series ran at least thirty-eight volumes, until 1928. The edition advertised its goal

to bring to light the works of the most interesting of the young group, and to make them known to those who are occupied with the organ. However, *l'Orgue Moderne* will not publish the compositions of only one school; its eclecticism will accept all those who present a [work of] real artistic interest. All young organists desirous of making contact with the public to affirm their personality may address themselves to the editorship. Manuscripts not published will be returned to their authors.[87]

To begin the first volume, Widor petitioned three of his finest students, Tournemire, Vierne, and Libert "to light the fire."[88] Several years later, Libert returned the honor by freely transcribing for two pianos the first, third, fourth, and fifth movements of his *maître*'s great Sixth Symphony. Libert inscribed a copy of the score "To my dear *maître* Mr. Widor / Respectful homage of the transcriber / and affectionately grateful remembrance / from his devoted student / H. Libert."[89]

—72—

"I found myself called to take [Dubois's] composition class"

In February 1896, Ambroise Thomas died, leaving the directorship of the Paris Conservatory vacant. Although the post should have fallen to Massenet by right, Théodore Dubois was named director.[90] Whether from resentment that he had been passed over for the directorial seat[91] or that he was too busy at the theater, Massenet resigned from his composition class.[92] This left the composition classes of Dubois and Massenet vacant. Widor applied for one. Although Fauré wanted the other, Dubois had someone else in mind. Saint-Saëns recommended privately to Fauré, "If I were you I should let Widor follow Massenet, and I'd take the organ class. It's done no harm either to him or to César Franck."[93] Fauré responded that Widor would undoubtedly be appointed to a composition class and that he had no interest in taking the organ class:

> [Widor] has already announced his appointment to different people with as much eagerness as the fact that he has contrived to forget that he *had promised me* not to come forward against me.
> But this matters little: all of us are more or less forgetful or fickle.
> As for the organ class it will be reserved for Guilmant. Besides I would not offer myself for the organ class in any case. Never will I undertake to teach students who do not even know harmony or how to improvise fugues.[94]

Saint-Saëns tried to be supportive: "I fear, not that D.[ubois] is against you, but [that he] is in favour of another, which amounts to the same thing; but I am convinced that you will get it."[95] Saint-Saëns was right; whatever may have been Dubois's desire, on October 1, 1896, the decision of the Conseil supérieur was that Widor would succeed Dubois, and Fauré would take the class of Massenet.[96] "I found myself called to take [Dubois's] composition class," Widor later recounted.[97]

Whereas his salary as professor of organ had been fifteen hundred francs a year, it doubled to three thousand francs as composition professor.[98] Vierne naively wondered why Widor so willingly abandoned his organ class for one in composition:

> Whence came this desire? Did he think that his influence there would be as positive as in the organ class, where he had gained it by the individuality of his teaching, or that he could broaden the horizons? I do not know whether the future justified this illusion. In any case he could not reform the spirit that limited the students' ambitions to winning the Prix de Rome.
> Occasionally he tried to make them write symphonic music, but most of his time was spent in serving up the "Cantata" and the "Chorus," in preparation for the trial examination. In the organ class he was a real innovator, but in composition he had to reckon with the students in the rival class and keep his own at the same level.[99]

The work of the composition class traditionally focused on preparing the students to compete for the Prix de Rome, a strenuous competition in which the contestant had to demonstrate mastery of music as both an art and a science. In a preliminary round (*concours d'essai*), contestants had to submit a fugue on a given theme and a short choral piece on an assigned text. Those progressing to the final round (*concours définitif*) were sequestered for about four weeks at the Château de Compiègne, where they had to compose an academically correct cantata on a given text for one or more voices with orchestra. Members of the music section of the Academy of Fine Arts made the preliminary judgment and then all the members of the Academy came together in a formal session to pronounce the final decision. The rewards were substantial: winners could spend at least two years at the Villa Médicis in Rome and another two either there or in another cultural center; the Academy paid the winner a moderate stipend, arranged for a performance and publication of the winning submission, afforded opportunities for travel, arranged for military deferments in appropriate cases, and provided other necessary support.[100]

Although Widor was not artistically opposed to the necessary focus of his composition class, he also viewed it as an equal opportunity to include a concomitant element in symphonic music. As customary, he used one of his weekly journal columns to vent his opinion on the matter:

> As for the reformers clamoring with hue and cry, and protesting against the system practiced to accord the Prix de Rome only to cantatas, to the exclusion of pure symphonic works, we will respond that the jury must truly not reward musicians who have not proved that they know how to write for voices as well as for instruments. . . .
>
> To conciliate all the opinions, to satisfy all the exigencies, it will suffice to add at the bottom of the competition program the following little remark:
>
> *The jury will accord a good mark to the candidates who show their symphonic skill either in an overture placed at the head of their score, or in some orchestral piece, if the vicissitudes of the poem permit it.*
>
> I speak all the more liberally of these things since, first of all, I am not a Prix de Rome laureate, and also, professionally, I defend the symphonic cause.[101]

Ultimately, only five of Widor's composition students succeeded in winning the coveted Prix de Rome, but he evidently did not feel stifled by the academic requirements of the class, as he retained the professorship for thirty-one years. Some of France's most illustrious and diverse young musicians passed under his prudent guidance: Gabriel Dupont—won Second Grand Prix in 1901; Hélène-Gabrielle Fleury-Roy (b. 1876)—the first woman candidate for the Prix de Rome won Third Grand Prix in 1904; Nadia Boulanger—won Second Grand Prix in 1908;[102] Marcel Dupré—won Premier Grand Prix in 1914; Darius Milhaud (1892–1974); Paul Paray (1886–1979); René Guillou (1903–58); Claude Delvincourt (1888–1954); Jean Déré (1886–1970); Arthur Honegger

(1892–1955); Germaine Tailleferre (1892–1983); Edgard Varèse (1885–1965); Olivier Messiaen (1908–92).

Curiously, one of Widor's last students denied ever having been his pupil at all. Maurice Duruflé (1902–86) entered the class in 1925 and remained there until Widor retired in October 1927; during those two years he won two prizes in composition (1926—*second accessit*; 1927—*second prix*).[103] In addition, when Duruflé was a candidate for the position of titular organist of Saint Étienne-du-Mont, he sought out recommendations from Widor, Tournemire, and Vierne.[104] He was certainly aware that an endorsement from his former composition professor, who also happened to be the most influential organist in Paris and the perpetual secretary of the Academy of Fine Arts, would seal the post for him. Widor wrote a flattering note to the curé on October 4, 1929, recommending "my former student (at the Conservatoire) . . . a consummate musician . . . remarkable performer."[105] For reasons unknown, Duruflé later disassociated himself from his *maître*. "I knew Widor the last year that he was professor of composition at the Conservatoire. I was not his student; I was a student of Paul Dukas [1865–1935], who was his successor."[106]

This is quite a unique case among Widor's students. Even the most avant-garde among them did not so flatly turn their back on the benefit gained from his teaching. Varèse was admitted to the class in January 1905 and referred to Widor as "one of his most important teachers,"[107] an assessment with which Messiaen could concur:

> Widor was my first composition teacher, with whom I had instruction six months after my introduction to the composition class. . . . Widor was a very old man with a small speech impediment, but very distinguished and intelligent, in no way a snob, as some might think. He was quite open to all opinions, a great spirit and well versed in a great many things. He was, not least of all, a very good teacher.[108]

Although Lili Boulanger (1893–1918) was not officially enrolled as Widor's student, she thought enough of what he had to offer that she often audited his classes, and in 1913 she became the first woman to win the Premier Grand Prix de Rome.[109] Even Hungarian nationalist Zoltán Kodály (1882–1967) went to Paris in 1907 for a year of study with Widor.[110]

Contact with foreign students was a musical lifeline that Widor valued highly. At a time when a group of French musicians were showing an aversion to Italian composers in particular and foreign music in general, Widor was one of several French composers queried about his viewpoint:

> What I can affirm to you is that never has a question come more inopportunely. What is this! People are going to set themselves up as an enemy of foreign musicians when French composers have received a welcome so cordial

and touching in Munich last September, when the expositions in Rome and Turin have called upon our musicians and painters!

In my class at the Conservatory, I have an Italian, two Germans, three Americans, and an Irishman as students. Each week these young musicians bring to me all there is of interest in the production of their countries. We study the works together; the students instruct themselves and I also get to know modern foreign music.[111]

Widor felt he had changed the course of the organ class and, upon leaving it to take a position as composition professor, he was concerned that the wrong successor would undermine his work. In Guilmant, he saw the appropriate torchbearer, and he threw the full weight of his influence on procuring the position for his colleague: "Lemmens was my *maître* as well as Guilmant's, and he left these traditions for us to hand down in our turn."[112] Widor expressed regret on leaving the class:

> Grievous was the sadness of leaving my students; the traditions that I had been able to convey to them were not at all established sufficiently, and I feared to see them soon forgotten. . . .
> The very day of my nomination as composition professor, I wired Guilmant, asking him to come spend some time with me: "We have drawn from the same source," I said to him, "we have the same sense of duty; there must be neither deviation nor interruption in the movement being instilled at the Conservatory; you alone must succeed me, carry on with my work, and make our school the best in the world."[113]

In matters of performance, they had received the same teaching from Lemmens; for improvisation, however, Widor felt Guilmant was not forward-looking enough. In 1878, Guilmant had presented one of the recitals at the inauguration of the Trocadéro organ, and while generally praising his performance of composed music, Widor found his improvisation entirely impoverished: "The least happy part of the program was the improvisation with tremolo, thunder, flashes of lightning, etc., etc. Such fantasias have had their time; to whom therefore, if not to artists, does it belong to form the taste of the public, to guide and elevate it?"[114]

Consequently, Widor wanted Vierne—his finest pupil, class assistant, and assistant at Saint-Sulpice—to be retained as the tutor for Guilmant's class.[115] With so much at stake, he told Vierne: "Since there are politics, I will set my political friends to work in order to assure that [Guilmant] obtains the professorship."[116] Widor's wish was soon realized, and Guilmant became the new professor of organ. Vierne described the new class:

> Physically he was as different from Widor as possible. He was short and stocky, with a ruddy complexion, long white hair, and a white beard; he used slight,

quick gestures, and was less eloquent than his predecessor. Neither did he have Widor's broad cultural background, originality of ideas, nor the same artistry in a critical sense. He was a man who knew his profession thoroughly, had absolute integrity, was a conscientious research scholar, hard-working, honest and, above all, good-hearted. . . .

[Guilmant] changed nothing in playing technique; a few additional points of articulation in certain Bach preludes and fugues, certain tempos a bit faster—those were his personal contributions in that area. As for improvisation, he turned his attention purely and simply to the forms required for the competition. His examples demonstrated a solid craft, but his imagination was incomparably less fertile than Widor's. . . . He appeared old-fashioned to his pupils, who were moving toward a more daring modernism. . . .

On the free subject his ideas were much vaguer than those of his predecessor. It was here that I had to intervene discreetly. I assigned myself the role of maintaining the Franck-Widor tradition, and the pupils agreed with me enthusiastically. It is true that le père Guilmant grimaced slightly on first hearing of some of the immature attempts, and he winced a bit, too, at certain fanciful rhythms, but basically he was liberal and, provided that common sense prevailed, he tolerated tendencies that were not his own.

"If you wish," he would say, shaking his head[,] "If you wish. That's a little disturbing, but it's interesting." . . . In that case he would look at me mischievously, seeming to say: "Are you satisfied? They're up to date!" I remained unperturbed, biting my lip so as not to laugh.[117]

Widor had correctly perceived the situation; in matters of execution Guilmant proved to be the perfect successor; but for free improvisation, the collaboration of Vierne was necessary to keep the class abreast of the times. With Vierne as an intermediary, Widor kept himself well informed of all that took place in the organ class:[118]

I was used by Widor as a liaison with Guilmant, and through me the continuity of the teaching begun in 1896 was maintained smoothly and in close harmony. I was delighted with the role of intermediary between two men whose most ardent desire was the growth of our national organ school. Through that go-between, Widor never lost contact with his former class. He knew what was happening and was highly satisfied in having recommended Guilmant as his successor. "Guilmant is conscience [conscientiousness] itself," Widor told me. "He loves the profession and acquits himself with great dignity. We were truly lucky that he was there at the right moment to take over the reins of the chariot. No one else could have guided it like him."[119]

The admiration and respect between Widor and Guilmant remained steadfast throughout their lives, and although Widor had not allowed his students to play any of his own music at the examinations, "Guilmant enthroned it there."[120]

—73—

"The grand race of liberal educators"

As a composition teacher, Widor was of "the grand race of liberal educators," refusing to permit his own personality as a composer to influence his judgment of a student's work, even when it differed radically from his own style:[121] "So much an artist, so little a formalist, and loving free imagination so much, he did not speak *ex cathedra*, but rather thought of his class as an open aesthetic chat around the piano."[122] Critiquing a score Edgard Varèse had brought to a lesson, Widor once quipped, "I can't say I'd advise that, Varèse, but perhaps the textbooks will have to be changed."[123] Varèse, who later pointed music in radical new directions, described the qualities in Widor's teaching that were particularly attractive to him:

> As all music students, I naturally began by learning the rules and I was submitted to the rigorous disciplines of counterpoint and fugue, as much at the Schola Cantorum under the direction of [Albert] Roussel [1869–1937] as in the master class of Widor at the Paris Conservatory. . . . My composition professor at the Schola Cantorum [1904] was Vincent d'Indy. He became a bitter adversary when I left his class in order to go study at the Conservatory [1905] with Widor. I left him because his conception of teaching consisted of training disciples. His vanity did not permit the slightest sign of originality or even personal reflection, and I was not keen on becoming a little d'Indy. One was enough. Widor, on the other hand, was very liberal and allowed me enough rope to hang myself or to escape from the prison of orthodox music. Therefore, I escaped.[124]
>
> Widor . . . encouraged me a lot. [He] was the most open and most understanding professor. Even if he didn't understand a piece of music, he knew how to reveal in it elements rich in promise for the future. One day I presented to Widor a score that excited him. He invited me to lunch.[125]

At the Conservatory, Widor's initial evaluation of Varèse was telling: "Intelligent, works now and then; leaving the 'Schola' where they taught him nothing."[126]

Darius Milhaud related much the same attitude on the part of Widor: "That charming teacher, a most brilliant conversationalist, would utter cries of alarm at every dissonance he came across in my works; as he listened he would exclaim: 'The worst of it is that you get used to them!'"[127]

Not above telling stories on himself, Widor traced a similar scenario around one of his students—likely Arthur Honegger:[128] "This intelligent student, very gifted, amazingly informed but somewhat bewildering, found himself at a soiree, and as a beautiful woman asked him, 'And Widor, your *maître*, what did he say about your audacities?' the young man responded, 'At first he winced a good bit, but we've trained him.'"[129] Indeed, Honegger and Milhaud enjoyed pulling one over on Widor when an opportunity presented itself. At Milhaud's urging and with Gedalge's permission, Honegger moved from Gedalge's class to Widor's late in 1915. Honegger reported to his parents an amusing incident: "I made my debut with two little songs, sung by my friend Milhaud. Widor said they were 'charming, intelligent, and ingenious,' and when Milhaud claimed that the second one was like a Neapolitan ditty called *Funiculì, funiculà*, Widor exclaimed indignantly, 'not at all!' Milhaud and I were splitting our sides with laughter because they were both old pieces (*Barcarolle* and one other)."[130]

Widor held that "the first duty of a professor is to respect the temperament, albeit excessive, of his students."[131] Georges Favre (1905–93) enrolled in Widor's composition class for the three last years that he taught at the Conservatory—1924 to 1927—and affirmed, "This role, Widor understood and practiced magnificently, either in the correction of our compositions or in the reading of and commentary on the great works of music."[132] For Favre, Widor was an oracle:

His class generally began with the examination of our manuscripts when one of us had a new, freshly written composition to submit to him. Then he listened scrupulously to the work and critiqued it, giving proof of a soundness of view and astonishing insight. He immediately underscored the weak point of the composition, the poor declamation of a melody, the lack of equilibrium in a sonata movement, the awkwardness of an orchestral page, or the misunderstanding and false accents in a theatrical scene. With a skilled hand, he put the faulty passage in its place, indicated to us the correction to improve the whole, or by example improvised for us remarkably and in a flash the development of a sonata-allegro that we were unable to succeed in putting solidly afoot.

The second part of the class was devoted to the reading, careful examination, and comparison of works by the great masters of music. By the chance of conversation or following the inspiration of the moment, Widor took whatever score, played it and commented on it, interspersing strong aesthetic considerations with the vastest historic and literary erudition. Of a truly encyclopedic culture, he had seen everything, read everything, and knew almost all that concerned the fine arts. Without being exclusive, for he cited all the important names in music, including the modern ones,[133] he had a marked predilection for Bach and Beethoven. Of the first, "our Holy Father Bach," as he sometimes called him, he frequently played the twenty-six organ Preludes for us, emphasizing their prodigious richness of form, since only two are conceived on the same plan. Of Beethoven, in addition to the Symphonies, he played—perhaps a bit too frequently for our taste—the piano Sonatas, insisting particularly on the wealth of themes and the perfection of form. This regard for solid and well established architecture dominated his teaching, and ensured an excellent formation for the young students, sometimes a little too inclined to treat form contemptuously and without due concern. "Of all the arts," he frequently affirmed, "none has more rapport with music than architecture." The art of the architect aims to materialize the dream in space, and to give it a form both harmonious and solid. The art of the musician also consists of raising in sonorous space an ideal structure, beautiful, expressive, and strongly built. And he then took pleasure in establishing precise parallels between the robust builders of medieval cathedrals and the great sonorous architects of the eighteenth and nineteenth centuries. "Go see," he advised us sharply, "the admirable façade of Notre-Dame de Paris, and tell me if there exists anything more closely resembling the plan of a first movement of a symphony than the conception of the central portal, sturdily framed by its two towers, as a development positioned between two symmetrical aisles." Music, he loved to repeat, lives from symmetries and recurrences. . . .

Aside from the complex study of construction, he knew perfectly and taught with an incontestable mastery the writing for and perilous handling of the orchestra. For an organist to know how to treat and adroitly proportion instrumental color seems rare enough that it needs to be emphasized. . . . He had attentively scrutinized Berlioz, Liszt, Wagner and all the masters of the modern orchestra. Also, when he opened and analyzed one of their scores, he knew how to show us the interesting page, the skillful disposition of a passage, the novelty, originality, and the unparalleled art with which the sonority was balanced and the timbres blended. . . .

If one wanted to give a complete picture of this teaching, many aspects would have to be recalled: the incomparable analysis of songs by Schubert and Schumann, the reading of great dramatic works, those of Gluck in particular that he encouraged us to read attentively at the time of the Rome competition, and many more things. But these few recollections suffice to evoke the lively and so special atmosphere of this class. It did not have, like so many others, the single goal of preparing for and succeeding in the competitions, but was rather a place of choice *where one learned about music.* . . . Although an unforgettable grand professorial figure, he knew how to mask his vast and stupefying erudition with the liveliest flashes of wit and humorous stories. . . . For these memories permitted him to evoke almost all the great musicians of the nineteenth century, Rossini, Berlioz, Liszt, Wagner, César Franck, Bizet, and others whom he had known personally. Thus, this contact and conversation with him were a continual enrichment for the student. Without any doubt, history will give to Charles-Marie Widor a just and important place in this great line of composition professors who, since [Étienne] Méhul [1763–1817] and Cherubini up to Gabriel Fauré and Paul Dukas, ensure the continuation, the brilliance, and the renown of the modern French school of music.[134]

For the most part, Widor had the ability to suspend his own sensitivities so that he could encourage and inspire students to explore their own, while at the same time enabling them to discriminate between clumsy errors and the intentional breaking of academic rules for the purpose of achieving certain effects. "Nothing requires more tact," wrote Widor, "than the essential duty of the professor to respect the most diverse tendencies, not to halt any progress, not to lock the doors that open on the future."[135] In this way he endeavored to shepherd his students, allowing them adequate freedom to express their own individualities. As one of his students put it, he was "a well of musical science, a psychologist, an impartial umpire, a kindly adviser . . . a diplomat."[136] Even when he seemed unable to digest a student's stylistic adventures, Widor endeavored to remain encouraging, which Honegger appreciated:

> I showed Widor my quartet, but so far he's only been able to take in the first movement, which is much the easiest to understand, being the oldest. He found it extremely extended . . . and thought the harmony was frighteningly "grimacing." I'm afraid the Adagio, which is much more polyphonic and polyharmonic, will cause him some nasty moments. But he's so nice, and afterward always tells you you have a lot of talent.[137]

On the other hand, Honegger did express impatience with his old professor when comparing the two counterpoint classes (those of Gedalge and Caussade) with the two composition classes (those of Widor and Vidal). He confided to his parents: "Widor's class is less academic [than Caussade's and Vidal's], but Widor is the kind of academic musician who can't understand anyone writing music different from his own."[138] Honegger also reported that Milhaud went to Widor's class "for appearance's sake but continues having private lessons with Gedalge because he regards him first of all as the best teacher and also the only one who, while teaching technique, doesn't influence a pupil's ideas and personality."[139]

When it came to the integrity of form and style, Widor was rigidly uncompromising; no music could be permanent without a proper balance of the constituent elements: melody, rhythm, harmony, counterpoint, proportion, architecture, and coloring; to each class he propounded the same creed:

> Musical history shows us that the great masters possessed these qualities in a superlative degree. It was owing to these qualities that they wrote in a way that defies time, that causes their works to stand up like a rock of ages.
>
> What, for instance, has preserved and will always preserve the names of Rameau, Bach, Mozart, Beethoven, Chopin, Schumann, Wagner, or Debussy? It is the fact that in their music we find an almost perfect blending of the elements available at their time, coupled with an individuality which bears the unmistakable stamp of each master.
>
> The great line of such masters offers a rich field of meditation and study to all young composers. It sets before their eyes an outline of the goal which is at the end of an arduous road. Their example is in itself a great teaching.[140]

Widor demanded no less of his students than he demanded of himself, and, perhaps above all else, sincerity had to be brought to the creative process. He wrote: "What all artists ought to hold as indisputable—a law that binds them all—is that there is no true art without reflective thought and purpose [*volonté*]."[141]

Widor defended these tenets above all else and had little patience for those who did not respect them. When police court proceedings were brought against three young men who had protested by booing the performance of a Beethoven concerto (with Paderewski as soloist) because they judged the form contrary to art, the lawyer for the young men consulted with Widor on the case. *Le Ménestrel* published Widor's letter to the lawyer:

> Your clients boo the virtuosos; the cook at [Restaurant] Foyot can't bear that they play tragedy at the Odéon; that of [Restaurant] Voisin only tolerates the cake-walk at the Nouveau-Cirque; Mr. Dejeante requires the expropriation of Sacré-Cœur; Mr. Jaurès wants no more army; Mr. Hervé no more country; the women of the telephone company no more foreign languages; a master mason called yesterday for the immediate demolition of the cupola of Saint-Peter's in order to consolidate the Franco-Italian alliance; previously, La Fontaine told us the story of a fox who wanted the tails of all the other foxes to be cut.
>
> Your clients are liable only to a medical treatment, for they have been attacked with a slight hypertrophy of "me," complicated by what our fathers commonly called "the spoil-sport."
>
> Bach, Handel, Haydn, Mozart, Beethoven, Weber, Schumann, Brahms, Liszt, Mendelssohn, Saint-Saëns, etc., have made the most eloquent response to the question you have been willing to ask of me, by producing these admirable works of inspired virtuosity that impassion the throngs for art.
>
> I very much allow your clients an ideal very superior to that of Bach or Beethoven, but it's not in booing that they will demonstrate this superiority.
>
> It is so simple not to go to the concert when the program displeases you![142]

—74—

"French" Bolsheviks at the Salzburg Mozart Festival

Ironically, in August 1922 when Widor learned that his former pupils Milhaud, Honegger, and some other cohorts were to appear in Salzburg at the Mozart Festival, his indignation wore thin. Widor described Mozart as "the most sublime of musicians," "a genius without parallel and one of the glories of humanity"[143]—descriptions that he could not confer upon this French delegation to the Festival.

Milhaud's music had long been a lightning rod for critical invective. The 1919 premiere of *Le bœuf sur le toit* was given in the company of works by Erik Satie (1866–1925), Georges Auric (1899–1983), and [Francis] Poulenc [1899–1963]; Milhaud reported that the newspapers treated the program as a "practical joke," and "both public and critics agreed that I was a clown and a strolling musician."[144] Audiences often reacted violently to his polytonal style with "animal noises" and shouts of "Take it away!" The police had to intervene at performances on more than one occasion.[145]

In like manner, audiences greeted the 1918 premiere of Honegger's *Le dit des jeux du monde* in the most disdainful manner. In the audience of one performance sat his former composition professor: Widor.[146] Honegger described the scandal provoked at the premiere: "The performances all led to a fearful uproar. The auditorium was filled with such a din of shouting, screaming, whistling, and clapping that on some evenings you couldn't hear a word of the text or a note of the music. There was even fighting and exchanges of cards."[147] For Widor, this bewildering new style of music was totally inappropriate to represent proper French culture at the Salzburg Mozart Festival. As an upholder of sane traditions, he took it as his duty to protest "against the vandalism that assails the monuments of the past, against the scandalous disrespect of the ignorant—in a word, against every offense to the eternal laws that have never stopped the most audacious demonstrations of the freest geniuses, to the laws whose care has been confided to us and for which we are responsible to our successors."[148] Widor caustically expressed his scorn to Robert Brussel, the French cultural attaché responsible for artistic exchanges between France and other countries:

Mozart celebrated by "Le bœuf sur le toit" and his companions—what an unseemly joke!

The program (that I read here at home) carries exclusively the names of blasphemers and those ignorant of Mozart. I wouldn't want the money you inherited from the *House of Music* to subsidize this delegation of "French" Bolsheviks; instead of Salzburg, one ought to send them to Lenin to give him a foretaste of the pains that certainly await him in the next world.

What a nice letter Saint-Saëns would have written on this sinister parody and the assistance offered to some malefactors by X and Y![149]

Indeed, Saint-Saëns had written a letter on the subject to Gabriel Pierné, who often included controversial new music on programs that the newspapers headlined: "Scandal at the Concerts Colonne."[150] Milhaud took Saint-Saëns's censure as a badge of honor, writing:

Much later I learned that Pierné's courageous attitude had earned him the unanimous disapproval of the musicians at the Institut[e], and delayed his own election to that august body. The *Ménestrel* reproduced a letter written to him from Algiers by Saint-Saëns. From it I took the following extract, which I had framed and hung on the wall of my studio in Aix: "I am grieved to see that you are opening the doors to all sorts of bedlam aberrations and trying to force them down the public's throat when it protests. Several instruments playing in different keys have never produced music, only a babel!"[151]

Although Widor and Saint-Saëns were like-minded aesthetically, Widor admitted that positive developments could emerge, even though he could not foresee what they might be: "Let's not be amazed. Let's wait. Even in times of decadence, I have said elsewhere [*Initiation musicale*], it is possible among the preposterousness and banality of the moment to discern some sane seeds, useful pursuits, and principles still unknown that, taking shape, developing, and linking up, sooner or later will be able to produce new forms and prepare the evolution."[152]

As can be seen, Widor allowed his composition students plenty of room to experiment, but at the same time he expected them to devote their highest level of thinking to their work; he had no patience for what he viewed as indifference, pretense, affectation, and airs.

—75—

"I admit only those who please me"

From 1900 until his move to the Mazarin Palace in 1914, Widor lived at 7 rue des Saints-Pères—a house in which Berlioz once resided.[153] There, he continued to teach privately on his beautiful *orgue de salon* in the spacious and lofty music room of his well-appointed apartment. Albert Riemenschneider, one of Widor's most industrious American pupils, often translated lessons for non-French-speaking pupils. Although Widor traveled frequently to England and Germany, he spoke almost no English and, as noted earlier, his German was not developed.[154] Normally, he seemed to have "unlimited patience in his teaching, and [would] repeat a phrase and even sing it over and over again in order that the pupil may grasp it beyond all doubt."[155] One day, however, from behind his shuttered windows that permitted him without being seen "to catch a glimpse of the identity of his visitors,"[156] he watched for a tardy and poorly trained student. At length, when the student failed to appear, Widor gruffly instructed Riemenschneider to tell the pupil, "I am gone, gone to England—no, tell him that I am dead and cannot give him any more lessons."[157] To Edmond Maurat, Widor confided, "I admit only those who please me."[158]

Alexander Russell (1880–1953) described the rigors under which he labored while studying privately with Widor in 1908, and he added an intriguing anecdote along the way:

> Tuesday morning found me ringing the bell at his door. His apartment was on the ground floor. He himself opened the door and ushered me into a little room facing the court through which I had just come. In front of the window looking on this court was a large flat table upon which were spread manuscripts. I was to learn to know that table well. Here were spread my

orchestration, fugue and composition manuscripts every week, and here Widor performed his drastic surgical operations, using blue and red pencils instead of scalpels, but operating none the less. I used to call the room the hospital and begged for anesthetic one day when one of my brain children underwent an appendectomy.

Beyond this room was Widor's salon which looked out through French windows on a charming garden. In this room was the little two-manual Cavaille-Coll organ on which he gave his organ lessons, and a grand piano. . . . In my first organ lesson I learned the fundamental principle of his organ playing.

I played his popular Fifth Symphony for him, the one with the Toccata at the end. He stopped me frequently, repeating over and over, "You play well, but everything is too fast! On an organ every note must have its full value of time and tone. The organ is not a percussion instrument like a piano where the tone dies away immediately. The piano speaks falsely, because the sound actually does not last as long as the printed notes indicate. The organ speaks truly. The sound lasts as long as the notes indicate. But you must give the organ *time* to breathe and speak." . . .

My lessons in composition, fugue and orchestration, while not flattering to my vanity, were full of bright spots entirely aside from the musical knowledge I absorbed. [There were g]limpses of Widor as a human being. For instance, one bright morning as we sat at the table in front of the window which looked out on the entrance court, I noticed that he was ill at ease. He kept looking apprehensively out the window towards the big door that opened on the street as if expecting someone whose arrival he anticipated with displeasure.

Presently, the bell at the gate rang vigorously. As the porter crossed the court to open the door, Widor reached up quickly, pulled down the blind, and peered through the shutters. So did I. There entered the court an aggressive looking female with chin thrust forward, who strode with determination towards Widor's door. With a whispered "Keep quiet . . . don't speak a word" he dropped suddenly to the floor and hid under the table. The door bell rang violently . . . one[ce] . . . twice . . . thrice. "Don't move! Quiet!" cautioned the Master from his retreat.

No servant was on duty during Widor's work hours, so the imperious summons at the door remained unanswered. Then came a shower of knocks on the panel . . . no response. Presently convinced that no one was at home the fair visitor strode away in high indignation. When the outer gate clanged shut, Widor arose from the floor, wiped the beads of perspiration from his forehead, and without a word of explanation proceeded with unusual good nature to dissect my poor manuscript. He was highly pleased with himself. There was a boyish twinkle in his eye. I never learned who this luckless female was. . . .

One day, apparently at his wit's end over my attempts at writing a fugue, he exclaimed, "You must write them constantly. For years I have written a fugue every night before going to bed. It keeps me in practice."[159]

American organist G. Huntington Byles (1908–98) met up with the same exacting standards when he went for lessons with Widor in 1933. Having gone to Paris initially to study with Marcel Dupré, Byles had not intended to seek out Widor as a teacher, but Dupré insisted:

Dupré wanted me to be sure to go see M. Widor at his home in Quai Conti [at the Institute], and I said I would, and straightway proceeded to forget it. I had so much that I had to do with Dupré. . . . The next week came around, and I went out for my lesson, and almost his first question was, "You have been to see M. Widor?" And I said no, I was busy. Well, he said, you be sure you go next week, and I said I would and of course, didn't. Then the third week came around and he asked me the third time. I rather shamefacedly admitted that I hadn't gotten there, and I got the command then to Go! And thereupon I went. I've always remembered the experience because at that time I had the Sixth Symphony (of Widor) pretty well under my fingers, and so I tucked that under my arm and started up the Seine, so to speak, to where he lived. . . . I got off the tram and went over and rang the bell and this gouvernante of Widor came to the door—a real old battleaxe—and I asked if M. Widor was there, and she said Yes, and to follow her, whereupon we went up some stairs and across some rooms and then down a flight of stairs into this enormous hall, with all these statues draped in sheets. At the far end of the hall there was this light, and this little bit of an organ, 2 manuals, and this elderly gentleman sitting at it and I went up to him. Once I had arrived at the hall, the gouvernante turned to me and said "Voila! M. Widor." I walked down, and he stopped playing, and looked at me. Of course, I was still fishing for words in French, and he spoke no English, but he had taught so many Americans for so long that he had come to use very simple and elementary French and speak very slowly, so that we got along very famously. . . . He told me that he wanted to see me the next day at 2:00, and he took out his watch and pointed to the dial. I had understood what he meant when he said "à deux heures," but he didn't seem to think I *had* understood it. Anyway, I went back the next day, and played for him for the first time. . . .

Well, he taught me a very great deal. One lesson, at least, that he taught me, was something that I very much needed to learn, . . . and that was to listen to myself. There was one section that I was working on in the (Widor) Sixth Symphony, and he kept complaining that this was not "equal." This bothered me, because to me it was quite "equal" but he kept complaining about it, and finally he asked me to get off the bench and he got on, and it took him some little time to get himself loosened up so that he could play this particular passage. He made several attempts at it before he finally did, and he said Now, and then he did play it. But he, perhaps more than anyone else that I ever studied with, taught me that lesson. . . .

Well, he just complained that I was not paying enough care to the detail of the passages that were not precisely equal, and that was the way he taught me, I guess.[160]

Through decades of practice and teaching, Widor set up strict and exact-ing standards that his students were expected to meet. His own training had been exceptionally rigid, and under his teaching, those standards became no less demanding. Widor admonished his students: "To defeat your rival, very simple is the way: do better than him."[161] And he dedicated himself to training his students to excel in every aspect of their craft. Saint-Saëns may well have been thinking of Widor when he wrote: "A virtuoso hardened to every difficulty, an ingenious improviser—such should the perfect organist be. It is to form such organists that they are laboring in the organ-class at the Conservatory of Paris, where execution and improvisation receive an equal meed of honor."[162]

—76—

Rome: "A thousand things to tell"

In the second half of the 1890s, Widor composed only four works: a set of five piano pieces Op. 71; Introduction and Rondo, Op. 72, for Clarinet and Piano; *Symphonie romane*, Op. 73, for Organ; Choral and Variations, Op. 74, for Harp and Orchestra. Of these, the last two were not premiered until 1900.

Written in 1898 as a trial piece for the Conservatory clarinet examination, the Introduction and Rondo became a *tour de force* for clarinet, and the Paris Opéra orchestra later adopted it as a requirement for clarinet applicants. Judg-ing Conservatory examinations could be a long and onerous task; Widor once referred to those "dreadful examinations . . . from noon to 7:30!"[163] The 1898 examinations were no different, and he confided to Marie Trélat that an exem-plary performance of his new work at the clarinet competition that year gave him his "only moment of joy."[164]

With a raft of opus numbers in his catalogue by this time, Widor continued to devote a good deal of time to conducting and performing programs of his music. In one instance, he conducted a performance of his Third Symphony for Organ and Orchestra at the Trocadéro,[165] and sixteen days later changed roles to become the organ soloist in a performance of the work at the Rouen Exposition.[166] Shortly after, Widor was invited to conduct his Second Sym-phony with the Imperial Society of Music in Moscow and then to perform an organ recital at the church of Saint Peter and Saint Paul.[167]

Travel was tiring and foreign organs rarely offered him any of the advan-tages of Cavaillé-Coll's splendid instruments, to which he had become accus-tomed; from Moscow, he wrote: "The thirty hours from Warsaw to Moscow, a horrible region of hopeless monotony, are an excellent preparation for the surprise that this indescribable city reserves. . . . I just worked two hours on the organ that is less bad than I feared."[168]

Audiences were always intrigued by the diversity of his talents, and he demonstrated them to the best advantage by offering a wide variety of works on his
programs. Although there were a few all-Bach programs, most were eclectic:
"Before a full house, Mr. Widor directed with a consummate art the Third Symphony of Beethoven, a Concerto of Bach, two pieces of Philipp, his beautiful
Fantaisie [Op. 62] and his *Ouverture espagnole*."[169] The public especially loved
the programs in which he was featured as both performer and conductor:

> Mr. Ch.-M. Widor left this week for Rome, where he is going to conduct . . .
> at the Academy of Saint Cecilia, a grand festival organized in his honor. . . .
> Here is the program, of the most varied and interesting: *Ouverture espagnole*;
> Chorale of Bach; Toccata and Fugue for Organ alone; Third Symphony for
> Orchestra [and organ]; Fifth Symphony for Organ alone; fragments from
> the score of *Conte d'avril.*[170]

Four articles for *Piano Soleil* resulted from this sojourn to Rome. For the
above program: "three rehearsals. Indeed, I found an orchestra so attentive,
so eager to do well and to follow the slightest indications of the baton, that
I would have been content with two rehearsals. A composer not begging for
additional preparation and finding that one works too hard—this is something
new."[171] At the conclusion of the concert, the gracious reception by Queen
Margherita (1851–1926) left a vivid impression: "Her Majesty loves and protects the arts. Her literary knowledge is as extensive as her musical erudition;
she plays the piano very well, speaks nearly all the European languages, and
even writes the language of Cicero with a rare elegance. She is blond and very
beautiful, very animated, and very popular in Italy."[172]

Among the highlights that Widor reported during his stay in Rome included
visits to the library of the Academy of Saint Cecilia, where he marveled at Monteverdi's *Orfeo*, first editions of Palestrina's works, and some polychoral music
that astonished him: "I remained imbued with admiration before the enormous score of a Mass for twelve choirs by Gregorio Bellabene, and before a
Fugue for six choirs by Raimondi."[173] At the Argentina Theater, Widor caught
a performance of *La Bohème* by Giacomo Puccini (1858–1924), whom he
described as "altogether remarkable and noticed all over the place, except in
Paris."[174] And then there was the awe-inspiring visit to the Sistine Chapel for a
service attended by Pope Leo XIII:

> It's quite difficult to get admitted to the ceremonies of the Sistine Chapel,
> the building being of relatively restricted dimensions, and the public, covet-
> ous of invitations, being more and more numerous.
>   Having been obligingly warned of this fact, I had applied to several influ-
> ential people, out of fear of missing the very rare occasion to see Leo XIII
> and the Roman curia. At the last moment, instead of one invitation—the

much awaited precious yellow ticket—five of them were brought to me, my five influential individuals having taken the trouble to solicit for me, and having been clever enough to succeed, everyone in his own way. . . .

I entered the chapel; a friendly guardian came to usher me into the space reserved for the chamberlains, right on the front row, to the right of the passage by which the cortege had to file.

. . . The uproar approached, one saw hands extended, handkerchiefs waving, and soon appearing in the distance, emerging into the Ducal Hall, carried on the sedan, a white form, a diaphanous figure, a sort of apparition, the real sight of the scene that painters and engravers have interpreted for us so often: it was Leo XIII. . . .

The sedan stopped at the foot of the altar, which was very simple, five candlesticks, no ornamentation, not one flower.

The Pope got out and knelt down; they took off his tiara and replaced it with a white miter, and then he mounted his throne to the right of the altar, and the Mass began.[175]

There were only thirty-two singers in that little gallery made famous by Palestrina, and since him, it has remained the same. Michelangelo died in 1564, Palestrina in 1594. One left a work without parallel on those walls of the Sistine Chapel; the other wrote immortal music for the ceremonies that they celebrate there. . . .

. . . The Mass was very well sung, as if the composer himself held the baton. In the *forte*, those thirty-two voices succeeded in giving the impression of absolute fullness and of filling the vast chapel as well as an orchestra or a powerful organ could.

The *Gradual* and the *Alleluia* were vocalized, as formerly, at the unison by two sopranists executing the ornaments of the text with a rare ensemble. In general, the choir sang perfectly in tune and, in spite of the length of the piece, remained faithful to the feeling of the mode. Never was there any instrumental accompaniment. It was just barely, if the choirmaster allowed himself to make the *la* of the tuning fork vibrate discretely before the beginning of the piece.[176]

The Offertory by Mustapha [the choirmaster] began well; the end seemed to me less good, a little long. It seemed that His Holiness was of my opinion, for I saw him twice stare at the gallery of singers, not without manifesting some restlessness. . . .

. . . During the whole duration of the service . . . I wasn't able to take my eyes off that extraordinary face.[177]

Deeply moved by the whole affair, Widor exclaimed: "When you attend a feast like that of the other day, you sense all at once, and not without emotion I admit, the idea of eternity."[178] Concluding his series of articles for *Piano Soleil*, there were still "a thousand things to tell" about Rome, including his search for Palestrina's tomb in Saint Peter's: "Baedeker seriously avouches to you that it is at the foot of the altar in the left transept. There remains no trace of it."[179]

Aside from those already mentioned, during this period Widor conducted or performed at festivals of his works throughout France: Lourdes, Dieppe, Lille, Lyon, Bordeaux, Versailles, Royan, Strasbourg, as well as numerous concerts in Paris. Usually, either Isidor Philipp or Francis Planté went with him as piano soloist, though occasionally Widor played the piano parts himself, as at the Salle Pleyel in Paris on March 21, 1899, when he performed in all four of his works on the program.[180] A review of the Royan concert typifies the manner in which Widor was received everywhere:

> The program, entirely composed of fragments from the works of the author of *La Korrigane*, was very brilliant from every point of view and crowned with complete success. Mr. Widor—recalled, applauded, and lauded—received a real ovation from an enthusiastic public, as much in the course of the performance of the program as at the end of the concert when the whole hall hailed his name.[181]

For a work requiring an organ soloist—such as his Op. 69 Third Symphony or later the *Sinfonia sacra*—Schweitzer, Vierne, or Dupré joined him, as in May 1899 when Vierne accompanied him to the neighboring German towns of Barmen-Elberfeld to play the solo part in the Third Symphony on the new organ of the Festival Hall: "The first day, the audience could not have welcomed the new work more favorably, and the next day the success took on the proportions of a real triumph, with cheering, wreaths, and orchestral fanfares."[182]

To Wallace Goodrich (1871–1952), then organist for the Boston Symphony and director of the New England Conservatory of Music, Widor described the organ in the Rome Academy of Saint Cecilia as "a German instrument from Ludwigsburg speaking slowly, pneumatic."[183] The Ludwigsburg firm of Walcker employed a tubular-pneumatic type of key action that was renowned for its sluggishness, especially when the wind chests were located a distance from the console.[184] As a vocal opponent to all but the sensitivity and precision of mechanical action, it is not surprising that Widor complained about the instrument's poor action.[185] And when the Academy of Saint Cecilia engaged Saint-Saëns to perform, he sought Widor's advice as to whether or not he could risk playing his *Rhapsodies bretonnes*, Op. 7, on that organ.[186] Widor delighted in being able to give his appraisal of the instrument:

> The organ of Saint Cecilia is quite complete; unfortunately its manufacture is very mediocre: a tubular system, asthmatic, albuminuric, ataxic, and all that you will want in "ic."
>
> The only passable reed stop in the récit expressif is the Trompette; as for the Hautbois, it's to it that I make reference in the Appendix of the Berlioz treatise—it's impossible to connect two sounds in a *moderato*![187]

After Widor's description, Saint-Saëns responded that he would not be performing his *Rhapsodies* in Rome![188]

Insofar as Widor represents the quintessential French romantic organ composer/performer, his thoughts on key action and touch are noteworthy:

> The solidity of the simple mechanism of the 18th century Organs has, so far, defied competition, and held its own against all modern systems, whether pneumatic or electric. Nothing can surpass it in principle, but if this principle has always been religiously respected by the great organ-builders, it is nevertheless true that its application has been greatly improved within the last 50 years.
>
> The ingenious invention of Barker, an English watchmaker, now allows of coupling together any number of keyboards without affecting the touch, which remains as light as that of an Érard Pianoforte. The sound is instantaneous; the will of the virtuoso encounters neither resistance nor surprise; his hand is in direct contact with the sonorous material, which he moulds at will, and which becomes his obedient servant.
>
> Could as much be said for the pneumatic or electric systems? Certainly not. They are like insulating bodies coming between the organist and the sound; he strikes a wooden keyboard, an unconscious piece of mechanism, which seems to transmit to another more distant piece of mechanism motions of only approximate precision. He can never be sure at what precise moment after the depression of a key a pipe will speak. The *virtuoso* is not in communication with a soul: he has to deal with an automaton. . . .
>
> Recently too, I stood dumbfounded before the wonderful invention of a Swiss inventor, who had conceived the idea of adapting the pneumatic action to the Swell. Of course, neither suppleness nor quick response was to be expected from this contrivance. It was impossible to execute a slow and progressive *crescendo*, or to stop the sound when it had reached a certain degree of strength. The barbarous bit of mechanism could only shut or open with a sudden jerk, like a shutter banging in a thunderstorm, and this was not the worst of it: the said mechanism was never up to time—the automaton was lazy. When he was needed, he put in an appearance two bars late. The wind began to blow when the storm was over.
>
> *Barbarous* seems too mild a term under the circumstances; such inventors should be brought before the assizes, and finish their days in prison. . . .
>
> However, what I am sure of, is that nothing equals a well-made mechanical action.[189]

—77—

"My 10th and last Symphony for Organ"

The ancient family home, constructed of the warm yellowish stone of the region, is located near Lyon, just outside the town of l'Arbresle at "Persanges,"

Savigny. Widor's sister, Marie, and her family lived there, and it provided him a welcome respite from the hectic pace of Paris and his travels about Europe and England. There, in the waning summer months, he could wander among nature's beauties and compose in peace. As his brother-in-law was often detained by his work in Lyon, "Widor assumed the role of master of the house, and his natural verve animated the conversations."[190] Though he lived with the family, his room was apart from the daily business of the household: "I appear at mealtime and then write as tranquilly as at rue Garancière," he wrote in 1886.[191] Widor described the countryside that inspired his thought during his familial summer sojourns:

> Every year, I spend the months of August and September in the department of the Rhône, in the middle of the mountains that separate the basin of the Saône from that of the Loire.
>
> The country is picturesque: some wooded summits in the most fanciful forms, some attaining close to a thousand meters in altitude; some pretty brooks running at the bottom of steep valleys; to the east, a vast indentation exposing the plateau of the Dombes, the great plane of la Bresse and, beyond the Rhône, the first foothills of the Alps; finally, in the far distance, closing the horizon is the massif of Mont Blanc.
>
> We are equidistant from a quite important market town, l'Arbresle, and a formerly famous village in the monastic records, Savigny. . . .
>
> . . . Stroll in the surrounding country; you will meet at each step the vestiges of a rich past: some astonishing remains, marvelously worked stones, faces, and compositions marked out by the chisel of skillful unknowns, from Charlemagne until Louis XIII.
>
> You will make a course in architecture for yourself.[192]

On one such stroll through the countryside Widor had the strange feeling of *déjà vu*—he had been there before. In his usual good-humored manner, he narrated: "Do you believe in the transmigration of souls? As for me, I have memories of having been a duck! Do you want evidence of it? Last autumn [1891] in the environs of Montereau, I was strolling in the woods in joyous and pleasant company. I had never been in the region that we were traversing, but I seemed to recognize it. I rediscovered some bushes, particularly some brooks, and with the instinct of an animal that comes back to the throw, I led my company to a certain pond where I recalled having paddled and splashed about."[193]

During his annual vacation in 1899, Widor completed Opuses 73 and 74.[194] Whereas he had introduced a plainsong theme into two movements of the *Symphonie gothique*, in the Op. 73 *Symphonie romane* he constructed a great cyclical organ symphony, permeating it with plainsong: the opening phrases of the Easter Gradual *Haec dies, quam fecit Dominus* (This is the day the Lord hath made) in the first, second, and fourth movements; the Easter

Sequence *Victimae Paschali laudes immolent Christiani* (To the Paschal victim let Christians offer songs of praise) in the third movement.

The idea of the *Symphonie romane* had germinated in the composer's thought for a considerable length of time; Dupré related: "The master often told us that this theme lay for more than a year on his table before he brought himself to develop it."[195] In a postscript to a letter dated November 2, 1898, Widor wrote to Wallace Goodrich: "I am beginning to work mentally on my 10th and last Symphony for organ, the *Symphonie romane*."[196] The autograph manuscript is dated July 20, 1899. In declaring this to be his last symphony, Widor must have felt it would represent his ultimate contribution to the solo repertoire of his instrument; it will be recalled, however, that he had stated a similar sentiment after completing the Eighth Symphony. Still, some twenty-five years after the *Romane*, he would find that he had yet something to express for his chosen instrument.[197]

Like the *Symphonie gothique* of 1895, the *Symphonie romane* is dedicated to a church—in this case, the remarkable eleventh-century Romanesque Basilica bearing the name of the first bishop of Toulouse: *Ad Memoriam Sancti Saturnini Tolosensis* (To the memory of Saint Sernin of Toulouse). Cavaillé-Coll had installed an exceptionally fine three-manual instrument beneath its barrel-vaulted ceiling in 1888 and followed it two years later with the large four-manual instrument at the Gothic church Saint Ouen. The musical style of Widor's last two symphonies not only reflect the architectural styles of the two churches to which they are dedicated, but they must also be viewed as homages to the organ builder whose unparalleled instruments provided the composer with a life of inspiration.

One of the problems that Widor faced in the *Romane* was how to incorporate a rhythmically flexible plainsong melody into a modern composition of rhythmic constraints. In the *Gothique*, he had largely treated the *Puer natus est* plainsong in a traditional cantus-firmus style—in long note values and pointed rhythms, mirroring the architecture of Saint Ouen. Upon further contemplation and study of plainsong, Widor formed the opinion that while the time-honored cantus-firmus treatment had validity, it generally opposed the very nature of fluid plainsong expression. In "La révision du plain-chant" (The revision of plainsong), he wrote:

> To divide the course of time according to the oscillations of the pendulum, to lean on the periodic return of the strong beat, to equalize the rhythms, to order, to specify precisely—all this is modern, of polyphonic necessity, [but] contrary to the ideal of plainsong.[198]

And in the "Avant-propos" to the *Symphonie romane*, he elaborated:

> The *Puer natus est*, of very pure lines and solid construction, lends itself—it couldn't be better—to polyphonic development; it's an excellent subject to treat.

Quite another is the *Haec dies*, an elegant arabesque adorning a text of a few words—about ten notes per syllable—a vocalization as elusive as a bird's song. . . .

The rhythmic independence of Gregorian chant conforms badly to the absolutism of our metronomic measure. Is there anything more delicate than to transcribe in modern notation the vocalizations of a Gradual or an Alleluia? So one turns to spoken explanations and commentaries for it: *Quasi recitative, rubato, espressivo, a piacere*, etc.[199]

Widor came to see that the "inexpressible suppleness" of a melismatic melody "as elusive as a bird's song" could not be served by cantus-firmus treatment; nor could it be served by casting it into a rhythmic mold governed by the strict rules and definitive practices advocated by some schools of thought on plainsong interpretation. In his article on plainsong revision, Widor argued vehemently against hard and fast rules of rhythmic interpretation, and in favor of rhythmic freedom as characterized by Dom Pothier's method. For Widor, Gregorian art was a "living tradition"—one that he had grown up with and loved his whole life.[200] He would not be swayed into any other interpretation.

In the *Symphonie romane*, Widor illustrated an ingenious handling of plainsong melody through a number of remarkably varied treatments, and he largely solved the innate stylistic conflict between free plainsong expression and traditional rhythmic constraint.[201] In the *Romane*'s preface, he explained his approach:

In order to impose so fluid a theme on the attention of the listener, there is only one means: to repeat it ceaselessly.

Such is the reason behind this first movement of the *Symphonie romane*, which, sacrificing all to the subject, risks here and there some timid attempt at development, only to abandon it quickly and get right back to the first idea.[202]

Consequently, Widor mostly treated appearances of the theme in the expressively free manner of a recitative—either in solo or pitted against only a pedal point. His "timid attempts at development" do not represent his central aim of retaining the fluid character, the "inexpressible suppleness" of the theme.

The spiritual ideal begun in the *Symphonie gothique* culminated five years later with the *Symphonie romane*. These two symphonies brought Widor's doctrinal beliefs full circle: in the *Gothique* he availed himself of the Christmas Introit—announcing the joy of the Nativity; in the *Romane* he chose the Easter Gradual—celebrating the wonder and glory of the Resurrection. Albert Schweitzer wrote of the profound impression created by Widor's last organ symphony:

When one May Sunday, still striving with technical problems he played for the first time in St. Sulpice the Symphonie romane, I felt with him that in this work the French art of organ playing had entered sacred art, and had experienced that death and that resurrection that every art of organ playing must experience when it wishes to create something enduring[203] (see fig. 15).

The Symphonie romane perfectly fits Widor's definition of a masterpiece: "The nature of a masterpiece is to remain eternally new; time glides by without leaving its mark on it."[204] As a complete synthesis of concert and liturgical styles in organ music, the Romane closed Widor's contribution to the symphonic genre of organ music. Albert Riemenschneider pronounced the following summation on the last two symphonies:

> Here the wealth of spiritual values as inherent in Widor come [sic] to a climax and we have before us masterpieces which will outlast any other organ compositions since Bach. Here particularly is the music of tomorrow and organists who are able to master the contents technically as well as spiritually have a field of investigation and study amazing in its outlook.[205]

In 1895 Widor remarked, "Since the beginning of the current season [in Paris], we have been able to hear I don't know how many 'Love-deaths' or 'Rides of the Valkyries.'"[206] Wagner's music was in the air, so to speak, and since his attendance at the premier of the Ring in 1876, Widor had been breathing the Wagnerian atmosphere deeply. As in parts of the Op. 42 Symphonies, several passages in the first and second movements of the Romane seem to stem, even if unconsciously, from Widor's knowledge of Wagner's music. Almost direct quotations from Tristan und Isolde are evident in the appearance of the "Isolde" motive—sometimes characterized as "full of sensuous yearning"[207]— and the arrival of the special sonority known as the "Tristan chord."[208] Coincidental with the completion of the Romane was the Paris premiere of Tristan und Isolde, on October 28, 1899.

In light of such passages, an appraisal that Vierne made of some of Widor's work seems particularly apropos: "one concedes in some scores an adulterated lyricism, dependent, almost to plagiarism, upon Franck and Wagner."[209] Even so, Widor always handled such passages in an individual manner and maintained dominion over the material by the assertion of his own strong musical personality. It should be recalled that he once wrote: "The brain of a composer is a sort of sponge that absorbs every day the multiple impressions of life, preserves them a longer or shorter period, and then, one day, reproduces them either spontaneously or under the influence of the will, with a relish, an intensity, a colouring, more or less powerful, or more or less personal."[210] As Beaumarchais pointed out, "one is always the son of someone."

In early January 1900, Widor traveled to Berlin with Isidor Philipp to conduct two orchestral concerts and a program of chamber music, and to play an organ recital—which seems to have been the premiere of the *Symphonie romane.*

An organ recital of Widor, at the "Gedächtniss Kirche" had drawn all that Berlin counts among serious musicians. Widor played marvelously the *Symphonie romane*, an unpublished work, and the *Fantaisie* and Fugue in G Minor [BWV 542] by Bach.[211]

As for the orchestral concerts, the Op. 69 Third Symphony, Op. 39 Piano Concerto, and *Ouverture espagnole* were among the works performed at the Philharmonic concerts.[212] The Prince of Hohenlohe (1819–1901) hosted Widor while in Berlin, and he dined with the upper echelon of titled folks.[213] By his own estimation, the concerts were everything he had hoped for:

The symphony was admirably performed and they recalled me three or four times after the Final.
The Piano Concerto had equally great success. There was a very large audience.
Yesterday there was an organ performance that went very well, and last evening a chamber music performance that was also very good.[214]

When Eugène de Bricqueville (1854–1933) reported the success of the Berlin concerts in the press, he made a poignant observation:

The endeavor of Messrs. Widor and Philipp is very interesting in the sense that the Germans believe they have the monopoly on the symphonic art and in chamber music, and readily persuade themselves that nothing of worth in this strict art has been produced elsewhere than in Germany.[215]

—78—

"I am willing to be hung"

An organist and collector/historian of musical instruments, Bricqueville had published a series of studies on the organ, and in 1899 he prevailed upon Widor to write a preface to his most recent monograph: *Notes historiques et critiques sur l'orgue.* Part of the preface aroused the ire of Alexandre Georges (1850–1938), a former student and harmony professor at the École Niedermeyer and the recently appointed organist of Saint-Vincent-de-Paul. A minor critical brawl ensued in the journal *Le Maître de Chapelle.* Out of strong personal conviction and because of his position and notoriety, Widor often felt empowered to state his views as though they were historical fact; and, like his former teacher, Fétis, his critique made law.[216] Of Widor, it was noted: "His general culture and the decidedness of his argumentation gave to his judgments an unquestionable authority."[217] The following excerpts from Widor's preface to Bricqueville's book sparked the controversy:

How long has it been since you regularly find pieces by Bach or Handel on the music rack of French organists? Do you see them on the first shelf of their little library in the organ loft? How long has it been since we have had some chance to hear, in entering a church, a chorale of the great Sebastian?

I hardly dare to admit the state of absolute virginity of the three immortal volumes of Chorales that I had the amazement to notice, ten years ago [1890], at the time of my first visit in one of our grand, national institutions. It was an old Richault edition; the binding had never been worked and resisted proudly; no prying hand had yet turned these immaculate leaves. They remained inviolate, no one having touched them.

The students knew nothing of the existence of this incomparable collection, a veritable breviary for musicians; they contented themselves to practice five or six fugues, always the same, like pianists practicing velocity studies, from the sole point of view of technique. . . .

. . . Thanks to the genius of Cavaillé-Coll and the authority of Lemmens, an organ school without rival in the world today was formed on the banks of the Seine. From this school of our national Conservatory have recently come Vierne, Libert, Tournemire, Runner, Bouval, Schmitt, Quef, Cœdès, Maquaire, Mulet, Jacob, etc. Vierne, who just produced his remarkable first symphony, of such elevated style, of such noble architecture, and of such profound artistic feeling; Libert, organist at Saint-Denis; Tournemire at Sainte-Clotilde; Runner at la Madeleine; Bouval at Saint-Pierre-de-Chaillot; Schmitt at Saint-Ignace; Quef at Saint-Laurent; Cœdès at Saint-Leu; [Auguste] Maquaire [1872–1906] at Gerson; Jacob at Notre-Dame-de-la-Gare; Mulet at Saint-Pierre-de-Montrouge; quite a pleiad of musicians of whom, moreover, one can appreciate the tendencies and observe the worth in the interesting periodic collection that Leduc publishes. . . .[218]

It's not without some chauvinistic pride that we mention the results obtained. It's not without a little thrill of ironic contentment—let's not let any of it show—that we see Americans, English, even Germans come here to study the art of the master of Eisenach. . . .

For ten or fifteen years, it is here that they come to perfect themselves and that they are little by little making the habit of pitching their tent without thinking of going farther. They now consider Paris as a musical last stop.[219]

Singling out the students of the Conservatory organ class as the torchbearers of an "organ school without rival in the world today," Widor tacitly ignored any others. Orpha Ochse points out, however, "Lemmens's techniques and his emphases on the performance of composed music and on Bach as the cornerstone of organ repertoire were the bases of organ instruction at the Niedermeyer School long before Widor promoted the same ideas at the Paris Conservatory in 1890."[220] Writing an indignant "Response to a Preface of Mr. Ch. Widor," Georges mauled Widor over what he took to be an out and out attack on the École Niedermeyer, an institution that, since its founding in 1853, had as its goal to train choir masters and organists for placement in the principal churches of French dioceses:

> I was astonished to read a short preface of Mr. Widor, where bad faith is displayed in a hurtful manner.
> It is really too easy for him to rest on a reputation as a great organist that brings him students, to claim the right to criticize, to cut and to want to tear to pieces some worthy and respectable things that are all the more respectable and worthy because they have always been above all the coteries of which Mr. Widor has sometimes known how to draw profit.
> These worthy and respectable things are, in their great simplicity, the École Niedermeyer and the musical education that the students receive there.[221]

Georges did not surmise that Widor's comment concerning the unopened volumes of Bach chorales at "one of our grand national institutions" was actually a reference to the Conservatory at the time he arrived in 1890 to take over César Franck's organ class. Georges mistakenly inferred that Widor was pointing to the Niedermeyer School and perceived lacunas in its teaching: "It's certainly not of the Conservatory that Mr. Widor wants to speak—he would not dare to think so ill of it *today*. Therefore, I don't see at this period any other grand musical institution in France than the École Niedermeyer."[222] Stating that the Niedermeyer students had "never played anything other than Bach, Handel, and Mendelssohn," Georges related:

> Richault's son told Mr. Gustave Lefèvre [1831–1910] thirty years ago that without the [Niedermeyer] School, he would not have sold a piece of S. Bach, which proved that the Conservatory—where Mr. Widor (since he is professor there) finds that everything is for the best—was still not familiar with [Bach]; moreover, it is simple to make inquiries and know that at that period Mr. Benoist was professor of organ there, and that other than his music or that of Baptiste, they knew nothing of the great Sebastian.
> The Niedermeyer School is absolutely the only school that made known the great classic masters in a time when people gave little attention to their existence.[223]

In his diatribe against "the malevolence of Mr. Widor," Georges continued at some length to justify the Niedermeyer School and its long tradition of teaching Bach, and to offer a list of its own celebrated graduates:

I still have a thousand things to say to prove the error in which Mr. Widor is found concerning what the Niedermeyer School has done and is still doing. Let him ask *Maître* Saint-Saëns, Mr. Clément Loret—organ professor in this school for forty years, Gabriel Fauré—his colleague in the composition classes at the Conservatory, Messager, Périlhou, Lippacher, Stoltz, Planchet, Letocart, etc., Gigout—one of the most celebrated organists and unquestionably the most skillful among improvisers, and many others, former students of the school such as A. Claussmann at Clermont-Ferrand, Kotzul, Meyer at Roubaix, Dubois at Tourcoing, Deplantay, Delaroqua at Lille, and all those whose names don't come to my pen, and who are *titulaires* of the *grandes orgues* of cathedrals around the country.

To finish, I will add that thanks to all the former students—today spread out to the four corners of France—a serious improvement has taken place in music education, and that when a school has had the honor of producing an artistic movement of that kind and a decentralization of that kind, one should think twice about it before putting on contemptuous airs to speak of it.[224]

Published in the next issue of *Le Maître de Chapelle*, a letter from Widor to Gustave Lefèvre, director of the Niedermeyer School, sought to clear the air:

The article of Mr. Alex. Georges of last January 1 just made me reread the preface to the Bricqueville brochure. Now, if an attack, an innuendo, or an implication chargeable to you or your institution is found there, I am willing to be hung.

In speaking of Cavaillé-Coll, in verifying the benefits of the tradition reestablished by Lemmens, I have no more thought of the Niedermeyer School—and that I affirm to you—than I would think of the Monge School, for example, if I had to make a lecture on Edison.

What? I do not have the right, without being accused of hostility toward X or Y, to certify that there are traditions, to tell where they come from and to show what they produce? I do not have the right, without being suspected of personal interest, to establish a list of organ pieces appearing each year and to publish the outcome? It would be an act of bad faith to point out this pleiad of composers of whom the oldest is not twenty-five years old; an act of coterie to dare to support, out of all that the publishers have given us in 1899, which work is the most merited, the most solid, the most made to honor the French school?[225]

Please understand, Sir, that I have never had the least desire to engage in controversy; artists have better things to do.

I remember in former days having written some laudatory things addressed to your institution. When I succeeded Franck, my first care was to form a library of the most necessary works for the organ class; you will be able to find there the collection of the *Maîtrise* and the treatise on the *Accompagnement du plain-chant* by d'Ortigue and Niedermeyer. Last year, solicited by your organ professor, Mr. Loret, I immediately set to work on his behalf to have the [Legion of Honor's] red ribbon bestowed on him, and a few days later I received the expected good news from the Head Office.

What more do you want? Doesn't this suffice? Don't you feel that I, no longer being an organ professor at the Conservatory or elsewhere, can say things without any constraint?

Reassure Mr. Alex. Georges, in speaking to him, that I have no recollection of having visited the Niedermeyer School; and, if politeness requires that I finally respond to him directly, I will not fear to let him know that I judge his collection of songs very superior to his prose.

Monsieur director, please accept again the assurance of my least hostile feelings and my very sincere consideration.[226]

Ill-contented not to have the final volley, Georges fired back:

Mr. Widor writes to Mr. Gustave Lefèvre, who at first had no hand in my first response to his preface; if it's to express to him his least hostile feelings and to relate that he employed his influence to have Mr. Cl. Loret decorated, it's quite weak! The wheels of his friendship lack oil, it seems to me.

. . . No one has ever disputed Mr. Widor's right to have his preferences, and even to believe that outside himself and his little clique there is no salvation.

But, when one wants to speak seriously of traditions, of their causes and their consequences, it is not permitted to ignore a school that has won the admiration of all the masters of such repute as to judge it, and that for the past fifty years has filled France with eminent artists, organists, and choir masters as seriously trained as are most students of the École Niedermeyer. . . .

All this would not have great importance if Mr. Widor were sincere and able to admit that the sun doesn't only shine for a few. . . .

. . . Today I want to speak only of the École Niedermeyer, which until now has always kept itself too much out of the way of flashy publicity. And in order to prove its superiority, if I were the director of it, I would propose for this year, in one of the great expositions halls, a *Grand International Match*, where all the students of the organ schools in the world would come to make themselves heard exclusively in the works of J. S. Bach.

What does Mr. Widor think of that? It's perhaps the best way to put everything in its place.[227]

Deciding not to respond further, Widor stepped out of the argument. History would confirm whether or not the line of Conservatory organ students was without rival.

Many years later Georges assumed quite a different attitude when he found himself needing to plead for Widor's help. Nominated for the Prix Rothschild in 1923, Georges found out that some members of the Academy objected to his candidature since he had won the prize before. He wrote to Widor that he had only been a partial recipient and that the war had left him in a financially precarious situation: "If in this circumstance I could hope for your support, I would be very honored and very happy for it, and with this hope I ask you, dear *maître*, to accept all my deepest gratitude."[228] Widor's response is not known, but it would have been in character for him to lend support to a struggling musician, regardless of any past enmity.

—79—

Choral and Variations: "The happiest arrival"

Widor's fascination with the harp, that "sort of magnificent piano that would not have dampers," as he once described it,[229] gave rise to his next important composition: Choral and Variations, Op. 74, for Harp and Orchestra. In 1897, the Parisian firm of Pleyel developed a chromatic harp—an instrument with one string for each semitone—as an alternative to the familiar pedal harp that Érard had introduced in 1810. Widor penned an article tracing the harp's history from antiquity, and initially described the merits of the new instrument.[230] Quite naturally, two camps immediately formed around each type of harp. The Brussels Conservatory—supplied by Pleyel—advocated the chromatic harp, while the Paris Conservatory—supplied by Érard—and its professor Alphonse Hasselmans (1845–1912), an eminent figure in the revival of harp playing at the turn of the twentieth century, defended the traditional pedal harp. Hasselmans succeeded in having several significant works composed for him, including one by his conservatory colleague Widor. Eventually the new chromatic harp lost favor, and by 1911 Widor had disavowed it: "no orchestra, no serious theater has been able to embrace it."[231]

Composed in 1899 during Widor's annual summer respite in l'Arbresle, the Choral and Variations received its premiere by Hasselmans in March 1900 at Érard's:[232]

> The great, very great success of the concert was for the Choral and varia-tions. . . . This piece is the happiest arrival. Of great allure or elegant charm in their free and easy form, the variations follow in succession, the harp sketching, the orchestra completing, or inversely, the theme broadly exposed by the orchestra and passing again to the harp, where it is embel-lished in fine arabesques, leading to a warm conclusion, colorful, full of strength and vigor.[233]

Widor's Choral and Variations was joined by future important contributions to the repertoire for harp and orchestra by Debussy, Maurice Ravel (1875–1937), and Pierné. He later arranged it for harp and piano, and Isidor Philipp arranged it for two pianos. Thirty years after the Concerto's premiere, audiences were still enraptured, and critic Henri de Curzon referred to it as "fresh, limpid, and full of light."[234]

—80—

"An organ *virtuoso* is only a savage among organists"

Louis Vierne succeeded Charles Tournemire as Widor's assistant at Saint-Sulpice in February 1892,[235] and he had assisted him with the Conservatory organ class; the bond between Widor and Vierne was as close as that usually reserved for father and son. Widor guided Vierne in every step of his career, much as Cavaillé-Coll had done for Widor. When Eugène Sergent, the old organist of Notre-Dame, fell ill, the cathedral officials asked Widor to recommend a substitute. There was only one choice in his mind, and he strongly encouraged Vierne to fill the temporary post:

> If I were considering only my own interest, I wouldn't suggest it, because you're accustomed to my organ, [and can be of use to me. B]ut we must think of the future, and there's every reason to believe that Sergent won't return to his post. It would seem to me that the title of organist of Notre-Dame, borne by an artist resolved to revive its prestige, ought to tempt you. I see it as a very important opportunity for the advancement of your career. You must accept it.[236]

At first, Vierne said he had little inclination to accept the offer, but he "finally gave in to Widor—Ah, yes, as always!"[237]

> I had been playing the organ at Saint-Sulpice for eight years, had become attached to it, and was proud of being the deputy of a man I admired and loved. However, as I did not want to disregard this advice any more than any other he had given me, I finally yielded to Widor's counsel.[238]

Sergent died soon after and the cathedral chapter announced a competition in order to cut short the intrigues that were being worked on a few of the clergy by some of the ninety-eight applicants. Widor knew his former pupil's playing to a tee and insisted that Vierne enter the competition, assuring him that he had every chance of succeeding.[239] The ten-member jury presided over by Widor included Dallier, Guilmant, and Gigout. After listening to the five anonymous applicants who ultimately registered to take part in the competition, the jury members cast their votes unanimously in favor of Vierne.[240] With his customary thick-nibbed pen, Widor scrawled the jury's recommendation to the chapter of Notre-Dame on the sheet of manuscript paper carrying the improvisation themes. He boldly signed his name as the first signatory, putting such finality to the decision that the nine other diminutive signatures appear superfluous.[241] Widor lost his assistant at Saint-Sulpice, but saw his pupil's superior potential rewarded.[242] In the person of Louis Vierne, Widor's precious tradition was installed in the most important cathedral position in France (see fig. 16). Tournemire noted, "Vierne, particularly, thoroughly assimilated Lemmens's pure technique transmitted by Widor; . . . In class, he was the absolute submissive vis-à-vis his maître, to whom he was extremely devoted."[243] Widor continued to shepherd his former student in the many years to come; to Vierne he was "an initiator and guide in all domains, as much spiritual and literary as musical."[244] Tragically, Vierne would die only four months after his *maître*.

When Widor visited Russia in 1896, he had become quite friendly with the director of the Moscow Conservatory, Vassily Safonoff. Safonoff planned to construct a new conservatory building with concert hall, and at Widor's suggestion, he went to Paris to order a new Cavaillé-Coll organ for the hall.[245] In 1898 Charles Mutin took over the Cavaillé-Coll firm and the new organ for the Moscow Conservatory marked the beginning of his illustrious career. Ready in mid-March 1900, the instrument was put through its paces when Widor went to the Mutin (formerly Cavaillé-Coll) factory and played his *Symphonie gothique* and Fifth Symphony before a select group of musicians invited by Mutin.[246] After its installation in 1901, Safonoff invited Widor to Moscow to play the inauguration on April 11:

> The new great hall of the Moscow Conservatory has just been musically inaugurated by Mr. Charles Widor. The excellent artist was the first to be heard on the superb organ that a rich citizen of Moscow offered to the Conservatory, and his success was extraordinary. Mr. Widor held the audience for more than two hours under the spell of his brilliant execution. Upon general demand, he had to give, in addition, a popular matinee, at the end of which he was hailed.[247]

Memberships in the Order of Saint Stanislas and the Imperial Society of Music were bestowed upon Widor at the inauguration ceremony for the great hall.[248] Upon his return to Paris, he wrote an article for Le Ménestrel entitled "Le nouveau conservatoire de Moscou" (The new Moscow Conservatory).[249] It is interesting for its description of the new facility and summary of the conservatory's innovative program of study. The twenty-five-hundred-seat concert hall and its organ earned Widor's highest commendation, and he modestly attributed the tremendous success of his recitals to the organ itself:

Of all the concert halls known, this one appears to me the most successful for acoustics. The power and attractiveness of the orchestra, the splendor of the organ, the delicacy and beauty of the voice, the fullness in sound of a piano or a harp are manifested there with an unparalleled intensity. Several times after rehearsing, I enjoyed playing the Schröder baby grand located on the platform, and not for an instant did I feel the need to force the attack of the key in order to augment its effect. In this enormous hall it was as in an ordinary salon—the same clarity and fullness of sonority. . . .

The organ that was just inaugurated . . . is of such mechanical perfection, attractiveness, and variety and richness of timbre that it has immediately been classed as among the most beautiful in Europe. . . . Its effect was extraordinary. After a long program composed exclusively of early and modern works special to the instrument, without any assistance from singers or foreign virtuosos, it was necessary, so to speak, to begin the performance afresh, and play on and on in order to respond to the calls of an insatiable audience. And the same two days later at the public concert: the performance, which was supposed to last an hour and a half, was prolonged in actual fact close to three hours. They scarcely knew in Russia anything but some mediocre instruments . . . : you can judge it from the surprise and emotion of those two thousand, five hundred listeners in the presence of the organ constructed by the most famous firm, the most justly admired in the entire world, the Cavaillé-Coll firm, which Mr. Charles Mutin currently directs and which is not declining under his direction: never a similar triumph for French industry.[250]

Widor attained a similar success in Warsaw on November 15, when, as part of the inauguration of a new concert hall there, he conducted the Warsaw Philharmonic Society in a performance of his Third Symphony, *Conte d'avril*, and the *Ouverture espagnole*; following this he went to the organ and closed the program with his Fifth Symphony and Bach's Passacaglia:[251]

The success of the festival organized in honor of Ch.-M. Widor . . . was very great. . . . The two thousand listeners who pressed into the elegant hall hailed Mr. Widor, who had to prolong the performance, upon general demand, by adding several pieces not listed on the program.[252]

The thought of an organist holding throngs of thousands entranced and demanding more is difficult to imagine in the twenty-first century. Although a different era, Widor had an artistic charisma that captivated audiences, as confirmed by one review after another. Yet, the flashy sort of performer that one might visualize as attracting public adulation is exactly what Widor was not; he once complained to Albert Schweitzer of having been labeled that kind of organist: "Just think, I have been insulted. I have been called in a magazine an organ *virtuoso*. But I am a genuine organist. An organ *virtuoso* is only a savage among organists."[253]

Critics for the Rome journal *Santa Cecilia* complained that French church music was too dramatic and not adaptable to religious functions: "It is a well-established fact that the [French] school often makes a deplorable confusion of styles. . . . Reform will be more difficult in Paris than elsewhere. The great masters like Widor understand only virtuosism, and the religiosity of music is for them boring."[254] Stunned, Widor fired back in a letter to *Le Ménestrel*:

> Permit me to protest in front of your readers, having nothing to say directly to an article of such bad faith. The *Santa Cecilia* is not at all unaware that I wrote against virtuosism in church music in general, and in plainsong in particular (*Le Correspondant*, July 10, 1901); as to the motets that I have published, their ideal is quite serious.
>
> A first year student can assure the *Santa Cecilia* that in Paris, as in Rome, we consider virtuosism as a means and not as an end; that the greatest artist, in our eyes, is the one who best covers his "devices."
>
> In the painting of Innocent X in the Doria Gallery, is it the person in the red cape or rather the painting's background that interests us?
>
> Is it the interior framework or rather the cupola of Saint Peter's?
>
> What a strange idea to attack contemporaries in order to attribute to them some theories in absolute contradiction to those that they spend their lives to defend! As long as they wander about this little planet, these contemporaries can reply: Don't be in such a hurry, wait at least until we are dead.[255]

In a rejoinder, the *Santa Cecilia* explained what it meant by the "virtuosism" of Mr. Widor: it was the feeding of his personal comforts in a place of sanctity by having the organ loft at Saint-Sulpice carpeted and electric lights installed! Of that, Vierne confessed: "I sinned with envy when I compared my set-up [at Notre-Dame] with that at Saint-Sulpice. His tribune was covered with a thick red wool carpet and the metal parts of his console were nickel-plated and shined like new. Thanks to his care, the organ at Saint-Sulpice looked like new, although it had not been touched up since 1862."[256] The editors of *Le Ménestrel* closed the journalistic argument with *Santa Cecilia*: "Good journal, you are right, these are abominable things. The damp straw of the jails and some little bit of smoky candle, this is all that is necessary to the right-thinking and truly orthodox organist. Widor, you are only a tyrant!"[257]

To Widor, a virtuoso consciously sought his own fame, an idea he personally held repugnant. He rather wanted "to hide behind the objectivity of the holy instrument and let it speak as if it spoke for itself, *ad majorem Dei gloriam* [to the greater glory of God]."[258] At a time when organ consoles were being placed so the audience could view the organist, Widor wrote: "the organist must not be visible because it is not he, but the spirit of the m*aître* [composer] that must speak to the listeners; the performer is only an anonymity, disappearing behind the work."[259] Widor's concept of organ playing far transcended the popular emotionalism that so many of his predecessors had displayed; for him, organ playing was a serious mode of musical expression not to be confused with entertainment. When once invited to dabble in a popular style, he flatly refused: "At the Théâtre des Champs Elysées, [there's] an evening with films and music by the Colonial Institute on the subject of . . . all the epidemics from the coast of Africa. They asked me to play the organ during the showing of the films; as that's not my 'element,' I asked Vallombrosa (a regular cinemagoer) to replace me."[260]

Schweitzer related Widor's concept of the true art of the organist:

"Organ playing," Widor once said to me on the organ bench at Notre-Dame as the rays of the setting sun streamed through the dusk of the nave in transfigured peace, "is the manifestation of a will filled with a vision of eternity. All organ instruction, both technical and artistic, has as its aim only to educate a man to this pure manifestation of the higher will. This will, expressed by the organist in the objectivity of his organ, should overwhelm the hearer. He who cannot master the great, concentrated will in the theme of a Bach fugue—so that even the thoughtless hearer cannot escape from it, but even after the second measure grasps and comprehends it whether he will or not—he who cannot command this concentrated, peaceful will imparting itself so powerfully, may be a great artist in spite of this but is not a born organist. He has mistaken his instrument; for the organ represents the *rapprochement* of the human spirit to the eternal, imperishable spirit, and it is estranged from its nature and its place as soon as it becomes the expression of the subjective spirit."[261]

That Widor was a "born organist" is indisputable; he knew how to exact every nuance from the instrument. Inspired by Widor's artistry, critic Alfred Herlé offered a poignant description of Widor's inauguration of Mutin's rebuild of the Merklin organ at Saint-Philippe-du-Roule in Paris:

Seated to the right of the master, in the organ gallery, I contemplated him in the transfiguration that took place in him when his fingers—lean and sinewy, almost diaphanous, having a disconcerting acrobatism (it's intentional that I did not say virtuosity, the word had been above my thought)—coursed over the keyboard, always with the same impeccable articulation—a very refined articulation—in playing the worst difficulties. Oh, the marvelous and brilliant artist! No one who has listened to him has heard perfection brought to a similar apogee. How all the details are enhanced; and what power, what vigor in the grand exclamation of the thousand united voices, gushing forth from the thunderous breath of the immense instrument! And what infinite sweetness when, on the *récit*, quietly supported by the *positif*, the dialogues on the string timbres interchange: the distant sounds of joyful angels in heaven above—one doesn't know from whence they are perceived.[262]

When Vierne became assistant organist at Saint-Sulpice, Widor urged him to come to the organ as often as possible to observe and learn. Widor's command of the instrument left an indelible impression on his young pupil and countless others as well:

I used and abused that invitation and profited from it immensely! There I heard performances I still marvel at today. He is certainly the greatest organist that I have ever heard. To be sure, there are organists today who have as fine a technique, but none with his authority, his sense of grandeur, his imperious mastery. And whether he played a piece or improvised, his formidable virtuosity never became other than a means of expression. What expression! What breadth of phrasing! What magnificent legato! What supreme taste in the use of light and shade! One always felt in him an unshakable will, fiercely intent on capturing the listener's attention through absolutely musical means. He could be majestic without grandiloquence, elegant without affectation, austere without coldness, fiery while remaining absolute master of the rhythm. His playing was "alive" without being hurried. His staccato was exact, but never too short. He attacked and released chords with precision, but he avoided detaching them quickly, a practice which reduces organ playing to a lamentably degraded imitation of the orchestra or piano. Even in rapid chords he always had "tone." . . .

He played the pedals marvelously without ever looking at his feet; nor did he look at them when activating the *pédales de combinaison*.[263]

In the eyes of many of his contemporaries, Widor appeared as merely an organ virtuoso, "like the Germans," some said. It was denied that he had the gift of improvisation. This is absurd and unjust. On the contrary, he improvised with splendid craftsmanship and a fertile imagination, served by a perfectly disciplined control of the elements he wished to put into it. I remember magnificent sorties at the end of High Mass or Vespers at Saint-Sulpice. I must say, moreover, that up to the final day of his incumbency he manifested the same lucid gift, and that the last sortie I heard him improvise last year (1934) [this would have been in 1933] left me marveling as always— with reason, I assure you.[264]

Mr. Widor demonstrates his inspiration still elsewhere than in his advertised works. I mean in the innumerable occasions that the Catholic liturgy offers him to exercise his talent as improviser. He excels in developing a theme; we have heard him at Saint-Sulpice take up such and such a motive by Handel—the Alleluia from *Messiah* or a chorus from *Judas Maccabeus*—that the choir was barely finishing. The organist then opened all the sails to the breath from on high, the harmony overflowed in broad waves and the hundred voices of the organ united in a sonorous and triumphal ensemble. The main phrase reappeared as appropriate in all the keys, with all the timbres and in all the forms, and all the series of the musical ideas were so logical and rigorous that it gave the illusion of a piece written all at once. This talent, let us not ignore, assumes on the part of the performer, besides the art of learned improvisation, an extraordinary power of adroitness and a perfect understanding of the instrument—virtuosity, in short. Mr. Widor possesses it, and one knows to what degree.[265]

At [Saint-]Sulpice I was . . . impressed by an improvisation by Widor. . . . One is tremendously affected by anything that he does on or for the organ; it is so broadly conceived, and executed in such an imposing manner, so woven polyphonically that its structure is fully assured and so colored with musical pigments that it meets the taste of even musical sensualists.[266]

In moments of softness, his harmonic language was consonant, very pure, and almost bare. In times of strength, his "sorties" were struck with the stamp of a deliberate and powerful rhythm. The modulations remained restrained, except towards the end of the improvisation when an "escape" in a distant key—as encountered in the works of Beethoven's "first style"—produced the greatest effect.[267]

Widor was one of the greatest of improvisers, and on several occasions I have heard him improvise movements of such splendour as to rival the greatest movements of his symphonies.[268]

Widor, Anton Bruckner, and Igor Stravinsky shared one prominent aspect as composers: they all tended toward revision, though for different reasons. None of them seemed to be concerned with retaining the stylistic integrity of a work's original conception. Widor affirmed, "it is necessary to be very severe on oneself and to criticize oneself much more rigorously than one would others."[269] A favorite anecdote that Widor enjoyed relating to his composition pupils concerned the famous pastelist and cartoonist, Charles Léandre (1862–1930), popular for his caricatures of celebrities. The story draws an interesting parallel to Widor's own process of molding a musical composition until he had fashioned it to suit his ultimate vision:

Once a lady told Léandre: "What an extraordinary talent you possess! Your last cartoon of King Edward VII is simply wonderful. But how can you catch the expression, the personality of your subject so admirably, in a few minutes and with so few strokes of your pencil?"

"A few minutes?" Léandre retorted, "You will be surprised if I tell you, Madame, that this caricature cost me a week of hard work. And I read six books in order to assimilate the king's character!"

Then he explained how he had worked it out gradually, reducing his original sketch, erasing one line here, one touch there, condensing, cutting down until indeed, seemingly a few strokes remained, but these were the essential ones that formed the synthesis and conveyed a lifelike impression.

"One can proceed musically in the same way," Widor said.[270]

And he did; but Widor's was a lifelong process of reducing, erasing, adding, condensing, and cutting, as clearly seen when one compares the various editions that he issued of his first eight organ symphonies. Not often did he feel the certainty that he expressed in a letter to Théophile Gautier, editor of the *Figaro Illustré*: "'Nuit d'été' is finished. It has four full pages. I hope that it will not be too long, for it would be impossible to cut one measure! If need be, I would give you something else."[271]

In 1901, Widor published a new edition of the Op. 13 and Op. 42 Organ Symphonies under the heading: "Nouvelle édition, revue, corrigée et entière-ment modifiée par l'auteur (1900–1901)" (New edition, revised, corrected, and entirely modified by the author [1900–1901]). Indeed, numerous modi-fications appeared in the new edition, including such major ones as the deletion of three movements (the Scherzo from the Second Symphony, the Fugue from the Third Symphony, the Prélude from the Eighth Symphony), and the addition of an entirely new movement (the *Salve Regina* to the Sec-ond Symphony). Changes of the broadest scope were effected in Opus 13, now in its fourth edition. Widor repeatedly imposed his mature style on these early works, and their nascent stylistic quality seems, at times, compromised under his all-too-constant scrutiny. The new *Salve Regina*, for instance, is a product of his late style—that which permeates the *Gothique* and *Romane*. With its plainsong theme, the movement seems ill-placed in the Second Sym-phony, a work conceived under the completely different aesthetic of thirty years earlier. This stylistic discontinuity seems to have escaped his otherwise discriminating judgment.

—81—

Technique de l'orchestre moderne

Widor's *Technique de l'orchestre moderne*, published in 1904, is a modernization of the *Traité d'instrumentation* by Hector Berlioz. Portions of the Berlioz *Traité*, written in 1843, eventually became superannuated as advances were made in the design of some instruments; consequently, Berlioz's publishers commis-sioned Widor to bring the work up to date. In its preface, Widor wrote:

> In the last fifty years or so, the mechanism of most instruments has under-gone notable progress, and at the same time the orchestral palette has been enriched with previously unsuspected sonorities. Whoever, after having stud-ied the *Traité* of Berlioz, wants to proceed from theory to practice, quickly notices inexactitudes and gaps that bear witness to the age of the book.
>
> Now, it is not necessary that such a work should grow old. . . .
>
> The present work is, therefore, only an appendix coming after a work that, above all, must be religiously respected and that we have not touched. It is a simple postscript establishing the current state of orchestral instruments, their range, and their means.[272]

A skilled orchestrator with a profound knowledge of the art gained through years of studying and listening to countless scores by masters past and present, Widor found the project to be a labor of joy:[273]

> Nothing has more interested me than to write this Technique; nothing [was] more instructive than to lay each instrument down as it were on an operating table in order to dissect and autopsy it: at every moment there were surprises, enigmas, acoustical problems, problems escaping analysis.[274]

Acoustical phenomena interested Widor a great deal, and he may have been the first to emphasize the importance of acoustical study to a true understanding of orchestration.[275] He poured painstaking care into the *Technique*; and, especially for its exhaustive examples for each instrument, it won high critical acclaim. Arthur Pougin, on the other hand, criticized Widor for not having consulted a violinist when writing the chapter on the violin, which resulted in some chords being given as practical when Pougin judged them not to be.[276] In response, Widor wrote to the editor of *Ménestrel* that he had consulted on every combination with Pierre Sechiari, concertmaster of the Lamoureux orchestra: "Permit me to defend myself: no more with the quartet than with the other instruments, I have not acted without surety and affirmed nothing without proof."[277]

Widor's familiarity with orchestral scores by a multitude of composers is greatly in evidence: there are excerpts by over thirty composers from Bach, Mozart, Beethoven, and Schumann to Wagner, Brahms, Strauss, and a plethora of French composers. Perhaps surprising is Widor's inclusion of at least ten excerpts from his own works: *Conte d'avril* (flute), Introduction and Rondo (clarinet), Symphony No. 2 (bassoon), Symphony No. 3 (horn), *Ouverture espagnole* (cornet), *La Korrigane* (trombone), Choral and Variations (harp), Violin Concerto (violin), Cello Concerto (cello), *Les pêcheurs de Saint-Jean* (double bass). Soon translated into several languages—including Spanish, English, German, and Russian—the *Technique* became a trusted orchestration handbook for many a composer. Such a master of orchestration as Maurice Ravel "always had at hand the *Technique of the modern orchestra* of Widor—an aid to memory where he found the list of trills and passages playable on each instrument."[278]

Of particular interest was the new chapter authored by Widor on the organ. In that area, he did not hesitate to assert his enlightened knowledge of the King of Instruments to correct the "inexactitudes and gaps" of Berlioz; he wrote:

> It is quite stinging to profess, in the appendix of a *Traité*, doctrines in absolute contradiction with the ideas in this *Traité*. This will not go without some astonishment on the part of the reader.

But, as Beethoven says: "*it must be*" [*es muss sein*]. I find myself forced to do it here in this chapter.

By whom was Berlioz informed, of what organist had he the misfortune to ask advice? I have not been able to find out, although I quite often endeavored to rouse the recollections of Aristide Cavaillé-Coll, even reproaching him for his indifference when being in frequent contact with the *maître* he would have been able, better than anyone else, to bring him up to speed.[279]

The chapter covers a variety of topics, the first of which is the amazing "Enregistreur Harmonique"—Cavaillé-Coll's invention for the study of harmonics, resultant tones, and their application to organ building.[280] Widor also discussed the need for a proper distribution of mixtures (he called them "mutations"), the virtues of the Barker machine, the worth of the expression box, and other mechanical systems that rendered the organ artistically manageable.[281] The relationship between the organ and orchestra that Berlioz described as adversarial, Widor healed into a harmonious union:

We are very far from the alleged antipathy between "the Emperor and the Pope" of whom Berlioz speaks. There's no longer anything like that today. Moreover, in pondering it a bit and thinking it over more carefully, has this antipathy ever really existed? Wouldn't this here again be the fault of the ignorant cicerone? . . .

If Berlioz were still living, he would repudiate his bygone ideas, or rather the ideas that someone so unjustly suggested to him.[282]

—82—

Second Concerto for Piano and Orchestra: "Refined and very modern"

A space of nearly thirty years separated Widor's two piano concertos. The intervening Op. 62 *Fantaisie* for Piano and Orchestra, premiered on February 28, 1889,[283] had received dozens of performances by Isidor Philipp, Francis Planté, Maurice Dumesnil (1886–1974) and others; the new Second Concerto, Op. 77, most likely came as a result of these pianists' urgings. Philipp found that "Widor's personality, at the same time sound and elegant, serene and noble, showed itself in its entirety" in these two works: "The Fantaisie . . . shows his unfailing good taste, the [Second] Concerto contains refined and very modern innovations."[284]

During his annual vacations at his family home in Persanges, cradled in the midst of the French countryside, Widor indulged his love of walking through the natural surroundings of the region with its craggy cliffs, rumbling rivulets, and peaceful ponds. The touch of nature fed his creative spirit. Shortly after the Second Concerto's composition, the press noted that it had been given the suggestive title "Tapage nocturne" (*Nocturnal Uproar*), and ventured that "it will certainly make an uproar in the world."[285] Philipp played the premiere under Widor's direction in 1905:

> Mr. Ch.-M. Widor gave the premiere of a Concerto for Piano and Orchestra, recently composed, and which will certainly count among the best modern productions. The work is complex, and one would not know how to analyze it in its details upon a simple hearing; the orchestra, well wrought, often plays a preponderant role; the piano is an integral part of the ensemble without ceasing to have its distinct personality as solo instrument. There emanates from this Concerto an altogether remarkable impression of fire, grandeur, and fullness. The first movement, in C minor, of an ardent and tumultuous expression, exposes the two principal themes on which the whole work will be constructed. . . . The Concerto of Mr. Widor obtained every approbation, and the composer and interpreter were justly and extendedly acclaimed. —J. Jemain.[286]

Widor penned this brief analysis of the Concerto:

> The work is of completely classical architecture: Allegro (C minor): First theme presented by the orchestra; second theme (G minor) entrusted to the piano. The two themes are presented and developed following the traditional form and in very sober proportions, for the real deductions of the main theme will be manifested in the Final.
> The Adagio sounded by the violins and cellos, and then taken up later by the solo violin on the crystalline sonorities of the piano treble, is only a parenthesis in the whole work, a sort of interlude inserted to rest from the persistence of the same themes. This Adagio suddenly takes us back and almost without transition to the beginning of the Allegro, slightly transformed and developing logically until the final peroration in C major, the main theme and almost alone being then presented in all its brilliancy.[287]

Philipp, Planté, and Émile Frey (1889–1946) each performed the Second Concerto several times, usually with Widor conducting; but the work never attained anything near the popularity of the *Fantaisie*.

—83—

Les pêcheurs de Saint-Jean: "Indeed, the opera is beautiful"

Fishermen and sea songs must have been somewhat of a preoccupation early in the first decade of the 1900s. The poetry of his cousin Paul Bourget had served Widor well for his song cycle *Soirs d'été*, and a set of Bourget's poems again attracted his attention in 1901. A set of fourteen songs forms Widor's largest cycle, *Chansons de mer* (*Sea Songs*), to which he apparently assigned no opus number, although the blank Opus 75 coincides exactly with the work. The expressive vocal writing fully captures the mood of Bourget's texts in drama and lyricism, while the demanding accompaniments amply demonstrate their full and equal partnership with the vocal line. Heugel published the cycle as a series in 1902, and following several acclaimed performances Widor realized the orchestral potential of six of the songs by orchestrating the accompaniments of numbers one, five, six, seven, ten, and fourteen, the latter of which was also arranged with a solo violin part.

The demands imposed on Widor for concerts did not ease during this period,[288] but his next opera, *Les pêcheurs de Saint-Jean* (*The Fishermen of Saint John*), had to have been in the forefront of his thought. He had been working periodically on the opera for several years, and in August 1895 he hoped to find "absolute meditation in a tranquil corner" to work on the third act.[289] Indeed, the following month, *Le Ménestrel* reported that Widor had gone to l'Arbresle "where he completed in tranquility the third act of his new opera, *Les marins* [*The Sailors*]," and that the premiere was imminent.[290] Still, four years later, in August 1899, Widor reported, "I'm going to [re]write the overture to *Pêcheurs de St. Jean* that I haven't felt very good about until the present, but which is taking shape."[291] Again, in September 1900, he wrote that he had worked out his Overture "which was very difficult to do because of the subject: a storm without discontinuity!"[292] By February 1903, the title of the opera had been changed definitively from *Les marins* to *Les pêcheurs de Saint-Jean*, and Widor performed some of the orchestral portions of the score in Saint Petersburg and Moscow, where he had been invited both to conduct orchestral concerts and to play organ recitals.[293]

The long-awaited premiere of *Les pêcheurs de Saint-Jean*, a "drame lyrique" in four acts on a libretto by Henri Cain, took place on December 26, 1905, at the Opéra-Comique in Paris (see fig. 17).

Act I is set at the seaport of Saint-Jean-de-Luz; a large number of sailors have assembled to drink toasts in celebration of the christening of the new fishing boat of their wealthy skipper, Jean-Pierre. He greets them all, shaking hands with Jacques, the young steersman who has worked with him for five years, and who more than once saved the boat and fishermen during heavy weather. Marie-Anne, the beautiful daughter of Jean-Pierre, soon arrives; she is to be the godmother of the new boat at the christening. Marie-Anne and Jacques are enamored with each other, but without having avowed it yet. While Jacques is arranging some nets, Marie-Anne quietly approaches; at first, they are timid, but they soon confide their mutual love. Then with great regret, Jacques laments, "Your father is rich, and I have nothing. He will never want us to marry." But Marie-Anne consoles him; her father loves her, and will not refuse anything to make her happy. Meanwhile, the sailors have begun their procession to the christening; happy children, young girls all dressed in white and carrying candles, the fisherwomen carrying their nets, the fishermen carrying the flag-draped new boat on their shoulders, and finally the priest, followed by some boys carrying the holy water, censer and cross, all proceed to the ceremony intoning the *Kyrie eleison* and a Basque hymn.

Act II takes place at the same scene, now three months later. Jean-Pierre, upon learning of the love between Jacques and Marie-Anne, had become furious and dismisses his steersman. Jacques, however, cannot decide to move away and leave behind the one who means everything to him. Moreover, he still holds strong rancor towards Jean-Pierre. By coincidence, Jacques and Marie-Anne meet and there is a scene of great love and emotion; they renew their affection, and without knowing what the future holds, vow to love each other forever. Suddenly, Jean-Pierre bursts in angrily and surprises them. He harshly accuses Jacques of courting his daughter only for her dowry. In great anger, Jacques runs out before he might do something regrettable, and he goes to the local tavern to drown his sorrows. A little later, Jean-Pierre passes by, and seeing Jacques completely intoxicated, makes some offensive remarks to him. After an exchange of words, Jacques pulls his knife on Jean-Pierre. In a rage, he wants to kill his former skipper; but the other sailors in the pub restrain him, and he soon exhausts himself, breaking into tears in the arms of his mother who has come running upon hearing the noise of the quarrel.

Act III is set in Marie-Anne's bedroom at Jean-Pierre's house; it is Christmas Eve. While all the neighbors go to church, Marie-Anne feels a terrible anguish: her father and younger brother have been gone at sea for two days; a bad storm is brewing, the seas are very heavy, and they no longer have Jacques to save them if they are in trouble. She seeks diversion from her anxious thoughts by working on some fishing nets and singing a folk song. Suddenly, there is a knock at the door; perhaps they have returned! No, it is Jacques's mother; she can only visit in Jean-Pierre's absence since he had also dismissed her from his service. The two women are consoling each other when Jacques suddenly comes in to get his mother, "Come with me, your place is not here." Jacques, believing that Marie-Anne has completely forgotten him, cruelly reproaches her for betraying their vows. But she softly answers, "To be so unkind, you must be suffering!" She tells him that she thinks only of him, and guards his memory in her heart. Asking her forgiveness, Jacques proposes that they flee away together. But when Marie-Anne refuses and his mother tries to make him understand that it is impossible, he goes mad with anguish: "Impossible! Well then, forget everything and stay here. Don't worry about me; I no longer love you! The one I loved was brave and proud. She is dead, do you hear, dead forever!" And he runs out, heartbroken.

Act IV opens with a horrible storm in the middle of the night. The thunderbolts rumble and the waves break with fury. Suddenly, a signal is seen from a great distance out at sea; it is from Jean-Pierre's boat. On shore, everyone feels helpless. Jacques arrives, and upon learning of the situation, wildly exclaims, "It is the sea that will avenge me. Jean-Pierre, merciless man, count your money now!" But Marie-Anne, desperate and in tears, looks at Jacques imploringly: "Jacques, it's my father who will die!" Her words transform him; he quickly rounds up some men, and, in spite of the danger, goes out to save Jean-Pierre and his men. Of course, Jacques is restored to Jean-Pierre's favor, and he and Marie-Anne are at last happily reunited.[294]

The story contains many colorful and dramatic elements of which Widor took full advantage. From the very first, the opera was declared a resounding success; Widor had finally achieved his full mark as an opera composer:

Mr. Widor has constructed a well-built, strongly bound together score that makes his remarkable talent stand out. From one end to the other, it is written with the conscience of a true artist, and we don't need to speculate whether the greatest care with the form makes of it a particularly distinguished work. We no longer meet here the peculiarities and oddities—that are in any case useless to point out—with which certain works are adorned. Mr. Widor does not believe it necessary to cut his dog's tail to draw a crowd of passers-by and arouse their attention. He restricts himself to searching for inspiration, giving it the nobility that it must have, and adorning it with a style that owes nothing to the quest of eccentricity, which some abuse under the pretext of originality.

He gives us a pleasant surprise from the start by beginning with an Overture, of which his broad developments and powerful sonorities obtained a great success. The first act is, moreover, particularly substantial. I will cite above all from it the entire scene between the two lovers and, especially in its last part, the beautiful phrase, full of breadth, built up by Marie-Anne and sustained by the harps: "When during the night the storm engulfs" . . . which is then repeated by the two voices together; the effect is excellent. Then, the entire long episode of the procession and christening, which is truly imposing and which gives rise to two choruses, one of which is full and of great character, and the other of beautiful tone and superb sonority.

We must again note the scene between Jacques and Marie-Anne in the second act; its pleasing design of violins and cellos bring out the charm of the scene; then the joyous chorus of the sailors and the dance of the women sardine fishers, the effect of its full spirit is impossible to miss; and, above all, the whole scene, so boisterous and dramatic, of the drunken Jacques rushing wildly at Jean-Pierre, which is truly, and as one would wish, powerful and exciting.

The third act begins with a charming symphonic piece, a Christmas march, the design of which is full of grace and freshness, with an orchestration as Mr. Widor knows how to write. The prayer of Marie-Anne to the Madonna: "Virgin Mary, lady of the waves," is absolutely moving; and we must note the intensely melancholy character that distinguishes her reply to the unjust reproaches of Jacques: "To crush me such with insulting words" . . . ; it is truly heartfelt, and this phrase, simply built and successfully developed, emits a sincere and truly penetrating emotion.

The last act required power and energy, and the composer lacked neither one nor the other. The situation is excessive from one end to the other from continual fury, and allowed no variety. Nothing can be abstracted from it; it must be taken as a whole. Mr. Widor has surmounted the difficulty, and his storm scene is imprinted with real magnitude.

In summary, the work is strong and vigorous as a whole, full of warmth and movement, always alive and well suited to the stage, with pages of tenderness and profound melancholy when the situation lends itself [to such emotion]. It does the greatest honor to its composer and it is worthy of the very brilliant success that has greeted it from the first hour. It will certainly raise Mr. Widor in the esteem of the public and artists.[295]

At the Opéra-Comique, the new score of Ch.-M. Widor . . . has been received with the greatest favor by artists. It has proven yet again what a vigorous and sound musician has written it. Indeed, one can count on the fingers of one's hand the number of contemporary composers capable of such a work.[296]

Italian opera composer Umberto Giordano (1867–1948), whose *Andrea Chénier* had achieved spectacular success throughout Europe, happened to be in Paris for the premiere of *Pêcheurs*. From the Elysée Palace Hotel he quickly penned a complimentary letter: "Passing through Paris, I went to the Opéra-Comique to applaud your new piece, *Les pêcheurs de Saint-Jean*, which I found ravishing. Accordingly, please accept, dear *maître*, my most sincere congratulations."[297]

The German composer/critic Otto Neitzel (1852–1920) made a German translation of *Pêcheurs* within a month of its Paris premiere, and it was soon readied for production in Frankfurt. The German press hailed the opera no less enthusiastically than did the French, and predicted: "the first production in Germany . . . is going to be the object of quite a series of German reprises. Indeed, the opera is beautiful; it obtained an extraordinarily great success."[298] One Munich correspondent praised the "great art" with which Widor treated the voices and the orchestra, and how the intensity of the sentiment of each situation was always perfectly expressed.[299] When Widor went to Frankfurt to conduct a few of the performances himself, the audiences gave him numerous and resounding ovations:[300] "In a word, an excellent work has arrived in Germany; it is also a glorious event for our Opera house."[301] Considering Germany's own operatic tradition, the acclaim given to *Pêcheurs* is especially notable.

The French Academy of Fine Arts awarded Widor the Monbinne Prize of three thousand francs for his new opera.[302] He truly gained in notoriety from it, but *Pêcheurs* turned out to be his only successful opera. An orchestral Suite excerpted from the opera is comprised of the Overture, the Prelude to Act II— "The calm of the sea," and the Prelude to Act III—"Marche de Noël." Widor dedicated the Suite to Albert Carré (1852–1938), director of the Opéra-Comique.

Over a period of a few years, *Pêcheurs* was produced in Geneva, Antwerp, Algiers, The Hague, and a dozen or more French cities, including Marseilles,

Rouen, Lyon, Pau, Dijon, Nice, Avignon, and Grenoble.[303] In spite of its burst of popularity, it fell into oblivion, along with the vast majority of late nineteenth-century French opera. Perhaps *Pêcheurs* would have remained in the repertory longer had it not been for an intrigue revolving around who would sing the leading female role in the productions at the Opéra-Comique. Widor had chosen a singer he deemed ideal for the role, but Carré's wife, Marguerite, wanted the role for herself; when Widor refused to take the role from his favored singer, Madame Carré took revenge through her husband by seeing that the opera was retired from the Opéra-Comique's repertory.[304] Such was the price that Widor paid for not bowing to political pressure and intrigue, all of which he resolutely endeavored to avoid throughout his life:

> It has been said that Widor . . . could have been a great diplomat . . . since he never mixed in any intrigues, never was part of any small "clique," never "played politics" in order to have his works performed nor to gain access to an official post. He never tried, either, to make himself the center of such cliques or groups. . . . For a man of Widor's caliber, friendship is neither an investment nor a calculation, and he expects no returns from it.[305]

Widor's approach to opera was rooted in nineteenth-century romanticism, which increasingly put him out of step with more recent trends. As early as 1892, he recognized a new direction in opera, but he hoped it might be only a passing fancy:

> Today, music is becoming an accessory; one declaims more than one sings. The "piece" no longer exists, it's the poem that one listens to; the musician must no longer be anything but a faithful echo, a translator word for word of the poet.
>   Such is the present conception of lyric drama in Paris. Such is the fashion of the day.
>   But you know well that fashion doesn't last long.[306]

—84—

Violin and Cello Sonatas:
"Two new works of the highest value"

From the grand dramatic landscapes of opera, Widor turned almost immediately to the intimacy of chamber music. On March 14, 1907, in the home of Madame Charles Max, "two new works of the highest value" received their premieres: Sonata in D Minor, Op. 79, for Violin and Piano; Sonata in A Major, Op. 80, for Cello and Piano.[307]

Widor sent a copy of the Violin Sonata to his old friend Jules Massenet, asking if he would accept the dedication. After reviewing the work, Massenet wrote back to Widor, using the familiar "tu" form of address: "I heartily embrace you great friend! I think that, since such a work is dedicated to me, I am *also* going to have desires to write beautiful and profound music! Ah! *I want: to my friend Massenet.*"[308] Widor revised the Sonata toward the end of his life and a new edition was published in 1937. The autograph manuscript of this work, dated October 7, 1906, resides in the Musikaliska Akademiens Bibliotek in Stockholm, Sweden. After Widor became perpetual secretary of the Academy of Fine Arts at the Institut de France, he worked tirelessly for various indigent causes; on the manuscript's cover is written, "for sale to the diplomatic mission of France, in Stockholm, for the benefit of French orphans of the war—Paris, February 10, 1921."

Widor performed the very demanding piano parts in both works with violinist Bilewski (b. 1884), 1903 first prize winner at the Paris Conservatory, and cellist Jules Lœb, cello professor at the Conservatory and dedicatee of that Sonata:

> The two sonatas . . . have been written the one immediately after the other, both obeying the same will, the same laws of construction, but in absolute contrast of ideas and sentiment: the Violin Sonata, very moving, very dramatic, its only two themes (which develop and transform during the three movements of the work) in minor tonality; the Cello Sonata, in major, on the contrary, of melodious and calm character, each of its three movements built on different themes. . . .
>
> . . . By the similarity of their proportions and the difference of the means employed, the study of these two twin works offers a real interest.
>
> No less interesting is the technique of the writing and instrumentation, always clear and sonorous.
>
> . . . two works so important and which do so much honor to their author, and consequently to the whole school of French music. The modern repertoire of chamber music numbers few of this class and of this high value.[309]

Whenever performed, these two Sonatas drew critical acclaim as contemporary masterpieces in their respective genres. Each exhibits the high level of inspiration and craftsmanship for which Widor was noted in this twilight of his compositional career.

—85—

Sinfonia sacra; foreign engagements and honors

Early in 1907, the Berlin Royal Academy of Fine Arts elected Widor an associate member; with Saint-Saëns and society painter Léon Bonnat, he became one of

three French members of that illustrious assembly.[310] As a token of his appreciation for the honor bestowed upon him, Widor composed the *Sinfonia sacra*, Op.
81, for Organ and Orchestra, and dedicated it to the Berlin Academy:

> When I was elected correspondent of the Academy of Berlin, Schweitzer
> hinted to me that I would do well to thank my confrères of the Spree.
>   I said to him, "Give me a particular text that does not require a great
> orchestral deployment, that can be performed in a church gallery." It's then
> that he suggested to me the text of Luther's chorale that the Lansquenets
> [German mercenary soldiers] sang to less liturgical words when rescued
> from the siege of Francis I.[311]

Like the *Symphonie gothique* and *Symphonie romane*, Widor infused the *Sinfonia
sacra* with melodic content borrowed from the context of the Church. Emil
Rupp (1872–1948), a great friend of Widor and one of his early biographers,
suggested it was as though Widor wanted to show "the way to salvation," and
"the way" was by returning to sacred melody, be it plainsong or chorale.[312] The
Sinfonia sacra is built on the Lutheran Advent chorale, *Nun komm, der Heiden
Heiland* (Now come, Savior of the heathen). The craftsmanship is consistently
high, and the serious religious sentiment and mysticism compare favorably to
Bach. Although the role of the organ in Widor's Op. 69 Third Symphony is
imposing, it does not take on the virtuosic character of a concerto partner to
the orchestra, as in the *Sinfonia sacra*:

> The special character of the work consists of a combination of great original-
> ity for the organ with a small orchestra—comprising an oboe, a clarinet, a
> trumpet, three trombones and string instruments. What has been pleasing
> here above all . . . is that the work is inspired from the genius of Sebastian
> Bach, and not, actually, by some reminiscences (as in the case for example
> with a musician of note, Mr. Max Reger), but by a higher and truly inventive
> influence that has not given any place to imitation, but has kindled the idea
> from a particularly personal conception.[313]
>   The Symphony of Mr. Widor . . . is one of the most distinguished and
> modern works of the composer; in his score he has condensed the essen-
> tial gifts of his conception of the organ and the effects that he expects from
> the instrument: elevated conception, engaging thoughts, masterful construc-
> tion even in its most intrepid liberties, opulent variety of means and develop-
> ments, mixed combinations of rhythms and sonorities, in which the organ
> always remains in the foreground when it comes in, thanks to the tact of the
> composer, who has known how to isolate it from the ensemble by employ-
> ing some essentially different tonal sonorities and in always maintaining the
> other orchestral parts at a certain distance from the principal part. All of
> this is found here, linked together, and unfolded with a perfect lucidity! The
> work has produced a grandiose effect, especially by the solemn spaciousness

and imposing splendor of its finale! . . . And when the last note was sounded, the public gave to the work, the orchestra, and the composer—recalled five times by the entire house—an ovation that seemed like it would never end.[314]

Widor especially enjoyed conducting the work, and most often either Albert Schweitzer or Marcel Dupré played the solo part. The Paris premiere featured Dupré at the organ, after which Widor assumed the bench to give a "delight- ful" performance of Handel's Concerto in F.[315] Dupré also accompanied his *maître* to performances in Barcelona, Wiesbaden, and Marseilles.[316]

The *Sinfonia sacra* came to be considered the model for its genre, and it provided a brilliant capstone to Widor's series of ten organ symphonies.[317] Not everyone found the work so brilliant, however. One French critic attending the 1910 festival of French music in Munich wrote that he had spent several days arguing the virtues of French music with the German critics, and then found the *Sinfonia sacra* completely lacking in the qualities he had exalted:

> In hearing the first pages of this dull composition . . . I thought I saw the ironic smile of my [German] contradictors from the preceding days: "So that's your French music." I was unable to withstand this distressing sensa- tion, and in the middle of the *Sinfonia sacra*, I fled the concert hall; I am still running. Never will I pardon Mr. Charles-Marie Widor for the humiliation that his music made me feel that day.[318]

To commemorate the centennial of Haydn's death, Jules Écorcheville (1872–1955), founder of the journal of the Société de musique indépendante, *SIM, Mercure musical*, selected Debussy, Dukas, Reynaldo Hahn (1875–1947), d'Indy, Ravel, and Widor to compose six pieces on Haydn's name in musical notation and in whatever form each cared to choose.[319] Although in the 1830s Robert Schumann had extended the musical alphabet beyond the traditional A through H by assigning a pitch to subsequent letters of the alphabet, the idea was still considered a novelty in 1909.[320] Widor offered a Fugue whose subject spelled Haydn (*H*=B natural, *a*=A, *y*=D, *d*=D, *n*=G).

Successes in Germany and England favored Widor with many return engage- ments. The French Embassy in Berlin devoted a concert to his chamber music in March 1909, but when at the last moment he was unable to make the trip, pianist Émile Frey, cellist Marix Loewensohn, and Romanian violinist Georges Enesco (1881–1955) performed "with great brilliance and feeling" the Op. 58 Suite for Piano, Op. 79 Sonata for Violin, and Op. 80 Sonata for Cello. Noted contralto Maria Freund sang "Nella's Ballade" from *Maître Ambros* and other *mélodies*. The press remarked, "The white and gold room, hung with magnifi- cent Gobelin tapestries, harmonized magnificently with the delicate and ten- der music of the French master."[321] Widor appeared in London two months later, on May 4, to conduct the London Symphony Orchestra at Queen's Hall in a program that featured the Op. 69 Third Symphony (Arthur Mason, organ soloist), Op. 62 *Fantaisie* (Olga Samaroff, piano soloist), and "Bacchanale" from *La nuit de Walpurgis.* The *Times* of London characterized Widor as "one of the most earnest of modern French composers," yet a composer whose music adhered to traditional qualities and spurned eccentricities:

> There is point in all the composer writes. . . . The appeal of all this music is exclusively to the intelligent, for it is free from effective tricks of every kind . . . the workmanship is sound and honest all through.[322]

In celebration of the beatification of Joan of Arc, the "Maid of Orléans," Widor returned from London immediately to conduct part of his *Jeanne d'Arc* in the Orléans Cathedral, with orchestra, military band, and a Berlioz-sized chorus of 800.[323]

Soon after Widor's election to the Berlin Academy, the Belgian Royal Academy of Fine Arts elected him—over Richard Strauss—as an associate member to replace the deceased Edvard Grieg.[324] And in 1910, Widor, Vincent d'Indy, and Claude Debussy were all elected as foreign members of the Swedish Royal Academy of Music.[325] But Widor's imminent election to the Académie des beaux-arts of the renowned Institut de France would soon irrevocably alter his life's focus.

Part Five

Mr. Widor, Member of the Institute of France (1910–37)

Il est des vieillards dont on finit par douter qu'ils soient mortels.

He is an old man whose mortality one can hardly believe.

—Jacques Heugel
Ménestrel 99 (1937): 104.

—86—

Institut de France: "A most courteous contest"

One of architect Louis Le Vau's masterpieces, the seventeenth-century former Mazarin Palace (Quai de Conti), with its distinctive cupola flanked by two square pavilions designed to harmonize with the Louvre on the other side of the Seine, was given over to the Institute of France in 1805. The most prestigious of French organizations, the Institute devotes itself to perfecting and protecting French arts and sciences. Five academies, the earliest founded in 1635 by Richelieu, comprise the illustrious body of the Institute: Académie française (French Academy), Académie des inscriptions et belles-lettres (Academy of Inscriptions and Literature), Académie des sciences (Academy of Sciences), Académie des beaux-arts (Academy of Fine Arts), Académie des sciences morales et politiques (Academy of Moral and Political Sciences). Each of the five academies includes several branches of specialty.

The Academy of Fine Arts—an elite body of forty "immortals," as they are known, plus a *secrétaire perpétuel* (perpetual secretary)—is divided into five specific areas: painting (fourteen members), sculpture (eight members), architecture (eight members), engraving (four members), and music (six members). There are also ten free members, ten foreign associates, and fifty correspondents. Luminaries in their respective fields incorporate the representative body of each academy. An academician is elected for life by majority vote of his peers in the academy to which his name has been proposed; a vacancy occurs only upon the death of a member. It is both a great honor and a symbol of considerable distinction to be elected a member of the French Institute.

A vacancy in the music branch of the Academy of Fine Arts occurred in 1909 upon the death of Ernest Reyer. Widor penned a letter of candidature to Henry Roujon (1853–1914), perpetual secretary of the Academy, on February 19, 1909; he briefly detailed his qualifications by citing what he considered to be some of his most important works:

> Mr. Perpetual Secretary,
>
> I am writing to ask you to be my spokesman to the Academy of Fine Arts, and to inform your illustrious colleagues of my candidature to the chair of the greatly missed Maître Reyer.
>   I believe I am complying with the customary practice in permitting myself to recall some of my works: La Korrigane, Conte d'avril, Les pêcheurs de St. Jean, four symphonies and numerous orchestral pieces, ten organ symphonies, sixty or more pieces of chamber music and music for various instruments, eighty songs, etc.[1]

Widor and "his perpetual rival"[2] Gabriel Fauré became the chief contenders among the nominees. In terms of the qualifications for membership, Widor seemed to have the edge; he had been one of five candidates considered for Delibes's chair back in 1891.[3] But Fauré was director of the Conservatory. The press was abuzz as to which candidate would win the chair; both musicians had an impressive catalog of works. After six rounds of voting, in which the numbers continually jockeyed in favor of one and then the other, an eighteen-to-sixteen vote finally elected Fauré.[4] As one journal pointed out, "Perhaps the authority that is tied to the position of director of the National Conservatory of Music decided the outcome of the contest in which the opponents both presented themselves so well armed."[5]

The Comœdia Illustré made a special point to demonstrate that it had been "a most courteous contest," that Fauré and Widor "have not ceased to have a high opinion of each other," and that the outcome was "favorably welcomed by the less fortunate of the two."[6] Each was asked to contribute a short article about the other to the journal. For his part, Widor concluded somewhat grandiloquently:

> No existence is happier than that of Fauré, an existence made of tranquil labor, constant success, and always the greatest and most merited satisfaction. Since the first days of his career, the maître has climbed with a steady and sure step the winding route that slopes gently up to the summit of the mountain, towards the plateau of supreme honors in the region of immortal glory.[7]

Fauré wrote in polite rhetoric, tracing their friendship back nearly forty years and lavishing high-flown "precious" praise on Widor's most successful works:

And this success, is it not perfectly justified by the character of elegant research, by the assured technique, by the personal touch, by the ensemble of so many precious qualities that mark the least as well as the most significant of his works?

One final trait in this thumbnail sketch: Widor is also a learned man, a man of wit and taste, a charming man.[8]

Officially, the Institute's charter proclaims it free from political shenanigans; historically, it has not always proven so virtuous. True enough, Fauré was the director of the Conservatory, but it did not hurt that the sculptor Emmanuel Frémiet, one of the illustrious members of the Academy and, coincidentally, Fauré's father-in-law, succeeded in swinging needed votes to Fauré.[9] Yet another player on the field turned out to be Saint-Saëns, "the guardian angel watching over Fauré's career."[10] Although Saint-Saëns also had a significant influence on Widor's career, vis-à-vis his appointment at Saint-Sulpice in 1870, on this occasion the elder statesman of the Institute threw his support to Fauré, his former pupil. Widor probably never knew the extent of it, as Saint-Saëns remained one of his closest friends to the end of Saint-Saëns's life.

On February 24, 1909, in anticipation of the March 13 election, Saint-Saëns wrote to Fauré:

> It's done; I've already written around forty letters and I've still more to write; and I shall do my utmost to be there [in Paris] at the critical moment.
>
> Your rival candidate has a dreadful trump card in his hand, the female charmer of rue Jacob; but you must have many women up your sleeve, and at their head Mme Greffulhe [Fauré dedicated to her his *Pavane*, Op. 50], for whose support you should certainly not hesitate to ask. It's women more [than] anything that get you into the Académie.[11]

Soon after the election, Saint-Saëns wrote to his close friend Charles Lecocq (1832–1918) expressing the intense anxiety he had suffered during the voting:

> On Saturday [March 13], the fight. It has been a rough one, and when I saw, on the fifth round, that Widor had gained two votes and Fauré had lost one, I believed the game was lost; it was all up to me and I had a chesty cough which had still not completely cleared up by Monday morning. I really did believe that I should have had a heart attack if he had lost.[12]

The closeness of Saint-Saëns to Fauré was again manifested when Fauré's father-in-law Frémiet passed away. Saint-Saëns responded with a huge memorial wreath, and Fauré wrote to thank him saying, "*You are one of the family!*"[13]

Two months later, on a tour to Finland and Russia, Fauré found enthusiastic audiences shouting his name. He gloated in a letter to his wife Marie, "What a pity that Dubois and Widor were not able to see it, from the outside! No doubt they would have found this welcome very excessive!"[14]

—87—

The new academician: "A rare personality"

Another vacancy in the music branch of the Academy of Fine Arts arose upon the death of Charles Lenepveu (1840–1910). Widor again submitted his name to Henry Roujon for candidacy.[15] This time he succeeded handily, receiving twenty-one of the thirty-two votes of the Academy.[16] He assumed his chair at the Institute toward the end of October 1910 (see fig. 18), in the company of Jules Massenet, Camille Saint-Saëns, Émile Paladilhe, Théodore Dubois, and Gabriel Fauré. The Institute records show that Widor had an excellent attendance record, whereas Fauré rarely attended meetings.

Shortly after Widor's election, many of his students, friends, and admirers gathered at a banquet held in his honor. Gabriel Dupont, one of Widor's favorite pupils, delivered a very touching salute to his *maître* on behalf of all:

I quite believe, my dear *maître*, that I am the youngest here of your former pupils. Consequently, I ought to keep quiet, since children don't have the right to speak at the table and as I don't have, furthermore, a reputation as an improviser. But what do you expect? I am a lad badly brought up, who doesn't know how to hold his tongue; and I absolutely want to say to you, before everyone, how much all of us love you.

We love you in your *teaching*, classical and liberal at the same time. As pupils, we were already your friends; and now that we are in our careers, you remain for us the amicable and sure guide.

We love you, we admire you in your *works* so diverse and so beautiful, where the vigor and richness of imagination unite in absolute mastery of the science. From your admirable organ works to your theater works, from your great orchestral symphonies to your chamber music and to your numerous songs, it is always the same flood of music, limpid and deep, which flows to the brim.

And we also love you, let me tell you, for the rare example of your *life*. It follows its road straight, valiantly, simply. It is noble, it is proud, it is fertile. It teaches us the uprightness, the work, the will of being men; and when we raise a toast to the new academician, we salute in you, my dear *maître*, with all our heart and with all our respect, the very character of the genuine artist, in the highest and most complete sense of this word.[17]

Along with the honor of being an academician, Widor felt the seriousness of his new obligations and a great sense of duty:

The Academy, I insist . . . , is not a society, but an essential organ of the home-land; it is therefore the usefulness of the State that guides us in the choice of our elected. Can personal feelings count before the general interest? Each carries here its quota of strength: talent, authority, character, fate. Twice at the demand of my confrères I went to look for modest individuals whose qualities we were missing.[18]

Widor resonated with a line from Molière: "I want people to be sincere, and as a man of honor, to utter no word that does not come from the heart."[19]

Possessing a big heart, beneficent and generous, Widor was like Liszt; he cared for people and helped them in whatever way, large or small, that he could. Albert Schweitzer had gone to study with Widor in the autumn of 1893 and recalled how, as a struggling student, he could barely afford to feed himself:

Many a time, if he got the impression that, concerned about the slenderness of my purse, I had not allowed myself enough to eat, he took me with him after my lesson to his regular haunt, the Restaurant Foyot near the Luxem-bourg, that I might once more, at any rate, eat my fill![20]

Marcel Dupré also related how Widor helped one of his composition pupils without the latter's knowledge. Albert Doyen (1882–1935) had written a very attractive Sonata for piano and violin that Widor urged him to have published. He had already prepared the way for his pupil by making the arrangements with the publisher Heugel; but it would be necessary for Doyen to put up a share of the three-thousand-franc expense. The poor boy's hopes were shat-tered; with only seventy-five francs to spare, the undertaking seemed hopeless. Widor explained that it did not matter; he would have three years to pay the full amount. Upon returning three years later to pay the sum, the publisher informed Doyen that Widor had paid off the full amount three years earlier.[21]

As a member of the Institute, Widor liberally exerted his influence to aid unfortunate and struggling artists, sometimes helping young painters get their work displayed:[22] "How many receipts he paid to keep some impecunious stu-dents from being evicted from their garret! His purse was always open to unfor-tunate comrades; to certain ones, he even paid a regular allowance."[23] For various war efforts, Widor extended his generosity to the fullest extent, for the most part anonymously; in one magnanimous gesture, he gave up a cherished collection of Rembrandt sketches for the work of the Fraternité des artistes.[24] As one tribute to him pointed out, "he is like those who deserve their success not only by their talent, but by their good grace and kindness."[25]

In spite of a busy schedule in Paris, Widor continued to travel surprisingly often outside the capital. Between 1908 and 1911, he fulfilled numerous engagements throughout France,[26] and appeared in Zurich, Liège, London, Rome, Berlin, Potsdam, Munich, and Brussels:[27]

The fact is that Widor, thanks to his activity, is known today all over Europe, and his talent is appreciated everywhere as it deserves to be. Thanks to him, the musical influence of France has spread out in all directions, and to a marked degree.[28]

Review after review confirmed Widor's remarkable talent as an organist. The review of his inauguration of the new Mutin organ in Rome at the Basilica of Santa Maria Trastevere is representative:

As performer and composer, he showed himself once again the powerful artist, endowed with a rare sensibility joined to the profound knowledge of all the secrets of musical technique. A smooth and velvety attack, an extraordinary agility, sureness, and precision in the chords, an interpretation always in perfect equilibrium: all this constitutes a rare personality.[29]

In league with many nineteenth-century composers, Widor adhered, even well into the twentieth century, to a more or less classical/romantic aesthetic, avoiding whatever he considered to be passing fashion or gimmickry. As he got older, he remained generally indifferent to current trends as an influence upon his own style. In a period bristling with innovative composers and rapidly changing styles, Widor's conservatism must have been conspicuous to many, and downright old-fashioned to the avant-garde. Still, his music retained its appeal to a public yearning to hold onto their comfortable past. After his London Symphony concert in 1909, the *Times* concluded:

The concert of yesterday must have shown a good many people how much we are apt to lose by our eager adherence to all that is eccentric in modern music, for such sane and really beautiful music as M. Widor's ought not to be neglected.[30]

In September 1910, a three day "Festival of French Music" in Munich brought Fauré, Saint-Saëns, Widor, and Dukas together to conduct their own works. Among those presented by Saint-Saëns was his famous Third Symphony for Organ and Orchestra, with Widor playing the organ.[31] For his own part, Widor conducted his new *Sinfonia sacra* and several orchestrated songs. Albert Schweitzer arrived from Strasbourg especially to perform the organ part, and a near fiasco ensued:

The day it was to be given[,] both were invited to dinner. Schweitzer declined with thanks. He wanted to be fresh for the symphony, which is very difficult. But Widor went. At eight o'clock, when they were to begin, Widor was not there. At five minutes past he had not arrived. At ten minutes past he appeared, rushed to the rostrum, and began at once to conduct the orchestra with one hand while he searched for his glasses with the other. He was unable to conduct the symphony without the score, and neither he nor the orchestra was thoroughly familiar with it. With his baton first in his right hand and then in his left he searched in his pockets, one after the other. They were a quarter of the way through before he found them. Had not Schweitzer been so sure of himself and supported so well with the organ, the whole thing would have been disastrous. Said Schweitzer afterwards, "You see, I was right in not accepting the invitation."[32]

Usually mindful of the weighty responsibilities of a conductor, Widor once wrote, "I don't know a profession that demands more presence of mind, will, and dominion over the nervous system than that of the conductor. Also, the remarkable individuals in this field are very rare, in the past no less than in the present. Very few great composers can be cited as such."[33] Widor conducted often and generally made a success of it, though according to Isidor Philipp it was not his strong card: "This supervirtuoso of the organ, this inspired improvisor was, like Debussy and Ravel, a mediocre, uncertain, timid orchestra conductor, yet he liked to conduct, as if he, of all people, was in search of applause."[34] Vierne confirmed this opinion: "Widor, who adored orchestra conducting, had interpretive gestures of which it was sometimes difficult to be absolutely certain."[35] Even Widor admitted that his interpretive ideas were not infallible:

One day [Francis] Planté gave me the great pleasure of playing at Sainte-Cécile de Bordeaux my Concerto in C [Op. 77], and invited me to conduct the orchestra. At the rehearsal, from the beginning, I asked him for a slight acceleration in the general tempo. "No," he told me, "let's go like this until the end; afterwards we'll see." Afterwards, I had seen, or rather heard. The nobility of his playing, the clarity, the enhancement of the episodes, and the result of the ensemble added singularly to the character of the piece, and the next day at the concert, it was he who here and there with a glance urged me to "move ahead."[36]

Regardless of whether Widor appeared as conductor or organist, he packed concert halls and churches with enthusiastic crowds; from Brussels:

This inauguration . . . has been a real event not only for Brussels, but for the entire country. For most of the organists of Belgium and Holland attended the ceremony; they flocked in from Liège, Gent, Brugge, Antwerp, Luxembourg, Maastricht, Tilbourg, Rotterdam, etc., and all will retain a profound impression.[37]

—88—

Conservatory reforms:
"Me, an anarchist! Me, a rebel! Nonsense!"

The Widor/Fauré rivalry had been longstanding, and each new episode only intensified the rift between the two men. The wound deepened when Widor agreed to represent a large faction of Conservatory professors protesting over reforms that had been instituted by Fauré.[38]

Fauré received his earliest musical training at the École Niedermeyer. When he was named director of the Conservatory in June 1905, consternation spread throughout Parisian musical circles. It was widely assumed that qualifications for the post included being a former student of the Conservatory and a winner of the prestigious Prix de Rome, distinctions held by the previous directors Auber, Thomas, and Dubois, but which Fauré could not claim. Consternation turned to rebellion when, within four months of his appointment, Fauré instituted a series of sweeping reforms at the Conservatory.[39] The fallout was immediate. Several professors complained of his "dictatorial despotism," even comparing him to Robespierre,[40] and appealed to the government secretary of the Fine Arts to reestablish the former regulations; at the same time, the two professors of dramatic oratory tendered their resignations.

One reform drew dissension like a lightning rod: admission juries would no longer include the Conservatory professors from the discipline to which a candidate was applying:

> It was well known that at the Conservatory, the candidates who took private lessons from the admission jurors had a greater chance of being admitted than those who did not take lessons. It was equally known that those who were able to pay generously for these private lessons had an even better chance.[41]

Clearly, Fauré wanted to break the unjust partiality between professors and their paying private students. To assure strict observation of this reform, he created a disciplinary council for Conservatory professors. The laissez-faire attitude of the Dubois administration had ended. Professors were no longer at liberty to do as they pleased in their classes and in the examination and admission juries. Those who were most unhappy with the new rules were those whose teaching had gone afield from their true discipline—voice and dramatic oratory.[42]

For nearly six years the reforms of Fauré simmered; classes of students had come and gone. In the spring of 1911 an eruption took place. Max Bouvet (1854–1943), a professor of voice, resigned in protest because his students did not suit him. He complained, "There is a lack of zeal, discipline, and exactitude that would exhaust the most patient of masters."[43] A movement quickly took foot to form a professors' union. Étienne Dujardin-Beaumetz (1852–1913), government undersecretary of the Fine Arts, responded to the roily situation:

> The Conservatory is in turmoil; a wind of revolt is blowing, they say. It is important to put things back in order.
>
> First of all, it seems to me improbable that the professors of the Conservatory have thought of forming a union. They well know, in fact, that a union of civil servants would be illegal, and they are civil servants. . . .
>
> Among the grievances they have formulated can be cited: political influence taints the decisions of admission juries and examination juries. I dispute the validity of this allegation. . . .
>
> As for the lack of diligence from the students, be informed of this: the day before the examinations, the professors remit to the administration a report on the diligence of the students. Now, I myself just scrutinized the reports relative to the voice class, and I noticed that, except for one class where some observations are made on two students, the professors point out absences only attributable to illness. . . .
>
> Don't think that I am unaware of the real causes of the discontent that the professors of the Conservatory have shown. Several of them wish—and it's my duty to say it—that their right be reestablished to take part on the admission and final examination juries. Now, in excluding the professors from these juries, I have stopped too much abuse to ever think of revoking my decision. On this point I remain inflexible.
>
> They deplore also, it seems, that artists not having studied at the Conservatory take part on these juries. In truth, this is bizarre. How can one challenge the right of free artists . . . to judge the merit of beginners? They have not been students at the Conservatory, it's true, but the public has recognized their worth in the courses of their careers. To exclude them from the juries would be to restrict the education of the Conservatory.
>
> Finally, although one knows that Mr. Gabriel Fauré has never been a student at the Conservatory that he directs today, the complaint of the malcontents is apparent on this immaterial question.[44]

Rumors circulated in the press that Fauré would resign: "People are already speaking of Mr. Bruneau and Mr. Dukas as candidates to the succession of [Fauré]."[45]

On the heels of this imbroglio, an apparent injustice in the final voice examinations further fanned the fires of indignation among Conservatory professors. One student, Mr. Toraille, sang brilliantly and received an ovation from the public. The jury, headed by Fauré, awarded him no prize, however, and gave a singer estimated by some as "vulgar and clumsy" the second prize.[46] Reynaldo Hahn, who was present at the examination, spoke of the incompetence of certain jury members; it was termed "an examination where mediocrity reigned."[47] Particularly scandalous was the fact that Toraille had also been blackballed the previous year, "the victim of an incomprehensible bias on the part of the jury."[48] The scene that followed the announcement of the prizes flashed across the press:

> Mr. Toraille . . . took part in the examinations and was not included in the distribution of awards. This young man, very displeased, went out on the stage, his hat on his head, and was so bold as to insult the jury, exclaiming: "It's shameful!"[49]

The first-prize winner refused to accept the award "given under such conditions."[50] The press heralded the disgrace with headlines like "Sabotage of awards at the Conservatory" and "Incidents of the Conservatory."[51] Georges Imbart de la Tour (1865–1911), Toraille's professor, resigned in anger and died a couple of months later. A couple of dailies did "their utmost every day to assure us that Mr. Gabriel Fauré is a 'great honest man.'"[52] The *Courrier Musical* wondered, perhaps sardonically, "Why proclaim this uncontested truth on every page?"[53]

At this point, Widor was drawn into the fray as "the head of a major movement of professors having for its goal to bring back . . . an era of tranquility made of logic and justice."[54] Widor explained:

> The Conservatory professors have the custom of dining together every year. I hadn't attended this little party for a long time. Last May, several of my colleagues came to find me and pointed out that the situation we were facing at the Conservatory obliged us to meet and come to a decision.
> So I went to this dinner, where we chatted in the most tranquil manner.[55]

It was decided at the dinner that a committee of professors would meet again to draw up a petition. The resulting document, "Resolutions expressed in the meeting of the Conservatory professors, June 16, 1911," was sent to some sixty professors. Forty-five of them signed it and several others told Widor that while they were not signing it, they fully approved of his campaign.[56]

Although leading the charge on behalf of the professors, Widor made some effort to separate himself from the protestors, and yet he still admitted that he agreed with their viewpoints: "Me, an anarchist! Me, a rebel! Nonsense! My colleagues and I, we are speaking to the contrary, in the name of discipline, order, and equity."[57] He made every effort to clarify his position in the argument:

> People continually throw the word "reforms" at my head. However, it is by no means reforms that we want. We are protesting only against this slow *deformation* of an admirably established institution that has been functioning wonderfully since *l'an III*.[58] If we are protesting only now a state of affairs that

began six years ago, it's because we cannot stand for another moment to see established around the Conservatory these shady dealings that have resulted in the admission of students without any merit. Because of this, the Conservatory has become "the upside-down house." It cannot continue for long in this most unstable equilibrium. In all this I am only a spokesman—a spokesman all the more free and independent since my class is one of the only ones (there are exactly *three* of them) around which this detestable pressure is not raging at all.

Clearly, [even] if I am only the "collector of viewpoints," I am taking my task to heart, for it's a matter of the vitality of musical art in France and it's a question in which I cannot be disinterested. The press and foreign artists who attended the last examinations observed the mediocrity of the students, and to my mind it's a state that cannot endure.[59]

And he explained to *Le Temps*:

I am one of the most unbiased in this conflict. As titular of a composition class, I am, with my colleague in the other composition class and with the organ professor, completely sheltered from these difficulties. In fact, we take all the students who show up in our classes. After some months of study under our direction, the students whom we judge capable of it or who themselves wish to submit to this test, pass before an evaluation jury that either confirms or annuls our opinion. Thus, I myself am in no way complaining about the current administration.[60]

The central issues delineated in the petition concerned the recruitment for classes, the makeup of admission and examination juries, the discipline of students, and the authority of professors. The most important question, putting Conservatory professors back on the admission and examination juries, received a unanimous vote. The very reason Fauré had excluded them from the juries had backfired; many of the outsiders who were appointed to the juries were unqualified to make appropriate determinations, and some took unscrupulous advantage of their situation. Widor decried what had been happening:

The recruitment of the classes is currently turned over to a jury having no part in the interests of the institution, a jury made up of individuals—always the same—openly making deals from their position, and promising admission into classes in October from the awards in July.

The concern of the professor is to form good students; as for the outside juror, for him it's a matter of getting his clientele admitted; good or bad, come what may, too bad for the professor!

The consequences of this baneful rule are a lowering of the level of the classes, lessening of the authority of the *maîtres*, disrespect and indiscipline from the students.[61]

In a comment on the situation, Widor explained further:

> Please note that when we ask for "the exclusion of outside professors," we mean to indicate only the shameless industrialists—professors without talent and without authoritativeness who took profit from their title as a member of the admission and examination juries at the Conservatory, who inscribed this title in large letters on their personal cards and who wrote letters like this one that we have: "Miss, your [Conservatory] professor has no influence. Study with me, and I will get you admitted to the Conservatory." . . .
>
> In my personal name, but being quite convinced nevertheless that I was the faithful interpreter for all my colleagues, I have written . . . that our resolution was the following: "Give back to the professors the right to intervene in the choice of students for whom they carry the responsibility in the public examinations and in the future." . . .
>
> How is it, you will ask me, that only today we thought about protesting against this state of things that has been going on for five or six years? It's very simple, and here is my response: if the Conservatory professors didn't make any protest when they were excluded from the admission juries, it's because at that moment they could not surmise the deplorable consequences that would come from this *deformity*—pardon! from this reform (and Mr. Widor smiled knowingly), and because although very humiliated, they reckoned in a spirit of discipline that they ought to keep quiet.[62]

The protest paid off only to a degree. Dujardin-Beaumetz and Fauré devised some concessions to pacify the faculty, but largely brushed the petition aside. *Le Temps* summarized the affair as "A lot of noise for nothing."[63] Although the composition of the juries still would not include Conservatory professors, the "outsiders" appointed to the juries could serve only one year and could not be reappointed until another three years had lapsed. No member of the jury could claim a title, privilege, or other advantage, and a disciplinary council consisting of the director, general secretary, and two or three Conservatory professors would be created to assure fairness in all controversies that might arise. In addition, Dujardin-Beaumetz planned to require everyone called to serve on a jury to give to the director his word of honor that he fulfilled all the conditions of the regulations.[64]

Outwardly, the thrust of the petition was to effect changes in the modus operandi of the Conservatory, but behind it all was a suppressed hostility that had been stewing for six years against Fauré, his administrative ideas, and even his artistic ideals. Critic Pierre Lalo (1866–1943), son of Édouard, widened the divide between Fauré and his staff when he wrote bluntly in support of the director:

> Mr. Fauré is *a musician*, and some of the professors of the Conservatory are not musicians, but only professors and civil servants. The idea of music, the taste

of music and the sense of music that are Mr. Fauré's and that he reveals in his works . . . are to these men disquieting, troubling, and threatening; these are disturbing to them in their conventional, superficial, and lifeless conception of music . . . ; they do not speak the same language as their director.[65]

Undersecretary Dujardin-Beaumetz went well beyond what was necessary to proclaim his staunch and unconditional support of Fauré in a *Temps* interview, of which the following is a short excerpt:

I would be pleased if you would make known clearly, in a way that all those who are interested in the Conservatory will understand, that I am in no way impressed by the campaign of malevolent insinuations aimed against the director of this establishment. I am resolved to do what seems just to me, and to do only that.

Now, what seems just to me, first of all, is to keep the *Maître* Gabriel Fauré as head of the Conservatory.

Gabriel Fauré, the composer of such beautiful and refined works, has all my admiration; Mr. Gabriel Fauré, director of the Conservatory, has all my confidence.

I am of the opinion that an artist like him honors the great establishment that he directs. I am determined to proclaim that Mr. Gabriel Fauré is a great honest man whose loyalty and frankness are unwavering. He is upright and noble in character, quite French, one could say.[66]

Although Dujardin-Beautmetz's statement obviously intended to lay the issue to rest, Widor penned a final volley to the editor of *Le Temps*. The letter was prefaced in supportive terms when republished in *Le Courrier Musical*:

Floods of ink have flowed; innumerable conflicting and fruitless interviews have been taken. So many schemes advocated, so many plans freely suggested—only one stands: that which Mr. Undersecretary of the Fine Arts conceives presently in his soul and conscience. . . . No change in the composition of the jury, from which the professors will be, as in the past, excluded.

This last point is of an extreme importance: the so legitimate demands of the majority of professors and their forbearance . . . have remained dead letters. The voices that were supposed to have been listened to are naturally those that [the administration] did not want to hear.

More than that, their spokesman, Mr. Widor, was nearly taken to task, at least from the malevolent insinuations that have been put forth with the objective of distorting the worthy and loyal role that this *maître* saw himself forced to play in the affair. Last, as the conclusion to this final news item so profoundly tainted with injustice, we make a point of publishing the letter that Mr. Widor just addressed to *Le Temps*:

Paris, July 25, 1911

Dear Editor,

Mr. Dujardin-Beaumetz, in an interview with *Le Temps* (July 14), attributes to an intrigue, indeed to a sort of rebellion, the desires expressed by most of the Conservatory professors—desires of which these professors asked me to be the interpreter to their director [Fauré] and the rue de Valois [the office of Dujardin-Beaumetz].

Yet, is there nothing more correct than their attitude and nothing more just than their request?

Universal reason, common sense, and the ways and customs of all the schools in the world have always assigned to the *maître* who is going to assume the very heavy responsibility of the formation of a mind, the right to choose this mind; people have never disputed the freedom to vote for the candidate who has promise, *as opposed* to the one who will achieve nothing.

Now, for the six years that this right has been taken from them, my colleagues in Paris are observing a progressive drop in the average of the students admitted into their classes, and sadly they are stating it.

Is it thus admissible that a common policy excuse can prevail against natural right, good sense, and conscience? This right, recognized at the School of Fine Arts and at quai Malaquais [the French Institute], is denied at rue de Madrid [the Conservatory]: a different legislation for the two banks of the Seine—liberal on the south, tyrannical on the north!

In the interview of Mr. Dujardin-Beaumetz, first of all I permit myself to call attention to a singular inexactitude: contrary to what he has affirmed, his repeal of the liberal edict from *l'an III* has not been able to facilitate any career or open any door, for never has the Conservatory been reserved *only* to young people residing in Paris; students from the country schools have always been admissible here. Second, the honorable Undersecretary of the Fine Arts attributes the desires that my colleagues have given me the honor to transmit to him some feelings that have nothing in common with the interests of the establishment, and these innuendos affect me personally.

I protest.

There are still some Frenchmen in France defending a cause of general interest, although they have no particular stake in it. I do not believe myself of an administrative aptitude; I am looking for neither title nor honor; I have no reason for animosity against anyone. This said, I share fully in his words: "It is just, it is good, it is necessary, it is edifying that Mr. Fauré, a musician of great talent, remain at the head of the Conservatory."

Vere, dignum et justum est, aequum et salutare [Truly, he is worthy and upright, equitable and beneficent], says the old liturgy; one cannot state it better.

And we will continue to demand the strict justice back, the right to choose the students for whom we carry the responsibility in the future. It's necessary. We must.

Most sincerely,
Ch.-M. Widor[67]

Widor had brought the full weight of his name and position to bear in this matter. When necessary, he did not hesitate to voice his disapproval of a perceived injustice, and such was the time. While he professed support for his director, his feisty role in the protest could not have pleased Fauré, who was undoubtedly not amused by headlines such as this one: "Mr. Ch. M. Widor 'Cries Out' Courteously about the Conservatory."[68] In his crying out, Widor concluded: "As we believe ourselves responsible for traditions that we have been left, as we passionately love our art, and as nothing that touches French interests leaves us indifferent, we met and drew up the most courteous and most urgent of requests. . . . And very courteously, we 'cry out.'"[69] Such rhetoric certainly must have offended Fauré in its implication that he was somehow callous to "French interests," and did not "passionately love our art." It would not be the last time Widor rubbed Fauré the wrong way.

—89—

Vierne and Dubois: "Widor junior" and "Dudu"

Usually known for his good graces and tact, Widor committed the great imprudence of speaking ill of Fauré in front of some "mutual friends," who needless to say hastened to report the insult to Fauré. The faux pas cost Vierne dearly: "Deeply hurt, Fauré felt a resentment of which I, by a special favor from heaven, had to bear the expense."[70] After Guilmant's death on March 29, 1911, Vierne—whom Widor referred to as his "alter ego"[71] and others sometimes maliciously called "Widor junior"[72]—had hoped to become the new organ professor at the Conservatory. Fauré blocked the nomination and appointed his old friend Eugène Gigout, "the direct heir of the doctrines of Niedermeyer."[73] Vierne did not lose on all counts, however; Guilmant had also held the professorship of the organ class at d'Indy's Schola Cantorum, and the organ professorship there was offered to Vierne. A long-standing rivalry had existed between the two institutions, and although Widor did not care for d'Indy or his school, he approved of the appointment, telling Vierne that it would provide "a chair from which you can preach the good word."[74]

From the beginning, Vierne seemed to have borne the brunt of jealousy directed toward his professor. Some who envied Widor's position in the world agitated against him by inhibiting the progress of his favored pupil.[75] Vierne's efforts to win first prize in the Conservatory organ competition failed for three years running. In 1891 Widor's students all played Bach, and he was criticized for not having them play something of Franck. In 1892 Vierne played Franck's *Grande pièce symphonique* "without an error," but its length seemed excessive to some jurors and his improvisation too daring; he was awarded only a second prize.[76] Widor furiously brandished harsh words toward those jurors who had derailed a just outcome: "I despise this bunch of failures," he snarled, and he vowed to get even one day.[77] Nonetheless, during these years Widor continually urged Vierne to persevere: "It's a question of will-power, and it's worth it, believe me."[78]

> What seems an injustice to you today, and with good reason, is perhaps a blessing. You'll probably never do better in a competition, but a longer stay in the class will be profitable from a much more important point of view than that of obtaining the coveted diploma. You'll form a critical sense that's always lacking in people who've left too soon. Believe me, your double career of virtuoso and teacher won't suffer from it.[79]

Vierne's fine performance of Bach's Passacaglia in 1893 failed to win even a second prize; this third failure stung sharply. Théodore Dubois had presided over the jury in the absence of Ambroise Thomas and done nothing to rectify the injustice. Vierne related that "Widor was in a terrible rage,"[80] but he still managed to encourage his downtrodden pupil:

> "Competitions don't mean a thing," Widor told me. "They're a small satisfaction for the families and an official stamp for the *bourgeois*. I don't have a prize for anything, and yet I can't complain. When you've made a name for yourself as a virtuoso and composer—and I'll help you—no one will ask whether you have a prize from the Conservatoire. Never mind, you must keep at it and see whether they'll dare to send you away without the famous diploma."[81]

The fourth year (1894), Thomas warned the jury that he would not tolerate this conspiracy against Widor's students, and Vierne finally obtained the first prize by the jury's unanimous judgment with Bach's Prelude and Fugue in B Minor.[82]

Widor had been waiting for an opportunity to reckon with Dubois, and planned a little celebration party for Vierne. Unsuspecting, Dubois himself would provide the entertainment. Widor invited several friends: Henri Dallier (1849–1934), Henri Libert, Guilmant, Émile Bernard (1868–1941), Hugues Imbert, Raoul Pugno, Carolus-Duran, and Jean-Louis Forain. Vierne arrived early and found his *maître* in conference with the headwaiter:

> "I've also invited," [Widor] told me, "Théodore Dubois, your former juror, for whom I hold in store a little trick. Oh! Not very spiteful, but from which you'll take some pleasure, I presume. I don't have a grudge against this poor man, who basically isn't malicious; but he hasn't any character. I know him to be an amateur when it comes to good wines, and I'm going to have him served a little more than he should drink, in order to inebriate him in a few

moments. It seems that, under the influence of Bacchus, he readily loses his self-control; I'll take some notes and serve them to him a little later. As he's deliberately very chaste, I'll enjoy the spectacle of these changes of complexion. For him, I'll leave it at that."

The guests arrived; . . . Dubois came last, and Widor introduced me. The author of the *Traité d'harmonie* blushed a little. We sat down at the table and the meal began in an atmosphere of unreserved good humor. From time to time, Widor made a sign to the headwaiter, who slyly refilled the glasses for "Dudu," as he called him. When he judged him to be "just right," Widor told a rather spicy story. Dubois, glowing, went one better, and began to relate some affairs to us with frightful realism, supplying the names in support. Dallier and Widor threw the ball back to him and, very excited, he started to sing some songs that would make a regiment blush. With amazement and delight, we watched this good man—always of stiff and formal bearing, the perfect model of an usher— who, without taking account of the number of glasses, emptied them and sang coarse songs. "What do you think of that?" Widor said to me as he adjourned to the drawing room, "he's in fine form, the man of direct octaves. . . . I'd give a lot for his students to have seen him just now."[83]

Dubois held the directorship of the Conservatory between 1896 and 1905. He apparently continued to blacklist Widor's students, perhaps in part to avenge himself of the little trick Widor had played on him. In 1903, the *Courrier Musical* complained:

> The composition class of Mr. Widor, at the Conservatory, is not really favored by the liking of Mr. Dubois. The Prix de Rome is unknown there, and the Conservatory prizes in fugue are almost unknown. This year, *not one* reward has been accorded to the students of Mr. Widor who presented themselves at these competitions! This is becoming alarming and gives rise to doubts, not about the teaching of Mr. Widor, but about the impartiality of Mr. Dubois.[84]

Despite these perceived injustices, letters from Widor to Dubois dating from 1910 and after exhibit a very cordial relationship between the two men, Widor addressing his colleague in the informal "tu" form.[85]

—90—

Symphonie antique:
"A lofty and proud work of a noble and pure ideal"

Widor's love of plainsong is exalted in his last orchestral symphony—his magnum opus. Although stylistically on the edge of post-romanticism, the title of the work is a bold, self-conscious admission that its thematic material, at least, represents another era. On the title page of one score, Widor wrote: "The author has not at all wanted to contrast the ancient world with the Christian world, but to blend them, as has history from the origins of Christianity."[86] The *Symphonie antique*, Op. 83, stands as a monumental testament to Widor's art in terms of the underlying idealism, compositional inspiration and technique, and the resources employed to carry it out. The use of plainsong as thematic material in a large work—begun timidly some fifteen years earlier in the *Symphonie gothique*—comes into full bloom. Through the *Symphonie romane* and the *Sinfonia sacra*, Widor's preoccupation with borrowed liturgical themes continued to exert itself. Turning to plainsong was the natural outgrowth of his vocation, and he wondered: "How is it that French organists having a talent for composing do not use more of these old legendary themes?"[87] In the *Symphonie antique*, two "admirable themes" (the *Te Deum* and *Lauda Sion*) underlie its vast musical edifice, the summit of Widor's spiritual vision.

As a model, Widor had surely cast an eye on Beethoven's Ninth Symphony— the "masterpiece of masterpieces," as he called it—with its choral Finale.[88] It is also noteworthy that Gustave Mahler conducted the premiere of his Symphony No. 2 (*Resurrection*) in Paris on April 17, 1910—eleven months before the premiere of Widor's new symphony. The resources required in the *Antique* are Mahlerian: piccolo, two flutes, two oboes, English horn, two clarinets, two bassoons, sarrusophone, four horns, four trumpets, three trombones, tuba, strings, timpani, triangle, tambourine, cymbals, bass drum, tamtam, harp, organ, and chorus with soprano and contralto soloists. A short explanatory note appears on the title page:

Legend attributes the theme of this Symphony to the improvisation of Sophocles on the eve of Salamis. The original words [of the Greek] Hymn that rendered thanks to the Gods of Victory have not come down to us; the Latin text (*Te Deum Laudamus*) by Saint Ambrose and Saint Augustine has been substituted for the Greek text.[89]

In his article "La révision du plain-chant," Widor referred to the ancient *Te Deum* as "one of the three or four most beautiful chants in the world."[90] He elaborated the context of its birth:

For five centuries, the first Christian bishops had selected carefully that which was most characteristic from the antique chant (Greek). Who were the authors of these chants? No one can say. One of the most beautiful cries that can come from the human chest is the intonation of the *Te Deum*; by whom is it? Once heard, one can no longer forget it. A legend maintains that it is by the greatest poet of all times and has attributed it to Sophocles on the eve of [the Battle of] Salamis. He was twenty-one years old, a citharist, chorus master, and lyric poet. Inundated by the host of Persians ten times more numerous than the Greek army, and astounded by their victory, he would thus have begun to sing . . . exhaling his soul in this sublime cry that belongs to two modes at the same time in the same tonality.[91]

Widor dedicated the *Symphonie antique* to Countess René de Béarn (1870–1939), a close friend, promoter, and organ pupil.[92] He conducted the premiere in her mansion's great hall—a reproduction of a room in the great pyramid of Egypt—on March 22, 1911.[93] The *Antique* premiered publicly at the Concerts Colonne on the day before Christmas 1911, under the baton of Widor's long-time friend Gabriel Pierné:[94]

The premiere of an important work figured in the Sunday concert; a lofty and proud work of a noble and pure ideal, without concessions nor compromise, a sincere work above all, inspired from an eminently original and fertile thought. The *Symphonie antique* of Mr. Ch.-M. Widor is built on two themes from the Christian liturgy, the *Te Deum* and *Lauda Sion*. . . . In the symphony of Mr. Widor, the [first] theme forms what people have agreed to call the cyclic motive. It is that motive that, by its returns or its transformations, gives the entire work its unity. The *Lauda Sion*, which intervenes at various places in an episodic manner, or is combined with the first theme, is of a less hieratic character, more human one could say, and it successfully stands in opposition to the first theme. The mastery of the learned professor of composition at the Conservatory is known; consequently, his symphony is constructed with logic, perfect clarity, and its developments abound in interesting and ingenious details. The use of religious themes as a frame gives the ensemble a gravity and an unction where some would be able to find a certain monotony, if some episodes full of passion, vigor, and brilliance didn't happily come to contrast with them. The third movement, corresponding to the customary Scherzo, is from this point of view particularly welcome and suggestive. The Finale, by the use of the chorus and two distant voices . . . that take up the liturgical themes again, blooms and concludes with a chorale of an impressive power and majesty. The work is severe in appearance, I have said, and one admits that in its lofty reserve it does not win the approbation of those who above all seek in music some rare or unprecedented sensations. The ideal pursued by Mr. Widor exceeds this narrow circle. Profound thinker, refined artist, but above all else a musician of tradition nurtured from pure classical sap, he has written, in conformity with his nature, a score which is certainly not a return backward nor an imitation of the masterpieces of the past, but the full blooming of a talent conscious of its strength, sure of itself, made of logic, emotion, and sincerity. The reception was not warm enough for the first two movements, but the third and especially the last obtained a unanimous success.[95]

The somewhat reserved audience response that greeted the symphony soon transformed into unabashed enthusiastic approval, and the work became highly respected as "one of the greatest of the contemporary period."[96] When programmed at the Concerts Colonne in 1929, one critic wondered what the concertgoers of 1911 had fussed about:

> Of noble architecture and yet very alive, the *Symphonie antique* of Widor is greatly interesting, and Mr. Pierné has been quite right to put it on the program. It aroused, they tell us, in 1911, some impassioned commentary. Nothing like it today, and all the public was in accord in applauding this beautiful work.[97]

Widor conducted the symphony in Strasbourg at the end of the war in the two-thousand-seat Sängerhaus, which he found of perfect proportions and admirable acoustics:

> At the end of the concert, the regret was expressed that this *Te Deum* of the *Symphonie antique* had not been performed in the Cathedral. . . . No, the work was not made at all for that, and the vast Gothic naves are hardly favorable to the orchestra. The organ is more fitting to them—the instrument of which the sound has neither beginning nor end and which evokes the religious idea by that of the infinite.[98]

With the *Symphonie antique*, Widor reached the apogee of his life's career as a composer, the following quarter century representing a sort of grand dénouement to a life rich in accomplishment and diversity.

—91—

Albert Schweitzer, "Super-doctor of music!" and the Bach edition

A particularly fortuitous teacher/student relationship arose between Widor and Albert Schweitzer (see fig. 19). In October 1893, the eighteen-year-old Schweitzer went to Paris to study privately with Widor: "[Schweitzer] asked if he could play something on the organ to me. 'Play what?' I asked. 'Bach, of course,' was his reply."[99] Over the next few years, Schweitzer returned for different periods of study. Although he characterized himself initially as "a poor scholar," he eventually excelled in four disciplines.[100] It was Schweitzer's superior intelligence, spirit of selflessness, and devotion to others that touched Widor deeply.[101] Writing a letter of introduction for him many years later, Widor enthused: "My Dear Minister, This is my friend Albert Schweitzer, from Strasbourg, doctor of philosophy, theology, medicine, and super-doctor of music!"[102]

While studying with Widor, Schweitzer enlightened his *maître* on an important facet of Bach's music that he had not understood before. Widor venerated the Leipzig cantor in every aspect of his art, though finding it sometimes enigmatic:

Bach is incontestably the mightiest of musicians; one is seized with a kind of terror in perusing the incredible catalogue of his works, in thumbing through those forty huge volumes, in pausing on any one of those pages where the least design seems always long considered and deliberate, where the idea—always original and profound—soars. Yet, on the other hand, was there ever a less enigmatic thinker?[103]

Widor described how Schweitzer taught him something about Bach:

Several years ago, I quite often received visits from a young Strasbourgian. . . . He came to ask my council on the interpretation of the masters; he sat at the organ and I listened to him; then we had discussions. As he knew the old Lutheran texts very well, I informed him of my uneasiness with certain chorales [of Bach] that passed abruptly from one order of ideas to another, from chromaticism to diatonicism, from the solemn to the pointed, without apparent reason or logical deduction:
    "What can be the thought of the composer here, what has he wanted to say? If he breaks the thread of his discourse, he therefore has an objective other than that of pure music, and without doubt he wants to put in relief a literary idea . . . but how do we know this idea?"
    "Quite simply by the words of the hymn," replied Schweitzer; and then he recited to me the verses of the chorale in question, which fully justified the musician, and showed the descriptive genius at grips with the text, word by word; I came to ascertain that it was impossible to appreciate the work when ignoring the sense of the implied words.
    And so we began to leaf through the three volumes of the collection [of chorale preludes] discovering the exact meaning of things. All was explained and clarified, not only in the overall lines but also in the smallest details. Music and Poetry closely embraced one another, each musical design corresponding to a literary idea. And it's thus that this collection, admired until then as a model of pure counterpoint, appeared to me as a suite of poems of an eloquence and emotional intensity without parallel.[104]
    The mysteries were all solved. During the next few afternoons we played through the whole of the chorale preludes. While Schweitzer—for he was the pupil—explained them to me one after the other, I made the acquaintance of a Bach whose existence I had previously had only the dimmest suspicion. In a flash it became clear to me that the cantor of St. Thomas's was much more than an incomparable contrapuntist to whom I had formerly looked up as one gazes up at a colossal statue, and that his work exhibits an unparalleled desire and capacity for expressing poetic ideas and for bringing word and tone into unity.[105]

Widor immediately suggested to Schweitzer that he write a book about the symbolism in Bach. Like all of Widor's students, Schweitzer was inclined to consider whatever advice was presented to him, and he undertook the project between 1899 and 1904.[106] In the preface Widor wrote for Schweitzer's book, *J. S. Bach: Le musicien-poète,* he described the importance of Schweitzer's revolutionary study; it literally unlocked the door to a new understanding of Bach's music:

> Better than all the discourses in the world, the pages that you are going to read will show the power of this extraordinary mind, for they will give you some examples and some proofs. From Mozart to Wagner, there is not a musician who has not judged the work of Johann Sebastian Bach as the most fertile of teachings. And rightly so! If such was the opinion of the Masters, when part of this work was lying unknown, buried under the dust of the libraries, when it was difficult to grasp from it the entire meaning, what will be our opinion today, when all of it is just now brought out? . . .
>
> In looking through the book of Mr. Schweitzer, it seems that we attended the inauguration of a monument; the last scaffoldings, the last veils just fell.[107]

In 1910, the publishing firm of G. Schirmer in New York asked Widor to prepare an edition of Bach's organ music, complete with instructions on the most suitable way of performing it. He agreed on the condition that Schweitzer collaborate with him on the project. The contract, signed and dated July 6, 1910, stipulated that "*les messieurs Widor et Schweitzer* were to deliver to Schirmer an edition of the Bach Organ Works in eight volumes."[108] During the next couple of years either Schweitzer traveled to Paris to meet with Widor, or Widor traveled to Gunsbach (Alsace) to meet with Schweitzer.[109] In this manner, they succeeded in completing the first five volumes, which were published in 1912 and 1913.[110] The remaining volumes, containing the chorale preludes, had been largely prepared except for some finishing touches, but the urgency that Schweitzer felt toward his African mission superseded their completion.[111] Widor had done everything to try to dissuade him from going to Africa, but to no avail. As he later told Dupré, "what can you do when a man says to you 'God calls me'?"[112] Schweitzer left for French Equatorial Africa in March 1913.

The remaining volumes were to have been completed during Schweitzer's first leave, but World War I broke out and other considerations inhibited further progress on the edition.[113] Not until 1919 did Schweitzer communicate a plan to Schirmer to complete the final three volumes; he concluded, "I promised the dear master Widor to begin and I will keep my word."[114] Unfortunately, Rudolf E. Schirmer (1859–1919), the head of the firm who negotiated the contract with Widor and Schweitzer, had just died and the new executive director had little interest in completing the edition. A curt "Dear Sir" letter was sent to inform Schweitzer that the remaining volumes would need to be "deferred and delayed."[115] By 1927, sales of the first five volumes had risen and attitudes at Schirmer had changed. The publisher showed interest in having Schweitzer complete the edition, but the damaged relationship endured and an internal Schirmer memorandum noted, "Dr. Schweitzer evidently is peeved and that makes the situation very embarrassing."[116] In 1930 Widor wrote to Schweitzer:

> Two weeks ago, I received a visit from the widow Schirmer, and today that of the director of the firm, Mr. Engel.
>   . . . I found myself in the position of complaining to the one and to the other about the halt in the publication of the last three volumes, (the *Chorales*), even though I believed all hope lost and all complaint useless!
>   "It's *necessary* that you come to terms with Schweitzer," I told them, "and publish his work, which will honor our times, our art, America, and the Schirmer firm."
>   I hope that you will be able to come to an agreement with this firm; it would be a joy without equal if it were given me to see the edifice completed thanks to you.
>   Engel appeared to me very intelligent and desirous to succeed.[117]

Relations normalized between the Schirmer firm and Schweitzer, yet he had occupied himself with his other work in the meantime, and Widor was becoming too old and ailing to continue an active role in the collaboration. Six more years passed without progress. Twice in 1936 Widor mentioned the edition of the chorales to Schweitzer: "how can I adequately express my regret over the delay of the edition of the chorales?"[118] And less than three months before his death, Widor pleaded, "If I have a prayer for you, it's that you don't forget the Bach chorales; the edition is urgent and for your glory and also a little for myself."[119] Only after Widor's death and another fourteen years had passed did Schweitzer find the time and energy, with the collaboration of Édouard Nies-Berger (1904–2002), to begin the completion of the Bach edition and finally to make good his promise to "the dear master Widor."[120]

From the outset, Schirmer desired that the edition be published in three languages; Schweitzer explained:

> The divergencies between the French text, on the one hand, and the German, together with the English which is based on it, on the other, arise from the fact that in respect of the details as to which our opinions differed, Widor and I had agreed that in the French edition his ideas, which fitted better the peculiarities of the French organs, should be dominant, while in the German and the English mine should, taking, as they did, more into account the character of the modern organ.[121]

In light of today's knowledge and scholarship concerning Bach performance practice, the Widor/Schweitzer concepts of interpretation quail.
Nonetheless, when one considers the almost total ignorance of Bach's music
during Widor's early life, his contribution to the Bach reawakening as we know
it, especially the organ works, must not be overlooked. He steadfastly carried the
torch from Lemmens, strictly adhered to teaching Bach at the Paris Conservatory, and consistently conducted and performed the music of Bach before it had
become popular. Bach was a god to Widor, "der Vater von uns allen" (the father
of us all), he would say, and he spent his life spreading the good word.[122]

—92—

Mr. Perpetual Secretary:
"I place myself at the disposal of the Academy"

Between 1912 and the outbreak of World War I, the focus of Widor's life
shifted dramatically to his official functions as an academician of the French
Institute. At the same time, his role as composer and touring artist waned to
a few select engagements. On December 22, 1911, he performed as pianist at
the Salle Malakoff in a special evening of his music that included the Op. 68
Quintet, Op. 34 Flute Suite, Op. 80 Cello Sonata, and Op. 52 *Soirs d'alsace*.[123]
Concerts outside of Paris included: Tournai, Rome, Dortmund, Rennes, and
Edinburgh.[124] In Rome, at the four-thousand-seat Augusteum, Her Majesty the
Queen of Italy counted among the throng that heard Widor conduct his Op.
69 Symphony and then play several organ works of Bach and Handel as well as
his *Symphonie gothique*.[125]

A trip to Liège with Gustave Charpentier to represent the Institute at the
official inauguration of the Grétry Museum typified the ceremonial roles
sometimes delegated to members of the Institute.[126] Widor greatly enjoyed
Charpentier's company, and he had taken an active role in his election to the
Academy upon the death of Massenet in 1912. As soon as the vote in favor of
Charpentier was certain, Widor had rushed to Montmartre by cab, "climbed
three steps at a time to the new 'immortal's' apartment on top of the house,
and took him in his arms to give him the great news."[127]

Because of his public visibility, Widor became a natural spokesman for various indigent causes, and he found himself in an influential office to that end
upon being elected president of the Association of Artists and Musicians in
1912.[128] The association provided its members pension funds and, at its discretion, contingency funds could be allotted to members in need due to illness
or lack of work.[129] In his official capacities, Widor's integrity and benevolence
overruled any past political rivalries or petty jealousies that may have been
aimed at him or his music. Isidor Philipp, as president of the Association of

Former Pupils of the Conservatory, found himself at Widor's door regularly: "I used and abused our friendship, for I became a sort of official beggar."[130] Marcel Dupré testified to one instance of Widor's benevolence:

> Beneath a cold appearance Widor had a warm and generous heart. I witnessed many of his acts of kindness to unfortunate artists. And he always forgot past disagreements. One day, arriving at his office in the Institut . . . I found him in a jovial mood. "Come here. Listen to this letter that I just wrote. 'Sir, I cannot thank you for the review you wrote of my last piece, but I have the pleasure of informing you that I have just given my approval for the aid you requested.'" The recipient of that letter never replied, but the essential point was that Widor had helped him.[131]

Widor's skill in working with people soon earned him the next star in his crown of achievements. Henry Roujon, perpetual secretary of the Academy of Fine Arts, had been in ill health for some time, and on June 6, 1914, Widor was designated as provisional secretary. Upon Roujon's death a few weeks later, Widor submitted the only letter of candidature, writing: "Some of my confrères have been good enough to think of me for the succession of our greatly lamented perpetual secretary. I place myself at the disposal of the Academy in case it would not have a candidature more authorized than mine."[132] He received the unanimous vote of the thirty-three voters present at the election:[133]

> It was my old friend Bonnat, then president of the Academy, who, on the death of Roujon, had the idea to make me his successor. However, I was never involved in business and knew no one, no more in the political world than in administration. Upon the insistence of Bonnat, who made me pose my candidature, and to my great surprise, lacking a rival, I was elected on July 18, 1914.[134]

When Widor assumed the office of perpetual secretary, he became virtually the highest official musician in France.[135] Saint-Saëns, who loved to compose short poems, sent one of congratulations to his friend:

Grand musicien, cher confrère,	[Great musician, dear confrère,
Doux et lumineux Secrétaire	Kind and luminous Secretary
Toi dont la perpétuité	You whose perpetuity
Nous remplit de joyeuseté	Fills us with joy
Puisse Minerve la guerrière	May Minerva the warrior
Patronne de notre Maison	Patroness of our house
Protéger ta belle carrière	Protect your splendid career
Étendre son bras sur ton front![136]	Stretch out her arm over your head!]

318 MR. WIDOR, MEMBER OF THE INSTITUTE OF FRANCE (1910-37)

Not since the opera composer Jacques-François Halévy (1799–1862) had the perpetual secretary been drawn from the ranks of his own academy; ordinarily, the secretary is elected from one of the other four academies. As perpetual secretary, Widor received a substantial salary of six thousand francs per year, and he was provided with a finely appointed apartment on the second floor of the west wing of the Palace of the Institute.[137]

Widor specifically chose a smaller suite of rooms than his predecessor in order to have direct access by a small interior staircase to the Salle de Caen on the first floor. There, he had his two-manual salon organ installed (see fig. 20), and after a fresh restoration of the hall at the end of the war he organized a series of concerts that took place the first Saturday of each month.[138] "His ability, his unselfish spirit of enterprise, and his generosity contributed to transform the Mazarin Palace into a living, humming bee-hive."[139] He delighted in drawing upon the talents of his colleagues and featuring seldom-heard chamber music on the monthly programs.[140] Comfortably situated in his new lodging, from his studio window he could view the cityscape he adored: the bustling activities on the Seine with its tugs and barges, the Pont des Arts, the grand Palais du Louvre, and the beautiful church of Saint-Germain l'Auxerrois with its magnificent bell tower.

The duties of the perpetual secretary encompassed a number of important activities during Widor's time: he served on the commission that administrated the Institute as a whole, as well as minding the functions of his own academy's affairs—which included the management of a considerable amount of correspondence, the preparation of numerous reports for the academy, the administration of the Prix de Rome and the Rome school, and whenever a fellow member died, the perpetual secretary had the duty of writing a historical notice on the life and work of the deceased member.[141] He also served as one of the Institute's official hosts when dignitaries visited Paris.

One such occasion arose when Queen Marie of Romania (1875–1938) attended a meeting at the Institute. The queen had taken a liking to Widor's music and, at a performance of *Conte d'avril* at the Odéon, she "frequently applauded it."[142] Widor became acquainted with the Romanian royal family and welcomed the king, queen, and one of their daughters to Sunday Mass at Saint-Sulpice on July 31, 1921. *Le Ménestrel* reported, "The sovereigns were received at the grand portal by Mr. Ch. Widor. . . . And in honor of Their Majesties, the eminent composer performed several pieces of sacred music with incomparable mastery."[143] Earlier in the year, an official reception was given at the Institute for Queen Marie with French President Alexandre Millerand (1859–1943; president 1920–24); Widor and Saint-Saëns availed themselves as escorts (see fig. 21). Widor related an unexpected incident that greatly amused everyone; the painter and engraver Auguste Frédéric Laguillermie (1841–1934) was presiding:

Laguillermie, who was not a man of the world, had never left his workshop and was not accustomed to speaking under such circumstances. He had made a speech of three points, written very largely, each paragraph having four lines. He had studied them with great care and had even included foreign affairs. He read the first four lines quite well, and then he realized he was losing his memory at the beginning of the second paragraph. He suddenly pulled out his lorgnon, hurled his speech into the air and exclaimed, "What the devil! I'm not used to speaking to royalty!" The sovereigns were delighted, Millerand convulsed with laughter, and Madame Millerand thoroughly enjoyed this incomparable moment.[144]

Needless to say, the qualities of organization and eloquence that Widor expressed to a superior degree made him an excellent choice for the post of perpetual secretary. For forty years, he had contributed countless reviews and articles to various publications; his scholarly and cultural acumen were well known by all. These writings shine for the depth of understanding and background information he brought to each subject. During his twenty-two years as perpetual secretary, Widor wrote dozens of articles and delivered scores of lectures at the Institute, each one reflecting the vast culture of its author; he was a "past master in the art of skillful speaking":[145]

As to the notices written by Widor, they are crisp, stirring, conserve the ease and quick-wittedness of his conversation, and contain numerous bits of information that will make them consulted by future historians.[146]

Isidor Philipp described them as "little masterpieces, distinguished by the linguistic elegance of an Anatole France."[147] Le Ménestrel praised Widor's election as the new perpetual secretary:

His colleagues well knew what they were doing in bringing together all their votes for him. Indeed, there is in Mr. Widor, aside from the composer, a very refined and tactful scholar—a scholar who knows how to handle the writer's pen with as much elegance as that of the musician. . . . And since to these qualities of a writer he joins a broad understanding of art in all its forms and in all its manifestations, one can rest assured that he will be up to the task that falls to him.[148]

In 1927, eighteen of his masterfully researched essays were published by the Academy of Fine Arts under the title Fondations, portraits, de Massenet à Paladilhe. By the articulate manner in which they are written, these writings speak as much of their author as they do of their subjects; Robert Brussel pointed out, "Those who have not known Widor will find him entirely in the work he titled Fondations, portraits."[149]

The unremitting success with which Widor would carry out his musico-political career lay in his integrity and humanity. He would say, "To know how to be of service to people—to know how to listen—is the great secret of politicians and also of artists."[150] Service was a theme that threaded itself through his life's work, and it continually earned him respect: "His kindness and generosity were inexhaustible. About himself, he didn't want people to speak. And if he was still hoping in life, it was in the desire to be able to serve music and musicians."[151] He made it his duty to be readily available to his constituents and his students: "When the *maître* is present, one is advised by this indication: his door is never closed."[152] Every one of his activities was equally important to him and he gladly took on whatever he needed to do. Dupré related: "He had the habit of saying, and this he repeated thousands and thousands of times: 'You have the duty to do a thing if you are sure it is necessary to the general interest!'"[153] Such sentiments were not empty philosophies.

—93—

"Censure on Mr. Widor"

When faced with a perceived injustice directed toward one of his composition students, Jean-Marie Déré, Widor went head to head with Fauré:

May 25, 1916

My dear Director,

I cannot protest strongly enough against the scandal that has been revealed to me this morning:
Two *second prizes*, two *honorable mentions* from 1915 judged unworthy to compete in 1916!
Is it possible that a prizewinner from one year not be allowed *by right* into the competition the following year?
Such an occurrence has never yet taken place.
It does no credit to the institution.

Sincerely,
Widor[154]

The following day, Fauré wasted no time filing Widor's complaint with the government undersecretary of the Fine Arts:

I received from Mr. Widor, professor of one of the composition classes at the Conservatory, a letter of which I have the honor to send you a copy.

I do not want to respond to this letter, which very much offends me, before you have had the kindness to let me know your opinion on its contents.

I am attaching to this letter an extract from the minutes of the examination meeting in question, in which you will find the list of committee members who were present and whose authority and competence is above all dispute, as well as the marks obtained by the students in the two composition classes.

You will also be able to see there that if the student Déré, from Widor's class, has obtained a second prize in fugue, it was in 1911, and that since then this student has competed two times without results, which demonstrates that his progress has been of no account and explains his failure today.

I might add that never in any of our regulations has it been specified that a student, having been awarded [previously], would be allowed by right to compete even if the examination committee no longer found him fit for it.[155]

Widor seems not to have had all the facts when he fired off his protest to Fauré, and as a result he got bloodied. The undersecretary wrote to Fauré, recommending strong discipline:

On May 26, you made known to me the tenor of a letter addressed to you from Mr. Widor, professor of a composition class at the Conservatory. . . .

The tone and wording of this letter are not acceptable; I would even say that they seem almost insulting to the examination committee that had the responsibility of pronouncing judgment and that was composed of the most competent and honorable people. . . .

This is not the first time, moreover, that Mr. Widor has permitted himself to judge the actions of the Administration inside the Conservatory or to review the regulations, and by doing so [also judging] the government that prepared and countersigned the decree and order that govern the Conservatory.

As for me, I have not forgotten the insult of which Mr. Widor was guilty in February 1916 by organizing, unknown to the Director and the Undersecretary of State [of the Fine Arts], a sort of petitioning or *referendum* of professors against the new regulations in force. . . .

The repetition of these facts, if unopposed, would soon infringe seriously on discipline by creating a situation in which anyone, following the example of one of the most prominent professors, would believe himself free to judge administrative actions.

I ask you, as much in my name as in the name of the government Secretary, whom I took care to inform about these two matters, to impose censure on Mr. Widor.[156]

Addressing a formal letter to Widor at the Institute, Fauré performed his duty—probably with some degree of satisfaction; the message must have been one of the most hurtful that Widor ever received:

June 17, 1916

The Director to Mr. Widor
Professor at the Conservatory
25, quai Conti

Mr. Professor,

I have the duty to transmit to you a copy of the letter that was addressed to me on June 16, 1916, by the Undersecretary of State of the Fine Arts.

In accordance with the instructions that I have received, the censure that is imposed on you will be inserted into your dossier as Professor at the Conservatory.

The Director of the Conservatory,
[Gabriel Fauré]
Member of the Institute[157]

That Fauré added "Member of the Institute" under his signature only added insult to injury—after all, he was addressing another member of the Institute, and the perpetual secretary of the Academy of Fine Arts at that.

When Fauré died in 1924, it would have been Widor's position to write an official eulogy for presentation at the Institute. In *Fondations, portraits, de Massenet à Paladilhe*, Widor inserted a "Nota Bene" before the eulogies that he had written by 1927:

[Each year] the perpetual secretary must read an essay on the life and works of one of his deceased confrères.

Such are the twelve following notices, from Massenet to Paladilhe.

One may be astonished not to find, after [the names of] Saint-Saëns and Th. Dubois, that of Gabriel Fauré. The reason for it is that the eulogy of Fauré has been so eloquently written by his successor Alfred Bruneau, the study of it is so documented and so complete, that it is difficult to add to it and very presumptuous to take it up again.[158]

Such was Widor's silence concerning his lifelong colleague with whom he had so often been at loggerheads.

—94—

Salvum fac populum tuum: "A bomb brushed past our ears"

In his new position as perpetual secretary, Widor quickly found his mettle tested with unimagined responsibilities:

I never suspected the situation in which I was going to find myself a few days later! On August 2, the mobilization—the War! The Villa Médicis closed its doors, the boarders returned in haste, and certain of them, despite the rules on celibacy, had married secretly and confessed to me that they had a wife and unforeseen expenses, and asked for aid and protection [for them] before leaving for the battlefront.

Imagine the frame of mind of the perpetual secretary![159]

Throughout World War I, Widor conscientiously worked with all the resources at his command to aid those unfortunate artists whose careers were devastated by the ravages of the war.[160] Adolphe Boschot, Widor's eventual successor as perpetual secretary, extolled his predecessor's resolve, resourcefulness, and courage:

During the four years of war, whatever were the dangers that fell on Paris, and even when the Germans approached so close, Widor, with zeal and resoluteness, fulfilled all the duties in his charge, and felt honor bound not to move away from the Institute.[161]

The dangers loomed very real indeed for the presidents and perpetual secretaries of the five academies, since they were responsible for monies apportioned to them by various foundations: "If Germany had entered into Paris," Widor later wrote, "we would have found ourselves exposed to its threats and, to extort these monies, we would have been taken as hostages."[162] Widor detailed those desperate times for the Institute's archives in two slightly differing accounts: "At a time when all the agencies in the country are fighting with generosity and energy to defend right, it is well not to leave our successors ignorant of what courage and to what extent the Institute of France took part in this heroic struggle."[163]

On September 2 [1914], Étienne Lamy [1845–1919], perpetual secretary of the Académie française, came to see me and said: "Poincaré [1860–1934; president of France 1913–20] is asking the perpetual secretaries to pack their bags in order not to be taken as hostages. I'm leaving this evening," he added. All day we deliberated. At 6:00 in the evening we held a meeting at [Albert] Sarraut's [1872–1962; French politician], at the Ministry of State Education. "I have no orders to give you," he said, "but the effect of your departure would be disastrous." While we visited with him, suddenly an intense fireball burst under our windows; it was one of the first German planes that dumped its bombs on the capital, and to which the battalion of Zouaves from the barracks at rue de Bellechasse responded.

We drew the shutters in order to hear ourselves, and we decided conclusively not to leave.

"As for me," the minister [Sarraut] said to us, "I'm leaving tonight for Bordeaux!"

In return, the minister of the interior had seventeen passes distributed to us permitting us to leave Paris. I remember the indignation of Bonnat when I took one of these passes to him: "You think that I'm going to give up my Fine Arts Institute for which I am responsible, my students, my collections? What do you take me for? Get out! Get out!"

Thus we remained in Paris, which became ominous as soon as night fell; everyone remembers that the boutiques and the restaurants closed early. Maxim's was our refuge. We went there often.[164]

Not since the Commune in 1871 had Widor seen Paris in such a chilling light:

The morning of [August] 31, some of us gazed with emotion on the nudity of the walls in the rooms of the Louvre, stripped of their paintings. More than seven hundred [770] canvases had been removed and sent to the south of France [Toulouse]. . . . In the evening, another unimaginable sight: sepulchral Paris—no more lights, neither gas nor electric; on the Champs-Elysées, on the quays, in most of our grand boulevards, nothing that might serve as a landmark to the German aviators, nothing that indicated the topography of the city. Crossing the Seine was unforgettable: lifeless water without reflections, bordered by dark masses of imprecise contours (trees or houses, you couldn't tell, everything blurred in the dark). It was frightful, but magnificent.[165]

At this moment, we were a certain number of bachelors uniting every evening for dinner at Chez Maxim's, rue Royale, not having a kitchen at home. We met regularly there at about 8:00. Those who came to dine were: André Tardieu, Flameng, Forain, . . . , Arthur Meyer, Maginot, . . .

We went there because we were across from the Admiralty, in the heart of Paris. We believed ourselves closer to the news there than elsewhere. It must be said that the female staff had followed the government to Bordeaux; thus Maxim's became a sort of club where one scarcely met anyone but men of canonical age. I still hear Grosclaude coming one evening to tell me: "Gallieni just left our house and told my wife what danger she risks staying in Paris; in spite of all the precautions of our defense, the Germans can break through, and if a gunshot sounds from a window it's the signal for the destruction of the whole neighborhood or the whole city. Leave immediately!"

Things weren't at all happy. We were very nervous and remained nearly a week or so under this rather distressing feeling. The government had left for Bordeaux and Paris seemed deserted, and the news was more than vague.

I breakfasted every morning at the restaurant of the Orsay rail station, living nearby, rue des Saints-Pères [Widor had not yet had time to move into his new quarters at the Institute]. There, I met very few patrons; at 12:30 Gallieni, minister of war, and his aide-de-camp arrived, and within twenty minutes they had eaten and returned to rue Saint Dominique. Sometimes Delcassé came to join them. I forbade myself to question the minister, but I never failed to salute at the passing of the man who was defending Paris.

In reality, we knew nothing about what was happening, nothing more of the battle of the Marne than what we had learned from [Élie] Berger [keeper of the castle at Chantilly] some days earlier.

In the evening, dinner at Maxim's was lively. As I had complained to Flameng of my loneliness, he responded: "Then come dine with us at Maxim's. We've formed a real club there, we make our own rules and we are quite at home, the women having left for Bordeaux with the government."[166]

Widor found good company and a source of news, albeit often not good, at his wartime dining haunt. At dinner on September 5 came the crushing prediction that Paris would fall: "Paris would be pillaged, plundered, burned," Widor recalled hearing predicted. "And on that mournful vision of our country, we parted without saying a word."[167]

The war would grind on for several more years. In two letters to Saint-Saëns in 1918, Widor sketched the nearly unbearable scene in Paris: "I received your letter . . . and respond to the noise of nearby detonations, German or French, I don't know. . . . My windows are vibrating violently."[168] "The heavy long-range gun is recommencing its din. There have been three successive detonations in a half-hour; how long is this going to last?"[169] Still, in a letter to the Duchess of Noailles on July 23, 1918, written from the Institute, Widor reaffirmed his resolute determination not to be intimidated by the dangers of war: "I am retained by *the duty not to leave the old house* [Palais Mazarin] where I am alone in this moment and for which I have moral responsibility. As long as we are under the menace of planes—there was one yesterday in *broad daylight*—I will remain here, where we have been bombed."[170] During the days of the bombardment, Widor and another member of the Institute, the sculptor Charles Waltner (1846–1925), were walking bravely on the Pont des Arts "in the wonderful moonlight at midnight. The whistling of a bomb brushed past our ears and I said to Waltner, 'Hey, that was for us!'"[171]

Saluting the tradition from revolutionary times of composing patriotic works, during the war period Widor dedicated to "Our Soldiers" his *chanson de route*, "Délivrance," a hymn of five strophes with refrain. Its cover depicts a troop of soldiers marching to the defense of the fatherland. His *mélodie* "Fleurs de France" and his *chant militaire* "France!" similarly reveal the nationalistic fervor Widor always so proudly displayed.

During the war, Widor composed little of substance, but he busied himself with writing, editing, and revising or correcting scores that had already been published.[172] In 1918, Durand published a new edition of Mendelssohn's organ works, edited and prefaced by Widor. Then, shortly after the end of the war, Hamelle issued yet another major revision of the Op. 13 and Op. 42 Organ Symphonies under the heading "New edition, revised, and entirely modified by the composer (1914–18, 1920)"; this became the fourth major edition of these works. No movements were added or deleted, but many of them reflect his most discriminating touch. Widor cited precedence in Bach and Beethoven for reviewing his works so frequently: "We all know that the Mass in B Minor was, for Johann Sebastian Bach, the leitmotiv of his entire life. A cantata or oratorio finished, he took up the Mass again to correct, modify, even to replace certain parts. The same process of gestation for Beethoven in the Ninth Symphony."[173]

In 1916, in anticipation of the end of the Great War and "trusting in the final result and the help from America,"[174] Widor composed one heroic work—a sort of grand march based on Psalm 28:9—to be performed at Notre-Dame Cathedral for the victory celebration.[175] *Salvum fac populum tuum* (*Lord, Save Thy People*), Op. 84, was originally scored for three trumpets, three trombones, three timpani (G–C–E flat), and organ, with the explanatory note: "In the case where the exiguity of the tribune permits only two timpani, one can suppress the highest one (E Flat), which has only six measures (letter E) and which the piece can do without if need be." The timpani were replaced by a drum (tambour) in the second edition, a year later. A freely revised version for full orchestra also exists in an undated manuscript in Widor's hand at the Bibliothèque nationale.[176] A solemn ceremony at Saint-Sulpice on December 19, 1916, in memory of Belgian soldiers killed for the fatherland included a performance of *Salvum fac populum tuum*, but the intended premiere at Notre-Dame had to wait another two years—until after the armistice. Finally, on November 17, 1918, Widor conducted a victory performance at Notre-Dame that also included the *Kyrie, Sanctus, Benedictus*, and *Agnus Dei* from his Mass, Op. 36.

> In a splendid setting that symbolized all the joys of the victory, the *Te Deum*— the grand evocation of religious gratitude—was sung this morning at Notre-Dame by more than fifteen thousand voices. . . . The ceremony began with the choral *Salvum fac populum tuum* by Mr. Widor, written for organ and trumpets, and which the distinguished *maître* had been eager to direct himself. Mr. Marcel Dupré, grand-prix de Rome, played the *grand orgue*, and Mr. Serre the *orgue de chœur*.[177]

In the face of many dangers, Widor had attended to his duties with dispatch, refusing to flee Paris. At the Institute, he continued to work in his studio at a small rustic wooden table lighted by a three-branched lamp, with an Érard upright piano situated perpendicularly to the left.[178] He often related how late one night, a shell fragment crashed through his window and landed on his work table. He never replaced the cracked windowpane, instead pasting a piece of paper over the hole to preserve it as a souvenir.[179] Walter Damrosch (1862–1950) visited Widor shortly after the perilous incident:

He showed me a hole in the window of his workroom and told me that a few days before he had just stooped down to pick up a musical score from the floor when a shell from Big Bertha burst in front of his apartment and a piece of it hurtled through his window, missing him only because he was in a stooping position.[180]

In another account, Widor was quoted as having been occupied with writing the very work he composed in anticipation of the armistice: "'A shell splinter fell on my table when I wrote my *Salvum fac*,' are the very words of the *maître*."[181] However, *Salvum fac* had already been composed and published two years earlier (1916). Another account reported that he was actually involved with the "corrections of proof sheets."[182] Years later, Widor's own telling of the terrifying moment lacked these specific details, but nonetheless indicated some horrific details:

June 27(?), a shell splinter from a bomb fallen on the Pont des Arts about 11:00 in the evening came through my window and crashed down on my desk at the very moment when I came into my apartment. It's that night that the poor news agent on the Pont des Arts had both legs cut off.[183]

At the onset of the Second World War, Madame Widor would find solace in recalling her husband's strength of spirit: "When I'm ready to lose heart, I think of the optimism of my husband at the height of the [First World] War and in the most anguishing hours. He was comforting and strong; in hearing him speak, one had the impression that in spite of everything, nothing was lost."[184]

During the war, *Le Ménestrel* ceased its publication (between August 1914 and October 1919); this period remains largely devoid of print information about Widor's activities. Nonetheless, it can be assumed there would have been very limited travel to foreign engagements.

After the war, Widor found himself invited to the Élysée Palace on several occasions:

In the time that followed the war, nearly all the allied kings and princes followed one another at the Élysée. Each sovereign read a discourse carefully prepared and [President] Poincaré responded to all of them by heart. There were also some more intimate dinners, notably the one given in honor of the Queen of Italy [Elena, 1873–1952] and her daughters, following which I permitted myself to dedicate to Her Majesty a "Petite suite pour violon et piano" that I had just written and that [Léon?] Pascal played for us. I dedicated it to her under the title of "Suite florentine."[185]

The *Suite florentine* for Violin and Piano is a reworking and expansion of an earlier work, the Suite, Op. 76, for Violin and Piano (d'après la musique de scène écrite pour la Sulamite, pièce en vers du Vte de Borelli), published in 1903 with three movements: Cantilène; Berceuse [Lullaby]; Danse de la Bayadère [Indian dancing girl]. These movements relate to the first, third, and possibly fourth movement of the revised and enlarged *Suite florentine*, dedicated to "Sa Majesté la Reine Hélène d'Italie" for a performance at the Élysée Palace on February 20, 1919. The four movements are titled in Italian: Cantilena; Alle Cascine (a Florentine park); Morbidezza (softness; titled "Berceuse" in the earlier version); Tragica (begins and ends in a strong folk-dance rhythm).

—95—

Debussy: "I weep . . . for a great artist, a French glory"

As perpetual secretary, Widor sponsored new candidates for election to the Academy whenever openings in any of the branches under his jurisdiction occurred, perhaps in spite of his personal estimation of their artistic work. Above all, he wanted illustrious artists as members, and he campaigned actively for the success of those he deemed worthy. So urgent was his desire to see Debussy elected to the Academy that he wrote to him the very day of his own election as perpetual secretary on July 18, 1914: "Your work honors our art in France and elsewhere; my chair is becoming vacant, do you want me for your sponsor?"[186] Although Widor had told Alexander Russell a few years earlier that he considered Debussy "a man with very few ideas,"[187] he either changed his opinion or at least recognized Debussy's importance to French music. On July 23, Widor received an amiable response:[188]

> I received the following note from Claude Debussy, whom I had known since 1884 at the Concordia Society, when the young composer who just won the grand prix de Rome with his *Enfant prodigue* came as accompanist, heartily recommended to me by Ambroise Thomas: "It was upon returning from London that I learned of your nomination; although anticipated, it is still very fortunate for the entire music world. Please count me among those that it particularly delights and believe in my affectionate devotion."
>
> I responded to Debussy, "Very touched by your kind thoughts, I would be very flattered to act as your sponsor to the Academy and to have you as my successor—with the dispensing of my eulogy—we will welcome you with open arms. Come and see me tomorrow, if possible."[189]

Customarily, a new member of the Institute had to eulogize the member whom he succeeded. This time-honored tradition often provided great sport for the other academicians as they observed how cleverly a new member would extol a predecessor who may have been his bitter enemy. In the present case, the tradition would be dispensed with, as Debussy would only be taking the chair that Widor had vacated.

Widor's invitation that Debussy visit him "tomorrow" had to be postponed. Unfortunately, it was the day of the mobilization of French forces at the onset of World War I. Artistic and political life in France quickly halted; there would be no more candidatures and no more elections at the Institute for the time being. Only in 1918 did the Institute resume its normal activities.[190] Widor later recounted:

> Paris depopulated. Debussy spent almost all of 1915 at Pourville. In 1916, the first attacks of the disease that would carry him away set in. In a letter of July 3, after taking an interest in a concert by Francis Planté, he spoke of his suffering and his will to recover. Now, chance had put me right next to him in the concert hall, and I was profoundly alarmed by his thinness and weakness. After a sojourn in Saint-Jean-de-Luz, in 1917 he returned to Paris very ill.[191]

Saint-Saëns, a long-time member of the Academy, was not at all in support of his colleague's efforts to secure a chair for Debussy, and he let him know it in a "scolding letter . . . filled with 'insults and injuries,' which gave Widor great delight."[192] Equally, Saint-Saëns endeavored to turn Fauré against Debussy's candidacy, writing, "I recommend you to look at the pieces for two pianos, *Noir et Blanc* [*sic*], which M. Debussy has just published. It's *unbelievable*, and we must at all costs bar the door of the Institut[e] against a man capable of such atrocities; they should be put next to the cubist pictures."[193] Nonetheless, Widor wanted Debussy as his successor, and he even insisted that he would personally manage the gathering of all necessary documents for him.[194] Widor renewed his efforts on Debussy's behalf:

> People began then to foresee the end of the war. The necessity arose to provide for the numerous vacancies that came about during those four tragic years. Desirous of news about my future "successor" and to know if anything had changed regarding his intentions, I believed it necessary to write to Madame Debussy, who was good enough to respond to me immediately:
>
> Dear Sir,
>
> May I permit myself to recall to you that a little before this terrible war, you had been kind enough to speak to my husband about his candidature at the Institute.
>
> Unfortunately, his frequent indispositions have prevented him from going to you to know if you thought that the moment had come to take up his candidature in an effective manner.

Having until now followed only your advice, he leaves everything up to you and asks you to let him know by a note if there is something to do.

Please accept, dear sir, the grateful memories of my husband and the expression of my best sentiments.

Signed: Emma-Claude Debussy.

Thus, Debussy presented himself to the Academy.

Nothing is simpler than the protocol of a candidature. Visits are pure courtesy; they are not obligatory. A few lines suffice to give evidence of the candidature, and here is the letter that I received, written in the same hand as the preceding one, but carrying the trembling signature of the author of *Pelléas*.

March 17, 1918

My dear perpetual secretary,

Since you are willing to help me pass through the doors of the Institute, I will be very happy to enter my name, even now, for the chair that you occupied there.

In renewing, dear *Maître* and Friend, the expression of all my gratitude, deem me faithfully yours.

Signed: Claude Debussy.[195]

Eight days later, alas, Debussy was carried away by the sickness that undermined him. Debussy's two letters of candidacy are found with the letters of Madame Debussy in our archives. The first is dated after my election as perpetual secretary when I left my chair free. The second is from the end of the war.

The death of Debussy thus prohibited him from being seated among us.[196]

Widor felt profound regret that Debussy was not to be his successor.[197] He addressed a hasty letter to Madame Debussy, "Pauvre chère Madame," the day after Debussy's death: "How can I express to you my pain! You know that for some months I had prepared an almost unanimous election. And now the disaster. Please believe in my feelings of profound and respectful sympathy. I weep with you for a great artist, a French glory."[198]

Equally lamentable was the same fate his efforts encountered in securing a seat for Auguste Rodin in the sculpture section of the Academy: "In his turn Rodin was carried away and was never able to take a place among us, having obtained twenty-seven votes in a single balloting. Three days after this memorable election, alas, he died."[199] Isidor Philipp claimed, "[Widor] knew that neither Debussy nor Rodin liked him. He forgot their unfriendliness and, wishing to have the most illustrious artists as members of the Institute, invited these two to become candidates, assuring them of complete success."[200]

During Widor's tenure as perpetual secretary, the music branch of the Academy welcomed seven new members: Henri Rabaud (1873–1949) in 1918, Georges Hüe in 1922, Gabriel Pierné in 1924, Alfred Bruneau in 1925, André Messager in 1926, Paul Dukas in 1934, and Florent Schmitt (1870–1958) in 1936.[201] The two latter candidates were admitted after Widor's health was failing. He had wanted Dukas admitted to the Institute for some time, even writing to him that if there were no other openings, "The only consolation for me is that you would succeed me there—a consolation mitigated by the fact that I would no longer be there. . . . Of our French art you are one of the most eminent and justly admired representatives."[202] Dukas told Philipp "how touched he had been by the friendliness and esteem with which he had been received. 'Widor,' he added, 'is the most delightful of men, and I can only admire his prodigious culture.'"[203]

Upon Dukas's death on May 17, 1935, Jacques-Émile Blanche and Gabriel Pierné encouraged Igor Stravinsky to submit his candidacy for the vacant seat. Since candidates were to pay a courtesy call to each member of the Academy, Stravinsky compiled an agenda of visits and scheduled a meeting around January 10, 1936, with Widor, to whom "under other circumstances, Stravinsky would not have extended his hand."[204] For a variety of reasons, Stravinsky wanted to withdraw, but the election went forward on January 25. Florent Schmitt was elected from the slate of four candidates that also included Samuel Rousseau and Büsser. When Widor died the following year, Stravinsky's name once again came forth as an obvious candidate, but Stravinsky retorted: "I will never undertake another act of candidacy. . . . I have no more taste for 'officials' than they have for me."[205]

—96—

"Choir masters and organists . . . are dying of hunger"

In 1922, Widor became president of the Association of Choir Masters and Organists (Union des maîtres de chapelle et organistes); in that capacity he carried the banner for his fellow church musicians, actively speaking out for improvement in the pitiful postwar church salaries and mediating grievances between musicians and clergy.[206] Founded in 1912, the union declared its worthy intentions "to contribute to the development of religious Art, and to aid its members in the achievement of their mission."[207] However, the union was unable to keep funds abreast of its needs. To the address the urgent matter of better salaries for church musicians, Widor decided to send form letters in November 1924 to parish priests, presumably throughout Paris, requesting substantial increases.[208] The parish priest of Saint-Sulpice wrote to the vicar-general that he had just received a form letter from Widor requesting a fifty percent raise in his salary![209]

Not having received a commitment from every person whom he had solicited, Widor sent out another, more insistent letter in which he detailed specific reasons for the request.[210] When this letter failed to obtain a sufficient response, a 1926 newspaper article sounded the alarm publicly: "it's a question of choirmasters and organists who, literally, are dying of hunger."[211] Citing the average organist's monthly salary as 250 francs, the article pointed out: "For this famine wage, [the organist] must ensure the services on Sundays and festival days, including masses and vespers, without mentioning other possible services, as well as the ordinary parish service, complicated by the annual grand ceremonies: midnight masses, first communions, perpetual adorations, confirmations, etc., and even greater are the preparations of the offices and the rehearsals."[212]

Although the union aided its members as best it could, the situation came to a head in 1933 when there were insufficient funds to carry forth its mission. On September 25, a subscription was opened to benefactors, and topping the list as the most generous contributors were Cardinal Verdier (two thousand francs), Widor (one thousand francs), and the minister of the fine arts (five hundred francs).[213]

—97—

d'Indy: "What a shame that such a man is not musical!"

In spite of an intense workload, Widor maintained an even temper and self-control.[214] Vierne related that he assumed a "half-serious, half-joking tone . . . that never left him during his whole life."[215] With keen and quick-witted humor he could disarm jealousies and hostilities. Edmond Maurat (1881–1972) narrated an episode illustrating Widor's wry sense of humor:

> As we were leaving his class one morning, Widor said to me, "If you're free, Maurat, come to lunch with me; we'll chat." Arriving on the sidewalk of the rue Bergère, he hailed a horse-drawn cab: "Chez Foyot." The horse set out, and Widor, with the slight lisp that was characteristic of him, told me the following story in nearly these words during the journey:
>
> "Last evening I read a part of the composition Treatise [*Cours de composition musicale*] by Vincent d'Indy. What an astonishing man! He knows everything. This work is remarkable; only he could manage such an undertaking."
>
> When the coachman had turned onto rue Richelieu, Widor continued: "For him, the pedagogue is equivalent to the musicologist. This, everyone knows; but there's more: d'Indy is a real schoolmaster. He has trained a pleiad of students and disciples; he exerts an attraction that goes beyond our borders."
>
> Passing under the gateways of the Louvre, Widor went on: "This man hasn't stopped being astonishing; when [Camille] Chevillard fell ill, he was

called to replace him at the head of the Concerts Lamoureux. He showed himself to be a great conductor. Have you seen him direct? He is sober, precise, efficient."

At the approach of the boulevard Saint-Germain, Widor began to speak of the organizer: "Not only does d'Indy direct the Schola [Cantorum], he teaches there and he publishes important works there; he revises and edits old works; even better, he discovers unknown manuscripts."

When the vehicle was at the bass of the rue de Tournon, Widor had not finished: "There is in d'Indy several great men; how many strings has he on his bow? His activity has no measure; it's an example, a phenomenon."

The coach, having stopped in front of the door of Foyot, Widor got out. Taking from his waistcoat pocket some money, he put it into the hand of the coachman and, turning his head towards me, he exclaimed, "What a shame that such a man is not musical!"[216]

Neither aristocrats nor the highest representatives of politics and finance intimidated the perpetual secretary.[217] He had rubbed elbows with the best of them and was every bit their equal in his own domain. Isidor Philipp witnessed an incident when Widor abruptly silenced the tart language of one of his interlocutors:

I recall that after a concert at Angers in which we had collaborated . . . we were dined by the president of the "Association des Concerts," the Comte de Romain. One of the guests, the Viscountess of Trédern, the daughter of the sugar merchant Say, a very rich little *bourgeoise* who did not like Widor, allowed herself to become rather disagreeable. Annoyed, he said to her with the greatest composure: "Madame, may I dare to ask you to mingle in your conversation a little of that sugar which M. *votre père* manufactures so well." The lady kept quiet.[218]

In his writings Widor was often given to moments of humor; even in the most serious contexts he will catch the reader off guard. Concluding his essay on Bach's G-Major *Fantaisie* (*Pièce d'orgue*, BWV 572), he quipped, "Whoever remains unmoved by the pathos of the peroration, whoever sees only a mechanical exercise there, had better abandon music for a post as signalman on a local branch line."[219]

—98—

The Franco-American School of Fontainebleau

One of the activities of the Academy of Fine Arts involved the operation of its renowned educational facility, the Villa Médicis in Rome. It offered outstanding

French students the opportunity to leave the routine of their Parisian lives and to work in an artistic atmosphere of beauty and peace, while at the same time absorbing the artistic riches of Italy.[220] The concept of the Villa Médicis greatly appealed to Widor, and he dedicated himself to maintaining and expanding that concept in the form of various additional educational institutions.

An offshoot of initiatives taken toward the end of World War I and after the armistice was the founding of the Conservatoire franco-américain. A collaborative idea between Widor and Francis Casadesus (1870–1954), it became the first such institution to be formed. In a promotional brochure, Widor wrote:

> As for us, directors, professors, lecturers, it is needless to assure that we most cordially undertake to accomplish a duty both artistic and fraternal.
>
> We shall never forget the assistance so generously given by America during the tragic days of 1918, the joint efforts and the sacrifices to defend the same ideas of justice and liberty.
>
> The best of our thoughts, all that experience has taught us, we will place at the disposal of the Franco-American School of Fontainebleau.[221]

The Ministry of Public Instruction and Fine Arts named Widor director on February 10, 1921,[222] and the Conservatoire Américain, as it came to be known, was officially inaugurated on June 26, 1921, by the minister of public instruction, the director of the Beaux-arts, Saint-Saëns, Widor, Walter Damrosch, and several professors.[223] As part of the opening celebration, Widor presented a recital at the town hall of some of his works as well as those of Saint-Saëns and Bach.[224] With state approval and funding from the city of Fontainebleau, the artistic surroundings of the Louis XV wing of the Fontainebleau Palace— a "veritable living museum"—became the school's facility.[225] Widor explained the background to its creation:

> In 1917, [American General] Pershing [1860–1948] came to France. As he didn't have enough bands [to play] for his troops, he spoke to the well-known conductor of the New York Symphony, Walter Damrosch, who immediately came over and, thanks to the assistance of our professors, organized a method of teaching compatible with the situation of an army in the field, which meant a traveling conservatory that followed the staff and settled with it in Chaumont. In that way, 240 leaders and 800 instrumentalists were trained; all chosen, moreover, among professional musicians: a pianist or violinist [in former civilian life], under the military jacket turned into a clarinetist or cornetist. From time to time, a furlough led them to Paris. Abandoning their clarinet or cornet, the pianists and violinists went to ask of French master pianists and violinists supplementary instruction in their true profession.
>
> Then came the peace, the return to their own country, and the exchange of correspondence: "How happy we would be," they wrote, "to stay in touch

with you. Are you in Paris during the summer? Would we have the luck to find you there during our vacations?"

From there, very naturally, came the idea of a summer school specially designed for the Americans.[226]

The American Conservatory convened for three months each summer (June 25 to September 25), offering American composers, instrumentalists, and vocalists the opportunity to pursue studies with the most eminent French teachers for a charge of only one hundred dollars (twenty-five hundred francs) per month.[227] Full scholarships were also available if the student merited it.[228] The first year, there was one class each in composition, fugue and counterpoint, harmony, cello, organ, harp, and conducting; four classes in piano, three in violin, and three in voice. Each class, limited to twelve students, met twice a week for three hours. Supplementary courses were also offered in music history, chamber music, old instruments, musical culture, acoustics, and the physiology of instruments and the voice. Examinations were given at the beginning and end of each session, with prizes awarded at the end. Concerts were given in the Palace's former Jeu de Paume, which was furnished with a two-manual, twelve-stop Cavaillé-Coll/Mutin organ donated by the New York Committee in charge of the school's publicity and recruitment.[229]

Stanley R. Avery (1897–1967), from Minneapolis, was one of six organists in the first group of one hundred American students to arrive in Fontainebleau the summer of 1921.[230] He described the routine of study that summer:

Once a week Widor comes down and hears us. While much of the work here in all branches is devoted to technique, M. Widor gives his whole attention to interpretation and keeps us almost entirely on Bach. He is very particular as to the turn of a phrase and sings or plays passages again and again. He goes down to the fundamentals, but they say that in the last few years he has made some radical changes in his Bach readings. Whether or not it is his long association with Bach . . . he as often talks to us in German as in French, which seems at least odd in France. . . .

We have gone right back to Bach, Mendelssohn and Widor, besides whom, says Libert, there is no other composer for the organ, except Franck. So we are going through the big preludes, toccatas, fantasias and fugues, the sonatas and the symphonies, and getting, besides directions for playing, most valuable analyses and scholarly interpretations of these master-works. The class method of teaching is excellent, as each man plays to an audience and also hears his fellow student's lessons.

. . . We are all professionals with a past, who recognized the opportunity here offered to get Paris Conservatoire ideas, methods and contacts in this splendidly equipped and managed American conservatory, instituted for the first time this summer in the beautiful Palace of Fontainebleau.[231]

Miss Charlotte Klein, from Washington DC, described the organ class of 1923:

> The organ class met on Tuesdays and Fridays from 10 o'clock in the morning
> until 4:30 in the afternoon, with recess for luncheon. It is customary for all
> the organ students to remain in class for the entire day, thereby getting inter-
> pretation, registration, etc., of the assignments of the other students. This
> is very helpful. Our first assignment was pedal and manual technique, with
> metronome. We then had Bach (each student doing a different number)
> and then the third part of the course was more Bach and Widor. M. Widor
> always gives his registration for a larger or "cathedral organ," as he calls it,
> together with the registration on the organ at the Conservatoire. We had les-
> sons with M. Widor about every ten days.
>
> M. Henri Libert, Widor's assistant, is a very fine organist and splendid
> teacher, and having studied with Franck as well as with Widor, it is possible to
> study Franck with Libert, but not with Widor. Widor plays and teaches noth-
> ing but Bach and Widor, and, as someone said, "mostly Widor."[232]

The great success of the Conservatory spawned the addition of an École des
beaux-arts two years later for painters, sculptors, and architects.[233] In view of
the American war effort in behalf of France, Widor felt great pride in being
able to offer this rich cultural association between the two countries.[234] After
the fourth year, he reported:

> The School increases each year. How interesting for the two nations, this
> intellectual communion, this transfusion of our old traditions into the veins
> of a new, sound, and strong people.[235]

Although Aaron Copland (1900–1990), who had come to study with Nadia
Boulanger, viewed Widor as "the ancient organist and composer,"[236] Fontainebleau became a mecca for American organists especially seeking the opportunity to study with Widor. Charlotte Klein reported, "Regardless of the fact that
practice time is divided between a pedal piano and a two-manual tracker action
organ with straight pedal board, it is possible to accomplish a great deal, provided one is not a beginner."[237] However, in 1925 it was noted: "The encyclopedic teaching that the young 'transatlantics' receive there, offered until now
but one gap—the insufficiency of the instrument assigned to organ study."[238]
Accordingly, a three-manual, seventeen-stop organ with electric action by
Auguste Convers (1884–1976) was installed prior to the 1925 season.[239]

The American Conservatory provided an outstretched arm to American
music students, and they came in ever increasing droves, many returning year
after year. In 1928 the number of students had to be limited because the facility
and its faculty had reached the maximum number. The success of the school
caught the eye of the Italian government, and in 1925 it planned to start its own

competing American Conservatory at the Villa d'Este. Irked by this "upstart," Widor nonetheless saw a bit of silver lining, and hoped its creation would coax the French government to increase its financial support of Fontainebleau.[240] In the end, he did not have to worry: "[The school] had established an excellent reputation, collected supporters and admirers, boasted an outstanding faculty, and was producing successful students, both male and female. . . . As America's 'summertime conservatory,' the Conservatoire Américain was succeeding in its mission."[241]

Twenty-five years had passed since Widor had composed for his chosen instrument, and the inauguration of the new organ at Fontainebleau offered him an opportunity. *Bach's Memento, Six pièces pour orgue*, had the unassuming byline "Transcription et registration de Ch. M. Widor." Far from being transcriptions, however, Widor's six favorite Bach movements are so freely arranged that they are arguably more Widor than Bach.[242] William Hays suggested that "paraphrases, freely based on themes by Bach" would be a more accurate description of the work.[243] Indeed, the "Mattheus–Final" is as "symphonic" in manner as any movement from the Op. 13 Symphonies.[244]

The credit "Orchestration de Ch. M. Widor" appears at the head of each movement and in those terms he briefly described the work to Albert Schweitzer: "I have recently 'orchestrated' six pieces of Bach for organ, *Bach's Memento*, drawn from the harpsichord works or the Cantatas; I wrote just five of them originally, but I did the sixth because the number *five* is lame."[245] Widor premiered the collection at the American Conservatory on June 30, 1925.[246] *Bach's Memento* represents his most direct tribute to the composer whose works—especially those for organ—had been the *cantus firmus* of his whole life. In Bach's organ music, Widor found the roots for all that followed:

> There are few musicians' careers whose education has not included the study of the organ, less with the goal of attaining a virtuoso's technique than to go deeply, by practice, into the work of Bach, of which this instrument is the expression; it's a colossal work, an astonishing synthesis of ancient homophony, medieval polyphony, and modern symphony.[247]

Reporting on the progress of the American Conservatory in 1928, *Le Ménestrel* noted: "The fugues of J. S. Bach and the symphonies of Ch.-M. Widor resound on the practice organs."[248] Widor touted the school's achievement:

> The brilliance of our organ school is due to its adherence to traditions and its spirit of discipline. These traditions are made out of respect for the texts and awareness of their import; and they have exerted their effect not only on our instruments but also on French symphonic output itself.
>
> If you want to know the state of French organ building three-quarters of a century ago, the banality of the compositions from the period will show you.

The influence of a master-virtuoso and the inspired understanding of a builder have brought about the miracle and resuscitated our art.[249]

By 1931, he reported that approximately three thousand students had attended the school since its opening.[250]

At a time when so many American musicians were traveling to Europe and numerous European artists to America, there were endeavors to entice Widor into making a tour. Felix Borowski (1872–1956), president of the Chicago Musical College, with its more than three thousand students, invited Widor to officiate as guest teacher in its 1919 six-week summer school at a minimum guaranteed fee of two thousand dollars plus other teaching fees. Borowski wrote, "You would enjoy, I am sure, coming to this great country, where your works are so much admired and you would find talent for organ playing here that would give you great satisfaction."[251] Alexander Russell also worked on Widor for years hoping to get him to America, but again to no avail: "We kept it up as a sort of joke between us. The last time I teased him about it, he patted me on the back and with the famous twinkle in his eye and his inimitable lisp, said, 'Be patient. Don't hurry me, Russell. I promise to come to America when I am one hundred years old!'"[252] Rumor had it that "the width (and depth) of the Atlantic prevented his even considering a trip to America."[253]

Widor's most outstanding students, Vierne and Dupré, did go to the United States and admirably represented their *maître*. In his article "La musique en Amérique," Vierne related that in some sixty welcoming speeches on his tour around America, "our national school was glorified in magnificent terms. My *Maître* Widor and I had the honor of being highly proclaimed the most prominent exponents and the most significant representatives of contemporary organ composition, the incontestable successors of Bach and Franck."[254]

In view of Widor's renown at home and abroad, he was dismayed and angered at a survey that arrived asking him questions appropriate to an apprentice. Alexander Russell thought it very amusing to watch Widor's reaction:

At a lesson one morning he handed me a big envelope postmarked "Chicago." It contained a letter and an elaborate questionnaire to be filled in. The letter announced that a certain publishing firm was preparing a World Biography of Musicians. Widor's name had been given them as a French musician of some prominence. Would he please fill in the questionnaire with his full name, address, age, with whom and where he had studied, what positions he had held, what instrument he played—if any—and (as a final affront) if he had ever composed anything would he kindly list the compositions by title, and tell whether he had ever had anything published? . . .

I hesitated to translate this idiotic request, but decided to do so just to get even with him for blue-pencilling my cherished manuscript. So I read the letter to him. He boiled visibly, and at the end exploded with Gallic violence, tore up the letter in a rage, and proceeded to initiate me into a hitherto unsuspected but extremely useful vocabulary. When he saw that I was laughing he laughed too, saying, "Well, after all, I asked you to read the letter to me, didn't I?" The blue pencil worked overtime that day.[255]

—99—

Mathilde: "It's my last nocturne"

Widor married quite late in life. It was said, "he adores bachelorhood, not that he has the least dislike for the daughters of Eve, but he considers that the real artist is little made for marriage. His work is too engrossing to him."[256] In fact, Widor once proclaimed that he was "possessed by the demon of music."[257] In spite of this, Edgard Varèse, who occasionally received extra composition lessons at Widor's apartment, enjoyed imitating Widor's lisp when relating a certain incident: "One morning when [Varèse] arrived for his lesson, after quite a long wait, Widor opened the door a crack, obviously without much on and 'his two hairs *en bataille* [disheveled].' 'Pardon, Varèse,' he said. '*Je ne peux vous recevoir, j'ai du monde* (Excuse me, Varèse, I can't receive you, I have company).'"[258]

As Widor entered his seventies, his work continued to be as pressing as ever, especially upon becoming perpetual secretary of the Academy of Fine Arts. His personal life, however, became more solitary in 1917 with the loss of his dearly beloved sister, Marie Widor Pierron.[259] Before long, the youngest and most persistent of his female admirers won her way into his heart and became his bride. At the age of seventy-six, Widor married a woman of noble birth and upbringing; she was thirty-nine years his junior. "It's my last nocturne," he told Joseph Trillat.[260] The couple joined in holy matrimony on April 26, 1920, in the private chapel of the Château d'Hauteville in Charchigné (approximately twelve miles northeast of Mayenne), an estate belonging to his intended bride.[261]

Mathilde-Marie-Anne-Elisabeth de Montesquiou-Fezensac (see fig. 22), born July 19, 1883, in Lorient (Morbihan) at Nouvelleville en Meurville (rue de Brest),[262] was the only child of Count Bertrand-Pierre-Anatole de Montesquiou-Fezensac (1837–1902) and Émilie-Gabrielle-Marie de Pérusse des Cars (1844–1901), who had married in 1874.[263] The marriage of Mathilde's parents brought together "two families traditionally bound to aristocratic values and to the sense of honor of service to their country."[264]

Bertrand de Montesquiou-Fezensac had joined the Imperial Naval Academy in Brest in 1853 at age sixteen, and except for a few leaves of absence he spent the better part of the next thirty years at sea earning the highest praises from his superiors: "excellent officer, perfectly brought up, intelligent and devoted, with all the desirable qualities to make a fine superior officer."[265] Émilie des

Cars was the grandniece and, most significantly, heir of Charles-Alexis du Hardas and Mélanie-Françoise Prudhomme de la Boussinière, whose estate included the Château d'Hauteville. Mathilde's father being absent for long periods at sea, her early upbringing became the responsibility of her mother, two aunts—Hélène des Cars Standish and Stéphanie des Cars (later, Bertier de Sauvigny)—and her maternal grandparents, Count Amédée des Cars and Countess Louise de Cossé Brissac des Cars. Time was divided between the family residence in Paris, at 91 rue de Grenelle, and their sumptuous summer residence in Charchigné, the Château d'Hauteville: "All surrounded the wonderful Mathilde with an attentive tenderness."[266]

A schoolmistress was engaged to begin her formal education at about age seven, and piano lessons became an essential part of her training.[267] She enjoyed every delight surrounding her privileged young life: "For the time being she went out between her grandparents, her little hands squeezed in their protective grasp, the coddled little girl of the manor."[268] The deaths of these beloved grandparents within two months of each other (Countess des Cars in November 1898 and Count des Cars in January 1899) brought the first of much deep sadness Mathilde was to know.[269] Still, she continued to lead a charmed life in Paris and especially at the Château d'Hauteville:

> Country life was full of appeal for the seventeen-year-old Mathilde, who dreamed under the trees, swayed to the melodies of her piano, read stories from the *Journal des Demoiselles*, and who didn't forget to discover each evening, before the bedtime prayer, the life of the next day's saint in *La vie des saints à l'usage des familles chrétiennes et des communautés religieuses.*[270]

The new century was christened with the excitement of the 1900 Universal Exposition in Paris. Marvels such as the modern Grand Palais, a "luminous cathedral of glass and iron" bathed in electric light, captivated exposition goers.[271] Among the host of attractions and festivities, Mathilde noticed one that drew upon her musical sensitivities more than others: to commemorate the Franco-Russian alliance and the inauguration of the Alexandre III bridge, Charles-Marie Widor was to perform a concert on Mutin's newly constructed organ destined for the Moscow Conservatory.[272]

By this time, Mathilde was certainly aware of the renowned organist of Saint-Sulpice. In 1939 she related, "I can say that my memories date from the last century because my mother, who preferred Saint-Sulpice to her parish, Sainte-Clotilde, always took me there."[273] Émilie de Montesquiou-Fezensac and her wide-eyed daughter Mathilde must have counted among the aristocratic visitors who occasioned the tribune of Saint-Sulpice. These visits awakened in Mathilde an infatuation for Widor, and, like Pushkin's impulsive Tatyana, the innocent Mathilde delivered a naïve proposal to the great organist. Ennemond Trillat related:

The organ bench [at Saint-Sulpice] was to play a fateful role in the private life of the *maître.* . . . It had served as the seat to a quite young girl, a descendant of the nurse of Louis XV: Mademoiselle de Montesquiou de Fezensac, orphan-girl, heiress of a great name and an imposing fortune. An ascetic duenna accompanied her—a protectress watching her steps.

"*Maître,* I want to marry you."

Widor was already of a certain age, and had an acknowledged mistress: Madame de Max, a socialite singer and very beautiful, of uncertain nobility moreover. With much kindness, Widor whispered to [the young girl]:

"We will speak of it again, Mademoiselle, when you have reached the age of reason."

"At what age, *Maître,* do you consider that a woman has the age of reason?"

"At forty-five [intended to be thirty-five] years, Mademoiselle."

Could he imagine that she would take him at his word and that his quip would oblige him at seventy-three [actually seventy-six] years to marry Mademoiselle de Montesquiou, who had, two years earlier, attained "the age of reason."[274]

Although Trillat made a couple of factual errors, this account is largely on track, as is a similar account given by Edmond Maurat.[275] Responding to a congratulatory note from his old friend Saint-Saëns, Widor himself confirmed the story.[276] The warmth shown by the letter's exaggerated greeting is typical of their correspondence.[277] "Illustrissimo Carissimo! [Most Illustrious Beloved!] Thanks for your charming [note of] sympathy for this abducted major—the law only punishes abductions of minors. Since the age of six, she's been saying to me: 'I want to be your wife.' And now thirty-two years later, it's happening!"[278] Because of the great difference in their ages—thirty-nine years—the marriage undoubtedly caused many a raised eyebrow, but over the years Mathilde's initial infatuation had developed into a lifelong adoration of Widor, and their marriage would be a happy affair lasting almost seventeen years.

While still in her teenage years, after the deaths of her maternal grandparents, Mathilde suffered the crushing losses of both parents—losses that left her an orphan and the direct heir to the huge family fortunes, which from the Pérusse des Cars side included the ninety-eight room Château d'Hauteville and its surrounding properties. Her mother died first, on March 1, 1901, and her father suddenly found himself unprepared to take on the role of a single parent:

Bertrand de Montesquiou was fully aware of the emotional and moral solitude in which his daughter found herself. He was aware of her beauty, charm, and artistic sensibility. He knew her musical gifts, but he did not know how to share with her the expression of despair. He who had faced the storms of so many victorious battles found himself totally unequipped before the duties incumbent upon him to perfect the education of a young girl. Fortunately,

Aunt Hélène was there and proposed to be the feminine supporter who would welcome and stand by her young niece during her visits to Paris.[279]

Then on July 24, 1902, Mathilde's father died, just five days before her nineteenth birthday. Quite naturally, Aunt Hélène—Lady Hélène-Marie-Aldegonde de Pérusse des Cars Standish (1847–1933)—and her husband, Lord Henry Noailles Widdrington Standish (1847–1920), became Mathilde's adoptive parents, having no children of their own.[280] Mathilde moved into their private residence at 3 rue de Belloy where the couple had been living since their marriage.

As Mathilde had not yet come of age, the Standishes took on a controlling role in her life. Their protective custody was such that she remained somewhat cloistered and naive to the ways of the world; a cousin judged Mathilde "childish" and "under-developed."[281] Lady Standish was reportedly strict with her niece, though only out of concern for her proper upbringing. She saw to it that Mathilde was religious and well educated—Mathilde wrote in a sure and elegant hand.[282] Mathilde had a good working knowledge of English, if not fluency; Albert Riemenschneider was able to write to Widor in English, saying, "Madame Widor can translate this letter to you."[283] One source described her as "an impassioned musician," and another stated that early on she wanted to learn to play the organ and that Widor taught her.[284] The extent of her accomplishments is not fully known, however, and the degree to which the Standishes were musically inclined cannot be fully determined.[285] Certainly, their home hosted the occasional "soirée mondaine" or "matinée musicale" so popular among the aristocracy of that era, and Henry Standish, Wagner enthusiast or not, once (in 1888) made the trek to a Bayreuth festival. As Albert Lavignac pointed out in Le voyage artistique à Bayreuth, "the pilgrimage to Bayreuth became fashionable, as it is fashionable to go to the spa or to Monte Carlo."[286]

Lord and Lady Standish were close friends of Edward VII and his wife Alexandra, and they received the royal couple regularly upon their visits to Paris, just as they were received at Windsor and Sandringham.[287] Although Widor does not mention Mathilde in the following account, it is clear that he was a welcomed dinner guest of the Standishes during the first two decades of the twentieth century, and Mathilde would certainly have been present:

When he came to Paris, King Edward VII [reigned 1901–10] always came to dinner here at Madame Standish's, née des Cars. At these always intimate dinners, the same table companions always attended: the king, the queen, the aide-de-camp of the king, the lady of honor of the queen, then three invited French guests, always the same: Sardou, who represented [the Academy of Inscriptions and] Literature, Detaille, the painting section [of the Academy of Fine Arts], and me, the music section. Whereas the sister of King Edward VII, the Princess Christian, accepted the hospitality every year of Baroness d'Erlanger, the sister of King George V [reigned 1910–36], the Princess Victoria, came here like a member of the family. She very much loved the arts and I was very honored to make myself her escort. I willingly accompanied her to the theater, for example, to see new plays. But one day, she said to me, "Instead of going to the theater, would you be willing to let me hear the organ of Saint-Sulpice? I find myself a little tired of the theater, but what I would like above all, is to hear Saint-Sulpice all alone by myself, in the night, in the barely lit church. Is it possible?" Naturally, I said to her, "All alone, it's a little difficult, for it's impossible for me not to forewarn the curé, who would find it very bad not to be alerted." "All right! That goes without saying," she said. So that's what we did.

The next day, the curé related to me his emotion in front of this kneeling woman, her head in her hands, in the midst of the mysticism of this sonorous wave—this voice of the organ that, if it can have a beginning, can have no ending, and by the idea of infinity gives us the idea of eternity.[288]

The Standishes were noted by the press in their role as host and hostess of visiting English dignitaries, and Widor fulfilled his customary role as piano accompanist (see fig. 23) for the evening entertainment:

Monsieur and Madame Standish entertained in their mansion at 3 rue de Belloy, at the corner of rue La Pérouse, the salon of which was adorned with a remarkable collection of art objects and ancient curios. Reputed for her particular elegance, Madame Standish . . . wore dresses that inspired her neighbor Marcel Proust (from his kitchen, the writer could see the Standish's mansion). In 1908, the Standishes gave a dinner in honor of the Prince and Princess of Wales, at the end of which Anita Kinen and Warmbrodt sang accompanied by Widor.[289]

The social goings-on at the Standishes did not escape the attention of the novelist Proust (1871–1922), either as an imagined guest or voyeur from his kitchen window, and he had to have known that Widor frequented their musical gatherings. In *Le côté de Guermantes*, volume three of his multitome novel *À la recherche du temps perdu*, Proust placed himself at a reception given by the Duke and Duchess de Guermantes for King Edward VII and Queen Alexandra. One of the novel's characters, Count Hannibal de Bréauté-Consalvi, was a guest at the reception and wondered about Proust's identity:

Having arrived late, [Count de Bréauté] had not had time to inquire about the dinner guests and when I entered the salon, seeing in me an invitee who was not part of the duchess's social circle and consequently to have some quite extraordinary titles in order to gain admittance there, he put in his monocle under the curved arch of his eyebrow, thinking this would help him greatly to discern what kind of man I was. . . . For an instant, the name of Mr. Widor crossed his mind; but he thought that I was quite young to be an organist, and Mr. Widor of too little prominence to be "received."[290]

The latter assumption proved to be false, as Widor was regularly "received" by nobles and aristocrats. As one of the most renowned musicians of the capital he moved in their circles with ease, he in their private salons and they in his organ gallery. Juggling social engagements, however, was something of an art that required the utmost tact and grace; as he somewhat grudgingly wrote to a friend: "It's a real fatality! *I am obliged* to dine with the Princess Schleswig-Holstein! But I hope to be free early and will meet up with you. . . . Life in Paris is complicated!"[291]

During the time Mathilde lived with the Standishes, from the death of her father in July 1902 until her marriage to Widor in April 1920, little is related about her. However, she enjoyed the closest familial relationship with her "adored" aunt and uncle, and she imparted the warmth and generosity of spirit that earned her the love and respect of those whose lives she touched.[292] Equally little is known of the contacts and eventual courtship between Mathilde and her "beloved Charles-Marie,"[293] but she must have expressed a good degree of intelligence and refinement of character to attract the attentions of so imposing a personality as the perpetual secretary of the Academy of Fine Arts. Aside from seeing Widor at the Standishes, Mathilde began to attend some of his performances, perhaps beginning with the March 1903 inauguration of the new organ of Saint-Philippe-du-Roule. The event has been sketched in a suggestive scenario befitting Mathilde's sensitivities:

> Still filled with a despair that [her father] had not allowed her to externalize, and isolated in a luxurious residence, without friends her own age, her attraction to music prompted her to accompany Lord and Lady Standish to the organ concert of their friend Widor. He was at the pinnacle of his art. The sweet, then sumptuously powerful sonorities overran the nave of the church, rolling over Mathilde and filling her being. She suffered, and at the same time a flood from the depth of her being swept over and freed her. Tears welled up that could only flow internally, in order not to show this mingled distress and happiness. Her sensitive soul vibrated with the rhythm of the organ, plunged into it with delight and came out of quenched. She did not know how to give a name to what had just been awakened in her, but she promised herself to find again this overwhelming flight, until then unknown.[294]

The day after Christmas 1905, Mathilde accompanied her aunt and uncle to the premier of *Les pêcheurs de Saint-Jean* at the Opéra-Comique.[295] She collected news items and learned everything she could about the idol of her life:

She knew that he was part of all Paris, that he kept company with the aristocracy, the political, artistic, and literary worlds. . . . A wave of admiration drowned Mathilde—an admiration that she knew how to transform into love. She stole into Saint-Sulpice often to see him and revel in his playing.[296]

For nearly two decades she nourished her juvenile love for Widor into the consummation of marriage. Although undocumented, one account offers possible circumstances that led to that end:

Charles-Marie Widor, at the time of regained euphoria [the end of World War I], lingered more and more in the salon of Hélène Standish. He sat close to Mathilde's piano, counseling her, noticing that she regularly took the place of her aunt for the organization of the house, the contacts with the servants, and the management of daily life. She was a woman who knew how to uphold her position, organize receptions, and lead a conversation while keeping a certain distance. What remarkable company she would be for a man alone in his apartment at the Institute, but who would love to see a spouse at his side to share in the honors, to allow him to receive worthily his friends and the numerous personalities who visited him![297]

A marriage contract, separating their estates, was signed in Paris at the notary establishment of Maître Desforges on April 13, 1920.[298] Although Mathilde was enormously wealthy, Widor never utilized her resources to his gain, and certainly he did not need her societal position to further his own professional or personal ends. In his will, he wrote: "Mathilde is rich. We are by marriage contract separated in our personal holdings, in such a way that there has never been a question of money between us . . . and the little money that I have been able to save must serve artistic interests."[299] A further testament to this statement is that shortly after his resignation from Saint-Sulpice, Widor lamented to the curé, "If I had been richer, I would have given to the parish the two pedal stops I have always wanted."[300] At the time of his death, Widor's personal estate holdings consisted of railroad stocks.[301]

—100—

"Dear husband and wife . . . Be happy!"

Mathilde's marriage to Widor brought her into the spotlight, perhaps for the first time. Something of her life can be gleaned from the allocution delivered by Abbé Augustin Sicard, curé of Saint-Pierre de Chaillot (avenue Marceau, 16th Arrondissement, Paris), where Mathilde and the Standishes were parishioners. The attentive wedding party included Widor's brother, Paul, Lord and

Lady Standish, uncles and cousins Montesquiou and des Cars, Aunt Stéphanie des Cars Bertier, and the cousins Béatrix and Isabelle Bertier.

Dear Husband and Wife,

Here we are, brought together for one of the greatest events in human life, for the marriage ceremony; and this marriage is going to be celebrated in this family chateau where it will have the enchantment of intimacy.

This chateau is familiar to me. It is familiar to Saint-Pierre de Chaillot by the hospitality that our young women's club has received here several times during the war. It's an act of kindness of which they have preserved the memory; they took some recreation and refreshment in this delightful place where the air is so pure, the welcome so kindly and so generous. The souls have found here nourishment for the body, and on this day, Mademoiselle, it seems to me that the prayers said in this chapel by the modest and good young women fall back at this moment on you in gratitude and blessings from heaven.

This hospitality, given to the humble, brings out in you, Mademoiselle, some qualities that quite particularly characterize you, and that have great reward before God and before men: CHARITY, KINDNESS.

To love to give, to take pleasure in good works, not to be able to witness a suffering without your heart being moved, without your hand opening wide, here is a feeling that you know well, and that constitutes the most noble use of wealth. To love like this is the surest means of being loved, and to sow sympathies and gratitude on one's way.

Without looking far away, I divine, I know what affection and what devotion your kindness has won for you from your tenants on this estate. I have noticed that on this day the table is also set for their benefit in order to have them participate in this grand event. . . .

I see here those who are united with you by blood ties, in particular your two witnesses, in whom the traditions of ancestry have revived bravery and the spirit of sacrifice for country in the last war. Nearest you, I see your dear uncle and your dear aunt, who have surrounded you with a so constant solicitude. Struck early with the great misfortune of losing your parents, you have had the joy of finding in them a father and a mother, and of giving to them in your person a darling and affectionate young daughter.

I have been able to observe several times in the language of [your aunt], who has been for you a second mother and who takes the place of her this day with such emotion, what affection she holds for you, and what fervent wishes she makes to heaven for your happiness. How much your presence in her home has been sweet for her! How much, also, has it been good for you to spend your youth with her whose tender affection you have felt every day, who by her perfect understanding of the world was able to give you precocious experience, who by a heritage of ancestry has kept among us, and at times in the most brilliant Courts, these grand manners that are a tradition of the highest French aristocracy.

You appreciate the value of such a gift. I know that you do not want to move away from those who have loved you so much. I know also that such is the thought of the one who today unites his life with yours. . . .

[After an equally lengthy description and praise of Widor's accomplishments, Sicard concluded:] I have said enough, Monsieur, about the public man. I finish by adding that you will bring to the home all the private virtues. You were anxious to tell Abbé Létourneau, at a festival celebrated recently in your honor, "I owe everything to Saint-Sulpice," forgetting, as it were, what you owe only to yourself.

Both of you are very Christian, and religion is the guarantee of durable happiness. You both have this conquering virtue that is called KINDNESS. . . . You will join to it devotedness, self-sacrifice, reciprocal amenity, which are the condiment and charm of daily life. I recalled earlier, Mademoiselle, your great charity. God has given you the means to exercise it very freely. And what a joy it is for the heart to be able to pour out blessings. This chateau will be the home of charity. Charity is above all the concern of the wife; work, more particularly that of the husband. I see you, Monsieur, strolling outside on this enchanting estate, and dreaming under its great inspiring trees of some symphony that will be a new masterpiece added to so many others.

Dear husband and wife, I finish in saying: Be happy! It is the prayer that we will address to God during this Mass. It is the wish that goes from my heart, and from the hearts of all the relatives and friends united here by this great day, and also, I love to declare it, from the hearts of the farmers and servants attached to the estate and to the family, who bring you the evidence of their attachment and their gratitude.[302]

Clearly, this must have been the happiest of days for Mathilde, but her uncle Standish was greatly fatigued and in ill-health. Three short months later, on July 31, Henry Standish died and Mathilde's life plunged once again into the grief of losing a cherished family member. As Abbé Sicard mentioned in his allocution, it was Mathilde's desire, and apparently Widor's too, that she be able to remain close to her aunt and uncle. Although Widor was provided with a commodious apartment at the Institute, the Standish mansion at 3 rue de Belloy became a second home that he and Mathilde shared with Lady Standish.

The marriage was, by all veritable accounts, a happy one.[303] Tales of domestic life fill a letter to Albert Schweitzer:

What to tell you of Paris that might interest you? The days follow one another without great variety. . . . Belloy sends you its affectionate remembrances— Madame Standish lost her Tonton from Pomerania, a frightful despair; with great sorrow we replaced it with a little puppy, exquisite in appearance. Well, impetigo just killed it! From that, a second despair. A real tragedy in the house, catastrophe upon catastrophe![304]

Mathilde traveled with her husband to many of his concert engagements, and she proudly accompanied him to Spain the month after their marriage for the laying of the cornerstone of the Casa Velásquez. The following August, Widor and Mathilde paid their first visit to his family home in Persanges. Arriving from Lyon by taxi at the Persanges terminus hotel, rooms were requested for the newlyweds and their chambermaid.[305] Letters from Mathilde to Widor's niece Marguerite "Guite" Reynard (1882–1937) in Persanges that first year have the tone of a young schoolgirl in love. Tearing herself away from her husband for a little time at the Château d'Hauteville, Mathilde posted a letter to Guite from Mayenne:

> I wanted to write to you before my departure from Paris, but I had so much anguish leaving your uncle that I didn't leave until the last moment.
>
> Alas, we are now separated again, supposedly for one month, but I'm already plotting—not without warning him in advance—a little visit to Paris. . . .
>
> P.S. You would give me pleasure by calling me Mathilde, because it wouldn't matter to your uncle.[306]

According to Widor's grandniece, Guite was quite pretty and outgoing. The friendship between Mathilde and her eventually cooled to the point that Mathilde grew extremely jealous and forbade her to visit. Guite's older sister, Gaby, was not as attractive, and Mathilde maintained a close relationship with her even in the years after Widor's death. In 1935 when Guite wanted to visit her uncle around the time of his ninety-first birthday, Marcel Dupré had to act as the intermediary between Guite and Widor to keep the visit a secret from Madame Widor. Dupré wrote to Guite that he had paved the way for her visit:

> I have seen your uncle just now and have read your letter to him. He was profoundly happy to have your news and told me that "with joy I will see her; she may come whatever day she would like between 2 and 6. She is sure to find me at the Institute. She may choose the day herself." I saw a great flash of joy on his face at the thought of your visit.
>
> I next saw the concierge who, from Madame Widor herself, is perfectly informed of the situation [Madame Widor's dislike of Guite]. [The concierge], a decent and honest woman, is indignant at this situation and at certain actions, and told me: "Let Madame Reynard come without the shadow of fear. I'll take charge of it. She will enter and leave without being seen or challenged."
>
> [The concierge] is completely won over by you and I had nothing to say to her about this, as she already had her opinion. She knows the pleasure that your visit will bring to your uncle, whom she reveres.
>
> Consider therefore that everything is wide open. The only precaution to take is preferably not to arrive before 3:00 and not to stay later than 5:00. . . .

In any case, come in complete confidence. At this moment, your dear uncle is doing really well, and his arm is better. Take advantage of the fact that you're sure to find him at the Institute. Simply tell me the day that you choose for your trip so I can alert the concierge, and be assured that you are expected with joy, without a shadow [of concern].[307]

—101—

Celebrity, original ideas, and rash notions

After World War I, Widor's concert appearances grew increasingly rare; when they did occur, they were especially noted events. He presided at the organ with Dupré and titular organist Abel Decaux for the consecration services of the Basilique du Sacré-Cœur de Montmartre on October 16, 1919.[308] When Widor and Mathilde visited Madrid in May 1920 for the cornerstone laying ceremony at the Casa Velásquez, he conducted several of his works at a "French Festival."[309] A month later, Her Majesty the Queen of Romania was charmed by a performance of *Conte d'avril* at the Odéon in Paris.[310] The citizenry of Wiesbaden thrilled to hear the Marktkirche resound with his Fifth Symphony during a program he shared with Dupré on September 7, 1921, and two days later Widor conducted an orchestral concert of his music at the Kurhaus:

Several minutes before the hour of the concert, it was impossible to find a seat in the vast nave of the church.

The expectation of the public was so earnest, and so justified by the celebrity of Mr. Widor . . . and this expectation was surpassed. . . .

. . . The Organ Symphonies of Mr. Ch.-M. Widor count among the most splendid masterpieces with which organ literature is enriched since J. S. Bach and Mendelssohn. . . .

Is it necessary to say in what masterly fashion Mr. Widor has brought forth all the beauties of his symphonies? It is said of the organ that it is a world; it is necessary to add then that Mr. Widor is the god of it, for he gives it a multiple life with nuances ranging from the most subtle finesse to the most imposing power. The composer and the performer blended here in a rare and precious union.[311]

On the orchestral program, Widor conducted his tried-and-true Third Symphony for Orchestra and Organ. The challenges encountered with the Wiesbaden organs prompted an article from him upon returning to Paris; he once again expressed his firm opinion on the superiority of mechanical action: "The tubular [pneumatic] organs of the Marktkirche and the Kurhaus lack precision and are slow—what a shame that Germany has abandoned the old mechanical action of Bach, which obeys instantaneously!"[312]

In a volume titled *Un demi-siècle de civilisation française (1870–1915)*, published in 1916 and with chapters contributed by twenty authors, Widor willingly fulfilled his assignment to write on music. In the space of barely twenty-one pages in "La musique," he undertook to distill into a short essay the history of music from its origins through the nineteenth century, and to sketch the historical backgrounds of the Conservatoire, Société des Concerts, Opéra, and Opéra-Comique. Though necessarily superficial in nature, the chapter reveals that its author had a surprisingly broad grasp of music history. In one paragraph he described his intellectual fascination and practical experience in grappling with some old music:

> Nothing is more instructive than to bring some singers together to try to interpret venerable texts. We did this last summer at the Conservatory. . . . We went up to the library and sight-read as well as possible these old masters of polyphony—Belgian, French, and Italian. Beneath the apparent simplicity of these pages, so clear, so unladed with notes and almost blank in appearance, at each moment a surprise arises, an emotion from the effect produced always by very simple means. Alone and without accompaniment, three or four voices evoke the idea of an incomparable grandeur and imperishable beauty; what a marvel, and what pride for us to be able to claim, as from our blood, some of the most illustrious of these "Fathers of music"![313]

From certain parallels, it is apparent that this brief chapter gave rise seven years later to Widor's 160-page music primer, *Initiation musicale*, whose preface begins by offhandedly proclaiming: "This little book contains the program of what is necessary to know in music."[314] Topics in the book include: the ear, sound, harmonics, timbre, wind and stringed instruments, keyboard instruments, scales, harmony (consonant and dissonant), counterpoint, composition, the origins of music, opera, acoustics, and various composers (Handel, Bach, Mozart, Beethoven, Weber, Schumann, Wagner). Everything is deliberately simplified and compressed—sometimes naively so: beginning his chapter on counterpoint, Widor casually observed, "Nothing is less complicated."[315] Émile Vuillermoz (1878–1960) pointed out in his review of the book, "There is in the manner of Ch.-M. Widor a characteristic element, sometimes enjoyable and sometimes irritating: offhandedness."[316] Widor certainly did not pretend to treat each topic exhaustively in his presentation; he simply wrote from his life experience and covered what interested him personally, as another critic confirmed:

> Of impulsive spirit, not lacking in imagination, the author has written in the quick manner of free conversation, and that excuses certain errors made in passing that an *authoritative* exposé would certainly have put right, and gives it an attractiveness that would be lacking in a more severe treatise. Original ideas and rash notions abound.[317]

Widor's "offhandedness" earned him a critical lashing from Joseph Bonnet, an organist colleague forty years his junior whom he had credited with carrying to America "the good word" of the French school.[318] Bonnet's review in *La Petite Maîtrise* of *L'orgue* by Alexandre Cellier and Henri Bachelin did not omit pointed criticism of the book's preface by Widor. After assessing that Cellier and Bachelin "too often abandon in an unfortunate manner the depth of their subject,"[319] Bonnet turned his sights on Widor: "Reminding us of those [prefaces] that we have read under the same signature . . . published during the last forty years, this preface brings to us some new ideas that, to tell the truth, have amazed us."[320] Bonnet enumerated six statements in which Widor was historically fanciful, factually inaccurate, or contradictory, and then asked, "Will we endorse this?"

Bonnet failed to appreciate the poetic synthesis of Widor's statement: "Blowing into a reed, the shepherd invented the flute. Cast in bronze, the wooden instrument became the trumpet. An artificial ventilation replacing the effort of the lungs created the hydraulis, the ancestor of the organ."[321] In another passage, Widor argued: "It's not the sensational pneumatic, electric, dyspeptic, ataxic, and other inventions that have transformed the eighteenth-century organ, but two very simple mechanisms: the *expression box* and the *Barker lever*."[322] Bonnet railed on this assertion, countering, "The very invention of Barker is that of the *pneumatic* lever! Furthermore, doesn't Mr. Widor himself own a salon organ furnished with a pedal clavier with electric transmission?"[323] Nor could Bonnet let pass Widor's assertion:

As for assigning controls of every type [appels de tout genre] to the manuals—couplers and registers—so as to force the player to interrupt himself in order to actuate with the right or left hand some buttons, to subordinate art to the machine—what an aberration! It's to this that electric means are directed.[324]

Having had considerable experience with electric-action organs, Bonnet readily pointed out Widor's specious argument:

So these electric means wouldn't allow us to actuate the couplers and registers with the foot as easily as on mechanical organs? For us the answer is not in question, since all the controls—couplers and combinations—exist in the two systems and are equally commanded by pedals. To see the player inexorably forced to actuate his registration by the right and left hands, it's necessary to go . . . to Saint-Sulpice, where the combination registers exist only for the hands and require the organist to operate two to three movements in order to draw a single stop. Now, is art thus more subordinated to the machine or do we find the real aberration?[325]

In a later issue of *La Petite Maîtrise*, in an article titled "Pro Vero" [For Truth], Widor responded to Bonnet's critique, which he found "a bit harsh."[326]

Instead of answering Bonnet point for point, however, Widor simply ignored him by adding further correlative commentary on Cellier and Bachelin's book and largely extolling Bach and Cavaillé-Coll along the way. Only at the end of his response, in a brief section headed "Pro domo mea" [For my defense], did Widor address Bonnet's caustic review of his preface: "The harsh criticism of Cellier and Bachelin is still more severe toward me, attacking the preface that the authors were good enough to ask of me." After pointing to one instance in which Bonnet had misconstrued his meaning, Widor scolded: "May the foolhardy individual go immediately to confess at Solesmes. I will continue my esteem and bestow my benediction on him: "Pax hominibus bonæ voluntatis, nec non et feminis" [Peace and good will to men, and also to women].[327]

The editors of *La Petite Maîtrise* submitted Widor's article to Bonnet for a follow-up response. Taking the elder statesman of French music to task, regardless of his perceived faulty reasoning, was tantamount to questioning papal infallibility; undaunted, Bonnet attacked Widor tit for tat in a lengthy self-justifying diatribe that got quite personal:

> I admire as much, if not more than anyone, the works of Bach and Cavaillé-Coll; they are not of concern for a moment in my article. It would be, contrariwise, difficult to discern the proof of heartfelt admiration for the Cantor of Leipzig in a certain *Bach's Memento* authored by my contradictor. In this collection, some noble pieces of Bach are mercilessly deformed and gain nothing from these tasteless treatments. . . .
>
> Not having sinned even venially in this circumstance, I do not have to go look for absolution at Solesmes. Moreover, why this invitation "to confess" at Solesmes? There is no lack of confessors in Paris, at Saint-Sulpice notably. But I have always believed that it was more convenient and more agreeable to invite others to confess than to confess oneself. . . .
>
> The benediction that he wants to "bestow" on me?
>
> In principle, I bow only before the representatives of God on the earth, and as he is not, that I know, "the anointed" of the Lord, his benediction can only be a benediction in a very broad sense.
>
> Finally, not wanting to be indebted in generosity to my eminent contradictor, I myself also conclude with a wish—his own; but I'm enlarging it further: "*Pax hominibus bonæ voluntatis, Nec non et feminis, Nec non et omni animali*" [Peace and good will to men, and also to women, and even to every animal].[328]

Although Widor did not respond further, he undoubtedly felt very hurt by Bonnet's inflammatory remarks. He soon received a supportive letter from Albert Riemenschneider that must have been greatly appreciated; it reads, in part:

> It grieves me to hear from Paris that history is repeating itself and that a "J. A. Scheibe" has again arisen to attack a "Bach." These things are always

unpleasant, but I am sure, my dear Master, that the historical result of 1737, when J. A. Scheibe made his infamous attack upon Bach, will repeat itself. This episode of 1737 has in the end served to make the figure of J. S. Bach stand out all the greater and the figure of Scheibe to be reduced to the roll of the merely ridiculous. I feel that the present situation has precisely the same background that the former situation had and that the result will be the same. I would therefore at this time like to add my suggestion that you cease to worry about this event, as I am confident that it will take care of itself to your advantage.[329]

—102—

Nerto: "A robust story, gorgeous setting, and 'safe' music"

The gestation period of Widor's last opera continued an incredible thirty-six years. The seeds of the project were sown in 1888 when Frédéric Mistral (1830–1914) asked Widor to consider writing an opera based on his poem Nerto.[330] Mistral had arranged for Massenet to compose the opera four years earlier, but when librettist Paul Mariéton (1862–1911) failed to deliver the libretto, Massenet dropped the project.[331] Widor found the poem filled with dramatic potency and agreed to the undertaking. A year later, however, nothing had progressed. Widor described how the logjam was broken:

> The difficulty was Mariéton, whom I did not care to have as theatrical poet. Mistral, who had lunch with me at Maupassant's place, having drunk a carafe of champagne, suddenly exclaimed: "So! It's because of Mariéton that our work isn't going forward? Let's drop Mariéton; he's a child. Two men of the theater are offering me their collaboration on Nerto. I will send them to you; Mariéton will know the news only when all is settled; I will know nothing about it, have known nothing, and we will be very astonished!" So there's the story; neither Mariéton nor the newspapers knew anything, temporarily.[332]

Mistral's poem was turned over to Maurice Léna (d. 1928), who was later the librettist of Massenet's Jongleur de Nôtre Dame. Work on the score began about 1891, but continued only sporadically.[333] Reportedly, Widor penned the final measures during his annual vacation in Persanges in 1912, and he completed the orchestration a year later.[334] Presumably ready to be premiered, the outbreak of World War I prohibited such plans; Nerto would have to wait another eleven years before it would be produced. In the intervening time, Widor continued to revise the score. He wrote to Albert Riemenschneider on April 25, 1916, "I just finished 4 acts of opera and at the same time the 4th volume of Bach (Schirmer)";[335] and he wrote to Imbart de la Tour from Persanges on September 12, 1919, that he was finishing Act IV.[336] Still one year later he wrote to his niece Gaby, "I am finishing *Nerto*, working without the doorbell ringing and without annoying visitors."[337]

Back in 1895 Widor had written to critic Charles Tenroc about getting *Nerto* accepted at the Opéra: "The directors perform the 'dead,' and they are quite right. Thanks to them, the passage from this earth to an unknown world— a passage so dreaded by ordinary mortals—is for musicians a sweetness that you don't suspect: 'Finally,' they say, 'we are now going to enter into eternity and perhaps rehearsals!'"[338] Although belated, *Nerto* did not have to wait until its author had passed from this earth; rehearsals began and the Paris Opéra mounted the premiere on October 27, 1924.

A lyric drama in four acts, *Nerto* is set in medieval times, and has but three characters of note:

Act I opens with the Baron Pons de Château-Renard on his deathbed, watched over by his daughter Nerto. As he exhales his last regrets to life, the horror of the situation unfolds: greedy for gold, he had once contracted with Satan to exchange his soul for the glitter of worldly riches—but not his soul alone, that of Nerto too! Now is the hour of the exchange, but he shows no remorse; as Nerto prays, the vision of his riches still illumines his demented eyes. Satan appears to claim the soul of Pons. What will become of Nerto, her innocence damned? A celestial chorus indicates that only the Pope can save her. Being the epoch of the Avignon popes, Nerto departs immediately for the papal city.

Act II begins with her arrival in Avignon, exhausted from the journey, and obsessed by her terrible condemnation. A popular festival is taking place in the market place. Some local gypsies ask her to join them in dance, but she declines, announcing that she is damned. Taking her for a witch, they begin to taunt her when the archer-police captain, Rodrigue de Luno, who also happens to be the Pope's nephew, interrupts them. He promptly falls in love with Nerto; but owing to the seriousness of her mission, she feels it difficult to return his affection. On learning of her purpose in Avignon, he pokes fun at her fears and continues to speak only of love; however, he finally agrees to present her to the Holy Father. The Pope is borne in with great ceremony, and, on hearing his nephew's story, points to a group of nuns who will attend to Nerto. She follows them away, but not without a look of regret cast towards Rodrigue.

In Act III, Nerto is within the nuns' convent praying. Rodrigue invades the convent to take Nerto away with him, but she only repels him in order to remain faithful to the endeavor of saving her soul. In great anger, Rodrigue decidedly calls on Satan to take his soul. Within a moment, the Devil appears and whisks him away.

Act IV opens with Rodrigue in the gorgeousness of Satan's magical house of the seven capital sins. Just before his soul is to be taken, Nerto enters; she could no longer resist being without his love—even though it means she will now lose her soul too. This ultimate proof of her love impels Rodrigue to summon his courage and defend her from this terrible fate. As Satan approaches, Rodrigue draws his sword in defiance. The palace collapses in demonic horror, and the two young lovers ascend to Heaven, where they are received by celestial voices proclaiming their pardon. United in death, they fall at the feet of the Virgin of Mercy, who appears.[339]

Critical opinion varied widely in the days following the premiere. If one appreciated it as "a very pleasant score, elegant and decidedly melodic, and of lovely orchestral coloring, without complications or useless subtleties,"[340] another condemned it as "a work that would have appeared stale in the 1860s."[341] Critic Jean Poueigh pronounced it "stillborn."[342] The following two critical excerpts indicate the ambivalence among the reviewers:

For the musical evocation of these scenes, a prime and fundamental quality was required: clarity. It is to this, it seems, that Mr. Widor has devoted himself from the outset. By the skillful and buoyant fashion in which he makes use of this process—having his characters tell the essential story almost openly, yet in an expressive and melodic declamation, with some discrete and equally expressive instrumental voices commenting on rather than just supporting them—he gives to his work a color as firm as it is appealing. . . . Unlabored, without insistence, with an orchestra of perfect equilibrium, the musical work progresses thus: united and faithful to the literary work, constantly sustaining and renewing the interest of the listener.

This conformity, this union of the music and the drama, is naturally not the sole attraction of the work. The freshness and the grace of certain inspirations are such that one is sometimes surprised. Perhaps one would wish for more transport and force in the action scenes, in certain diabolic evocations; but the contrast would then risk being more abrupt than it should be in this "mystery" in stained glass, whose fine colors need harmony first of all. —Henri de Curzon.[343]

It is impossible to guess the objective of this "retrospective." . . . If the operatic genre had not already been attacked by the pitiless illness that will one day kill it, practitioners like Mr. Widor would be enough to send it to a better world. . . . It seems the intention was to assemble in this work all the elements representative of the old operatic formula of 1860, whose anachronism no longer needs to be demonstrated. —Émile Vuillermoz.[344]

According to Isidor Philipp, *Nerto* had been doomed from the start by "the caprice of the pretty prima donna and by a foppish and unintelligent impresario."[345] Aside from the sundry intrigues, it seems the main reason for *Nerto*'s failure came from its indisputably nineteenth-century style, as pointed out in most reviews: "Mr. Widor's music voices the French lyrical tradition as developed by Gounod and Massenet, but preserves its distance from all recent contributions in this art."[346] "The new opera . . . will appeal to those who love a robust story, gorgeous setting, and 'safe' music."[347] Maintaining that Widor had purposely not moved beyond the traditions of his youth, André Messager concluded: "I don't think he can keep a public long tired of the form called Grand Opera close to him with that method. . . . This is why the score of Mr. Widor has disappointed some of his listeners, musicians especially."[348] When baritone Rouard, who sang the part of Baron Pons, asked Widor if he was happy with his interpretation of the role, Widor jested, "I would not have sung better than you."[349] Philipp remarked, "Widor accepted everything with a smile on his lips."[350] From long experience, the composer knew that "the career of an artist is not without some resemblance to a roller coaster: ups and downs."[351]

—103—

"Has music reached its pinnacle?"

Widor undoubtedly realized that his effectiveness as a composer was drawing to a close; indeed, only three further works, all for organ, were composed in the years that remained to him. He had passed over a threshold that defined his artistic ideals, and consequently his art, as anachronistic. Perhaps he took some solace in knowing that he was not alone in feeling the artistic divide between himself and the current styles of the time. Saint-Saëns, at the very end of his life, had written to him:

> I see with great pleasure that I am not forgotten at the Concerts Widor [in the Salle de Caen at the Institute]. It is not the same at the Concerts Colonne, which have not deigned to make a place for me in three months; only at the end, two concertos certainly imposed by the virtuosos, while in chamber music concerts one never sees my name. People prefer to play Debussy and Ravel. The rest of us are not *advanced* enough![352]

When Alexander Russell requested from Widor a note of introduction to Saint-Saëns, Widor chuckled, "You won't need it, just go to see him and tell him you admire his compositions. He will see you and talk for hours."[353] Widor delighted in relating an anecdote about Saint-Saëns and a commemorative statue of him that had been erected in Dieppe in 1907: "Every year on his birthday Saint-Saëns would take the train to that city, hang a wreath on his own statue, and make a deep bow."[354]

Although amusing, these vignettes reveal the sad truth that some of the older generation felt neglected and forgotten. Widor, however, did not have time for self-absorbed pity. Fully engaged in his duties at the Institute, he had visionary plans including an expansion of its presence and influence both inside and beyond French borders. His mental and physical energy seemed limitless: "Endowed with ironclad health, Widor was a great worker."[355] Russell recalled a time when Widor led him on a wild dash to the Institute on foot:

> When he was over seventy-five years old, I called one day by appointment. He told me that he had just received word of a special meeting of the Academy. As secretary, he must be present. "Come along," said he, "we will talk on the way." No taxi for Widor. Walk he would, and did. Perhaps he played Bach too slowly, as some think, but there was nothing slow about his walking.
>
> In and out of traffic we wound, dodging buses, motor cars and pedestrians, block after block, across the Seine, up winding streets, with me half his age and with legs almost twice as long, trailing a full yard behind him. At the door of the Academy he bade me good-bye and disappeared up the stairs leaving me breathless on the sidewalk.
>
> I shall always think of him like that. His amazing vitality of mind, body and spirit; his monumental achievements in all lines of music; the tremendous impact of his personality on people of all sorts and conditions; his wit; his active participation in world affairs; his executive as well as musical genius; his generous, kindly nature; and his unfailing charm.[356]

In a brief article written in 1923, Widor subtly disclosed his view of current trends in music:

> La Musique, is it in a state of progress or in a state of decadence? Those who view purely sensory effect as the ultimate aim of music will contend that we are progressing. Those, on the contrary, who seek, in the art of music, ideas and their highest development, will feel that music is retrogressing.
>
> "Has music reached its pinnacle?" I am asked. Certainly. It reached its pinnacle with Mozart, afterward with Beethoven, afterward with Wagner; and it had reached it with Bach. You see, musical progress is a long succession of pinnacles.[357]

From his deeply rooted nineteenth-century aesthetic, much of the music of 1923 must have seemed devoid of all that he held sacred—"ideas and their highest development." If Widor failed to cite a pinnacle after Wagner, it is perhaps that he did not want to make a public judgment of the period he was in, but not of. Through the years, Widor had suffered bitter and discouraging comments from critics who had neither understood nor appreciated him; and in a lecture at the Institute, he warned against callously judging the artistic expression of other generations by one's own idealism: "We must be careful when we judge the tastes of our elders according to our own, the needs of the imagination and of sensibility change so much with the generations."[358] Widor had always stood steadfastly by his younger colleagues, usually respecting their right of expressive freedom and heralding their causes; he expected no less from others.[359] Gustave Doret (1866–1943) understood: "Posterity will judge impartially the certain value of [Widor's] scores, victims of a severity that without doubt comes from the quality of high integrity of the artist who never stooped to compromises of conscience, who always defended music for itself and never feared to state straightforwardly, but with courtesy, his opinion on all and everything."[360]

As in some other forms of art, not all music is destined to endure the volatile tastes of time, and by its very nature much of it is bound to be consigned to forgotten library shelves and museum basements, if it even survives. Widor understood all that quite well:

> While painters and musicians have to submit to the caprices of opinion and the ravages of time, architects and sculptors benefit from a more independent and certain life.
>
> What do we know of the painters of antiquity or the musicians of the Hellenic period? Well, the Acropolis dates back twenty-four centuries, and London jealously retains the marbles of Phidias.
>
> Isn't he enviable: the architect called to construct a palace right in the heart of Paris, in such a beautiful space that for centuries one is fully aware of it.[361]

In truth, Widor lived through several style periods; although the son of early nineteenth-century romanticism, his life span equaled or exceeded those of Debussy, Dukas, Satie, Roussel, and Ravel. Widor witnessed the formation and artistic thrust of the anti-impressionist group "Les Six," which included two of his own pupils—Honegger and Milhaud. He saw the rise of post-romanticism, primitivism, neoclassicism, expressionism, atonality, serialism; all these styles occurred within his lifetime.

As to the changing tides in organ music, Widor's insatiable intellectual curiosity would have led him to examine new works by his former students. He most likely heard Dupré perform at Saint-Sulpice the *Symphonie-Passion* (1924), *Seven Pieces* (1931) and *Le chemin de la croix* (1932), and Vierne's latest organ symphonies would not have escaped his attention. While it is not known how much he knew of the music of Olivier Messiaen, Widor was his first composition teacher and Messiaen did visit him at Saint-Sulpice.[362]

From *fin de siècle* romanticism into the new century, the face of French music was changing so rapidly and radically that Widor saw his own aesthetic tastes and traditions pass away right before his eyes. With the passing of Saint-Saëns in 1921—in Widor's words, "an irreparable loss for French art,"[363]—and Fauré in 1924, Widor lived to see himself become the venerated doyen of French music for still more than a decade. Born during the reign of Louis-Philippe (1830–48), he had survived more transitions in French government, more wars, crises, and changes in the social fabric than perhaps any other French musician in history.

Widor became one of the most decorated men in France. In 1890 the Archevêché d'Alger named him "Commandeur de Saint-Grégoire"; in 1893 the Belgian king named him "Chevalier de l'ordre de Léopold"; in 1901 he was made "Commandeur de l'ordre de St. Stanislas IIe classe"; in 1906 the Société de Sainte Cécile de Bordeaux gave him the title of "Vice-Président d'Honneur de Ste. Cécile"; in 1918 the Ministerio de Instrucción pública y Bellas Artes in Madrid named him "Comendador de número de la Orden Civil de Alfonso XII."[364] The Royal Academy of Florence elected him a member in 1923, as did the Academy of Bologne in 1924, and the Belgian Order of the Crown named him "grand-officier" in 1935.[365] The French Légion d'honneur named him "chevalier" in 1892, "officier" in 1922, "commandeur" in 1929, and "grand-officier" in 1933.[366] Concerning the latter distinction, Widor was unaware initially that he had been given the rank of grand-officier:

I returned home at the end of a meeting at the Institute when I was caught by my concierge, who told me: "A minister—he didn't give his name—just telephoned me: 'Mr. Widor isn't there? When he arrives, embrace him for me!'" Thinking it a joke, I immediately replied: "Fine, in return, you embrace the minister for me." It wasn't until the next morning, by the newspapers and the congratulations that began to flow, that I learned what you know and what I was far from suspecting. The telephone call really came from the Minister of National Education.[367]

In spite of all his honors, the humility of the man remains legendary. "He didn't want people to speak of him"; his sole desire was "to serve music and musicians."[368] In France, where the love of decorations reached considerable proportions, Widor wore his only at the annual meeting of the Academy; "he is content with wearing these distinctions morally," wrote Maurice Dumesnil.[369]

—104—

Retirement: "An old man without age"

After thirty-seven years as a professor at the National Conservatory, Widor wrote to Director Henri Rabaud in June 1927 of his desire to retire on October 1; the official ministerial decree recognized his long years of service and fixed his pension at 6,659 francs per year.[370] The choice of Paul Dukas as his successor could not have been more pleasing to Widor; they had been long-time friends and he held Dukas in very high esteem.[371] Widor did not relinquish all responsibility, however; the Academy of Fine Arts immediately appointed him as its representative to the Council for Higher Education in the music studies section of the Conservatory.[372]

Improved music education at the public school level had long been one of Widor's theme songs. Over the years, he had spoken out in condemnation of a deplorable practice used in French public schools—that of teaching music by rote:[373] "It is inadmissible that we are still treating the French little ones like parrots."[374] As early as 1883, Widor had compiled a charming collection of thirty-three children's songs that he harmonized in the simplest manner: *Vieilles chansons et rondes pour les petits enfants* (Old Songs and Rounds for Little Children). A well-known artist of the time, Boutet de Monvel (1851–1913) colorfully illustrated each song. And partially under Widor's patronage, a free weekly concert series for the public school children of Paris was begun in 1909.[375] Still, he insisted, "Too many people confuse *song* and *music*. They believe they have taught music to children when they have made them learn some school songs by heart."[376]

In a 1923 preface written for a book by André Sarnette, Widor exhorted the importance of music in public education:

The study of music is a social necessity.

While the language of words specifies thought, that of sound expresses the infinite subtlety of the movements of soul—movements that words cannot translate.

It's a wonder, in the symphony, to notice the impression produced by the return of the theme. This theme [may be] abstract, a group of some notes more rhythmic than melodic; it corresponds to no word in the dictionary; major or minor, sad or happy, even devoid of all pathos, it is enough for it to have remained in our memory for us to look forward to it and celebrate its return. What is happening in our brain? Why are we moved? The episodes of the musical novel have unfolded having no rapport with those in life, in the real world. [Yet,] we have understood what the word cannot make understood; no one needs an explanation; art alone has captivated us.

Antiquity wasted no time in recognizing the social necessity of music: Plato, Aristotle, Plutarch, and Aristoxenus devote long chapters to its role in the education of the young.

Heir of Greece and Rome, the Christian world continued the ancient tradition: it is in the shadow of the monasteries that civilization developed. The people were soon allowed to sing with the deacons in the sanctuary, and then a new era for our art began, that of vocal polyphony, the two great notables of which were Palestrina and Victoria.

Where are we today?

In the North, the South, the West, in Sweden, Spain, England, Italy— everywhere there are admirable choirs. [But] we don't have them in Paris!

Recently, in a commission of the Ministry of State Education, they discussed music education in our schools, the method of this teaching and its results: "Progress or retrogression?" they asked. "Somewhat retrogression" was the response. This "somewhat" was a euphemism. It is much easier to learn to read seven notes than twenty-four letters. . . .

It is inadmissible that we are still treating our French little ones like parrots. The [music] theory that is satisfactory in primary school can be formulated on one leaf of letter paper, small size.

Unfortunate the one who has no music in his soul said the poet of *Conte d'avril*. The trouble comes from what the teacher lacks in artistic sensibility. How do you vaccinate him?

Formerly, in the time of the choir schools, the kids of seven to eight years knew how to read, write, count, and sing. The choirmasters imparted to them a little of what they had in them—the love of the beautiful. All worked together well and kindly. Some great artists came out of these schools.

Music education must begin at an early age; it's from infancy that the soul must be touched. . . .

. . . All efforts must be united in order to lift the soul of the people. Is there a more efficacious way, a lever more powerful than art?[377]

As perpetual secretary, Widor, along with several other influential musicians who included Vincent d'Indy (director of the Schola Cantorum) and Henri Rabaud (director of the Conservatory), signed a petition in 1924 requesting that music "become obligatory in all the classes of primary and secondary teaching, and that it be taught with the greatest seriousness by competent instructors having taken exams appropriate for that [duty]."[378] Shortly thereafter, Widor severely scolded the Council for Public Education for omitting music from its program; he addressed a letter to one of its members:

Last year I protested against the ineptness of the musical methods of elementary education, which, they have been obliged to write back to me, "is rather backward."

Recently, I wrote to the Director of Secondary Education to point out to him the absence of the word *Music* from the programs in which Architecture, Sculpture, Painting, etc. are mentioned.

It is clearly demonstrated that there are holes in the brains of the authors of these programs. These pedagogues are ignorant of the origins of our art, which is closely tied to that of classic literature, at the same time that they remain deaf to the singing all around them.

Please sir, count on my devotedness to the service of a cause that I have already defended, and which your support will help me to defend even better.[379]

Two years later, the Institute saw fit to delegate Widor as its representative on the Council for Higher Education.[380]

Widor never really looked his age, and throughout his octogenarian years he remained a potent force—"an old man without age"[381] (see fig. 24). Still, his advancing years were a constant reminder of his mortality; in 1925 he wrote to Riemenschneider about a projected sojourn to Paris two years hence: "If I'm still living in '27 I'll be happy to see you again."[382] And on March 13, 1927, he wrote to A. M. Henderson, "As for myself, I am a little nearer the end of life's journey."[383] Widor underwent an operation in December 1928 to remove a cataract in his left eye, after which *Le Ménestrel* reported that he was in "perfect health."[384] G. Huntington Byles noted: "[Widor] wore these glasses with the bulls-eye lens coming out toward you, which I had never seen before—the one eye was apparently very poor, as there was this one lens which stuck way out. He was very kindly. He had of course become somewhat stooped."[385] Jean Jacque interviewed him in April 1934—his ninetieth year—and observed a "lively and youthful expression behind shell-rimmed glasses, his face of an extraordinary liveliness of expression enlightened by a nice smile."[386] Responding to a question concerning his boundless energy, Widor said, "What do you want[?] . . . Providence has completely forgotten me; I have to keep busy."[387]

—105—

Suite latine: "A definitively purified
and spiritualized sentiment"

Though Widor's life centered largely on his multiple activities at the Institute and the weekly services at Saint-Sulpice, he made one or two concert appearances a year. Paul Bertrand rightly observed, "He provided the example of a devouring activity."[388] He also found that the creative urge had not yet yielded entirely. After several declarations that the *Symphonie romane* would be his last organ work—just as the Eighth Symphony was to have been—to the surprise and delight of all organists, at the age of eighty-three Widor composed the six-movement *Suite latine*, Op. 86.[389] In both the Eighth Symphony and the *Symphonie romane*, Widor felt that he had exhausted what he had to say in terms of organ composition; but with each recrudescence, he brought the expression of new concepts to his instrument.

The impetus for the *Suite latine* came from his devoted American pupil, Albert Riemenschneider, who championed his *maître*'s organ music in America by performing complete cycles of the symphonies.[390] Riemenschneider studied in Paris with Widor in 1904–5, 1914, 1924, 1927, and, finally, in 1930.[391] Widor refused to take remuneration from Riemenschneider in 1924, insisting they work together as colleagues,[392] and he praised Riemenschneider as "an accomplished musician, one of the contemporary *masters* of the organ."[393] Touched by his American student's devotion, Widor wrote to him on November 21, 1924: "I cannot give you more eloquent thanks than to declare to you that I'm going to make myself write again—and you will be the cause of it— some new compositions for organ."[394]

For three of the movements of the *Suite latine*, Widor returned again to the wellspring of plainsong to draw forth familiar Gregorian melodies: "Beatus Vir," "Ave Maris Stella," "Lauda Sion." Each is treated with a fresh hand, and the medium is managed with new efficiency as the registration "color" is kept to a minimum. This music exhales "a definitively purified and spiritualized sentiment," to use Dupré's words,[395] and for Riemenschneider, "Here the music assumes a sort of Greek philosopher state in which truth and perfection of thought are paramount."[396] Widor premiered the new work on January 13, 1928, for the inauguration of the restored organ at La Madeleine in Paris.[397] One critic began: "*Maître* Widor played the organ: that says it all"; after describing each movement, he had difficulty finding the words to summarize his emotions:

> The splendid communion of faith, art, and sacred dream that we owe *Maître* Widor cannot be interpreted by words. On the infinite summits where meditation loses itself in the ideal and where the hymn becomes diluted in prayer, how do you thoughtfully express praise, even the highest?[398]

Riemenschneider described the work as "the wonderful product of a man old in years, but who seems to keep eternally young through his work and interest in the progress of others."[399] After receiving the first edition of the *Suite latine*, he wrote to Widor pointing out about fourteen errors in print.[400] Widor responded: "I don't know how to thank you enough for your insight to discover and point out to me the errors in the *Suite latine*. Thanks to you, the next printing will be correct. Since you crossed the Atlantic in order to study Bach with me, you have made the voyage five [*sic*] times; you have asked me details about the feeling, the color, and the movement of my symphonies, which proved the insufficiency of my indications. You are, therefore, my collaborator."[401]

A few of the concert appearances that Widor made during his eighties included: the inauguration of the newly restored French classical organ at Saint-Sauveur in Petit Andely; a performance of the Beethoven *Missa Solemnis*, Op. 123, at Notre-Dame, with Gabriel Pierné conducting; the inauguration of the newly restored choir organ at the church of the Sorbonne in Paris; the inauguration of the new organ at the church of Saint-Ferdinand des Ternes (see fig. 25); and he conducted at the festival at Orléans for the five hundredth anniversary of the martyrdom of Joan of Arc.[402]

Widor's long life often tied together events that occurred decades apart. One such instance was the inauguration of the choir organ at the church of the Sorbonne. Félix Raugel described the details surrounding the restoration of this instrument and Widor's role in its history:

> During 1927, the furnishings of the church of the Sorbonne were enriched with a handsome organ case, designed and realized in 1865 by the master sculptor Liénard, containing an excellent instrument built by Aristide Cavaillé-Coll. This organ, which has fourteen stops, two manuals, and pedal, was built for the music room of baron Émile d'Erlanger, where it was inaugurated on February 1, 1866. It has been given to the city of Paris by baron Rodolphe d'Erlanger (1872–1932)

and his brothers, who, being settled in London, wanted leave this precious instrument in France in memory of their father. Mr. Widor, who had already participated, in the presence of Rossini, in the first trials of this organ during its [original] construction, will watch over its setting up in the choir of the church of the Sorbonne, where it is to be restored by the technicians and voicers of the Cavaillé-Coll/A. Convers firm.[403]

Because of Widor's lifelong friendship with Cavaillé-Coll, his daughter Cécile enlisted Widor to help her with the book she was writing about her father: *Aristide Cavaillé-Coll: Ses origines, sa vie, ses œuvres* (1929). For some reason she had second thoughts, which left Widor puzzled: "Mlle Cavaillé-Coll wrote an unreadable book and, having requested me to put her manuscript on its feet, I worked on it every evening for nearly two months. . . . Then, at the moment of having it printed, she didn't agree to it and prevented it by a *veto*. (The book that she published was elaborated thanks to outside assistance that I don't know)."[404]

One of the most important temporal accomplishments of Widor's career came as he completed sixty years as organist of Saint-Sulpice, on January 18, 1930. The members of the Institute, professors of the Paris Conservatory, and many other notabilities gathered together in the Caen Pavilion at the Institute for a grand celebration in his honor. After numerous tributes, the President of the Municipal Council of Paris concluded:

In the name of the City of Paris, as evidence of its recognition of this magnificent jewel that the Master [Widor] has added to his crown of light; the greatest distinction that it has at its disposal: its grand gold medal; and it asks him to receive it from [our] hands as a just homage rendered by some mortals to an Immortal.[405]

The following day at Saint-Sulpice, friends and admirers thronged the church, Cardinal Verdier came especially to preside at the service, and a long receiving line formed to greet Widor when he descended from the organ gallery. Perhaps Widor had lived to see his compositional style outmoded by present trends, but he also lived to see himself revered as the "grand old man of French music"—a veritable living legend.

—106—

Organ restoration at Notre-Dame:
"My dear Vierne, calm down!"

In May 1932, the Institute delegated Widor to be its official representative at the centennial commemoration of the founding of the Brussels Conservatory.[406]

It had been nearly seventy years since Widor had studied in Brussels under Lemmens and Fétis. Then, a month later, on June 10, Widor joined Vierne at Notre-Dame for the reinauguration of the newly refurbished organ that he had helped inaugurate sixty-four years earlier.

The restoration of the Notre-Dame instrument had been a long and arduous process. Since World War I, the instrument had been allowed to deteriorate to an alarming state. The Notre-Dame clergy, overwhelmed by the cost of the restoration, refused to open its coffers. Deciding to take matters into his own hands, Vierne undertook an American tour in 1927 to solicit financial aid from interested parties in the United States. He succeeded in gaining the support of the American Guild of Organists and the National Association of Organists. American organ builder Ernest Skinner agreed to furnish a modern console. With the funds in place, however, some unscrupulous tactics by a "third party" derailed the whole endeavor.[407] Vierne wrote, "They thought in America that I had tried over there to finance an operation that could have been done just as well by us."[408] The incident left him "so disheartened that [he] did nothing to pick up the broken pieces."[409]

In 1928, Widor wrote a booklet entitled *L'orgue moderne: La décadence dans la facture contemporaine* (*The Modern Organ: Decadence in Contemporary Building*). He had hoped to enlist the assistance of Albert Schweitzer, urging him, "If you can have a breathing space for an instant in your world travels, think about a notice on organ building, on the obligations to impose on the builders who at this moment are forgetting all traditions. In September, I hope you will be here— then we can compose the ordinance."[410] When September came around, the notice had already been written by Widor alone, Schweitzer being too occupied with other business.

Finding a little breathing space of his own, Widor joined Madame Widor and Lady Standish for a respite near Geneva. In a note from the Grand Hotel Divonne, Madame Widor informed Schweitzer that the notice was soon to be published and that her husband needed rest: "Charles-Marie finally came to join us in Divonne. It's a delightful place near Lake Geneva, where we are going to go for a boat ride on the water without tiring him, according to your recommendation."[411]

In the *L'orgue moderne*, Widor made a special point about the deplorable condition of the Notre-Dame Cathedral organ:

> In 1900, one could write: "If our French organ school is today so highly placed in the general esteem, it is to our instruments that it is owed." . . .
> We cannot coldly witness the decline of our art.
> Poor Cavaillé, poor great man, so scrupulous, so modest, so stricken with his duties, going out each Sunday to hear his instruments here and there, the experience gained from the old ones serving him for the future! What would he say of the current abandonment, of the lack of maintenance, of all cares, of the simplest probity with regard to his masterpieces!

The organ at Notre-Dame is sounding its death rattle. During the war, the rose windows were dismantled, and cold or hot, dry or humid, the temperature has freely been able to attack the bellows, the mechanism, indeed even the pipes of the façade.[412]

Vierne later described, in similar terms, the desperate state of the instrument:

Dust now reigned supreme in the organ. Mold had crept into many parts, numerous leaks occurred, and some of the pipes were giving way. . . . I fought continuously for eleven years to save the most beautiful gem of nineteenth-century organbuilding, the organ whose worldwide reputation I had succeeded in restoring, which had returned to the church some of its prestige, and which now attracted all foreigners who were in any way interested in the arts.[413]

Roused by the alarm that Widor sounded, the Beaux-Arts and Cathedral officials edged toward releasing funds for the renovation. An organ committee was formed and Widor was appointed chairman. Although he invited Vierne to be on the committee, the latter claimed never to have received the invitation and firmly believed there was a plot perpetrated by Charles Mutin to prevent his participation.[414] In February 1931 Widor informed the exasperated Vierne of the latest progress:

My dear Vierne,

Calm down! The B. Arts have asked my advice about the reports on the restoration of the organs of Notre-Dame and Versailles, about which I have informed you—when we have the necessary funding—let's wait and hope.[415]

The sum of 270,000 francs was soon appropriated for the renovation, but almost none of Vierne's wishes for the organ were to be realized. To clear his name of all responsibility of what he called "the monstrous blunder that was about to be so brazenly perpetrated upon [the organ]," he protested in a report to the Beaux-Arts.[416] The director immediately had the work postponed just as it was about to begin on February 14.[417] Discussions that now included Vierne started anew, and the long-overdue work finally commenced in September.[418] Vierne described Widor's keen interest in the project:

During the period of rebuilding, Widor often came to the tribune. His criticisms and endorsements coincided with mine. He would improvise on the stops that were in place and it was extraordinary to see how the brain of that eighty-eight-year-old man was still fertile with musical ideas and ingenious progressions. When the subject of the inauguration ceremonies arose, I was in complete agreement with Canon Favier, administrator of Notre-Dame . . . that Widor should be invited to participate. He had inaugurated the original instrument in 1868 with Guilmant, Franck, (Saint-Saëns, Chauvet, Loret, Durand), and the incumbent (Eugène Sergent). He accepted and we made up a program intended to demonstrate, in a limited time, the principal resources of the rejuvenated and augmented organ. . . .

The majority of the readers of the *Bulletin des Amis de l'Orgue* who were present at that ceremony [June 10, 1932] must certainly remember it. I do not want to go into detail; however, those who were in the tribune were simply astounded watching Widor, coming to grips with an instrument he scarcely knew, play without the slightest slip the *Symphonie gothique*, perhaps his masterpiece, which harbors in every movement such snares as give young organists considerable trouble in performance.[419]

One can only wonder what Widor's thoughts must have been on that auspicious occasion; more than six decades had elapsed since he had participated in the inauguration—Vierne had not yet been born.

—107—

Recording at Saint-Sulpice:
"I'm closer to the grave than the organ"

Two months earlier, at the end of April 1932, Widor reluctantly consented to make his one famous recording at Saint-Sulpice. Forty-three years earlier, he had had direct contact with Thomas Alva Edison (1847–1931) and the phonograph. Edison had gone to France in August 1889 as an exhibitor at the Paris Exposition and to receive the red sash of Commander of the Legion of Honor. After the Eiffel Tower, Edison's phonograph was the most popular attraction of the Exposition.[420] Besieged with endless invitations to "dinners, dinners, dinners," Edison apparently accepted one from Widor, who briefly recalled the occasion, though inaccurately (Liszt had died three years earlier).

In 1889, I had invited Liszt, Mistral, Edison, and [Gustave] Lyon [1857–1936; director of the piano firm Pleyel] to lunch. After this meal, which had been very cordial, Edison proposed that we attend one of the first phonographic recording sessions. This took place at Pleyel's. The session must certainly be in the archives of the firm. I remember that despite the imperfections of this beginning, Mistral was enthused. What progress since then![421]

The vast potential of the phonograph and the Aeolian player organ impelled Widor to muse wistfully:

How interesting for us, if we could only consult a phonograph from the time of Molière or an Aeolian [organ], [the] contemporary of Bach! What uncertainties and errors [could be] avoided if the distant echo of the *Matthew Passion*, for example, directed by the composer, could reach us still! . . .

So, we must welcome gratefully every means, every instrument, that permits us to specify and to be explicit. Isn't it truly admirable to be able to record the interpretation of a musical work with absolute exactitude, and to expect that this record will remain an unalterable document, a sure testimony, rigorously and unalterably true, now and forever![422]

Widor made his first known recording for Pathé (X 8792) around 1929 when he conducted two selections from *La Korrigane*: "La Sabotière" and "Entrée d'Yvonette." At the end of the recording he spoke briefly: "L'œuvre qui vient d'être exécuté sous ma direction a été composée par moi sur le scénario de François Coppée. La création a eu lieu à l'Opéra en décembre 1890." (The work that was just performed under my direction was composed by me on the scenario of François Coppée. The production took place at the Opéra in December 1890 [it actually took place in 1880]).

When Piero Coppola (1888–1971), manager of His Master's Voice Gramophone Company, approached Widor with the idea of preserving the renowned art of the old master organist on disc, Widor drolly explained that Coppola was taking a big risk:

Look here, my friend, take into account that I no longer have my technique, and at my age I'm closer to the grave than the organ; but if this gives you a good time, I'm willing—we'll have a good time together.[423]

During the recording sessions Widor grumbled a bit to his niece that he was swamped "putting all my organ music back under my fingers and feet."[424] For three consecutive evenings, April 28 through 30, the church was closed to the faithful and turned over to the recording engineers.[425] Placement of the microphones created a considerable problem because of the long reverberation time. Nonetheless, the warmth of Widor's personality and his unflagging energy deeply impressed Coppola:

We commenced at 9 o'clock p.m. and, pitilessly, we made him work until midnight. I had some remorse about it; but I got over it when I saw him briskly descend the stairway and, going out on Saint-Sulpice Square, taking me by the arm, he said: "Let's go for a little stroll." In spite of the rain that was falling . . . we went around the square several times, while waiting for the car that came to meet him and drive him back to his residence. A dear and great friend! So simple, so good and understanding towards the young;

astonishing in life, enthusiasm, and geniality, making fun of all the Swedish exercises, violent sports, and some other modern inventions of hygiene. "In order to live well and long," he told me, "it is sufficient to work well, eat and drink well, and not to turn your head before a pretty face."[426]

Although failing technically, from Coppola's recording sessions Widor left the remarkable recordings of his famous Toccata from the Fifth Symphony, and the first two movements and part of the fourth movement of the *Symphonie gothique*.[427] To Coppola's extreme disappointment, there was not much demand for Widor's recordings:

> The disks of the prince of French organists sold ten times less (and I am [being generous]) than the discs of some star from the Casino de Paris or the Folies Bergères that I had been forced to put in our catalogue in order to cater to present tastes.[428]

When Coppola related his bafflement to Maurice Ravel, he consoled him, "My poor Coppola, you give yourself much trouble over this, but don't forget that the French don't like music!"[429]

Widor gave his final foreign concert on July 31, 1932, when he opened the Salzburg Festival. At the Salzburg Cathedral, he performed the *Symphonie gothique, Salvum fac populum tuum,* and *Suite latine*:

> The prince-archbishop . . . had expressed the desire to hear me interpret in person my *Symphonie gothique* before my death. I say "in person" rightly, since it is possible today, and I did not say "No" a little while ago to a recording at Saint-Sulpice to assure some posthumous hearings.
>
> [The prince-archbishop] welcomed me in Latin with these words: "*Pro me honor et gaudium*" (It's for me an honor and a joy). "*Pro me, Excellentia*" (For me, Excellency), I responded.[430]

Those who came in touch with Widor's legendary art glimpsed again and again the special aura of a great artist—one who can triumph even when circumstances are less than favorable. The audience would not suspect the sustained effort he had made in preparing the concert; the organ did not please him at all. The archenemy—electricity—being applied to the organ, Widor complained once again: "After having practiced four days at the organ that all the electric improvements have deprived—for one who is accustomed to classical mechanisms—of the simplest means, I would have been very inferior to my task without the truly fraternal aid of the choirmaster Joseph Messner"[431] (see fig. 26). The press hailed the concert:

It was a unique impression. The man of eighty-seven years [*sic*], this famous master, this composer known around the world, this artist of high culture, playing his own works on the organs of Mozart. . . . One felt there the spirit of a Very-Great, a contemporary not only of his own greatness but also someone who has lived in contact with Richard Wagner, Franz Liszt, Verdi. . . . And nevertheless, in spite of these proximities, Widor has remained, in that which he creates and created, essentially himself. How lyric the *Suite latine*, of which the Adagio evokes a brother of Bruckner, for Widor has also known him. But there was a general excitement, an outpouring of enthusiasm, to hear the illustrious master play his Toccata, fantastic, dazzling in movement . . . a unique musical case in his genre and of ingenious inspiration. This concert [was] unforgettable in the historic annals of the Salzburg Cathedral. . . . At the exit, an enthusiastic and dense crowd waited for *Maître* Widor to hail him with its admiring veneration.[432]

At the Concerts Pasdeloup in Paris, Widor made a brief appearance in November 1933 to conduct the orchestral Suite from *Les pêcheurs de Saint-Jean*. *Le Ménestrel* paid him charming homage:

The 26th of December, it will be exactly twenty-eight years since the Opéra-Comique [first] staged *Les pêcheurs de Saint-Jean*. . . . The composer was then sixty years old, almost sixty-one [*sic*]. Well, last Saturday, this composer went to the podium to conduct three fragments of his work. He did it with quite youthful fire and, long applauded, came back to bow to the public in the most gracious manner. Dear *Maître* Widor, you must have, without saying anything about it, found on Parnassus, in company with Euterpe [the Greek muse of music], the famous spring that prevents aging! And you have baptized your music with its water, for it doesn't have a wrinkle. It is straightforward and knows how to wear the most varied robes, those of strength, grace, and sorrow. Please find here the salutation, affectionate no less than respectful, from those whom you have known as children. —J. H. Moreno.[433]

—108—

"I was named to Saint-Sulpice *for one year.* That has lasted long enough"

Widor once asserted, "God has forgotten me. Do you know how Leo XIII answered Rampolla when the Cardinal told him he would live to be a hundred years old? 'Set no limits, my son, set no limits.' Perhaps it will be that way with me."[434] In December 1905, Stockholm's *Dagens Nyheter*, reporting on a performance of *Pêcheurs de Saint-Jean* in that city, stated, "the composer Charles-Marie Widor, organist of Saint-Sulpice, dead since 1887, was able to have his only lyrical drama, *Maître Ambros*, performed the year preceding his death." Quoting the report, *Le Ménestrel* added: "It's Widor who is going to be vexed upon learning that news."[435] Due to his iron health and youthful attitude, Widor seemed largely to have escaped the claims of old age. But during 1933, he began to feel his eighty-nine years. Though he continued to climb the long winding stairway to the organ gallery each Sunday, when Dupré was present Widor asked him to play the greater portion of the Mass[436] (see fig. 27). The summer of 1933, G. Huntington Byles paid weekly visits to the tribune of Saint-Sulpice; the admiring throngs that had once frequented that famous organ gallery had long since disappeared:

> I used to see him Sundays at the organ loft. I used to go up there. He'd be all alone sitting there at the great organ, and he always seemed very glad to have company. . . . I can imagine that in Widor's prime the organ loft used to be filled with people, just as it is today [1966] with Dupré.
> . . . [Widor] never [gave recitals] while I was there. He just played the vespers.
> . . . Of course, his playing at this time was all improvised—the sersets [*sic*] that come between the psalms, for instance, were all improvised, and when they got to a certain point in the service, after they got to the benediction, he never bothered with the Postlude, he just packed up and left. He'd just go in and play for the service itself.[437]

Byles judged Widor's improvisations characteristic of the style of the *Suite latine*.

In the fall of the year, Dupré left for his sixth American tour, and during his absence Widor realized that he could no longer sustain the rigors of playing the services. Dupré recalled, "I left him in excellent health, playing still with an exactitude and an astonishing purity in spite of his eighty-nine years, but came back some months later to find him very changed and tired."[438]

Lady Standish had died on October 12; that she was three and a half years younger than Widor certainly brought his mortality home to him.[439] She, Mathilde, and Charles-Marie had been living in the same household and taking vacations together to their favorite spots around Lake Geneva in Switzerland for more than thirteen years. Her death was a profound loss. Numerous photos taken during these sojourns show the trio looking very correct and exhibiting the characteristics of a family (see fig. 28). Some of the snapshots of Widor were used on their greeting cards (see figs. 29–31). Now, for the first time in their marriage, Charles-Marie and Mathilde were alone at 3 rue de Belloy.

After the Mass on December 31, 1933, Widor took Dupré back to the Institute with him. In a very calm manner, he confided:

You are going to replace me at Saint-Sulpice next Sunday; I want to see you succeed me at my post during my lifetime. In your absence, I've lost the strength
in my arms, hands, and legs. Consequently, I've lost my technique.[440]

Quite shaken, Dupré tried to dissuade him: "But maître[,] why? I am here to
help you."[441] Widor remained resolute that his time to step down had come;
and he drafted his letter of resignation on the spot.[442] He explained his decision to the press in these words:

> In January 1870, I was named to Saint-Sulpice *for one year.* That has lasted
> long enough: sixty-three years [actually only two weeks short of sixty-four
> years]! The last Sunday of 1933, I wrote to the curate that my lungs no longer
> permitted me to climb the sixty-seven steps and I asked him to please consent
> to annulling my duties. They have named me "honorary organist"—just as
> there are some honorary Canons. It's the first time that this title has been
> conferred.[443]

Albert Schweitzer had seen it coming; as he wrote to Dupré in 1962: "When
our dear *Maître* Widor invited you to the service to play in his place and he
managed the expression box, I suspected that he no longer felt in top form
because his feet no longer obeyed him as easily as before."[444]

For Dupré to follow in his master's footsteps was perhaps the most momentous step of his career; his mind wandered back to 1906:

> While I was still a member of the organ class, Widor's assistant at Saint-Sul-
> pice died. I was summoned by Widor himself, who, to my great suprise [*sic*],
> asked me to be his assistant.
>   "But maître, I do not yet have my first prize in organ."
>   "I know that, but you will have it soon!"
>   Since he had to leave on a trip, he entrusted me with his instrument for
> two Sundays. He also asked me to play for a wedding the very next day at
> eleven o'clock.
>   "Be at the church a half-hour ahead of time so that I can give you the nec-
> essary instructions."
>   "What shall I play?"
>   "Improvise."
>   The next day he showed me the various characteristics of the organ. "I
> leave you now. You are going to have some fun!"
>   After he left, I looked down into the nave to be sure he had gone. Then I
> took my place at the organ, filled with an indescribable feeling. Just think of
> it, I was going to play this organ of a hundred stops. . . . That evening I saw
> Vierne, who said to me,
>   "This morning your prelude was in the key of B-flat, your recessional in E
> minor, and your postlude in B."

"How did you know that? You were there?"

"No, but 'he' reentered the church, heard everything; and said to me later, 'I shall take him,' and he even added, 'Are you sure he improvised? It seemed written.'"[445]

Dupré readily acknowledged what he owed Widor: "In 1906, at the age of twenty, I was already his assistant at Saint-Sulpice, and all the great events of my life are tied to his name."[446] Dupré entered Widor's composition class in 1907, and from the very beginning Widor found no fault with Dupré's work; his evaluations of his pupil rarely went beyond the word "*excellent*."[447] Since his appointment as Widor's assistant, Dupré had been a steady presence, and his succession was the natural outcome of years at Widor's side—years in which he had received exacting attention from his *maître*. In an unidentified news clipping, "Charles-Marie Widor," written shortly after Widor's death, author N. Darros recounted that he was present at the Salle Gaveau, Paris, when Widor was rehearsing his Symphony for Organ, with Dupré at the organ: "Although still quite young, the current organist of Saint-Sulpice [Dupré] was already an admirable artist. But the *maître* made him repeat certain musical phrase[s] several times, even tormenting him with some brusqueness until he succeeded in interpreting perfectly the thought of the author."[448]

American organist Arthur Poister (1898–1980) related a similar anecdote about Widor having to take a strong stand to assure that Dupré would adhere faithfully to his score. At a performance of the *Suite latine*, the composer made a last minute emendation that Dupré said he could not observe. During the performance Widor went to the organ, tapped his pencil on the score as the revision approached, and told Dupré, "get ready, here it comes!"[449] Jean Bouvard noted a happy collaboration between Widor and Dupré on Sunday, May 12, 1929: "During the offertory, Dupré played one of Widor's works for organ, trumpets and trombones, written in 1916 [*Salvum fac populum tuum*]. The composer, facing the organ, directed the composition himself. Dupré was attentive to the gestures of his aged master—it was touching. . . . During the communion, Widor improvised a very elegant and refined improvisation. It was good to see how respectfully Dupré listened to the improvisation of his master."[450]

Although no longer able to climb to the organ gallery by the steep narrow corkscrew stairs that some compared to "the stairway of paradise,"[451] Widor continued to attend the services whenever he could until the spring of 1935, listening below to the instrument that had given him a lifetime of joy—a lifetime in which "He seem[ed] to pour out a marvelous shower of light, from the organ loft down onto our heads!"[452] Dupré said he would see Widor seated in the nave, in his favorite listening spot near the pulpit;[453] "and in my turn, I try to pour on him a little light and harmony."[454]

Widor continued to practice daily on his own salon organ that had been installed in the Salle de Caen at the Institute. From there he continued to give "some remarkable organ performances during which he astonishes, as always, his numerous admirers."[455] Even then, he said he was discovering something new in organ playing and writing for the instrument.[456] At the age of ninety, from this indomitable exploring mind came his last musical testament: *Trois nouvelles pièces*, Op. 87. Each piece is individually titled: (1) Classique d'hier; (2) Mystique; (3) Classique d'aujourd'hui. Dedicated to three of his former American pupils—Albert Riemenschneider, Charlotte Lockwood, and Frederick Mayer—this final triad of pieces, undaunted by modern trends, shows a mind still fertile with ideas and artistic sensitivity.

—109—

The Farewell Concert at Saint-Sulpice:
"One of my greatest artistic joys"

In the spring of 1934, two farewell concerts marked the end of Widor's professional career: one at Saint-Sulpice on April 19, and another at the Salle Érard on May 9. To honor Widor for his long years of service, the Saint-Sulpice clergy authorized a special festival of his works. The orchestra of the Concert Society of the Conservatory was engaged and placed on a specially constructed dais under the tribune. Marcel Dupré played the *grand orgue* and Widor conducted his Third Symphony, Op. 69 (see fig. 32). He would later say of that concert, "One of my greatest artistic joys was to conduct my symphony at Saint-Sulpice, owing to the magnitude of the place and the assistance of the most beautiful of orchestras and organs."[457] A couple of weeks before the concert, Dupré wrote to an abbé at Saint-Sulpice concerning this symphony and the momentousness of the occasion: "Its performance under the vaults of Saint-Sulpice, of which the marvelous acoustic is universally renowned and admired, constitutes a major event in the history of religious music in France."[458] And in the same letter, Dupré referred to Widor's last organ pieces—from which he was to perform the "Mystique"—as "of an elevated inspiration, in some way the spiritualization of the *maître*'s style."

During the rehearsal with the orchestra, it became apparent that the performance was courting disaster on account of the long reverberation time of the church acoustic and the distance between the organ and orchestra. Widor insisted on conducting, but his strength was failing and he managed to finish the performance only with a desperate effort. Isidor Philipp described the performance as a "catastrophe." After the concert, Widor was led fainting to his car; that evening Philipp and Schweitzer visited him: "Widor seemed to suffer bitterly and said to us immediately: 'I feel that it is ended.'"[459] The reviews were charitable and failed to betray any of the difficulties that may have marred the concert:

Festival in honor of Mr. Ch.-M. Widor (April 19).

In this church of Saint-Sulpice, which was, during more than half a century, the center of one of the most brilliant manifestations of his prodigious and multiple artistic activity, the *Maître* Ch.-M. Widor has just been solemnly honored in the course of a festival devoted to his works, and which brought together a considerable throng.

It was absolutely not, as has been said, a "goodbye concert," for the *maître*, in spite of his ninety years, conserves—this performance has moreover proven it—a vitality that will without doubt allow him to play a role in the musical movement for a long time and to pursue, as perpetual secretary of the Institute, his benevolent activity. The festival was a touching homage to the long career of a musician whose name honors French art and towards whom a testimony of respectful and fervent admiration was shown.

Yet again, in one of those generous initiatives that are customary for him, the *maître* gave this festival for the benefit of the rebuilding of the organ of Saint-Louis-des-Invalides, thus emphasizing his attachment to the organ, the prestigious instrument that he has made, with incomparable brilliance, famous.[460] And this performance furnished the occasion to emphasize the significance that the name of Widor represents from the point of view of the evolution of "vertical" writing in organ music, especially when it is coupled with the orchestra.

The program, indeed, comprised the Third Symphony of the *maître*, directed by him with a precision and a stupefying energy, notably marked by the vigorous distinctness with which he stressed the attacks and accents. It was executed by the orchestra of the Concert Society of the Conservatory and Mr. Marcel Dupré. . . . As prelude and postlude, Mr. Dupré, moreover, performed the Variations from the Fifth Symphony and the Allegro from the Sixth Symphony of the *maître*.

He performed, as well, the *Miserere mei* (*Bach's Memento*, no. 4 [*sic*]) and premiered a *Pièce mystique* (Op. 87). It was an elegance from the *maître*, and one was wonderstruck at the fresh suavity of this composition.

Finally, a solemn Benediction service, under the direction of Mr. Ch. Pineau [1877–1958], choirmaster of Saint-Sulpice, brought together a certain number of the motets of the *maître*: *Ave verum* and *Ave Maria . . .* , *Tu es Petrus* [Op. 23] and *Tantum ergo* [Op. 18] . . . and *Da pacem*.[461]

This ceremony will leave an imperishable memory in the hearts of all those who were present. —Paul Bertrand.[462]

This final program closed Widor's career at Saint-Sulpice, which had begun with a recital nearly seventy-one years earlier. Widor lamented that he was not wealthy enough to give the parish two pedal stops that he had always wanted. In honor of his life's service, the parish presented the stops in Widor's name. The addition of the two pedal Principals (16' and 8') enlarged the great instrument to 102 stops.

At the Salle Érard concert a few weeks later, some songs, the Opp. 39 and 77 Piano Concertos, and the Op. 62 *Fantaisie*, were performed by the Orchestre du Châtelet under the baton of Widor's former pupil Paul Paray. At the conclusion of the concert, the crowd that had squeezed into the hall paid a last tribute to the renowned composer in a lengthy ovation.[463]

Until the Salle Érard concert Widor's health had held up fairly well. However, three days later, on May 12, the Widors checked into the Hôtel du Grand Condé in Chantilly, where they were to remain until November. Widor was ailing and badly in need of rest. Although his regular physician, Dr. Lereboulet (sometimes spelled Lereboullet), was in attendance, a flurry of letters to Albert Schweitzer from Madame Widor—either in her hand or typed, though usually signed by Widor himself and some obviously dictated by him—brought almost daily updates on his condition and also sought additional advice. In one card, Madame Widor asked Schweitzer to counsel her on a couple of medicines prescribed by Dr. Lereboulet because "[my husband] won't take one or the other until you have counseled him."[464] A sampling from the letters the Widors sent to Schweitzer clearly indicates the very tenuous condition of Widor's health that summer:[465]

—May 17: Implore supreme counsel—to the point of being sluggish, I remain on my back from morning to night. Is this good? Feet normal, forearm painful.

—May 23: Believing in you, I arrived in Chantilly May 12 after lunch. Following your orders, I put myself in a horizontal position, observed until yesterday, Tuesday 22, when we made a half-hour trip by auto to visit a house. How long must I keep this horizontal position?

An extraordinary phenomenon, a vision from beyond: on the evening of the emotional sensation of the Third Symphony, still holding the bow [*sic*, Madame Widor meant baton], I see the modern Apostle [Schweitzer] arrive, not dressed like Brahms, but with his hospital jacket, bringing me glass ampoules. I laugh without understanding well. And I understand even less today how I have been able to house a lake that flows without stop night and day [a condition of edema]!

Today my legs have dried, the swelling took refuge in the left forearm.

Seeking to recognize my ailment, and seeing my hand swollen and my fourth finger not bending, Lereboulet exclaimed: "But it's the ailment of pianists that you have there!"

So now, dear Friend, Grand Apostle, great benefactor, made of simplicity and grandeur, don't forget me, send me a few words.

—June 20: Beginning to be impatient. Rules implicitly followed; state of forearm almost the same; left hand half paralyzed; mouth persists in remaining bituminous; absence of appetite; horror of meat; soup and cream almost the only nourishment. Can we hope for change soon? I dare not . . .

—June 27: I realize that Ch. M. hasn't given you the news about his health, which continues, anyhow, to get better. His ankles are completely reduced in swelling now. *Deo gratias*!!

—July 2: Charles-Marie continues to do better, his ankles are all normal but swell a little toward the evening. His appetite is better. And now it will be necessary to defend him against this useless and noxious clique called "The Friends of Widor," which has already worked so much havoc.[466]

—August 23: What good news you give us, and how we both will be happy to have you here for 24 hours!

You will find Charles-Marie still better; I hope that he will make up his mind to go out, something he has refused to do until now. He is revising his *Symphonie antique*—between us, I foresee nothing good from these alterations—he works at it from 9 o'clock in the morning until dinner. It's true that his window is open, but that's not worth as much as the air outside.[467]

—August 28: Your presence, your counsel, and your concern not to let me pass away as long as my old carcass can draw breath, have allowed me to believe that, except for and in spite of a persistent swelling of my feet, I [can] still hope to go to Madrid next October 20.

—November 5: We are leaving Chantilly tomorrow morning;[468] one month ago the swelling of my legs absolutely disappeared, the ailment took refuge in my forearms, my right elbow generated a slight abrasion that is already healing and the left elbow is very probably going to follow its example, which bothers my writing.

I just finished my 20th Academic Notice that I'm going to read at the Public Meeting [at the Institute] on the 1st of December and that Bonnaire had the kindness to write under my dictation.

I was very surprised, given my condition when I arrived in Chantilly last May 12, that I would still have a 20th Notice to write—for my confrères elected me Perpetual Secretary in 1914 on the eve of the war.

In seeing me arrive, the people of Chantilly declared that I wouldn't see the 1st of June; they are astonished today, and I tell them that I have faithfully followed your prescription.

In a typewritten letter of November 17, 1934, hand-corrected by Widor, he summarized to Riemenschneider those long and frustrating months of recuperation:

Indeed, I had two concerts admirably performed: one at Saint-Sulpice with the Conservatory Orchestra (my Third Symphony for Organ and Orchestra); the other at the Salle Érard with the Châtelet Orchestra had for the program my three concertos for piano and orchestra, recalling three periods of my life—at a distance of ten years from each other [First Piano Concerto, Op. 39, 1876; *Fantaisie* for Piano and Orchestra, Op. 62, 1889; Second Piano Concerto, Op. 77, 1905].

Eight days after the Érard concert, I showed, it seems, the outward signs of the approaching end. The doctors, Albert Schweitzer among them, told me: "Don't stay in Paris another three weeks, even if you have work to finish; abandon all your work, leave for the country and right away, start by staying in bed for more than two months, having your feet more elevated than your head so the swelling of your legs doesn't rise to your heart." Thus, my wife took me to Chantilly, from where I have returned only these recent days.

Except for my arms, which are still half paralyzed, which restricts me from writing, and my legs, which have rendered me no service for six months and are weak, I can consider myself as relatively saved or rather profiting from the reprieve promised by the Doctors.

Marcel Dupré has succeeded me at Saint-Sulpice.

Naturally, I don't dare make any plans for the coming year, being at the end of a life that passes the average span, but believe me very grateful for the idea that I could see you again in Paris and hear you![469]

Back in Paris, Widor read his 20th Annual Notice at the Institute on December 1: "[I had] to take care of myself in order to have the strength to read it, which happened without too much fatigue."[470] Although commencing on the topic "Honorary Devotees of the Royal Academy; Free Members of the Academy of Fine Arts" (Amateurs honoraires de l'Académie royale; Membres libres de l'Académie des beaux-arts), Widor suddenly broke off his discourse: "I'm stopping here, regardless of interest, for it's not the past that I am concerned with today, but the last twenty years that we've just lived, *et quorum pars parva fui* [and of which I have been a small part]. I want first of all to address a deserved thanks to my confrères for the support they have lent me and for their comforting fellowship."[471] Widor somehow knew this would be the last time he would address his colleagues, and he needed to express his gratitude for the service with which he had been so graciously entrusted. He then retraced the history of what he considered his two greatest accomplishments for the Institute: the Casa Velásquez in Madrid and the Maison de l'Institut de France in London.

Still complaining to Schweitzer of various health problems, he wrote, "Dr. L. stakes his reputation on being triumphant; he comes two or three times a week. Let's not lose hope."[472] Faced with such serious health challenges, Widor had resigned the directorship of the American Conservatory at Fontainebleau before the 1934 season. One press notice simply read: "Mr. Maurice Ravel has just been named General Director in replacing Mr. Ch.-M. Widor who, for personal reasons, had given his resignation."[473]

With the exception of very limited work at the Institute and a few rare appearances, Widor retired from public life. Madame Widor worried about his health almost constantly: "Charles-Marie, in going out to the concert at the Institute on the first Saturday of the month, caught a chill of course; there resulted a cold that sent me into a panic, but happily it lasted only a few days; today it's almost over."[474] There was quite a commotion when he appeared on March 16, 1935, at a banquet at the Hotel Majestic to confer the decoration of "Officer of the Legion of Honor" on Marcel Dupré:

The great moment of the evening was the entrance of Charles Marie Widor at dessert. Everyone stood up and there was a tremendous ovation. He seemed to be much moved and walked up the huge hall to Dupré's place, read aloud the official announcement of the decoration, pinned the cross on Dupré's coat, and embraced him. After this Widor made a charming speech.[475]

Madame Dupré wrote to Widor's niece, "The dear *maître* was remarkably well that evening; he had an air so happy and so moved too!"[476] (see fig. 33).

A few days later, Charles-Marie and Mathilde set out for Brussels, where the Belgian Order of the Crown was to name him "grand-officier." Mathilde worried that her husband would be "induced to take some imprudent risks, which happens to him too often."[477] The Brussels Société Philharmonique under the direction of Joseph Jongen (1873–1953) presented a festival program of Widor's works at the Brussels Conservatory on March 27: Ouverture to *Pêcheurs de Saint-Jean*, *Sinfonia sacra* (Charles Hens, organist), "Le calme de la mer," "Marche" from *Pêcheurs*, three songs, and finally Widor himself conducted the Op. 69 Symphony for the final time.[478] For the occasion, the photographic studio of Malivez(?) made what was certainly the last professional photo of Widor. A few days after his return to Paris, an inscribed copy arrived: "To Maître Ch. M. Widor, in cordial remembrance of his visit to the union of the students and former students of the Royal Conservatory of Brussels. 2 April 1935. Jos. Jongen."[479] The trip was a resounding success and gave him the hope that he could make one more trip to Madrid the following month.

—110—

The Madrid Casa Velásquez:
"With order and will, what can't one do?"

One project that Widor had been shepherding since 1916—one very close to his heart—had yet to be brought to full fruition. To help build stronger relations with its southern neutral neighbor during World War I, the French government had asked Widor and three members from different academies of the Institute to make a trip to Spain as goodwill ambassadors.[480] Widor would end up taking the lead among his colleagues:

Towards the end of April 1916, Mr. Jules Cambon [1845–1935], former French ambassador to Berlin, then director of Foreign Affairs, asked some of us at the Institute to leave for Spain, to visit intellectuals of note, government officials, politicians, academicians and teachers, to inspect scientific and literary institutions, laboratories, historic research centers, and art schools. "What do they think of us down there? What is their opinion of the war . . . ?

Whatever the fierce propaganda made against us . . . is it still possible for them to believe in the decadence of our people, as the Germanophiles never cease proclaiming?"

Such was the mission entrusted to Imbart de la Tour (of the Académie des sciences morales et politiques), Bergson (of the Académie française), Edmond Perrier [1844–1921] (of the Académie des sciences), and to the perpetual secretary of the Académie des beaux-arts.[481]

I hesitated, considering myself little suited to fill this mission. But [Cambon] insisted, "I will send Imbart de la Tour to you tomorrow." I knew him only by name. [La Tour] said to me, "After the services rendered by Cambon at Berlin, can you say 'no' to him? We must go. . . . Are you familiar with Spain?" I told him that I was not, to my great regret. "Then," he said, "come with us, it would be unwarrantable to refuse!"[482]

Those of us who had never crossed what Louis XIV left us of the Pyrenees marveled at Burgos, its cathedral, its fortress gate, and its old manor houses. How could we know nothing of such beautiful things in such a state of preservation? How is it that our painters, sculptors, architects, and even musicians, don't come to admire them? This first impression only increased in roving through the country: Toledo, Salamanca, Avila, Grenada, Seville. . . . And it's this impression that I allowed myself to speak of at the Aténéo in Madrid.

. . . A vast hall where we came [to speak] was crammed with an audience of more than fifteen hundred to listen to Edmond Perrier, Imbart de la Tour, Bergson [and me].

Must I confess my very legitimate anxiety to have to speak after [them]? . . . I had to do it. I plunged into history, referring to the benefit of the old Spanish contrapuntists and speaking of their work, which is equal to that of the great Italians of the Renaissance. Then it was the moderns' turn, the young school of Albéniz, Granados, and de Falla. And to finish: "You have a most picturesque country, a blue sky without parallel; you have monuments, living testaments of three or four civilizations; palaces, incomparable cathedrals; you possess treasures, museums containing unique masterpieces: Velásquez, Titian, Goya. Well, we send our young painters, sculptors, and architects to Rome [the Villa Médicis] to study the classics, to inspire themselves with the greatness and nobility of the Raphaels and Michelangelos. . . . Why shouldn't France have a hostel here, a branch of the Villa Médicis, where our laureates would complete their studies, and which they would remember all their lives?[483]

Numerous young composers were in the company of the young painters, sculptors, and architects who sojourned at the Villa Médicis; the list of those who won the Prix de Rome reads like a *Who's Who* of French musicians.[484] Widor had long felt that music students were overly cloistered in their studies and that they needed broader sources of inspiration than their own discipline provided: "The education of a musician is made almost as much with the eyes as with the ears."[485] From this aspect, he became impassioned by the idea of yet another venue of study sponsored by the Institute.

By the cordiality and sincerity of Widor's lecture, "for this audience [he] was immediately a *maître* and a friend."[486] Newspapers reproduced the lectures delivered at the Aténéo, and a few days later, on May 8, King Alphonso XIII (1886–1941) accorded the French envoy an audience. Having learned of Widor's idea, he conceived a plan forthwith and presented it to him:

> "If your students come here," he said, "the example will without doubt be followed by [other countries]; . . . Spain will only gain from it. Not far from the palace, on the hill of Moncloa, a large piece of land overlooks the valley of the Manzanarez. . . . This is the scenery that you will recognize in the background of the paintings of Velásquez, whose country house was quite nearby. Go see this piece of land; I am giving it to you . . . : you will be able to construct a beautiful villa with studios and annexes there on one of the most beautiful sites in the world."[487]

What had come as an idea only a few days earlier quickly became a possibility. One writer viewed it as "an eleventh 'Symphony' that he was going to add to [his] ten sumptuous monuments."[488] The enormous task of financing the project had to be undertaken, but Widor always believed, "With order and will, what can't one do?"[489]

Along with his generous gift of land, the Spanish King made a substantial request of Widor: "I would like you to put together an exhibition of fine contemporary French painting in Madrid." Widor was overwhelmed by the enormity of the tasks that lay ahead of him: "And there I was, returning to Paris some weeks later, charged with finding the money to construct a palace as well as [gathering] the best paintings for the exhibition of contemporary French art."[490] It would be more than a year before the King's wish would be fulfilled, but Widor knew the benefits such an exhibition could garner for his Casa Velásquez project:

> I didn't hesitate to go to the Minister of Foreign Affairs who was then Stéphen Pichon [1857–1933]. Immediately, Pichon asked a Beaux-Arts colleague to lend us the best canvases from the Luxembourg Museum, and he had the sum of 40,000 francs allocated to us. I went to the most famous collectors in Paris. This exhibition had to be worthy of France, and it was upon [the exhibition] that our success down there depended.[491]

In December 1917 Widor and la Tour returned to Madrid with the French minister of the interior and the director of the Beaux-Arts to determine the precise location of their future domain:[492] "At 10:00 in the morning, we were struck by a horrible glacial north wind on the plateau, and we were quick to admire the beautiful view and to appreciate its location."[493] Because wartime placed severe risks on travel, Widor wondered if the time was right to proceed with shipping to Madrid the valuable paintings he had procured for the exhibition:

> In order to be put into the hands of the forwarding agent, the canvases had been collected at the Institute, in the Caen pavilion; several of the most justly famous had been kindly loaned by some collector friends; that was a grave responsibility for me. Now, at this moment—the beginning of March [1918], Big Bertha [a long-range gun] and bombs raged; the shells whistled above my head (one even sent a splinter onto my work table); and then, all of a sudden, the 27th, our front line broke at Montdidier; there was panic in Paris; people feverishly wrapped up precious knick-knacks and family records. A confrère came to tell me, "Give back your holdings, clear out the Caen pavilion; free yourself; let's think about ourselves; can there be a question of Madrid!"
>
> After reflection, I said, "Since we escaped, brushing disaster in the onrush of 1914, and then we 'held' in 1915, 1916, and 1917, we ought to hold again in 1918; the *Salvum fac populum tuum* that I wrote for the great day of the *Te Deum* of Notre-Dame will certainly be performed there at the specified hour. Have faith, let's prepare our two-hundred paintings for the forwarding agent; nothing will be changed in the program."[494]
>
> For five days Big Bertha boomed. The Duke of Alba [1878–1953] was supposed to come to chat with me about the exhibition. I hurried to his house to tell him that it was dangerous to go out. It was Easter Day. From fear of endangering the crowd, the services of Saint-Sulpice had been reduced to the minimum. The evening service, very simple, lasted fifteen minutes. For its security, the clergy set up a dormitory in the vaulted room of the façade situated between the two towers, in which the organ of the Dauphin resided.[495]

In May 1918, about two hundred canvases were sent to Madrid for the "Exhibition of French Painters (from 1850 to 1918)." Widor traveled there again as part of a French delegation for the opening at the Palacio del Retiro on May 12, 1918. And, as he had foreseen, his *Salvum fac* resounded under the vaults of Notre-Dame on November 17.[496]

At the request of the Spanish King, an exhibition of Spanish paintings opened at the Petit-Palais in Paris a year later. Widor had become the cultural spokesman for the Franco-Spanish Committee, and he duly recognized the importance of the cultural exchanges between the two countries:

> Spain is with France on the top rung of contemporary painting. It is therefore natural that the artists of these two countries join hands and work in common to tighten the lines that must unite the two peoples. Moreover, it is on our part to pay a debt—a debt of gratitude. France will never know sufficiently all of the generous assistance that it has received from Spain and its King during the course of this long war.[497]

During a fourth trip to Madrid, on May 22, 1920—four years after the idea of the Casa Velásquez had been conceived, Widor and three colleagues from the Institute had the supreme joy of officially accepting the land on the Moncloa and attending the cornerstone-laying ceremony for the Casa:

> Under a tent: Queen Victoria, Queen Maria-Cristina, the Court, the ministers, the Bishop of Madrid, the intellectual and social elite of the capital. Deployment of the troops with music and flags. Three very brief speeches: by the Duke of Alba—president of the French-Spanish Rapprochement Committee; the perpetual secretary of the Academy of Fine Arts; and Mr. de Saint-Aulaire—French Ambassador. Then, the response from the King, and the blessing of the stone. After their Majesties, we were invited to sign the record of the ceremony on a parchment that is sealed within this stone.[498]

During the trip, Widor also conducted his *Symphonie antique* at the Madrid Opera.

Baron Edmond de Rothschild, Widor's close friend and confrère, had contributed 150,000 francs to initiate the construction of the Casa Velásquez. The entrepreneurial spirit of the Rothschilds deeply touched Widor: "I have never met friends more reliable, simple and true, than the Edmond de Rothschild couple. Having the power of money at their service, they considered that their fortune had to serve the general interest; from this, an inexhaustible generosity towards individuals and works."[499] In addition to the Rothschild's contribution, Widor had raised 750,000 francs on his own. Still, it was estimated that at least another two million francs would be needed to complete the villa, which was to include an interior patio, more than twenty guest rooms, a library, dining hall, director's apartment, and so forth.[500] In reality, the postwar financial instability would drive costs far beyond the original three million franc estimate to build the Casa.

—111—

Maison de l'Institut de France à Londres

While baron Rothschild had already contributed generously to the Casa Velásquez, he was more interested in founding a similar educational facility in London under the administration of the Institute—a Maison de l'Institut de France à Londres (Fondation Edmond de Rothschild). Rothschild felt impelled to strengthen intellectual ties between France and England by allowing deserving French scholars and artists to imbibe English culture by taking courses from its most distinguished professors, and by frequenting English museums, libraries, and laboratories.[501] When Widor went back to Rothschild for more money to support the Casa Velásquez, he was turned down:

When the King [of Spain] gave me the land in Madrid, I asked a hefty sum from Rothschild. He told me, "No! Whatever the interest for us in Spanish art, it is far from being worth that of the rapport existing between England and France. Without the English fleet, we were lost in 1914. . . . Therefore, we need to unite with Great Britain by all possible means and to establish an endless bond between the two groups of youths!"[502]

Widor readily agreed that another branch of the Institute would only strengthen its cultural outreach, and that London would provide an excellent intellectual and cultural milieu.[503] The students, however, were not to be limited to "youths." The school would be open to "scholars or artists, young or old, desirous of devoting themselves to the study of any genre."[504] They could stay a maximum of two years and a minimum of two months.[505] Widor set out on his new mission with enthusiasm:

From May 26 to 30, 1919, I went to London with Edmond de Rothschild in order to find a house that he desired to give to the Institute. Somebody had indicated a house to us, that of Thomas Morris [*sic*: More], that was supposed to be torn down to put a street through and to be transported stone by stone to the banks of the Thames. The house was very interesting, but it was impossible to transform it for our purposes; its name was Crosly [*sic*: Grosby] Hall.

Faced with the impossibility of finding what we wanted, I had the idea of asking a correspondent [of the Academy of Fine Arts], Sir [John William] Simpson [1858–1933], president of the Royal Society of Architects, an architect whom we just named. He came the next morning and said, "Don't waste your time and trouble, I will look for you; nothing is easier for me, for I am informed daily of all that is here to rent or to buy. Go back to Paris; I will advise you when I have found something."[506]

Rothschild and Widor found themselves returning to London in short order—on July 17, three days after the memorable Paris celebrations of Bastille Day, 1919. Similar festivities were to take place in London on July 19 and the trip to England unfolded like a series of stirring snapshots, all colorfully described by Widor:

The staff of General Debeney was on the train that carried us. In Boulogne, the boats and transports were filled with English troops packed onto the decks, returning to their country. *Rule Britannia* responded to *God Save the King*. We sailed surrounded by a number of ships, a real flotilla. At Dover, we had to wait for the disembarkation of the brigades coming from the Rhineland, some thousands of men who, barely on the pier, formed into columns and marked the time. In London, a French troop camped in Hyde Park. Foch was at Buckingham Palace.[507]

Sir Simpson had understood the needs of the Institute perfectly and discovered a spacious house with garden, central hall, library, dining room, and two upper floors having some twenty rooms; in short, it was the "house dreamed of."[508] Located in an area well known to Widor—behind Royal Albert Hall—it was separated from the Royal College of Music by a lovely garden:[509]

The next day, Sir Simpson came to take us to Queen's Gate to inspect the house that he intended for us. It surprised us by its condition and its furnishings, which were French. Corneille and Racine were represented in the library, as well as a certain number of engravings of our chalcography and some models or small-scale copies of statues of our French school. I was astonished and made inquiries from the owner, Madame Vivian, mother of Colonel Vivian—military attaché at the English Embassy [in Paris], faubourg St. Honoré—and she told me, "My husband was impassioned with art. He had worked ten years at Dalou's [a French sculptor]. During this time, the house was built and we inhabited it when we came back to London. My husband is dead, my son is in Paris, and I'm retiring to my Scottish properties where I was born, having had enough of the city."

The discussion on the price of the house between Edmond de Rothschild and her was quick. At noon, our confrère was the owner of 185 Queen's Gate.[510]

The next day, Widor was treated to the "unforgettable spectacle" of the victory parade of allied troops: "In the morning, I was awakened by the bugle calls of the French troops who were camping in Hyde Park. We watched the parade from the balcony of Lady Rothschild, the cousin of Edmond de Rothschild. And I still have the cheers of the people in my ears when the sailors from the battle of Jutland passed before them—the sailors under [British] admirals Beatty and Jellicoe."[511]

Considerable work was necessary to ready the London house, and its delayed inauguration took place inauspiciously, yet years ahead of its sister branch in Madrid:

On his last trip as president of the Republic, Raymond Poincaré asked if he could include the inauguration of the London house. Simpson put himself immediately to work to organize the house to suit the needs of its new purpose, including about twenty rooms, without counting the director's quarters and the reception hall, which took a considerable amount of time.

I told Poincaré that unfortunately the work was not finished and that it was still necessary to count on some months [of work].

This inauguration took place without any ceremony and in a fashion completely unexpected [nearly two] years later. Léon Bérard [1876–1960] was minister of public instruction. He went to London one day to inaugurate a French grammar school. The ceremony over, he was chatting with our ambassador, de Saint-Aulaire, when I asked him if he knew the Maison française in London. *Neither he, nor the ambassador knew of it!* So, I proposed to them to pay a visit to it. My old friend Émile d'Erlanger, president of the society for the tunnel under the English Channel, who lived in London, was there. I asked d'Erlanger to take us. The director of the house, Robert Cru, correspondent of the *Times*, was amazed when I introduced him to the minister and the ambassador. Bérard was filled with admiration: "What luck for French students to have such a house!" he said. We inspected it. There were already some boarders there. On the Érard piano in the central hall, I played *God Save the King* and the *Marseillaise*. Thus, on a foggy afternoon [February 26, 1921], the London house was inaugurated, in the absence of the donor, whom we didn't have time to notify.[512]

Widor had just cause to be proud of his far-reaching initiatives for the Institute; in its first six years, 233 students passed through the London house.[513]

People have often reproached the Academies for their alleged idleness, if not their inactivity; people reproach them for living far from reality, without regard for the necessities of the times or the changes in things.

Can they address this reproach to the Academy of Fine Arts? We had the Rome school since Colbert [1666]. Well, since 1916, we have added Madrid and London to it, and now our ambitious activity is already causing a stir from the other side of the Atlantic, from New York.

In this manner, we want to enclose in intellectual ties the allied and sympathetic neutral nations—intellectual ties more solid than those created by the chance of commercial interests or the vicissitudes of politics.[514]

Funds were always short of what was needed for the Casa Velásquez; construction had to be halted several times, and one delay followed another—all critical situations to which, Widor complained, "I owe long nights of insomnia."[515] The final blow came when architect Léon Chifflot died in the middle of the project. A new architect had to be engaged, but he wanted to make many changes costing yet more money. In 1922, during an evening party at the Dutch foreign ministry in Paris, Widor happened to dine with Raymond Poincaré, then French prime minister. The occasion was too tempting. Widor plucked up his courage and sketched the precarious situation of the Casa Velásquez, dramatically imploring financial assistance from him.

Aid, Mr. President, it is urgent that you grant us aid, official support! —Don't hope for anything, don't expect anything, the Chambers will do nothing. — But we are pledged, it's a question of honor, you are condemning me to suicide! —I've already seen Gounod die. —But Gounod didn't commit suicide!

—You have the Villa Médicis and, thanks to Rothschild, the House at Queen's Gate; what more do you want? —We have Rome and London, indeed, but we still need Madrid and New York for our intellectual expansion, which, from the Tiber to the Hudson and from Paris to Fez, works tirelessly for world peace. *Pax hominibus bonæ voluntatis*" [Peace to men of good will].[516]

Although Poincaré had not encouraged his solicitor, he did indeed study the matter and sent it on to the Chambers. By the end of 1923, the French government granted 3.5 million francs to support the Casa's construction.[517] Further vagaries in the financial markets continued to plague the project, however. In *Écho de Paris* (June 1926), Widor decried the international financial "game" that kept forcing costs up due to the increasingly poor exchange rate between France and Spain.[518]

A portion of the Casa was finally completed in late 1928, and Widor went to Madrid for the inauguration ceremony on November 20.[519] King Alfonso lauded Widor's persistence with the project, and expressed his sincere gratitude for the efforts that had so heightened the ties between the two neighboring countries.[520] Widor's mind reflected vividly on the past eleven years of unremitting toil that led to that day: "During his address to His Majesty, Pierre Paris, director of the Casa, recalled the vicissitudes of the construction; I relived that cold December morning in 1917 on the plateau of the Moncloa, then bare as a slope leading up to a fortress."[521] In 1929 the French government allotted fifteen million francs to complete the Casa.[522] Widor made trips to Madrid as further portions of the Casa were finished, first in 1932 and last in 1935 (see fig. 34).[523]

On the last trip, he arrived in Madrid the morning of May 15. Friends waiting to greet him at the railroad station assumed the *maître* would want to rest after his long train trip from Paris, but Widor had no intention of wasting a minute of his precious time in Madrid and asked to visit the Prado. The museum director, Sanchez Canton, took the party on a two-hour guided tour. Despite having spent a substantial part of 1934 struggling to recuperate in Chantilly and still in very frail health, Widor displayed remarkable stamina, sitting down for only a few minutes. Later that afternoon they went to the Casa Velásquez for the formal ceremony. The beauty of the monumental building was profoundly moving to the ninety-one-year-old perpetual secretary.[524] Shortly after returning to Paris, Widor proudly wrote to his niece, "The trip to Madrid was a success for me. . . . The Casa is truly an honor for us."[525] Reflecting on his years as perpetual secretary, he once mused, "What a strange adventure! I expected to administer an academy, keep the records of our meetings, and respond to correspondence as our charter prescribed, but could I have imagined that I was successively going to construct a chateau in Spain and a Maison de France in London?"[526]

—112—
"I am revising all of my works a little"

In the late spring of 1935, Widor's doctor again sent him to Chantilly for rest. While visiting Paris, Schweitzer went with Dupré to have dinner with Widor. Afterward, Dupré inquired of Dr. Schweitzer what he thought Widor's condition to be: "He is suffering . . . from a very slow blood poisoning; the tissues no longer have the capacity to reconstruct themselves. I think that he could live about two more years."[527] Schweitzer's prognosis turned out to be quite accurate. In spite of his failing health, Widor returned to Paris and continued to work, maintaining his energetic attitude toward life. Those who saw him were amazed: "What sprightliness of spirit and even body, upon my word, for such an age! And always this affability, this courteousness."[528]

During his last visit with Schweitzer in Strasbourg in July 1935, Widor exhibited the indomitable spirit that gave him such a zest for life. He visited the Church of Saint-Paul where Emil Rupp, one of his early biographers, was organist; the press noted that Widor "performed one of those admirable improvisations of which he has the secret."[529] He also visited the Cathedral of Notre-Dame in Strasbourg:

> Schweitzer went to his office . . . Widor having made an appointment at the cathedral with the Canon Mathias. I still hear Schweitzer saying to Widor: "Don't climb up to the organ, you have been there a hundred times, you know it, it would be pointless to fatigue yourself. Moreover, it's your doctor who forbids you to do it!" Widor was as a matter of fact ninety years old [*sic*], and even though he had remained astonishingly alert, Schweitzer thought rightly that he should avoid such an effort. Well, when we met for dinner together, Widor, triumphant, proclaimed: "You know, I climbed up to the organ. . . ." Schweitzer immediately blew up, and with vigor stated in no uncertain terms to him that it wasn't worth being so old to show oneself so foolish! Widor tried to defend himself: "But Mr. Mathias, who is fatter than I, also went up there!" Schweitzer shrugged his shoulders: "Mr. Mathias is at home, and does what he pleases. But you! . . ." This profound affection expressing itself with crude sincerity was infinitely touching.[530]

The filial relationship between Widor and Schweitzer had extended over more than four decades. During the war, when he learned that Schweitzer was being detained at Saint-Rémy as an enemy alien, Widor anxiously wrote, "Give me some news of yourself very quickly and tell me what I can do for you."[531] He could also scold him, "What's becoming of you? I haven't heard anything more from you for centuries! That's bad."[532] And he could be tender, signing letters: "From the heart," "Your devoted," "Yours affectionately," or "Do I need to tell you of my long-standing and admiring affection?"[533] Widor happily assumed the role of godfather to Schweitzer's daughter, Rhena (1919–2009).

A visit to Mont Ste. Odile in August 1935 offered a refreshing retreat to the Widors.[534] By the end of the year, however, he was again flat on his back: "For three days now I get up only one hour for lunch—that's to tell you how infirm I am. My right arm is still immobilized, as is my foot—for three days it has been enclosed to the calf in a plaster. They tell me that recovery is certain, but how slow to come!"[535]

In April 1934, Widor had explained to an interviewer, "I am revising all of my works a little, I touch up, something like a stock-taking or a last will. Oh yes! I am old and suffering a little!"[536] In spite of the later stroke that left his right side paralyzed and forced him to write with his left hand, the process of "touching up" his works continued until his final days. Widor's personal bound volumes of his published scores, now in the Bibliothèque nationale de France, carry numerous corrections and revisions made over the years. Many bear witness to the attention he gave to this last "stock-taking," and his hand-writing often betrays his pitiful physical condition. Even after being confined to his bed, he continued to dictate changes to Dupré, Jean-Jacques Grunen-wald (1911–83)—Dupré's eventual successor at Saint-Sulpice, and pianist Mar-celle Herrenschmidt (1895–1974), who would then play them at the piano for him.[537] When Henri Potiron visited the bed-ridden composer in his last months, Widor proudly announced that he had found a compositional error in one of his orchestral works and corrected it: "Yes," Widor said, "it lacked a few measures to bring back the main theme."[538] He had admitted, "I would not be possessed by the demon of music . . . if in spite of my great age I was no longer busy with what has been my whole life.[539]

It seemed that the Casa Velásquez would have a bright future, but a cruel fate soon descended upon the fledgling institution. The Spanish Civil War broke out. The Casa, located on the front line, was bombarded during the bat-tle of Madrid and mostly destroyed on November 20, 1936, eight years to the day after its inauguration. Again, Widor's cherished Casa Velásquez brought him terrible anguish:

Even though [Widor] scarcely spoke of a preoccupation so distressing, [he] preserved the confidence of true idealists: "If the Casa is in ruin," he declared, "we will rebuild it." For in him lived an ever alive and active thought—a thought fortified by twenty years of struggles and finally recog-nized by success. For him, faithful to his generous enterprise, he considered that our young artists and litterateurs who sojourn to the Casa Velásquez, all coming in contact with the secular genius of Spain, would be of service to the peaceful brilliance of France.[540]

Widor was now almost ninety-three, in gravely ill health and no longer able to take up any cause, let alone that of rebuilding his dream. After the Casa's destruction, the artists and students moved to Fez, in Morocco, not returning to Madrid until 1940. A hotel on Serrano Street served as the school's home until the Casa was reconstructed on its original location in 1958. The Casa Velásquez reopened in 1959.[541] Widor's plan for an analogous educational facility in New York has never materialized.

—113—

"This was our last time together"

Although 1936 may have shown a glimmer or two of hope—"I am doing better and beginning to walk,"[542]—Widor's last letters to Schweitzer indicate that it was a miserable year for him:

> —August 6: Thanks for your letter, happy man who can work from morning to evening with the full use of his limbs!
>
> If my legs permit me some steps, in return my feet remain swollen in spite of my efforts to keep them at the height of my nose—the only remedy, they tell me. From time to time I interrupt this uncomfortable situation to do some five-finger exercises on a piano keyboard.
>
> Useless to tell you how much I envy your muscular freedom and grieve to not be able to write still.
>
> —August 24 [from Versailles, Hôtel Trianon]: What's happening here is ultra poor. . . .
>
> My elbow and my arm are not healed, and if I don't work harder to walk, it's because the bit of fatigue that results from it provokes the swelling of my feet.
>
> —December 30: I'm doing a little better and [Dr.] Lardenois assures my return to the Institute in the spring.

Despite everyone's best hopes and wishes, this was not to be. Spring would not bloom again for him. Though Widor suffered cruelly, his mind remained clear to the end and he seemed serenely prepared for death. Schweitzer related that at his last visit with Widor at the end of 1936, "Both of us knew that his days were numbered. His feet were already so swollen that he could no longer put on shoes but had to be in slippers. And we evoked once again the memories we had in common, and we realized the great attachment we felt for each other. And when I left him, he shook my hand and said in a low voice: 'This was our last time together.'"[543]

Dupré related his final visits with Widor and the remarkable coincidence of the date of Widor's death with the one hundredth anniversary of Guilmant's birth:

> Two months before his death, he still had me correcting the proofs of three orchestra pages from his *Symphonie antique* that he just revised.

One month after, in the course of one of my visits, with calm he told me: "If you can do it, come to see me a few moments every day. In three or four weeks, I won't be here any longer. I am quite conscious of the end. But I cannot complain, I have had a beautiful life."

He died March 12, 1937, at nine o'clock in the evening, while at the church of la Trinité the former pupils of the great organist Alexandre Guilmant . . . and myself gave a recital to commemorate the centenary of his birth. Guilmant was born, as a matter of fact, in Boulogne-sur-Mer, March 12, 1837.

These two great virtuosos, these two founders of the French organ school which made Bach known and loved in France, who both held the most fervent admiration for their master Lemmens, and who profoundly esteemed each other, are placed day for day within a century.[544]

As reported at the beginning of this biography, the date of Widor's birth was never clarified during his lifetime, and evidence exists that he was not certain of the correct date: February 21, 1844. Ninety-three years later, yet another document carries a false date of birth. Widor's death certificate was registered as number 528 at the Mairie du 16ème Arrondissement in Paris:

The twelfth of March, nineteen hundred thirty seven, at eight o'clock in the evening, is deceased in his residence, 3 rue de Belloy, Charles Marie Jean Albert WIDOR, born in Lyon (Rhône) the twenty-fourth of February, eighteen hundred forty five. Composer of music, Perpetual Secretary of the Academy of Fine Arts, Grand Officer of the Legion of Honor; son of Charles WIDOR and Fanny, deceased spouses; spouse of Mathilde Marie Anne Elisabeth de MONTESQUIOU FEZENSAC. Drawn up the fourteenth of March, nineteen hundred thirty seven, at eleven thirty in the morning, upon the declaration of Marcel SPITE, thirty-four years old, employed 3 rue Mesnil, who, having read, has signed with us Gaston ERNEST, deputy mayor of the sixteenth district of Paris, Chevalier of the Legion of Honor.[545]

Madame Widor, described as "one of the most gracious of ladies" by Wallace Goodrich,[546] must be credited for her total devotion to Charles-Marie—her "Love" [*mon Amour*];[547] in his last years and months, her solicitous tender care could only have helped extend his already long life. When Edmond Maurat visited Widor at the end of the summer of 1936, he met Madame Widor for the first time:

She entered and thanked her husband for having let her know [I was there]. Her welcome, warm and simple, made me at ease. . . . When I got up to go, she accompanied me to the ground floor. While slowly descending the two floors, she told me of all her love for her husband, all her admiration, her personal happiness, and her pride! She made allusion to their late union in such moving terms and with such passionate sincerity that I found myself in the street with a handkerchief in my hand.[548]

At her husband's death, on stationery with the familiar address "3, rue de Belloy," but now heavily bordered in black, she wrote a most touching and revealing letter to Schweitzer:

Dear Doctor and Friend,

The letter that I received from you is sweetness in my immense grief and I thank you for your compassion in these, the most painful, days of my life!

You have known me in my happy days, you have seen me between my two Loves,[549] no one better than you can understand the intensity of my pain.

The end of my beloved Charles-Marie was beautiful; he received the last Sacraments in full lucidity and with joy, and his resignation to the will of God is a memory that I will keep until my death.

I am sure that you will love to know that he reposes in the burial vaults of Saint-Sulpice and that he will remain definitively in this church that he so loved!

Toward the middle of February his work slowed, and Professor Lereboulet told me that the weather was very bad for the sick, but he hoped in any case, as did you, that his robust constitution would one more time allow him to recover his health. Alas! it was not that way. God didn't want it, he had to give in!

My life has become atrocious now that I have lost all that gave interest, charm, and radiance to it!

Three years ago, I lived only in the thought "Vita mutatur non tollitur" [Life is changed, not taken away], but now my pain is so sharp that I remain as one petrified. My poor head has been completely lost, and during the long nights that I spent without sleep, I thought how you would be afflicted in learning the sad news.

I see now that I should have telegraphed you, excuse me for not having done that, but I was persuaded that you would be notified by wireless.

Your grateful friendship, a thing so rare, was a joy to him, and we spoke often of you and of all the beautiful works that you did together.

The magnificent homage that was given him and that arrives from every-where is also a consolation to me; you add a eulogy to it that goes right to my heart!

Please believe, dear Doctor and friend, in my most grateful and affection-ate feelings.

Your, [signed] Montesquiou Widor[550]

With a few faithful and caring servants, Mathilde experienced the first soli-tude she had ever known at 3 rue de Belloy. Shortly after the first anniversary of

Widor's death, she wrote to Gabrielle Guibaud of the grief that would accompany her the rest of her life:

> Your broken heart foretold it; I have indeed been distressed by the sad anniversary, which was a simple and moving ceremony. The coffin of my dearly beloved Charles-Marie, beside which I loved so much to go to pray, has now disappeared forever from my eyes; this last adieu was heartbreaking, but it is a comfort to me, nevertheless, to know that he rests in Saint-Sulpice, where during a long life he gave the best of his heart and his talent! . . . I would like, after your example, to have a death image made; I found in the works of Charles-Marie three beautiful thoughts on art and the organ, but I don't see anything to describe his devotion to the Holy Virgin. . . . Perhaps you could help complete my project by searching in his letters to his mother or his sister for some phrases that could figure on an image?[551]

The second anniversary found Mathilde still grappling with her loss and, as soon as the spring weather permitted, wanting to visit Persanges, which she described as "so filled with Charles-Marie . . . and of which I hold a charming memory!"[552] Later in the summer she confessed, "I really ought to leave Paris, but you can imagine how difficult it is for me to resign myself to leave Saint-Sulpice, where my Beloved rests!"[553]

After her husband's death, Madame Widor suffered inconsolable grief, and it proved to be the beginning of a state of mental dissolution that left her vulnerable. Ennemond Trillat, director of the Lyon Conservatory (1941–63), related an incident that would seem to confirm a certain instability on her part; it purportedly occurred around 1945, after a "Widor competition" commemorating the centennial of Widor's birth had taken place:

> On the occasion of a little competition, the Pierron family [that of Widor's sister] lent us a bust of Charles-Marie by one of his confrères in the Academy and naturally 100 percent academic.[554]
>
> They undoubtedly forgot about it, and I found a place for it in my office on my grand piano. Well, a year went by. I was lingering at the end of a morning's work, enjoying the silence that prevailed over the Conservatory, our students and their professors having gone to lunch.
>
> There was a knock at my door; our concierge came to inform me that a woman was asking for me, "It's Madame Widor." I had totally forgotten her existence and believed her dead! We had written to her before the competition suggesting that she offer, if not a supplementary prize, at least a memento of the *maître* that we would have entrusted in his name to the holder of the Widor Prize. No response.
>
> I dashed into the atrium and found myself in front of a sort of tall pipe with two supplemental arms covered in astrakhan from head to foot. The pipe came to life and knelt at my feet; Madame Widor took my hand and

kissed it three times. The concierge had disappeared; we had no witness but the statue of the Slave of Michelangelo, which set my mind at rest.

Fearing the arrival of a student, I led her *prestissimo* into my office. The door barely opened, she discovered on my piano the bust of her husband. She rushed over, wrapped her arms around it and gave it a new triplet of kisses on the skull. I didn't know if I should call the emergency police or the Bron asylum.

"I have come to Lyon," she told me, "to draw the royalties of Charles-Marie."

I knew from Isidor Philipp that, in his will, Widor had left [the royalties] to his Lyon nephews. She had been rejected [by family members] in Paris and supposed, undoubtedly, that they would be more understanding in Lyon.[555]

"That's not all," she added. "I am staying at the Hotel des Beaux-Arts and ask you to send one of your young students to me so that I can transmit to him the sacred fire that I have in me."

With kindness and firmness I escorted her as rapidly as possible to the sidewalk of the rue de l'Angile.

The concierge waited for me in front of his lodge, a little annoyed: "I must tell you, Monsieur Director, that this woman borrowed five hundred francs from me to pay the taxi." These were unimportant francs and I do not regret it, for from high heaven Widor must have been smiling if, that is, a smile is authorized there.

Philipp let me know subsequently that she had squandered her fortune, mortgaged her mansion at the Place des États-Unis, and sold the furnishings that she possessed in Paris to benefit her lady companion, who undoubtedly must have left her to die at the Sisters of the Poor or in an asylum for the deranged.[556]

—114—

Le crime de Mathilde

Madame Widor lived twenty-three years after the death of her husband, mostly in seclusion. Many unfortunate events in her life during that period can only be described as bizarre, and they have given rise to a host of stories—some invented, some speculative, some apparently true. It is difficult to determine the whole truth, however, especially in light of a sensational novel, *Le crime de Mathilde*, by her famous author cousin, Guy des Cars (1911–93). The author of some sixty-six novels, Guy des Cars's first novel, *L'officier sans nom*, was an immediate success and was followed by a "series of works that all present the profoundly human study of a psychological or pathological case."[557]

Le crime de Mathilde, published in 1983, found its inspiration in the life of Mathilde Montesquiou Widor. The fact that she inherited the des Cars fortune through both her mother and her aunt, and then lost it to an unscrupulous mother superior, a cleric, and his paramour (her nurse), caused an outrage in the family. Through his novel, Guy des Cars spins a tale that exposes the crookery by rising from time to time above the clouds of fiction. In the forward to *Le crime de Mathilde*, des Cars alerts the reader:

> Because this book is a novel, I have been obligated to modify the family names and the names of certain places where the action took place. Not everything has been modified, however. . . . I also needed, in the interest of the story, to slip in some episodes, but as few as possible, so much has the raw material—that is to say the real events—appeared to me surprisingly rich in the retelling. The first name of the heroine, Mathilde, was also that of my cousin, and it's to her memory that I dedicate this story.[558]

The names are, in fact, so little disguised as to make one wonder why he bothered with the charade. In the book, Charles-Marie Widor becomes Jean-Marie Bardor; Mathilde Montesquiou-Fezensac becomes Mathilde Raviroux-Luzensac; Lady Standish becomes Lady Wandish, and so forth.

Early in the novel, des Cars makes an observation that may be just on the verge of the truth and that provides the point of departure for what seems to have been reality in Mathilde's later years:

> The real tragedy in the life of Mathilde was that never, from her infancy to her decease, was she able to use her own free will. She always had beside her—with the exception of some years when she was finally able to live alone with her husband—some implacable women whose overwhelming personality and even hidden cruelty ended in annihilating her will to the point of making her believe that she was only an incompetent person.[559]

Guy des Cars paints an unflattering picture of Lady Standish as one of the "implacable women": "[she] was a terribly authoritative woman: everyone had to yield before her and she was always persuaded that her words and her decisions were Gospel truths."[560] Although Lady Standish had an admittedly strong character, Mathilde adored her, and there is no evidence to suggest that Widor held her in anything but the warmest regard. They were a family, often traveling together, for more than thirteen years. It was only after the deaths of Lady Standish and Widor, and all alone for the first time in her life, that Mathilde became particularly susceptible to outside agents and, apparently, ultimate domination.

One version of the story assembled by Alain Hobbs alleges that in the depths of her sorrow Madame Widor sought solace in the church, as she had always maintained a sincere and profound faith. Having gone to visit a young distant cousin who was a nun in a convent in Normandy, she met the mother superior. Avariciously impressed by the sight of Mathilde's fancy automobile, chauffeur, maid, jewels, and so forth, the scheming mother superior worked her way into Mathilde's confidence. Leaving her convent for the luxurious life in Paris at 3 rue de Belloy, the mother superior began to take control of Mathilde's daily affairs. After a devotional excursion to Lourdes one day, they stopped at a village church where they met the curé [allegedly one Roger Labat-Bérot (d. 1964)] who, also dazzled by all the outward signs of Mathilde's wealth and as unscrupulous as the mother superior, wiled his way into Mathilde's life. He too soon left his church to live at 3 rue de Belloy. Now in cahoots, the mother superior and the curé began to isolate Mathilde from her friends and relatives. They mistreated and abused her and slowly gained control over her wealth and properties. Eventually the mother superior became very ill and needed nursing care. The curé engaged a nurse [allegedly one Juliette Jean-Petit Matile (b. 1904)] whom he knew from his village. There was a romantic entanglement between the two, and tired of waiting for the old mother superior to pass out of the picture, they relieved her sufferings with a fatal injection. Using money swindled from Mathilde, the curé purchased property in the tiny village of Madaillan, near Prayssas (Lot-et-Garonne), where, from 1958 on, he and the paramour nurse were able to keep Mathilde totally guarded and under their control: "Madame Widor appeared willing, indeed, to live somewhat sequestered. She came to Mass in the church of Doulougnac . . . but always supported by the abbé and her 'housekeeper-nurse.' No one was able to approach her and speak to her privately."[561] Mathilde passed away there, her fortune having been extorted by the two of them.[562]

Though less embellished, Hobbs's account follows some of the storyline related in Guy des Cars's fanciful novel. If entirely true, however, one would have to wonder that there had been no police investigation!

A second, more credible, version of the story by Marie-Thérèse Pelatan, Jean Pelatan, and Odette Tournier,[563] states that Mathilde arrived at the convent with her traveling companion, Aline Léger—a longtime employee in the Standish household—and that it was Mathilde's cousin who left the convent, not a mother superior. Little by little, her cousin—a "defrocked" nun—took control of Mathilde's affairs and pushed out Madame Léger. The cousin, considered "mean" by some, soon manifested an incurable cancer. Mathilde hired a nurse—one Madame Dervo—who came to live with them in order to care for her ailing cousin, who soon died, and before long Mathilde submitted to the strong-willed Madame Devro. On a devotional pilgrimage to Lourdes, Madame Devro introduced Mathilde to a priest friend "on leave"—one Labat-Bérot. During the 1950s, Devro and Labat-Bérot took control of Mathilde: "the two 'nurses,' under the pretext of protection, rapidly became guardians. There were no more visits with cousins Montesquiou or Bertier, and no more contacts with the Widor family"; those who saw Mathilde judged her "naïve, fragile, weak, and even deranged."[564] The two "guardians" fleeced Mathilde of her estate and purchased a property in Combelle (Lot-et-Garonne) where she remained more or less secluded until her death.

Regarding the first version of the story, authors M.-T. Pelatan, J. Pelatan, and O. Tournier state definitively:

> A novelist can invent the last years: mistreatment and a death accelerated by hypodermic injections. The reality is not so sinister. It is certain that some residents neighboring Combelle testified to Alain Hobbs that "Madame Widor seemed a bit secluded, that she came to mass in the church of Doulougnac, always supported by the priest and her housekeeper-nurse," and that no one could speak to her face to face. The parish priest of Madaillan considered such a "family," whose head was a "defrocked" priest, with suspicion. But bodily mistreatments, if they had taken place, would have been noticed by her doctor, who visited her every week and pointed out no physical violence.[565]

As a final point, the resolution of Mathilde's estate took an interesting turn. Her "guardians" had pressured her into signing everything over to Labat-Bérot, making him her sole legatee:

> Mathilde had always proven her attachment to her cousins Montesquiou and Bertier de Sauvigny. Deprived of all contact with her for many long years, they could not understand to what extent this seclusion had led to a will that transferred all the bank accounts, houses, properties, chateau, and all the family keepsakes to the priest Labat-Bérot. The natural heirs came together to contest the will that they thought did not reflect the wishes of Mathilde, who was so attached to kindred ties and to what a patrimony represents. . . . A lawsuit was filed. The Lourdes notary, counsel of the priest and the nurse, would be dismissed for malpractice. The family agreed to a compromise that allowed [the priest] to recoup a part of the inheritance from Mathilde. The priest Labat-Bérot continued for a few years in common-law marriage with the nurse on the Combelle property that he kept and that he left to her upon his unexpected decease in April 1964. She departed very soon and sold it along with the contents. Mathilde's piano is still in the house, a moving evocation of her love for music and her passion for her famous organist-musician, Charles-Marie Widor.[566]

A final letter to Albert Schweitzer, dated September 23, 1957, and not written in Madame Widor's hand, expresses regret not to have seen him for a very long time and hopes that a visit might be arranged.[567] Mathilde passed away on September 11, 1960, in Madaillan (Lot-et-Garonne).[568] After two exhumations, first from a cemetery near Combelle and second from the Montmartre cemetery in Paris, her body was finally interred in the family crypt in Charchigné.[569]

—115—

"'He came late to heaven.' We who loved him are thankful"

The year 1937 turned out to be a sad one for French music in general. Henri Libert, Louis Vierne, Gabriel Pierné, Albert Roussel, Maurice Ravel, and the composer who immortalized the French spirit in American music, George Gershwin, would also die that fateful year. Widor had no regrets, however; he left a legacy rich in accomplishment and deed. His fame had spread all over the European continent and beyond: organist and improviser par excellence, venerable teacher of organ and composition, celebrated composer, benevolent and farsighted administrator. He had commanded the respect of great men, musicians, litterateurs, artists, politicians, the socially elite, and royalty.[570] All had come to genuflect at the tribune of Saint-Sulpice:

> Indeed, it was necessary to see Widor before the five manuals, pedal clavier, and stops—arranged in hemicycles—of the great Saint-Sulpice organ. There, dominating some 20 meters above the nave that extended in front of the gigantic instrument, Widor was king. He reigned, and he had his court of musicians, the faithful, friends, and the inquisitive.[571]

Widor had helped to prepare the plans for his funeral. He may have envisioned that had he not specified everything to be conducted in the simplest way, his own famous Mass for double choir and two organs would have been performed—something he did not want.[572]

> The Mass was said by Canon Merré, choirmaster of Notre-Dame, and the absolution was given by His Eminence Cardinal Baudrillart, rector of the Institut Catholique. The bereavement was shown by Madame Ch.-M. Widor, widow of the deceased, Count de Bertier de Sauvigny, his uncle, Mr. Guibaud, his nephew. Following the wishes expressed by Ch.-M. Widor, no discourse was pronounced. After the ceremony, the body was placed in the burial vault of the church.[573]

He had thought of Saint-Sulpice as his home, and it was fitting that the funeral service and subsequent interment took place there on March 17 at eleven o'clock in the morning, where the body had been taken the day before. Dupré played Bach's Prelude and Fugue in E Minor[574] before the Requiem—sung in plainchant at Widor's request—then Widor's Andante Cantabile from the Fourth Symphony at the consecration, and from the *Symphonie gothique* during the procession to the crypt.[575] Cardinal Baudrillart of the Académie française conducted the ceremony. Numerous bishops and church dignitaries, including an emissary from the pope, were seated in the choir. With his usual humility, Widor had requested that the Institute of France not be represented officially, so its members attended only in a private capacity. Notabilities from the world of art, literature, and society, and the ministers of France and foreign ministers representing their respective countries filled the vast nave of the church.[576]

A great life had come to a close: born three years before the death of Mendelssohn, five years before that of Chopin, and twelve before that of Schumann, Widor lived to know all the renowned nineteenth-century French musicians, and countless others as well—many were his close friends; yet, alas, he had seen them all pass from his sight.[577] In 1934 Widor reflected, "When I dream about the third of a century just passed, I cannot say what sadness grips me in thinking about all the great people who have passed away in this period. . . . What sadness to survive all that! If there is one consolation, it's to think that others are going to continue our work and assure its future, for they will be responsible for it, bringing it to a young generation more and more eager to learn"[578] (see fig. 35).

Throughout his long life, Widor maintained a gentle humility, never vainglorious; perhaps he harbored a deep inner satisfaction that he had remained faithful to his highest ideals. He once wrote, "Since the beginning of the world, man must choose between good and bad, virtue and vice, art and vulgarity. Happy are those who have sought only light!"[579] From that sentiment, he could feel contentment at what others recognized in him: "An iron constitution, an invariably beautiful spirit, an extraordinary competence in all his labors, and a charming kindness won all hearts to him. . . . No man has rendered more service. He seemed a bountiful flame that illuminated and animated all around it."[580]

Isidor Philipp expressed dismay that Widor had not been even more celebrated at the end of his life: "I was able to realize, in reading his will, how much this great artist had suffered from insufficient recognition, without ever uttering a murmur of complaint."[581] And in the obituary Vierne submitted to L'Orgue, he protested, "The ostracism that banishes Widor's music from performances of all kinds, reducing it to the minimum, seems perfectly unjust to me."[582]

Eight years before his death, Widor eulogized his fellow confrère André Messager with words that are an equally fitting tribute to him:

Death does not at all carry away those who . . . have consecrated their life to the service of the Beautiful. They leave behind them the best of their thought. Even in the lightest parts of their work, in their sketches and improvisations where their imagination but scarcely plays, one still recognizes the reflections of Beauty: Elegance, Charm, and Grace.[583]

In his *Notice sur la vie et les œuvres de M. Charles-Marie Widor*, Adolphe Boschot, Widor's successor as perpetual secretary of the Academy of Fine Arts, concluded:

Let's not forget the example of a mind and will that neither age nor illness had been able to subdue. During the last months in which he paid his debt to suffering—and when the affection and devotion of his very loving wife surrounded him with an attentive tenderness—he preserved in his infallible memory the best recollections of a long life gone by. By his ever-generous narratives, he taught us to direct our attention not to the shadows, but rather toward the light side of things—not to the inevitable pettinesses of men or the disillusions that events sometimes carry, but rather toward the beautiful works and the good deeds that enrich our intellectual and moral heritage.

All of you, gentlemen, last March, attended his funeral with emotion. You noticed that this famous artist, rightly bestowed with every honor, had wanted that people forget all that, and that no speech was delivered rendering homage to him. In fact, when he had understood that death was soon going to free him from all that supports a human personality, that is to say all that is perishable, he listened only to the humbleness of Christianity: preparing his own funeral service, he turned down the display of all secular music; he asked only for plainsong for a Requiem in this church where his talent and his faith had for such a long time participated in the celebration of the divine office.

In spite of its dignified austerity, his funeral, as you have seen, brought together a large and meditative crowd. But it is also necessary to recall that the wake took place almost unseen. Towards the end of the afternoon, the coffin had been . . . placed in the crypt. In the evening, some relatives and friends gathered in the church. . . . They were alone, in a very small group, in the deserted nave that darkness made more vast. The towering pillars were scarcely visible, and the vaults became indistinct. The night that encompassed the church no longer let any distant noise penetrate inside; and the man who just fell asleep forever, withdrawing from our unrest, entered into the continuity of silence. But his friends were gathered at Saint-Sulpice still to draw near to him. Then the majestic voice of the organ, awakened by a disciple whom Widor cherished, repeated one of the most radiant meditations of the great Sebastian Bach. This sublime prayer, so familiar to the artist who just died, carried that last farewell to him, the farewell from a music that was the initiator of his youth and the love of his entire life.[584]

—116—

Poetic Epilogue

Charles Marie Widor: In Memoriam
by Minnie McIlrath

The white flame of a life rich in length of years
And accomplishment burned low . . . then disappeared
Leaving mankind richer in that he lived
And shall ever live in enduring fame.
Thrice blest are we who in such age have lived
And blest the generations that shall come
After to reap the fruit of his creations:
To sit beneath the master hand of one
Versed in the Art of interpreting the majesty
Of harmonies which flowed as by magic
From the unremitting font of his genius

In symphonies of strength and classic beauty
And dedicated to the instrument
He so loved. He wrought better than he knew.[585]

Strophes à la Mémoire du Maître Ch.-M. Widor
By Hector Reynaud
Ancien élève de Saint-Sulpice
Curé de Saint-Jean de Valence.
March 19, 1937

Soixante ans tu régnas sur des légions d'âmes,
Dominateur insigne, au royaume des sons,
Sous tes doigts s'élançaient en des gerbes de flammes,
Préludes envolés aux derniers horizons.

Nous écoutions ravis ces fugues gigantesques,
Ces strophes d'harmonie ouvrant leurs ailes d'or,
Elles nous entraînaient aux paradis-dantesques,
Notre guide céleste était Charles Widor;

Des hymnes s'essoraient au zénith, la prière
S'élevant vers les cieux à l'appel de ton art.
Ta symphonie ardente, enthousiaste et fière
Ressuscitait Haëndel, Sébastien Bach, Mozart.

Ton cœur se répandait en ces accents sublimes,
Nos esprits et nos fronts ployaient sous tes accords,
Mais soulevés soudain jusqu'aux plus hautes cimes
Ensemble, ils frémissaient d'harmonieux transports.

Maintenant que la mort, pour l'éternel silence
A fait taire ta voix et t'a fermé les yeux,
Ne restera-t-il rien de cette pure essence
Harmonisant ta lyre au Cantique des Cieux?

Ton corps gît au tombeau, mais ton âme immortelle
Évadée à jamais de sa prison de chair,
S'est unie à son Dieu dans un puissant coup d'aile
Et sa note d'amour émeut l'Infini clair.

Or ton œuvre demeure, ô lyrique, ô poète
Ton orgue aux voix sans nombre en retient les accents,
Les voici réveillés par ton sûr interprète,
Marcel Dupré, l'aède aux envols frémissants.

Quand, sous son doigt vainqueur vers la voûte sonore
Tes chants retentiront—harmonie et clarté—

Le peuple émerveillé croira t'entendre encore
Glorifiant le Christ en son éternité![586]

[*Verses in Memory of Maître Ch.-M. Widor*
By Hector Reynaud
Former student at Saint-Sulpice
Curé of Saint-Jean de Valence.
March 19, 1937

For sixty years you reigned o'er legions of souls,
Illustrious ruler in the kingdom of sound;
From your fingers sprang bursts of flame—
Preludes flown off to farthest horizons.

We listened enchanted to those gigantic fugues,
Those harmonious verses opening their wings of gold,
They swept us to Dantesque paradise,
Where our celestial guide was Charles Widor.

Hymns soared to the zenith, prayer
Rising to the heavens at the call of your art,
Your symphony, ardent, vibrant, and proud
Awakened Handel, Bach, and Mozart.

Your heart poured out in accents sublime,
Our spirits and our heads bowed 'neath your chords,
But suddenly rose to the highest peaks
Together, they trembled in harmonious joy.

Now that death, for eternal silence
Has stilled your voice and closed your eyes,
Will nothing remain of that pure essence
Tuning your lyre to the Heavenly Hymn?

Your body lies in the tomb, but your immortal soul,
Escaped forever from its prison of flesh,
Has flown to its God on a mighty wing
And its song of love moves the bright Evermore.

Yet your work lives on, oh lyric, oh poet,
Your organ of numberless voices reechoes its strains
Now wakened by your faithful interpreter,
Marcel Dupré, bard of shimmering flights.

When, to the sonorous vault his conquering hands
Raise your songs of harmony and light,
The wondering crowd will hear you once more
Glorifying the Christ in his Eternity.]

Appendix I

Published Literary Works

The following is a selected bibliography of Widor's published writings, including a sampling of the more than 225 critical reviews and articles in *Estafette* and *Piano Soleil*.

Widor, Charles-Marie. "A. Cavaillé-Coll." *Piano Soleil* (March 13, 1892): 1–2.
———. "L'Académie des beaux-arts." *Piano Soleil* (May 24, 1896): 1–2.
———. "L'accent tonique et la psalmodie." *Piano Soleil* (December 22, 1895): 1.
———. "Æolian." *Revue Éolienne* 1 (May 1899): 17–19.
———. *Amateurs honoraires de l'Académie royale; Membres libres de l'Académie des beaux-arts*. Paris: Firmin-Didot, 1934.
———. "Ambroise Thomas." *Piano Soleil* (March 1, 1896): 1–2.
———. "L'art du chef d'orchestre." *Piano Soleil* (October 22, 1893): 1–2.
———. "L'Association des artistes musiciens." *Piano Soleil* (April 12, 1896): 1–2.
———. "Association des concerts de l'école moderne." *Piano Soleil* (May 5, 1893): 1–2.
———. "Audition des œuvres de Liszt." *Estafette* (March 25, 1878): 2.
———. "Autour de Saint-Sulpice." *Piano Soleil* (October 25, 1891): 1–2.
———. "Avant-propos." *Symphonies pour orgue*. Paris: Hamelle, [1887].
———. "Avant-propos." *Symphonie romane*. Paris: Hamelle, 1900.
———. "La Casa Velásquez." Paris: Académie des Beaux-Arts, Bulletin No. 2 (July–December 1925): 3–10.
———. "Chant sacré." *Piano Soleil* (February 28, 1892): 1–2.
———. "Chez nos compositeurs." *Piano Soleil* (June 12, 1892): 1–2.
———. "La classe d'orgue du conservatoire." *Ménestrel* 83 (1921): 237–38.
———. "Les concerts du Châtelet." *Piano Soleil* (November 15, 1891): 1.
———. "Concerts du Trocadéro: Première séance d'orgue." *Estafette* (August 12, 1878): 2.
———. "Concours." *Piano Soleil* (August 12, 1894): 1–2.
———. "Concours du conservatoire." *Estafette* (July 30, 1877): 2.
———. "Le concours Rubinstein à Berlin." *Ménestrel* 61 (1895): 274–75.
———. "Conservatoire de musique." *Piano Soleil* (April 14, 1892): 1–2.
———. "Consultation sur la musique contemporaine." *Courrier Musicale* 26 (January 1 and 15, 1924): 10.
———. "Contemporains." *Piano Soleil* (January 10, 1892): 1–2.
———. "Discourse [No. 3]." In *Les cinq académies. Le quatrième centenaire du Collège de France (18 et 19 juin 1931)*, 27–30, discours de Bédier et al. Paris: Firmin-Didot, 1931. Reprinted in *Le quatrième centenaire du Collège de France*. Paris: Presses Universitaires de France, 1932.

————. "La distribution des prix au conservatoire." *Piano Soleil* (August 16, 1891): 2.

————. "L'école d'orgue en France." *Ménestrel* 65 (1899): 131–32.

————. "Les écoles d'art américaines de Fontainebleau." *Beaux-arts* (November 1931): 1–2.

————. "L'édition Vaticane." *Correspondant* (October 25, 1905): 237–45.

————. *Edmond de Rothschild*. Paris: Firmin-Didot, 1935.

————. *Fantaisie pour piano et orchestre, Op. 62: Notice analytique et thématique*. Paris: Durand, [1894].

————. "Felix Mendelssohn-Bartholdy." *Mendelssohn: Œuvres d'orgue*, edited by Charles-Marie Widor. Paris: Durand, 1918.

————. *Fondations, portraits, de Massenet à Paladilhe*. Paris: Durand, 1927.
Contents: Préface (Debussy, Rodin); Origine et fonctions de l'Académie des beaux-arts; La Casa Velásquez; La Maison de l'Institut à Londres; Nota bene [explains absence of Gabriel Fauré from this collection]; Massenet; Aimé Morot; Antonin Mercié; Carolus Duran; Georges Lafenestre; Jean-Louis Pascal; Jean-Paul Laurens; Camille Saint-Saëns; Léon Bonnat; Théodore Dubois; Les procès-verbaux de l'Académie royale d'architecture (1671–1793); Émile Paladilhe; Beethoven, architecte; Fontainebleau: Les Fondations franco-américaines (1927).

————. "Fortieth Anniversary Prophecies and Greetings." *Etude* 41 (1923): 661–62.

————. "The French Organ as Seen in Year 1932." Translated by M. Vigneras and W. Holtkamp. *Diapason* 33, no. 2 (1942): 18–19; no. 3 (1942): 12.

————. *Funérailles de M. Edmond Paulin*. Paris: Firmin-Didot, 1915.

————. *Funérailles de M. de Saint-Marceaux*. Paris: Firmin-Didot, 1915.

————. "G. Cavaillé-Coll et Kastner-Boursault." *Piano Soleil* (July 31, 1892): 1–2.

————. "M. Gabriel Fauré." *Comœdia Illustré* 1, no. 7 (1909): 202–3.

————. "Gounod." *Fortnightly Review* 54 (1893): 837–41.

————. "Gounod." *Piano Soleil* (November 19, 1893): 1–2.

————. "Un homme heureux [Charles Malherbe]." *Comœdia Illustré* 1, no. 17 (1909): 482.

————. "Inauguration de la salle des fêtes du palais du Trocadéro." *Estafette* (June 10, 1878): 1.

————. *Inauguration du monument élevé par l'Institut de France à la mémoire de Mme Jacquemart-André à Chaalis*. Paris: Firmin-Didot, 1926.

————. *Initiation musicale*. Paris: Hachette, 1923.

————. "Instrumentation de l'orgue d'autrefois." *Piano Soleil* (July 5 and 19, 1896): 1–2.

————. "Jean-Sébastien Bach." *Piano Soleil* (September 9, 1894): 1–2.

————, ed. *Jean-Sébastien Bach—Œuvres complètes pour orgue: Édition critique et pratique en huit volumes*. French prefaces by Ch.-M. Widor, vols. 1–4. New York: Schirmer, 1914–16.

————. "Johannis Brahms." *Estafette* (May 19, 1879): 1.

————. "Une lettre de M. Ch.-M. Widor à M. Gustave Lefèvre." *Maître de Chapelle* 2, no. 7 (1900): 4–6.

————. "*Lohengrin* à l'Opéra." *Piano Soleil* (September 27, 1891): 1–2.

————. "*Lohengrin* et *Faust*." *Piano Soleil* (October 11, 1891): 1–2.

———. "Madrid et Londres: La Villa Velásquez à Madrid; La Maison de l'Institut à Londres." *Ménestrel* 82 (1920): 349–50.

———. "La *Messe* en si mineur au conservatoire." *Piano Soleil* (January 27, 1895): 1–2.

———. "La musique." In Baillaud et al., *Un demi-siècle de civilisation française (1870–1915)*. Paris: Hachette, 1916.

———. "La musique dans l'antiquité." *Piano Soleil* (July 21, 1895): 1–2.

———. "Musique française." *Piano Soleil* (November 1, 1891): 1–2.

———. "La musique en France et à l'étranger." *Estafette* (July 9, 1877): 2.

———. "Musique et musiciens." *Piano Soleil* (November 24, 1895): 1–2.

———. "La musique grecque et les chants de l'église latine." *Revue des Deux Mondes* 131 (1895): 694–706.

———. "Notes sur Lemmens." *Méthode d'orgue: Lemmens-Widor.* Paris: Hamelle, 1924.

———. *Notice sur l'École des beaux-arts, Jean-Pierre Laurens.* Paris: Firmin-Didot, 1932.

———. *Notice sur la vie et les œuvres de M. André Messager.* Paris: Firmin-Didot, 1929.

———. *Notice sur la vie et les œuvres de Charles Girault.* Paris: Firmin-Didot, 1933.

———. *Notice sur la vie et les travaux d'Auguste Patey (la gravure, la monnaie, les médailles).* Paris: Firmin-Didot, 1930.

———. *Notice sur la vie et les travaux de M. Jean-Louis Forain.* Paris: Firmin-Didot, 1931.

———. *Notice sur la vie et les travaux de M. Moreau-Nélaton.* Paris: Firmin-Didot, 1927.

———. "Le nouveau conservatoire de Moscou." *Ménestrel* 67 (1901): 149–50.

———. "Nouveaux organistes." *Piano Soleil* (November 28, 1897): 1–2.

———. "Nouveau système d'éclairage de la scène." *Ménestrel* 72 (1906): 117.

———. "L'œuvre de Gevaert." *Revue des Deux Mondes* (September 15, 1908): 393–410.

———. "L'œuvre de Gounod." *Piano Soleil* (December 3, 1893): 1–2.

———. "À l'Opéra." *Piano Soleil* (July 2, 1893): 1.

———. *L'orgue de la chapelle du château de Versailles.* Paris: Imprimeries Renouard, 1933.

———. "L'orgue de la salle des fêtes au Trocadéro." *Estafette* (April 8, 1878): 1.

———. *De l'orgue de la Sorbonne au Théâtre de Bayreuth, et retour.* Paris: Académie des Beaux-Arts, Bulletin No. 9 (January-June 1929).

———. "L'orgue du Dauphin." *Piano Soleil* (April 4, 1897): 1.

———. "L'orgue et l'électricité." *Piano Soleil* (November 8, 1891): 1–2.

———. *L'orgue moderne: La décadence dans la facture contemporaine.* Paris: Durand, 1928; rev. ed. 1932.

———. "Les orgues de Saint-Sulpice." In Gaston Lemesle, *L'église Saint-Sulpice,* 124–40. Paris: Bloud & Gay, [1931].

———. "Phonographes et programmes." *Piano Soleil* (June 2, 1895): 1–2.

———. "Plans d'orchestres au théâtre." *Piano Soleil* (July 29, 1894): 1.

———. Preface to Jérôme Gross, *Accompagnement des cantiques du Manuel Paroissial.* Paris: P. Lethielleux, 1923.

———. Preface to Paul Ginisty, *Les artistes morts pour la patrie.* Paris: F. Alcan, 1916.

406   PUBLISHED LITERARY WORKS

————. Preface to Francis-Salomon Waël-Munk, *Causes de l'ébranlement de la tonalité produit par l'altération descendante de la quinte dans les accords de septième et de neuvième placés sur la dominante des deux modes.* Paris: J. Vieu, 1920.

————. Preface to Charles Bouvet, *Les Couperin.* Paris: Delagrave, 1919.

————. Preface to Paul Pierre de Fleury, *Dictionnaire biographique des facteurs d'orgue nés ou ayant travaillé en France.* Paris: Office Général de la Musique, 1926.

————. Preface to Jean Huré, *L'esthétique de l'orgue.* Paris: M. Senart, 1923.

————. Preface to J.-A.-André Sarnette, *Étude d'esthétique musicale et d'éthique.* Paris: Au Ménestrel, Heugel, 1923.

————. Preface to L.-E. Gratia, *L'étude du piano.* Paris: Delagrave, 1914.

————. Preface to Auguste Lenoir and Jean de Nahuque, *Francis Planté, doyen des pianistes.* Hossegor, France: D. Chabas, 1931.

————. Preface to *Frédéric Chopin: Exposition de tableaux, gravures, manuscrits, souvenirs (1810–1849); Organisée par la Bibliothèque polonaise sous le patronage du Comité des fêtes du centenaire de l'arrivée en France de Chopin.* Paris: Bibliothèque Polonaise, 1932.

————. Preface to Georges Jacob, *Les grands organistes français de XVIIe et XVIIIe siècles.* Paris: Procure Générale, 1928.

————. Preface to René Brancour, *Histoire des instruments de musique.* Paris: Henri Laurens, 1921.

————. Preface to Albert Schweitzer, *J. S. Bach: Le musicien-poète.* Leipzig, Germany: Breitkopf, 1905. Also: Albert Schweitzer, *J. S. Bach.* Translated by Ernest Newman. 2 vols. New York: Macmillan, 1911.

————. Preface to Félia Litvinne, *Ma vie et mon art (souvenirs).* Paris: Plon, 1933.

————. Preface to Félix Raugel, *Les maîtres français de l'orgue aux XVIIe et XVIIIe siècles.* Paris: Schola Cantorum, 1927.

————. Preface to *Manufacture d'orgue d'église et de salon A. Cavaillé-Coll, Charles Mutin, successeur.* Paris: Aragno, n.d.

————. Preface to Eugène de Bricqueville, *Notes historiques et critiques sur l'orgue.* Paris: Fischbacher, 1899.

————. Preface to André Pirro, *L'orgue de Jean-Sébastien Bach.* Paris: Fischbacher, 1895. Also: *Johann Sebastian Bach: The Organist and His Works for the Organ.* Translated by W. Goodrich. New York: G. Schirmer, 1902. Preface only: "John Sebastian Bach and the Organ," translated by B. L. O'Donnell. In *Studies in Music,* edited by Robin Grey, 52–68. London: Simpkin, Marshall, Hamilton, Kent, 1901.

————. Preface to Alexandre Cellier and Henri Bachelin, *L'orgue: Ses éléments, son histoire, son esthétique.* Paris: Delagrave, 1933.

————. Preface to Félix Raugel, *Les orgues de l'Abbaye de Saint-Mihiel.* Paris: L'Écho Musical, 1919.

————. Preface to *Palace of Fontainebleau: French High School of Musical Studies.* Melun, France: Imprimerie Administrative, 1921.

————. "Le Prix de Rome." *Piano Soleil* (July 16, 1893): 1–2.

————. "Pro vero," *Petite Maîtrise* 243 (1933): 38.

————. "Profession de foi." *Piano Soleil* (June 16, 1895): 1–2.

————. "Réformes au conservatoire." *Piano Soleil* (May 29, 1892): 1–2.

————. "La réforme du conservatoire." *Piano Soleil* (September 10, 1893): 1–2.

———. "La réforme du Prix de Rome." *Piano Soleil* (March 29, 1896): 1.

———. "La révision du plain-chant." *Correspondant* (July 10, 1904): 55–66.

———. "M. Richard Wagner." *Estafette* (April 28, 1879): 2.

———. "Richard Wagner à Paris." *Piano Soleil* (August 23, 1891): 2.

———. "Saint-Ouen." *Piano Soleil* (May 19, 1895): 1–2.

———. "*Samson et Dalila*, de M. Saint-Saëns." *Estafette* (January 14, 1878): 2.

———. *Les sept premiers secrétaires perpétuels de l'Académie des beaux-arts (1803–1903)*. Paris: Firmin-Didot, 1914.

———. "À Solesmes." *Piano Soleil* (December 27, 1891): 1–2.

———. "Souvenirs autobiographiques," 1935–36. Family arch.; a photocopy is in the author's possession.

———. *The Symphonies for Organ*. Edited by John R. Near. Vols. 11–20. Recent Researches in the Music of the Nineteenth and Early Twentieth Centuries. Madison, WI: A-R Editions, 1991–97.

———. *Symphonie pour orgue et orchestre*, Opus 42bis. Edited by John R. Near. Vol. 33. Recent Researches in the Music of the Nineteenth and Early Twentieth Centuries. Madison, WI: A-R Editions, 2002.

———. *Technique de l'orchestre moderne faisant suite au traité d'instrumentation et d'orchestration de H. Berlioz*. 5th ed. Paris: H. Lemoine, 1925.

———. *The Technique of the Modern Orchestra*. Translated by E. Suddard. London: J. Williams, 1906.

———. "Thaïs." *Revue de Paris* 1 (1894): 217–24.

———. "Les Troyens." *Piano Soleil* (July 17, 1892): 1–2.

———. "Vieille musique." *Piano Soleil* (December 20, 1891): 1–2.

———. "Virtuoses célèbres." *Piano Soleil* (November 29, 1891): 1–2.

———. "Was ist mir Johann Sebastian Bach und was bedeutet er für unsere Zeit?" *Die Musik* 5, no. 1 (1905/1906): 19–22.

Appendix 2

List of Musical Works

It is unlikely that a definitive list of Widor's works can ever be established. He did not keep a complete or accurate record of his works and their dates of composition or revision; this is affirmed by a notation in his "Souvenirs auto-biographiques," p. 61: "Ask my publishers: Hamelle, Heugel, Durand, Schott, for the titles and dates of my different works." Few autograph manuscripts have been discovered, and published scores (sometimes having multiple arrangements) are not always easily located.

Known opus numbers are taken either directly from a score or from publishers' listings of Widor's works. Arrangements made by Widor or others during his lifetime are indicated, as known. Eight opus numbers are not filled and many works do not carry an opus number at all. An opus number may be found serving two works (indicated by a bracketed letter following the opus number), or a second opus number may serve a slightly revised work. The works designated by opus numbers are sometimes inexplicably out of chronological order. The dates given are the earliest discovered and are taken from the manuscript or score, calculated from publishers' plate numbers, or taken from press reports.

Since Widor continually revised his music, oftentimes decades after the original date of composition, the works listed may have appeared in more than one version; this is not consistently indicated on the covers or by the plate numbers and can only be determined by painstaking comparisons made between several, apparently same, editions of a work. Because surviving copies rarely exist in the same location, such comparisons are burdensome at best. The author undertook this comparative process for the organ symphonies and determined eight different levels of revision for Opuses 13 and 42 during Widor's lifetime, with further emendations for a future printing indicated on his personal scores—see *Charles-Marie Widor: The Symphonies for Organ*, 10 vols.; vol. 11, "Preface," contains a complete history of Opuses 13 and 42; vols. 19 and 20 have Opuses 70 and 73, respectively. Most of Widor's personal scores reside in the Bibliothèque nationale de France (Mus. Don 381–74) and carry many layers of corrections and emendations in his hand. Selected references to manuscripts in the Bibliothèque nationale are indicated as BN, and in the Bibliothèque de l'Opéra as BO.

As the sets of *mélodies* were eventually collected into four increasingly larger volumes, opus numbers were mixed, songs revised, new songs added, some titles altered, and so forth; this has been indicated as completely as possible for each collection. A similar situation exists with the collections of piano works. A number of miscellaneous works, exam pieces, exercises, unpublished manuscripts, transcriptions, and cadenzas are found at the end of this appendix; these are not exhaustive. Finally, a list of known works by François-Charles Widor is given.

Opus	Date	Title	Publisher/plate no.	Comments	Dedicatee
1	1867	Variations de concert sur un thème original, pour piano	Heugel: H.4653	Probably published in late 1866; the British Library copy is stamped "12 Jy [January] 67." Later revised as Op. 29. Pages intimes is advertised on the cover.	M. Alfred Jaëll
2	1867	Pages intimes, six pensées musicales pour piano 1. Nocturne 2. Valse 3. Rêverie 4. Sicilienne 5. Mazurka 6. Scherzettino	Heugel: H.4647 (1)–4652 (6)	Although titled the same, this work is completely different from Op. 48. The Nocturne was later issued by Hamelle: J.4950H.	1. unknown 2. unknown 3. M. G. Mathias 4. F. Planté 5. Mlles Lefébure-Wély 6. C. Saint-Saëns
3	1867	Six duos, pour piano et harmonium (orgue) 1. Canzona 2. Allegro cantabile 3. Nocturne 4. Allegro vivace 5. Sérénade 6. Variations	Renaud (1867); Régnier-Canaux (1868): R.C.2660–65	The autograph manuscript came up for sale in January 2009: Les Autographes, 45 rue de l'Abbé Grégoire, Paris, catalogue #127 "Orgue," item 261.	1. M. D. Pinto de Faria 2. M. Lefébure-Wély 3. Mme la V^{sse} de Balsemont 4. M. Amédée de Boissieu 5. Mme la Bar^{ne} de Gérando 6. M. Lemmens
3[a]	n.d.	Six duos, pour piano et harmonium 1. Humoresque 2. Allegro cantabile 3. Marche nuptiale 4. Nocturne 5. Sérénade 6. Variations	Schott's Söhne: 24863.1–6	Six duos 1. Former Canzona, revised 2. Revised 3. New, replaced former No. 4 4. Former No. 3, revised 5. Revised 6. Revised	

(continued)

Opus	Date	Title	Publisher/plate no.	Comments	Dedicatee
[3b]	1886–91	Quatre pièces en trio, pour piano, violon, et violoncelle 1. Humoresque 2. Cantabile 3. Nocturne 4. Sérénade Arrangements: 2. Cantabile, pour violon et piano (L. Vierne) 2bis. La même, pour violoncelle et piano (L. Vierne) 4. Sérénade, pour violon et piano (L. Vierne) 4bis. La même, pour violoncelle et piano (L. Vierne)	Schott's Söhne (1886–91?): 24805.(1–4); Pérégalli & Parvy (1893): P.P.4458–61; Heugel (1925, 1929): H. et Cie 28374, 24460, 22422, 22438. Pérégalli & Parvy (1897): P.P.4622–25	These are arrangements of Six duos, Nos. 1, 2, 4, 5.	
[3c]	1909	Quatre pièces, pour piano (I. Philipp)	Heugel	Transcription of Quatre pièces en trio	
4	1868	Airs de ballet, pour piano	Maho: J.811 M.; Hamelle: J.1938 H.; simplified version (1909) J.5553.H.	Three revisions are marked "nouvelle édition." There is an arrangement for piano 4-hands (F. Linden) J.5519 H. (1907).	Monsieur le Chevalier X. Van Elewyck
5	1868	Scherzo-Valse, pour piano	A. Magnus: A.M.C. 115; Durand, Schœnewerk (1877): D.S. et Cie 2338; Hamelle [authorized by Durand] (1903): J.5021.H.; Hamelle (before 1923)	Originally titled Scherzo-Caprice. There are three revisions.	Mlle Blanche Gaulot
6	1868	2 Suites italiennes, pour piano 1. La barque 2. Le cabriolet [later: Le corricolo]	A. Magnus: A.M.C. 117/118; Durand, Schœnewerk (1877): D.S. et Cie 2336/2337	In the edition of 1877, each piece is subtitled "Fantaisie Italienne" and the title 2 Suites italiennes was deleted;	

7	1868	Quintette (Quintetto) en *ré* mineur, pour piano, 2 violons, alto, et violoncelle 1. Allegro 2. Andante 3. Molto vivace 4. Allegro con moto	Maho: J.802 M.; Hamelle: J.802 H.	La barque was revised, and the title of Le cabriolet changed to Le corricolo. Le corricolo, La barque, and Scherzo-Valse are advertised on the cover of the Durand, Schoenewerk edition of Op. 5, D.S. 2338.	*Charles Gounod*
8	[1882–84]	O salutaris, pour une voix avec accompagnement d'orgue (ou piano) et violon (ou violoncelle) *ad lib.*	Hamelle: J.1966 H. (cover); J.5638 H. (music)	In Fétis's *Biographie universelle* (1880), Arthur Pougin gave the title "*l'Orientale*, scherzo, pour piano" as Op. 8, but this work is most likely the *Scherzo oriental* by François-Charles Widor. O salutaris first appeared as Op. 8 in a Hamelle listing of Widor's works. Also, O salutaris appeared in *L'Illustration*, supplément musical, 2671 (May 5, 1894), and *Piano Soleil* (January 17, 1897): 17–18. Four later manuscripts carry the same title: BN Ms 18172, dated March 24, 1901, is scored for SATB and organ; Ms 18173 is scored for voice and organ, and appears to predate the following: Mss 18170 and 18171 scored for one voice and organ, and dated November 5,	*M. Taskin*

(continued)

Opus	Date	Title	Publisher/plate no.	Comments	Dedicatee
9	1869	Caprice en *ut* mineur, pour piano	Maho: J.822 M.; Hamelle: J.2679.H.	1931, with the note, "Sung for the first time by Mme Delprat at St. Ferdinand des Ternes."	*M. Patÿn de Kloetinge*
10	1870	Sérénade en *si* bémol, pour piano, flûte, violon, violoncelle, et harmonium (orgue)	Maho: J.986 M.; Hamelle: J.1532 H.		*Mme Achille Picard-Marix*
		Arrangements:			
		—piano à 4 mains (Arthur Napoléon)	Hamelle: J.1531.H.		
		—2 pianos à 4 mains (H. Frêne)	Hamelle: J.3508 H.		
		—piano seul	Hamelle: J.2841.H.		
		—violon (ou flûte) et piano (Ch. Bordes)	Hamelle: J.2842 H.		
		—violoncelle et piano (J. Delsart)			
		—deux violons et piano			
		—flûte, violon, et piano			
	1896	—violon, violoncelle, et piano (Fr. Hermann, Widor)	Hamelle: J.4023.H.		
		—piano et harmonium			
		—orchestre (Widor)			
		—instruments à cordes avec piano	Hamelle: J.2183.H.		
11	1871	Trois valses, pour piano	Maho: J.987.1–3.M. Hamelle: J.1938.H.	No. 2 was revised for the second edition. Arrangements: all three for violon et piano (J. Danbé); No. 1 for violoncelle et piano (C. Casella).	
		1. en *ré* bémol			
		1bis. Édition de concert (Th. Ritter)			
		1ter. Édition simplifiée			
		2. en *sol* majeur (Valse Lændler)			
		3. en *la* bémol (Valse-caprice)			

12	1871	Impromptu en *ré* bémol, pour piano	Maho: J.990 M; Hamelle	A simplified arrangement is advertised.	*Mme La Baronne Le Pin*
13	1872	Symphonies, pour orgue, 1ère Série: 1. en *ut* mineur 2. en *ré* majeur 3. en *mi* mineur 4. en *fa* mineur	Maho: D.J.M.A.; then J.1214 M. (1–4)	II/2 was transcribed for harmonium, Hamelle: J.5986 H. (ca. 1910); IV/3 was transcribed for piano as "Cantabile," Hamelle: J.4527.H. (1900). When II/4 (Scherzo) and III/5 (Fugue) were deleted from early editions, they were reissued as Deux pièces pour grand orgue, Hamelle: J.5899–5900.H. (ca. 1910). A-R Editions: Recent Researches in the Music of the Nineteenth and Early Twentieth Centuries, vols. 11–14, ed. John R. Near.	*M. A. Cavaillé-Coll;* the dedication appeared only on the 1879 edition.
14	1872	Six mélodies, chant et piano 1. Nuit d'étoiles (Th. de Banville) 2. Adieu (Mme Desbordes-Valmore) 3. Chanson indienne (Méry) 4. À cette terre (V. Hugo) 5. Guitare 6. Le doux appel (Mme La Barre)	Maho: J.1090 (1–6) M.; Hamelle: J.1090(1)H.–J.1095(6)H.	Widor orchestrated Nuits d'étoiles in 1910 (rev. 1915): BN Ms 18155. Le doux appel is also arr. "pour voix de soprano (en *ré*) avec accompagnement de violon (ou violoncelle) et de piano," Hamelle: J.3050.H.; Widor orchestrated it in 1930: BN Ms 18148. An edition containing "Guitare" has not been found.	*Mme Marie Trélat*
14[a]		Huit mélodies, chant et piano 1. Nuit d'étoiles (Th. de Banville) 2. Adieu (Mme Desbordes-Valmore) 3. Chanson indienne (Méry) 4. À cette terre (V. Hugo)	Same Maho plate nos. as above, without taking the two additional songs into account.		

(continued)

Opus	Date	Title	Publisher/plate no.	Comments	Dedicatee
		5. Guitare			
		6. Le doux appel (Mme La Barre)			
		7. Avril (Lucien Paté)			
		8. Tristesse des choses (Sunt lacrimæ rerum)			
14[b]		Six mélodies, chant et piano	Hamelle: J.1090 (1)–1095 (6) H.		
		1. Nuit d'étoiles (Th. de Banville), pour contralto			
		1 bis. La même, pour soprano ou ténor			
		2. L'abeille (Elie Cabrol)			
		3. Chanson indienne (Méry)			
		4. Avril (Lucien Paté)			
		5. Enfant de Catane, Sérénade (N. G.) pour ténor, en *fa* dièse	Hamelle: J.1708.H.		
		5 bis. La même, pour soprano, en *fa*	Hamelle: J.1709.H.		
		5 ter. La même, pour mezzo-soprano, en *ré*	Hamelle: J.1710.H.		
		6. Sunt lacrymæ rerum (Mme Blanchecotte)			
		Trente mélodies; Quarante mélodies; Quarante-quatre mélodies	Hamelle: J.1585 H.		
		1. Nuit d'étoiles (Th. de Banville)			
		2. L'abeille (Elie Cabrol)			
		3. À cette terre (V. Hugo)			
		4. Avril (Lucien Paté)			
		5. Enfant de Catane, Sérénade (N.G.)			
		6. Sunt lacrymæ rerum (Mme Blanchecotte)			

No.	Year	Title	Publisher	Notes	Dedicatee
15	1872	Six morceaux de salon, pour piano Livre 1. Scherzando; Allegro cantabile; Andantino Livre 2. Allegretto; Moderato; Vivace	Maho: J.1096.1 M; J.1097.2 M	Livre 2, Moderato appeared separately as "Fileuse," Hamelle: J.5825 H. (1909); Vivace appeared separately as "Valse-Impromptu," and was also arr. for piano and violon (A. Bachmann), Hamelle: J.5639 H. (1909).	*Mme L. D'Eckmühl, Marquise de Blocqueville*
16	1872	Première symphonie en *fa*, pour orchestre 1. Allegro con moto 2. Andante 3. Scherzo 4. Finale	Durand, Schœnewerk: D.S. et Cie 1595	Widor wrote on his copy: 20 June–20 August 1872. Portions were performed by the Conservatory orchestra in November 1872. Widor also made a piano 4-hands arrangement, D.S. et Cie 1524 (1873).	*Répertoire de la Société des Concerts du Conservatoire*
17	1874	Prélude, andante, et final, pour piano	Maho: J.1131 M.		*M. É. Delaborde*
18		Deux motets, pour double-chœur avec accompagnement d'orgue 1. Tantum ergo (1re strophe: solo de baryton ou unisson par le séminaire; 2e strophe: chant par le séminaire accompagné par le chœur.) 2. Regina cœli	Hamelle: J.4503.H. Hamelle: J.2834.H.	"Tantum ergo" is also listed separately as for "chœur à 5 voix avec accompagnement d'orgue." "Regina cœli" is also arr. "en duo ou chœur à 2 voix [soprano et contralto] par l'auteur," Hamelle: J.4594. "Tu es Petrus" (Op. 23, no. 2) was listed later on the cover (by mistake?) as Op. 18, no. 3.	
19	1874	Trio en *si* bémol, pour piano, violon, et violoncelle 1. Allegro 2. Andante con moto quasi moderato	Maho: J.1180 M. (1st ed.) Hamelle: J.1180 H. (2nd ed.)	There are two versions.	*M. le Baron É. d'Erlanger*

(continued)

Opus	Date	Title	Publisher/plate no.	Comments	Dedicatee
		3. Scherzo 4. Presto			
20	1874	Scènes de bal, pour piano Livre 1: 1. Fanfare 2. Entrée de la reine 3. Prélude d'orchestre 4. Clair de lune Livre 2: 5. Chanson 6. Malesch? 7. Le bal 8. Souvenir	Maho: J.1181(1)M.; J.1182(2)M. Hamelle	Clair de lune was also arr. pour violon (ou violoncelle) avec accompagnement de piano (ou harpe) by Claude Fiévet (1917), Hamelle: J.6941 H. Chanson appeared in 1908 as "Chanson pour piano" (Hamelle).	Mme M. Molinos
21	1875	Trois pièces, pour violoncelle avec accompagnement de piano 1. Moderato (Romance) 2. Vivace (Allegro appassionato) 3. Andante (Cantabile)	Maho: J.1213 M; Hamelle: J.1213.H.	Paris, BO Res 232 is Widor's undated orchestration of the Appassionato. Res 233 is a copyist's undated manuscript with Widor's corrections of Trois pièces pour violoncelle et orchestre.	1. M. Delsart 2. M. Loÿs 3. M. J. Gallay
21[a]	1913	Suite en mi mineur, pour violoncelle et piano 1. Méditation 2. Appassionato 3. Canzonetta 4. Final	Heugel: H & Cie 25,741 (1–4)	Movements 1–3 are slight revisions of Trois pièces; mvt. 4 is new. Le guide du concert refers to this as a new work when performed in January 1913. The Suite also appeared in 1913 as "Orchestre (Suite complète)," H & Cie 25,739. An arrangement (first three movements only) for violon et piano appeared in 1900, Hamelle: J.4604 H., J.4605 H., J. 4606 H.	Joseph Hollman

22	1875	Six mélodies, pour chant avec accompagnement de piano 1. L'abeille (Elie Cabrol) 2. Sonnet d'Arvers (d'Arvers) [later titled: Mon âme a son secret] 3. L'aurore (V. Hugo) 4. Sois heureuse (V. Hugo) 5. Dans la plaine (F. Coppée) 6. Aubade (V. Hugo)	Durand, Schœnewerk W.P.3010 W.P.2914	Individual dedications vary from one edition to another and include: *Mme Vaudoyer, Mme la Comtesse de Bresson, Mme de Marval, M. L. Valdec, M. Théodore Robin*
22[a]	1876	Six mélodies, pour chant avec accompagnement de piano 1. Sois heureuse (V. Hugo) 2. L'aurore (V. Hugo) 3. Aubade (V. Hugo) 4. Mon âme a son secret (d'Arvers) 5. Dans la plaine blonde (F. Coppée) 6. Adieu (Mme Desbordes-Valmore)	Maho: J.1303 (1)–1308 (6) M.	
23		Trios motets 1. Psaume 83 "Quam dilecta tabernacula tua," pour 4 voix, 2 orgues, quatuor à cordes *ad lib.* 1bis. Le même, pour chœur à 2 voix, avec 1 orgue 2. Tu es Petrus, pour double-chœur et 2 orgues 3. Surrexit a mortuis (Sacerdos et Pontifex) [double texte] pour chœur à 4 voix mixtes et 2 orgues	Hamelle: J.5084 H. J.5084 H. J.5396.H.	Tu es Petrus was shown on the some covers of Op. 18 (by mistake?) as no. 3. Widor orchestrated Tu es Petrus in October 1923: BN Ms 18179; he also composed brass parts to be added to the original version about 1934, probably for the Farewell Concert at St. Sulpice: BN Ms 18180. *1. M. Lebas* *3. M. le Chanoine R. Moissenet*

(continued)

Opus	Date	Title	Publisher/plate no.	Comments	Dedicatee
24	1877	Ave Maria [I, en sol mineur], pour mezzo-soprano ou baryton avec accompagnement de piano, (d'orgue et de harpe)	Hamelle: J.1396 H.	Premiered at Orléans, 1877.	Mme Marie Bataille
25	1876	Trois chœurs, à quatre voix (soprano, contralto, ténor, basse), sans accompagnement 1. Barcarolle (Mme Desbordes-Valmore) 2. Au matin (L. Nigra) 3. Rêverie (Mme Blanchecotte)	Maho: J.1309 (1) M. Maho: J.1310 (2) M. Maho: J.1311 (3) M.	Another pressing has plates: W.P. 3198 W.P. [?] W.P. 3192	Mme Théodore Robin
26	1876	Six valses caractéristiques, pour piano 1. Introduction: Presto 2. Moderato quasi Romanza 3. Andantino 4. Allegro deciso 5. Largamente cantabile assai 6. Tempo giusto	Maho: J.1325 M.	No. 2 is also arranged for violon et piano, and appeared as Valse lente in Supplément Musical du Dimanche 8 (September 2, 1894): 73–74; No. 4 is also arranged for violoncelle et piano (C. Casella); No. 5 is also arranged for piano 4-hands, and violon et piano: J. 6287 H.	M. Le Comte d'Osmond
26[a]	1903	Six valses caractéristiques, pour piano 1. Rhapsodie-Valse 2. Valse romance 3. Valse rêverie 4. Valse slave 5. Valse élégante 6. Rhapsodie-Valse			
27				Op. 27 unassigned or unknown.	
28	1876	Trois mélodies, pour baryton (ou mezzo-soprano) et piano	Maho: J.1312–14 M.	Another pressing has plates: W.P. 3199–3201	Variously: M. Théodore Robin; Mme Théodore Robin; Mme

No.	Year	Title	Publisher	Notes	Dedicatee
		1. À toi (V. Hugo) 1bis. La même, pour ténor ou soprano 2. Invocation (V. Hugo) 3. Lamento (Mme Blanchecotte) [Sunt lacrymae rerum, Op. 14, no. 6]			*Marie Bataille*
29	[1892]	Variations sur un thème original, pour piano	Hamelle: J.3428.H.	This is a revision of Op. 1.	*Émile Bernard*
30	1876	Deux duos, pour soprano et contralto avec accompagnement de piano 1. J'étais seul près des flots (V. Hugo) 2. Je ne croyais pas au bonheur (M. W.)	Hamelle: J.1315.1316.H.		*Mlles Agnès et Isabelle Marshall*
31	1876	Douze feuillets d'album, pour piano Livre 1. Lilas; Papillons bleus; Chanson matinale; Drame; Nuit sereine; Valse lente Livre 2. Solitude; Bruits d'ailes; Pensée; Ciel gris; Marche américaine; Myosotis	Maho: J.1323–1-M.; J.1324–2-M.	"Papillons bleus" and "Ciel gris" were arranged for violin and piano (V. Balbreck) 1908, and for cello and piano (Delsart) 1908; "Chanson matinale" was arranged for cello and piano (C. Casella) 1908. "Marche américaine" was arranged for piano 4-hands (I. Philipp) 1897 and also by Widor and A. Hignard J.1324 2/11–2284.H.; also for organ (M. Dupré) 1939, Hamelle: J.7886 H.; also for two pianos 8-hands.	*Miss Leila Morse*
[31a]	1923	March américaine, pour orchestre	Hamelle: J.7210.H.		*Walter Damrosch*

(continued)

Opus	Date	Title	Publisher/plate no.	Comments	Dedicatee
32	1877	Trois mélodies italiennes, chant (soprano) avec accompagnement de piano 1. Lia è morta (Canto popolare) 2. Il tempo passato (Canzone toscana) 3. Il primo amore (Canzone napolitana) 3bis. La même, pour baryton ou contralto	Maho: J.1345(1)–47(3) M.	Op. 32 was soon combined with Op. 35 and titled Six mélodies italiennes, pour une voix avec accompagnement de piano, J. Hamelle: J. 2440(1)–2445(6) H.	Miss Reed
33	1877	Six valses, pour piano 1. Neuilly-Valse 2. Valse flamande 3. Valse tzigane 4. Valse chantante 5. Valse légère 6. Valse noble	Hamelle: J.4968.5021 H. J.4969.5021 H. J.5021 H. J.5021 H. J.5021 H. J.5021 H.	Op. 33 is also found in 2e Recueil de Valses, 1903. Valse légère also appeared in Piano Soleil (February 6, 1898): 41–43. Valse noble is a revision and expansion of Op. 31, no. 6.	M. le Docteur Paul Segond
34	1884	Suite, pour flûte et piano 1. Moderato 2. Scherzo 3. Romance 4. Final	Heugel: H. & Cie 18909	Widor arranged the Romance for Violin and Piano, Hamelle: J.2452.H. The Romance is also found in Conte d'avril.	Paul Taffanel
35	1878	Trois mélodies italiennes, pour mezzo-soprano avec accompagnement de piano 1. Dimmi perchè (Aleardo Aleardi) 2. Rude maèstro (Aleardo Aleardi) 3. La bianchina (Canzone Toscana)	Maho: J.1348(1)–1350(3) M.	Op. 35 was combined with Op. 32 and titled Six mélodies italiennes, pour une voix avec accompagnement de piano, J. Hamelle: J. 2440(1)–2445(6) H.	Mme la Princesse Caradja
36	1885	Messe, à deux chœurs avec accompagnement de deux orgues	Hamelle: J.2343 H.	Cette messe a été écrite pour la Chapelle de l'Eglise St.-Sulpice, à	

		1. Kyrie 2. Gloria 3. Sanctus 4. Benedictus 5. Agnus Dei Arrangements : —Trompettes et trombones (en location) —Instuments à cordes remplaçant le 2e orgue, ch. —La meme, pour un chœur et un orgue		Paris; c'est à dire pour un double chœur composé, l'un des deux cents voix, environ, du Grand-Séminaire, l'autre, des quarante exécutants de la Maîtrise. The Kyrie is shown in the Dépôt Légal in 1877. The arrangements were listed in one of Hamelle's "Musique Religieuse" catalogues; they have not been discovered.
37	1877	Six mélodies, pour mezzo-soprano avec accompagnement de piano: 1. Le soleil s'est couché (V. Hugo) 2. S'il est un charmant gazon (V. Hugo) 3. Soupir (Théophile Gautier) 4. Aimons toujours (V. Hugo) 5. Le chasseur songe dans les bois (V. Hugo) 6. Le bouquet (Elie Cabrol)	Maho: J.1356(1)–1361 (6) M.	In Quarante-quatre mélodies, No. 5 has a few new phrases of text by A. Dorchain and is titled L'enfant rêveur au fond des bois. No. 5 was also arranged for piano and titled Chanson du chasseur, Hamelle: J. 5609.H.	Mlle Mathilde de Kervéguen
38				Op. 38 is unassigned or unknown.
n.op.	1877	Concerto, pour violon et orchestre		BN Ms 18142, Ms 18143, Ms 18149 (the full score is dated September 20, 1894), Vma ms 598. The Concerto was premiered on November 18, 1877, at the Châtelet, Paris. Widor intended to revise it, but never did; it remains unpublished.

(continued)

Opus	Date	Title	Publisher/plate no.	Comments	Dedicatee
39	1876	[Première] Concerto, pour piano avec accompagnement d'orchestre 1. Allegro con fuoco 2. Andante religioso 3. Final	Hamelle: J.1377.M. (full score); J.1378.M (piano part)		*Louis Diémer*
40	1876	Deux duos, pour soprano et contralto avec accompagnement de piano 1. Nocturne (A. Dorchain) 2. Qu'un songe au ciel m'enlève (V. Hugo)	Hamelle: J.2082.2083 H.		*Mesdames Rosita Stern et Anita Kinen*
41	1876	Concerto, pour violoncelle et orchestre 1. Allegro 2. Andantino (Romance) 3. Final	Hamelle: J.1887/3172 H.	The autograph ms is located in the Boston Public Library. Premiered by Jules Delsart in 1877. Reviewed in *L'Art Musical* 15 (1876): 372. Réduction pour violoncelle et piano, Hamelle: J.1887 H.	*Mme la Comtesse de Beaumont-Castries*
42		Symphonies pour orgue, 2ème Série:	Hamelle:	Several arrangements from these symphonies appeared:	*M. Auguste Wolff*, the dedication appeared only on the 1879 edition.
	1879	5. en *fa* mineur	J.1459 H.	—V/2 served as the basis of an independent piano work, "Conte d'automne," Hamelle: J.5023 H. (1904).	
	1878	6. en *sol* mineur	J.1460 H.	—V/5: piano à 2 mains, J.4566.H. (1900); piano à 4 mains, J.5774.H. (1909); 2 pianos à 4 mains (I. Philipp), Hamelle and republished by Schirmer 40206 (1943); piano et violon (A. Bachmann), J.5113 H. (1904)	
	1887	7. en *la* mineur	J.2660 H.	—VI/3 and VIII/2: piano et violoncelle (J. Delsart), in his "Six	
	1887	8. en *si* mineur	J.2663 H.		

No.	Date	Title	Publication	Manuscript / Notes	Dedicatee
				transcriptions pour violoncelle et piano" of works by Widor, J.3010.1.H. and J.3011.2.H. —VIII/2: piano et violon "Romance pathétique" (V. Balbreck), J.3940.2.H.; piano et alto "Andante" (Van Waefelghem), J.3796.2.H. —6me Symphonie pour orgue, transcrite pour 2 pianos (H. Libert), J.5016 H.; the transcription does not include the second movement of the symphony. A-R Editions: Recent Researches in the Music of the Nineteenth and Early Twentieth Centuries, vols. 15–18, ed. John R. Near.	*M. Louis Diémer*
42[a] (42 [bis])	1882	Symphonie, pour orgue et orchestre 1. Allegro maestoso [from Sixth Symphony, mvt. 1] 2. Andante [from Second Symphony, mvt. 3] 3. Final [from Sixth Symphony, mvt. 5]	A-R Editions: Recent Researches in the Music of the Nineteenth and Early Twentieth Centuries, vol. 33, ed. John R. Near.	Numerous manuscript materials exist: BN Ms 18135; Vma ms 603–5. Eastman School of Music, accession no. 1560996. The Riemenschneider Bach Institute at Baldwin-Wallace College, R4011.	
43	[1877]	Six mélodies, pour une voix avec accompagnement de piano 1. Je ne veux pas autre chose (V. Hugo) 2. Le vase brisé (Sully-Prudhomme) 3. Contemplation (V. Hugo) [titled: Mon bras pressait in Trente mélodies] 4. Le plongeur (M. Vacquerie)	Hamelle: J.1416(1)–1421(6) H.	No. 5 was given a new musical setting in Quarante-quatre mélodies. Widor orchestrated Nos. 3, 4, and 6: No. 3, BN Ms 18146 (March 5, 1923); No. 4, BN Vma ms 591; No. 6, Ms 18150.	*Mme la Comtesse de Mercy-Argenteau*

(continued)

Opus	Date	Title	Publisher/plate no.	Comments	Dedicatee
		5. N'avez-vous point su les comprendre (Sautter de Beauregard) 6. Vieille chanson du jeune temps (V. Hugo)			
44	1878	Dans les bois, cinq pièces pour piano 1. Par monts et par vaux 2. Feuilles mortes 3. Chanson du ruisseau 4. Grillons et sauterelles 5. Au soir	Hamelle: J.1455 H.		*Mlle Olga de Lagrené*
n.op.	1878 (1900)	Le capitaine Loys, comédie héroïque en cinq actes et six tableaux d'Édouard Noël et Lucien d'Hève.		BN Ms 18130 (incomplete piano score). Mélodrame, transcription pour piano, *L'Illustration*, supplément musical, 2994 (July 14, 1900): 109–10. This two-page transcription is the only published piece that has surfaced from the score.	
n.op.	1879	Psaume 112 "Laudate, pueri Dominum," pour orchestre [3 cornets, 3 trombones, 2 harpes, cordes], chœur, orgue de chœur, grand orgue, et orchestre de tribune [3 cornets, 3 trombones]		BN Vma ms 582. Composed for the solemn inauguration of the *grand orgue* of St. François-Xavier, Paris. Premiered February 27, 1879, with 220 performers. Widor considered the work "improvised, poor" and never published it.	
45	1880	La Korrigane, ballet fantastique en deux actes de François Coppée et Louis Mérante	Heugel: H. 6880 (piano reduction)	BO A.636 includes the full manuscript dated October 23, 1880.	*M. Vaucorbeil, Directeur de l'Académie Nationale de Musique*
45[a]	1880	La Korrigane, Suite d'orchestre 1. Prélude alla marcia 2. Tempo di mazurka (la Sabotière)	H. 7043		

No.	Date	Title	Publisher	Notes	Dedicatee
		3. Adagio 4. Scherzando 5. Valse lente 6. Finale			
45[b]		La Korrigane, Suite pour piano 1. Danse d'Yvonnette 2. La lutte aux bâtons 3. La Sabotière, mazurka 4. Contredanse bretonne 5. Lutte des danseuses 6. La revanche d'Yvonnette 7. L'épreuve, valse lente	Heugel		
46	1889	Romance en *mi*, pour violon avec accompagnement de piano	Durand/Schœnewerk: D.S. 4075	BN Ms 1544, dated April 25, 1889. A revised edition appeared in 1912, D.&F. 8393. Orchestrated version by Widor: BN Vma ms 600.	M. A. *Lefort* (1889); *Bilewski* (1912)
47	1879	Six mélodies, pour une voix avec accompagnement de piano 1. La captive (V. Hugo) 2. J'ai dit aux bois (Lucien Paté) 2bis. La même, pour ténor ou soprano 3. Les étoiles (Lucien Paté) 4. Je pense à toi (Sautter de Beauregard) 5. Albaÿdé (V. Hugo) 6. Prière (Sautter de Beauregard)	Hamelle: J.1547(1)–1552(6).H.	Widor orchestrated J'ai dit aux bois: BN Mss 18161 (dated March 5, 1935), 18162, Vma. Ms 584.	Mlle *Alice Boissonnet*
48	[1891]	Pages intimes, six pièces pour piano 1. Romance 2. Agitato 3. Valse légère	Hamelle: J.3103.1–3108.6.H.	Although titled the same, this work is completely different from Op. 2. The Romance also appeared in *Piano Soleil* (November 20, 1898): 161–64.	

(continued)

Opus	Date	Title	Publisher/plate no.	Comments	Dedicatee
		4. Crépuscule 5. Novelette 6. Mazurka			
49	1881	Chant séculaire, pour soprano, chœur, et orchestre (après une poème de Albert Grimault) L'air de soprano [Peuple, ta voix] transposé en *sol, séparé*	Hamelle: J.1885.H. J.1886.H.		*Mme Henriette Fuchs*
50	1881	Sonate [en *do* mineur], pour piano et violon 1. Allegro con fuoco 2. Andante 3. Allegro-vivace—Moderato—Allegro vivace	Hamelle: J.1870 H.		*Son Altesse La Princesse Bassaraba de Brancovan*
51	1881	Suite polonaise, pour piano 1. Polonaise 2. Scherzando 3. Romanza 4. Volkslied 5. Appassionato	Hamelle: J.1877.1.H–J.1881.5.H.		*La Comtesse [Emmanuela] Potocka*
n.op.	1881	Deux scènes-mélodiques, 1. Hier et aujourd'hui (Baron Imbert de St. Amand) 2. Reviens! O pauvre fleur (Édouard Noël)	Heugel: H.5291.(1, 2) H.5315.(1, 2)	No. 1 appeared in *Figaro*, September 21, 1881.	1. *Victor Maurel* 2. *Talazac*
52	[1885]	Deux duos, chant (soprano et contralto) avec piano 1. L'hiver (V. Hugo) 2. Guitare (D. Marval)	Hamelle: J.2084 H. J.2085 H.		*Mmes S. Pérouse et H. Guichard*

52[a]	1908	Quatre duos, pour violon et violoncelle avec accompagnement de piano 1. En route! 2. Ciel d'orage 3. Le calme renaît 4. Promenade sentimentale	J.5727.1.H.–J.5730.4.H.		*Messrs Bilewski et Bazelaire*
52[b]	1908	Soirs d'alsace, quatre pièces en trio pour violon et violoncelle avec accompagnement de piano 1. En route! 2. Ciel d'orage 3. Le calme renaît 4. Promenade sentimentale	J.5727.1.H.–J.5730.4.H.	Revision of Quatre duos; although the copyright date still reads 1908, this revision is certainly later.	*Messrs Bilewski et Bazelaire*
53	1885	Six mélodies, pour une voix avec accompagnement de piano 1. Dis, le sais-tu, pourquoi (Mme de Pressensé) 2. Prière au printemps (Sully-Prudhomme) 3. Je respire où tu palpites (V. Hugo) 4. Quand vous me montrez une rose (F. Coppée) 5. Ne jamais la voir, ni l'entendre (Sully-Prudhomme) 6. Songes-tu parfois, bien-aimée (F. Coppée)	Hamelle: J.2087(1)–2092(6)H.	A different order is given in Cinquante-quatre mélodies.	*A[nita] Kinen*
54	1882	Deuxième symphonie en *la*, pour orchestre	Heugel: H. 8149 (1885)	Second edition, revised: Durand: D. & F. 4312 (1892). An arrangement	

(continued)

Opus	Date	Title	Publisher/plate no.	Comments	Dedicatee
		1. Allegro vivace 2. Adagio [Moderato in 2nd ed.] 3. Andante con moto 4. Scherzando-final [Vivace in 2nd ed.]		for piano 4-hands (A. Benfeld): D. & F. 4689 (1893), and another for two pianos, 4-hands.	
n.op.	[1882]	Ballade, pour une voix avec accompagnement de piano (*ut mineur* pour soprano ou ténor, *si-bémol mineur* pour mezzo-soprano ou baryton), poésie de Auguste Dorchain	Hamelle: J.1940 H.		*Mlle Ella Lemmens-Sherrington*
55				Op. 55 is unassigned or unknown.	
n.op.	1883	Vieilles chansons et rondes pour les petits enfants	E. Plon, Nourrit	33 songs with illustrations by Boutet de Monvel.	
n.op.	1885	Les Jacobites, marche et 3 airs		Incidental music to a drama by François Coppée; November 21, 1885.	
n.op.	1885	Marche gauloise, pour piano	No. 29 in *Album du Gaulois* (1885): 120–25		
56	1886	Maître Ambros, drame lyrique en 4 actes et 5 tableaux de François Coppée et Auguste Dorchain	Heugel: H. 6175 (piano vocal score)	Premiered May 6, 1886, at the Opéra-Comique. BN Vma ms 671 (1–2). Nine numbers from the opera were issued as "Morceaux détachés avec accompagnement de piano," Heugel: H. 6182 (1)–6194 (9); four of the numbers are given in two keys.	*Son Altesse la Princesse Bassaraba de Brancovan*
56[a]		**Suite d'orchestre:** 1. Ouverture 2. Intermezzo 3. Marine	Heugel: H.8296		

		4. Ronde de nuit (d'après Rembrandt) 5. Kermesse			
57	1887	Cavatine, pour violon et piano	Hamelle: J.2676 H.	The melody is based on the Eighth Organ Symphony, Adagio.	*Victor Balbreck*
58	1887	Suite en *si* mineur, pour piano 1. Moderato assai 2. Scherzo (Trio andante) 3. Recordare 4. Final	Hamelle: J.2767.1H.–J.2769.3H.	The third and fourth movements are printed under the same plate number.	*Mme W. Szarvady*
n.op.	1887–88	N.-D. d'Espérance (Loire), pour 4 voix avec accompagnement d'orgue ou harmonium	V. Durdilly & Cie	*Maîtres Contemporains: Recueil de litanies à la St. Vierge, écrites à 3 ou 4 voix par des maîtres français*, recueillies par E. Grivet. This collection also contains a Kyrie by Ch. Widor (père), N.-D. de la Platière (Lyon).	
59	1884	Ave Maria [II, en *mi* bémol] pour mezzo-soprano ou contralto avec accompagnement d'orgue et de harpe (piano)	Hamelle: J. 2753 H.	In Quarante-quatre mélodies, the title indicates "avec accompagnement d'orgue et de harpe"; the parts, however, indicate "chant" and "harpe," the accompaniment being made of arpeggiated sixteenth notes with a bass that sometimes extends below the keyboard range of the organ; there is no pedal part. In Cinquante-quatre mélodies, vol. 2, the parts also indicate "chant" and "harpe." This Ave Maria is also found in *Recueil de*	Variously: in Quarante-quatre mélodies, *Mme la Comtesse de Mailly-Nesles*; in Cinquante-quatre mélodies, vol. 2, *Mme Jean de Reské*

(continued)

Opus	Date	Title	Publisher/plate no.	Comments	Dedicatee
				motets à une, deux, trios, quatre, et cinq voix avec accompagnement d'orgue ("Humblement dédiés à Notre Saint-Père le Pape," Toulouse: Musica Sacra, 1889). BN Ms 18164 is a chordal reduction for organ on two staves. Ms 18165 is a chordal reduction for organ on three staves, with registration. BN Ms 18166 is for voice and orchestra.	
60	1880 (1888)	Walpurgisnacht (Nuit de Sabbat), poème symphonique 1. Ouverture 2. Adagio 3. Bacchanale	Heugel: H. & Cᶦᵉ 23491 (1908)	Premiered February 8, 1880, at the Châtelet, Paris. BN Ms 1541, Ouverture is dated February 26, 1888.	*Société Philharmonique de Londres*
n.op.	1888	Gaillarde, pour piano		In *La danse* (Le gaulois à ses abonnés, 1888), 85–87.	
61	1889	Carnaval, douze pièces pour piano: 1. Timbales et trompettes 2. Flirt 3. Bal masqué 4. Rosita 5. Entrée turque 6. Zanetto 7. Viennoise 8. Entrée polonaise 9. Hongroise 10. Bohémienne	Hamelle: J.2953.1.H–J.2964.12.H.		*Mme Georges Durand (née Dubois)*

		11. Francesca 12. Final			
62	1889	Fantaisie, pour piano et orchestre	Durand: D.S.4135 (full score); D.S.4136 (orchestral reduction); D.S.4094 (piano solo)	Premiered February 23, 1889. BN Ms 1547: sketches, irregular pagination.	*I. Philipp*
63	1889	Soirs d'été, poésie de Paul Bourget 1. Quand j'aimais 2. Silence ineffable de l'heure 3. Brise du soir 4. L'âme des Lys 5. Près d'un étang 6. Le soir et la douleur 7. Cœur gai, cœur triste 8. Pourquoi ?	Durand: D.S.4142 (1–8); Hamelle: J.1585 H. (II)	Widor orchestrated Nos. 1 and 2: BN Ms 18149, dated November 23, 1931, and No. 8: Ms 18152, dated January 6, 1922, revised 1931 (?). Soirs d'été is also included in Cinquante-quatre mélodies, vol. 2.	*La Comtesse de Mailly Nesles*
64	1885,	Conte d'avril, comédie en quatre actes, vers de Auguste Dorchain	A. Lemerre (1885); Heugel: H. & Cᵢₑ 9141 (full score, 1892); H. 8690 (piano reduction, 1891)	Premiered September 22, 1885, at the Odéon. The score was revised and greatly expanded in 1890. Marche nuptiale originated in Six Duos, No. 3. Romance was taken from the third movement of Suite pour flûte et piano Op. 34. Schott's Söhne also published individual movements under plate 25163. Jules Delsart transcribed four movements for cello and piano: Andante, Sérénade illyrienne, Mélodrame, Guitare. (Heugel: H. & Cᵢₑ 9113 [Mélodrame] and 9114 [Guitare]).	
64[a]	1890	Première Suite d'orchestre: 1. Ouverture 2. Romance 3. Appassionato 4. Sérénade illyrienne 5. Marche nuptiale Deuxième Suite d'orchestre: 1. Presto scherzando 2. La rencontre des amants 3. Guitare 4. Aubade 5. Marche nuptiale			

(continued)

Opus	Date	Title	Publisher/plate no.	Comments	Dedicatee
		Pièces détachées:			
		1. La rencontre des amants, andante			
		1bis. La même, pour violoncelle et piano			
		2. Sérénade illyrienne			
		2bis. La même, à quatre mains	Hamelle: J.2459H.		
		3. Aubade	Heugel: H. & Cie 9125		
		3bis. La même, pour piano, violon, violoncelle et alto			
		4. Guitare			
		4bis. La même, à quatre mains			
		4ter. La même, pour violon et piano			
		5. Romance			
		5bis. La même, à quatre mains			
		5ter. La même, pour flûte et piano			
		5quater. La même, pour violon et piano			
		6. Marche nuptiale			
		6bis. La même, pour piano à quatre mains			
		6ter. La même, pour piano et orgue			
		6quater. La même, pour orgue seul	Heugel: H. & Cie 8960		
64[b]	1891	Suite concertante pour deux pianos, en deux livres:			Mlles G. Molinos et S. Perrot
		Premier livre	Heugel: H. & Cie 8834		
		1. Ouverture			
		2. Sérénade illyrienne			
		3. Adagio			
		4. Presto			
		Deuxieme livre	Heugel: H. & Cie 8840		
		5. Guitare			
		6. Appassionato			

Op.	Year	Title	Publisher	Notes
65				Op. 65 unassigned or unknown.
		7. Romance		
		8. Marche nuptiale		
n.op.	1890	Jeanne d'Arc, grand pantomime en quatre tableaux, poésie de Auguste Dorchain	The full score indicates: "This score has been printed to facilitate the rehearsals and performance of Jeanne d'Arc at the Hippodrome; it cannot be put up for sale." No publisher, place, date, or plate number is indicated. Hamelle: J.3171 H. (piano vocal score).	Premiered June 26, 1890, at the Paris Hippodrome. The arrangement of "Chant militaire" for two voices and piano indicates Orléans May 8, 1929; BN Ms 18160 has further corrections dated 1930; BN Ms 18181 is an arrangement made in 1909 by M. A. Soyer "pour musique militaire, chœur à 3 voix et harmonie."
	1911	Pavane Guerrière, extraite des Airs de Ballet	Hamelle: J.6358.H.	
	1929	Chant militaire, transcrit pour piano à 4 mains (I. Philipp)	Hamelle: J.3161 H.	
	1929	Chant militaire, pour deux voix et piano	J.3143 H.	
n.op.	1890	Non credo, pour chant et piano, poésie de Stéphan Bordèse	Durand & Schoenewerk: S.B.2–12	From Contes mystiques (poésie de S. Bordèse), which includes music by Augusta Holmès, Diet, Dubois, Fauré, Lecocq, Lenepveu, Maréchal, Massenet, Paladilhe, Saint-Saëns, Viardot, and Widor; premiered December 27, 1890 (January 11, 1891, Concerts Colonne). Stockholm, Stiftelsen Musikkulturens Främjande, MMS 1488, Nydahl Collection. Widor also orchestrated Non credo, BN Vma ms 588, 589, 590 (dated April 1932).

(continued)

Opus	Date	Title	Publisher/plate no.	Comments	Dedicatee
66	1891	Quatuor, pour piano, violon, alto et violoncelle 1. Allegro moderato 2. Adagio 3. Vivace 4. Allegro ma non troppo	Durand & Schœnewerk: D.S. 4364	Completed in November 1890 (*Monde Musical* 2, no. 37 (November 15, 1890): 6. Second edition, Durand & Fils: D. et F. 4364.	*Mme la Comtesse Emmanuela Potocka*
n.op.	1891	Air en style ancien [en *la* mineur], pour piano	*Supplément Musical du Soleil du Dimanche* 6 (December 20, 1891): 193–94.	Revised in 1912 and titled Pastorale Louis XV, Hamelle: J.5295 H.; *Le Gaulois du Dimanche* 169 (February 26, 1912).	
n.op.	1891, 1904	Credo, pour baryton, poésie de Édouard Noël	Heugel: H. & Cie 21,949		
n.op.	1892	Prélude [en *sol* mineur], pour piano	*Supplément Musical du Soleil du Dimanche* 6 (May 29, 1892): 171–72.	This Prélude was composed specifically for *Piano Soleil* and is described in its issue of May 29, 1892: 2.	
67				Op. 67 unassigned or unknown.	
n.op.	1893	Laetáre puérpera, Séquence pour le temps de Noël, chant avec accompagnement d'orgue	Baudoux Éditeur	In 2ème Livraison: Mélodies de chant gregorien tirées des anciens missels pour les Saluts du T.S. Sacrement, avec accompagnement d'orgue par: MM. Ch. Widor, Eug. Gigout, F.J. Brault, Gevaert, L. Vanhoutte, Stéph Morelot.	
n.op.	1894	Marche française [en *ré* majeur], pour piano	René Godfroy, Éditeur (Supplément au *Paris-Piano*, 72)		

68	1894	Quintette, pour piano, deux violons, alto, et violoncelle 1. Moderato—Allegro 2. Andante 3. Allegro con fuoco 4. Moderato	Schott's Söhne: 25731	Widor submitted corrections to Schott's Söhne for the second edition in January 1912.	M. le Comte G. Zichy
69	1893	Troisième symphonie, pour orgue et orchestre 1. Introduction [Adagio]—Allegro—Andante 2. Scherzo—Final	Schott's Söhne: 25801	BN Ms 1542, dated September 15, 1893. Widor gave the manuscript to his friend Malherbe, December 24, 1902.	à la memoire de Daniel Fitzgerald Barton, consul général d'Angleterre.
70	1894	Symphonie gothique, pour orgue 1. Moderato 2. Andante sostenuto 3. Allegro 4. Moderato—Allegro—Moderato—Andante—Allegro	Schott's Söhne: 25798;	A-R Editions: Recent Researches in the Music of the Nineteenth and Early Twentieth Centuries, vol. 19, ed. John R. Near.	Ad memoriam Sancti Andoëni Rothomagensis
n.op.	1894	Pâle étoile du soir, pour chant et piano, poésie de Alfred de Musset	Heugel: H & Cie 8095.(1)	This mélodie became one of Cinquante-quatre mélodies in 1906. 1. mezzo-soprano or baritone; 2. soprano or tenor.	Mme Anita Kinen
n.op.	1894	Noël, pour chant et piano	Supplément Musical du Soleil du Dimanche 8 (December 16, 1894): 193–95.		
n.op.	1913	Noël ancien, pour chant et piano	Heugel: H & Cie 8360	Noël was revised as Noël ancien in Le Gaulois du Dimanche 207 (December 6, 1913): 32–33.	
n.op.	1895	La nuit, pour chant et piano, poésie de Paul Bourget		1. mezzo-soprano or baritone; 2. soprano or tenor. Mentioned in a letter (July 1, 1895) to Théophile Gautier, editor of Figaro.	Mme Lambert de Rothschild

(continued)

Opus	Date	Title	Publisher/plate no.	Comments	Dedicatee
n.op.	1896	Pièce en style ancien, [en *sol* mineur] pour piano	*Figaro* (June 20, 1896): 6	This is different from "Air en style ancien" (1891).	
n.op.	1897	Ouverture espagnole, pour orchestre	Heugel: H. & Cie 18404	Originally planned to be the first movement in a five-movement Suite pittoresque (premiered 1893); [second mvt.: Mélancolie(?)]. A reduction for piano 4-hands (E. Alder) was published in 1898, Heugel: H. & Cie 19,163. Ch. Foaré made an arrangement for military band: BN Vma. Ms 602.	
71	1903	[Cinq pièces], pour piano 1. Valse gaie 2. Valse triste 3. Kermesse carillonante 4. Valse oubliée 5. Après la fête	J. Hamelle: J.5021 H. J.5021 H. J.5004.5021 H. J.4998.5021 H. J.4999.5021 H.	Op. 71 is also found in 2e Recueil de Valses; a revised edition is dated 1923. No. 3 was also issued separately: Hamelle: J.5991 H.	
72	1898	Introduction et rondo, pour clarinette avec accompagnement de piano	Heugel: H & Cie 19231	Morceau de concours pour le Conservatoire de Paris 1898. Widor created a version for clarinet and orchestra, BN Ms 18141, dated June 8, 1935.	*M. Cyrille Rose*
73	1899	Symphonie romane, pour orgue: 1. Moderato 2. Choral 3. Cantilène 4. Final	Hamelle: J.4518.H.	BN Ms 20825. A-R Editions: Recent Researches in the Music of the Nineteenth and Early Twentieth Centuries, vol. 20, ed. John R. Near.	*Ad Memoriam Sancti Saturnini Tolosensis*
74	1900	Choral et variations, pour harpe et orchestre	Heugel: H & Cie 20361 (full score)	Premiered March 12, 1900, at the Salle Érard, Paris.	*Alphonse Hasselmans*

Opus	Date		Publisher	Dedicatee	Notes
75	1900 1903	Arrangements: Harpe et piano (Widor) Deux pianos (I. Philpp)	H & Cie 20063 H & Cie 21248		Op. 75 unassigned or unknown.
n.op.	1902	Chansons de mer, pour chant et piano, poésies de Paul Bourget 1. La mer 2. A mi-voix 3. Sérénade italienne 4. Encore un soir qui tombe 5. La petite couleuvre bleue 6. A l'aube 7. Ce monde meilleur 8. Rosa la rose 9. Seul dans la nuit 10. Les nuages 11. Douleur précoce 12. Le ciel d'hiver 13. Les yeux et la voix 14. Repos éternel	Heugel: H & Cie 20964–20977	*Mme Jeanne Ch. Max*	In 1902 and 1903, Widor orchestrated the accompaniments to Nos. 1, 5, 6, 7, 10, and 14 (BN Vma ms 586, 587, 592, 595; Mss 18154, 18156, 18157, 18158). No. 14 was arranged with a solo violin part (BN Ms 18151).
n.op.	1902	La chanson des enfants: Le petit pauvre, mélodie pour chant et piano, poésie de Paul Gravollet	Hamelle: J.4815 (8) H.		This appears to be the eighth mélodie in a series by Gravollet. 1. mezzo-soprano or baritone; 2. soprano or tenor.
76	1903	Suite, pour violon et piano, d'après la musique de scène écrite pour la Sulamite, pièce en vers du Vte de Borelli 1. Cantilène	Hamelle: J.4914 H.		Widor arranged Cantilène for solo violin, harp, and strings (BN Ms 18136); this movement was also revised to become the first movement of Suite florentine. The Berceuse was revised to

(*continued*)

Opus	Date	Title	Publisher/plate no.	Comments	Dedicatee
		2. Berceuse	J.4924 H.	become the third movement, Morbidezza, of Suite florentine.	
		3. Danse de la Bayadère	?		
n.op.	1903	Nuit mystérieuse, mélodie pour chant avec accompagnement de piano, poésie de Paul Gravollet	Hamelle: J.5005 H. (single copy); J.5234 H. (in Les Frissons)	From Les Frissons, Vingt-deux mélodies, poésie de P. Gravollet; 22 composers contributed to this collection: Bemberg, Büsser, Caplet, Chaminade, Debussy, Duvernoy, Fontenailles, Hess, d'Indy, Lassen, Lecocq, Leroux, Levadé, Maréchal, Marty, Missa, Pessard, Puget, Ravel, Thomé, Vidal, and Widor. The collection (1906) is J.5213 H.–J.5234 H.	
n.op.	1904	En route, pour piano	*Figaro Illustré*, November 1904	The 4-page facsimile, dated August 20, 1904, was published in *Figaro Illustré*.	
n.op.	1904	Conte d'automne, pour piano	Hamelle: J.5023 H.	This independent piano piece is based partially on the second movement of the Fifth Symphony, Op. 42.	
n.op.	[1904]	Trois duos, pour soprano et baryton avec accompagnement de piano, poésie de Gabriel Vicaire 1. Au bois joli 2. [blank] 3. [blank]	Hamelle: J.5158.1.H	The cover leaves the opus number blank, but assigns plate numbers to blank nos. 2 and 3: 5159 and 5160.	
77	1905	Deuxième concerto, pour piano avec accompagnement d'orchestre: 1. Allegro con moto e patetico 2. Andante—Allegro	Heugel: H. 22,517 (full score); H. 22,264 (piano solo); 22,277 (orchestral reduction)		*Francis Planté*

n.op.	1905	Les pêcheurs de Saint-Jean, scènes de la vie maritime en quatre actes, poème de Henri Cain	Heugel: H & Cie 21,599 (full score); 21,758 (piano vocal score)	Premiered December 26,1905 at the Opéra-Comique under the direction of Albert Carré. BN Ms 18123 (1–4). Marche de Noël is also arranged for piano, H & Cie 22,702 (1905).	*Albert Carré*
n.op.	1904	Orchestral Suite: 1. Ouverture 2. Le calme de la mer (prélude du 2e acte) 3. Marche de Noël (prélude du 3e acte)	Heugel: H & Cie 21,598 Heugel: H & Cie 21,612 Heugel: H & Cie 21,661		
n.op.	1908	Prière des Pêcheurs de Saint-Jean, avec accompagnement de violon, orgue, et harpe (ou piano)	Heugel: H & Cie 23,995	Also an English version (Selma M. and A. Riemenschneider), H. 30,273 (1932).	
78	1905	Suite écossaise (Scotch Suite), pour piano 1. Sur la falaise (On the Cliff) 2. Chevauchée matinale (A Morning Ramble) 3. Spleen (Spleen) 4. Roses d'avril (April Roses) 5. Nuit d'hiver (A Winter's Night) 6. Marche écossaise (Scotch March)	Joseph Williams: J. W. 14353	Marche écossaise was reissued in a new and revised edition in 1930: J. W. 14353a.	
79	1907	Sonate en *ré* mineur, pour violon et piano 1. Allegro 2. Andante 3. Moderato—Allegro	Heugel: H & Cie 23,280	Stockholm, Musikaliska Akademiens Bibliotek, Ms x:134:1, dated October 7, 1906. A second edition was published in 1937.	*Jules Massenet*

(continued)

Opus	Date	Title	Publisher/plate no.	Comments	Dedicatee
80	1907	Sonate en *la* majeur, pour violoncelle et piano 1. Allegro moderato 2. Andante con moto 3. Allegro vivace	Heugel: H & Cie 23,292		*Jules Lœb*
81	1907	Sinfonia sacra, pour orgue et orchestre	Hamelle: J.6177 H.	Stockholm, Stiftelsen Musikkulturens Främjande, MMS 1489. Nydahl Collection; the manuscript is signed: "à Monsieur Rudolf Nydahl 1 June 1922."	*L'Académie des beaux-arts de Berlin*
82				Op. 82 unassigned or unknown.	
n.op.	1909	Trois pièces en *la* mineur, pour hautbois avec accompagnement de piano 1. Pavane [arr. from Pastorale Louis XV] 2. Elégie [arr. from First Symphony, Op. 13, Méditation] 3. Pastorale [arr. from Second Symphony, Op. 13, Pastorale]	Hamelle: J.5296–98.H.	The transcriptions are by Albert Rey.	
n.op.	1910	Fugue sur Haydn, pour piano	*Société Internationale de Musique* 6, no. 1 (January 15, 1910): 13–16.	This piece is No. 6 of *Hommage à J. H.*	
83	1911	Symphonie antique, pour orchestre et chœur 1. Allegro moderato 2. Adagio 3. Moderato—Allegro 4. Moderato	Heugel: H & Cie 24,910 (full score); H & Cie 25,001 (Chœurs)	Premiered March 22, 1911, in the hall of the mansion de Béarn.	*Mme la Comtesse R. de Béarn*

n.op.	1913	Chanson du fou, pour piano et 4 voix mixtes, poésie de Victor Hugo	*Gaulois du Dimanche*, 207 (December 6, 1913).	The score is in a copyist's hand, with emendations by Widor: BN Vmg 18335.	*Nos soldats*
n.op.	1916	Délivrance! Chanson de route, poésie de A. Chuquet	Heugel: H & Cie 26,787 (refrain and strophe) and 26,788 (insert with 5 strophes)		
n.op.	1916	Fleurs de France, mélodie, poésie de Miguel Zamacoïs	Heugel: H & Cie 26,819		*Miss Alice O'Brien*
84	1916	Salvum fac populum tuum, pour trois trompettes, trois trombones, [3] timbales et orgue	Heugel: H & Cie 26,888	The first edition (1916) calls for 3 timpani (G–C–E flat) with the note: "In the case where the exiguity of the tribune permits only two timpani, one can suppress the highest one (E-flat), which has only six measures (letter E) and which the piece can do without if need be." Widor used the first version in a concert in St. Sulpice as late as January 19, 1930 (the sixtieth anniversary of his appointment). The second edition (1917) substitutes tambour in place of timpani. Performed in Notre-Dame, November 17, 1918. Widor orchestrated this work in a freely revised version for full orchestra (BN Ms 18505).	*Son Eminence Monseigneur le Cardinal Amette*
n.op.	1917	Pater Noster, pour soprano et ténor avec accompagnement d'orgue	Heugel: H & Cie 27,203	Sung by Mme Charles Max and M. Plamondon in the chapel of the Palais de Versailles, July 20, 1917. The organ part is on three staves, with registration.	

(continued)

Opus	Date	Title	Publisher/plate no.	Comments	Dedicatee
85				Op. 85 unassigned or unknown.	
n.op.	1919	Suite florentine, pour piano et violon (ou flûte) 1. Cantilena 2. Alle cascine 3. Morbidezza 4. Tragica	Hamelle: J.6985 H	Premiered February 20, 1919, at the Palais de l'Elysée.	*Sa Majesté la Reine Hélène d'Italie*
n.op.	1920	France! Chant militaire pour sopranos, ténors, basses, poésie de A. Dorchain Arrangements: —piano seul —piano à quatre mains —piano et chant —chœur à 4 voix —chant seul —chœur à 2 voix avec piano	Hamelle: J.3143.H. (cover); J.7052.H. (music)	BN Ms 20824: "Hymne à la France" performed November 11, 1920, by a chorus of 300 at the Hôtel-de-Ville, Paris, at a ceremony in honor of "Nos grands ancêtres de 1790."	
n.op.	1924	Hymne à l'épée, pour chœur d'hommes: 1er ténor, 2e ténor, 1re basse, 2e basse, poésie de Victor de Laprade	Buffet Crampon et Cie: B.C. 2371-V (Evette et Schaeffer, Successors)	BN Ms 18163, dated February 29, 1924.	
n.op.	1924	Nerto, drame lyrique en quatre actes de Maurice Léna, d'après le poème de Mistral	Heugel: H.27,973 (piano vocal score)	Premiered at the Paris Opéra, October 20, 1924. BO: A.753 includes 2 vols. of manuscript; Ms 18125, 4 vols. of manuscript.	
	1927	Morceaux détachés: —Ouverture	H.29,454		
	1924	—le Baron, "O mon épée!"	H.28,849		
	1924	—la Zingarella, danse pour piano	H.28,850		
	1924	—Marche des escholiers, pour piano	H.28,851		

	Year	Title	Publisher	Notes
	1924	—Nerto, "Le château du Saint-Père!"	H.28,852	
	1924	—Nerto, "L'amour?"	H.28,856	
	1924	—Nerto et Rodrigue, "Ah! Ne blasphémez pas!"	H.28,853	
	1924	—Nerto, "La prière me fuit"	H.28,854	
	1924	—Les indolences, pour piano	H.28,857	
	1924	—Ballet, pour piano	H.28,855	
n.op.	1925	Bach's Memento, six pièces pour orgue 1. Pastorale, flûte et hautbois 2. Miserere mei domine 3. Aria en e-moll 4. Marche du veilleur de nuit 5. Sicilienne 6. Mattheus-final	Hamelle: J.7310.H.–J.7315.H.	Premiered by the composer at the American Conservatory of Fontainebleau, June 30, 1925. The arrangements are based on the following: No. 1, Pastorale, third movement, BWV 590; No. 2, Prelude in D Minor (from WTC, book 1), BWV 851; No. 3, Prelude in E Minor (from WTC, book 1), BWV 855; No. 4, "Wachet auf, ruft uns die Stimme" (from Cantata 140), BWV 140; No. 5, "Siciliana" (from Sonata for Flute in E-flat Major), BWV 1031; No. 6, "Wir setzen uns mit Tränen nieder" (from *St. Matthew Passion*), BWV 244.
n.op.	1925	Ecce Johanna Alleluia! Choeur à quatre voix mixtes	Librairie de l'art Catholique	"Alleluia en l'honneur de Jeanne d'Arc." Performed at the Trocadéro, April 1925.
86	1927	Suite latine, pour orgue 1. Praeludium 2. Beatus vir 3. Lamento 4. Ave maris stella	Durand: D & F.11,221	Premiered by Widor January 13, 1928, at La Madeleine, Paris. There are two editions; the first appeared with several errors.

(continued)

Opus	Date	Title	Publisher/plate no.	Comments	Dedicatee
		5. Adagio 6. Lauda sion			
n.op.	1931, 1932	Da Pacem, pour 4 voix mixtes et orgue	Durand: D. & F. 12,047 (full score); D & F 12,048 (choral part)	Widor made an arrangement with the addition of 3 trumpets and 3 trombones, and wrote on the folder: "1st version destroyed 1931. The 2nd version dates from 1932 after the first performance in Notre-Dame, birthday of the Pope." BN Vma ms 583 and Ms 18167–69; Vmg 18323.	*Son Eminence le Cardinal Verdier*
87	1934	Trois nouvelles pièces, pour orgue 1. Classique d'hier 2. Mystique 3. Classique d'aujourd'hui	Durand: D. & F.12,393 (1–3)		*1. Albert Riemenschneider* *2. Charlotte Lockwood* *3. Frédérick Mayer*
Collections					
[1881]		Trente mélodies pour une voix avec accompagnement de piano Op. 14: Nuit d'étoiles; L'abeille; À cette terre; Avril; Sérénade [Enfant de Catane]; Sunt lacrymæ rerum. Op. 22: Sois heureuse; L'aurore; Aubade. Op. 28: À toi; Invocation. [Op. 24]: Ave Maria. Op. 37: Le soleil s'est couché; S'il est un charmant gazon; Soupir; Aimons toujours; Le chasseur songe; Le bouquet. Op. 43: Je ne veux pas autre chose; Le vase brisé; Mon bras pressait; Le plongeur; N'avez-vous point su les comprendre; Vieille	Hamelle: J.1585 H.; also, an edition showing a change of title to Sérénade (Enfant de Catane): J.1585 (1708) H.	141 pages	

chanson du jeune temps. Op. 47: La captive; J'ai dit aux bois; Les étoiles; Je pense à toi; Albaÿdé; Prière.

[1885] Quarante mélodies pour une voix avec accompagnement de piano Op. 14: Nuit d'étoiles; L'abeille; À cette terre; Avril; Enfant de Catane (Sérénade); Sunt lacrymæ rerum. Op. 22: Sois heureuse; L'Aurore; Aubade. Op. 28: À toi; Invocation. [Op. 24]: Ave Maria. Op. 37: Le soleil s'est couché; S'il est un charmant gazon; Soupir; Aimons toujours; Le chasseur songe dans les bois; Le bouquet. Op. 43: Je ne veux pas autre chose; Le vase brisé; Contemplation [Mon bras pressait]; Le plongeur; N'avez-vous point su les comprendre; Vieille chanson du jeune temps. Op. 47: La captive; J'ai dit aux bois; Les étoiles; Je pense à toi; Albaÿdé; Prière. [Op. 14]: Chanson indienne. [Op. 22]: Mon âme a son secret [or Peuple, ta voix . . . (extrait du Chant séculaire Op. 49)]. [Op. 22]: Dans la plaine blonde. [Op. 14]: Le doux appel. Op. 53: Dis, le sais-tu pourquoi; Prière au printemps; Je respire où tu palpites; Quand vous me

Hamelle: J.1585 H.; Enfant de Catane (Sérénade): (1708) J.1585 H.; Peuple, ta voix: J.1585 H. (3148)

192 pages; a second edition (after 1885) substituted Peuple, ta voix in place of Mon âme a son secret. In 1888, G. Schirmer issued a two volume edition of these songs in an English version by Eugène Oudin; each volume was issued in two ranges: soprano/tenor (nos. 119, 120) and mezzo-soprano/baritone (nos. 138, 139).

(continued)

22: Dans la plaine blonde. [Op. 14]: Le doux appel. Op. 53: Dis, le sais-tu pourquoi?; Prière au printemps; Je respire où tu palpites; Quand vous me montrez une rose. [Op. 14 and 22]: Adieu. [Op. 59]: Ave Maria avec accompagnement d'orgue et de harpe (en *mi* bémol). Op. 53: Ne jamais la voir, ni l'entendre; Songes-tu parfois, bien-aimée. [Op. 22]: Mon âme a son secret. [n.op.]: Ballade scandinave (A. Dorchain).

1907

Cinquante-quatre mélodies, pour une voix avec accompagnement de piano, 1er volume [1st edition, 130 pages]

Same order as Quarante-quatre mélodies through Op. 43; then Tristesse infinie (Paul Bourget); Ballade scandinave; Pâle étoile du soir (Alfred de Musset)

Cinquante-quatre mélodies, pour une voix avec accompagnement de piano, 2ème volume [1st edition, 135 pages]

Op. 47: La captive; J'ai dit aux bois; Les étoiles; Je pense à toi; Albaÿdé; Prière. [Op. 14]: Chanson indienne. [Op. 49]: Peuple, ta voix . . . (extrait du Chant séculaire).

Hamelle: J.1585 H.

There is a mixed array of mélodies from different opus numbers in this collection, which appeared in two volumes and two editions. The first edition (1907) contains revisions of Quarante-quatre mélodies, and the second edition (1926) contains revisions of the first edition of Cinquante-quatre mélodies. Widor's copy of the second edition carries emendations planned for a third edition.

(continued)

Opus	Date	Title	Publisher/plate no.	Comments	Dedicatee
		Op. 53: Dans la plaine [formerly Op. 22]; Le doux appel [formerly Op. 14]; Dis, le sais-tu pourquoi?; Prière au printemps; Je respire où tu palpites; Quand vous me montrez une rose; Adieu [formerly Opp. 14 and/or 22]; Op. 59: Ave Maria (en *mi* bémol); Ne jamais la voir, ni l'entendre [also shown as Op. 53, no. 5]; Songes-tu parfois, bien-aimée [also shown as Op. 53, no. 6]; Mon âme a son secret [Op. 22]; Op. 63: Soirs d'été			
	1926	Cinquante-quatre mélodies, pour une voix avec accompagnement de piano, 1er volume [2nd edition] Same order as 1st edition, with revisions, until final three melodies, which are: Ballade scandinave; Les cloches de la côte bretonne (I. Le Bratz); Pâle étoile du soir. Cinquante-quatre mélodies, pour une voix avec accompagnement de piano, 2ème volume [2nd edition] Same order as 1st edition, with revisions.			
	[1884]	Six duos, pour soprano et contralto avec accompagnement de piano, comprenant les œuvres 30, 40, et 52	Hamelle: J.1315.1316 H.; J.2082.2083 H.; J.2084.2085 H.		

n.d.	Six mélodies italiennes, pour une voix avec accompagnement de piano, comprenant les œuvres 32 et 35	Hamelle: J.2440 à 2445.H.; transpostions: J.2440.1–2445.6.H.	
n.d.	Quinze valses, pour piano, comprenant les œuvres 4, 11, et 26; le No. 6 des Morceaux de salon [Op. 15]; le No. 2 des Scènes de bal [Op. 20]; les Nos. 2 et 10 de Feuillets d'album [Op. 31]; et une Introduction. Nouv. édit. revue et corrigée.	Hamelle	
1903	Valses, 1er Recueil, pour piano Introduction (Andantino) 1. Valse, Op. 11, no. 1 (Allegro con spirito) Intermezzo 2. Valse lændler, Op. 11, no. 2 (Allegro ma non troppo) 3. Valse caprice, Op. 11, no. 3 (Allegro vivace) 4. Valse rêverie, Op. 26, no. 3 (Andantino) 5. 1er Rhapsodie-Valse, Op. 26, no. 1 (Presto) 6. Valse romance, Op. 26, no. 2 (Moderato quasi romanza) 7. Valse slave, Op. 26, no. 4 (Allegro deciso) 8. Valse élégante, Op. 26, no. 5 (Largamente cantabile assai) 9. Papillons bleus, Op. 31, no. 2	Hamelle: J.1938 H.	Nouvelle édition revue et corrigée; the Intermezzo was added.

(continued)

Opus	Date	Title	Publisher/plate no.	Comments	Dedicatee
		(Vivace scherzando)			
		10. Ciel gris, Op. 31, no. 10 (Moderato)			
		11. Valse-Impromptu, Op. 15, no. 6 (Vivace)			
		12. 2ᵉ Rhapsodie-Valse, Op. 26, no. 6 (Allegro con fuoco)			
		13. Entrée de la reine, Op. 20, no. 2 (Dolce e tranquillo)			
		14. Airs de ballet, Op. 4 (Presto scherzando)			
	1903	Valses, 2ᵉ Recueil, pour piano	Hamelle: individual plate numbers are the same as for the opus numbers except as noted for Nos. 7, 13, and 14, which were reengraved.	Valse noble is indicated on the score as Op. 31, no. 6, and is a revision and expansion of Valse lente (from Douze feuillets d'album). Valse oubliée also appeared in L'Illustration, Supplément Musical 3281 (January 13, 1906).	
		1. Neuilly-Valse, Op. 33, no. 1			
		2. Valse flamande, Op. 33, no. 2			
		3. Valse tzigane, Op. 33, no. 3			
		4. Valse chantante, Op. 33, no. 4			
		5. Valse légère, Op. 33, no. 5			
		6. Valse noble, Op. 33, no. 6			
		7. Scherzo-Valse, Op. 5	J.5021 H.		
		8. Valse gaie, Op. 71, no. 1			
		9. Valse triste, Op. 71, no. 2			
		10. Kermesse carillonante, Op. 71, no. 3			
		11. Valse oubliée, Op. 71, no. 4			
		12. Après la fête, Op. 71, no. 5			
		13. Valse de l'épreuve (de La Korrigane)	J.5021 H.		
		14. Yvonette-Valse (de La Korrigane)	J.5021 H.		

Miscellaneous Works

n.d.	Ave verum corpus, à 4 voix mixtes a cappella	Procure Générale: P.3507 G.	Widor published the second version of this work under his own mark.	
n.d.	Ave verum, mixte chœur à 4	Widor: W		*La Gilde Sainte-Cécile et aux chanteurs de la Sainte-Chapelle; Mr. Hawkins, St. John's College, Hurstpierpoint (Sussex).*
n.d.	Impromtu, en *mi* bémol, pour piano		Proof sheets carry small corrections: BN Vmg 18300 and Vmg 18300 A.	
1894	Morceau de déchiffrage du concours de piano (hommes)	*Piano Soleil* (August 12, 1894): 4		
1894	Morceau de déchiffrage du concours de piano (femmes)	*Piano Soleil* (August 19, 1894): 4		
1894–1907	Morceaux de lecture à 1ᵉ vue de concours de piano au Conservatoire de Paris (1894–1907).		BN Vmg 18433 (1–11).	
1908	Morceaux de lecture à vue donnés aux concours du Conservatoire, année 1908. Concours des élèves hommes.		BN Vm12.34460 bis.	
1880	Contribution to *Solfège universel avec accompagnement de piano*, leçons de style et de perfectionnement composées par les plus célèbres auteurs et réunies par Émile Artaud.	Paris: Léon Grus	Widor's contribution appears on p. 159.	

(continued)

Opus	Date	Title	Publisher/plate no.	Comments	Dedicatee
	1900	Contribution to *Collection complète des leçons d'harmonie par Albert Lavignac*, augmentée de nombreuses leçons écrites spécialement pour cet ouvrage (en 3 Recueils).	H. Lemoine & Cie	Widor's contribution appears in Recueil 3, Nos. 207 and 208 (pp. 52, 53, 116, 117). These were for the "Concours de 1899."	
	1900	Contribution to *Basses et chants donnés aux examens et concours des classes d'harmonie et d'accompagnement* (Années 1827–1900), par [auteurs divers] recueillis par Constant Pierre.	Heugel	Widor's contribution, "chant donné" for "1899 (femmes)," is No. 147, p. 124.	
	1896	Pa-Hos et Zu'ella		Incidental music with François Thomé and Michel (?) performed at the Théâtre des Poètes, March 9, 1896.	
		Unpublished complete manuscripts:			
	n.d.	Oubliras-tu, pour chant et piano, [poésie de Paul Bourget?]		BN Ms 18185, 3 pages. On the cover of the manuscript are two different orders of the songs in Soirs d'été.	
	1898	Sub Tuum, pour chant [soprano] et orgue		BN Mss 18175 (dated July 15, 1898), 18176, 18177.	
	1903	Pour charmer le cœur, pour chant et orchestre		BN Ms 18153.	
	1908	Te Christe, qu ce sumus famulis subveni, pour chœur à 4 voix et orgue		BN Ms 18178, 5 pages signed and dated January 1, 1908.	
	1916	Dormez, Melité, pour chant et piano		BN Ms 18144, dated January 30, 1916, and ms 18145.	

[1918–20]	Le chêne du souvenir, pour chant et piano, poésie de Jules Casadesus		BN Vma ms 596, Ms 18147. The post–World War I text is in three strophes; the first strophe tells of planting an oak born on American soil in France "in order that the memory of our American glory may live."	
1930	Salve galliæ patrona, pour chœur à 2 voix et solo		BN Ms 18174, dated April 2, 1930.	les Sœurs de St. Sulpice
	Transcriptions and Cadenzas:			
1907	"Les larmes" [en *mi* bémol] (Beethoven: "Wonne der Wehmut": *Drei Gesänge*, Op. 83, no. 1), transcribed for voice and orchestra by Widor		BN Ms 18159, dated December 10, 1907.	
n.d.	"La jeune religieuse" (Schubert: "Die junge Nonne"), transcribed for voice and orchestra by Widor		BN Vma ms 593.	
1926	Henry d'Ollone, *Devant le mausolée*, poème symphonique pour orchestre, transcription pour orgue par Ch. M. Widor	Sénart: E.M.S.6985		
n.d.	Cadence du Concerto, Op. 4, no. 4 (1er mvt.), pour orgue et orchestra de Hændel		BN Ms 18138.	
n.d.	Cadence pour le final du Concerto, Op. 4, no. 7, pour orgue et orchestre de Hændel		BN Ms 18139.	

(continued)

Opus	Date	Title	Publisher/plate no.	Comments	Dedicatee
		Works by François-Charles Widor			
6	1852	Sérénade, pour piano	Lyon: J. Benacci et Peschier: B&P.853	Ch. Widor, père	*Stephen Heller*
8		Scherzo oriental		Ch. Widor, père	
12	1859	Chant du meunier, pour piano	Heugel: H.5016	Ch. Widor, père	*Marmontel*
13	1856	La voix du cœur, nocturne-caprice	G. Brandus, Dufour et Cie: 9664	Ch. Widor, père	*Joséphine Martin*
	1858	Souvenir de Lyon, barcarolle, pour piano	Heugel	Ch. Widor, père	
17	1859	Aux Alpes, impromptu-caprice, pour piano	G. Flaxland: A.R.471	Ch. Widor, père	*Louise et Julienne Rémi Charrin*
18	1859	Petits anges (Caprice)	Benoit, ainé: 1303	Ch. Widor, père	*Marie Longin*

A Cross-Section of
Musicians during Widor's Life

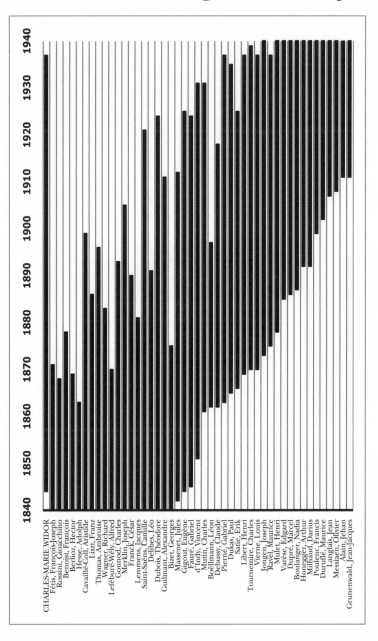

Appendix 4

Chronology

1844　February 21: Birth of *Charles*-Marie-Jean-Albert Widor, first child of François-Charles Widor and his wife Françoise-Elisabeth Peiron, 19 rue Sala, Lyon.

1847　February 5: Birth of Marie-Joseph-Albert-*Paul* Widor.

1848　April 20: Birth of Jeanne-*Marie*-Françoise Widor.

1850　Jacques Lemmens performs in Paris for the first time.

1862　April 29: Inauguration of Cavaillé-Coll organ at Saint-Sulpice by Saint-Saëns, Franck, Bazille, Guilmant, and Schmitt. August 12: Charles-Marie Widor awarded *Diplôme de Bachelier ès Lettres*.

1863　Late February to July 9: Studies in Brussels with Fétis and Lemmens. May 1: Lefébure-Wély becomes *titulaire* of Saint-Sulpice. July 28: Widor performs a recital at Saint-Sulpice.

1864　January 9: Participates in inauguration of Cavaillé-Coll organ at Sainte-Perpétue, Nîmes.

1865　May: Performs at Salle Pleyel as pedal-pianist and at Cavaillé-Coll's factory (rue de Vaugirard) as organist. September: Performs at International Exposition of Porto, Portugal.

1866　April 13: Among select group who hears Franck perform for Liszt at Sainte-Clotilde. May 22: Named "Chevalier de l'Ordre du Christ" by Napoléon III in the name of Portuguese King Luís I. July: Accompanies Cavaillé-Coll and Guilmant for his first trip to England.

1867　April: Premieres youthful piano concerto (not extant) in Lyon. Publishes first works, including Six Duos, Op. 3. May: Performs harmonium concerts at Universal Exposition, Paris.

1868　March 6: Participates in inauguration of Cavaillé-Coll organ at Notre-Dame de Paris with Saint-Saëns, Franck, Loret, Durand, Chauvet, Guilmant, and Sergent. March 22: Performs music for organ and piano with Franck at Cavaillé-Coll's new establishment, 13 and 15 avenue du Maine. May 26: Inaugurates Cavaillé-Coll *orgue de chœur* in Toulouse Cathedral.

1869　March 11: Attends Berlioz's funeral at La Trinité, Paris. March 16: Participates in inauguration of Cavaillé-Coll organ at La Trinité with Saint-Saëns, Franck, Durand, Chauvet, and Fissot. March 25: Premieres Quintet, Op. 7, at Pleyel, Wolff & Co. Early December: Widor and Chauvet inaugurate Cavaillé-Coll organ in Notre-Dame, Épernay. Late December: Substitutes for Saint-Saëns at La Madeleine, Paris. December 31: Lefébure-Wély dies.

1870　January 16: Begins as "provisional" organist at Saint-Sulpice. Takes up residency at 8 rue Garancière. February 28: Performs several of his piano works and Sérénade, Op. 10, at Salle Érard. March 6: Performs with Saint-Saëns at Cavaillé-Coll's audition hall on piano and organ (three-manual, forty-one stop organ destined for residence of music publisher Mr. John Turner Hopwood in Bracewell, England). March 13: Performs with Guilmant at Cavaillé-Coll's. July: Outbreak of Franco-Prussian War; joins mobilized artillery.

1871 Endures severe hardships of Paris Commune. Saint-Sulpice is shelled, but the massive portico protects the organ.

1872 Publishes Four Symphonies for Organ, Op. 13, various piano pieces, songs, and First Symphony for Orchestra, Op. 16. Late February: Performs in Rouen as pianist, and inaugurates organ in the chapel of Bon-Secours. March: Performs some of his organ compositions at Cavaillé-Coll's. June 5: Inaugurates Cavaillé-Coll organ in Saint-Jean-Baptiste, Chaumont. November: Parts of First Symphony, Op. 16, are given a hearing by Société des concerts du conservatoire.

1873 February 21: Inaugurates, with Saint-Saëns and others, the organ restored by Cavaillé-Coll in the chapel of the Palace of Versailles. May: Saint-Saëns and Widor play programs at Cavaillé-Coll's on new organ destined for Sheffield.

1874 Achieves published works through Opus 20. March: Premiere of Piano Trio, Op. 19. July: Member of Conservatory organ jury. December: Performs with Lemmens the latter's new compositions (*L'organiste catholique*) at Cavaillé-Coll's.

1875 January 25: Premier of Opus 21. July: Member of Conservatory organ jury.

1876 Achieves published works through Opus 31. August: Attends premiere of Wagner's *Der Ring des Nibelungen* in Bayreuth. November 19: Premiere of Piano Concerto, Op. 39, with Diémer, pianist.

1877 January: Succeeds Saint-Saëns as music critic for *Estafette*; writes seventy-seven articles of musical criticism before relinquishing the position after June 5, 1882. Member of Conservatory organ jury. November 18: Premiere of Violin Concerto with Marsick, violinist. December: Inaugurates Cavaillé-Coll organ in the chapel of Saint-Paul des Pères Barnabites, Paris. J. Hamelle takes over the publishing firm of J. Maho, Widor's main publisher.

1878 March 31: Tests new organ for the Trocadéro at Cavaillé-Coll's audition hall. June: Demonstrates Trocadéro organ for Liszt and spends a week listening to Liszt play the piano at Madame Érard's. Member of Conservatory organ jury. August 24: Premieres Symphony in G Minor, Op. 42, at Trocadéro during Universal Exposition.

1879 February 27: Participates in inauguration of Fermis & Persil organ at Saint-François-Xavier with Franck, Gigout, and Renaud; premieres part of Symphony in F Minor, Op. 42, and *Psaume* 112. June: Publishes Fifth and Sixth Symphonies for Organ. July 16: Performs his new symphonies in private concert at Trocadéro. Member of Conservatory organ jury. October 19: Performs Fifth Symphony at Trocadéro. December 3: Inaugurates Cavaillé-Coll organ in the chapel of the Hôtel-Dieu, Vitry-le-Français, "in spite of the exceptional cold."

1880 February 8: Premiere of *La nuit de Walpurgis* at the Châtelet. March: Assumes directorship of the choral group "Concordia." December 1: Premiere of *La Korrigane*, Paris Opéra. December 16: Inaugurates Cavaillé-Coll organ in Saint-François-de-Sale, Lyon.

1881 April: "Concordia instrumentale" established with Widor as conductor. May 1: Performs Fifth Symphony on Cavaillé-Coll organ destined for Martinique.

May 31: Premiere of *Chant séculaire*, Op. 49, by Concordia. August/September: Composes Violin Sonata, Op. 50, and *Suite polonaise*, Op. 51, during annual vacation in l'Arbresle.

1882   April 13: Premieres Symphony in G Minor for Organ and Orchestra, Op. 42[a], at Trocadéro. May 11: Conducts Concordia in complete performance of Haydn's *Seasons*. May 20: Performs Symphony in G Minor for Organ and Orchestra at Royal Albert Hall, London. December: Travels to Vienna for performances of chamber music and *La Korrigane*; attends numerous other performances. Awarded the Prix Chartier by the Academy of Fine Arts for his Violin Sonata.

1883   March: Performs at a festival of his music at the Palais des Beaux-Arts, Brussels. April 10: Death of his mother Françoise-Elisabeth Peiron Widor; Charles and his brother-in-law, Eugène Pierron, sign the death record. September 8: Inaugurates the organ in the church of Lion-d'Angers. September 11: Inaugurates Cavaillé-Coll organ in the church of Saint-Jean, Château-Gontier.

1884   May 8: Inaugurates Cavaillé-Coll organ at Saint-Godard, Rouen. Dedicates Flute Suite, Op. 34, to Paul Taffanel. November 30: Conducts premiere of Second Symphony, Op. 54, Cirque d'Hiver, Paris. December 3: Tests Cavaillé-Coll organ for Notre-Dame d'Auteuil.

1885   February 11: Inaugurates Cavaillé-Coll organ in Notre-Dame d'Auteuil. April 21: Conducts Concordia in Bach bicentennial concert: Magnificat and two Cantatas.

1886   May 6: Premiere of *Maître Ambros*, Opéra-Comique. November 28: Conducts and performs at a festival of his music, Amsterdam.

1887   April: Publication of Seventh and Eighth Symphonies for Organ, Op. 42, along with revisions to the earlier symphonies. May 7: Benefit concert with cellist Delsart for Association des artistes-musiciens, Salle Érard, Paris.

1888   April 19: Conducts London Philharmonic Society in a performance of the revised *La nuit de Walpurgis*, Saint-James's Hall. May 16: Directs Concordia's performance of Bach's *Saint-Matthew Passion*, Paris Conservatory. July 2: Inaugurates Cavaillé-Coll organ at Saint-Michel du Havre. October: Concert of his works in Barcelona; performs Symphony in G Minor for Organ and Orchestra. November 9: Concert of his works in Salle Valette, Marseille. November 22: Inaugurates Puget organ in Notre-Dame de la Dalbade, Toulouse. December 16: Performs at a concert of his works presented by the Association Artistique d'Angers.

1889   February 23: Premiere of *Fantaisie*, Op. 62, with Philipp, pianist. July 3: Premieres Eighth Symphony, Op. 42, at Trocadéro; the program also includes the Fifth Symphony. November 17: Inaugurates restored Marie-Antoinette organ in Saint-Sulpice with works by Mozart, Gluck, and an arrangement for cello and organ of the second movement from his Eighth Symphony.

1890   Named "Commandeur de Saint-Grégoire," Angers. March 2: Widor and Mailly inaugurate Schyven organ at Liège Conservatory. March 13: Conducts London Philharmonic Society in performance of *Fantaisie*, Op. 62, with Philipp, pianist. March 14: Performs organ concert at Royal Academy of Music, London. April 17: Inaugurates Cavaillé-Coll organ at Saint-Ouen,

Rouen. June 3: Premiere of *Jeanne d'Arc* at Paris Hippodrome. November 8: Franck dies. November 23: Named Franck's successor as professor of organ, Paris Conservatory; first class meets on December 11.

1891 January: Plays organ at funeral of Léo Delibes. January 18: Inaugurates Cavaillé-Coll organ at the church of Charenton. February: Premiere of Piano Quartet, Op. 66. March 12: Premiere of revised version of *Conte d'avril* at the Odéon. May: Inaugurates Cavaillé-Coll organ in Saint-Jean-Baptiste, Roubaix. May 23: Inaugurates organ in Newcastle Cathedral. August: Accepts artistic directorship of *Piano Soleil*; writes over 150 articles by 1898; retains directorship through at least 1906. August 15: Attends production of *Conte d'avril* in Aix-les-Bains. November 15: Inaugurates Cavaillé-Coll organ in the Temple de Pentemont, Paris. December: Participates in inauguration of Schyven organ at the Antwerp Cathedral.

1892 Named "Chevalier" in the French Legion of Honor. February: Vierne becomes his assistant at Saint-Sulpice. March 17: Inaugurates with Vierne the restored organ at Saint-Germain-des-Prés, Paris. June: Performs two-piano version of *Conte d'avril* with Berthe Max in London. July 31: Writes an article in *Piano Soleil* describing the perceived demise of Cavaillé-Coll's firm; orders ten-stop *orgue de salon* from Gabriel Cavaillé-Coll. October: Moves to 3 rue de l'Abbaye.

1893 Named "Chevalier de l'Ordre de Léopold," Belgium. January: Travels to Budapest for premiere of *La Korrigane* (January 20) and to conduct a concert of his works (January 25). April 12: Concert of his works at the Jardin d'Acclimatation: premiere of *Suite pittoresque* for Orchestra. Albert Schweitzer begins study with Widor.

1894 Initiates *L'orgue moderne*, a quarterly publication of new organ compositions. Premiere of Piano Quintet, Op. 68. April: Participates in inauguration of the restored Cavaillé-Coll organ at Saint-Vincent-de-Paul with Dubois, Gigout, Guilmant, and Boëllmann. July 31: Participates in reinauguration of the Notre-Dame organ with Guilmant, Gigout, and Sergent. November 28: Premiere of Third Symphony for Organ and Orchestra, Op. 69, in Victoria Hall, Geneva.

1895 February: "Société de musique nouvelle" formed under Widor's patronage. March: Festival of his works in Monte Carlo. March 28: Performs Quintet in Frankfurt. April 28: Premieres *Symphonie gothique* at Saint-Ouen, Rouen. May 12: Conducts Piano Concerto with Philipp at the Jardin d'Acclimatation. July 23: Festival of his works in Ostende; popular demand requires repeat performance on July 25. August: Ambroise Thomas sends Widor as a juror to the International Rubinstein Competition, Berlin (Diémer and Busoni are co-jurors); Widor performs on Sauer organ at the church of Apostel-Paulus, Berlin.

1896 February 12: Ambroise Thomas dies. April: *La Korrigane* achieves its one-hundredth performance at the Opéra. June 11: Conducts Third Symphony, Op. 69, at Trocadéro with Vierne, organist. June 27: Performs as soloist in the Third Symphony in Rouen. July 28: Presides over jury for the post of organist at Saint-Denis; Libert appointed. November 16: Conducts Second Symphony, Op. 54, in Moscow and later performs at the church of Saint

Peter and Saint Paul. October 1: Becomes professor of composition, Paris Conservatory, succeeding Dubois who was named director.

1897 May 7: Conducts Bach's Magnificat and *Actus tragicus*, Salle Érard, Paris. May 30: Inaugurates Cavaillé-Coll organ at Église du Rosaire, Lourdes. August 14: Conducts concert of his works in Dieppe.

1898 February 6: Conducts concert of his works in Lille. February 28: Conducts and performs in a concert of his works in Rome; attends Mass in Sistine Chapel with Pope Leo XIII. Early December: Conducts Beethoven's Third Symphony, a Bach Concerto, and some of his own works, in Angers. Mid-December: Conducts Cello Concerto, Op. 41, in Lyon.

1899 February: Conducts *La Korrigane* Suite and performs at Saint-Ferdinand in Bordeaux. March 27: Conducts program in chapel of the Palace of Versailles. April 7: Death of his father François-Charles Widor. August: Conducts at a concert of his works in Royan. October 13: Death of "père" Aristide Cavaillé-Coll. October: Returns from vacation having completed *Symphonie romane*, Op. 73, and Choral and Variations for Harp and Orchestra, Op. 74. December 5: Conducts Third Symphony in Cologne. December 8: Conducts Third Symphony in Strasbourg.

1900 January: Conducts and performs in Berlin; premieres *Symphonie romane* at Gedächtniss Kirche. March 12: Conducts a concert of his works, including premiere of Choral and Variations for Harp and Orchestra, Salle Érard, Paris. March 28: Premiere of *Le capitaine Loys*, Théâtre des Célestins, Lyon. April: Inaugurates Puget organ at Lille Conservatory. May 21: Presides over jury for the post of organist at Notre-Dame, Paris; Vierne appointed. August 14: Moves to 7 rue des Saints-Pères.

1901 February: Conducts concert of his works in Bordeaux. April 11: Inaugurates Cavaillé-Coll/Mutin organ at the Moscow Conservatory. Named "Commandeur de l'Ordre de St. Stanislas IIe Classe." Publishes new edition of Organ Symphonies Opp. 13 and 42. November 15: Conducts and performs his works in Warsaw.

1902 January 5: Publication of the song cycle *Chansons de mer* is advertised. August 4: Conducts concert of his works in Dieppe.

1903 February: Conducts and performs in Moscow and St. Petersburg. February 19: Inaugurates rebuilt organ in the church of Saint-Philippe-du-Roule, Paris. March 25 and 28: Conducts program for benefit of the "Union mutualiste des femmes de France"; program includes excerpts from Schumann's *Manfred* and Bizet's *Carmen*, works by Gluck, Mendelssohn, Massenet, and his own *Danse Byzantine*[?]). July 28: Performs works of Bach and Handel at memorial Mass for Pope Leo XIII at Notre-Dame, Paris. August 17: Inaugurates Cavaillé-Coll/Mutin organ at Notre-Dame, Metz. August 21: Presides over jury for the post of organist at Sacré-Cœur, Montmartre; Decaux appointed.

1904 Publication of *Technique de l'orchestre moderne*, a revision of Berlioz's *Traité d'instrumentation*. November 17: Inaugurates Mutin organ at Saint-Jean-Baptiste, Neuilly. December 6: Performs in Third Symphony, Op. 69, and plays several solo organ works in Mannheim.

1905 February 26: Conducts premiere of Second Concerto for Piano, Op. 77, with Philipp, Concerts Colonne, Paris. March 6: Conducts program of his works including both piano Concertos and the *Fantaisie*, Salle Érard. June 8: Performs program at Cavaillé-Coll's on a large Mutin organ. December 26: Premiere of *Les pêcheurs de Saint-Jean*, Opéra-Comique.

1906 Early March: Conducts Second Piano Concerto with Planté, Bordeaux. April 16: Attends premiere of *Les pêcheurs de Saint-Jean* in German translation, Frankfurt. May: Academy of Fine Arts awards Widor the Prix Monbinne (three thousand francs) for *Les pêcheurs de Saint-Jean*. Named "Vice-Président d'Honneur de Ste Cécile," Bordeaux. Dupré becomes Widor's assistant at Saint-Sulpice.

1907 March 14: Premieres Sonatas for Violin, Op. 79, and Cello, Op. 80. March: Elected associate member of Berlin Royal Academy; composes *Sinfonia sacra*, Op. 81, as token of appreciation. June: Inaugurates Didier organ in Sacré-Cœur, Nancy.

1908 Elected associate member of Belgian Royal Academy. February: Conducts Second Piano Concerto, Op. 77, in Zurich with Frey, pianist. Early September: Inaugurates Mutin organ at Notre-Dame, Guebwiller (Alsace).

1909 February 19: Submits his name for a chair in the music section of the Academy of Fine Arts at the Institute of France; Fauré elected. May 4: Conducts Third Symphony, *Fantaisie*, and other works at Queen's Hall, London. June: Karl Straube performs Eighth Symphony for Organ at Saint-Thomas Church, Leipzig. November 12: Inaugurates Mutin organ at Santa-Maria del Trastevere in Rome. November 15: Widor and Mutin have an audience with Pope Pius X. December 4 and 5: Conducts *Sinfonia sacra*, with Schweitzer, organist, for inauguration of the Saengerhaus, Strasbourg.

1910 January 28: Conducts Berlin Philharmonic in performance of Second Piano Concerto, with Frey; accompanies Second Violin Sonata in Potsdam. March: Elected associate member of Swedish Royal Academy. July: G. Schirmer commissions Widor and Schweitzer to prepare an edition of Bach's organ works. August: *La Korrigane* achieves its 138th performance at the Opéra. September 18–20: Participates in Festival of French Music in Munich; performs in Saint-Saëns's Third Symphony, Saint-Saëns conducting; conducts *Sinfonia sacra*, Schweitzer, organist. October 29: Elected member of the Academy of Fine Arts, succeeding Charles Lenepveu.

1911 January 29: Conducts a program of his works in Lille. March 22: Premiere of *Symphonie antique*, Op. 83, in the concert hall of Countess René de Béarn. March 29: Guilmant dies. April 13: Inaugurates Kerkhoff organ at Saint-Michel, Brussels. May 13: Inaugurates rebuilt organ at Notre-Dame de la Gloriette, Caen. Becomes spokesman for Conservatory reforms.

1912 March 10: Conducts a program of his works in Tournai, Belgium. December 22: Conducts and performs in the Augusteum, Rome. Elected president of the Association des artistes-musiciens.

1913 July 14: Widor and Charpentier represent the Institute at inauguration of the Grétry Museum in Liège, Belgium. Late November: Conducts *Symphonie antique* and other works in Dortmund, Germany.

1914   February 21: Performs organ concert at the Métropole in Rennes, France; conducts *Symphonie antique* and other works the next day. June: Performs organ concert in Uhser Hall, Edinburgh. July 18: Elected perpetual secretary of the Academy of Fine Arts, succeeding Henri Roujon. September: Refuses to leave Paris at the onset of World War I and during the bombardment.

1916   April: Completes fourth volume of Bach edition. April: Travels to Madrid as part of delegation from the Institute to build stronger relations with Spain; proposes a branch of the Institute in Madrid. May 8: Meets Spanish King Alphonse XIII, who offers land for "Casa Velásquez." June: Composes *Salvum fac populum tuum*, Op. 84; narrowly escapes shell fragment bursting through his apartment window. December 19: *Salvum fac populum tuum* premiered at Saint-Sulpice.

1917   May 28: Death of his sister, Marie Widor Pierron. December: Returns to Madrid to further plans for Casa Velásquez.

1918   March 17: Debussy accepts Widor's sponsorship of his candidacy to the Academy of Fine Arts. March 25: Debussy dies. Widor organizes Exposition of French Painters for showing in Madrid. May 12: travels to Madrid for opening. Named "Comendador de Número de la Orden Civil de Alfonso XII," Madrid. November 17: Conducts *Salvum fac populum tuum*, Notre-Dame. Publishes his edition of Mendelssohn's Sonatas for Organ.

1919   February 20: Performs *Suite florentine* for the queen of Italy at the Élysée Palace, Paris. May 26–30: Travels to London to find a location for a branch of the Institute. July 17: Returns to London to approve location for the Maison de l'Institut de France à Londres. October 16: Participates in consecration ceremony of Sacré-Cœur de Montmartre. November: Performs at Promenade Concerts in London.

1920   April 26: Marries Mathilde-Marie-Anne-Elisabeth de Montesquiou-Fezensac in Charchigné (Mayenne), in the chapel of Château de Hauteville. May 22: Attends cornerstone laying of Casa Velásquez, Madrid, and conducts at the French Festival. Publishes new edition of Organ Symphonies Opp. 13 and 42.

1921   February 10: Named director of American Conservatory at Fontainebleau. February 26: Inaugurates Maison de l'Institut de France à Londres. July 31: King Ferdinand I and Queen Marie of Romania, with one of their daughters, visit Widor at Saint-Sulpice for the Sunday Mass. September 7 and 9: Conducts and performs in Wiesbaden.

1922   Named "Officier" in the Legion of Honor. Becomes president of the Association of Choir Masters and Organists.

1923   December: Elected to the Royal Academy of Florence. Publishes *Initiation musicale*.

1924   August: Elected to Academy of Bologne. October 27: Premiere of *Nerto*, Paris Opéra.

1925   June 30: Premieres *Bach's Memento*, American Conservatory at Fontainebleau.

1926   November 16: Program of Widor's chamber music at Salle Érard.

1927   April 30: Gives lecture, "Beethoven, architecte." October 1: Retires from Paris Conservatory. Appointed to Council for Higher Education in the music section of the Conservatory. Publishes *Fondations, portraits, de Massenet à Paladilhe*.

1928 January 13: Premieres *Suite latine*, Op. 86, for inauguration of restored organ at La Madeleine, Paris. January 29: Inaugurates restored organ at the church of the Sorbonne. Publishes *L'orgue moderne: La décadence dans la facture contemporaine*. November 20: Attends inauguration ceremony for first completed part of Casa Velásquez. December: Undergoes successful operation to remove a cataract.

1929 February: Named "Commandeur" in the Legion of Honor.

1930 January 18: Celebrates sixty years of service at Saint-Sulpice; receives "Grande Médaille d'Or" from the City of Paris. June 4: Death of his brother, Paul Widor.

1931 April 26: Performs organ concert at Saint-Sulpice for Amis de l'orgue. November 5: Inaugurates organ at Saint-Ferdinand des Ternes, Paris.

1932 April 28–30: Represents Academy of Fine Arts at centennial of the founding of Brussels Conservatory. April 28–30: Records at Saint-Sulpice. June 10: Participates with Vierne in reinauguration of the Notre-Dame organ. July 31: Performs at Salzburg Cathedral. Travels to Madrid for inauguration of another portion of Casa Velásquez.

1933 May: Named "Grand-officier" in the Legion of Honor. October 12: Aunt Hélène Standish dies. November 18: Conducts orchestral Suite from *Les pêcheurs de Saint-Jean* at Concerts Pasdeloup, Paris. December 31: Retires from Saint-Sulpice.

1934 Publication of final work: *Trois nouvelles pièces*, Op. 87, for Organ. April 19: Conducts Third Symphony at Farewell Concert at Saint-Sulpice. May 9: Attends second Farewell Concert, Salle Érard. May 12: Retreats to Chantilly for much needed rest. July: Resigns as director of the American Conservatory; Ravel named general director. December 1: Reads final notice as perpetual secretary at the Institute.

1935 Named "Grand-officier" of the Belgian Order of the Crown. March 16: Appears at Hotel Majestic, Paris, to confer on Dupré the decoration of "Officier" in the Legion of Honor. March 27: Conducts Third Symphony, Op. 69, on a program of his works with the Symphony Orchestra of Brussels; Joseph Jongen conducts remaining works: *Sinfonia sacra*, with Charles Hens, organist; orchestral Suite from *Les pêcheurs de Saint-Jean*; three songs. May 15: Travels to Madrid for completion of Casa Velásquez. Returns to Chantilly for rest. July: Travels to Strasbourg to visit Schweitzer and Emil Rupp.

1936 November 20: Casa Velásquez bombarded in Spanish Civil War; Widor declares, "If the Casa is in ruin, we will rebuild it."

1937 March 12: Dies at home, 3 rue de Belloy, Paris. March 17: Funeral and interment at Saint-Sulpice.

1960 September 11: Madame Widor dies.

Abbreviations

A.B-A.	Archives de l'Académie des beaux-arts, Institut de France, Paris.
A.D.	Archives de la maison diocésaine, Paris.
A.N.	Archives nationales de France, Paris: Archives du Conservatoire AJ37.
A.N.(a)	Examen: Rapports des professeurs: AJ37 292–303.
A.N.(b)	Dossier individuel (Widor): AJ37 484.
A.N.(c)	Personnel: Candidatures et nominations AJ37 65.
A.S-S.	Archives de Saint-Saëns, Château-Musée de Dieppe, France (53 letters).
B.I.	Bibliothèque de l'Institut de France, Paris.
B.I.(a)	Correspondance de Widor (207 letters): Ms 4124.
B.I.(b)	Lettres autographes à Imbart de la Tour de Widor: Ms 4168.
B.I.(c)	Lettres autographes à Widor de Saint-Saëns (85 letters): Ms 4123
B.N.	Bibliothèque nationale de France, Paris.
B.N. Fonds Mont.	Fonds Montpensier (Widor). A file of 53 miscellaneous news clippings and programs not having complete bibliographic information.
B.N.(a)	Lettres autographes de Cavaillé-Coll (nos. 146–74 to Widor).
B.N.(b)	Lettres autographes à Lamoureux: W39.
B.N.(c)	Lettres autographes à Widor: L. A. Widor.
B.N.(d)	Lettres autographes de Widor (72 letters).
B.N.(e)	Nouvelles lettres autographes—Nouveau Fonds: N.L.A.
B.O.	Bibliothèque de l'Opéra, Paris, Dossier d'artiste (Widor).

B.T.	Bibliothèque Thiers, Paris, Fondation Dosne Thiers: Ms Thiers 680.
Family arch.	Documents held in the Family archive, l'Arbresle, Persanges, France.
M.S.	Maison Schweitzer, Gunsbach, France. Widor file.
N.E.C.	Harriet M. Spaulding Library, New England Conservatory of Music, Boston.
P.M.L.	Pierpont Morgan Library, Department of Music Manuscripts and Books, New York. Mary Flagler Cary Music Collection, MFC W641.X2.
R.B.I.	Riemenschneider Bach Institute, Baldwin-Wallace College, Berea, Ohio. Correspondence of Ch.-M. Widor and Albert Riemenschneider, 1905–34.
R.M.A.	Rouffach Municipal Archives, France.
S.M.L.	Sibley Music Library, Eastman School of Music, University of Rochester. Ruth T. Watanabe Special Collections. Letters of Ch.-M. Widor, 1880–1903 (59 letters; all letters cited are from Widor to Marie Trélat).

Notes

Preface

1. Wilson, "Organ Symphonies of Widor," 69. The quotation is found in Buhrman, "Music to Survive," 228.

2. Harding, *Saint-Saëns and His Circle*, xii.

3. Ibid.

4. Dupré, "En parlant de Ch.-M. Widor."

5. P.M.L. Widor letter to unknown addressee, December 4, 1914.

6. Documentation concerning this 103-page typed manuscript, dictated between 1935 and 1936, was transmitted in a letter dated December 30, 1971, to Gabrielle Guibaud, Widor's niece, from Madame Marcel Dupré, who eventually found the manuscript among her husband's papers after his death in May 1971. Madame Dupré wrote: "I remember the time when our friend Édouard Monet, cousin of the great painter [Claude Monet], deceased a long time ago, went to the Institute to write the memoirs of your illustrious uncle under his dictation. I also know that this work was interrupted after a certain time, Madame Widor being opposed to its publication. Mr. Monet had indeed given what he had written to my husband, and I promise you that I am going to make a search to try to find these pages. This will perhaps take some time." A separate cover, likely in the hand of Monet, specifies: "1. A complete reproduction of the notes taken, without corrections. It is on this text without any editing that the volume will be constructed. 2. Certain chapters remain that I must do myself, or reproduce certain articles." The translations used in the present work maintain, as much as possible, the spontaneous quality of the original, though in some cases they have had to be less literal. A photocopy of the original typescript was sent to the author on April 6, 1989, by Madame Marie-Ange Guibaud, grandniece of Charles-Marie Widor.

7. Lehman, "Charles-Marie Widor," 497.

8. Widor, Preface to *J. S. Bach: Le musicien-poète*, ix.

9. When giving them a piece of cake, he would say coaxingly, "Qu'est-ce qu'on dit? M e r r r r ... [ci / de?]."

Part One

1. Jacque, "Ch.-M. Widor."

2. This document and other information tracing the family lineage are found in the Family archive, l'Arbresle, France, hereafter referred to by the abbreviation "Family arch." The author is deeply indebted to Marie-Ange Guibaud (b. 1922), the grandniece of Charles-Marie Widor, for generous access to this collection over a period of many years. Complete birth, marriage, and death information for Jean-Baptiste Widor and Marie-Anne-Eve Frey, both of whom died in Rouffach, was provided by the R.M.A. in a letter to the author, April 27, 2009.

3. Meyer-Siat, *Les Callinet*, 27. Documentation from the R.M.A. identifies Jean Widor first as a wood worker, then an organ builder, and finally a supervisor with Rabiny-Callinet.

4. Recollections given by Widor to *L'Alsace Française* (October 25, 1924), cited in Louchart, "Charles-Marie Widor," 103. Sambre-et-Meuse was one of the most important armies during the French Revolution. Count Géza Zichy (1849–1924) directed the Budapest Opera.

5. Dupré, "M. Charles-Marie Widor," 1.

6. R.M.A. Letter to author, April 27, 2009.

7. Meyer-Siat, *Les Callinet*, 27.

8. Ibid., 57. This information is also transmitted in a letter of August 6, 1930, from Widor to Gustave Helbig. Helbig, "La grande pitié," 4:139. In the Archives municipales de Lyon, Registres paroissiaux et d'état civil (Lyon–2ème Arrondissement), Décès 1899, entry number 993 is François-Charles Widor.

9. R. Dumesnil, *Portraits de musiciens français*, 197.

10. Meyer-Siat, *Les Callinet*, 27. In a letter of February 11, 1931, Widor affirmed that Kienzl was his father's teacher and that he wrote masses and hymns. Kienzl had many pupils, including Jean-Baptiste Weckerlin (1821–1910) who was born in Guebwiller and later became librarian of the Paris Conservatory. Family arch.

11. Barthalay, "Notes." Jacques Simon Herz (1794–1880); Henri Herz (1803–88).

12. Meyer-Siat, *Les Callinet*, 27.

13. R. Dumesnil, *Portraits de musiciens français*, 197; Meyer-Siat, *Les Callinet*, 27.

14. Barthalay, "Notes"; http://orguesaintfrancois.free.fr/index.php/les-titulaires (accessed May 7, 2010). Charles-Marie Widor recalled, "My father . . . during part of his life brought his artistic gifts to the works of the organ builder Callinet, whose reputation had conquered the whole eastern region, and he played the instruments of the celebrated artisan on the occasion of their inauguration. It's thus that he inaugurated the *grand orgue* of Saint-François, of which he was to become the *titulaire*." Widor, "Souvenirs autobiographiques," 1–2.

15. Meyer-Siat, *Les Callinet*, 27; also Family arch.

16. *Revue et Gazette* 11 (1844): 369. Several works published in the 1850s by François-Charles Widor (identified only as Charles Widor on the covers) are preserved at B.N., and incorrectly catalogued with the works of his son Charles-Marie: *Sérénade pour piano*, Op. 6 (1852); *Chant de meunier pour piano*, Op. 12 (1859); *La voix du cœur pour piano*, Op. 13 (1856); *Aux Alpes pour piano*, Op. 17 (1859); *Petits anges pour piano*, Op. 18 (1859); *Souvenirs de Lyon (Barcarolle pour piano)*, no opus (1858). A Kyrie for mixed chorus and *Scherzo oriental* for piano are also preserved. The latter work appears to be the one attributed mistakenly to Charles-Marie Widor as "*L'Orientale*, Scherzo," Op. 8, in Arthur Pougin's 1880 supplement to Fétis's *Biographie universelle*.

17. *Ménestrel* 11 (1844): 3–4.

18. *Revue et Gazette* 19 (1852): 330.

19. *France Musicale* 24 (1860): 201–2.

20. *Revue et Gazette* 27 (1860): 169.

21. *Revue et Gazette* 27 (1860): 169; 28 (1861): 190–91; *France Musicale* 26 (1862): 15.

22. *Revue et Gazette* 30 (1863): 246.

23. *Ménestrel* 31 (1864): 54.

24. *Revue et Gazette* 31 (1864): 23.

25. *France Musicale* 25 (1861): 189.

26. *Le Plain-Chant* 2 (1861): 171.

27. *Ménestrel* 28 (1861): 231.

28. Rupp, *Ch.-M. Widor*, 6. The Mairie d'Annonay, Service Archives Documentation, confirmed Françoise-Elisabeth Peiron's date of birth in an email to the author, April 9, 2009. In the Archives municipales de Lyon, Registres paroissiaux et d'état civil (Lyon–2ème Arrondissement), Décès 1883, entry number 936 is Peiron's death certificate; it is signed by her son Ch.-M. Widor and her son-in-law, Eugène Pierron (August 23, 1842–May 24, 1906). Upon Madame Widor's death, the considerable proceeds of her estate (101,438 francs) were divided between her husband and their three children. Family arch.

29. Family arch. Thomas, "Organ Loft Whisperings" (November 29, 1893): 19.

30. Rupp, *Ch.-M. Widor*, 6. The Peiron genealogy was researched back to 1574 and documented in 1896 by E. Nicod, librarian of Annonay; Family arch. Widor's recollections were anecdotal: "Born in Rouffach, the son of an organ builder and destined to build organs, my father preferred to play them. An excellent musician, called to Lyon to play an instrument that came out of the workshops in Rouffach, he was greatly appreciated there; he moved there and married there. My mother, from Annonay (Cévennes) was related to the Seguins, inventors of the steam boiler, and to the Montgolfiers, creators of aeronautics." Recollections given by Widor to *L'Alsace Française* (October 25, 1924), cited in Louchart, "Charles-Marie Widor," 103.

31. Fétis, *Biographie universelle*, Supplément, 2:669.

32. Landormy, "Widor," 3564.

33. Archives municipales de Lyon, Registres paroissiaux et d'état civil (Lyon–2ème Arrondissement), Décès 1883, entry number 936.

34. B.I. In 1934 Widor told Jean Pédron, "very exactly," that his birthday was February 22. Pédron, "Charles Widor."

35. Bret, "Symphonies pour orgue," 13.

36. Family arch.

37. Near, "Letters"; the author found and photographed this document in 1983.

38. Widor, "Souvenirs autobiographiques," 1. Widor's birth certificate gives his birthplace as 19 rue Sala, which is the cross street with the former rue de Bourbon.

39. Marie Widor's marriage to Eugène Pierron, on December 19, 1878, produced two children: Gabrielle "Gaby" (1880–1979; married Louis Guibaud) and Marguerite "Guite" (1882–1937; married Jean Reynard). The eighth and youngest child of Gabrielle and Louis Guibaud is Marie-Ange Guibaud.

40. Dupré, "M. Charles-Marie Widor," 1.

41. *Courrier de Lyon* 49 (December 18, 1880): 1.

42. Gavoty, *Louis Vierne*, 67; *Dictionnaire de lyonnaiseries*, Lyon, 1932.

43. *Salut Public* 33 (December 18, 1880): 2; *Salut Public* (December 19, 1880): 2.

44. http://orguesaintfrancois.free.fr/index.php/les-titulaires.

45. Dupré, "M. Charles-Marie Widor," 1.

46. Boschot, *Charles-Marie Widor*, 5; Malherbe, "Charles-Marie Widor."

47. Vierne, "Ch.-M. Widor," 75.

48. "As for the organ of the school where I studied up through my baccalaureate, I played it Sundays, mass and vespers. It was also by Callinet (of Rouffach) where my grandfather directed the work." Letter dated August 8, 1930, to Gustave Helbig, Helbig, "La grande pitié," 2:73. As of 1930, this sixteen-stop instrument built in 1847 was in Saint-Chef, Isère.

49. Widor, "Souvenirs autobiographiques," 2. Typical of the "Souvenirs," Widor loved to embellish details of which he had unbounded knowledge; he continued to describe the school: "Today this beautiful chapel has been converted into a gymnastics room. The old Collège des Jésuites, which raised its architecture on the banks of the Rhône

opposite the quai Saint-Clair, contained a magnificent library. The room still exists. One can see in it a globe of ten feet in height that also has a story: witness to the siege of Lyon, the globe received in the middle of its Pacific Ocean the blow of a shell fired by the artillery of Canteloube, which had established its positions on the Croix-Rousse and sprayed Lyon [with artillery fire]. The other hemisphere, on which one could see perfectly designed the sources of the Nile, Ethiopia, and the great discoveries of Stanley, remained intact" (2).

50. *L'Orgue* 164 (1977): 74–75.

51. M. Dumesnil, "Widor," 143.

52. Douglass, *Cavaillé-Coll*, 363.

53. Dupré, "M. Charles-Marie Widor," 1.

54. Dupré, "Souvenirs sur Ch.-M. Widor," 28. There has been some disagreement as to when Guilmant studied with Lemmens. From Dupré's recollection of what Widor told him, it would have been before 1858; and a report in 1861 would seem to confirm it: "At twenty years old [1857] he [Guilmant] met Mr. Lemmens, the famous Belgian organist. The latter adopted him as a student." P. Bernard, "Alexandre Guilmant," 389. However, Fétis's *Biographie universelle* (1878 Supplement, 433) states that Guilmant studied with Lemmens in 1860; a recent source also maintains that Guilmant had "lessons taken for one month with J. Lemmens in 1860." Vanmackelberg, "Alexandre Guilmant," 152. Kurt Lueders has finally confirmed that Guilmant was in Brussels between March and July 1860. Lueders, "Alexandre Guilmant," 55–61. Widor simply recalled, "It's to Lemmens that the young Guilmant came one fine day to seek the holy tradition. Some years later, I followed his example." Widor, "La classe d'orgue," 238.

55. Boschot, *Charles-Marie Widor*, 5.

56. Family arch. This diploma carries the correct date of Widor's birth and confirms the date of his graduation, which has also long been in dispute: Louis Vierne affirmed that Widor received his Baccalauréat at age fifteen [1859]. Vierne, "Ch.-M. Widor," 75. Another usually reliable source—although it incorrectly gives his date of birth as 1845—states that he graduated at age seventeen, which yields the correct date of 1862, though from the wrong date of birth. Rupp, *Ch.-M. Widor*, 6.

57. Widor, "Souvenirs autobiographiques," 2–3.

58. Jurine, *Joseph Merklin*, 3:42.

59. At this time, Cavaillé-Coll was endeavoring to get Lemmens to move to Paris to take the position of organist at Saint-Sulpice.

60. Dufourcq, "Lemmens et Cavaillé-Coll," 58–59 (1951): 60.

61. Ibid., 60 (1951): 85–86.

62. Vierne, "Ch.-M. Widor," 75. Born into a family of musicians, Fétis had studied piano and harmony at the Paris Conservatory, and later taught composition and was librarian there.

63. Widor, "Richard Wagner à Paris," 2.

64. Widor, *L'orgue moderne*, 12.

65. Widor, "Notes sur Lemmens," 2.

66. Guilmant, "La musique d'orgue," 1155.

67. Widor, "La classe d'orgue," 238.

68. Kooiman, "French Bach Tradition," 62.

69. Dupré, *Méthode d'orgue*, 74.

70. Ochse, *Organists and Organ Playing*, 176. Ewald Kooiman described Fétis as an "unbelievably prolific publicist." Kooiman, "French Bach Tradition," 56.

71. Widor, Preface to *L'esthétique de l'orgue*, ix.

72. Widor, Preface to *J. S. Bach*, xi.

73. Cited in Ochse, *Organists and Organ Playing*, 261 n. 11.

74. Fétis, "Lemmens, Jacques-Nicolas," 267. Widor perpetuated this story: "The clarity, grandeur, and simplicity of Lemmens's playing have provided us the example that we owe ourselves to transmit to our descendants. . . . This example of clarity—it's Lemmens who has given it to us. With him it was a gift so remarkable that at the end of a year of study in Germany, Hesse wrote to Brussels that 'he had nothing more to teach Mr. Lemmens.'" Widor, "Souvenirs autobiographiques," 5–6.

75. Kooiman, "French Bach Tradition," 58. Hesse wrote, in part: "As I can in no way see my judgments ridiculed without reacting, I want here to restore the truth: I never gave such a letter to Mr. Lemmens." Cited in Ferrard, "La 'sainte tradition,'" 49.

76. Ferrard, "La 'sainte tradition,'" 47, 50. Again, Widor certainly knew nothing of this, always affirming the transmission of the Bach tradition from Hesse to Lemmens: "[Lemmens] had been in his youth the most brilliant student of the new Conservatory of Brussels, which dated from 1830. Endowed with a State scholarship for having achieved his musical studies and carried off all the *prix de virtuosité*—his organ competition had been sensational—he went to Germany to study with the most prestigious master in organ technique and the traditions of J. S. Bach; I have described Hesse, the famous master of Breslau, who himself had known the sons of Johann Bach." Widor, "Souvenirs autobiographiques," 5. It would have been impossible for Hesse to have known any of Bach's sons; Widor is certainly speaking figuratively here, meaning the "musical descendants" of Bach.

77. Quoted in Ferrard, "La 'sainte tradition,'" 49.

78. A portion of this letter, owned by the late Lowell Lacey, is quoted in Soderlund, *How Did They Play?*, 516. The letter goes on to say: "I must tell you also that I have massacred Mr. Hesse rather without pity at the piano. One must know that he is also the first pianist of Breslau. One Sunday we went together to a piano maker, the best in this city. There, naturally, I had Mr. Hesse play first. After he had played, thin and poorly as a child would play, I fell on this poor piano like a lion and overwhelmed Mr. Hesse as well as the maker and the other people who were there."

79. Kooiman, "French Bach Tradition," 63.

80. Widor, "Notes sur Lemmens," 2.

81. Ochse, *Organists and Organ Playing*, 177–78; Kooiman, "French Bach Tradition," 63.

82. Kooiman, "French Bach Tradition," 63.

83. Ferrard, "La 'sainte tradition,'" 47.

84. Widor, Preface to *Les Couperin*, v.

85. Ibid.

86. Ibid., vi. Widor especially singled out the following composers as harpsichordists composing intelligently for the organ: Nicolas Gigault (1627–1707), François Roberday (1624–80), Nicolas-Antoine Lebègue (1631–1702), Nicolas de Grigny (1672–1703), François Couperin (1668–1733), Louis-Nicolas Clérambault (1676–1749), André Raison (1645–1719), Pierre du Mage (1674–1751), and Louis Marchand (1669–1732).

87. Ibid., v.

88. Ibid., viii.

89. Widor, Preface to *Les maîtres français*, [ii].

90. Widor, Preface to *Les Couperin*, viii.

91. Douglass, *Cavaillé-Coll*, 1.

92. Widor, Preface to *Notes historiques*, 6.

93. Widor, "Les orgues de Saint-Sulpice," 126.

94. Ibid.
95. Cheronnet, *L'église Saint-Sulpice*, 12.
96. Raugel, *Les grandes orgues*, 146.
97. Widor, "Les orgues de Saint-Sulpice," 126.
98. Douglass, *Cavaillé-Coll*, 1.
99. Wallace, *Letters of Felix Mendelssohn-Bartholdy*, 335.
100. *Revue et Gazette* 1 (1834): 197.
101. *Revue et Gazette* 5 (1838): 430.
102. Sumner, "The French Organ School," 285.
103. Widor wrote of Boëly in the preface to his edition of Mendelssohn: *Œuvres d'orgue*. "A strange thing in France, the imitation of Mendelssohn was more modest [than elsewhere]. It is true that organ study was quite neglected and the publications for the instrument very rare; from 1830 to 1860 Paris barely counted but one representative of the classical art, Alexandre-Pierre-François Boëly, organist of Saint-Germain-l'Auxerrois. Esteemed by a small number and not at all popular, his conscientious and cold compositions attracted [only] a few amateurs from time to time." Widor, "Felix Mendelssohn-Bartholdy," 5.
104. Cellier and Bachelin, *L'orgue*, 181. Always ready to share an anecdote, Widor enjoyed relating an amusing incident concerning Boëly and Giacomo Meyerbeer (1791–1864) that had been related to him by Emmanuel Vaucorbeil (1821–84), the director of the Opéra:

> Old Boëly, organist of Saint-Germain-l'Auxerrois, one day invited Vaucorbeil to come and hear him play a recently completed sonata at the end of the Office: "You won't at all regret your afternoon," [Boëly] told him.
> The piece was quite interesting, it seems, and interpreted with all the conviction of a pure soul.
> The two were returning to the boulevard when, at the detour of the rue de Richelieu, they found themselves nose to nose with Meyerbeer: "Hello there, Monsieur Boëly," said the author of *Les Huguenots*, "what a cheerful look you have!" —"It's quite natural, Monsieur Meyerbeer, I just heard some very beautiful music, very magnificently performed." —"Oh! And by whom is this music, Monsieur Boëly?" —"By me, Monsieur Meyerbeer." —"And who played this music, Monsieur Boëly?" —"I did, Monsieur Meyerbeer," —"Ah! How I regret that you didn't invite me! It's unkind for one to forget his friends, it's truly very unkind, my dear Monsieur Boëly; I am very irritated with you. Well, I am going to take my vengeance: this evening we have the first full rehearsal of *Pardon de Ploërmel*; do me the kindness of coming to listen to it; here is my card" —"Are you thinking, Monsieur Meyerbeer, to ruin my day! You don't know how theater music is an inferior art! Thank you for the offer, but keep your card, and good health to you!"
> "It's really unfortunate," [Boëly] continued to say to Vaucorbeil, "that this man persists in writing for the stage; he will be lost there." Widor, "Les Troyens," 2.

105. Widor related that Ambroise Thomas (1811–96) told him about his visit with Boëly at Saint-Germain-l'Auxerrois soon after receiving his first prize in organ at the Conservatory (Thomas actually received a first prize in piano in 1829):

> —"So! You have obtained the first prize; do you know how to play?" —"Oh! Mr. Boëly!" —"There's no 'Mr. Boëly'; sit on this bench and show me what you can do during the sortie of the mass." Thomas started a Bach prelude. —"Ah! But that's very good. Ah! So it's true that you can play the organ! Then one works seriously at

the Conservatory? Go pay my compliments to your professor. Come here whenever you wish; you are my friend." Fromageot, *Pierre-François Boëly*, 3.

106. Cellier and Bachelin, *L'orgue*, 180. Boëly's tenure at Saint-Germain-l'Auxerrois lasted only eleven years, from August 1840 to October 1851.

107. *Revue et Gazette* 11 (1844): 232.

108. Ibid., 231.

109. *France Musicale* 7 (1844): 197. The review continued, "he is the king of the pedals; for him, the hands are only accessories."

110. Douglass, *Cavaillé-Coll*, 36–37.

111. Ibid., 70.

112. Ibid., 108.

113. Cellier and Bachelin, *L'orgue*, 183.

114. Pearce, "Alex. Guilmant," 211.

115. *Revue et Gazette* 12 (1845): 232.

116. Cellier and Bachelin, *L'orgue*, 183.

117. Douglass, *Cavaillé-Coll*, 82.

118. Monter, "Lefébure-Wély," 11.

119. Prosper-Charles Simon (1788–1866) became organist of Saint-Denis Cathedral in 1840.

120. Eloi-Nicolas-Marie Miroir (1746–1815), organist of Saint-Germain-des-Prés, Paris.

121. Fétis, "L'orgue mondaine," 105–6.

122. Dufourcq, "Lemmens et Cavaillé-Coll," 55 (1950): 44.

123. Douglass, *Cavaillé-Coll*, 76–77. One prominent French organist did not agree with this assessment of Lemmens, however; purportedly, "Saint-Saëns could not bear the great Belgian master." Huré, "Eugène Gigout," 6.

124. Douglass, *Cavaillé-Coll*, 276.

125. d'Ortigue, *Musique à l'église*, 181, 185.

126. Douglass, *Cavaillé-Coll*, 315.

127. C. Cavaillé-Coll and E. Cavaillé-Coll, *Aristide Cavaillé-Coll*, 92.

128. Widor, *L'orgue moderne*, 11.

129. *Revue et Gazette* 21 (1854): 175.

130. Douglass, *Cavaillé-Coll*, 102.

131. Dufourcq, "Lemmens et Cavaillé-Coll," 65 (1952): 112. The four pupils to whom Lemmens referred were: Clément Loret (1833–1909), St. Louis-d'Antin; Auguste Andlauer (1845–89), Notre-Dame-des-Champs; Guilmant, La Trinité; and Widor, Saint-Sulpice.

132. Widor, "Notes sur Lemmens," 2.

133. Widor, *L'orgue moderne*, 11.

134. Ibid., 6–7.

135. Douglass, *Cavaillé-Coll*, 76.

136. Dufourcq, "Lemmens et Cavaillé-Coll," 58–59 (1951): 58.

137. Widor, "Souvenirs autobiographiques," 6. Lemmens's wife, Helen Sherrington was greatly sought after as a singer. At the time of this recollection, Widor reported that one of the daughters, likely Ella, was residing in Mechlin, Belgium, and the other was a nun in Africa.

138. Ibid., 4.

139. Ibid., 3. Widor wrote further: "Fétis, after having been professor of composition at the Paris Conservatory, was called to the directorship of the new Brussels Conservatory.

A musicologist of the first order (all musicians know his remarkable *Dictionnaire des musiciens* [*Biographie universelle des musiciens et bibliographie générale de la musique*]), and he collaborated at the same time on the *Gazette Musicale*. You can get an idea of the authority and reputation that he brought to this unrivalled publication from the teaching of his conservatory" (6).

140. Lehman, "Charles-Marie Widor," 494.

141. Widor, Preface to *L'orgue de Jean-Sébastien Bach*, xiv.

142. Valbelle, "Quelques souvenirs," 1.

143. "La mort du maître Ch. M. Widor," *La Semaine Religieuse de Paris* (March 27, 1937): 429; see also Curzon, "Charles-Marie Widor," 1.

144. Widor, "Notes sur Lemmens," 2.

145. Boschot, *Charles-Marie Widor*, 5–6. Bach had been Widor's daily bread since childhood; at the age of ninety-one, he boasted that he still had his first Bach volumes: "At the age of six or seven, I came to grips with the music of Bach for the first time; I still have in my library the editions of Naegeli, Bâle, . . . Richault." Widor, "Souvenirs autobiographiques," 27.

146. Widor, "Souvenirs autobiographiques," 3. Widor used the word "nursery" quite accurately. At that time, César Thomson [Thompson in "Souvenirs"] (1857–1931)—a pupil of Hubert Léonard (1819–90) and Henri Vieuxtemps (1820–81)—was but a lad of six, and Eugène Ysaÿe (1858–1931)—a pupil of Vieuxtemps—was little more than an infant, not yet aged five.

147. Ibid., 4. Charles-Auguste de Bériot (1802–70), a composer, famous violin virtuoso, and later professor at the Brussels Conservatory, toured Europe with Mme Felicità García-Malibran (1808–36) in the years 1830–35; she, the daughter of the eminent tenor and singing teacher Manuel del Popolo Vicente García (1775–1832), was considered one of the greatest singers of the nineteenth century. When her first husband, Malibran, went bankrupt, she divorced him and in 1836 married de Bériot, with whom she had been living since 1830; the marriage was very short lived, however, as she died from singing too soon after having been thrown and dragged by a horse. Her younger sister, Pauline Viardot-García (1821–1910), was a famous mezzo-soprano and singing teacher. Peter [Pierre-Léonard] Benoît (1834–1901) was a prolific Flemish composer and writer.

148. Ibid., 4. Widor continued, "Hadn't I put my hands on the same keyboards some months before,'full of confidence in myself and happy to show Lemmens the progress that I had made in his absence? He had accompanied his wife, an excellent singer, to London, where her contracts sometimes called her to sing at Covent Garden. I profited from these days, working hard at a stretch to play the little fugue in C minor of Bach. Although always seeking more perfection, I felt satisfied in my effort and I waited impatiently for the master's return, eager to play for him my fugue. 'It's worthless,' he exclaimed to his dismayed pupil. 'No rhythm, no will, no breath.' Lemmens wanted to hear all the notes, such as the composer had heard them himself. He had an admirable sense of rhythm and grandeur" (4–5).

149. Raugel, "Widor, Charles-Marie," 398.

Part Two

1. When Widor retired in 1934, two pedal stops that he had always wanted were added, bringing the total number of speaking stops to 102 and the pipe count to 6,706. Sources varied as to the number of pumpers. A. M. Henderson queried Widor about the draw

stops marked "sonnette haut" and "sonnette bas": "That's for the blowers, to tell them to start," replied Widor. —"Not human beings?" —"Well yes, why not?" And at the end of the service, Henderson said four perspiring men appeared. Henderson, "Memories of Widor," 659. Frederic Stiven reported that one blowing apparatus on the main floor required five men, and another on a level twenty-five feet higher required two more men. Stiven, *Organ Lofts of Paris*, 55. Daniel Roth, the current *titulaire* at Saint-Sulpice, affirms that the number was five: three on the lower level and two on the upper level. Email to author, February 26, 2009. An electric blower became the wind source in 1922.

2. Hamel, *Saint-Sulpice*, 374.

3. *Revue et Gazette* 30 (1863): 246.

4. Dufourcq, "Lemmens et Cavaillé-Coll," 60 (1951): 86–87. What constituted Widor's "Sonate" is unknown today, although it is quite possible that he appropriated or revised part of it for inclusion in the Op. 13 Symphonies for Organ. Throughout his life, Widor was reluctant to discard an idea. As will be seen, he repeatedly reviewed his works, if not to effect a major revision, at least to adjust a few minor details. He never hesitated to revise his music, and this often led to multiple published versions of a work.

5. Jurine, *Joseph Merklin*, 3:44. The "sonata manuscript" referred to in the letter was likely the unknown work from which he played a movement on his Saint-Sulpice program the preceding July.

6. Widor, "Souvenirs autobiographiques," 18.

7. Jurine, *Joseph Merklin*, 3:44. The cause of such belated disparagement of Widor can likely be attributed to Merklin's controversial use of electricity in his organs, specifically for the playing action, beginning in 1884. Although Merklin thought he had found the wave of the future in electric action, Widor was an outspoken critic of it and remained a staunch supporter of Cavaillé-Coll and mechanical action. When brother Paul Widor's criticisms of Merklin's electric-action instrument in the Église Saint-Nizier in Lyon were invoked against him during a contentious pamphlet war (1:247–50), Merklin may certainly have suspected collusion between the brothers, and in any case he knew exactly where the organist of Saint-Sulpice stood on the issue of electricity in organ building. His letter denouncing Widor to the parish council of Notre-Dame de Valenciennes came at an important moment of decision; the council had before it Merklin's proposal for a new instrument. Whatever role the letter played, the church ordered a four-manual, fifty-three-stop electric-action organ from the Merklin firm the next day (1:250).

8. *Revue et Gazette* 31 (1864): 23; also *France Musicale* 28 (January 17, 1864): 18.

9. Dufourcq, "Lemmens et Cavaillé-Coll," 62 (1952): 22.

10. Widor, "Souvenirs autobiographiques," 6–7. *L'Africaine* was produced at the Paris Opéra in 1865, the year after Meyerbeer's death.

11. Boschot, *Charles-Marie Widor*, 6.

12. Widor, "Virtuoses célèbres," 1–2.

13. *Revue et Gazette* 32 (1865): 151.

14. Widor, "Souvenirs autobiographiques," 7. Widor continued, "It would be too long and sometimes without interest to recall here each of these trips. Their great number will lend itself, on the other hand, to a simple list that I will give later in an appendix." He never did this, as his "Souvenirs autobiographiques" were not completed.

15. One later such occasion occurred on June 10, 1891; Cavaillé-Coll wrote to Widor: "We just finished the rebuilding, or rather the restoration, of the Ste-Clotilde organ that we built thirty years ago. The curé has given me an appointment for Wednesday, the 10th, at 1:00 at the church, for the work to be appraised by Mr. [Gabriel] Pierné [1863–1937; organist] and Mr. [Samuel] Rousseau [1853–1904; choirmaster]. I hope

on my behalf that you will be willing to assist us in this little exam, if you are free. I also asked [Eugène] Gigout [1844–1925] to join us. I would be very glad for you to be able to test this organ, which is one of the best instruments that we have built. Therefore I'm counting on you, if possible, even though this makes a very small committee." B.N.(a), letter 166, dated June 8, 1891. On another important occasion, Cavaillé-Coll brought Widor and Gigout together to demonstrate his instruments for representatives from the Vatican, when a monumental project was under consideration for Saint-Peter's Basilica. *Musica Sacra* 10 (1887): 16.

16. Ochse, *Organists and Organ Playing*, 86.

17. *Ménestrel* 37 (1870): 120, 135–36.

18. L. Compagnon, "L'orgue de l'Hôtel-Dieu de Vitry-le-François," *Musica Sacra* 5 (1879): 131.

19. Ibid.

20. Dupré, "M. Charles-Marie Widor," 1.

21. Widor, "Souvenirs autobiographiques," 7–8.

22. Family arch.; *Revue et Gazette* 33 (1866): 102.

23. *Revue et Gazette* 32 (1865): 337.

24. Dufourcq, "Lemmens et Cavaillé-Coll," 64 (1952): 88.

25. Ibid., 62 (1952): 25.

26. Ibid., 65 (1952): 111; 67 (1953): 59–61; 68 (1953): 85.

27. *Organ* 1 (1893): 269.

28. Widor, "Souvenirs autobiographiques," 8. On July 3, 1866, the Austro-Prussian War (Seven Weeks' War) was decided in favor of Prussia in the Battle of Sadowa (Königgrätz), a small Bohemian village; some forty-four thousand Austrian troops and nine thousand Prussian troops perished.

29. Raugel, *Les grandes orgues*, 264.

30. Widor, "Souvenirs autobiographiques," 10–11; Widor related this story in exactly the same way in Widor, *L'orgue de la Sorbonne*, 3–4. Dupré also narrated the story, but the details are slightly more specific and likely reflect what Widor had related to him orally:

> Mr. Cavaillé-Coll, who went Sundays to hear Widor at Saint-Sulpice, found the works of the young master a little daring. "It will be expedient," he said to him, "that I accompany you to Rossini's home. He will certainly have the same impression as I." Widor had to comply one day and play the Finale of his Second Symphony for organ on a pitiful upright piano. Charitably, Rossini took charge of the pedal part, then turning towards Cavaillé-Coll: "But no, this piece is very interesting and pleasing to me. Carry on, young man." Widor, in going down the stairs with the famous builder, took care not to rub in this unhoped-for success. Dupré, "Souvenirs sur Ch.-M. Widor," 30.

The story is quaint; one can easily picture the aged and corpulent Rossini huddled next to Widor on the same piano bench, Cavaillé-Coll keenly awaiting the patriarch's verdict. But while there is certainly truth to Dupré's account, there is also a problem: Rossini died in November 1868, more than three years before Widor's Symphonies were published, and well over a year before Widor became the organist of Saint-Sulpice. Although the title of the work was not specified by Widor in his telling of the incident, other accounts of this occasion agree that the piece Rossini delighted in was the Finale to the Second Symphony (M. Dumesnil, "Widor," 143; Dupré, "M. Charles-Marie Widor," 2); nonetheless, it could not have been known as such at the time, nor could Cavaillé-Coll have heard Widor play it at a Saint-Sulpice service. Any number of explanations could account for the above narrative. One explanation might be that the work eventually known as the Finale to the Second Symphony was one of those early compositions that Widor later included in the Second; it does quite closely mirror the style of Lemmens (the *Fanfare* in D Major, for example). In that case, perhaps Cavaillé-Coll did hear Widor perform the work somewhere, and perhaps Widor did play it with Rossini.

One other piece of evidence is found in a newspaper notice ("Des anecdotes sur Rossini") announcing a new biography of Rossini by Giuseppe Radiciotti [published 1927–29]. The clipping, from an unknown source and dating from about 1928, had been saved by Widor. In it, the writer related how Widor had told him that Cavaillé-Coll took him to meet Rossini when he was fourteen and that Rossini had taken a liking to him and invited him to visit from time to time: "One time, [Widor] heard Rossini comment on the countryside, where he always went without enthusiasm: 'Yes, the countryside is very nice, but I like it with a sidewalk, a gaslight and a policeman.' One day at the home of the famous musician, the 'petit Widor' played one of his early compositions. 'Bravo!' exclaimed Rossini, 'there's will and rhythm in it. Continue on!'" Family arch.

31. *Revue et Gazette* 33 (1866): 102. After Lefébure-Wély's demonstration, he offered the bench to Liszt, who replied humbly that "he only permitted himself to play village organs." *Ménestrel* 33 (1866): 142.

32. *Ménestrel* 33 (1866): 166. The review noted, "The different compositions performed by Mr. Franck, conceived in a very strict style which did not, however, exclude variety, lent themselves marvelously to the numerous resources of the organ of Sainte-Clotilde. . . . Abbé Liszt, in honor of whom this performance was given, warmly complimented Mr. Franck on the elevated style of his works and his authoritative performance."

33. Widor, *Initiation musicale*, 126.

34. Opus 8 has been problematic since at least 1880; as mentioned earlier, some of François-Charles Widor's works—he being identified only as "Ch. Widor" on the editions of his music—have been falsely attributed to his son, and it seems that his *Scherzo oriental*, Op. 8, has sometimes been wrongly identified as his son's Opus 8.

35. Dupré, "M. Charles-Marie Widor," 1. Widor had quite a reputation for relating anecdotes from his abundant experience, and Dupré followed the same tradition, undoubtedly in the spirit of his *maître*. As one of Widor's most important pupils and, later, closest associates—Dupré became Widor's assistant at Saint-Sulpice in 1906 and eventually succeeded him in 1934—he certainly heard Widor recount many fascinating incidents; but in their retelling, Dupré's own tendency to color a narrative may have entered in, especially if his memory was a bit vague. His re-narrations have not always proven to be completely accurate. See note 30.

36. *Ménestrel* 34 (1867): 183.

37. Dupré, "En parlant de Ch.-M. Widor."

38. Dupré, "M. Charles-Marie Widor," 1. An obituary of Widor repeated the notion that he had composed the concerto as a mere child: "The precocity of the young Charles-Marie was such that, as early as the age of eleven, he was named the sole organist of the Lycée de Lyon and he composed a Concerto for piano and orchestra, the slow movement of which was to make up, with all the necessary modifications, the Andante of the Fourth Symphony." Malherbe, "Charles-Marie Widor."

39. See the author's critical edition of Widor's Symphonies for a complete history of their composition, revision, and publication: *Charles-Marie Widor: The Symphonies for Organ*, 11: xi–xvii.

40. Imbert, *Portraits et études*, 38.

41. *Ménestrel* 37 (1870): 135–36.

42. Douglass, *Cavaillé-Coll*, 276. This revealing statement indicates that, at least in Cavaillé-Coll's opinion, some traditional organ music was inappropriate for church use.

43. *Ménestrel* 34 (1867): 192. Also popular as salon pieces, Widor performed some of the Duos with Albert Lavignac (1846–1916) at a reception for the Comte de Nieuwerkerke. *Ménestrel* 36 (1869): 127. Today it is hard to imagine that the harmonium ever had a high profile among instruments. Indeed, *The New Grove Dictionary of Music and Musicians* devotes only three slim paragraphs to this ingenious instrument—initially little more than an expansion of the accordion. Yet, in its heyday the harmonium enjoyed considerable popularity in the salons of French high society and, because of its highly expressive organlike character and modest price, in the newly emerging post-Revolution Catholic Church. Lueders, "A Captivating Repertoire," 7. Alexandre Debain, a French piano builder who excelled in mechanics and cabinetry, claimed a series of patents for an "orgue-expressif" that he later called "harmonium." Dieterlen, "The Harmonium," 3. His instruments usually contained four sets of reeds, divided mid-keyboard and controlled by eight stops. At the 1867 Universal Exposition in Paris, daily concerts were given on Debain's refined harmoniums, which capably evoked the most "delicious effects," to quote a contemporary review. *Ménestrel* 34 (1867): 192.

In spite of a period of favor, original music for solo harmonium is not plentiful. Berlioz, reportedly moved to tears by the harmonium playing of Sigismund Thalberg (1812–71), composed three pieces (his only keyboard works) for the instrument in 1845. Pilling, "Harmonium and American Organ," 814–15. Among the most notable contributors of original solo literature were Guilmant, Franck, and the Vierne brothers (Louis [1870–1937] and René [1876–1918]); the latter's harmonium works specify the more marketable "orgue ou harmonium" in their titles. Most of the solo repertory appears to have been made up of arrangements. Perhaps more interesting are concerted works in which the harmonium was a part—the Duos for piano and harmonium by Saint-Saëns and Widor being especially notable. A few non-French composers also showed interest in the instrument. To name but a few, Dvořák composed his Bagatelles, Op. 47, for Harmonium and String Quartet; later, Mahler used it in the Eighth Symphony and Strauss in *Ariadne auf Naxos*. Essentially, though, the harmonium had its currency in nineteenth-century France. That the instrument also found utility in poor rural French parishes cannot have helped its image. Michel Dieterlen bemoaned the eventual status of the harmonium in these words: "Today the harmonium is mostly found lying dormant, like a recumbent tombstone figure, in church sanctuaries—a drab fate indeed for an instrument that so greatly captivated the 19th century." Dieterlen, "The Harmonium," 2.

44. Widor, "Souvenirs autobiographiques," 18–19. Widor continued: "As I drew his attention one day to the fact that it was quite simply the theory of the ancients that he was reviving, that all the ancient theaters have a rectangular stage, he replied to me with the charming naiveté of the plain and good man that he was: 'I didn't know that the ancients had so much experience!' The remark was charming."

45. Rupp, *Ch.-M. Widor*, 8–9.

46. Widor, "Souvenirs autobiographiques," 8–9. The autograph manuscript of the Duos came up for sale in January 2009; the asking price was thirteen thousand euros! Les Autographes, 45 rue de l'Abbé Grégoire, Paris, sales catalogue no. 127 "Orgue," item 261.

47. *Revue et Gazette* 35 (1868): 366.

48. Widor, "Souvenirs autobiographiques," 27.

49. Widor struck the deal with Maho in a letter written from Lyon dated May 16, 1868:

As a conclusion is necessary for everything, and as I don't want to condemn you to a correspondence without result, I give you my Quintet, and furthermore I pledge, in consideration of the sum of *six-hundred* francs, to buy twenty-five copies of it the day the first edition appears.

Is this matter concluded?

You will be able to have my manuscript in a week or so.

I put myself completely at your service for [proofreading] this edition. . . .

B.N.(e), N.L.A., 12.

50. *Revue et Gazette* 35 (1868): 392.

51. Sabatier, "Widor (Charles-Marie)," 12788.

52. *Revue et Gazette* 35 (1868): 85.

53. Widor, "Souvenirs autobiographiques," 9–10. That Gounod continued to have utmost confidence in Widor is evidenced in a letter in which he affirmed that one of the conditions under which he would approve a performance of his motet *Gallia* was "with you at the organ." B.I.(a), letter 88, dated May 2, 1881.

It appears that a similar request from Gounod brought on an ugly incident between Widor and Louis Bruneau (1822–92), founder of the International Society of Composers. In a letter to Widor, Gounod attempted to appease both sides. Reporting to Widor that Bruneau "is resolved to call upon another organist, and that he suspects on your part some malcontent with the season's programs on which your name doesn't appear," Gounod concluded in exasperation: "My God! how it's difficult to please one's fellow man! It would be, however, so simple with a little good will! A thousand regrets then, and all my best to you. —Ch. Gounod" B.I.(a), letter 90, dated March 10, 1884.

54. *Revue et Gazette* 35 (1868): 94.

55. *Revue et Gazette* 35 (1868): 157. Widor once described Saint-Saëns's gifts as a pianist: "Precision as writer, precision as virtuoso. Saint-Saëns had stout, short hands; one scarcely saw the knuckles of those marvelous fingers moving, always in contact with the keyboard. 'Thundering execution,' said Berlioz? The epithet could apply to Liszt, but not to Saint-Saëns, not to his always well-considered mastery. If it is true, as Baudelaire said, that fragrance and sound respond to each other, from Mozart played by him [Saint-Saëns] emanated the fragrance of violet; Beethoven under his fingers had an expressive intensity, and Liszt a sparkling one. He was not from the big and 'noisy' school of bangers. He handled the instrument considerately, and this very reserve, which did not drain away the sonority, evoked an impression of rare quality for the listener. Saint-Saëns was content to move the listener by the charm of rhythm, the absolute consciousness of chronometric values, and the nobility of style. *It's Truth that one heard.*" Widor, *Fondations, portraits*, 156–57.

56. *Revue et Gazette* 35 (1868): 175.

57. *Revue et Gazette* 36 (1869): 101.

58. Ibid.

59. Widor, "Souvenirs autobiographiques," 15. Elsewhere, Widor was quoted as saying, "The themes, the developments, the execution were equally admirable: he never wrote better!" Raugel, *Les grandes orgues*, 220.

60. *Ménestrel* 36 (1869): 128.

61. Fétis, *Biographie universelle*, 8:10.

62. Ochse, *Organists and Organ Playing*, 31.

63. Dufourcq, "Lemmens et Cavaillé-Coll," 58–59 (1951): 58.

64. Ibid., 59.

65. Louchart, "Les interprètes," 12.

66. C. Cavaillé-Coll and E. Cavaillé-Coll, *Aristide Cavaillé-Coll*, 125.

67. Dufourcq, "Lemmens et Cavaillé-Coll," 58–59 (1951): 58. Despite Hesse's preference for the Sainte-Clotilde organ, he did assess the Saint-Sulpice organ as "the most perfect, the most harmonious, the largest, and really the masterpiece of modern organ building." Cited in Ochse, *Organists and Organ Playing*, 75.

68. Dufourcq, "Lemmens et Cavaillé-Coll," 58–59 (1951): 59.

69. C. Cavaillé-Coll, "Les orgues et les organistes," 318; also Dufourcq, "Lemmens et Cavaillé-Coll," 60 (1951): 85–86.

70. Douglass, *Cavaillé-Coll*, 358.

71. Minutes of the Vestry Council meeting concerning Lefébure-Wély's hire show that Schmitt was being replaced because the renowned Lefébure-Wély was available to take the position. Although paying Schmitt his full year's salary, the vestry terminated his services at the end of April 1863. Their outward decision to hire Lefébure-Wély at that moment was rationalized as a purely artistic one: such a great organ should have a great organist. A.D., "4ème Registre des Délibérations du Conseil de Fabrique," meeting of March 30, 1863.

There was, however, another compelling reason that was not mentioned, at least not in the official "Registre des Délibérations." Lefébure-Wély was on the verge of taking the organist's post at the nearby church of Saint-Germain-des-Prés, raising "a veritable state of crisis." This simply would not do, either for the Vestry Council, which was not about to risk losing this most popular organist to a smaller parish, or to Cavaillé-Coll, who desired to see "the maximum artistic and commercial benefit drawn from his costly masterpiece." Lueders, "Georges Schmitt," 39.

72. C. Cavaillé-Coll and E. Cavaillé-Coll, *Aristide Cavaillé-Coll*, 125.

73. Upon Saint-Saëns's resignation from La Madeleine in 1877, Widor wrote: "The personality and musical intelligence of Mr. Saint-Saëns are of the first order; the composer and the virtuoso are on equal footing, the one on the level with the other, equally admirable; no human mind has come from the hands of the creator more suited to the complex requirements of our art. Since Bach, Mozart, and Mendelssohn, no one has known better than he how to improvise in four voices in the purest style and with a more irreproachable correctness. . . . The history of music scarcely offers us but these three examples of a similar spontaneity. I do not fear at all to write here that Mr. Saint-Saëns is the direct heir of these three illustrious models. When the church of La Madeleine had the honor to have him as organist, on many occasions we saw him contending with the texts of the sacred chant that he developed under a form and in a style that did not disavow Bach, Mozart, or Mendelssohn. Difficulties of execution not existing for such an artist, the conception and interpretation were elevated to the same level; the written piece was not at all different from the improvised piece. The resignation of Mr. Saint-Saëns from La Madeleine is a great loss for art. We have in Paris the premier organ builder of the world, Mr. Cavaillé-Coll, and we have in most of our churches some marvelous instruments; but good organists are rare, and it is regrettable to see the most brilliant musical incarnation in our country give up the organ and *militant* religious music [musique religieuse *militante*]." Widor, "Revue musicale," *Estafette* (July 9, 1877): 2.

74. Saint-Saëns, "Music in the Church," 7; see also Widor, *Fondations, portraits*, 160. Widor wrote to Saint-Saëns in 1908: "Don't be surprised with regard to the ignorance of the crowds—even the elegant ones—still believing L[efébure]-W[ély] at La Madeleine!" A.S-S., letter 7, dated October 22, 1908. The author is deeply indebted to Professor Yves Gérard who, in 1991, graciously transcribed the fifty-three letters from Widor that Saint-Saëns had conserved.

75. Monter, "Lefébure-Wély," 11.

76. Dupré, "Souvenirs sur Ch.-M. Widor," 29; Launay, "I Knew Him," 202; Murray, "The Pure Tradition," 6; Smith, "Widor's Symphonie gothique," 43.

77. Harding, *Saint-Saëns*, 62.

78. Family arch. The family letters quoted were written hastily and informally, without careful regard to spelling and grammatical syntax. Remarks are sometimes made in a rather cryptic manner. For the ease of the reader, the author has opted for idiomatic English translations.

79. Abbé Pierre Henri Lamazou (1828–83) was quite an expert on organ construction. In 1863, he authored a study on the Saint-Sulpice organ and modern trends in organ building (Lamazou, *Saint-Sulpice*); in 1868, he wrote a similar monograph on the Notre-Dame organ (Lamazou, *Notre-Dame de Paris*).

80. *Ménestrel* 37 (1869): 16.

81. Leray, "Souvenirs d'un maître."

82. Widor, "Souvenirs autobiographiques," 16. The celebrated Frenchmen mentioned here are: Léon Foucault (1819–68), physicist; Baron Paul Thénard (1819–84), chemist and agronomist; Jules Lissajous (1822–80), physicist.

83. Harding, *Saint-Saëns*, 29. In a 1934 interview, Widor repeated the same mistake, saying: "In 1869, I replaced Saint-Saëns at La Madeleine while he was in Weimar, where Liszt produced *Samson et Dalila.*" Valbelle, "Quelques souvenirs," 1.

84. Dupré, "Souvenirs sur Ch.-M. Widor," 29.

85. Louchart, "Les interprètes," 11. Albert Schweitzer recalled Cavaillé-Coll's regular visits to Saint-Sulpice: "I can never forget him; I can still see him today with his little cap, and with the good, true eyes in which so much of art and intelligence lay, sitting every Sunday beside Widor on the organ bench at St. Sulpice, and caressing with his hand the console of his darling organ." Joy, *Albert Schweitzer*, 151.

86. Cheronnet, *L'église Saint-Sulpice*, 11.

87. Family arch. Widor was, in fact, appointed that Thursday, January 13, and began the following Sunday.

88. C. Cavaillé-Coll and E. Cavaillé-Coll, *Aristide Cavaillé-Coll*, 125.

89. Louis Vierne affirmed, "I have never heard anything that could compare with Franck's improvisation from the point of view of purely musical invention." Smith, *Louis Vierne*, 43.

90. Cellier and Bachelin, *L'orgue*, 242.

91. Dupré, "M. Charles-Marie Widor," 1.

92. C. Cavaillé-Coll and E. Cavaillé-Coll, *Aristide Cavaillé-Coll*, 126; R. Dumesnil, *Portraits de musiciens français*, 198.

93. A.D., "Procès-verbal des séances du Bureau de la fabrique de l'église paroissiale S. Sulpice de Paris," 67.

94. Leray, "Souvenirs d'un maître."

95. Valbelle, "Quelques souvenirs," 1.

96. Dupré, *Recollections*, 46.

97. Dupré, "Souvenirs sur Ch.-M. Widor," 29.

98. Widor, "Souvenirs autobiographiques," 17. Vierne discovered he had similar problems after he became *titulaire* at Notre-Dame in 1900: "The chapter was divided into two camps about me: one, headed by Monsieur Pisani, was not startled by my way of doing things; the other, disturbed in its habits, reproached me for the audacious things I was doing. . . . Widor advised me to close my ears and to make no concessions. 'The same thing happened to me when I was appointed to Saint-Sulpice. I turned a deaf ear,

and you see that I'm no worse off. As a matter of fact, the clergy of my church congratu-
lated me on making you my assistant because you came from the same tradition. My
troubles go back thirty years, but don't think that I had to wait until 1892 for people not
only to leave me alone but [also] to use me as a shining example. Hang on and you'll
see!'" Smith, *Louis Vierne*, 245; Vierne, "Memoirs of Louis Vierne" (July 1939): 8.

99. The minutes read: "The committee of the Vestry Council, in view of the numerous applications submitted to the parish priest and in keeping with the report that was
made on the subject by Mr. Cauchy, had determined that judgment on the definitive
replacement of Mr. Lefébure-Wély as organist of Saint-Sulpice would be postponed until
January 1871, and that Mr. Charles Widor would be provisionally charged to hold the
post for 1870, reserving to the Vestry Council the care of fixing the salary allotted to this
temporary office." A.D., "4ème registre des délibérations du conseil de Fabrique de la
paroisse St. Sulpice 1855–1888," meeting of January 24, 1870.

100. From the beginning of his appointment on May 1, 1863, to the end of the year,
however, Lefébure-Wély was to be paid only fifteen hundred francs. By comparison,
the salaries of the choir organist and choir master were eight hundred francs per year
(notes of council meeting on December 5, 1866). In order to help attract Lefébure-Wély
to Saint-Sulpice, it is likely that the council set his salary artificially high; they doubled
the salary of his predecessor, Georges Schmitt.

101. Because of severe financial constraints on the church budget, undoubtedly the
aftereffect of the Paris Commune, Widor's salary was soon subject to further reduction.
At its meeting on December 29, 1871, the council "on the proposition of Messrs. Widor
and Cavaillé-Coll themselves" reduced Widor's salary to two thousand francs per year,
beginning January 1, 1872; and the budget for tuning and maintenance of the organ
was cut in half—from twelve hundred to six hundred francs per year. At least Widor
could be pleased that in its meeting of November 4, 1872, the council agreed to repair
the carpet around the organ, to purchase lanterns to light the pedal clavier, and to put a
heating stove in the organist's chamber in case the fireplace could not be repaired. At its
meeting of January 28, 1873, the council reinstated, at Cavaillé-Coll's request, an annual
allotment of twelve hundred francs to maintain and tune both organs, but this would
last only two years. On May 19, 1874, because the budget was in a deficit state, the council decided to reduce Widor's annual salary to seventeen hundred francs, and the organ
maintenance budget to nine hundred francs beginning January 1875; in addition, it was
noted that chandelier candles, flowers, and wall hangings for ceremonies were being cut
back. Curiously, in contrast to all the reductions, there was an augmentation of the choir
master's salary. Mr. Bleuzé (d. 1884?) had been named choir master of Saint-Sulpice on
October 10, 1867, at an annual salary of two thousand francs; the Vestry Council raised
this to twenty-four hundred francs on December 12, 1873, thus putting his salary significantly higher than that of Widor. A.D., "4ème registre des délibérations du Conseil de
fabrique"; also "Procès-verbal des séances du Bureau de la fabrique de l'église paroissiale S. Sulpice de Paris," 49. By 1897, Widor's salary had been raised to only twenty-four
hundred francs. Eddy, "Great Frenchmen," 14.

102. *Ménestrel* 37 (1870): 55.

103. "Mr. Ch.-Marie Widor was just called to succeed Mr. Lefébure-Wély in the functions of organist of the *grand orgue* of Saint-Sulpice." *Revue et Gazette* 37 (1870): 30.

104. Undated letter, but from its contents it is evident that it was written on the eve of
the Franco-Prussian War. Family arch.

105. Dupré, *Recollections*, 46.

106. Dupré, "Souvenirs sur Ch.-M. Widor," 29.

107. A number of letters from Cavaillé-Coll to Widor are preserved in B.N.(a); some of these are transcribed in Noisette de Crauzat, *Cavaillé-Coll*. Most of the letters carry greetings such as "Mio Caro," "Mio Caro Maestro," or "Mio Caro Widor," and have an affectionate, fatherly tone. In one, Cavaillé-Coll writes, "I have learned from Mr. Blondel of your success in Lille as composer and conductor. It seems that they found you *too modest*. I told Mr. Blondel that they didn't know you." B.N.(a), letter 150, dated March 14, 1890. In another letter addressed to Widor in Lyon, Cavaillé-Coll closes, "Good-bye and remember me kindly to Papa and all the Widor family, and accept my affectionate greetings." B.N.(a), letter 169, dated September 11, 1891.

108. Although Widor was seven years younger than Guilmant, he always looked much younger than his years, making the disparity in their ages seem even wider.

109. Widor, "Souvenirs autobiographiques," 18.

110. Widor, "Chez nos compositeurs," *Piano Soleil* (June 12, 1892): 1.

111. Widor, "Autour de Saint-Sulpice," *Piano Soleil* (October 25, 1891): 1.

112. It was also reported that he lived on the "fifth floor." Philipp, "Charles-Marie Widor," 126.

113. Fanny Thomas described the painting as "Rembrandt colored" and "so singularly life-like that with it in the room, one would not be without a host." Thomas, "Organ Loft Whisperings" (December 13, 1893): 12. Today, the location of the painting is unknown.

114. Imbert, "Charles-Marie Widor," 222–24. Thomas identified the subject as Miss Lee Robbins, of New York. Thomas, "Organ Loft Whisperings" (December 13, 1893): 12. The badly damaged painting, dated 1891, is in the Family arch.

115. Imbert, "Charles-Marie Widor," 225.

116. C. Cavaillé-Coll and E. Cavaillé-Coll, *Aristide Cavaillé-Coll*, 126. Fenner Douglass refutes this claim: "With this explanation Cécile seems to excuse her father for passing over Franck for the most important organ position in France. We doubt that this is correct. [Here, Douglass inserts a footnote, citing a memoir of Théodore Dubois to substantiate his doubt.] Widor was chosen because he was the most promising young virtuoso in Paris, who was, significantly enough, a pupil of Lemmens." Douglass, *Cavaillé-Coll*, 109.

117. Douglass, *Cavaillé-Coll*, 109 n. 4.

118. Widor, *Initiation musicale*, 126. Vincent d'Indy (1851–1931), in his unctuous book on Franck, wrote: "In 1872 a very curious event happened in the master's career: he was appointed, nobody knows how—and he himself, a stranger to all intrigue, understood it less than the rest—Professor of Organ at the Conservatory. . . . The mystery has never been elucidated." d'Indy, *César Franck*, 46–47. In his "Souvenirs," Widor railed against d'Indy's profession of ignorance as well as his involvement in what Widor perceived to be spiteful intrigues and rumor-mongering:

> Against Ambroise Thomas—composer of *Hamlet* and *Mignon*, a delightful man (modesty itself) and an excellent musician (knowing the orchestra to the core)—a school of amateurs came together with the purpose of usurping his position and primarily dishonoring him as a musician. Thomas was incapable of defending himself, he was so guileless and modest. This school called itself the Schola Cantorum, and they only ceased their attacks against the Conservatory the day when its head [d'Indy] was named a professor there. Vincent d'Indy relates in his book on Franck that he didn't know to what to attribute the nomination of Franck as organ professor at the Conservatory, whereas no one had any doubts, including d'Indy. Franck was accompanist at Sainte-Clotilde. When Cavaillé-Coll

built the organ there that we hear every Sunday, Théodore Dubois, upon coming back from Rome, was named choirmaster, and Franck switched over to the *grand orgue* that was just built. Upon the death of Father Benoist, organ professor at the Conservatory, Thomas asked Théodore Dubois whom to appoint to the post. Therefore, despite the assertions of Vincent d'Indy, the nomination of Franck is due to Ambroise Thomas.

Speaking too of the burial service of César Franck, d'Indy has written, "All the Conservatory was at the burial service of Franck except Ambroise Thomas[";] he was stricken with an attack of eczema and had himself replaced by Delibes, professor at the Conservatory and member of the Institute. I still see, near the door of the sacristy, Delibes and Franck's son shaking hands. The assertions of d'Indy must not be taken into serious consideration; moreover, the day when d'Indy ended up being named professor of the orchestra class at the Conservatory, his attacks suddenly ceased. To be said in passing, he could not arm himself with sufficient authority, and the greatest lack of discipline reigned in his orchestra class. Widor, "Souvenirs autobiographiques," 53–54.

Widor quite obviously held Thomas in high esteem and always spoke well of him. After one such occasion, some eleven years after Thomas's death, Widor received a kind letter from his widow: "Dear *Maître*, you have spoken to me of your former Director in terms so touching, by which I have been greatly moved, that I permit myself to send his photo to you! I hope that it will bring you pleasure! It will be sweet for me to think that you will look at it with feeling and that his memory will be recalled now and then in a circle as artistic as yours." B.I.(a), letter 193, dated July 22, 1907.

119. C. Cavaillé-Coll and E. Cavaillé-Coll, *Aristide Cavaillé-Coll*, 126.

120. Widor, "Souvenirs autobiographiques," 62–63. Widor repeated the story more than once; see also Valbelle, "Quelques souvenirs," 1.

121. Dupré, "Souvenirs sur Ch.-M. Widor," 31.

122. Widor, "Souvenirs autobiographiques," 56, 63.

123. Reynaud, *Œuvre de Ch.-M. Widor*, 7.

124. Saint-Saëns, *Harmonie et mélodie*, 207.

125. Widor, "Revue musicale," *Estafette* (January 14, 1878): 2.

126. Ibid. Hoping that the Théâtre-Lyrique might fulfill the role of a national theater, Widor continued: "the young musicians are asking for a hall, an orchestra, and a satisfying ensemble of singers; give them the means to produce their work in conditions sufficient to make themselves heard, and above all that they might *hear themselves*."

127. Widor, "Revue musicale," *Estafette* (April 23, 1877): 1.

128. Ibid. (August 13, 1877): 1.

129. Ibid. (July 9, 1877): 2.

130. Ibid. (January 14, 1878): 2.

131. Widor, "Vieille musique," 1. Widor found much to be learned from the study of early music, and he felt his composition students would benefit from practical exposure to the repertoire: "During the war of 1914, I was still professor of composition, rue de Madrid; the class was naturally more than reduced, and the competitions were suppressed. I took the students who remained with me to the library, and there we read—I dare not say we sang—the old counterpoints and all this detail of the old music, so important for us and that one cultivates so little." Widor, "Souvenirs autobiographiques," 59.

132. Widor, "La musique," 460.

133. Widor, *Amateurs honoraires*, 18.

134. R. Dumesnil, *Portraits de musiciens français*, 199.

135. In like manner, Widor undoubtedly arranged for the premiere of Saint-Saëns's *Requiem* at Saint-Sulpice in May 1878. A large work for soloists, orchestra (including four trombones that played from the tribune), choirs, and two organs, Saint-Saëns conducted the orchestra, choirmaster Bleuzé directed the choirs, and Widor played the *grand orgue* in an "irreproachable performance." Widor, "Revue musicale," *Estafette* (May 27, 1878): 2.

136. *Ménestrel* 37 (1870): 120.

137. *Ménestrel* 58 (1892): 127. Jules-Étienne Pasdeloup (1819–87), Charles Lamoureux (1834–99), and Édouard Colonne (1838–1910) each founded concert organizations in Paris.

138. *Ménestrel* 37 (1870): 111. Another significant later example is *Conte d'Avril*, a work that spawned numerous arrangements; in its arrangement for two pianos, Widor enjoyed performing it with various second pianists. *Ménestrel* 58 (1892): 152, 197. On the first of these two concerts Widor and Isidor Philipp (1863–1958) gave "a very brilliant performance," and on the second Widor and Mlle Berthe Max performed the suite in London for the benefit of a relief fund for ill-fated foreign artists living in England.

139. The performers at that December 23, 1871, concert were impressive: Charles Lamoureux, violin; Auguste Tolbecque (1830–1919), cello; Paul Taffanel, flute; Gabriel Fauré (1845–1924), harmonium; Widor, piano. Blakeman, *Taffanel*, 40.

140. *Revue et Gazette* 37 (1870): 83–84.

141. Landormy, *Franck à Debussy*, 171.

142. Family arch., letter to a family member, dated April 13, 1902.

143. *Musica Sacra* 19 (1897): 92–93. The concert took place on May 29, 1897, in Lourdes; the following day Widor inaugurated the Cavaillé-Coll organ in the Église du Rosaire.

144. *Revue et Gazette* 39 (1872): 190.

145. On March 16, 1889, Widor, Gabriel Pierné, César Franck, Raoul Pugno (1852–1914), Marie Jaëll (1846–1925), and Clara Janizewska performed as pianists for the chamber music society "La Trompette." Fauquet, *César Franck*, 598.

146. Smith, *Louis Vierne*, 65, 67; Vierne, "Memoirs of Louis Vierne" (November 1938): 10.

147. *Revue et Gazette* 39 (1872): 71.

148. Gavoty, *Louis Vierne*, 54.

149. A passport issued to Widor on January 22, 1903, gives his height as 172 centimeters, or about 5'6½".

150. Bret, "Symphonies pour orgue," 14.

151. Smith, *Louis Vierne*, 91; Vierne, "Memoirs of Louis Vierne" (December 1938): 6.

152. Dupré, "M. Charles-Marie Widor," 2.

153. Potiron, "Widor," 83.

154. Widor, Preface to *L'orgue de Jean-Sébastien Bach*, xvii–xviii.

155. Brogan et al., *Short History of France*, 156.

156. Family arch.

157. Hamel, *Saint-Sulpice*, 382.

158. Bertrand, "Widor: Conteur d'anecdotes," 3. Also Riemenschneider, "Tribute to Widor," 26: "as I belonged to the 'garde nationale,' I was imprudent enough to play with my spurs on and received a very severe wound in my leg thereby." Also Dupré, "En parlant de Ch.-M. Widor."

159. Family arch., undated letter.

160. In one letter dated February 7, 1871, Widor reported that he just received a letter from his mother dated October 28, 1870.

161. Paul Widor was imprisoned in Leipzig.

162. Many years later, Widor declared that "if a bomb had fallen on his beloved instrument he would have wished to have been there and have died with it." Bidwell, "Widor and St.-Sulpice," 422.

163. Food shortages in Paris were such that dietary needs had to be met in the most unappetizing ways; *Le Figaro* of November 30 ran an ad: "Butcher's Shop Open: DOGS, CATS & RATS." The chef of one hotel had to put his culinary skills to the test with such menu items as: Consommé of horse, with millet; Skewers of dog liver à la maître d'hôtel; Minced saddle of cat, with mayonnaise; Ragoût of rats à la Robert; and the like. Jones, *Gabriel Fauré*, 26–27.

164. Family arch.

165. In an interview, Widor elaborated: "Everything around us was burning. And everyday we expected to be roasted. But we looked at the fleche of Sainte-Chapelle, always standing upright in the smoke. It was like a symbol of France remaining above these terrible events!" Pédron, "Charles Widor."

166. At Saint-Sulpice, many of the windows together with their iron tracery were blown in as a result of the explosion at the Luxembourg powder mill; though showered with some debris, the organ sustained no real damage. C. Cavaillé-Coll and E. Cavaillé-Coll, *Aristide Cavaillé-Coll*, 126.

167. Here, Widor briefly changed the topic to the Saint-Sulpice organ. Then follows a gap in the text with the notation: "Communards et la Notice orgue: livre St. Sulpice."

168. Widor, "Souvenirs autobiographiques," 22–26.

169. Libert, "Charles-Marie Widor," 113.

170. Eymieu, *Études et biographies musicales*, 14.

171. Widor, "Souvenirs autobiographiques," 27–28. Widor did concede, however, that "the composers who imitated Mendelssohn are very numerous! For more than fifty years, most of the works written for organ were inspired by him." Widor, "Felix Mendelssohn-Bartholdy," 3. Widor edited an edition of Mendelssohn's Six Sonatas for Durand about 1918, and Albert Schweitzer noted: "Widor considered the fourth of these the most interesting and most important, because in it Mendelssohn was daring enough to write for the organ in a thoroughly orchestral manner." Schweitzer, Jacket Notes.

172. Unidentified news clipping, B.N. Fonds Mont.

173. This descriptor is found on the back cover of Widor's "Trois chœurs à 4 voix," Op. 25, published in 1876.

174. Widor, *The Symphonies for Organ*, 11: xiii.

175. Widor related the beginning of Cavaillé-Coll's career in his own inimitable fashion in his "Souvenirs":

> He received his early education at the University of Toulouse, where he was interested only in the sciences.
> The Cavaillés were originally from [blank space in the manuscript]. Both brothers were organ builders. One Cavaillé had built organs not only in the Midi but also in the north of Spain two hundred years ago. He married a Miss Coll in Barcelona. There were Cavaillé instruments and Cavaillé-Coll instruments.
> As for the history of the illustrious Aristide Cavaillé-Coll, it is no less colorful.
> His mathematics professor at the University of Toulouse, who was delighted with his disposition toward the sciences, went one day to tell his father: "My son is leaving for Paris. I have former Polytechnic colleagues there: [Charles]

Cagniard-Latour [1777–1859], [Félix] Savart [1791–1841], etc. Let your son go with mine; it may be very helpful to him. At the same time, I will introduce him to all my former colleagues. . . .

The young Aristide presented himself on Monday, a quarter hour before a meeting of the Academy of Sciences and delivered his letter of introduction to Cagniard—inventor of the siren—who read the letter, looked Aristide straight in the eyes, and, discerning his intelligence, said: "You are coming no doubt about the organ of Saint-Denis. Have you drawn up a proposal? The competition closes next Friday. Are you ready?"

The young Aristide, without showing concern, responded: "I'm unaware of the competition for the organ of Saint-Denis. In any case, I must ask permission from Papa!"

"If you have any brains, any new ideas, if you are capable of expressing them clearly and all this work can be done by Friday at 7 o'clock, then on Saturday you ask your Papa!"

Aristide Cavaillé-Coll returned home as soon as possible and went to work. He had, as the son of an organ builder and as a student of the faculty of sciences, acquired a certain stock of knowledge, and he conceived a certain number of new plans for the organ, notably from the point of view of the bellows, the mechanism, the timbres, the wind pressures, etc. This represented quite an experiment, but he lacked the practical experience.

Meanwhile, he knew how to put forth in his plan, naively perhaps, but clearly, all that he had in his head in such manner that the jury that met the following week judged his report "No. 1."

The government of Louis Philippe had decreed the construction of a *grand orgue* in the Basilica of Saint-Denis.

The jury requested the author of the report that it had just classed outstanding to appear. When this provincial young man of twenty-one years, a bit bewildered and astonished, appeared before the jury, he was asked to tell about the projects he had already done. "I have never made anything," he responded. "It's my father who builds organs; I am still studying at the university!"

The minister who had decreed the construction of a *grand orgue* for Saint-Denis was the young Mr. [Louis-Adolphe] Thiers [1797–1877], then minister of commerce. The jury related its amazement and also its embarrassment in confiding the largest instrument in France to a young man without practical experience. Thiers asked the jury: "Have you indeed rated the project unanimously?" —"Yes, Mr. Minister." —"Well then," continued Thiers, "I immediately wrote to the prefect, who responded that the Cavaillés are very decent men who have built many organs in the south of France and in the north of Spain. As for him [Aristide], he is full of very ingenious ideas from the point of view of mechanical theory. Very well, gentlemen, everything is arranged; we are going to give the first prize to Messrs. Cavaillé, father and son, and ask them to move to Paris."

A short time later, the Cavaillés moved to Paris, rue Notre-Dame-de-Lorette, building the organ of Notre-Dame-de-Lorette right away before beginning that of Saint-Denis.

I never pass in front of no. (23?) quai Voltaire without stopping, struck with a sort of hallucination that makes me see the young Cavaillé spending night and day in a little cramped room amending his report; in this same building I see, many years later, [Theodor] Mommsen [1817–1903], the illustrious historian, who came to Paris for a congress, and Wagner, finishing his *Meistersinger* [this would have been *Der fliegende Holländer* (1841)]. . . .

The organ of the basilica was an unprecedented triumph for Cavaillé-Coll. The application of his theories from the point of view of the sonority, the equilibrium of the forces, and the mechanism made a sensation.

When Cavaillé moved to the avenue du Maine, he constructed a theater in his house. He had trained two eminent voicers: the Reinburg brothers. The eldest of the two, Gabriel, had married [Cavaillé-Coll's niece, Berthe Cavaillé-Coll]. It's to the voicing of the Reinburg brothers, Gabriel and Félix [1837–97], that all his beautiful instruments owe the quality of their timbres. Cavaillé himself had trained all the masters of his industry. Widor, "Souvenirs autobiographiques," 19–22.

176. Widor, "Les orgues de Saint-Sulpice," 138. Of all Cavaillé-Coll's instruments, Widor considered that of Saint-Sulpice to be "one of the three most beautiful masterpieces, together with Notre-Dame de Paris, and Saint-Ouen de Rouen." Widor, "Souvenirs autobiographiques," 26.

177. Widor, Preface to *Notes historiques*, 6.

178. Widor, "Pro vero," 38.

179. Information identifying specific movements from Opus 13 as extant in some form during the 1860s is compelling, if not abundant. Examples already mentioned are the Scherzo and Finale of the Second Symphony, and the Andante Cantabile of the Fourth Symphony. Curiously, this last example was not included in the first edition of the symphonies. Primary evidence that Opus 13 contains at least some music composed in the 1860s is found in Paul Widor's letter, cited earlier, to Marie on June 20, 1869: "[Guilmant] asks me to thank Charles for having promised to copy for him his Chasse or Fanfare that begins like or nearly: [Paul then wrote out a theme of sixteen notes]." Although notated a fourth higher, Paul's sketch is unquestionably the opening of the Scherzo that appeared in the first four editions of the Second Symphony. Family arch.

180. Malherbe, "Charles-Marie Widor."

181. Widor, Preface to *L'orgue: Ses éléments*, 2.

182. Reynaud, *Œuvre de Ch.-M. Widor*, 13.

183. Bret, "Symphonies pour orgue," 14.

184. Widor, *L'orgue moderne*, 5.

185. Widor, "Les orgues de Saint-Sulpice," 128.

186. Widor, Preface to *Les maîtres français*, i.

187. Widor, Preface to *Les Couperin*, xi.

188. Widor, *Initiation musicale*, 53–54.

189. Widor, "La musique," 460.

190. Widor, Preface to *L'orgue de Jean-Sébastien Bach*, xxxv. In a footnote, Widor offered one suggestion: "We still must require our organ builders to use a uniform model of pedal claviers going up to *G*, like the manuals."

191. Widor, Preface to *Les maîtres français*, ii.

192. Widor, Preface to *L'orgue de Jean-Sébastien Bach*, xxxiv.

193. Raugel, *Les grandes orgues*, 123. The specifications as defined by the organ builder and adopted by the commission provide an early model for respectful restorations of antique instruments (123–25).

194. Widor, Preface to *Les maîtres français*, ii.

195. Widor, "Les orgues de Saint-Sulpice," 128. In this passage, under the term "mixtures"—stops that combine a selection of high-pitched unison and usually fifth-sounding

pipes for each note of the keyboard—Widor included "mutations"—stops of a single pitch corresponding to one of the harmonics of the fundamental pitch. Smith, *Louis Vierne*, 81; Vierne, "Memoirs of Louis Vierne" (December 1938): 6. In this sense his description is accurate; aside from a generous supply of mixture stops, Cavaillé-Coll supplied his largest instruments with mutation stops representing the harmonic series to an unprecedented degree. The harmonic series was represented in the Notre-Dame organ as follows (the harmonic partial is given in parentheses): 32' (1), 16' (2), 10 2/3' (3), 8' (4), 6 2/5' (5), 5 1/3' (6), 4 4/7' (7), 4' (8), 3 1/5' (10), 2 2/3' (12), 2 2/7' (14), 2' (16), 1 3/5' (20), 1 1/3' (24), 1 1/7' (28), 1' (32). Although Widor knew the colorful effect of mixing mutations and unison-sounding stops, he did not call for such combinations in his organ symphonies, and only rarely did he call for the gap registration of 16' and 4' stops.

196. Widor, "Les orgues de Saint-Sulpice," 128. The pneumatic machine that Charles Spackman Barker (1806–79) applied to mechanical action made large instruments easily managed without unnecessarily heavy key action. Cavaillé-Coll's first use of it was for his monumental instrument in the royal church of Saint-Denis in 1841.

197. Moderate-sized instruments may have had a Barker machine only for the grand-orgue keyboard, rendering the coupling of the manual divisions comfortable to the player.

198. Widor, "Les orgues de Saint-Sulpice," 128.

199. Widor, *Initiation musicale*, 52.

200. A "swell" mechanism, first applied to harpsichords in the eighteenth century, was soon adapted in a limited way to some English and Spanish organs. Cavaillé-Coll made the first practical use of the swell box in France.

201. Widor, Preface to *L'orgue: Ses éléments*, 3.

202. d'Indy, *César Franck*, 41.

203. Dupré, "M. Charles-Marie Widor," 1.

204. Widor, Preface to *Dictionnaire biographique*, 10.

205. *Musica Sacra* 12 (1890): 64.

206. Dufourcq, "César Franck," 8.

207. Boschot, *Charles-Marie Widor*, 9.

208. R. Dumesnil, *Portraits de musiciens français*, 200.

209. Lang, *Music in Western Civilization*, 995.

210. Robert, "Organistes," 55.

211. Widor, "Gounod," 837.

212. Cellier and Bachelin, *L'orgue*, 190; see also: M. Dumesnil, "Widor," 143; Riemenschneider, "Program Notes," 262.

213. Vierne, "Symphonies de Ch.-M. Widor," 320.

214. Dupré, "M. Charles-Marie Widor," 2. Dupré stated elsewhere, "Widor has brought about a great revolution in organ music that can now be represented by two eras, two testaments: the previous with Johann Sebastian Bach and Handel, and the new with César Franck and Ch.-M. Widor." Dupré, "En parlant de Ch.-M. Widor."

215. Favre, "Grande figure d'éducateur," 33.

216. Widor, "Avant-propos," *Symphonies pour orgue*, 2.

217. One can point to certain early twentieth-century American organs that did strive for that goal. Many of the instruments of Ernest Skinner (1866–1960) and certainly the great John Wanamaker organ in Philadelphia fulfill that aim.

218. Boschot, *Charles-Marie Widor*, 9.

219. Widor, "Avant-propos," *Symphonies pour orgue*, 2.

220. Smith, *Louis Vierne*, 73; Vierne, "Memoirs of Louis Vierne" (November 1938): 11.

221. *Revue de la musique religieuse, populaire et classique* 3 (1847): 37. Although the Saint-Sulpice organ was replete with these stops, and Cavaillé-Coll eventually came to understand their place in the tonal scheme of his large instruments, in only one movement of his organ symphonies does Widor call for a cornet by name, and then it is in combination with the foundations and mixtures (*Symphonie gothique*, movement 3).

222. Gavoty, *Louis Vierne*, 55.

223. Dupré, "M. Charles-Marie Widor," 2.

224. Widor, Preface to *Les Couperin*, ix.

225. Ibid.

226. Ibid., x.

227. Widor, Preface to *Notes historiques*, 5.

228. Widor, Preface to *Les Couperin*, xi.

229. Widor, Preface to *Notes historiques*, 6.

230. Widor, Preface to *L'orgue de Jean-Sébastien Bach*, xxxv.

231. Widor, Preface to *Les Couperin*, x.

232. J.-K. Huysmans, *En Route* (Paris: Imprimerie Nationale, 1954), 383–84.

233. Cellier and Bachelin, *L'orgue*, 242–43; in Locard, "Maîtres contemporains," 134, the Huysmans quote is mistakenly attributed to his 1891 book, *Là-bas*. Huysmans acerbic style of criticism was not limited to Widor; he likened the Wagner tubas in Siegfried's Funeral March to "intestines ravaged by some exotic disease." Brody, *Paris: The Musical Kaleidoscope*, 54. While such a comparison might be drawn to Fafner's purposefully "dragonesque" motif in *Siegfried*, the description does not apply to Siegfried's funeral music in *Götterdämmerung*.

234. Locard, "Maîtres contemporains," 134.

235. Widor, Preface to *Les Couperin*, x.

236. Widor, *L'orgue moderne*, 11. Writing in 1895, Widor praised Boëly's standards: "Do you know that sixty years ago you would have looked in vain in Paris for two virtuosos who knew the B-Minor Fugue [of Bach]? With the exception of the conscientious Boëly, of Saint-Germain-l'Auxerrois, I know of no one; the published compositions testify to the ideal of the time—an ideal without a name." Widor, Preface to *L'orgue de Jean-Sébastien Bach*, xxxv–xxxvi. In relating the charming account of the meeting between Ambroise Thomas and Boëly—given earlier—Widor quoted Boëly's personal judgment of the work of his contemporaries: "these abominable potpourris of Fessy, Danjou, and [Jacques-Claude-Adolphe] Miné [1796–1854]: pompous marches, carnival marches, sacristans on the spree." Widor, "Ambroise Thomas," 1.

237. Ochse, *Organists and Organ Playing*, 21. The manuscript is found in the Bibliothèque nationale, Ms 13356(5).

238. Klein, *Le grand orgue*, 39–40.

239. Goodrich, *The Organ in France*, 41.

240. Dufourcq, *Jehan Titelouze à Jehan Alain*, 147.

241. Riemenschneider, "Widor; An Estimate," 4.

242. Bret, "Symphonies pour orgue," 16; see also Sabatier, "Widor (Charles-Marie)," 12789.

243. An autographed score (B.N.: D.13.267) dated February 18, 1872, verifies that the symphonies were in print very early in the year. Guilmant's *Première Sonate* for organ followed Widor's *Symphonies* by nearly three years; he first advertised it in February 1875 [*Ménestrel* 41 (1875): 96].

244. *Ménestrel* 38 (1872): 279.

245. *Ménestrel* 39 (1873): 111.

246. *Ménestrel* 37 (1870): 135–36.

247. Of the two remaining fugues in Opus 13, the monumental double-fugue Finale of the First Symphony stands out in the last of its four versions, which is contemporaneous with Widor's last organ symphony—the *Symphonie romane* of 1900. In its original version, this fugue reflects a rather classical orientation, but as it was revised it took on all the romantic rhetoric of the composer's maturity at the end of the century. Widor later wrote of the form: "The *fugue* is a monument whose proportions must be reasoned and justly balanced; it's the ideal of musical 'form' adopted and recognized by the masters since the beginnings of instrumental polyphony." He also noted, "all the great musicians come back to the fugue or fugal style towards the end of their life." Widor, *Initiation musicale*, 88–89.

248. Widor, "Profession de foi," 1.

249. Grace, *French Organ Music*, 132.

250. Widor, *Initiation musicale*, 94.

251. A few extra francs could also be picked up from weekly music journals that published short pieces (for example, *Figaro Illustré* or *Piano Soleil*). B.T., letter 274 (from Widor to Théophile Gautier, editor of *Figaro Illustré*), dated December 7, 1891.

252. Dufourcq, "Panorama," 375.

253. Dufourcq, *Jehan Titelouze à Jehan Alain*, 180.

254. Reynaud, *Œuvre de Ch.-M. Widor*, 13–14.

255. Ibid., 14.

256. Ibid.

257. Widor, Preface to *Manufacture d'orgue*, 3.

258. Widor, *Fondations, portraits*, 227.

259. Sumner, "Paris Organs and Organists," 53; Joy, *Albert Schweitzer*, 25.

260. Bret, "Symphonies pour orgue," 14.

261. Widor, "Revue musicale," *Estafette* (January 8, 1877): 2.

262. Ibid. (December 3, 1877): 2.

263. B.N.(d), letter 44.

264. *Ménestrel* 38 (1872): 407.

265. *Revue et Gazette* 40 (1873): 77; See also *Ménestrel* 39 (1873): 126.

266. Widor, "Revue musicale," *Estafette* (January 14, 1878): 2.

267. Widor, "Souvenirs autobiographiques," 28.

268. Writing in his "Souvenirs" about one of his inaugural concerts, Widor was suddenly reminded of some interesting tangential details; it is typical of that document that his narration is often like a stream of consciousness: "On March 20, 1877, I inaugurated the *grand orgue* in the church of Notre-Dame-des-Champs in Paris. It's an excellent organ, but hasn't the size of that of Saint-Sulpice or Notre-Dame. It had as titular organist an outstanding musician, [Auguste] Andlauer, who died one Sunday [in 1889] while playing the Magnificat. Suddenly, in the middle of the service, people heard a horrible thunder; Andlauer had collapsed onto the pedals with all the stops drawn. It was a brother of Louis Vierne (organist of Notre-Dame) [René Vierne] who succeeded him." Widor, "Souvenirs autobiographiques," 34–35. Widor had been a member of the jury (along with Gounod, Franck, Guilmant, and Gigout) that selected Andlauer in January 1877 to be organist of Notre-Dame-des-Champs. *Ménestrel* 43 (1877): 53; *Musica Sacra* 3 (1877): 32–33.

269. *Ménestrel* 39 (1873): 183, 191, 199, 207. Of this organ, Widor later wrote: "In 1874, Cavaillé-Coll took me to inaugurate the organ of Sheffield—a very beautiful instrument. For about a week, there were organ performances. People came from all

regions to hear it. Unfortunately, the organ has [subsequently] been spoiled, it seems, by the exaggeration of the wind pressure—a mannerism that rages in England. . . . . The true pressure of the Sheffield organ has not been respected, and, following the current trend—under pretext of forcing the sound—they have augmented it to unjust proportions." Widor, "Souvenirs autobiographiques," 32–33.

270. *Ménestrel* 41 (1874): 22.

271. Van Ausdall, Jacket notes.

272. Widor, "Souvenirs autobiographiques," 63–64.

273. *Ménestrel* 49 (1882): 22. Widor also performed as pianist in his Trio, Op 19, and Violin Sonata, Op. 50. In two lengthy letters dated December 6 and December 9, 1882, he described this sojourn in Vienna to Marie Trélat. In the first he mentions, "I'm staying in a superb palace in the elegant suburbs [of Vienna], next to the German Embassy and the Hotel Metternick; it's of a spacious luxury unknown in modern Paris—one could hold a ball in 'my drawing-rooms.'" B.N.(d), letters 35 and 36.

274. Lehman, "Charles-Marie Widor," 497.

275. *Ménestrel* 69 (1903): 255.

276. Philipp, "Charles-Marie Widor," 126.

277. Vierne, "Journal (Fragments)," 168.

278. Henderson, "Memories of Widor," 657.

279. Smith, *Louis Vierne*, 83; Vierne, "Memoirs of Louis Vierne" (December 1938): 6.

280. Vierne, "Ch.-M. Widor," 76.

281. Philipp, "Charles-Marie Widor," 129. Gabriel Pierné is being quoted.

282. Widor, "La réforme du Prix de Rome," 1.

283. Imbert, *Portraits et études*, 38.

284. Widor once described the hands of Saint-Saëns and Fauré as "short and fleshy," and he observed, "Bizet also belonged to this velvet paw [*patte de velours*] school; in listening to him, one imagined hearing an invisible quartet sustaining and being able to prolong the sounds of the piano; he seemed immobile at the keyboard, almost petrified, his fingers scarcely moving, riveted, so to speak, to the keys." Widor, "Contemporains," 1.

285. Widor, "Souvenirs autobiographiques," 35–38. Many personages are mentioned in this narrative: Dr. Ulysse Trélat (1828–90), professor on the faculty of medicine and surgeon of Napoléon III; his wife Marie Trélat (1837–1914), mezzo-soprano and vocal teacher; "Father [Ulysse] Trélat" (1795–1879), physician and politician; Louis-Nicolas Davout (1770–1823), marshal of France; his daughter Marquise Adelaide-Louise de Blocqueville (1815–92); Jules Ferry (1832–93) statesman and minister of public instruction and fine arts; Charles Ferry (1834–1909), politician and business man; Émile de Girardin (1802–81), journalist and politician; Ernest Renan (1823–92), philosopher and writer; Léon Gambetta (1838–82), lawyer, statesman, and French prime minister; Emmanuel Vaucorbeil, director of the Opéra; Agénor Bardoux (1829–97), statesman; Étienne-Jules Marey (1830–1904), who aside from Widor's description of him was a pioneer in cardiology.

286. *Ménestrel* 48 (1882): 86. Rosita Mauri was the principal ballerina in Widor's ballet.

287. B.N.(d), letter 25.

288. S.M.L., letter 9.

289. B.N.(d), letter 26.

290. S.M.L., originally consulted in 1992; missing in 2009 and presumed lost.

291. Ibid.

292. S.M.L., letter 39.

293. S.M.L., letter 38.

294. S.M.L., letter 45.

295. At a distance of several decades from the actual events, Widor sometimes confused a few facts in his "Souvenirs"; the author has endeavored to correct only the most blatant of them.

296. Jean-Auguste-Dominique Ingres (1780–1867) made numerous studies, drawings, and a splendid oil portrait of Countess Louise d'Haussonville (1818–82) that is now part of the Frick Collection, New York. In her memoirs, she described her secret dream for "a life of society, of triumphs, of flirtation." Tinterow and Consibee, *Portraits by Ingres*, 402. Claude Bernard (1813–78), scientist and physiologist; Louis Diémer (1843–1919) pianist and composer; Eugène Guillaume (1822–1905).

297. Act III, Scene 2 of *Manon* by Jules Massenet (1842–1912) is set in Saint-Sulpice and fueled an episode that greatly amused Widor. Earlier in the opera, Manon and the impecunious Chevalier des Grieux had been living together in Paris, but she decided to leave him for a wealthy nobleman and a life of luxury. Heartbroken, des Grieux decided to enter the priesthood; but when Manon later learns of her lost lover's fate, she hurries off to Saint-Sulpice to try to get him back before he takes his vows. In the Saint-Sulpice scene, she asks to speak to des Grieux and breaks into a heartfelt prayer to God to restore him to her. He comes to her side and struggles with his emotions until she sings, "N'est-ce plus ma main que cette main presse?" (Is this no longer my hand pressing yours?). Her urgent blandishments crumble his resolve to take the holy vows, and he falls into her arms vowing eternal love.

This passionate operatic love scene provoked an encounter in Saint-Sulpice that, according to Paul Bertrand, Widor relished recounting: "Very welcoming, he [Widor] had received the visit of an English woman of respectable age, brought up on our literature and music. She had asked him—the *maître* for whom Saint-Sulpice held no secret—where Abbé Prévost's heroine had met des Grieux, where he had fallen into her arms and was revived by a love that Massenet expressed so beautifully. Widor looked at the woman with a stupefied air. But she renewed her questions with explicit words, and she asked him where the exact place in the church was that Manon and des Grieux had been reconciled. Widor, more nonplused, didn't know how to respond. He directed the woman to the verger of Saint-Sulpice, who was well equipped, he said, to inform her. The verger became indignant upon hearing her words: 'Madame, you should know that we do not concern ourselves with these matters here! And besides, this Manon and des Grieux, they are parishioners whose names I have never heard spoken.' The woman, insisting again, twisted the buttons of the poor man's coat. He thought he was dealing with a crazy person, for this woman was at the height of excitement. He made up his mind what to do and hurled an expletive [*le mot de Cambronne*] at her. This exclamation had the effect of a shower bath. When he tells the story, Widor says he never would have believed in such an immediate effect." Bertrand, "Widor: Conteur d'anecdotes," 3.

298. The portrait is actually of Édouard's father, Louis Bertin, and now hangs in the Louvre.

299. Widor, "Souvenirs autobiographiques," 44–49.

300. Philipp, "Charles-Marie Widor," 130.

301. Malo, "Centenaire de Charles Widor." Foyot closed its doors in 1937.

302. Street, *Where Paris Dines*, 27.

303. Ibid., 30.

304. Burnand, *Paris Restaurants*, 19. (Author Robert Burnand wrote under the pseudonym Robert-Robert.)

305. Dupré, *Recollections*, 46.

306. Philipp, "Charles-Marie Widor," 129–30; Philipp, "Paris," 9. Ennemond Trillat (1890–1980) recalled, "From my first Sunday [in Paris], Widor took my brother and me to lunch at Foyot's, in the shadow of the Senate, in the company of his confrères at the Institute, Carolus Duran and Bonnat, two academic bigwigs of the paintbrush. I remember my embarrassment faced with some French fries cut into enormous slices: 'That is eaten with the fingers,' Widor told me. My brother, Joseph Trillat, was invited every Sunday. Widor liked him, appreciating his nonconformism, caustic spirit, and marvelous culture. He even designed to have him marry one of his nieces in Lyon, Mademoiselle Pierron." Trillat, "Charles-Marie Widor," 3.

307. Vierne, "Journal (Fragments)," 175.

308. B.N.(d), letter 30, dated August 1896, to Marie Trélat.

309. Brindejoint-Offenbach, "Avant *Nerto.*"

310. Dupré, "Souvenirs sur Ch.-M. Widor," 28.

311. Dupré, "Marcel Dupré nous conte," 2.

312. Philipp, "Paris," 9.

313. Widor, "Gounod," 837–38.

314. Widor, Preface to *Frédéric Chopin*, 13, 15.

315. Widor, "Profession de foi," 1.

316. Ibid.

317. Widor, *L'orgue de la Sorbonne*, 3. D'Erlanger had helped bankroll Wagner's Paris production of *Tannhäuser* in 1861, and despite the debt Wagner still owed him over the debacle, d'Erlanger remained true to him and his art.

318. Widor, "Souvenirs autobiographiques," 34.

319. See, for example: Widor, "*Lohengrin* à l'Opéra," 1–2; Widor, "*Lohengrin* et *Faust*," 1–2. Of the performers in Bayreuth, Widor was impressed with the theatrical abandon of Amalie Materna (1845–1918), who created the role of Brünnhilde: "Madame Materna, magnificent on her black mare, descended from the flies as a consummate horsewoman, without showing any fear." Widor, "Souvenirs autobiographiques," 34.

320. Widor, *L'orgue de la Sorbonne*, 4.

321. Goudeket, "L'institut croule."

322. Widor, *L'orgue de la Sorbonne*, 4.

323. Soubies and Malherbe, "Salle Favart," 65.

324. Schweitzer, Jacket Notes.

325. Gaudefroy-Demombynes, *Histoire de la musique*, 322.

326. Landormy, *Franck à Debussy*, 172.

327. Widor, "La musique dans l'antiquité," 1; also Widor, "Revue musicale," *Estafette* (April 28, 1879): 2.

328. Widor, "Musique française," 2.

329. See the author's discussion of this in: *Charles-Marie Widor: The Symphonies for Organ*, 20: xiii.

330. Widor, "À l'Opéra," 1. Widor suggested a solution: "The ideal would be to raise or lower at will, by means of a simple pedal placed under the foot of the conductor at the level of the orchestra; nothing would be easier, given the hydraulic motors that we have at our disposal today."

331. Widor, "Revue musicale," *Estafette* (January 28, 1878): 2.

332. Widor, "Les concerts du châtelet," 1. Widor wrote of this incident a second time, when he included the bracketed phrase, in Widor, *L'orgue de la Sorbonne*, 5.

333. Dupré, "Souvenirs sur Ch.-M. Widor," 30. In another telling, Dupré changed the story a bit: "Liszt took Widor to Germany. At Bayreuth, during the tetralogy, he wanted to introduce him to Wagner; but the two musicians had the misfortune to find the great master between two uprights in the scenery during *Rhinegold*, wild with anger and shaking his fist at one of his performers. At that, Widor said, 'Let's get out of here, this is not the time!'" Dupré, "En parlant de Ch.-M. Widor."

334. Widor, "Souvenirs autobiographiques," 33. Another of Wagner's staunchest financial supporters to whom he also owed enormous debts, Ludwig II, refused to attend the performance—but not out of any enmity against Wagner. Widor recalled, "The day of the premiere of the tetralogy, I noticed . . . the Kaiser, surrounded by a certain number of princes, though not Ludwig II of Bavaria, who had attended the rehearsal the day before and had refused to encounter the German Emperor who had unified Germany and thus confiscated his state." Widor, "Souvenirs autobiographiques," 33–34.

335. Widor, "Les concerts du Châtelet," 1.

336. Widor, "Souvenirs autobiographiques," 34.

337. Widor, *Fondations, portraits*, 153.

338. Dupré, *Recollections*, 50.

339. In his review of the inauguration, Widor described at some length the unfavorable acoustical properties of the Trocadéro hall and methods for improving them:

The hall is immense, very lofty and very deep; it assumes the shape of a circus on three of its sides; the fourth is a sort of shell intended to house the organ, the choruses, and the orchestra.

The sonority of the new temple consecrated to musical art resembles a little that of our gothic cathedrals; the sound floats in it. The melodic or harmonic design being ceaselessly blurred, its profiles lack clarity and its contours remain too vague; it seems like one is looking through glasses dimmed by water vapor or in fog. A space of this amplitude is generally excellent for broad and simple music, but much less suited to symphonic works of rapid movement and complicated texture. These works become incomprehensible if one cannot comprehend their rhythm.

. . . Witness the struck chords . . . that arrived to us in echoes, some directly, others by reflection, as if another orchestra, placed behind us, had sent them to us.

We hasten to add that it is very possible to remedy these partial defects either by an awning, or by some strings hung under the dome; and it is certainly worth more to have a hall too resonant than a hall too absorbent, since there is no known remedy in the latter case.

The system of strings hung at a certain height, intersecting at right angles or quite simply parallel—a sort of artificial spider's web, quite fine and distant enough one from another to stay almost imperceptible to the glance and not to harm anything from the perspective of the building—this system, invented by the Dutch, was applied for the first time this winter in Paris, and gave excellent results. We saw it experimented with in the church of Notre-Dame-des-Champs on the occasion of an organists' competition; being empty, the church was too reverberant, and the members of the jury sitting in the nave could not distinguish anything across this chaos of great indistinct sonority. The builder of the instrument, Mr. Cavaillé-Coll, had the idea of hanging throughout the nave, at the height of the entablature, a series of cotton strings, spaced a little less than a meter, one from the other; the eye, not warned, could not suspect the stratagem.

The means succeeded marvelously; all the details of the most complex pieces of Bach and Mendelssohn were perceptible to the most distant listeners, and they could judge securely.

A great awning, like the Romans made for their theaters and circuses, fulfills the same end, attaining an analogous result; it can even have a favorable decorative effect. . . .

Patient studies and numerous experiments will be necessary in order to adjust the numerous details that make a good music hall, that permit a perfect working out. Paris was not built in a day. Widor, "Revue musicale," *Estafette* (June 10, 1878): 1.

340. Fauquet, *César Franck*, 572; see also *Musica Sacra* 4 (1878): 56, 81.

341. *Ménestrel* 44 (1878): 158.

342. Widor, "Revue musicale," *Estafette* (April 8, 1878): 1.

343. Ibid. (August 12, 1878): 2.

344. Widor, *Initiation musicale*, 135.

345. This was Widor's reminder to himself to fill in some further details, but he never did.

346. Widor, "Souvenirs autobiographiques," 67–68. Dupré related, "For six consecutive mornings Widor heard from Liszt's fingers an important portion of the piano literature, from Bach to Liszt, touching upon Mozart, Beethoven, Schubert, Schumann, Chopin, and even certain new pieces, such as *Islamey* of Balakireff." Dupré, *Recollections*, 50.

347. Widor, "Revue musicale," *Estafette* (March 25, 1878): 2.

348. In his "Souvenirs," Widor identified two of the others as: Jules Delsart (1844–1900), cellist, and Ernest Hébert (1817–1908), violinist and painter, whose friendship with Liszt dated from Rome. Widor, "Souvenirs autobiographiques," 68.

349. Widor, "Les concerts du Châtelet," 2.

350. *Revue et Gazette* 42 (1875): 37.

351. *Revue et Gazette* 44 (1877): 76.

352. Widor also singled out Joseph Joachim Raff (1822–82) in this regard. Widor, "Revue musicale," *Estafette* (July 9, 1877): 2. In a letter to conductor Édouard Colonne, Widor recommended violinist Hugo Heermann (1844–1935), informing Colonne, "It's for him that Raff wrote his last concerto and Brahms one of his sonatas." B.N.(d), letter 34, dated October 1880.

353. Widor, "Revue musicale," *Estafette* (July 9, 1877): 2.

354. Riemenschneider, "Widor; An Estimate," 4.

355. Riemenschneider, "Program Notes," 263.

356. Miller, "L'école Widor," 488.

357. Vierne, "Memoirs of Louis Vierne" (November 1938): 10.

358. Widor, *Initiation musicale*, 95. He went on to compare music and architecture on a more metaphysical level, saying, "Like architecture, music obeys the conventional rules of number, proportion, and symmetry, and if it operates in the impalpable, it lives, meanwhile, in a reality, a substance—*the sound wave*. It is *true* or *false* according as it does or does not respect the natural and immutable laws of vibration. Architecture makes the material sing, and it is from the material itself [e.g., stone] that it demands the *la* of its song." Widor, *Fondations, portraits*, 207.

359. Boschot, *Charles-Marie Widor*, 9. In his chapter "Composition" in *Initiation musicale*, Widor used sonata form to illustrate how architectural form applies to music: "Music has its architecture. Symphony, overture, quartet, trio, sonata, every serious piece is constructed on the same plan: *a central development framed by two wings*; such is the portal of

Notre-Dame between the two towers. Of course, it's a matter here only of the first move-ment, the *Allegro* of a symphony. On a blackboard, with chalk, let's design a chateau. Left wing: two themes in *two relative keys*; right wing: these two themes in *the same key*, that of the beginning. . . . Music and architecture obey the same laws of number, following the same rhythm. Look at Versailles, where everything is conjugated by three. . . . Let's repeat it again: music, like architecture, lives from symmetry and returns." Widor, *Initiation musicale*, 91–93, 95. "Between the two similar arts, Architecture and Music, there is one essential dif-ference. One (which lives in the Material) works in *Space*, the other (in the Impalpable) in *Time*. We know what a sonata or a symphony endures; from exposition to recapitulation, our developments cannot compare better than to a round trip: in a time and determined direction, we must travel over a certain number of kilometers with the option of stopping at good places, but with the obligation of arriving at the appointed time." Widor, *Bach—Œuvres complètes pour orgue*, 4: viii.

360. Sumner, "The Organ Class," 427.
361. Boschot, *Charles-Marie Widor*, 7.
362. *Revue et Gazette* 43 (1876): 77.
363. *Revue et Gazette* 45 (1878): 190.
364. Léna, "Auditions d'œuvres," 222.
365. Waters, *Letters of Franz Liszt*, 371. Hans Bronsart (1830–1913) was a pupil of Liszt.
366. *Revue et Gazette* 45 (1878): 190.
367. Widor, "Souvenirs autobiographiques," 33.
368. Widor, "Revue musicale," *Estafette* (March 3, 1879): 1.
369. Widor, "Revue musicale," *Estafette* (February 18, 1878): 1. In another descrip-tion, Widor related his total astonishment at the great virtuoso's prowess:

I recall one morning when, before lunch with him, I arrived a few minutes ahead of the hour and found him in the vast and elegant studio that served as his practice room, in the course of reading a concerto of vertiginous difficulty, every novelty displayed; it was sent by a publisher in Saint Petersburg. The work was bristling with double sharps and triple flats; at each measure the tonality defied suspicion; the tempos oscillated between *appassionato con fuoco* and *pres-tissimo agitato molto*; the thirds, sixths, and octaves indulged in furious combat; the hands of the virtuoso traced some parabolas so rapid and designs so com-plex that the very form of his fingers grew blurred in the frantic whirlwind. The execution was so bold, so clean, and so impeccable, that I remained in the doorway, mouth agape, waiting for it all to finish. "Good day!" he exclaimed to me, without interrupting a series of fantastic octaves in sixty-fourth notes or sex-tuplets. "What do you say about this music?" And he continued, "It's quite good, it's brilliant, but it seems to lack a bit of depth." At this moment, a double scale of chromatic thirds furrowed the keyboard. "Ingenious, isn't it? Ah, this passage is pretty; this is getting better, but here it is really good! If the last part is of the same power, perhaps it will be possible to present the work to the public." And some trills in sixths descended little by little to the bass, preparing the perora-tion. "What?" I hazarded at the favor of a delicate and fleeting *pianissimo*, "you don't know the end? You're sight-reading?"

The peroration burst forth like a bouquet of fireworks; the arpeggios, scales, octaves, thirds, sixths, tenths, crossed and crackled from right and left in a curi-ous entanglement, at the minute indicated, and in the order desired by the com-poser, with a powerful sonority, a precision without parallel, an extraordinary sureness, and an unbelievable masterly skill.

"Have you a good appetite?" he said to me on the final chord. "Good! I have suffered from liver-complaint these days, and am convalescing; they have condemned me again this morning to a simple soup. You will not be angry with me if I don't make you a more earnest table partner; I am very weak, and can barely drag myself outside my bedroom!" Widor, "Virtuoses célèbres," 1.

370. *Messe*, Paris: Hamelle, [1877?]. Saint-Sulpice served not only as a parish church; it also had a seminary where priests received training.

371. Knauff, *Three Great Organists*, 15. T. Carl Whitmer (1873–1959) found the Saint-Sulpice choir organ and boys' choir completely deficient in tone quality: "I have never heard more acid-like voices, more destructive tone-production than I heard among the boys in St. Sulpice in Paris . . . ; nor such monstrously asthmatic organs as the chancel organ in the said St. Sulpice." Whitmer, "European Organs and Organists," 14. In 1892, Fannie Edgar Thomas had a different impression: "The chancel organ is played by Mr. [Jérôme] Gross [1852–1924?], while the maître de chapelle is Mr. [Philippe] Bellenot [1860–1928]. The music is mostly choral, and the regular choir is augmented by the students of the college, numbering about 100, and is well rendered." "Organs and Organists in the French Capital," *The Musical Courier* 25 (October 8, 1892): 12.

372. Landormy, *Franck à Debussy*, 171; Launay, "Louis Vierne," 14.

373. Henderson, "Memories of Widor," 659.

374. Knauff, *Three Great Organists*, 15.

375. Stiven, *Organ Lofts of Paris*, 58–59.

376. Thomas, "Organ Loft Whisperings" (December 13, 1893): 11. W. H. Miller left another description of a Saint-Sulpice service:

The choir and gorgeously robed priests were filing in, candles were being lighted on the altar, and the small organ in the choir already in full blast. Then a priest intoned a few words, and suddenly the great instrument all about us crashed and thundered, lifting one clear off one's feet and removing all sense of gravity. Then the organ down in the choir answered, and again Widor pressed down the five ranks of keys and we were riven with vast peals of sound. The ritual proceeded at the altar, while organ answered organ, rumbling and rolling through the long nave and wafting up into the one hundred and eight foot arches of the clerestory. The music was all Gregorian, upon the tones of which Widor harmonized freely.

Then the choir organ and choir settled down to a long *decanti-and-cantoris* chant of the *Benedictus*, and our pumpers were rung off, while friends and pupils of the master dropped in to pay their respects. He was not called until the *Salutaris*, when we had an opportunity to hear some fine voxes and strings. The offertory was a thing of Bach's, played with exact and metronomic precision and yet phrased so sympathetically as to make it a thing of beauty, constant shading of sections and half notes even, by lightning-like adjustments among the rows of stop handles.

The Mass ended, the priests and choir formed a sort of recessional, a *sortie* it is called, and Widor began a wonderful thing, a canon or plain-song, moving along in the midst of swirling arpeggios of left and right hands alternately. I looked at the pedals, for the air moved along as majestically as if double octaves were being played; but no, the pedal was occupied solely with foundation work. I looked again at his hands in amazement, for the rippling fingers were carrying four-octave arpeggios and yet that powerful air must come from *somewhere*! And then I saw that the wonderful hands were not only carrying the whirling arpeggios but

NOTES TO PP. 106–112 499

also supporting one another in giving out the legato theme of the piece. Always the right or left thumb or forefinger would pass along the note amid the rush of the figuration. And then the sonorous pedal trumpets took it up, but the hands merely added a counterpoint besides the rollicking arpeggios rolling up from the bass, six notes to the beat! And all this was a mere improvisation, harmony and all. I looked at the author of it expecting to see Promethean fire starting from his brows. He was simply calm and earnest about it, and now and then found time to drop a word to a friend seated at his side. Miller, "L'école Widor," 488.

377. Duchen, *Gabriel Fauré*, 32. Although Widor did not comment specifically on Fauré's organ technique, he did leave the following account of his bearing at the piano: "Like Saint-Saëns, his *maître*, Fauré plays the piano marvelously; like Saint-Saëns, he has short plump hands that play lightly into the keys, articulating effortlessly, almost without apparent movement, scarcely leaving the ivories, even for the most energetic attack." Widor, "Contemporains," 1.

378. R. Dumesnil, *Portraits de musiciens français*, 198.

379. Nectoux, *Fauré: A Musical Life*, 18.

380. R. Dumesnil, *Portraits de musiciens français*, 198.

381. Widor, "Contemporains," 1.

382. R. Dumesnil, *Portraits de musiciens français*, 198.

383. Thomas, "Organ Loft Whisperings" (November 19, 1893): 19.

384. Widor, *André Messager*, 7.

385. Havard de la Montagne, "Les maîtres de chapelle," 25.

386. Widor, Preface to *Accompagnement des cantiques*. Both Widor and Vierne wrote prefaces for Gross's *Accompagnement des cantiques du Manuel Paroissial.*

387. Erb, "Philippe Bellenot," 100; also Havard de la Montagne, "Philippe Bellenot."

388. For a complete table of the Saint-Sulpice organists, assistants, choir organists, and choir masters, see Havard de la Montagne, "Les maîtres de chapelle," 25–26.

389. Widor, "A. Cavaillé-Coll," 2.

390. Reynaud, *Œuvre de Ch.-M. Widor*, 14–15, 17.

391. Ibid., 17.

392. *Ménestrel* 56 (1890): 32.

393. *Musica Sacra* 12 (1890): 63. Writing about the performance of the Mass on January 19, 1890, Henry Eymieu reported that Widor played the first movement of the Fifth Symphony for the Offertory. *Ménestrel* 56 (1890): 32.

394. One would more correctly begin with Claudio Monteverdi.

395. Widor, *Fondations, portraits*, 226–27.

396. *Revue et Gazette* 43 (1876): 382.

397. *Musica Sacra* 3 (July 6, 1877): 95.

398. *Revue et Gazette* 45 (1878): 53.

399. *Ménestrel* 42 (1876): 407.

400. *Ménestrel* 44 (1878): 127.

401. *Ménestrel* 69 (1903): 117.

402. Philipp, "Charles-Marie Widor," 125.

403. *Revue et Gazette* 44 (1877): 373–74; see also *Ménestrel* 43 (1877): 416.

404. Fauquet, *Édouard Lalo: Correspondance*, 117–18.

405. Widor, "Souvenirs autobiographiques," 35.

406. S.M.L., letter 5.

407. *Ménestrel* 44 (1878): 127.

408. See *Revue et Gazette* 45 (1878): 78.

409. *Ménestrel* 66 (1900): 86.

410. *Revue et Gazette* 45 (1878): 78.

411. *Revue et Gazette* 44 (1877): 76.

412. Widor, *Initiation musicale*, 94–95.

413. *Ménestrel* 44 (1878): 127.

414. Reynaud, *Œuvre de Ch.-M. Widor*, 20.

415. *Ménestrel* 44 (1878): 305.

416. *Revue et Gazette* 45 (1878): 285–86.

417. The author discovered this review in 1982 when reading through *Revue et Gazette Musicale de Paris* and *Ménestrel* at the Boston Public Library.

418. *Ménestrel* 45 (1879): 248. This report is signed with the initials "E. G."—Eugène Gigout?

419. *Revue et Gazette* 45 (1878): 321.

420. Widor reported Lemmens's visit to Paris in the course of one of his reviews in *Estafette*: "One of the greatest artists of our time, the leader, the founder of the great modern organ school has come to Paris in recent days to present to the specialists and to those interested in sacred art a new theory on the constitution of plainsong and its accompaniment. Mr. Lemmens set forth his tenets in an interesting meeting that took place last week, at the Salle Érard, which all our organists and choir masters attended." Widor, "Revue musicale," *Estafette* (March 4, 1878): 1.

421. Widor, "Souvenirs autobiographiques," 40–41.

422. The critic for *L'Univers* complained, "Why an orchestra when it's a matter of hearing, in its varied and sacred applications, an organ . . . and why these pieces foreign to the worship service, as if one inaugurated an organ in an auditorium, instead of entry marches, offertories, communions, and postludes that are obligatory and that would otherwise have interested the audience? . . . The organists, more preoccupied with making their incontestable talent shine, have made the instrument heard only very incompletely. . . . It would have been very different, surely, if at the beginning Mr. Georges Schmitt or Mr. Alex. Guilmant had been there to charm the audience with a real improvisation, as we have heard them do in other circumstances, or to run through all the stops in turn, from the little to the grand, to uncover all the sonorous parts of the organ and show it successively in all its force and sweetness." Le Guillou, "Inauguration du grand orgue," 3.

423. J. Raynn, "Inauguration du grand orgue," 32.

424. Le Guillou, "Inauguration du grand orgue," 3.

425. *Ménestrel* 45 (1879): 103; Knauff, *Three Great Organists*, 16. Some descriptions reported "two orchestras"; however, the second orchestra consisted only of three cornets and three trombones in the tribune.

426. Raynn, "Inauguration du grand orgue," 32.

427. *Ménestrel* 45 (1879): 118.

428. Widor, "Souvenirs autobiographiques," 38.

429. Ibid., 60. Across the top of a manuscript copy (Bibliothèque nationale de France, Vma ms 582), Widor wrote, "improvisé, mauvais" [improvised, poor].

430. Widor, "Souvenirs autobiographiques," 39.

431. *Ménestrel* 45 (1879): 270.

432. *Estafette* (October 20, 1879).

433. *Ménestrel* 45 (1879): 384.

434. Barthalay, "Notes"; *Courrier de Lyon* 49 (December 18, 1880): 1; *Salut Public* 33 (December 18, 1880): 2; *Salut Public* 33 (December 19, 1880): 2.

435. Robilliard, "Charles-Marie Widor," 8.

436. *Ménestrel* 44 (1878): 342. This report is signed with the initials "E. G."—Eugène Gigout?

437. A well-respected organist and composer in his own right, Gigout had been *titulaire* of Saint-Augustin, Paris, since 1863; Widor described him as "a musician with as much talent as artistic devotion; . . . [he] does not have the popularity to which he would have the right if he were more egoistic and more occupied with his own glory." Widor, "Revue musicale," *Estafette* (July 5, 1880): 6.

438. Gigout, "Quelques publications nouvelles," 44. This statement by Abbé Lhoumeau, choirmaster at Niort, was quoted at the beginning of Gigout's article.

439. Widor himself referred to the "three periods of my life" in a letter to Riemenschneider on November 17, 1934. R.B.I.

440. For reasons unknown, opus numbers 27 and 38 seem not to have been assigned; and a couple of works—Opuses 34 and 36—appear to be later than their opus numbers would suggest. In addition, Opus 42 had yet to be filled out with the Seventh and Eighth Symphonies for solo organ.

441. Lehman, "Charles-Marie Widor," 497.

442. *Estafette* (March 19, 1877): 2.

443. *Ménestrel* 47 (1880): 6.

444. Landormy, *Encyclopédie de la musique*, 3564; *Piano Soleil* (August 9, 1891): 2.

445. Sol, "Widor et Messager," 5.

446. Widor, "Revue musicale," *Estafette* (May 26, 1881): 3.

Part Three

1. Widor, *Initiation musicale*, 93–94.

2. Widor, "Revue musicale," *Estafette* (January 15, 1877): 1. Thirty-nine years later, Widor had changed his mind, writing: "What place can one assign [to Berlioz] on the Olympus of music? Orlando di Lassus faces up to Palestrina, Bach to Handel, Rameau to Gluck, Mozart to Beethoven; but Berlioz, to whom does he face up? Today, because he sets the fashion and his disciples are without number, we count him among our national glories and we class him near the greatest. If he imitated no one, on the other hand many seek to imitate him." Widor, "La musique," 456.

3. *Revue et Gazette* 47 (1880): 53.

4. *Ménestrel* 46 (1880): 85.

5. Romain, *Essais*, 1.

6. B.N.(b), letter 313, dated November 2, 1883. Widor had also written to Lamoureux earlier to remind him about the work: B.N.(b), letter 276, dated January 15, 1883.

7. "Last night's Philharmonic concert [April 19, 1888] introduced yet another distinguished foreign composer to an English audience. Having done honour to Russian music by inviting M. Tschaikowski to conduct a work of his own, the Philharmonic directors were well advised in paying a similar compliment to the rising school of France, and their choice could not have fallen upon a better musician than M. Charles Widor. M. Widor is far from being, and probably would not care to be, the most popular of modern French composers—for his aims are serious, and he is apt to write over the heads of general audiences—but he is certainly one of the most individual among them. . . . M. Widor's music shows no direct or indirect reminiscence of [Berlioz, Boito, or Gounod]." "M. Charles Widor," *Times* [London] (April 20, 1888): 10. The large audience of English

concertgoers in attendance barely knew of Widor, and one critic admitted that they were more eager to hear the child piano prodigy Otto Hegner (1876–1907), who appeared on the same program, than a new work by a French composer with whom they were unfamiliar. *Ménestrel* 54 (1888): 140–41.

8. Widor, "Souvenirs autobiographiques," 59–60.

9. "Philharmonic Society," *The Musical Times*, 29 (May 1, 1888): 278–79.

10. Boston Public Library; two reviews of unknown origin, both dated April 28, 1888, are attached to score **M358.13.

11. "M. Charles Widor," *Times* [London] (April 20, 1888): 10.

12. *Salome* premiered in Paris on May 8, 1907.

13. *Ménestrel* 73 (1907): 76.

14. *Courrier Musical* 10 (1907): 169.

15. Widor, "Revue musicale," *Estafette* (January 15, 1877): 1.

16. "M. Charles Widor," *Times* [London] (April 20, 1888): 10; see also *Musical Standard* 34 (1888): 258.

17. B.N.: Vma 2940 A–D, copies B and D. Copy C contains the program from the February 8, 1880, premiere.

18. *Ménestrel* 44 (1878): 127.

19. *Ménestrel* 44 (1878): 314; see also *Journal de Musique* (August 31, 1878): 4.

20. B.N.(b), letter 193, n.d.

21. *Ménestrel* 66 (1900): 96. "*Le Capitaine Loys* is a heroic comedy in verse that shows us the mastery of weapons of the [sixteenth-century] lyonnaise poetess Loyse Labé, known by the nickname of "la belle Cordière," who serves in the army of the Dauphin of France, earns the rank of captain, and saves Perpignan from the Spanish who laid siege to it. The action is spirited, the verses have allure, the language is colorful, and often the epithet is felicitous. . . . Mr. Ch. Widor has composed several orchestral numbers for this work that have been greatly appreciated" (103).

22. S.M.L., letter 1, dated August 3, 1880.

23. *Journal de Musique* 5 (June 12, 1880): 2–3.

24. Widor, "Revue musicale," *Estafette* (January 8, 1877): 2.

25. Strapontin, "Une première à l'Opéra," *Estafette* (December 3, 1880): 2.

26. S.M.L., letter 2, dated August 28, 1880.

27. Beaumont, *Complete Book of Ballets*, 619. The original interview with Coppée appeared in *Figaro Illustré*, February 1895.

28. Coppée, "Centième de *La Korrigane*." 3.

29. Widor, "Souvenirs autobiographiques," 39.

30. Beaumont, *Complete Book of Ballets*, 621.

31. *Ménestrel* 46 (1880): 403.

32. S.M.L., letter 2, dated August 28. 1880.

33. The scene design for Act 1, "La place du village," depicting Yvonnette's dance appears in Rohozinski, *Cinquante ans de musique*, 1:55.

34. *Ménestrel* 47 (1880): 3.

35. *Revue et Gazette* 47 (1880): 385–86.

36. *Ménestrel* 47 (1880): 20.

37. *Ménestrel* 47 (1881): 35.

38. Widor, "Souvenirs autobiographiques," 41–42. The Prince of Wales loved Paris and, according to Widor, he amused himself by going to the Opéra every evening (39).

39. Ibid., 63. See also Stiven, *Organ Lofts of Paris*, 60–61.

40. Schwerké, "Composers as Human Beings," 78.

41. Anonymous news clipping, "Inapte à la danse." M.S.

42. *Ménestrel* 48 (1882): 229.

43. *Ménestrel* 62 (1896): 103.

44. *Ménestrel* 60 (1894): 18.

45. *Ménestrel* 74 (1910): 272. In 1925, Louis Laloy reaffirmed, "*La Korrigane* was very favorably appreciated by connoisseurs, whose opinion to this day has not changed." Rohozinski, *Cinquante ans de musique*, 1:55.

46. Curzon, "Reprise de *La Korrigane*."

47. *Le Guide Chorégraphique* (1934): 93–96.

48. Barthalay, "Notes," 2.

49. Paul Bertnay, "Lyon, 17 décembre—à Saint-François-de-Sales," *Courrier de Lyon* 49 (December 18, 1880): 1.

50. *Salut Public* 33 (December 18, 1880): 2; (December 19, 1880): 2.

51. The unpublished *Symphonie pour orgue et orchestre*, Op. 42[a], was edited by John R. Near and published as volume 33 in the series of Recent Researches in the Music of the Nineteenth and Early Twentieth Centuries, Madison, Wisconsin: A-R Editions, 2002. It was prepared in anticipation of the 2002 national convention of The American Guild of Organists in Philadelphia, where it was performed by the Philadelphia Orchestra on July 2, with Rossen Milanov, conductor, and James David Christie, organist.

52. Widor used the salon as a retreat for himself and his company during the sermon. The elegant little room contained a cheery wood-burning fireplace with a mirror above the mantle, a small writing desk, and several cushioned chairs; there were pictures of former organists, Cavaillé-Coll, a pope, the etching of Handel from the Prince of Wales, and various documents; a small gilded bust of Bach overlooked the room in approval. Hamel, *Saint-Sulpice*, 480; Thomas, "Organ Loft Whisperings" (November 29, 1893): 19. The salon appears essentially unchanged today.

53. Widor, "Souvenirs autobiographiques," 39. Press reports of the concert do not mention "two pieces of Bach," but, rather, an improvisation.

54. "Easter Thursday, April 13, a grand festival given by the conductor Lointier with the assistance of . . . Mr. Charles Widor, who will perform for this occasion, for the first time, a symphony for organ and orchestra." *Ménestrel* 48 (1882): 151.

55. Ibid., 166.

56. Ibid., 214.

57. *Times* [London] (May 20, 1882): 1.

58. Widor, "Souvenirs autobiographiques," 40.

59. Ibidl, 39–40. Widor also mentioned, "I made the acquaintance of [Sir Arthur] Sullivan [1842–1900] at that time. He was the author of charming pieces, among others the *Two Gondoliers*." During his many trips to England, Widor became acquainted with Gilbert and Sullivan's operettas; though he understood little English, he found them enchanting. Sullivan once thanked Widor for a "charming and flattering letter" and expressed regret for having missed him in London, but he hoped to see Widor at Easter in Paris. B.I.(a), letter 186, dated March 19 [no year].

60. Widor, "Revue musicale," *Estafette* (June 5, 1882): 2. Widor was endowed with perfect pitch, and in reviews he often commented on how a singer handled a specific note.

61. *Ménestrel* 48 (1882): 214.

62. Widor, *Technique of the Modern Orchestra*, 139.

63. Ibid., 144.

64. Widor, *Technique de l'orchestre moderne*, 178.

65. The program also included the Suite from *La Korrigane*, Sérénade (the orchestral version of Opus 10), and the First Piano Concerto, Op. 39, with Isidor Philipp performing "with extreme brilliance and remarkable sureness." *Ménestrel* 54 (1888): 343; also Widor, "Souvenirs autobiographiques," 61. The Palace of Fine Arts housed a five-manual instrument by the Spanish organ builder Amezua. The French press noted, "On this beautiful instrument, Mr. Eugène Gigout and Mr. Ch.-M. Widor have given several concerts that have been quite a success for our famous organists." *Musica Sacra* 11 (1888): 22.

66. *L'Art Musical* 29 (1890): 38.

67. For instance: the first movement was performed at a "Widor Festival" in Ostende, Belgium, where the composer was present but only conducted his Op. 69 Symphony [*Ménestrel* 61 (1895): 239]; and Eugène de Bricqueville peformed the Andante with Widor conducting in the chapel at the chateau of Versailles [*Ménestrel* 65 (1899): 112].

68. Published by B. Schott's Söhne, this symphony follows the sequential numbering of Widor's orchestral symphonies.

69. *Ménestrel* 70 (1904): 174.

70. *Opera News* 10 (April 14, 1919): 1–2; *Musical America* 29 (April 5, 1919): 1. Courtesy of the Philadelphia Orchestra Association Archives. At that time, the Philadelphia Wanamaker organ had grown to 18,144 pipes and 232 stops; it was touted as "the noblest musical instrument in the world." *Opera News* 10 (April 14, 1919): 3. In a lecture presented in 1925 at the Convention of the National Association of Organists in Cleveland, the rising wave of interest in organ-orchestral programs in America was traced to that seminal performance of Widor's Symphony at the 1919 Wanamaker concert. Palmer Christian, "The Organ and Orchestra: A New Orientation in Music," *Diapason* 16, no. 10 (1925): 19.

71. *Ménestrel* noted the makeup of the organization: "We learn of the formation of a new choral society of devotees: *Concordia*, founded and directed by a committee composed of fashionable society, with the assistance of Mr. C. M. Widor." *Ménestrel* 46 (1880): 142.

72. Chimènes, *Mécènes et musiciens*, 282.

73. *Ménestrel* 48 (1882): 167.

74. Widor, *André Messager*, 15n. Paul Vidal (1863–1931) was the first accompanist (1880–83). Ambroise Thomas sent Debussy to Widor in 1884, possibly in 1883, after Vidal's departure. "Charles-Marie Widor et Claude Debussy," *Le Matin* (March 20, 1934), B.N. Fonds Mont.

75. Widor, "Revue musicale," *Estafette* (January 15, 1877): 1.

76. Fauquet, *Dictionnaire de la musique*, s.v. "Concordia."

77. *Ménestrel* 47 (1881): 160.

78. Widor, "Souvenirs autobiographiques," 52–53. A competing amateur choral society, the Société Guillot de Sainbris, was Catholic, and the rivalry between it and the Protestant Concordia was apparent in that their memberships were mutually exclusive. Fauquet, *César Franck*, 563.

79. Chimènes, *Mécènes et musiciens*, 282–83.

80. For program examples, see *L'Art Musical* 27 (1888): 15, 55; 28 (1889): 15, 76.

81. Schweitzer, *J. S. Bach*, 1:259. The only other time the *Saint Matthew Passion* had been performed in Paris was some fourteen years earlier under the direction of Charles Lamoureux. In his preface to Schweitzer's Bach book, Widor incorrectly recorded the date of Concordia's performance as November 1885. Widor, Preface to *J. S. Bach*, vii. For the Bach bicentennial in 1885, Widor conducted two cantatas and the *Magnificat*.

82. Widor, Preface to *L'orgue de Jean-Sébastien Bach*, xxxvi.

83. B.I.(a), letter 105, dated March 12 [1888].

84. Julien Tiersot, "La 'Passion selon Saint Matthieu' de Jean Sébastien Bach," *Ménestrel* 54 (1888): 164.

85. Widor, "Liège," *Piano Soleil* (March 27, 1892): 2.

86. Widor, *Bach: Œuvres complètes pour orgue*, 1: xxv.

87. N.E.C., letter to Wallace Goodrich, dated March 23, 1898. And elsewhere, Widor referred to his idol as "notre saint-père le Bach" [our Holy-Father Bach]. Widor, "La classe d'orgue," 238.

88. Widor, Preface to *J. S. Bach*, xi–xii.

89. *Ménestrel* 47 (1881): 215.

90. *Ménestrel* 48 (1882): 78.

91. Ibid., 86; also 199.

92. Joy, *Albert Schweitzer*, 48–49. Schweitzer especially bemoaned the fate of Concordia's fine library of music; its holdings, although put up for sale at a very low price, failed to be sold.

93. *Monde Musical* 12, no. 5 (1900): 84.

94. Stiven, *Organ Lofts of Paris*, 54.

95. Leray, "Souvenirs d'un maître"; "M. Ch. Widor évoque pour nous ses souvenirs," *L'Intransigeant* (January 20, 1930), in Helbig, "La grande pitié," 4:136. In this recollection, Widor also mentioned the brothers Jules and Charles Ferry and César Franck as frequent visitors to the organ tribune.

96. R. Dumesnil, *Portraits de musiciens français*, 196–97.

97. Smith, *Louis Vierne*, 225.

98. Sumner, "Paris Organs and Organists," 53; see also Philipp, "Paris," 9.

99. B.N.(a), letter 169, dated September 11, 1891.

100. Paderewski and Lawton, *The Paderewski Memoirs*, 139–40; see also Sumner, "Paris Organs and Organists," 53.

101. Paderewski and Lawton, *The Paderewski Memoirs*, 139–40.

102. Widor, "Souvenirs autobiographiques," 103. The remainder of the notation continues: "Speak also of the charity concert for Jews chased from Germany. Anecdote of the little girl throwing herself to her knees and kissing his hands while offering him a bouquet." Widor's "Souvenirs" contains many such reminders for material to be filled in later; unfortunately, the manuscript ends abruptly after 103 pages with the following reminiscence of Paderewski:

With a most inquiring mind, rare artistic nature, and superior intelligence, Paderewski had refused credit for all his generous works, having accomplished through his virtuosic talent a work more effective in its moral force than would be winning a great battle for Poland.

As president of the Republic at Warsaw, Paderewski was acquainted with the papal legate who was to become Pope Benedict XV [1854–1922; pope 1914–22]. The Pope, having learned that Paderewski was in Rome, asked him to come reawaken his heroic memories of his time as papal legate in Warsaw. The cardinals, who had never seen a piano at the Vatican, were astonished.

103. Barnes, "Organ Student," 25. Barnes also noted that Charles Mutin (1861–1931) was usually in the loft "ready to go out and blow up the four or five men pumping the organ if they didn't give sufficient wind. . . . Mutin and his whiskers were terribly fierce when he did that."

104. d'Andigné, "Remise à Widor," 3. Another similar incident involved the son of Widor's friend Émile d'Erlanger; when the young boy tumbled onto the pedals, he did

not earn the approval of his parents or Widor, who was in the middle of the Offertoire! Thomson, *Charles-Marie Widor*, 20.

105. d'Andigné, "Remise à Widor," 2. The organ that had belonged to Marie-Antoinette found its way to Saint-Sulpice shortly after the Revolution; it was eventually restored by Cavaillé-Coll and located in the Chapelle de Notre-Dame des Étudiants— a long room above the front portico of the church. A report of Widor inaugurating it on November 17, 1889, appeared in "L'orgue de Marie-Antoinette," *Musica Sacra* 12 (1889): 39. He adored showing the little instrument to visitors, often playing some Gluck, Lully, or the first movement of Mozart's A-Major Sonata while one of his guests pumped the bellows; of Mozart, he would say over and over, "Yes, yes, he was the god of music." *Ménestrel* 55 (1889): 376; Bouvard, "My Recollections," 43; Philipp, "Charles-Marie Widor," 131. Widor related what he knew about the instrument in Lemesle, *L'église Saint-Sulpice*, 138–40; see also Smith, "Marie Antoinette." The instrument was relocated in 1926 to the circular chapel beneath the south tower, next to the Chapelle des Saints-Anges containing Delacroix's famous murals, and the organ was returned to the Palace of Versailles in 1975.

106. Blanche, *La pêche aux souvenirs*, 145. To be sure, the Countesse Potocka (1852–1930), daughter-in-law of the minister to François II in Saint Petersburg, had considerable physical allure. Jacques-Émile Blanche reckoned, "She received the divine gift: *beauty*," and he found that "Emmanuela's gaze was everything in a face polished like an apple" (163). Blanche interviewed Widor in 1935 and recorded that "[Widor] reminded me of the grand Sunday Mass and 'la Sirène' at the music stand" (145); see also A.D., Widor file. Widor once described her as "very beautiful, a born musician, [of] quick-witted verve." Widor, *Jean-Louis Forain*, 17. One upper-crust visitor to the tribune, Comte Robert de Montesquiou (1855–1921), wondered if the Countesse Potocka might be Widor's undoing: "[Widor] was dazzled; was Seraphitus going to burn his wings for this demon?" Jullian, *Robert de Montesquiou*, 108. Although undocumented, Andrew Thomson claims that Widor's Opus 66 Quatour (dedicated to Potocka) was "inspired by his passionate affair with Countess Emmanuela Potocka." Thomson's titillating prose has more the air of a romance novel than scholarly writing when he fancies: "[The] expression of intimate erotic feeling in the slow movement is enhanced by the piano's Lisztian flutterings and tremblings." Raugel and Thomson, "Widor, Charles-Marie," 360. Without documentation of any such multiple dalliances, Thomson conjectures, "[Widor] was a highly-sexed man who indulged in a number of affairs." Thomson, *Charles-Marie Widor*, 26.

107. See A.D., "4ème registre des délibérations du Conseil de Fabrique de la paroisse St. Sulpice: 1855–1888."

108. Trillat, "Charles-Marie Widor," 1–3.

109. Valbelle, "Quelques souvenirs," 1.

110. Trillat, "Charles-Marie Widor," 5–6. Trillat's reference to "C major" is apt in that it implied there were no daring harmonies, but there may be another reason; Widor agreed that "nothing surpasses the power of the chord of C sustained for a long time from low to high." Widor, Preface to *Les Couperin*, vi. And Henri Büsser (1872–1973) recalled about Gounod, "Didn't he say that God was in C?" Büsser, *Pelléas aux Indes galantes*, 61. Love for the organ remained a common thread in the friendship between Widor and Saint-Saëns. One of Saint-Saëns's letters carries the closing: "May S[ain]te Pédale protect us!!!!! and also Ste Gambe and St. Salicional, without forgetting Ste Fourniture and St. Prestant." B.I.(c), letter 3, dated June 28, 1896.

111. A.S-S., letter 2, dated November 14, 1895.

112. Widor, *Jean-Louis Forain*, 17.

113. *Ménestrel* 48 (1882): 382. Widor stated that he published this sonata at the same time as his first four organ symphonies (1872). Widor, "Souvenirs autobiographiques," 28. As no earlier version has surfaced, this is clearly an example of an error of recollection.

114. *Ménestrel* 48 (1882): 230.

115. Ibid., 95.

116. Ibid., 86.

117. Philipp, "Charles-Marie Widor," 126.

118. Trillat, "Charles-Marie Widor," 11.

119. Whitmer, "European Organs and Organists," 15.

120. B.I.(a), letter 87, dated September 10, 1884.

121. B.N.(d), letter 43, dated October 20, 1885.

122. *Ménestrel* 57 (1891): 104.

123. Cited in Thomson, *Charles-Marie Widor*, 41.

124. *Ménestrel* 69 (1903): 5.

125. *Ménestrel* 60 (1894): 376. The concert took place November 10, 1894. Widor, "Souvenirs autobiographiques," 69.

126. Blakeman, *Taffanel*, 105.

127. *Monde Musical* 2, no. 18 (January 30, 1890): 4.

128. Blakeman, *Taffanel*, 75.

129. Blakeman, *Taffanel*, 78, 105.

130. N.E.C., letter dated November 21, 1896.

131. Widor also arranged the Romance for violin and piano: "I have, it is true, arranged the Romance (flute), Op. 34, for violin." B.N., letter 14, dated December 4 [no year, no addressee].

132. Toff, *Monarch of the Flute*, 164.

133. Ibid.

134. Quoted in Blakeman, *Taffanel*, 106.

135. Ibid.

136. Dupré, *Marcel Dupré: Interview*, side 1.

137. Widor, "Un poète," *Piano Soleil* (December 6, 1891): 2.

138. *Ménestrel* 49 (1882): 22.

139. S.M.L., letter 4, dated September 29, 1883.

140. *Ménestrel* 52 (1886): 189–91.

141. Ibid., 183.

142. Widor, "Un poète," 2.

143. Curiously, although *Maître Ambros* had already been mounted in May at the Opéra-Comique, he wrote to Marie Trélat from Lyon on September 6, 1886: "I am working here fifteen hours a day—I just finished my *overture* to *Maître Ambros* that I will conduct for the first time in Amsterdam at the end of October." He likely meant the completion of the extracted Orchestral Suite. S.M.L., letter 5.

144. *Ménestrel* 53 (1886): 5.

145. Ibid.

146. Ibid. Many years later, Widor postulated, "If it is good to paint in order to judge a painting, it is not bad, I think, when one wants to be an art critic, to be familiar with the country of the artists of whom one speaks and the riches of their museums." Widor, *Moreau-Nélaton*, 10–12.

147. *Ménestrel* 53 (1886): 5.

148. Marie-Ange Guibaud, conversation with the author, 1990.

149. *Ménestrel* 56 (1890): 95.

150. Conway, "Widor's organ symphonies," 57 (1933–34): 540.

151. Family arch.

152. *L'Art Musical* 26 (1887): 20; *Ménestrel* 53 (1887): 72.

153. Author's collection.

154. *Biographie Musicale Française* 14 (January–March 1888): 7. Gustave Bret correctly dated these symphonies even though he has the dates of the Opus 13 Symphonies confused. Bret, "Symphonies pour orgue," 16. Also, on January 23, 1888, Widor wrote a letter to a Mr. Schœffer, the secretary to Queen Antonia (1845–1913) of Romania, in which he responds to the Queen's desire to know his organ music: "I have thus given the order to my publisher to send my *eight symphonies* and several other pieces to Romania; I think the publisher will have addressed them quite simply to the palace [in Bucharest], and I know that etiquette does not authorize me to offer them to the Queen without authorization. Thus, I am asking you to intercept the delivery of the parcel of music and to please present it to Her Majesty." Les Autographes, 45 rue de l'Abbé Grégoire, Paris, sales catalogue no. 127 "Orgue," January 2009, item 264.

155. *Ménestrel* 55 (1889): 207. Widor evidently considered this performance one of his most significant, as he made special mention of it in his "Souvenirs": "On July 3, 1889, I gave a concert at the Trocadéro, where I played my Eighth Symphony, the Aria of Bach with Delsart, the Fifth Symphony, and the Toccata and Fugue in D Minor of Bach." Widor, "Souvenirs autobiographiques," 61.

156. Ibid., 224.

157. *L'Art Musical* 28 (1889): 100.

158. Whitmer, "Widor's Organ 'Symphonies,'" 311.

159. Riemenschneider, "Program Notes," 267.

160. *Ménestrel* 75 (1909): 198.

161. M.S., letter dated January 20, 1939, from Mathilde Montesquiou Widor to Albert Schweitzer in Lambaréné. Although Widor played his Fifth Symphony and later the *Symphonie gothique* in concert very often, he did perform three movements from the Eighth Symphony in 1905 when he demonstrated a large Mutin organ (perhaps the rebuilt Cavaillé-Coll instrument destined for Sacré-Cœur) still set up in the factory. He also played Bach's Toccata, Adagio, and Fugue in C Major (BWV564), and he accompanied Madame Charles Max, who sang a Handel aria, a Schumann *Lied*, and an Ave Maria by Widor. *Ménestrel* 71 (1905): 208.

162. B.I.(c), letter 54, dated September 29, 1919. Harold D. Phillips confirmed, "When . . . I think of Widor, I am reminded of Liszt and the piano, not only because Widor has brought about innovations in methods of composition, but because he has converted the technique of the organ into something nearly identical with that of the piano . . . with the result that organists who play his pieces must be, we may almost say, the equals of pianists in mechanical facility of hand." "'Widor and the organ': An interview with Harold D. Phillips," *Christian Science Monitor* 13 (March 26, 1921): 12. Although Widor's hands were apparently not large, he was capable of wide stretches that made it easy for him to attain the strictest legato. M. Dumesnil, "Widor," 143.

163. Eymieu, *Études et biographies musicales*, 15.

164. Widor, *Fondations, portraits*, 53.

165. Widor, *Bach: Œuvres complètes pour orgue*, 2: v.

166. Ibid., 3: iii.

167. *Ménestrel* 54 (1888): 376.

168. *Ménestrel* 56 (1890): 94.

169. *Ménestrel* 55 (1889): 72; Widor, "Souvenirs autobiographiques," 60.

170. Widor, "Souvenirs autobiographiques," 35.

171. *Ménestrel* 75 (1909): 191. Olga Samaroff Stokowski (1880–1948), wife of the famed conductor, who studied organ with Widor in the 1890s and whom Widor referred to as "Mme Grande Artiste," performed the *Fantaisie* in an all-Widor concert with the composer conducting the London Symphony Orchestra in Queen's Hall in May 1909. Kline, *Olga Samaroff Stokowski*, 23, 68, 71.

172. *Ménestrel* 60 (1894): 343.

173. *Times* [London] 32,959 (March 14, 1890): 10, col. 4.

174. *Ménestrel* 58 (1892): 36–37. The Paris Conservatory was located at the corner of rue Bergère and Faubourg-Poissonnière.

175. *Musical Times* 31 (1890): 207. Widor mentioned this performance in passing in his "Souvenirs," 62.

176. *Musica Sacra* 12 (1890): 79.

177. Widor, "La musique à Sidney," *Piano Soleil* (March 5, 1893): 1.

178. Hugounet, *Musique et la pantomime*, 58–59, 61, 65. For another account, see Widor, "'Jeanne d'Arc' à l'Hippodrome," *Piano Soleil* (August 30, 1891): 2–3.

179. Widor, "'Jeanne d'Arc' à l'Hippodrome," 2–3. In a related anecdotal account, Widor related: "Do I smoke? . . . Certainly. [Georges] Clemenceau [1841–1929] advised that I use tobacco to contend with the effects of the heat and unpleasant smells of the ring in the Hippodrome on the Avenue de l'Alma. The bankers Berthier had built this circus where one gave performances with choruses and orchestra. After Massenet's *Roi de Lahore*, my *Jeanne d'Arc* was performed [there] for two years during the summer months. The rehearsals were toilsome because my two orchestras were a hundred meters apart and I had to bring them together by crossing a ring roasted by the sun. To cross it, people suggested a roman chariot, then the carriage of the Duke of Brunswick, and finally a smart horse that bowed to the women. My horsemanship greatly amused Clemenceau, who came to see me every day and taught me how to smoke cigarettes. I have continued." "Les histoires de Charles Widor," *Jour* (March 14, 1937), B.N. Fonds Mont. Widor confided that since that time he had never been able to correct himself of the habit. Spencer, "Widor," 222. However, he reserved smoking for special moments of relaxation. A survey on "Tobacco and its Influence" taken of famous writers and musicians posed three questions: "(1) Do you smoke? (2) Pipe, cigar, or cigarette? (3) How does the tobacco act on your body and your creative faculties?" Widor responded, "(1) Yes; (2) Three cigarettes when drinking my coffee, if the coffee is good. If no coffee, no cigarettes. Never when working, never when going for a walk; (3) Influence unknown." *Comœdia Illustré* 22 (1910): 645; 24 (1910): 706.

180. Widor, "'Jeanne d'Arc' à l'Hippodrome," 3.

181. Widor, "Souvenirs autobiographiques," 62.

182. Hugounet, *Musique et la pantomime*, 62.

183. *Ménestrel* 56 (1890): 191.

184. Ibid., 203.

185. *L'Art Musical* 30 (1891): 116.

186. *Ménestrel* 57 (1891): 253.

187. Hugounet, *Musique et la pantomime*, 119–21.

188. Ibid., 65.

189. *L'Art Musical* 29 (1890): 190.

190. Widor, "Nécrologie," *Piano Soleil* (May 22, 1892): 1.

191. Delibes died in January 1891, leaving his chair in the Academy of Fine Arts vacant. Both Guiraud and Lalo were favored as possible successors. Widor wrote, "For

what reasons did Lalo fail to respond? I can scarcely say, the author of *Roi d'Ys* having never very clearly explained it to me when I found myself charged with presenting the subject to him by some friends who were part of the illustrious assembly and who were desirous of voting for him." Widor, "Nécrologie," 1.

192. Vierne, "Memoirs of Louis Vierne" (October 1938): 13.

193. Widor, *Initiation musicale*, 126. Regarding Franck's funeral, Widor observed:

In the course of the funeral ceremony of Franck, it is true that two blunders were committed (I will cite, however, the very moving funeral oration of curé Gardey):

1. The grand organ, which was supposed to be silent and on which was hung a great velum awning, was played to the surprise of everyone by Mr. Gigout, whom no one had asked to play. [According to Fauré, Gigout played the organ at the request of the Franck family. Fauré, *Hommage à Eugène Gigout*, 17.]

2. It was, in my opinion, wrong to perform the *Libera* of the choirmaster Samuel Rousseau, which is too decorative and too theatrical, and which had the added effect of shocking many friends of the *maître*. Widor, "Souvenirs autobiographiques," 64.

194. Smith, *Louis Vierne*, 53; Vierne, "Memoirs of Louis Vierne" (October 1938): 13.

195. Smith, *Louis Vierne*, 33.

196. Ibid.; Vierne, "Memoirs of Louis Vierne" (October 1938): 13.

197. Smith, *Louis Vierne*, 55; Vierne, "Memoirs of Louis Vierne" (October 1938): 13.

198. B.I.(a), letter 49, dated October 10, 1891. Widor himself, on the other hand, found much to praise in Franck's *Béatitudes*: "The very serious organ professor at the Conservatory has put the best of his talent, all the faith of his soul in the *Béatitudes*; there are pages of the first order, all is balanced, reasoned, and calm." Widor, "Revue musicale," *Estafette* (July 15, 1878): 2. Widor did admit later, however, that while he was fond of the mystic and religious Beatitudes, he thought that the dramatic and satanic ones were very tame and uninteresting; he explained, "Franck was too good, too religious a man to write music depicting the evil one." Stiven, *Organ Lofts of Paris*, 60. In view of Dorchain's harsh opinion of Franck, it is all the more understandable that he asked Widor to play the organ at his wedding in Sainte Clotilde in 1887, while Franck was still *titulaire*. *Ménestrel* 53 (1887): 87.

199. Fauquet, *César Franck*, 959. Constant Pierre cites Widor as a member of the organ jury from 1878 to 1888. Pierre, *Conservatoire national de musique*, 406. In the intervening year of 1876 Widor served on the organ jury for the Niedermeyer École de musique religieuse. *Musica Sacra* 2 (August 1876): 98.

200. Widor, "Concours du Conservatoire," *Estafette* (July 30, 1877): 2.

201. Vallas, *César Franck*, 259. Thomas was said to have been somewhat hostile to Franck, but Théodore Dubois protested otherwise: "This was not true; . . . he appreciated fully the exceptional worth of César Franck." From *Discours de M. Théodore Dubois, souvenir de César Franck du 22 Octobre, 1904*; cited in Douglass, *Cavaillé-Coll*, 174.

202. Widor, "La classe d'orgue," 238. Rather than the death of Victor Massé, Widor's recollection may date from the death of François Bazin (1816–78). On July 10, 1878, Guilmant addressed a letter to Thomas stating that he had read in the papers that Franck might succeed Bazin as professor of composition, in which case he (Guilmant) was offering his candidacy for the succession of Franck as professor of organ. A.N.(c).

Concerning Dupré's narrations of incidents from Widor's life, the following analogous account is offered for comparison to Widor's own, given above; Dupré reversed one substantial piece of information: "[Franck] often stopped at Saint-Sulpice and waited for his friend at the foot of the stairway of the organ. One day, Franck, with his candor and legendary modesty, declared to him [Widor]: 'I would like very much to obtain a composition class at the Conservatory. I believe that I would know how to counsel these young men very well. Perhaps I have some chance, for certain of my works are beginning to be known. If my desire is realized, I will speak of you to the director (Ambroise Thomas in that period) for my succession to the organ class.'" Dupré, "Souvenirs sur Ch.-M. Widor," 31.

In his "Souvenirs," Widor offered yet another version of the account:

In coming down from the organ gallery at Saint-Sulpice one day in the summer of 1881 [1878 (Bazin's death) or 1884 (Benoist's retirement)?], I still see César Franck; [I was] very astonished to see him there. [He informed me], "The professor of composition has died; it is necessary to replace him." Franck was much less an organist than a composer. "Go ask your friend the Minister [Thomas] to have you appointed professor of organ in my place, and I will take the composition class."

Not being wealthy, Franck tried to pry some students away from the other classes. Ambroise Thomas, on the complaint of several professors, reproached him for it. His organ class broke down; Büsser tells about it. (Put here the anecdote of Büsser [the anecdote is lacking]).

I abstained from taking any steps, fearing intrigues.

Franck had called on Théodore Dubois, upon [the latter's] return from Rome. He relinquished the baton of choirmaster for Dubois, and became organist of Sainte-Clotilde. It's thus at the solicitation of Théodore Dubois that Franck was appointed professor of the organ class at the Conservatory upon the death [actually retirement] of Benoist. Franck had never specially studied the organ and his ideal was to become professor of composition rather than professor of organ. He was a very fine musician, but not a specialist and was not especially endowed with a true organistic classicism. Now, father Thomas, who was kindness itself, had been a little shocked to see that Franck, becoming professor of organ at the Conservatory, solicited a bit in various classes, looking to attract to himself the composition students. Widor, "Souvenirs autobiographiques," 55–56.

Further on, Widor continued:

César Franck had aroused the animosity of certain of his Conservatory colleagues by going to fish for students in the classes of his colleagues. Poor Franck was the only wage earner in his family; he had a son, and he was looking to earn as much money as possible. He worked very hard, but without an organ, which did not prohibit him from writing some masterpieces. He had no organ in his home, he had never studied the organ—it's absolutely false [to maintain that he did] (d'Indy maintains the contrary), and he had never been an organ student, nor won any organ prize. Widor, "Souvenirs autobiographiques," 62.

Widor either chose not to acknowledge or was ignorant of the fact that Franck was indeed a pupil in Benoist's organ class at the Paris Conservatory in 1841 and that he did win a second prize.

203. Widor, "Souvenirs autobiographiques," 58.

204. Smith, *Louis Vierne*, 59; Vierne, "Memoirs of Louis Vierne" (November 1938): 10.

205. Widor, "Souvenirs autobiographiques," 58.

206. In addition to Widor's letter of candidacy came those of Guilmant (November 10), Loret (November 11), and Gigout (November 13), each offering his qualifications at some length. Guilmant's letter closes: "I have not forgotten, dear *maître*, that it is you who obtained employment for me at the church of La Trinité, and that your support has been mine in all circumstances." A.N.(c).

207. Smith, *Louis Vierne*, 39.

208. B.N.(d), letter 8. The date "Nov. 1890" and addressee "à Imbert" have been penciled onto the top of this letter; while the first notation is correct, the second certainly is not (all other letters in the collection addressed to Hugues Imbert are marked "Legs, H. Imbert"). Other evidence might suggest the addressee was J.-B. Weckerlin, Conservatory librarian. However, after discovering the letter quoted next, and in view of the note Widor wrote at the top of the present letter, the author feels that the addressee was most likely Léo Delibes, professor of composition at the Conservatory and renowned composer of ballets and operas. Certainly, if Delibes was not the true addressee of this letter, he must have received a similar one.

The reference to Guilmant as "the blind one" seems a bit puzzling. Before a successful eye operation, however, he did have a disorder that for years prohibited him from facing intense light. On the other hand, this may simply be an artistic slur.

209. B.I.(a), letter 45.

210. Six letters, 65–70, from Ferry to Widor are conserved in B.I.(a); each bears witness to a very warm friendship between the two men. Letter 68 begins, "My dear Widor, you are an angel! And your friends are as celestial."

211. B.I.(a), letter 190. Not only Widor sought the entreaties of influential people. In turn, and apparently unbeknownst to each other, both Guilmant and Gigout went to Pauline Viardot, the great diva and former professor of voice at the Conservatory, asking her to speak in their favor to Thomas. Writing to the director on November 19 (already too late to affect his decision), she concluded: "I have promised nothing [to them], quite certain that what you do will be well considered." A.N.(c).

212. A.N.(c), 1-A.

213. A.N.(b).

214. Vierne, "Journal (Fragments)," 166.

215. Reynaud, *Œuvre de Ch.-M. Widor*, 8.

216. Smith, *Louis Vierne*, 59.

217. Widor, "La classe d'orgue," 238. As mentioned earlier in this biography, one of the weak links in this chain of descendants is that Hesse was only a child of eight when Forkel died; another is Lemmens's avowal that "Mr. Hesse has taught me very little." Soderlund, *How Did They Play?*, 516.

218. Hensel, "Charles-Marie Widor."

219. Thomas, "Organ Loft Whisperings" (November 29, 1893): 19.

220. Family arch. Note that Hensel thought his eyes were grey, Thomas found them brown, and the passport agency described them as dark.

221. Stiven, *Organ Lofts of Paris*, 53–54.

222. A.N.(a). Students not previously mentioned: Achille Runner (1870–1940); Paul Ternisien (b. 1870); Jules Bouval; André Burgat (b. 1865); Henri Büsser; Georges Guiraud (1868–1928); Charles Tournemire (1870–1939); Georges Berger (b. 1871).

223. Years later, Dupré confirmed the same impression: "I still see [Widor] with his eternal polka-dot lavallière, his ex-officer's countenance with the little moustache and tuft of whiskers below his lower lip, and stern look, even when he was joking." Dupré,

"Marcel Dupré nous conte," 1. Albert Riemenschneider similarly described Widor, but attributed his demeanor to the depth of his character: "Widor is usually considered by most persons who have come in contact with him to be rather severe and even austere. This may be true. No organist ever had higher ideals or tried to live up to these ideals with more definiteness than did Widor. . . . His sternness and austerity are simply the by-product of his high idealism and unyielding devotion to the highest standards with him." Riemenschneider, "Widor: An Estimate," 4.

224. The "antique 'bagpipe'" apparently lacked almost any redeeming qualities. The entire organ was enclosed in a single swell box with a two-notched hitch-down pedal. There were three reversible pedals (Grand-orgue Trompette, Récit Trompette, Pédale Basson) and three couplers (Récit/Grand-orgue, Grand-orgue/Pédale, Récit/Pédale). Vierne gave its specification, noting that the Grand-orgue Dessus de Montre and Prestant were "unusable":

> *Grand-orgue* (54 notes): Bourdon 8', Flûte 8', Dessus de Montre 8', Prestant 4', Trompette 8';
>
> *Récit* (54 notes): Flûte 8', Gambe 8', Voix céleste 8', Flûte 4', Hautbois 8' (free reeds), Trompette 8';
>
> *Pédale*: Soubasse 16', Flûte 8', Flûte 4', Basson 8'. Vierne, *In Memoriam Louis Vierne*, 22.

225. Even in his later years, Widor demanded no less than perfection from his students. Albert Riemenschneider described hearing an organist from Sweden begin his lesson with Widor: "It was the E Flat Prelude of Bach. A number of requests to repeat the opening measure drew [my] closer attention to the episode and before the organist went on there were seventeen repetitions by actual count of the opening measure until it was considered satisfactory." Riemenschneider, "Tribute to Widor," 26.

226. Smith, *Louis Vierne*, 55–69; Vierne, "Memoirs of Louis Vierne" (November 1938): 10.

227. Smith, *Louis Vierne*, 93; Vierne, "Memoirs of Louis Vierne" (January 1939): 8.

228. Smith, *Louis Vierne*, 73.

229. Smith, *Louis Vierne*, 91, 93. *Ménestrel's* review of the concert does not indicate if this happened.

230. Ibid., 92, 93, 95.

231. Trillat, "Charles-Marie Widor," 8.

232. Henderson, "Widor and His Organ Class," 341; see also Barnes, "Organ Student," 25. Although this observation is basically accurate, Widor did play some organ music by other composers, such as Lemmens, Mendelssohn, and Saint-Saëns.

233. Eddy, "Great Frenchmen," 14.

234. Thomas, "Organ Loft Whisperings" (November 29, 1893): 19.

235. *Musica Sacra* 7 (1882): 83.

236. Fauquet, *César Franck*, 474.

237. Widor, "La classe d'orgue," 238.

238. Fauquet, *César Franck*, 476. Fauquet points out, "Franck observed to the letter . . . the program such as was already in force from the time when he was a student. The rules [established in 1848] stipulated that 'the study of organ, principally designed for improvisation, is essentially bound up with the study of harmony and composition, which is indispensable to the organist.'" In 1870, the description of the class was officially expanded: "The teaching will be given from the technical and liturgical point of view." Franck claimed to adhere to this stipulation as well (476).

239. Widor, "La classe d'orgue," 238.

240. Quoted in Fauquet, *César Franck*, 477.

241. Ibid.

242. Widor, "Revue musicale," *Estafette* (July 30, 1877): 2.

243. W. H. Miller confirmed, "The least deviation from the written score, the least roughness in the handling of a phrase, the smallest vagaries in fingering—even the pedal held an instant longer than the manuals on the last chord of a piece—will bring from him that well-known trick of his of the sharp drawing-in of his breath, as if someone had hurt him,—and you have." Miller, "L'école Widor," 488.

244. Widor, "Souvenirs autobiographiques," 54–55.

245. This quotation from Tournemire's "Mémoires inédits" is cited in Fauquet, *César Franck*, 477.

246. Widor, "Souvenirs autobiographiques," 58.

247. *Maître de Chapelle* 2, no. 7 (February 1, 1900): 5.

248. Of those volumes, Widor wrote: "[Richault] was the first French publisher who dared to publish Bach. He published three volumes of the preludes and fugues, then three books of the chorales, which he gave to the Conservatory. The three volumes of preludes and fugues were put into practice, but not the three volumes of chorales." Widor, "Souvenirs autobiographiques," 27. Further on he reckoned that the Bach volumes preceded Franck's tenure: "I took the organ class in succession of Franck in 1890, a class that he whom people called 'Grandfather Benoist' had directed, and who during innumerable years [1819–72], without ever having been *titulaire* of any church, was organ professor at the Conservatory. He was, moreover, very much up to his task, having some excellent musicians in his organ class. He made them improvise. He attached, most certainly, more importance to bearing than to technique, and it's thus that in this organ class was found, next to the blower, a cupboard that contained the entire necessary organ library, which included the six books of Richault—three books of preludes and fugues, and three books of chorales by Bach" (57–58). Indeed, Benoist trained such admirable musicians as A. Adam, Alkan, Bazin, Bizet, Chauvet, Danjou, Félicien David, Delibes, Diémer, Th. Dubois, César Franck, Lavignac, Lecocq, Lefébure-Wély, H. Maréchal, Massenet, Paladilhe, Pugno, Saint-Saëns. Benoist would certainly have introduced some of the organ works of Bach to the classes. Bourligueux, "Benoist, François," 121. That the books of chorale preludes were ignored bewildered Widor:

> A strange thing, at the Conservatory, they didn't then know the three books of chorale preludes of J. S. Bach: they neither played them at the competitions nor at the exams. I will never forget the impression of Ambroise Thomas who, no matter what people may have said, was a very fine musician, listening to Libert (today organist of the Basilica of Saint-Denis) play one of the chorale preludes of Bach. He remained dumbfounded, pressing the book between his hands, returning it: "What is this? How is it that people don't play these chorale preludes? Could this pupil play one more of them for us?"
>
> Thus, the whole of Book One of the Chorale Preludes was played by the pupil Libert, to the great joy of the jury, most of whose members, let's admit, did not know it. Since Richault had published these chorale preludes, people had never played them, and when by chance you dared to open one of [the books], it cracked between your fingers like a work just issued from the printer (15).

249. Smith, *Louis Vierne*, 103; Vierne, "Memoirs of Louis Vierne" (January 1939): 8.

250. Widor, Preface to *L'orgue de Jean-Sébastien Bach*, xxxvi.

251. Ibid., xxxvi–xxxvii.

252. Widor, "Souvenirs autobiographiques," 64–65.

253. Smith, *Louis Vierne*, 65.

254. Widor, "Souvenirs autobiographiques," 65.

255. Smith, *Louis Vierne*, 65.

256. Widor, "Conservatoire de musique," 1–2. In music for the theater, Widor insisted dogmatically, "it's the poet's text, the precise sense of the *word* that must be translated; the musician is only an interpreter." Widor, *Fondations, portraits*, 237.

257. Widor, "Conservatoire de musique," 2.

258. Widor, "Réformes au Conservatoire," *Piano Soleil* (May 29, 1892): 2.

259. Ibid., 1.

260. Ibid.

261. Pierre, *Conservatoire national de musique*, 375.

262. Ibid.

263. Widor, *Fondations, portraits*, 188.

264. Widor, "Chronique," *Piano Soleil* (December 8, 1895): 1. Although complaining about the facility at that time, Widor later remembered it with some fondness: "All of us recall, not without emotion, the little hall at the rue Bergère where [Luigi] Cherubini [1760–1842; the Conservatory's first director] had performed some of Beethoven's symphonies for the first time, and also where Fétis later performed the Concerto in G. This hall was supposed to hold five to six hundred people at most. It was formed with a half balcony and a row of boxes, and it was in the official box, at the back of which a very awkward staircase, incredibly narrow, that Bonaparte climbed, coming to attend the distribution of prizes so that he himself might present a memorial bassoon to a bassoonist [a musician of the Consular Guard] to replace one that had been cut in half [between his hands by gun fire] at Marengo. It's certainly thanks to his slenderness that [Bonaparte] could get up there! It's in this same hall that our organ courses took place. The organ was fed by a blower, and next to this blower was a little cabinet containing the few works constituting the special library of the school. Widor, "Souvenirs autobiographiques," 27–28; also Widor, *Fondations, portraits*, 188–89.

265. A.N.(b), letter dated April 29, 1903, to F. Bourgeat.

266. This synopsis is found in the Family arch.

267. Widor, "Souvenirs autobiographiques," 59.

268. *Ménestrel* 57 (1891): 83.

269. Widor, "Un poète," *Piano Soleil* (December 6, 1891): 2.

270. Widor, "Souvenirs autobiographiques," 40.

271. B.N.(d), letter 19, to Mr. Schatté. Curiously, Widor did not possess the complete score, as he made another urgent request of Mr. Schatté for the score on July 15, 1891. B.N.(d), letter 18.

272. S.M.L., letter 7, dated August 14, 1889.

273. *Ménestrel* 57 (1891): 83.

274. Widor, "Souvenirs autobiographiques," 68.

275. Widor, *Conte d'avril*, Paris: Au Ménestrel, Heugel & Cie., 1892.

276. *Ménestrel* 57 (1891): 375.

277. *Ménestrel* 61 (1895): 348.

278. *Ménestrel* 58 (1892): 197. Berthe Max was likely the daughter of Mrs. Charles Max, whose "five o'clock musicales" were frequented by numerous members of the Academy of Fine Arts, especially Widor. Chimènes, *Mécènes et musiciens*, 185.

279. Widor, "Souvenirs autobiographiques," 68.

280. *Ménestrel* 59 (1893): 183.
281. Reynaud, *Œuvre de Ch.-M. Widor*, 21, 23.
282. B.I.(a), letter 30, dated September 30, [1889].
283. B.I.(a), letters 202 and 203, dated November 1898.
284. Widor, "Marsick et Lefort," *Piano Soleil* (November 20, 1892): 1–2. The members of the string quartet: Narcisse-Augustin Lefort (b. 1852) violinist; Victor Balbreck (b. 1862) violinist; Louis Van Waefelghem (1840–1908) violist; Jules Delsart, cellist.
285. *Ménestrel* 88 (1926): 222–23; see also *Ménestrel* 57 (1891): 46.
286. Widor, "En Belgique," *Piano Soleil* (January 3, 1892): 1.
287. Ibid.
288. *Ménestrel* 60 (1894): 69.
289. Ibid., 208; also *Ménestrel* 61 (1895): 45.
290. B.N.(d), letter 21, dated February 28, 1894.
291. *Ménestrel* 88 (1926): 501.
292. Widor, "Wilder et Mozart," *Piano Soleil* (October 23, 1892): 1.
293. Widor, "G. Cavaillé-Coll et Kastner-Boursault," 2.
294. B.N.(a), letter 165.
295. B.I.(a), (Ferry letters: 65–70), letter dated October 19 (no year, but likely 1891); cited in Shuster, "Orgue de Charles-Marie Widor," 27.
296. C. Cavaillé-Coll and E. Cavaillé-Coll, *Aristide Cavaillé-Coll*, 145. For example, when the organ of Saint-Ouen, Rouen, was completed, Cavaillé-Coll told Albert Dupré (1860–1940) that the instrument had cost him personally eighteen thousand francs: "But I am not sorry to have lost money. I wanted to create something beautiful." Murray, *Marcel Dupré*, 12.
297. Cited in Shuster, "Orgue de Charles-Marie Widor," 27.
298. Puget, "Widor et Cavaillé-Coll," 61.
299. Widor, "G. Cavaillé-Coll et Kastner-Boursault," 1.
300. Roth, *Sacré-Cœur de Montmartre*, 13.
301. Cited in Roth, *Sacré-Cœur de Montmartre*, 14.
302. Puget, "Widor et Cavaillé-Coll," 61.
303. Roth, *Sacré-Cœur de Montmartre*, 14.
304. Puget, "Widor et Cavaillé-Coll," 61. On March 18, 1893, the commerce court forbade Gabriel to unite the name Coll to Cavaillé. Shuster, "Orgue de Charles-Marie Widor," 28.
305. Following is the organ's disposition:

Grand-Orgue expressif (56 notes): Montre 8', Flûte harmonique 8', Prestant 4'
Récit expressif (56 notes): Bourdon 8', Gambe 8', Voix céleste 8', Flûte octaviante 4', Basson-hautbois 8', Trompette 8'; Widor had the Trompette replaced by a Plein-Jeu III about 1900.
Pédale (30 notes): Soubasse 16'
Pédales de combinaison: Appel Soubasse 16', Appel Basson-hautbois, Tirasse G.-O., Tirasse Récit; Copula Octaves graves du Récit sur le G.-O. Expression Récit, Expression G.-O.

This organ was restored to its original disposition in 1985 and is now located in the church of Selongey (Côte-d'Or). Clerc, "L'orgue de Charles-Marie Widor," 11–13; the disposition is given a bit differently in Riemenschneider, "Widor's Organ," 213.
306. Miller, "L'école Widor," 488; Pierre, *Les facteurs d'instruments*, 218–20.

307. Puget, "Widor et Cavaillé-Coll," 61; C. Cavaillé-Coll and E. Cavaillé-Coll, *Aristide Cavaillé-Coll*, 147. In 1894 Kastner-Boursault moved to the United States, where he lived until his death in 1913. Shuster, "Orgue de Charles-Marie Widor," 32.

308. Puget, "Widor et Cavaillé-Coll," 61.

309. Ibid.

310. C. Cavaillé-Coll and E. Cavaillé-Coll, *Aristide Cavaillé-Coll*, 146.

311. Ibid.

312. Brussel, "Ch.-M. Widor."

313. Philipp, "Paris," 9.

314. Widor, "Souvenirs autobiographiques," 49. During his residency, Widor reported that the bedroom of his apartment had been redecorated in new wallpaper "without screeching parrots; the new paper isn't bad, but the rest of the apartment seems quite dirty! Too bad, I only see it at night." Letter to his sister, Marie, dated August 7, 1897. Family arch. At the time of his move to 7 rue des Saints-Pères, Widor wrote to Marie Trélat: "I've fully moved and I'm sleeping at l'Abbaye tonight for the last time. The organ itself is installed and all is ready over there. This will be very good, but all the same I am a little crazy to leave my old walls where I have been so comfortable! My brother and sister-in-law are here. . . . Tomorrow morning they will help me carry away little knick-knacks in the last small cart and move me into my new room." S.M.L., letter 53, dated August 13, 1900.

315. Thomas, "Organ Loft Whisperings" (December 13, 1893): 12.

316. Ibid.

317. Ibid.

318. Landormy, *Franck à Debussy*, 171.

319. Thomas, "Organ Loft Whisperings" (December 13, 1893): 12.

320. Landormy, *Franck à Debussy*, 170–71.

321. *Ménestrel* 59 (1893): 125.

322. *The Organ* 2 (May 1893): 18.

323. *Ménestrel* 68 (1902): 136.

324. *Ménestrel* 58 (1892): 256.

325. B.N.(d), letter 33, dated November 14, [1892]. Widor had also written to Marie Trélat that he would soon be thinking about the *Marriage of Figaro*. S.M.L., letter 15, dated September 2, 1893.

326. Widor, "Souvenirs autobiographiques," 69–70.

327. Thomas, "Organ Loft Whisperings" (December 13, 1893): 12. Widor wrote to Marie Trélat on June 12, 1893: "Only yesterday I finished the second part of the Symphony; all of it must be sent to Geneva. . . . The Conservatory, where the examinations are taking place, is leaving me alone from this day on and free to compose without interruptions. . . . I haven't seen anyone these days except for the class that I had work in the evenings at my organ." B.N.(d), letter 29.

328. Thomas, "Organ Loft Whisperings" (December 13, 1893): 12.

329. *Ménestrel* 60 (1894): 381–82.

330. B.N.(d), letter 5, dated December 8, 1894, to Hugues Imbert.

331. Widor, "Victoria-Hall à Genève," *Piano Soleil* (December 16, 1894): 1. Widor greatly admired Saint-Saëns's Third Symphony, placing it among the highest manifestations of Saint-Saëns's compositional mastery, and he referred to Saint-Saëns as "the greatest French symphonist." Widor, *Fondations, portraits*, 155, 161; Widor, "La musique," 457. Soon after the premiere of Saint-Saëns's Third Symphony, Widor wrote to him: "I was wonderstruck at your symphony. What a beautiful work! What manner of expression and

what style! It's truly great art that refreshes and invigorates. It's superb, and owes nothing to anyone." A.S-S., letter 1, dated January 17, 1887. In 1905, Widor was to conduct Saint-Saëns's Symphony at the mansion of the Countess de Béarn; he wrote to Saint-Saëns giving him the schedule of rehearsals and asked, "Would you like to conduct it? I would then play the organ. The orchestra [of seventy musicians] is first-rate." A.S-S., letter 3, dated January 19, 1905. In 1910, both Saint-Saëns's and Widor's Third Symphonies were performed at the French Festival in Munich; Saint-Saëns reported, "Mr. Widor, who with a sure hand conducted his beautiful symphony with organ, did not disdain to take the organ part in mine." "Ce que pense M. Camille Saint-Saëns du Festival Français de l'Exposition de Munich," *Musica* 9 (November 1910): 173.

332. *Organ* 2 (August 1893): 92.

333. *Ménestrel* 61 (1895): 239. Vierne was organ soloist in two performances at the Paris Opéra on December 8 and 15, 1895, and again on June 11, 1896, when Widor conducted the symphony at the Trocadéro; "the success was complete." *Ménestrel* 61 (1895): 397; *Ménestrel* 62 (1896): 189.

334. Vierne, "Ch.-M. Widor," 76. Vierne provided a brief analysis of the work in Eymieu, "Nos grands organistes," 215–17.

335. *Ménestrel* 49 (1882): 22. In his "Souvenirs autobiographiques," Widor reported, "In December 1882, I went to conduct *La Korrigane* in Budapest. I went through Vienna. I was very much celebrated on this occasion" (53). And in a letter to Marie Trélat, he offered impressions of some performances he attended in Vienna: "I have spoken to you of *Lohengrin*; the next day at the same theater I heard an abominable ballet whose music people would have hissed at the Folies-Bergère, but Thursday I had a slight compensation with Mlle Bianchi in *Lucia* . . . ; she sings like a violin without any difficulty. . . . I [also] heard *Meistersinger*; in spite of some slowness, it is admirable—it's the incontestable masterpiece of Wagner. Furthermore, the performance of the men was no less magnificent than that of the women, and the perfection of the orchestra was hard to believe. We will never obtain anything like it in Paris. . . . Alas! Alas! We no longer have poetry in our country, nor do we even know how to listen anymore. During the four hours duration of *Meistersinger*, the hall, filled from top to bottom, observed a religious silence . . . and these people, following the musician in his course across the clouds, did not even look aside! I notice that I'm beginning a sermon." B.N.(d), letter 36, dated December 9, 1882.

336. *Ménestrel* 59 (1893): 31. B.N.(d), letter 27, dated January 19, 1893, to Marie Trélat from Budapest; letter 28, dated January 24, 1893, to Marie Trélat from Budapest.

337. Widor, "À Budapest," *Piano Soleil* (February 12, 1893): 1–2.

338. *Ménestrel* 56 (1890): 240; 58 (1892): 119; 59 (1893): 125, 168; 60 (1894): 399; 61 (1895): 80, 239.

339. *Ménestrel* 60 (1894): 348; see also 65 (1899): 56.

340. *Ménestrel* 61 (1895): 95; see also Widor, "Francfort-sur-le-Mein," *Piano Soleil* (April 21, 1895): 1–2.

341. *Ménestrel* 62 (1896): 271.

342. *Ménestrel* 58 (1892): 239.

343. *Ménestrel* 59 (1893): 192.

344. *Ménestrel* 59 (1893): 150; see also Widor, "Association des concerts de l'école moderne," 1–2.

345. Widor, "Association des concerts de l'école moderne," 2.

346. *Ménestrel* 61 (1895): 39. Some of the young composers in the group were Widor's students: Vierne, Libert, Tournemire, and Eymieu.

347. *Monde Musical* 2 (June 30, 1890): 7; *Ménestrel* 57 (1891): 95; *Ménestrel* 59 (1893): 48.

348. *Ménestrel* 57 (1891): 271.

349. *Ménestrel* 60 (1894): 221.

350. *Ménestrel* 72 (1906): 117.

351. *Musica Sacra* 12 (1890): 63. "The success of Mr. Widor has been especially great; the large audience that attended this festival greatly applauded the performance of the Sixth Symphony for Organ and Orchestra by the brilliant young composer." *L'Art Musical* 29 (1890): 38.

352. *Ménestrel* 56 (1890): 135. The inaugural concert included: Bach's Toccata, Adagio, and Fugue in C (BWV 564); Handel's Allegro from the Concerto in F; movements from his own symphonies [the Allegro from the Eighth Symphony had been programmed, but an Allegretto Pastorale (Second Symphony?) was substituted]; Marche Pontificale and Méditation (First Symphony); improvisations: Magnificat (versets composed for the occasion); Toccata (Fifth Symphony) for the Sortie. *Journal de Rouen* (April 9 and 17, 1890). Many years later, Widor did not recall the exact program, as he wrote a reminder in his "Souvenirs" to "Ask Albert Dupré [*titulaire* of Saint-Ouen] for the program of this inauguration." Widor also noted that the French society painter Léon Bonnat, who had painted his portrait in 1887 (this painting is owned by the author), was present at the inauguration. Widor, "Souvenirs autobiographiques," 61.

Concerning the "Magnificat versets," the program specified: "Fragments d'une symphonie gothique composée pour la circonstance par M. Widor" [Fragments from a *symphonie gothique* composed for the occasion by Mr. Widor]; this surprising indication suggests that Widor had already begun to conceive Opus 70 as early as 1890, and one might imagine that the "Puer natus est" variations served as versets. However, the mention of "certain storm effects" in one press description does not correspond with the character of the variations as they appeared in 1895: "Contrary to his strict and pure customs, [in the versets] he agreed to show some virtuosity with certain storm effects in opposition to a very pretty oboe tune. In his improvisations as in his written pieces, however, one always feels the superior organist whose style is austere, elevated, and personal, perhaps offered to all artists, to his emulators, and to his confrères as an irreproachable model." *Musica Sacra* 12, no. 11 (1890): 87. Another reviewer, S. Frère, summarized: "We do not have to judge the eminent organist of Saint-Sulpice from the compositional viewpoint. Mr. Widor is the incontestable leader of the French organ school; everything that comes from his pen is marked with originality and variety. His worth as performer is no longer in question; he juggles his keyboards without concern for the complications of the pedals, without anxiety over the stop combinations. He is there on the bench, as at home, following effortlessly his musical thought, interpreting Bach, Handel, and his own works with the grand style of a master and the elegance of a virtuoso." *Monde Musical* 2 (May 15, 1890): 7.

353. Philbert, *Causerie*, 76.

354. Widor, "Souvenirs autobiographiques," 61–62. With this trio of Cavaillé-Coll organs, Widor would boast eloquently, "In France we have the most beautiful instruments in the world; it's not matter-of-factly or without awe that, under the vaults of Notre-Dame, Saint-Sulpice, and Saint-Ouen, we have at our command their power, their grandeur, this mastery of sound singing eternity *ad astra* [to the stars]." Widor, *L'orgue de la chapelle du château de Versailles*, 4. And it was to Cavaillé-Coll that Widor always sang praises: "We have in Europe only one single and unique organ builder who is a great artist, an honest and industrial man whose works are absolutely worth the price that he

asks: Mr. Cavaillé-Coll. The others are as far from him as the prose of an apprentice literary man to that of Pascal or Bossuet." Philbert, *Causerie*, 10.

355. Widor, "Souvenirs autobiographiques," 68; also *Musica Sacra* 13 (1891): 86. Widor presented two different recitals for the inauguration. The afternoon program included: Toccata and Fugue in D Minor (BWV 565), Bach; Fifth Symphony, Widor; Largo (Sonata, Op. 2, no. 2), Beethoven; Allegro in F (Concerto, Op. 4, no. 4), Handel; Meditation (First Symphony), Widor; Marche Pontificale (First Symphony), Widor. The evening program included: Prelude and Fugue in E Minor (BWV 548), Bach; Andante Cantabile (Fourth Symphony), Widor; Concerto in A Minor (BWV 592), Bach; Adagio (First Sonata), Mendelssohn; Sixth Symphony, Widor; Scherzando (Fourth Symphony?), Widor; Fugue in D Major (BWV 532), Bach. Beechey, "Organ Recitals," 109.

356. *Musica Sacra* 13 (1891): 85.

357. *Ménestrel* 58 (1892): 95.

358. *Ménestrel* 60 (1894): 120.

359. Ibid., 240.

360. *Musica Sacra* 17 (1894): 6.

361. Ibid. Guilmant performed a Bach Prelude and Fugue in E Minor, his own *Marche sur un thème d'Hœndel*, and an improvisation. Gigout performed his *Grand chœur dialogué*, a Communion, and his Toccata. Sergent provided the Introduction and Sortie.

362. Edward Shippen Barnes related, "Widor, at St. Sulpice, I heard play only Bach, his own works and improvisations. All three he does beautifully." Barnes, "Organ Student," 25.

363. Widor, "Revue musicale," *Estafette* (January 15, 1877): 1.

Part Four

1. Van Wye, "Gregorian Influences," 1.

2. Joy, *Albert Schweitzer*, 174.

3. Ibid., 25.

4. Ibid., 169.

5. Aubry, "Idées de Pie X," 54. On these ideas, Saint-Saëns expressed much more conservative thinking than Widor ever would when he excluded the organ works of Bach from church use: "I will astonish many people in saying that I would exile from the Catholic Church almost all the work of Sebastian Bach. His marvelous chorale preludes are of Protestant essence; and, except for a few, his preludes and fugues, fantasies, and toccatas are pieces where virtuosity holds a great place: it's music for concert and not church." Saint-Saëns, "La réforme," 151. Quite the contrary, Widor wrote in his preface to Schweitzer's *J. S. Bach*, "What speaks through [Bach's] works is pure religious emotion; and this is one and the same in all men, in spite of the national and religious partitions in which we are born and bred." Widor, Preface to *J. S. Bach*, x.

6. Widor, *Bach: Œuvres complètes pour orgue*, 3: xxvii.

7. S.M.L., letter 17.

8. Widor, "Saint-Ouen," 1.

9. Philbert, *Causerie*, 76; Widor, "Souvenirs autobiographiques," 61–62.

10. M. Dumesnil, "Widor," 143.

11. R. Dumesnil, *Portraits de musiciens français*, 200.

12. *Journal de Rouen* (April 9 and 17, 1890). The program listed: "Fragments d'une symphonie gothique composée pour la circonstance par M. Widor." (See the earlier discussion in part 3 concerning the inaugural recital.)

13. Henderson, "Memories of Widor," 657.

14. Geer, *Organ Registration*, 217–18.

15. The oft-cited omission of the variation by Marcel Dupré from his circa 1958 recording of the Symphony (variously: Westminster WST-14871; XWN-18871; Westminster Gold WGM-8172), cannot be considered definitive evidence, especially since primary sources offer no supporting evidence. It should be noted that Widor's Fifth Symphony appears on the flip side of Dupré's LP recording; there, the entire third movement is omitted and the end of the Toccata is considerably altered, partly by omitting four measures. The amount of time available on each side of the LP would appear to be a reasonable explanation for these omissions; Dupré's playing of the *Gothique* runs twenty-six minutes, and that of the Fifth Symphony runs twenty-six minutes, twenty-five seconds.

Dupré's own strong musical personality, as a great composer/organist, did not necessarily make him the most faithful interpreter of other composers' music. In the case of his recordings of Widor's works, Dupré sometimes veered dramatically from the composer's published registration directives. His 1957 recording (Mercury Living Presence CD 434 311-2; LP SR90169) of Widor's *Salve Regina* (Second Symphony) has particularly blatant disregard of Widor's requested registration. The liner notes quote Dupré: "The Gregorian melody on which it is built is treated as a chorale, interrupted twice by a polyphonic episode played on foundation stops. Then the melody breaks through again and rises to an impressive climax which gradually dies away in an atmosphere of mystic serenity." The final part was Dupré's interpretation, not Widor's notated intention. Yet, regarding another performance of the *Salve Regina*, Dupré wrote to Widor's niece, Gabrielle Guibaud, about "the admirable paraphrase that [Widor] wrote for organ on the 'Salve Regina.' During my whole recital, I thought with all my heart of you and my dearly-loved *maître*. . . . Do I need to tell you if the greatly-cherished memory of my *maître* lives each moment in my heart?" Family arch., letter dated April 19, 1969.

16. Widor, "Æolian," 17.

17. *Ménestrel* 61 (1895): 87.

18. Ibid., 143–44.

19. Widor, "La *Messe* en si mineur au Conservatoire," 1.

20. Grace, *French Organ Music*, 142.

21. Eddy, "Great Frenchmen," 14.

22. Ibid.

23. An unidentified news clipping, "Charles-Marie Widor," by N. Darros, written shortly after Widor's death. Family arch.

24. Widor, "Les Troyens," 2. See also Widor, *Initiation musicale*, 105: "Time makes masterpieces."

25. Thomas, "Organ Loft Whisperings" (December 13, 1893): 12.

26. When Widor inaugurated the new Cavaillé-Coll organ for the Église du Rosaire in Lourdes, both symphonies appeared on the program, along with Bach's Toccata and Fugue in D Minor and Mendelssohn's Sonata no. 1. He reported, "The large audience that crowded into the Church of the Rosary listened in the most absolute silence to these works, almost all of very severe character." Widor, "Le nouvel orgue de Lourdes," *Piano Soleil* (June 20, 1897): 1. For the inauguration of Mutin's rebuild of the Merklin organ at Saint-Philippe-du-Roule in Paris, he performed the two Symphonies, Bach's

Passacaglia, and two chorale Preludes: "In dir ist Freude" (BWV 615), "O Mensch, bewein dein Sünde gross" (BWV 622); and he concluded with a portion of the *Symphonie romane*. *Piano Soleil* (March 1, 1903): 2–3. He also paired the Fifth and *Gothique* on the program he played on the new Moscow Conservatory organ while it was still in the Mutin factory. *Courrier Musical* 3, no. 12 (March 24, 1900): 9.

27. Bret, "Symphonies pour orgue," 16. Widor said that he played the Symphony "every year at Saint-Sulpice for Christmas." Anonymous news clipping: "À 88 ans, le maître donne à la cathédrale de Salzbourg un magnifique concert d'orgue," B.N. Fonds Mont. Henry Eymieu reported that Widor also had the custom of playing the pastoral Cantabile from the Fifth Symphony at the Midnight Mass. *Musica Sacra* 14 (1892): 71.

28. *The New Harvard Dictionary of Music*, s.v. "Gregorian chant."

29. Widor quoted Peter Wagner for his thesis: "It is not possible," said Wagner, "to reflect even a bit deeply on our art without discovering its statements of solidarity with that of the Greeks. Modern art is in truth only a link in the chain of the aesthetic development of the whole of Europe, a development which has its point of departure among the Hellenes." Widor, "La musique grecque," 694.

30. *Ménestrel* 61 (1895): 336.

31. Aubry, "Idées de Pie X," 38.

32. Widor, "L'édition vaticane," 243.

33. Aubry, "Idées de Pie X," 42. Of the public taste, Pierre Aubry wrote: "In the abuses the Holy Father combats, part of the responsibilities justly lies with the common mentality of the parishioners. . . . In Paris, the poor taste of the faithful is usually shown at the marriage masses: instead of allowing the organist to perform at the processional or recessional some chosen piece from the beautiful classical repertoire, they request of him . . . some march from *Lohengrin* or *Roméo et Juliette*. Master Guilmant relates . . . that it has been necessary for him on several occasions to refuse to the parishioners of La Trinité the minuet from *l'Arlesienne*" (45).

34. The author has a copy of the typewritten letter, originally enclosed in a sleeve signed in Widor's hand and titled: "Le plain-chant des Solesmes," 1.

35. Ibid.

36. Widor, "L'édition vaticane," 240–41. Elsewhere, Widor expressed a similar sentiment: "The venerable Dom Pothier and his followers, the Benedictine archivists, have translated [the neumes] with an almost exaggerated conscience, for their editions reproduce the good and the bad. As archivists, they have collected the texts; well, these texts are music, and it's up to musicians to judge them." Widor, *Fondations, portraits*, 218.

37. Widor, *Initiation musicale*, 107.

38. "Le plain-chant des Solesmes," 6; see also Widor, "La révision du plain-chant," 60.

39. "Le plain-chant des Solesmes," 6–7; see also Widor, "La révision du plain-chant," 60–61.

40. Widor, "L'édition vaticane," 241.

41. *Ménestrel* 88 (1926): 529–30; also Widor, *Fondations, portraits*, 229.

42. "Le plain-chant des Solesmes," 3; see also Widor, "La révision du plain-chant," 58.

43. "Le plain-chant des Solesmes," 2; see also Widor, "La révision du plain-chant," 57–58.

44. "Le plain-chant des Solesmes," 11–12, 13; see also Widor, "La révision du plain-chant," 64–65.

45. Widor, "L'édition vaticane," 241.

46. Widor penciled the name of Gevaert into his copy of the article, and he was also thinking of Saint-Saëns, Dubois, and Paladilhe. Dézelan, "Le chant grégorien," 4.

47. Widor, "La révision du plain-chant," 65–66.
48. Widor, "L'œuvre de Gevaert," 399 n.
49. Widor, "La révision du plain-chant," 58–59.
50. Potiron, "Widor," 85.
51. *Ménestrel* 75 (1909): 374.
52. C. Cavaillé-Coll and E. Cavaillé-Coll, *Aristide Cavaillé-Coll*, 133–36.
53. Widor, *Initiation musicale*, 107.
54. Ibid., 107.
55. Bas, *Rythme grégorien*, 76–77.
56. Widor, *Fondations, portraits*, 228, 230.
57. Dézelan, "Le chant grégorien," 4.
58. David, "M. Widor, l'édition vaticane," 81.
59. Ibid.
60. Ibid., 89.
61. *Ménestrel* 61 (1895): 87.
62. Ibid., 239.
63. Ibid., 248.
64. B.I.(a), letter 191, dated August 6, 1895. Widor reported back to Thomas in two letters from Berlin in which he described all the interesting details of the competition. See B.I.(a), letter 192, dated September 26, 1895. His health failing, Thomas died on February 12, 1896.
65. Widor, "Le concours Rubinstein à Berlin," *Ménestrel* 61 (1895): 274. Widor wrote in a letter of appreciation to the German organist/composer Alexander Wilhelm Gottschalg that he had begun studying German "to remain less left out of what is said in our country. I can barely write it yet; that's why I ask you to please pardon me for not *thanking* you in your language. [Signed] Sehr erkenntlich, Carl Maria Widor." Author's collection, letter dated April 10, 1887. Twenty years later, T. Carl Whitmer reported his conversation with Widor at Saint-Sulpice: "I sat on the organ bench and conversed [during] a large part of the service. Our conversation was entirely in German as he limps worse in English than I do in French." Whitmer, *My Heart and Mind*, 244.
66. Widor, "Berlin (Suite)," *Piano Soleil* (November 10, 1895): 1; see also *Ménestrel* 61 (1895): 274–75.
67. Widor, "Berlin," *Piano Soleil* (October 27, 1895): 2.
68. *Ménestrel* 61 (1895): 278.
69. Widor, "Berlin (Suite)," 2.
70. Widor, *Fondations, portraits*, 193–94. This statement evidences a change of heart on Widor's part, as in another source published just a year earlier (1923), he had written: "At the Bibliothèque nationale, at the Arsenal, and at Sainte-Geneviève, treasures are found. Let's hope that an intelligent initiative will one day unite them in a suitable building. Then we will possess the richest music library in the world." Widor, *Initiation musicale*, 122–23.
71. Widor, *Fondations, portraits*, 194–95. The Conservatory moved from its location on faubourg Poissonnière to a vast building at 14 rue de Madrid, formerly occupied by a Collège des Jésuites. It opened its doors in the new location on January 3, 1911, and Widor was assigned to classroom no. 9 on the third floor. Although much larger and better ventilated than the old Conservatory building, Widor still described the new spaces provided for the library and museum as "badly arranged . . . already insufficient," and without the "necessary comfort. The dwelling is unworthy of the treasures that it contains" (194). How Widor would have loved the ample new Cité de la musique complex,

where the Conservatory, a concert hall, library, studios, and the Musée de la musique share a corner of Paris's Parc de la Villette!

72. Widor, Preface to *Orgues de l'Abbaye de Saint-Mihiel*, xi–xii.

73. In addition to the original ten students inherited from Franck (Berger, Bouval, Burgat, Büsser, Guiraud, Libert, Runner, Ternisien, Tournemire, Vierne), several new ones enrolled in subsequent years. 1892: Charles Quef (1873–1931); 1893: Gustave Galand (1872–98); 1894: Alfred Marichelle (1866–1919), Charles-Marie Michel (1876–97), Henri Mulet (1878–1967), Harnisch [also spelled variously Harnick; Harnish; Harnich] (b. 1874), Rottembourg (b. 1875); 1895: Gabriel Dupont (1878–1914), Cœdès (b. 1871) and Alphonse Schmitt (1875–1912).

74. Widor, "Notes sur Lemmens," 2.

75. Ibid.

76. Widor, *Initiation musicale*, 127. Those not already mentioned: Joseph Bonnet (1884–1944); Henri Libert; Georges Jacob (1877–1950); Paul Fauchet (1881–1937); Achille Philip (1878–1959); Henri Letocart (1866–1945); Abel Decaux (1869–1943).

77. On January 24, 1891, Widor entered the first evaluations of his students; ten additional students eventually came under evaluation during his tenure as organ professor. A.N.(a), AJ37 292–95.

78. A.N.(a), AJ37 292 [1891], 403–4. Vierne's official admission to the class may have been delayed through some negligence, perhaps a result of Franck's final incapacity, as Vierne reported that he became a student in the class on October 4, 1890. Vierne, *In Memoriam Louis Vierne*, 24; Ochse, *Organists and Organ Playing*, 258 n. 13.

79. A.N.(a), AJ37 292 [1891], 553–54.

80. A.N.(a), AJ37 293 [1892], 83, 239; AJ37 293 [1893], 391, 533; AJ37 294 [1894], 83, 233; AJ37 295 [1896].

81. Thomas, "Organ Loft Whisperings" (December 27, 1893): 12.

82. Gavoty, *Louis Vierne*, 57–58. Widor taught Schweitzer gratuitously as well. Schweitzer, *My Life and Thought*, 28.

83. Gavoty, *Louis Vierne*, 71.

84. *Le Ménestrel* published the official requirements of the competition for obtaining the post of organist of the Basilica of Saint-Denis: "The fixed tests are: (1) accompaniment of a plainsong either in the bass or in the upper part; (2) improvisation of a fugue; (3) improvisation of a symphonic piece; (4) performance from memory of a piece by Bach." *Ménestrel* 62 (1896): 240.

85. In a letter to Marie Trélat, dated July 31, 1896, Widor wrote, "Tuesday, we spent the afternoon at the competition for organist of the Basilica of St. Denis, where I had Libert appointed." B.N.(d), letter 31.

86. Widor, "Nouveaux organistes," 1–2.

87. *Musica Sacra* 17 (1894): 32.

88. Smith, *Louis Vierne*, 518.

89. B.N., Vmg 18278.

90. Gavoty, *Louis Vierne*, 68.

91. Nectoux, *Camille Saint-Saëns and Gabriel Fauré*, 56 n. 93.

92. In his memoirs, Massenet related: "The directorship of the Conservatoire was offered [to] me. I declined the honor as I did not want to interrupt my life at the theater which took my whole time." Massenet, *My Recollections*, 215–16. Occasional unexcused absences from his composition class bore testimony to this devotion. Widor related:

> Massenet having left one day for Aix-les-Bains without taking leave of absence from his director Ambroise Thomas, Réty [the general secretary of the Conservatory] said

to him: "Mr. Director, I present to you the students of Massenet's class—professor: Mr. Gedalge."

Then, Ambroise Thomas: "But what are you saying, Réty? Explain yourself!"

"Massenet has left for Aix-les-Bains; I told him to pay a visit to you, but he responded to me: 'Bah! That will take me too much time.'"

"He is perfectly right; I prefer that he come to see me when he comes to teach his class!!"

The class, thus taught by Gedalge, gave rise to a general claim in all the competitions, since, in sum, Gedalge knew all the fugue subjects in advance. One can therefore suspect that he made them known to his students, but let's not provoke a quarrel, because Gedalge must have had an attack of conscience.

Moreover, Massenet taught an excellent class that produced some glorious results. Widor, "Souvenirs autobiographiques," 57.

93. Nectoux, *Camille Saint-Saëns and Gabriel Fauré*, 56.
94. Ibid., 57.
95. Ibid., 58.
96. *Ménestrel* 62 (1896): 343.
97. Widor, "La classe d'orgue," 238.
98. A.N.(b).
99. Smith, *Louis Vierne*, 113, 115; Vierne, "Memoirs of Louis Vierne" (January 1939): 9.
100. See Rosenstiel, *Lili Boulanger*, 54–55.
101. Widor, "La réforme du Prix de Rome," 1–2. In this regard, Widor was somewhat at odds with the late Conservatory Director Ambroise Thomas, who had declared: "No musician of standing would condescend to become a mere teacher of symphony." Calvocoressi, *Musicians Gallery*, 19.
102. On the advice of Raoul Pugno, Nadia Boulanger abandoned Fauré's composition class in favor of Widor's because she thought "[Fauré] didn't listen to much!" Duchen, *Gabriel Fauré*, 126.
103. Frazier, *Maurice Duruflé*, 40–41.
104. Ibid., 185.
105. Cited in ibid.
106. Cited in ibid., 40, from an interview with Duruflé by George Baker. While writing his doctoral dissertation on Widor, the author wrote to Duruflé around 1983, inquiring of any recollections he might share about Widor; there was no response.
107. Hambraeus, "Aristide Cavaillé-Coll," 187.
108. Lade, "Olivier Messiaen," 81. When asked in a 1968 interview if there was a connection between him and César Franck, Messiaen laughed, "None at all. He's dead." Rößler, *Olivier Messiaen*, 37.
109. Rosenstiel, *Lili Boulanger*, 88–90, 266.
110. Austin, *Music in the 20th Century*, 226.
111. Louis Schneider, "La musique étrangère et les compositeurs français," *Gaulois* 46 (January 10, 1911): 4.
112. Widor, Preface to *J. S. Bach*, xi.
113. Widor, "La classe d'orgue," 238.
114. Widor, "Revue musicale," *Estafette* (August 12, 1878): 2.
115. Smith, *Louis Vierne*, 117; Ochse, *Organists and Organ Playing*, 185. Widor, preferring to concentrate on performance and free improvisation in the organ class, had charged Vierne with two aspects of instruction that did not particularly excite him: accompanying plainchant and fugal improvisation. Gavoty, *Louis Vierne*, 59.

116. Vierne, "Journal (Fragments)," 174.

117. Smith, *Louis Vierne*, 117, 119; Vierne, "Memoirs of Louis Vierne" (January 1939): 9.

118. Smith, 129; Vierne, "Memoirs of Louis Vierne" (February 1939): 8.

119. Smith, 319.

120. Ibid., 121; Vierne, "Memoirs of Louis Vierne" (January 1939): 9.

121. Malherbe, "Charles-Marie Widor." Even as a music critic, Widor was open minded. Reviewing Benjamin Godard's *Le Tasse*, a dramatic symphony with soloists and chorus that took the City of Paris Prize in 1878, Widor wrote: "The general tendency of *Tasse* is anti-classical, in the sense that it deviates as much as possible from forms in common use and procedures admitted by the old masters. Is this, then, a reproach? Certainly not! One cannot too much encourage and support these noble efforts toward the unknown, this arbitrary choice to struggle on a new terrain." Widor, "Revue musicale," *Estafette* (December 30, 1878): 2.

122. Favre, "Grande figure d'éducateur," 34.

123. L. Varèse, *Varèse*, 42.

124. Charbonnier, *Entretiens avec Edgard Varèse*, 83. Varèse stated further, "Widor was the opposite of d'Indy: human, unpretentious, open-minded, and . . . he had a sense of humor." He grouped Widor with Massenet, Roussel, and Debussy as the keenest and most intellectual people, while he thought of d'Indy, Saint-Saëns, and Fauré as having "constipated" Paris. L. Varèse, *Varèse*, 41–42, 47.

125. Charbonnier, *Entretiens avec Edgard Varèse*, 24–25.

126. A.N.(a), AJ37 300 [1906].

127. Milhaud, *An Autobiography*, 51.

128. Bertrand, *Souvenirs d'un éditeur*, 91–92.

129. Widor, *Fondations, portraits*, 191.

130. Letter dated December 15, 1915, cited in Halbreich, *Arthur Honegger*, 33–34.

131. Widor, *Fondations, portraits*, 191; also: Favre, "Grande figure d'éducateur," 34.

132. Favre, 34.

133. Favre inserted a footnote here: "His eclecticism was great, and he knew how to appreciate in their right value the works of his contemporaries, not without irony sometimes, it's true. His opinion on some of his confrères didn't lack pungency, but that can't be reproduced here."

134. Favre, "Grande figure d'éducateur," 34–35.

135. Widor, *Fondations, portraits*, 48–49. Widor's liberal attitude was oft repeated by those familiar with his teaching: "In his composition class at the Conservatory, Mr. Widor does not impede the tastes of modernism; a number of our youngest, his disciples, testify to it. The master, who possesses a perfect technique, leaves the field open to the investigations of the future composers. A part of his glory—the most genuine—is there. And, if he himself does not take part in the current evolution, at least he channels it with a sureness of view that infinitely honors him and assures our unalterable respect for him." Raymond Charpentier, "*Nerto*," *Comœdia* 18 (October 25, 1924): 1.

136. Lehman, "Charles-Marie Widor," 450.

137. Letter from Honegger to his parents, dated June 18, 1916, cited in Halbreich, *Arthur Honegger*, 36.

138. Letter dated April 28, 1915, cited in Halbreich, 31. When Honegger presented a "sensible, classical little trio" in Widor's class, the *maître* was particularly delighted; Honegger, on the other hand, did not appreciate that Widor thought so highly of the work that he kept referring to it: "Widor had the crust to tell me it was the best thing of mine he'd heard, and he keeps on mentioning it at every class!" Letter from Honegger to his

parents, dated December 23, 1916, cited in Halbreich, 39. Still, Harry Halbreich proffered that "Honegger never lost his belief in the virtues of the sort of traditional technique he had learned from Gedalge and Widor." Halbreich, 608.

139. Letter dated April 28, 1915, cited in Halbreich, 31.

140. Lehman, "Charles-Marie Widor," 450, 494.

141. Widor, *Fondations, portraits,* 146.

142. *Ménestrel* 70 (1904): 191. Victor Dejeante (1850–1927), revolutionary socialist; Jean Jaurès (1859–1914), socialist leader; Gustave Hervé (1871–1944), antimilitarist socialist leader; Jean de La Fontaine (1621–95), fabulist.

143. *Estafette* (January 8, 1880): 3; *Estafette* (April 7, 1879): 2.

144. Milhaud, *An Autobiography,* 104.

145. Ibid., 105–6.

146. Halbreich, *Arthur Honegger,* 56.

147. Letter, dated December 24, 1918, from Arthur Honegger to Arthur and Julie Honegger, cited in Halbreich, *Arthur Honegger,* 56–57.

148. Widor, *André Messager,* 16.

149. B.N.(d), letter 48, dated June 30, 1922. In addition to Milhaud and Honegger, the "delegation of 'French' Bolsheviks" may have included Francis Poulenc and perhaps Charles Koechlin (1867–1950), each of whom was also represented on two programs. Edward Evans, critic for *The Musical Times,* wrote: "Great interest was aroused by the visit of the Société moderne d'instruments à vent, their chief contributions being . . . a melodious and somewhat rural-sounding Rhapsody by Honegger; and a militant Sonata by Milhaud which, coming as it did in the first program, startled both the seasoned critics and the less sophisticated inhabitants of Salzburg, and gave them alarms which the later concerts proved to be, on the whole, unfounded." Edward Evans, "The Salzburg Festival," *Musical Times* 63 (1922): 628–29.

150. Milhaud, *An Autobiography,* 107.

151. Ibid.

152. *Courrier Musical* 26 (1924): 10.

153. Henderson, "Memories of Widor," 657.

154. Russell, "Widor," 13. Widor found that "people of different languages *en rapport* on a subject may understand each other." Thomas, "Organ Loft Whisperings" (November 29, 1893): 20. Some English-speaking visitors to Saint-Sulpice reported that Widor explained everything "very carefully in French" so they could follow what he was doing. *Diapason* 16, no. 10 (1925): 36.

155. Bidwell, "Widor and St.-Sulpice," 422.

156. Trillat, "Charles-Marie Widor," 4.

157. Riemenschneider, "Charles M. Widor Dies," 2. Lucy Hickenlooper (later Olga Samaroff Stokowski) had some organ lessons with Widor and found them to be "cursory and boring." He mustered little enthusiasm for routine players; Hickenlooper reported that he simply corrected the wrong notes of each girl in the class. Kline, *Olga Samaroff Stokowski,* 23.

158. Maurat, *Souvenirs musicaux et littéraires,* 79. Henri Gagnebin (1886–1977) concurred that Widor did not open the door for everyone: "If you wanted to visit him, you had to ring three times at his door, then to go back into the courtyard so he could look from the window and decide if he was going to open or not." Gagnebin, "Guy Bovet joue Widor."

159. Russell, "Widor," 13, 65.

160. Ramsey, "An Interview," 14–15.

161. *Courrier Musical* 19 (1917): 245.
162. Saint-Saëns, "Music in the Church," 8.
163. B.N.(d), letter 31, dated July 31, 1896, to Marie Trélat.
164. B.N.(d), letter 32, dated 1898, to Marie Trélat.
165. *Ménestrel* 62 (1896): 189.
166. Ibid., 208.
167. Ibid., 312, 374.
168. S.M.L., letter 29, dated November 11, 1896.
169. *Ménestrel* 64 (1898): 391.
170. Ibid., 70.
171. Widor, "À Rome," *Piano Soleil* (April 3, 1898): 2.
172. Ibid.
173. Ibid. Gregorio Bellabene (ca. 1720–1803); Pietro Raimondi (1786–1853).
174. Ibid. Widor was, in fact, an great admirer of Puccini. He had written to him a few months earlier and received a cordial response: "I received your kind letter of November 19, 1897, which I was unable to answer because I was away. I thank you sincerely for your flattering comments about me and I hope for the pleasure of shaking your hand during my trip to Paris, which I hope is soon. Accept, my dear confrère, my cordial greetings. Yours faithfully, Giacomo Puccini." B.I.(a), letter 160, dated December 12, 1897.
175. Widor, "À Rome (Suite et fin)," *Piano Soleil* (May 8, 1898): 2.
176. Widor, "À Rome (Suite)," *Piano Soleil* (April 17, 1898): 2.
177. Widor, "À Rome (Suite et fin)," 2.
178. Widor, "À Rome (Suite)," 2.
179. Widor, "À Rome (Suite et fin)," 2.
180. Quintette, Op. 68; Sonate, Op. 50; *Soirs d'été*, Op. 63; Trio, Op. 19. B.N. Fonds Mont.
181. *Ménestrel* 65 (1899): 271.
182. Ibid., 158.
183. N.E.C., letter dated March 23, 1898.
184. Williams, *A New History*, 167.
185. For large instruments Widor approved the application only of the pneumatic Barker machine, which mechanically draws the trackers with exacting precision—thus carrying over many of the artistic advantages of the straight mechanical-action organ: sensitivity without heaviness of touch, immediacy of response, and subtlety of control over the instrumental forces. Joy, *Albert Schweitzer*, 154–55.
186. B.I.(c), letter 10, dated November 9, 1905.
187. A.S-S., letter 4, dated November 9, 1905. The letter continues by inviting Saint-Saëns to lunch after the Sunday Mass at Saint-Sulpice: "The Viernes will be there; it's useless to tell you of the joy you would bring us! [Signed] *With all admiration, yours affectionately*, Widor." For the reference to the Hautbois, see Widor, *Technique de l'orchestre moderne*, 181.
188. B.I.(c), letter 11, dated November 10, 1905.
189. Widor, *Technique of the Modern Orchestra*, 142.
190. Maurat, *Souvenirs musicaux et littéraires*, 94.
191. S.M.L., letter 5, dated September 6, 1886.
192. Widor, "L'Abbaye de Savigny," *Piano Soleil* (September 11, 1892): 1.
193. Imbert, "Charles-Marie Widor," 224.
194. *Ménestrel* 65 (1899): 359.

195. Dupré, "M. Charles-Marie Widor," 2.
196. N.E.C.
197. *Bach's Memento* (1925); *Suite latine* (1927); *Trois nouvelles pièces* (1934).
198. Widor, "La révision du plain-chant," 62.
199. Widor, *The Symphonies for Organ*, "Widor's Avant-propos," 20: xxiii.
200. *Revue du Chant Grégorien* 41 (1937): 125.
201. Van Wye, "Gregorian Influences," 21–24.
202. Widor, *The Symphonies for Organ*, "Widor's Avant-propos," 20: xxiii.
203. Joy, *Albert Schweitzer*, 174.
204. Widor, "Revue musicale," *Estafette* (February 10, 1879): 1.
205. Riemenschneider, "Widor; An Estimate," 4.
206. Widor, "Programmes de concerts," *Piano Soleil* (January 13, 1895): 1.
207. Harewood, *Kobbé's Complete Opera Book*, 186–87.
208. For further discussion, see the author's Introduction to the *Symphonie romane* in: *Charles-Marie Widor: The Symphonies for Organ*, vol. 20.
209. Vierne, "Ch.-M. Widor," 76.
210. Widor, "Gounod," 837.
211. *Ménestrel* 66 (1900): 14. Curiously, when Widor inaugurated the Puget organ at the Lille Conservatory just three months later, it was not the new *Symphonie romane* that appeared on the program, but the standard Fifth Symphony along with Bach's Toccata and Fugue in D Minor, BWV 565. Ibid., 127. Widor knew his audience in Lille, and they responded: "The audience greeted Mr. Widor with warm bravos as soon as he entered to sit at the console. As always, he showed himself to be an unrivaled performer and great artist; one doesn't know what is to be most admired about him: his impeccable and prodigious virtuosity or his qualities of style." *Monde Musical* 12 (1900): 189.
212. *Courrier Musical* 3, no. 4 (January 27, 1900): 8.
213. S.M.L., letter 49, dated January 7, 1900.
214. Ibid.
215. *Ménestrel* 66 (1900): 14.
216. See: Widor, "Richard Wagner à Paris," 2.
217. Doret, "Widor: 1845–1937."
218. In January 1894, Leduc began publishing *L'Orgue Moderne* under Widor's direction.
219. Widor, Preface to *Notes historiques*, 6–8; also *Ménestrel* 65 (1899): 131–32.
220. Ochse, *Organists and Organ Playing*, 211.
221. Georges, "Réponse à une préface," 3.
222. Widor, "Lettre de M. Ch.-M. Widor à M. Gustave Lefèvre," 6.
223. Georges, "Réponse à une préface," 4.
224. Ibid. Those not already mentioned: Clément Lippacher (1850–1934); Jules Stoltz (1848–1906); Charles Planchet (1857–1946); Aloÿs Claussmann (1850–1926). The others (Kotzul, Meyer, Dubois, J. Deplantay, Henri Delaroqua) left little or no record.
225. Widor had extolled Vierne's First Symphony; see Widor, Preface to *Notes historiques*, 7–8.
226. Widor, "Lettre de M. Ch.-M. Widor," 5.
227. Widor, "Lettre de M. Ch.-M. Widor," 5–6.
228. Family arch., letter dated June 22, 1923.
229. Widor, Preface to *Histoire des instruments*, 46.
230. Widor, "La harpe sans pédales," *Piano Soleil* (February 21, 1897): 1–2.

231. Author's collection, letter dated February 23, 1912, to "Mr. Escudier." In 1923 Widor reiterated that the chromatic harp "remained without usefulness for our orchestras." Widor, *Initiation musicale*, 45.

232. S.M.L., letter 45, dated August 26, 1899.

233. *Ménestrel* 66 (1900): 86.

234. *Ménestrel* 91 (1929): 548; 96 (1934): 103.

235. Gavoty, *Louis Vierne*, 60.

236. Smith, *Louis Vierne*, 215; Vierne, "Memoirs of Louis Vierne" (June 1939): 8.

237. Smith, *Louis Vierne*, 221.

238. Ibid.; Vierne, ibid.

239. Smith, *Louis Vierne*, 221.

240. Ibid., 223; Vierne, ibid.

241. See plate 75, "Official report of the Notre-Dame organ competition," in Smith, *Louis Vierne*, 222.

242. When Vierne became *titulaire* at Notre-Dame, Lazare-Auguste Maquaire became Widor's assistant at Saint-Sulpice. As a student in Widor's composition class, Maquaire received fine evaluations: "Worker; writes fugues very well"; "very interesting"; "excellent fuguist," and so forth. A.N.(a), AJ37 295 [1897]; AJ37 296 [1898–99]; AJ37 297 [1900–1901].

243. Quoted in Smith, *Louis Vierne*, 68.

244. Gavoty, *Louis Vierne*, 160. Widor premiered Vierne's *Messe solenelle* at Saint-Sulpice on December 8, 1901. Gavoty, 299.

245. *Ménestrel*, 63 (1897): 287.

246. *Courrier Musical* 3, no. 12 (March 24, 1900): 9. Referring to the Fifth Symphony, the reviewer wrote, "I would almost say that it's a popular work, if this word were not unfortunately improper for organ music."

247. *Ménestrel* 67 (1901): 143.

248. Ibid., 135.

249. Ibid., 149–50.

250. Ibid., 149.

251. *Courrier Musical* 4 (December 1, 1901): 254.

252. *Ménestrel* 67 (1901): 375.

253. Joy, *Albert Schweitzer*, 151.

254. *Ménestrel* 71 (1905): 79.

255. Ibid., 87.

256. Smith, *Louis Vierne*, 229.

257. *Ménestrel* 71 (1905): 136.

258. Joy, *Albert Schweitzer*, 151.

259. Widor, *Bach: Œuvres complètes pour orgue*, 1: xxviii.

260. M.S., letter dated April 18, 1930, from Widor to Schweitzer. Amédée de Vallombrosa (1880–1968) was a pupil of Widor and organist at Saint Leu, near Paris. An interesting footnote on this subject is that in April 1927, Marcel Dupré was booked by Harry Portman, the European impresario for Loew's theaters, to play twice daily for a period of time at the Gaumont Palais Theatre in Paris. Billy Nalle, "Theatre Organ Perspective," *Music: The AGO and RCCO Magazine* 9 (January 1975): 47.

261. Joy, *Albert Schweitzer*, 168–69.

262. *Piano Soleil* (1 March 1903): 3.

263. Smith, *Louis Vierne*, 89, 91; Vierne, "Memoirs of Louis Vierne" (December 1938): 6.

264. Smith, *Louis Vierne*, 65; Vierne, "Memoirs of Louis Vierne" (November 1938): 10.

265. Reynaud, *Œuvre de Ch.-M. Widor*, 18.

266. Whitmer, "European Organs and Organists," 14.

267. Delestre, *L'œuvre de Marcel Dupré*, 20–21.

268. Henderson, "Memories of Widor," 659.

269. Widor, "Profession de foi," 1.

270. Lehman, "Charles-Marie Widor," 497.

271. B.T., letter 275, dated July 1, 1895.

272. Widor, *Technique de l'orchestre moderne*, i.

273. Lehman, "Charles-Marie Widor," 494.

274. *Ménestrel* 72 (1906): 39.

275. Hambraeus, "Aristide Cavaillé-Coll," 186.

276. *Ménestrel* 72 (1906): 31.

277. Ibid., 39.

278. Manuel, *Maurice Ravel*, 249–50. Discussing a question of orchestration with Charles Koechlin, Francis Poulenc acknowledged seeking the solution in Widor's *Technique de l'orchestre moderne*—"The worthy Mr. Widor, that I sometimes consult . . ." Cited in Chimènes, *Francis Poulenc*, 212.

279. Widor, *Technique de l'orchestre moderne*, 176.

280. The device contained thirty-two pipes sounding the first thirty-two harmonics based on the "A" of the 8' octave; the pipes could be made to sound individually, in any combination, or all together. Widor described the result: "If beginning with the most acute pitch you put into vibration little by little all the pipes of the instrument, the synthetic "A" will increase in proportion until it becomes thirty-two times more powerful than the sound from the low pipe itself. If you put into action all thirty-two pipes together, you will hear a single fundamental tone of a strength with no other parallel and of an absolute exactness." Widor, *Technique de l'orchestre moderne*, 177.

281. Widor commended the Germans because they had the "good sense never to disregard the mixtures." Widor, *Technique de l'orchestre moderne*, 180.

282. Ibid., 184.

283. Widor, "Souvenirs autobiographiques," 59; also *Ménestrel* 55 (1889): 72.

284. Philipp, "Charles-Marie Widor," 127.

285. *Ménestrel* 69 (1903): 255.

286. *Ménestrel* 71 (1905): 77.

287. Undated ms in the author's collection.

288. *Ménestrel* 68 (1902): 136, 256, 369; 69 (1903): 5, 56, 101, 117, 175, 271–72, 381; 70 (1904): 93, 396; 71 (1905): 84.

289. S.M.L., letter 24, dated August 14, 1895.

290. *Ménestrel* 61 (1895): 278.

291. S.M.L., letter 45, dated August 26, 1899.

292. S.M.L., letter 55, dated September 19, 1900.

293. *Ménestrel* 69 (1903): 40.

294. *Ménestrel* 71 (1905): 417–18.

295. Ibid., 418.

296. *Ménestrel* 72 (1906): 13.

297. B.I.(a), letter 86, dated December 30, 1905.

298. *Ménestrel* 72 (1906): 130.

299. Ibid.

300. Ibid., 122.

301. Ibid., 130.

302. Ibid., 163.

303. *Ménestrel* 73 (1907): 39, 109, 112, 383; 74 (1908): 407; 76 (1910): 376.

304. Philipp, "Charles-Marie Widor," 127.

305. M. Dumesnil, "Widor," 144.

306. Widor, "Théâtres," *Piano Soleil* (June 5, 1892): 2.

307. *Ménestrel* 73 (1907): 95.

308. B.I.(a), letter 124, dated December 14, 1906. Numerous letters between the two men show their warm relationship; in one, Massenet closed: "I remain touched and proud of your feelings for your old comrade and fervent admirer!"; and in another: "Great friend, I thank you so *affectionately!*" B.I.(a), letter 122, dated November 25, 1897; letter 126, n.d. Dupré recalled, "I still see [Widor] with his habitual carafe of Vouvray [wine] and his indispensable bottle of mineral water, for he was very temperate, in discussion with Massenet, a big drinker and big eater, and an inexhaustible chatterer, but so witty." Dupré, "Marcel Dupré nous conte," 1.

309. H. Moreno, "Ch.-M. Widor: Deux sonates nouvelles," *Ménestrel* 74 (1908): 188–89; a lengthy description of each work is included in the review.

310. *Ménestrel* 73 (1907): 95, 271.

311. Widor, "Souvenirs autobiographiques," 43–44.

312. Rupp, *Ch.-M. Widor*, 52.

313. *Ménestrel* 76 (1910): 317.

314. *Ménestrel* 74 (1908): 69.

315. Ibid., 21.

316. Dupré, *Recollections*, 48. Performances were not limited to Europe; in Chicago, Wilhelm Middelschulte (1868–1943) made such a success with a memorized performance of the *Sinfonia sacra* that a second performance had to be given. *Ménestrel* 77 (1911): 55.

317. Widor, Preface to *L'esthétique de l'orgue*, 174.

318. *Revue Musicale de Lyon* 8 (1911): 689–90. It might be said that this same critic found Mahler's music to be "brilliant mediocrity."

319. The contents of the collection are: *Hommage à Haydn* (Debussy); *Prélude élégiaque* (Dukas); *Thème varié* (Hahn); *Menuet* (d'Indy); *Menuet* (Ravel); *Fugue* (Widor).

320. Nectoux, *Camille Saint-Saëns and Gabriel Fauré*, 88–89. Apparently, Saint-Saëns and Fauré were also invited to make submissions. Saint-Saëns wrote to Fauré protesting, "never, absolutely never have I seen Y and N in musical notation. . . . I am writing to M. É[corcheville] to convince myself that the two letters Y and N can mean D and G. I encourage you to do the same yourself. It would be annoying to get dragged into a ridiculous undertaking that could make us the mockery of musical Germany." Neither composer submitted a piece on Haydn's name.

321. *Ménestrel* 75 (1909): 87. Widor returned to Berlin to conduct the Berlin Philharmonic on January 28, 1910, in a performance of his Op. 77 Piano Concerto (Émile Frey, soloist), and in Potsdam he appeared as pianist in the Op. 79 Violin Sonata; his Berlin sojourn concluded with a concert, comedy, and supper at the French Embassy in honor of the Emperor, Empress, and court attendants. *Ménestrel* 76 (1910): 46.

322. "M. Widor's Concert," *Times* [London] 38,951 (May 5, 1909): 13, col. 2.

323. *Ménestrel* 75 (1909): 143.

324. *Ménestrel* 74 (1908): 22.

325. *Ménestrel* 76 (1910): 110.

Part Five

1. A.B-A.
2. Nectoux, *Camille Saint-Saëns and Gabriel Fauré*, 4.
3. *L'Art Musical* 30 (1891): 15.
4. *Ménestrel* 75 (1909): 95. For the first two rounds thirty-three voters were present and a majority of seventeen was needed to elect. First round: Fauré 11, Widor 8, Lefebvre 6, Maréchal 4, Pierné and Pessard 2 each. Second round: Widor 12, Fauré 11, Pierné 5, Lefebvre 4, Pessard 1. For the next four rounds thirty-four voters were present and a majority of eighteen was needed to elect. Third round: Fauré 14, Widor 13, Lefebvre 4, Pierné 3. Fourth round: Fauré 15, Widor 14, Pierné 3, Lefebvre 2. Fifth round: Widor 16, Fauré 14, Pierné 3, Lefebvre 1. Sixth round: Fauré 18, Widor 16. "Procès-verbal, Séance 13 mars 1909," Institut de France, Paris.
5. Widor, "M. Gabriel Fauré," 202.
6. Ibid.
7. Ibid., 203.
8. Fauré, "M. Ch.-M. Widor," 203.
9. Philipp, "Charles-Marie Widor," 128.
10. Nectoux, *Fauré: A Musical Life*, 18–19.
11. Nectoux, *Camille Saint-Saëns and Gabriel Fauré*, 84–85. Saint-Saëns was likely referring to Madame Charles Max as the "female charmer": "During the Belle Époque, a number of the members of the Academy of Fine Arts attended the *five o'clock* musicales of Madame Charles Max in her salon at 26 rue Jacob, which looks out on the garden of Racine. Massenet, who dedicated two songs . . . to this society singer . . . compared her to a 'Norwegian soufflé, burning-hot on the outside and cold on the inside.'" Chimènes, *Mécènes et musiciens*, 185.
12. Nectoux, *Camille Saint-Saëns and Gabriel Fauré*, 4.
13. Ibid., 92. Letter dated September 18, 1910.
14. Jones, *Gabriel Fauré*, 141. Letter dated November 14, 1910. Jean-Michel Nectoux identified Dubois and Widor as those with whom Fauré found himself "up against . . . at every stage of his career." Nectoux, *Fauré: His Life*, 224.
15. A.B-A. Widor's letter of candidature was written on October 15, 1910:

> Monsieur le Président
> I dare to solicit the great honor to become part of your illustrious company, and pose my candidature for the chair left vacant by my greatly lamented confrère and friend Charles Lenepveu.
> A short time ago, after the decease of Reyer, I permitted myself the same presumptuous application and joined to my letter a list of published works to which it seems needless today to tire the Academy with a new perusal.
> To this list can be added some new pieces and a symphony with chorus—which is being published at this moment.
> After a wordy formal closing and his signature, Widor added a little postscript: "Associate of the Academy of Berlin; Correspondent of the Academies of Brussels and Stockholm."

16. *Ménestrel* 76 (1910): 359. For the five rounds of voting, thirty-two voters were present and a majority of seventeen was needed to elect. First round: Widor 13, Lefebvre 7, Messager 4, Pierné and Maréchal 3 each, Pessard 2. Second round: Widor 14, Lefebvre 9, Pierné 6, Messager 2, Pessard 1. Third round: Widor 15, Lefebvre 8, Pierné 7, Messager 2.

Fourth round: Widor 16, Lefebvre 8, Pierné 6, Messager 2. Fifth round: Widor 21, Lefebvre 7, Pierné 4. "Procès-verbal, Séance 29 Octobre 1910," Paris, Institut de France.

17. *Ménestrel* 76 (1910): 414. Dupont competed for the Prix de Rome when he was a student of Widor, and while quarantined at the Chateau of Compiègne, a teenage misstep disqualified him from the competition. Widor related:

> [Léon] Bonnat and Paul Dubois [1829–1905], director of the École des beaux-arts, burst into my place. "It's appalling," they said to me at the same time.—"What are you talking about?"—"He is your student?"—"Who?"—"Gabriel Dupont."—"Yes, one of the best; I like him a lot."—"Well, your Dupont, working [for the Prix de Rome] in Compiègne, escaped during the night, climbed onto the roof of the chateau, descended by the rain pipes and did some damage that laid him open, first to be excluded from the competition, and second to the Police Court."—"My dear *maîtres*, I will telegraph Dupont; what he will tell me will be the exact truth."
>
> Now, here's the response:
>
> "Well, yes! Some charming young women came under our windows to listen to some waltzes that we were playing after dinner. I wanted to acknowledge their graciousness. Some roses were wilting uselessly in the rose garden. I went to pick a bunch of them, in the night like a robber and by way of the rooftops. It was very dark. One false step, my leg got scraped by a window glass that I broke. There you have it. I might have killed myself, but I brought back some roses and we decked out the young women with flowers." Widor, *Fondations, portraits*, 178–79.

In 1903, Widor was honored to go to Milan to accept the Sonzogno Prize for Dupont and to hear the first performance of his opera, *La Cabrera*. M. Dumesnil, "Widor," 192.

18. Widor, *Amateurs honoraires*, 17. Two individuals Widor especially sought out to become members were Auguste Rodin (1840–1917) and Debussy.

19. "Je veux qu'on soit sincère, et qu'en homme d'honneur, on ne lâche aucun mot qui ne parte du cœur." Molière, *Le Misanthrope*, Act 1.

20. Schweitzer, *My Life and Thought*, 30–31.

21. Dupré, "Souvenirs sur Ch.-M. Widor," 32.

22. Sumner, "The Organ in St.-Sulpice," 104.

23. *Avenir* (November 25, 1923), B.N. Fonds Mont. In a 1970 taped interview, Widor's niece Gabrielle Guibaud recalled that Widor was known to pay the expenses of his students when they were ill. Family arch.

24. *Avenir* (November 25, 1923), B.N. Fonds Mont.

25. Pougin, "Nouvelle académicien," 357.

26. It is not feasible to take account of all Widor's concerts, but a few references from *Ménestrel* follow: Nancy, 73 (1907): 191; Guebwiller, 74 (1908): 287; Orléans, 75 (1909): 143; Strasbourg, 75 (1909): 224; Lille, 77 (1911): 40; Paris, 77 (1911): 141–42; Caen, 77 (1911): 160. The program in Caen (Notre-Dame) represents Widor's typical offering: *Symphonie gothique*, movements from the Fifth and Sixth Symphonies; between the organ pieces, a Mlle Thébaud sang an *Ave Maria*, *O Salutaris*, and the "Prière" from *Les pêcheurs de Saint-Jean*.

27. Reviews of these concerts are cited respectively: *Ménestrel* 74 (1908): 63, 69; 75 (1909): 157, 374; 76 (1910): 46, 237; 77 (1911): 117.

28. Pougin, "Nouvelle académicien," 357.

29. *Courrier Musical* 12 (1909): 677–78. The program included the first movement of the Fifth Symphony, and Bach's Concerto in A Minor and the Toccata and Fugue in D Minor.

30. *Times* [London] 38,951 (May 5, 1909): 13, col. 2.

31. *Ménestrel* 76 (1910): 237.

32. Joy, *Albert Schweitzer*, 181.

NOTES TO PP. 298–300 535

33. Widor, "Revue musicale," *Estafette* (January 28, 1878): 2. In an anecdote, Widor related the clear difference between one conductor who did not exhibit authority and one who did:

> One can only vaguely imagine the influence of a man on an orchestra. Chance had me attend recently, in a foreign capital, at an interval of two days, a performance of the same work in the same hall with the same orchestra; only the conductor was different. The first day, no ensemble, no precision, no sonority, neither *forte* nor *piano* . . . everyone doing as he pleases, putting his feeling where and how it suits him, reasoning following the fancy of the moment—or falling asleep. The day after, another maestro—the real one. Everything was different: superb rhythm, nuances of an infinite delicacy, suppleness and power, unity, discipline, life, art at last! Such is the influence of this little end of the baton that moves about above the music stands, seeming so easy to wield, and that so few musicians, even eminent ones, handle well. Widor, "Revue musicale," *Estafette* (January 17, 1882): 2.

Widor sometimes borrowed his own anecdotes from earlier reviews; this same account had appeared four years earlier in a slightly different manner in the "Revue musicale," *Estafette* (January 28, 1878): 2.

In yet another article, Widor presented the role of the conductor a bit naïvely, betraying an attitude that confirms why Philipp considered him a weak conductor:

> In reality, the profession of conductor requires only a little practice, an exercise of a few months when one is a composer. Then, it suffices to make his arm supple and to smother his nerves. The more or less elegant gestures that the audience admires serve absolutely nothing. The real work is done at the rehearsal, simply, wisely, clearly; this work consists of demonstrating to each his role in the ensemble, to indicate to each the best way to fulfill it. . . . As to the concert, the role of the conductor is very simple: "don't forget anything, and be sure that no one forgets"; that's all. The grand movements of the arm and the lofty attitudes are destined only to dazzle the naïve; they annoy rather than lead the artists to whom they seem to be addressed. Widor, "Liège," *Piano Soleil* (27 March 1892): 2.

34. Philipp, "Charles-Marie Widor," 131.
35. Smith, *Louis Vierne*, 315.
36. Widor, Preface to *Francis Planté*, iii.
37. *Ménestrel* 77 (1911): 117.
38. Fauré and Widor had known each other for some forty years—at least since the time when Fauré served as choir organist at Saint-Sulpice in the early 1870s. Still, underlying jealousies between the two men continually simmered just below the surface. In 1896 when it seemed that Widor would edge out Fauré by being appointed a composition professor at the Conservatory, Fauré saw his chances of eventually becoming a member of the Institute diminish; he complained to Saint-Saëns, "it's the Institut[e] which will be put back indefinitely for Widor will have a title in addition, and a very considerable title. My only hope would be to succeed you in forty years, and I swear to you that I like you much more than the Institut[e]!" Nectoux, *Camille Saint-Saëns and Gabriel Fauré*, 57. Still, Widor had been involved with performances of Fauré's music from time to time: Fauré once wrote to an unspecified woman, "Hasselmans told me that Widor had made [my] *Elégie* rehearsed with a very special and amicable care. I would be pleased, Madame, if you would tell him how much I am touched by it." B.I.(a), letter 60, no date. In spite of perceived hard feelings, Fauré was able to sign one letter to Widor: "Your very affectionately devoted, Gabriel Fauré." B.I.(a), letter 62, dated January 26, 1918.

39. Hilson-Woldu, "Gabriel Fauré," 200.

40. Ibid., 199.

41. Ibid., 201.

42. Ibid., 203.

43. *Courrier Musical* 14 (1911): 364.

44. "Les professeurs du conservatoire," *Temps* 51 (June 2, 1911): 6.

45. *Courrier Musical* 14 (1911): 456. Alfred Bruneau (1857–1934).

46. Ibid., 506.

47. Ibid., 506, 511.

48. Ibid., 510.

49. *Ménestrel* 77 (1911): 219.

50. *Courrier Musical* 14 (1911): 525.

51. Ibid., 524, 525.

52. Ibid., 525.

53. Ibid.

54. Ibid.

55. "Les professeurs du conservatoire," *Temps* 51 (July 11, 1911): 4–5.

56. Ibid., 5.

57. Ibid., 4.

58. The Conservatory was founded under the *Constitution de l'an III*, the establishment of the Directoire in 1795.

59. A.N.(b), unidentified news clipping.

60. "Les professeurs du conservatoire," *Temps* 51 (July 11, 1911): 4.

61. *Ménestrel* 75 (July 15, 1911): 223.

62. "Les professeurs du conservatoire," *Temps* 51 (July 11, 1911): 4.

63. "La musique," *Temps* 51 (July 25, 1911): 3.

64. "Les incidents du conservatoire," *Temps* 51 (July 14, 1911): 4.

65. "La musique," *Temps* 51 (July 25, 1911): 3.

66. "Les incidents du conservatoire," *Temps* 51 (July 14, 1911): 4.

67. *Courrier Musical* 14 (August 1–15, 1911): 551–52.

68. *Matin* 28 (July 10, 1911): 4.

69. *Ménestrel* 77 (1911): 223.

70. Gavoty, *Louis Vierne*, 108.

71. Ibid., 69.

72. Ibid., 61.

73. Ibid., 107–8; Fauré, *Hommage à Eugène Gigout*, 11. In an April letter to *Le Ménestrel*, Gigout declared that he would not be a candidate for the succession of Guilmant at the Conservatory because of "professional obligations." *Ménestrel* 77 (1911): 119. But on May 11 he wrote back: "My 'professional obligations' have *disappeared suddenly*; some serious considerations have made me go back on my word." Ibid., 160. *Le Ménestrel* editorialized, "How Gigout changes! But we would love to know what these 'serious considerations' were." Ibid. Undoubtedly, they came from Fauré, who requested that Gigout take Guilmant's professorship. In his monograph on Gigout, Fauré related that "the day when the candidature of Gigout for the succession of Guilmant was discussed before the Superior Council, I thought I noticed on the part of some of the members, perhaps not well informed with regard to the organ and organists, a certain indecision. Absent from Paris at that moment, Saint-Saëns had expressed to me by letter his desire for the success of Gigout. I didn't miss conveying this letter to the Committee. It closed with these words: 'It would be deplorable if Gigout were not named, for he is without possible dispute the

premier organist of Paris.' Such an appreciation on the part of he who, at the time when he amazed his listeners at the Madeleine, was himself the premier organist of Paris, such an appreciation, I tell you, could only be conclusive, and to my great joy Gigout was named organ professor at the Conservatory." Fauré, *Hommage à Eugène Gigout*, 11–12.

74. Gavoty, *Louis Vierne*, 115.

75. Philipp, "Charles-Marie Widor," 127.

76. Vierne, "Journal (Fragments)," 166.

77. Ibid., 166–67.

78. Smith, *Louis Vierne*, 85.

79. Smith, *Louis Vierne*, 95. Vierne suffered from nervousness throughout his career (see Smith, *Louis Vierne*, 259, 311, 315). In Widor's written comments about his pupils, he had noted about Vierne on January 18, 1894: "knows his craft *perfectly well*; has nothing to learn except through experience. He lacks coolness [*sang-froid*]." A.N.(a), A37 294.

80. Vierne, "Journal (Fragments)," 168.

81. Smith, *Louis Vierne*, 105.

82. Ibid., 107; Vierne, "Memoirs of Louis Vierne" (January 1939): 8. Vierne, "Journal (Fragments)," 169.

83. Gavoty, *Louis Vierne*, 62–63; see also Vierne, "Journal (Fragments)," 171–72, and Smith, *Louis Vierne*, 106, 108.

84. *Courrier Musical* 6 (1903): 212. A few weeks later, the *Courrier Musical* carried an interview with Dubois, "M. Théodore Dubois a parlé"; the interviewer, Mr. Trilby, took a concluding swipe at the composer: "In sum . . . Mr. Dubois loves the music of Bach and Beethoven; but, on the other hand, he can't bear *music that bores him* (except his own, most probably)." Ibid., 231.

85. B.N.(d), letters 52–56.

86. R. Dumesnil, *Portraits de musiciens français*, 201.

87. Widor, "Souvenirs autobiographiques," 87.

88. Widor, "Revue musicale," *Estafette* (February 6, 1882): 1.

89. *Symphonie antique* (Paris: Heugel, 1911).

90. Widor, "La révision du plain-chant," 60.

91. Widor, "Souvenirs autobiographiques," 86–87.

92. An unidentified news clipping states: "People know that [the Countess's] music salon counts among the most important in Paris, not only by the name of the woman who presides . . . but also by the exceptional taste of the programs that are performed." Family arch. The countess was one of several socialites with whom Widor had close ties, and with her perhaps even more. In one letter she signs off: "Write to me dearest friend, you don't know how much I have need of you. Affectionately, MB." And eleven days later: "I beg you write to me quickly and very lengthily. Yours, MB." B.I.(a), letters 8 and 9, dated October 4 and October 15, 1914, respectively. For his part, Widor was no less effusive, addressing a letter to her, "Dear darling adored patroness!" Chimènes, *Mécènes et musiciens*, 130.

93. *Ménestrel* 77 (1911): 92; Maurat, *Souvenirs musicaux et littéraires*, 81–82.

94. Widor had played the organ at Pierné's wedding some twenty years earlier, on May 19, 1890, at Saint-Sulpice. *L'Art Musical* 29 (1890): 78.

95. *Ménestrel* 77 (1911): 411; for other reviews, see *Guide du Concert* 3 (1911): 188–90 for a brief analysis of the symphony, and pp. 319–20 for a summary of reviews from six different sources. Widor wrote to Robert Brussel, critic for *Le Figaro*, the following day: "You have spoiled me in your fine article of this morning. The *Symphonie antique* doesn't

know how to thank you! It retains an *intense gratitude* for you." Author's collection, letter dated December 25, 1911.

96. *Ménestrel* 79 (1913): 381.

97. *Ménestrel* 91 (1929): 123.

98. "Strasbourg," 3; five-page undated manuscript, author's collection. This concert is also mentioned in Widor, "Souvenirs autobiographiques," 86.

99. Widor, Preface to *J. S. Bach,* 1: vi.

100. Schweitzer, *My Life and Thought,* 13.

101. Philipp, "Charles-Marie Widor," 131.

102. M.S., letter dated December 4, 1923, from Widor to an unnamed person.

103. Widor, Preface to *L'orgue de Jean-Sébastien Bach,* v–vi.

104. Widor, Preface to *J. S. Bach: Le musicien-poète,* vii–viii.

105. Widor, Preface to *J. S. Bach,* 1: vi.

106. Joy, *Albert Schweitzer,* ix.

107. Widor, Preface to *J. S. Bach: Le musicien-poète,* xiv–xv.

108. Heinsheimer, "Schweitzer's Bach Edition," 30.

109. Schweitzer, *My Life and Thought,* 154.

110. Volumes 1 through 4 included the Preludes and Fugues, and volume 5 contained the Concertos and Sonatas.

111. Widor spoke at some length in his "Souvenirs" regarding the Bach edition on which he and Schweitzer collaborated:

During this time, in order not to forget my primary vocation, I occupied myself, with Albert Schweitzer, with an edition of the preludes, fugues, and chorales of J. S. Bach that the New York publisher Schirmer had asked of us. The five volumes of preludes and fugues have appeared, each piece with its preface, indications of style, registration, and tempos. . . . The Schirmer firm, having had to go through some turmoil, still exists, but we are still waiting for the edition of the chorales— the original publishers, alas, being dead.

Now, I had asked Mr. Delagrave—Schirmer having not published the chorales—if he would publish the French translation of the chorale texts in a little book [in order] that all French organists could have it in hand, each chorale annotated, studied, and detailed. Unfortunately, this publisher feared to launch into an affair that would not be profitable enough, and we left it at that. I am awfully sorry about it because only a man like Schweitzer can give us the true sense of this singular work of J. S. Bach, the musician-poet.

The Preludes and Fugues:

I don't have to retrace the performance of Bach on which many naïve musicians have permitted themselves so much license and fancy. They forget that of all instruments, the only one on which the sound can "last indefinitely" is the organ, whose sound gives us the example of good breathing, exempt from all agitation and all change. As for the articulation of repeated notes, this articulation must have, in a moderate tempo, half the value of the note.

What is style? It's the absolute sacrosanctity of the composer's text, of which each printed note must be rendered as he has conceived it.

Schweitzer came in the winter to complete his liturgical studies in Paris (he [also] profited from studying the organ with me), I went myself every summer to Gunsbach, near Colmar, to complete the chapters not finished in Paris. Widor, "Souvenirs autobiographiques," 42–43.

112. Dupré, *Recollections*, 54. It was not without a bit of resentment that Widor saw Schweitzer disappear to Africa for long periods of time: "With regard to the Schirmer Edition, all that will prove to you how much we think about you, Africa, Gabon, and your hospital, but also your blacks, who concern us less since they keep you so far away." M.S., letter dated August 13, 1926, from Widor to Schweitzer.

113. Schweitzer, *My Life and Thought*, 161–62.

114. Heinsheimer, "Schweitzer's Bach Edition," 30.

115. Ibid.

116. Ibid.

117. M.S., letter dated July 31, 1930, from Widor to Schweitzer.

118. M.S., letter dated August 24, 1936, from Widor to Schweitzer.

119. M.S., letter dated December 19, 1936, from Widor to Schweitzer.

120. Volume 6 appeared in 1954, and volumes 7 and 8 in 1967, after Schweitzer's death. "Edouard Nies-Berger [was] then staff organist of the New York Philharmonic. Some thirty years younger than Schweitzer, he was the son of one of Schweitzer's most intimate friends, an organist of one of the churches where Schweitzer had played the organ in his early days. Alsatian by birth and American by choice, the junior Nies-Berger was fluent in German, French, and English and steeped in the secrets of Bach's organ world. He was the logical man to assist Schweitzer in the completion of the work." Heinsheimer, "Schweitzer's Bach Edition," 31. See also Murray, *Albert Schweitzer, Musician*, 75–77.

121. Schweitzer, *My Life and Thought*, 162.

122. Miller, "L'école Widor," 488.

123. *Guide du Concert* 3 (1911): 182.

124. *Ménestrel* 78 (1912): 86, 414; 79 (1913): 381; 80 (1914): 71, 183.

125. *Ménestrel* 78 (1912): 414.

126. *Ménestrel* 79 (1913): 222.

127. M. Dumesnil, "Widor," 192.

128. *Ménestrel* 78 (1912): 158.

129. *Ménestrel* 79 (1913): 343.

130. Philipp, "Charles-Marie Widor," 128.

131. Dupré, *Recollections*, 50.

132. A.B-A., letter dated June 27, 1914; a copy is also found in the Family arch.

133. Pougin, "Les secrétaires perpétuels," 235.

134. Widor, *Amateurs honoraires*, 6.

135. M. Dumesnil, "Widor," 144.

136. At the end of the poem, Saint-Saëns noted: "the rhyme is weak but 'one can take license in order to express a beautiful thought.' Molière, *La Comtesse d'Escarbagnas*." B.I.(c), letter 14, dated July 1914.

137. As has been noted regarding each of Widor's residences, he was accustomed to such amenities; his previous apartments had also been what one might describe as somewhat posh. At 7 rue des Saints-Pères: "The [music] room was hung with fine paintings and embellished with statuary, for the master has many friends among the artists and sculptors of France; and it was altogether finished as one would expect in a man of such prominence and capabilities—a very far cry indeed from the composer's garret that the poets seem to insist upon as the accompaniment of musical greatness." Miller, "L'école Widor," 488.

138. M. Dumesnil, "Widor," 144; Boschot, *Charles-Marie Widor*, 14.

139. *Guide Hayet* 1, no. 4 (June 17, 1922), B.N. Fonds Mont.

140. Philipp, "Charles-Marie Widor," 130.

141. Widor loved to relate the story of a letter he received from a painter who had received a prize from the Academy of Fine Arts. It began: "Sweetie! The old fogies of the Institute just granted me a prize of two thousand bucks. Come this evening to eat and drink to their health." It appears "Sweetie" received the official letter of appreciation that had been placed in the wrong envelope by the sender. The painter eventually became a member of the Academy, and Widor relished reciting to him the opening words of his letter: "Sweetie! The old fogies . . ." Louis Schneider, "Charles-Marie Widor," B.O.

142. *Ménestrel* 82 (1920): 324.

143. *Ménestrel* 83 (1921): 324.

144. Widor, "Souvenirs autobiographiques," 90–91.

145. *Gaulois* (November 26, 1923), "M. Widor Conférencier," B.N. Fonds Mont.

146. Boschot, *Charles-Marie Widor*, 12.

147. Philipp, "Charles-Marie Widor," 130. Widor was also a careful editor of his work. When readying a notice for publication, nothing escaped his scrutiny. His proof copy for the notice on Massenet has many corrections of punctuation, spelling, verb tense, and other minute details. Family arch.

148. Pougin, "Les secrétaires perpétuels," 235.

149. Brussel, "Ch.-M. Widor."

150. Widor, *Fondations, portraits*, 53.

151. Doret, "Widor: 1845–1937."

152. Valbelle, "Quelques souvenirs," 1.

153. Dupré, "En parlant de Ch.-M. Widor."

154. A.N.(b).

155. A.N.(b), letter from Fauré to A. Dalimier, dated May 26, 1916.

156. A.N.(b), letter from A. Dalimier to Fauré, dated June 16, 1916.

157. A.N.(b).

158. Widor, *Fondations, portraits*, 39.

159. Widor, *Amateurs honoraires*, 6–7.

160. Prod'homme, "Charles-Marie Widor," 219–20.

161. Boschot, *Charles-Marie Widor*, 10.

162. Widor, *Fondations, portraits*, 175.

163. Widor, "Note sur les faits de guerre intéressant l'Ac. des B.-Arts en 1914," Ms 4123, dated December 31, 1914, B.I.

164. Widor, "Souvenirs autobiographiques," 75.

165. Widor, "Note sur les faits de guerre intéressant l'Ac. des B.-Arts en 1914"; see also B.I.(a), document 158.

166. Widor, "Souvenirs autobiographiques," 72–73. The personages mentioned in this excerpt: André Tardieu (1876–1945), French statesman; François Flameng (1856–1923), French academic painter; Jean-Louis Forain, French impressionist painter; Arthur Meyer (1844–1924), director of *Le Gaulois*; André Maginot (1877–1932), member of Parliament and soldier, advocated concrete fortifications—the "Maginot Line"; Étienne Grosclaude (1858–1932), French writer and political commentator; Joseph Galieni (1849–1916), French soldier and military governor of Paris at the outset of the war; Théophile Delcassé (1852–1923), French statesman.

167. Widor, "Note sur les faits de guerre intéressant."

168. A.S-S., letter 20, dated March 23, 1918.

169. A.S-S., letter 21, dated March 29, 1918.

170. Les Autographes, 45 rue de l'Abbé Grégoire, Paris, Summer 1983 sales catalogue, item 301.

171. Widor, "Souvenirs autobiographiques," 81.

172. He simply told Robert Brussel, "from 1914 to 1920 I worked on my opera in 4 acts, *Nerto*. . . . So that's what I did as a musician since the beginning of the War that shook the world." Author's collection, letter dated August 24, 1920.

173. Widor, *Fondations, portraits*, 236.

174. Author's collection, letter dated August 24, 1920, to Robert Brussel.

175. Widor wrote to Wallace Goodrich, "I will soon send to you my 'Domine Salvum fac populum tuum' for Notre-Dame the day of the *Te Deum* of victory. The 'Salvum' is for three trumpets, three trombones, drums, and organ. It is currently being engraved." N.E.C., letter dated September 17, 1916.

176. B.N., Ms 18505.

177. "Le 'Te Deum' à Notre-Dame," *Journal des Débats* 130 (November 18, 1918): 2. The article went on to report, "the *Te Deum* was sung by the choirs and crowd with indescribable enthusiasm. Then the singing of the *Magnificat* swelled every chest; on the *grand orgue*, Marcel Dupré, in the middle of a grandiose improvisation, started to play the *Marseillaise*, and it was in singing the national hymn that the crowd spilled out onto the square."

178. Carvalhos, "Charles-Marie Widor." A picture taken by *Excelsior* shows Widor seated at this table. Adorning its surface are piles of papers, an ink well, the three-branched lamp, and a half-empty wine bottle!

179. Boschot, *Charles-Marie Widor*, 10.

180. Damrosch, *My Musical Life*, 257–58.

181. Launay, "Charles-Marie Widor," 277.

182. M. Dumesnil, "Widor," 144.

183. Widor, "Souvenirs autobiographiques," 86.

184. M.S., letter dated January 20, 1939, from Madame Widor to Schweitzer.

185. Widor, "Souvenirs autobiographiques," 88. Widor wrote to Robert Brussel, "President Poincaré graciously asked me to dine with Her Majesty, who was passing through Paris incognito, and afterward to play a little music for her in the strictest intimacy, with violinist Pascal; we played these four pieces that were still in manuscript." Letter dated August 24, 1920, author's collection. On another occasion, in May 1929, Widor recalled: "I lunched at the Elysée. I allowed myself to ask President [Gaston] Doumergue [1863–1937; French president 1924–31] for the grand cross to be bestowed . . . on the former [prime minister] of the Republic of Poland. . . . One knows all that he did for the resurrection of his country. Doumergue did not hesitate. 'When leaving here,' he said to me, 'you can go to the telegraph [office] and announce to Paderewski that we just gave him the grand red ribbon (grand cross).'" Widor, "Souvenirs autobiographiques," 103.

186. Widor, *Fondations, portraits*, 176.

187. Russell, "Widor," 65.

188. Widor, *Fondations, portraits*, 6.

189. Widor, "Souvenirs autobiographiques," 74.

190. Ibid.

191. Widor, *Fondations, portraits*, 6.

192. Russell, "Widor," 65.

193. Nectoux, *Camille Saint-Saëns and Gabriel Fauré*, 108. After reading through the score of *Pelléas et Mélisande*, Saint-Saëns later wrote to Widor, "It isn't worthy of us, and I shudder from head to toe when I think that we have to have it." In the same letter, he

referred to *Pelléas* as an "incomprehensible piece," and concluded, "We are in a period of madness, one must admit." B.I.(c), letter 49, dated May 22, 1919.

194. M. Dumesnil, "Widor," 192.

195. Widor, *Fondations, portraits*, 6–8.

196. Widor, "Souvenirs autobiographiques," 74.

197. Prod'homme, "Charles-Marie Widor," 220.

198. Lesure, *Claude Debussy: Correspondance*, 2191.

199. Widor, "Souvenirs autobiographiques," 75. In his eulogy of Léon Bonnat in 1923, Widor expanded upon the interesting details of Rodin's candidacy:

> Bonnat was a member of the Institute since 1881 and his influence there was considerable. He brought all of it to bear in sponsoring the candidature of Rodin in 1917. On two previous occasions, his name had been put forth: first by Jean-Paul Laurens [1838–1921] and then by [François] Flameng. Many of our confrères considered it, and the rumor began to circulate of a possible election. It was then that a hostile group (foreign to the Institute, we hasten to say) was conceived, in the manner of a protest, to go all over artistic Paris, and even in the Institute, to seek dissenting signatures. It was rejected. Rodin, informed, expressed to me his gratitude. This malevolent campaign had, moreover, an excellent effect. It provoked the hatching of a list in which twenty-seven academic signatures expressed the desire that the vacant seat be offered to the celebrated artist. It's from the very hands of Bonnat that Rodin received this list. . . . Alas! Twenty-five days later, Saturday, November 24, the day scheduled for the election, I had the sad honor of making, in front of Rodin's coffin, the announcement of his candidature and his success. Widor, *Fondations, portraits*, 175–76.

In his discourse at Rodin's funeral Widor expressed his disdain for the "vanity of old quarrels" that were brought forth by outside dissenters to Rodin's candidature. "Agreement is easy between true artists when it's a matter of the general interest. At a time when, without concern for divergences of opinion, so many brave men are going off hand in hand to be killed for their country, what are quarrels between schools worth?" B.I., "Procès-verbal," November 24, 1917.

200. Philipp, "Charles-Marie Widor," 128.

201. http://www.academie-des-beaux-arts.fr/uk/membres/index.html; Philipp, "Charles-Marie Widor," 129.

202. B.N.(d), W.48, letter 565, dated December 29, 1932, to Paul Dukas.

203. Philipp, "Charles-Marie Widor," 129.

204. Craft, *Stravinsky: Selected correspondence*, 483.

205. Ibid., 486.

206. R. Dumesnil, *Le monde des musiciens*, 66. In one instance, Widor penned a plea, dated January 31, 1927, apparently to the archbishop of Paris, requesting that "His Eminence" intervene in "an unfortunate situation that interests all Catholic artists—devoted servants of the church" between the parish priest of Saint Ambroise and its choirmaster, Mr. Schlosser. A.D., Widor file.

207. A.D., Widor file, document dated December 13, 1933.

208. A.D., Widor file, letter dated November 12, 1924.

Monsieur le Curé,

The Union of Choir Masters and Organists, encouraged by His Eminence the Cardinal and approved by the Diocese Administration, has the honor of soliciting from your high eminence a favorable welcome to the request that it comes to make of you, and begs you to examine with kindness the respectful demand that it addresses to you with a view to the examination of the salaries of the Choirmasters and Organists.

The present conditions of life are becoming more and more difficult for all. They are particularly disturbing for the category of zealous and devoted servants of the Church to which we belong.

For a long time, the members of the Union have hesitated to ask for sacrifices from their parishes; but today, despite the resources that they can scarcely raise, such as from private lessons, and despite their voluntary sacrifices in a real spirit of devotion and attachment to the Church, the resources of the Choirmasters and Organists are absolutely insufficient; and from this fact they see, with sadness, their dignity and their moral authority threatened, and their legitimate and modest well-being less and less assured.

Under these conditions, Monsieur Curé, the Union of Choirmasters and Organists asks you to be willing to hear its voice and examine with condescension its present and very respectful proposition for the augmentation of their fixed salary.

Here is a plan that we are permitting ourselves to submit to you:

Augmentation of 75% *in their fixed salary* [italics indicates a handwritten insertion]; or

For your Maître de Chapelle _____Fr.
For your Organiste du Grand Orgue _____Fr.
For your Organiste accompagnateur_____Fr.

In the hope that you will receive its request favorably, the Union of Choirmasters and Organists, awaiting your good response, asks you to accept, Monsieur Curé, the assurance of its profound respect and its entire devotion.

President,
[signed] Widor
209. A.D., Widor file, letter dated December 2, 1924.
210. A.D., Widor file, letter dated January 25, 1925.
Monsieur Curé,

The Union of Choirmasters and Organists is duty bound to address all its thanks to those Curés who have already given a favorable response to the request formulated by the Union in its letter of last November 12.

We permit ourselves, Monsieur le Curé, to insist that you notice the disproportion that exists between the functions of the Choirmaster and those of the Singers placed under [his] directions. The Choirmaster, responsible for the service, must think about it constantly, and devote about 3 hours *per day* to it. The Singers have only a personal responsibility, and their Association has limited the time of required rehearsals to *26 hours per year.*

There is no less disproportion between the long and multiple studies necessary to a Choirmaster or an Organist (both composer and improviser) and a Singer.

Now, the salaries currently corresponding to the functions and duties of the one and the other seem equitable to you; that is what we permit ourselves, Monsieur le Curé, to submit to your benevolent attention.

Hoping that you will be willing to give us a favorable response, and sending to you our most heartfelt thanks in advance, we have the honor of offering to you, Monsieur le Curé, the expression of our most profoundly respectful and devoted sentiments.

President,
[signed] Widor
211. A.D., Widor file, anonymous news clipping, "Les maîtrises sont menacées."
212. Ibid.
213. A.D., Widor file, undated document [1933].

214. Philipp, "Charles-Marie Widor," 128.

215. Smith, *Louis Vierne*, 299. Upon returning from a series of concerts Widor had arranged for him in Holland in May 1895, Vierne was welcomed home by his *maître*, who teased him: "If your progress continues in this steadily accelerated rhythm, there's little chance you'll be fat. It's a regimen that could well be recommended to pretty women worried about their figures" (313).

216. Maurat, *Souvenirs musicaux et littéraires*, 81.

217. Trillat, "Charles-Marie Widor," 4.

218. Philipp, "Charles-Marie Widor," 129.

219. Widor, *Bach: Œuvres complètes pour orgue*, 1: xlii.

220. *Ménestrel* 84 (1922): 309. Though extolling the virtues of the opportunity for winners of the Prix de Rome to study there, Widor admitted that not everyone took appropriate advantage of it. "People have said, and I repeat it: there are two categories of boarders at the villa; on the one hand are the indifferent who live as they would live in Paris and who, boring themselves in Rome, dream only of getting back to the street; on the other hand are minds curious to see and learn, who become impassioned about antiquity and the Renaissance, who grow richer with all the great memories." Widor, *Fondations, portraits*, 219.

221. Family arch.

222. Family arch., letter dated February 23, 1921, from the Ministère de l'instruction publique et des beaux-arts to Widor. Also *Ménestrel* 83 (1921): 384.

223. Widor, *Fondations, portraits*, 249.

224. Leonard, *The Conservatoire Américain*, 4.

225. R. Dumesnil, *Le monde des musiciens*, 191.

226. Widor, *Fondations, portraits*, 248. In an interview for the *New York Herald*, Damrosch stated, "The French have the gift for teaching: they have clarity and enthusiasm; with these two qualities one makes miracles." R. Dumesnil, *Le monde des musiciens*, 190.

227. Widor, *Fondations, portraits*, 250. The professors were all to be French and chosen from those who were "the most prominent, the former winners of the Prix de Rome, and the most brilliant laureates of the National Conservatory or School of Fine Arts." Those familiar with the English language or the United States were given preference. *Fondations, portraits*, 251.

228. B.N.(d), letter 23, dated June 19, 1925, to Robert Brussel.

229. Widor, *Fondations, portraits*, 250; Avery, "Fontainebleau," 2.

230. Avery, "Fontainebleau," 1–2.

231. Ibid., 1. Widor made the weekly trip to Fontainebleau by train and trolley; the students felt his devotion to their lessons and one reported that he "won our love and admiration by his kindly interest and cordial manner." Pearson, "Organ Study in France," 22.

232. Charlotte Klein, "Fontainebleau School: Its Work for Organists and Story of Inception," *Diapason* 15, no. 4 (1924): 31.

233. Widor, *Fondations, portraits*, 249. For Americans awaiting repatriation after the war, educational centers had been set up in several French cities and various disciplines were taught by French professors. Near Paris, the Pavillon de Bellevue was divided into workshops for painters, sculptors, and architects; there, some three hundred students worked with their professors and made weekly visits to workshops of master French artisans in Paris. When the time came for the students to return to America, although 80 percent of them voted to be allowed to continue their studies in France, they had to

depart. Widor was anxious that they be offered the same opportunity afforded musicians to return to France for professional study. *Fondations, portraits,* 247–48.

234. Widor, Preface to *Palace of Fontainebleau,* 3.

235. *Ménestrel* 86 (1924): 408.

236. Copland and Perlis, *Copland: 1900 through 1942,* 52.

237. Klein, "Fontainebleau School," 31.

238. Locard, "L'orgue du conservatoire," 462.

239. Ibid. Convers succeeded Mutin in 1924 and "displeased his clients with mass-produced instruments whose electric note transmission system was unreliable." http://www.culture.gouv.fr/culture/cavaille-coll/en/bas_muttin.html.

240. Leonard, *The Conservatoire Américain,* 15.

241. Ibid., 17.

242. The movements are as follows: (1) "Pastorale," from Pastorale in F Major, third movement, BWV 590; (2) "Miserere mei," from Prelude in D Minor (WTC, book 1), BWV 851; (3) "Aria," from Prelude in E Minor (WTC, book 1), BWV 855; (4) "Marche du veilleur de nuit," from Cantata 140 ("Wachet auf, ruft uns die Stimme"), BWV 140; (5) "Sicilienne," from Flute Sonata in E-flat Major, second movement, BWV 1031; (6) "Mattheus-Finale" final chorus from the *Saint Matthew Passion* ("Wir setzen uns mit Tränen nieder"), BWV 244. Hays, Review, 5.

243. Hays, Review, 5.

244. Of this remarkable movement, Widor wondered, "Who among us has been able to listen to . . . the entrance of the double-chorus Final of the *Matthew Passion* without a thrill?" Widor, *Initiation musicale,* 88. For the one-hundredth anniversary of Beethoven's death, a commemoration concert took place at Notre-Dame Cathedral on March 17, 1927. Three hundred performers, soloists, chorus, and orchestra, presented Beethoven's *Missa Solemnis* under Gabriel Pierné's direction. Widor chose to play Bach's Prelude and Fugue in E Minor before the program and the "Mattheus-Final" at the conclusion. Widor, *Fondations, portraits,* 245.

245. M.S., letter dated August 13, 1926. Widor also used the term "orchestration" to indicate "registration": "He spoke of stop-changes as 'orchestration' always." Thomas, "Organ Loft Whisperings" (December 27, 1893): 12.

246. *Ménestrel* 87 (1925): 376.

247. Widor, *Fondations, portraits,* 227.

248. *Ménestrel* 90 (1928): 337.

249. Widor, *Fondations, portraits,* 253.

250. *Ménestrel* 93 (1931): 376.

251. B.I.(a), letter 27, dated October 21, 1918.

252. Russell, "Widor," 13. Many spoke of Widor's lisp; Hugues Imbert referred to it more as the "diction from the end of the lips peculiar to Widor." Imbert, "Charles-Marie Widor," 224.

253. Buhrman, "Widor Career is Closed," 128.

254. *Courrier Musical* 29 (June 15, 1927): 355. He went on to say, "I admit that my modesty, submitted to an ordeal so unforeseen, incited me angrily to hide under the table."

255. Russell, "Widor," 65.

256. Imbert, *Portraits et études,* 38.

257. Leray, "Souvenirs d'un maître."

258. L. Varèse, *Varèse,* 42.

259. Widor closed a letter on August 7, 1897, to his sister: "I love you like I loved mama, and I hug you close, very close." In a 1970 taped interview with Marie's daughter Gabrielle Guibaud, she stated that her mother so loved her brothers Charles and Paul that she told her fiancé Eugène Pierron that she wouldn't marry him unless her brothers were "adopted" too. Family arch.

260. Trillat, "Charles-Marie Widor," 8.

261. A facsimile of the signed marriage covenant is published in Pelatan et al., *Trois dames*, 88; there, Widor's date of birth is given as February 22, 1845. Separate notations in the left-hand margin of Widor's birth record indicate details of his marriage, and later the date and place of his death. Lyon Municipal Archives, birth records of 1844, entry number 700.

262. Pelatan et al., *Trois dames*, 69–70. Her baptism was celebrated on August 15 at the parish church of Sainte Jeanne d'Arc.

263. The family heritage is traced in "La maison de Montesquiou Fezensac depuis la fin de l'ancien régime" (see page 56) by Comte Armand de Montesquiou Fezensac; exemplaire 277 was consulted at the M.S. Mathilde's mother was born on February 23, 1844, just two days after Widor.

264. Pelatan et al., *Trois dames*, 67.

265. The appraisal of Rear Admiral Dupré, quoted in Pelatan et al., *Trois dames*, 68.

266. Ibid., 70.

267. Ibid., 71.

268. Ibid.

269. Ibid., 71–72.

270. Ibid., 74.

271. Ibid.

272. Ibid.

273. M.S., letter dated January 20, 1939, from Mathilde Montesquiou Widor to Schweitzer in Lambaréné.

274. Trillat, "Charles-Marie Widor," 3–4. Trillat's reference to Widor's "maîtresse en titre," Madame Charles de Max, raises an interesting question. In no other source is such a relationship mentioned, though it is certain that Widor was close to her. See Chimènes, *Mécènes et musiciens*, 185.

275. Maurat, *Souvenirs musicaux et littéraires*, 130.

276. B.I.(c), letter 60, dated March 25, 1920, from Algiers.

277. Saint-Saëns once addressed Widor: "Very illustrious and very venerable confrère in Pallas Athene, protectress of the Academy! I kiss the shadow of your respectable sandals." B.I.(c), letter 31, dated May 5, 1918. In letters between the two men, the informal "tu" was the usual form of address. Saint-Saëns had been a longtime close friend of the entire Widor family. Marie-Ange Guibaud related an amusing story about Saint-Saëns during a visit to the family in Lyon in the early 1900s; he played a charade on the family by donning one of Marie's dresses—Widor's sister had become somewhat heavy, about the size of Saint-Saëns.

278. A.S-S., letter 38, dated March 30, 1920.

279. Pelatan et al., *Trois dames*, 76.

280. Henry Standish, whose mother was French (family of Noailles), was the last Lord of the Standish Manor (1883–1920). He married Hélène Pérusse des Cars on October 17, 1870, and spent most of his life in France, where he was "very well known in high Parisian society." When he died in Contrexéville, on July 31, 1920, he left a fortune of approximately eight hundred thousand francs, in addition to properties. Madame

Standish and Mathilde (now Madame Widor) were his sole heirs, except for some members of the Noailles family to whom he left some valuable paintings. His desire to be interred in the village of Mouchy, near Noailles, was perhaps the most evident sign of embracing his maternal family. In turn, when Madame Standish died in Paris, on October 12, 1933, "Madame Widor became the single heiress of the immense fortune left by the couple. In France . . . Madame Widor became owner of a townhouse located at [3] rue de Belloy; three apartment houses, one at Place des Etats-Unis and rue Galilée, the second rue Villaret-Joyeuse, the third rue de Bellechasse; and the Château d'Hauteville property inherited from her aunt, while she was already usufructuary of the English property of her uncle." Manouvriez, "Le testament perdu." The chateau more likely passed to Mathilde upon her mother's death in 1901; it was gutted by fire in 1922 and never restored. See Pelatan et al., *Trois dames*, and Hobbs, "Madame Widor," 413, 416. Until the fire, the Widors enjoyed visits to the property. Family arch., card dated September 10, 1920, from Widor to his niece, Marguerite Reynard.

281. Hobbs, "Madame Widor," 414.

282. The author has read numerous letters of hers, and her manner of verbal expression gives solid evidence of the quality and refinement of her education and character.

283. R.B.I., letter dated March 27, 1934.

284. Maurat, *Souvenirs musicaux et littéraires*, 130.

285. Manouvriez, "Le testament perdu." A photo of Mathilde as a young woman playing the piano is found in Pelatan et al., *Trois dames*, (unnumbered) vi, between 80 and 81.

286. Chimènes, *Mécènes et musiciens*, 462–63. Lavignac, *Voyage artistique à Bayreuth*, 57; the quotation is cited in Chimènes.

287. Undated obituary of Henry Standish from *Le Figaro*, found in a collection of miscellaneous news clippings collected by Widor. Family arch.

288. Widor, "Souvenirs autobiographiques," 96. Victorien Sardou (1831–1908); Jean Baptiste-Édouard Detaille (1842–1912); Princess Christian (1846–1923); Princess Victoria (1868–1935).

289. Chimènes, *Mécènes et musiciens*, 423; *Le Figaro* (April 6, 1908) is referenced.

290. Proust, *Le côté de Guermantes*, 2:109–10.

291. Author's collection, letter dated February 27, 1914, to Mr. Blanck.

292. M.S., letter dated January 11, 1935, from Madame Widor to Schweitzer.

293. M.S., letter dated January 20, 1939, from Madame Widor to Schweitzer.

294. Pelatan et al., *Trois dames*, 78–79. Soon after, Widor returned from a trip to Russia. "[Mathilde] dreamed of hearing him recount his travels and of attending a new concert" (79).

295. Ibid., 79.

296. Ibid., 79. This source offers 1905 as the date of Mathilde's marriage proposal, but this is not credible by Widor's own account, and such a guileless proposal would more certainly have come from a young child than a sheltered twenty-two-year-old woman educated strictly in social conventions.

297. Ibid., 86.

298. Ibid., 87.

299. Hobbs, "Dernières années," 18.

300. Dupré, *Recollections*, 52. In honor of his sixty-four years of service, the curé proposed that the parish present the stops in his name.

301. A Paris notary, Mr. Ader, carried out the distribution of Widor's estate. Documentation in Family arch.

302. A copy of this allocution given by Monsieur l'Abbé Sicard is in the Family arch.

303. The following account maliciously paints quite a different picture:

Widor had to endure this world, where one feels dull with a burdensome flunky, [and] a very disappointing and authoritative wife, [who] isolat[ed] him from his Lyon family: his brother—"Mr. Court Clerk," fine pianist, magnificent citizen—his sister, Madame Pierron, and his nieces. He no longer had the right to spend his summer days at the family property in Persange[s]. . . . There remained to him an escape on the Left Bank: his Institute, his organ at Saint-Sulpice, the American Conservatory at Fontainebleau, and his most faithful friend and confidant, Isidor Philipp . . . whom he had named executor. Trillat, "Charles-Marie Widor," 9.

Ennemond Trillat's statement contradicts all other evidence; also, his mention of Widor's sister in this context is incorrect, as she had died three years before his marriage. Trillat also incorrectly states that Widor named Philipp his executor. Hobbs, "Dernières années," 18. In July 1930, Widor named as his executor Amédée Mancat-Amat de Vallombrosa who had studied composition with him, and temporarily acted as his assistant at the *grand orgue* in 1908 and choirmaster in 1928. Havard de la Montagne, "Les maîtres de chapelle," 16, 25.

304. M.S., letter dated April 18, 1930, from Widor to Schweitzer.

305. Family arch., letter dated September 1, 1920.

306. Family arch., letter dated November 8, 1920.

307. Family arch., letter dated February 18, 1935, from Marcel Dupré to Marguerite Reynard.

308. Widor, Guilmant, and Vierne had constituted the jury when Decaux was chosen organist of the Basilica in 1903. *Ménestrel* 69 (1903): 271. For the consecration, Widor performed the seventeenth-century *Messe royale* of Dumont and the second movement from the *Symphonie romane* in the morning, and at Vespers his motet *Tu es Petrus; Salvum fac* sounded under the great dome of the Basilica the next day. *Ménestrel* 81 (1919): 20.

309. *Ménestrel* 82 (1920): 291.

310. Ibid., 324.

311. *Ménestrel* 83 (1921): 379.

312. Ibid., 415.

313. Widor, "La musique," 453.

314. Widor, *Initiation musicale*, 5.

315. Ibid., 87.

316. *Temps* (October 14, 1923), B.N. Fonds Mont.

317. Tiersot, "Widor, *Initiation musicale*," 86.

318. Widor, "La classe d'orgue," 238.

319. *Petite Maitrise* 239 (April 1933): 13.

320. Ibid., 15.

321. Ibid.; Widor, Preface to *L'orgue*, 1.

322. Widor, Preface to *L'orgue*, 3.

323. *Petite Maitrise* 239 (April 1933): 16.

324. Widor, Preface to *L'orgue*, 3.

325. *Petite Maitrise* 239 (April 1933): 16–17.

326. *Petite Maîtrise* 243 (August 1933): 37–38.

327. Ibid., 38.

328. *Petite Maîtrise* 239 (April 1933): 39–40.

329. R.B.I., letter dated March 27, 1934.

330. S.M.L., letter 7, dated August 14, 1889.

331. Véran, "L'histoire de *Nerto*."

332. S.M.L., letter 7, dated August 14, 1889. On the same day that Widor wrote to Marie Trélat of his lunch at the home of Guy de Maupassant, the short story writer wrote to Widor: "I had a terrible headache all night, resulting in a fiercely bad temper, and I spent my morning writing some disagreeable things to all my friends. I don't know if I'll be in a state to dine this evening. I don't believe so and don't expect me at all. If I could come, I ask you not to tell anyone that I have dined with you, for my migraine made me blurt out something I shouldn't have; and this could bring me some trouble. In sum, I'm spending my life unable to hold to my commitments. . . . So, if I'm up I'll come, if I'm not up I'll stay in bed." B.I.(a), letter 129, dated August 14, 1889, from Maupassant to Widor. Two other letters, 130 and 131, from Maupassant indicate a hearty friendship between the men. In undated letter 130, Maupassant invites Widor to "dinner in the country with some beautiful ladies"; and in undated letter 131, Maupassant, describing himself as "the most serious and most perseverant joker," enlists Widor's help to play a hoax on "the Countess." The unnamed countess may have been Countess Emmanuela Potocka, with whom Widor was well acquainted, and who appears to have been Maupassant's mistress at the time. Chimènes, *Mécènes et musiciens*, 209.

333. *Ménestrel* 57 (1891): 272.

334. *Ménestrel* 78 (1912): 319; 79 (1913): 263.

335. R.B.I.

336. B.I.(b).

337. Family arch., letter dated September 20, 1920, to Gabrielle Guibaud.

338. *Courrier Musical* (November 1924): 518.

339. *Ménestrel* 86 (1924): 447–48.

340. Souday, "*Nerto*."

341. "*Nerto*," *Le Progrès* (November 5, 1924), B.N. Fonds Mont.

342. B.O., dozens of miscellaneous news clippings are found in "Dossier d'œuvre (*Nerto*)."

343. *Ménestrel* 86 (1924): 448.

344. Vuillermoz, "*Nerto* à l'Opéra."

345. Philipp, "Charles-Marie Widor," 128. Notwithstanding Philipp's appraisal, Widor and Léna wrote to the director of the Opéra praising the singers, the sets, the orchestra, and every other facet of the production, "Our work owes so much to you!" Letter printed in *Figaro* (October 31, 1924), B.N. Fonds Mont.

346. *Musical Times* 65 (1924): 1131.

347. *Times* [London] 43,794 (October 28, 1924): 10, col. 2.

348. Messager, "Les premières: *Nerto*." Messager went on to reminisce a bit: "Listening to [*Nerto*], I can't prevent myself from recalling long ago years when, as modest accompanist of the choir of Saint-Sulpice, I had the pleasure each Sunday to hear Mr. Widor at the *grand orgue*, and I found again in his instrumentation exactly the registration methods that he used back then." Henry Malherbe concurred in his review: "Mr. Widor . . . has without doubt deemed that in his music novelties were not permitted. He has subordinated all his inspirations to the immovable laws of tradition." Malherbe, "*Nerto* à l'Opéra."

349. M.S., anonymous clipping, "Rosserie."

350. Philipp, "Charles-Marie Widor," 128.

351. Widor, *Fondations, portraits*, 168.

352. B.I.(c), letter 76, dated April 8, 1921.

353. Russell, "Widor," 65.

354. Ibid.

355. Vierne, "Ch.-M. Widor," 76.

356. Russell, "Widor," 65.

357. Widor, "Fortieth Anniversary Prophesies," 661.

358. Philipp, "Charles-Marie Widor," 130.

359. M. Dumesnil, "Widor," 192.

360. Doret, "Widor: 1845–1937."

361. Widor, *Charles Girault*, 3.

362. Bouvard, "My Recollections," 43. *L'Ascension* (1933) was published before Widor retired from Saint-Sulpice.

363. Family arch., telegram copy, dated December 17, 1921.

364. All these documents and decorations are preserved in the Family arch.

365. *Ménestrel* 85 (1923): 547; 86 (1924): 367; 97 (1935): 124.

366. *Ménestrel* 84 (1922): 356; 91 (1929): 80; 95 (1933): 220.

367. Pons, "Charles-Marie Widor." A lunch in honor of Widor brought together about two hundred politicians, academicians, and musicians—among whom were Dupré, Pierné, Dukas, Hahn, Hüe, Milhaud, Honegger, Charpentier, Dubois, Samuel-Rousseau, and many others. "Un déjeuner en l'honneur du Maître Charles Widor," *Comœdia* (June 30, 1933), B.N. Fonds Mont.

368. Doret, "Widor: 1845–1937."

369. Philipp, "Charles-Marie Widor," 132; M. Dumesnil, "Widor," 192.

370. *Ménestrel* 89 (1927): 432; also A.D.(b). The Conservatory pay ledger for February 1915 indicates Widor's annual salary was three thousand francs, but it also indicates that it was "in the time of war." Author's collection.

371. Philipp, "Charles-Marie Widor," 129.

372. *Ménestrel* 89 (1927): 467, 551.

373. R. Dumesnil, *Le monde des musiciens*, 172–73.

374. *Ménestrel* 84 (1922): 453.

375. *Ménestrel* 75 (1909): 79.

376. R. Dumesnil, *Le monde des musiciens*, 172.

377. Widor, Preface to *Étude d'esthétique musicale*, v–vii.

378. *Courrier Musical* 26 (1924): 416–17.

379. Letter to Ed. Lavagne, dated March 6, 1925, J&J Lubrano, Great Barrington, Massachusetts, catalogue 45, item 626.

380. *Ménestrel* 89 (1927): 467.

381. Boschot, *Charles-Marie Widor*, 4. Well known for his sarcastic wit, Erik Satie, in a quip to Roland-Manuel, enlarged his oft-repeated signature quotation to mention Widor, who must have seemed the oldest in a pleiad of nineteenth-century musicians: "I came too young into a generation too old," wrote Satie, "from which, of course, I except at least Widor."

382. R.B.I., letter dated September 9, 1925.

383. Henderson, "Memories of Widor," 659.

384. Bouvard, "My Recollections," 43; *Ménestrel* 91 (1929): 20.

385. Ramsey, "An Interview," 14.

386. Jacque, "Ch.-M. Widor." One of Widor's editors wrote: "He seemed to have received from some beneficent fairy the gift of eternal youth. . . . He came to see me often, always without topcoat even during the severe cold, quickly climbing my stairway, and I felt rejuvenated by the presence of this old man—always of a supreme courtesy

and smiling affability—on whom the years had not taken hold." Bertrand, *Souvenirs d'un éditeur*, 60.

387. Doret, "Widor: 1845–1937."

388. Bertrand, *Souvenirs d'un éditeur*, 61.

389. Riemenschneider, "Tribute to Widor," 26.

390. Riemenschneider performed his first complete cycle in 1924. However, John H. Earnshaw claimed to have been the first American organist to perform the complete symphonies of Widor at his Sunday evening recitals at St. James's Episcopal Church in Atlantic City, New Jersey, in 1913. *Diapason* 15, no. 6 (1924): 18.

391. Riemenschneider gave a photo of himself to Widor with the inscription: "Fond memories to my very dear Maître, *Charles M. Widor, King of Organists*, to whom I owe most of my musical inspiration. Albert Riemenschneider, Paris, 1 August '27." Family arch.

392. *Diapason* 16, no. 6 (1925): 4.

393. R.B.I., letter dated August 15, 1924, to Riemenschneider.

394. R.B.I.

395. Dupré, "M. Charles-Marie Widor," 2.

396. Riemenschneider, "Widor; An Estimate," 4.

397. *Ménestrel* 90 (1928): 44. In a letter to Riemenschneider, dated January 16, 1928, Widor mentioned that at the same concert "Dupré accompanied *Salvum fac* [Op. 84] that I directed." R.B.I.

398. Gaëtan Sanvoisin, "Le maître Widor à l'orgue de la Madeleine," *Gaulois* (January 14, 1928).

399. Riemenschneider, "Letter," 14.

400. Riemenschneider, "Letter," 14.

401. R.B.I., letter dated August 21, 1927.

402. *Ménestrel* 88 (1926): 520; 89 (1927): 103; 90 (1928): 44; 93 (1931): 416; 91 (1929): 80.

403. Raugel, *Grandes orgues des églises de Paris*, 265.

404. Family arch., letter dated August 20, 1931, from Widor to a family member; accompanying the letter was an envelope containing Widor's work on the book.

405. *Ménestrel* 92 (1930): 39; also d'Andigné, "Remise à Widor," 6.

406. *Ménestrel* 94 (1932): 196.

407. Rollin Smith writes, "Vierne partisans claim that this third party was either Mutin or Dupré." Smith, *Louis Vierne*, 272. Mutin had succeeded Cavaillé-Coll in 1898 and naturally wanted the restoration of the most prominent French organ to be accomplished by a French builder; an American console would be out of the question. Vierne was convinced that Mutin worked an intrigue behind his back in order to bring the contract to the successor of his firm, Auguste Convers (who took over in 1924), and to exclude Vierne from the organ committee (see Smith, *Louis Vierne*, 274–75). Relations between Vierne and Dupré had soured years earlier. For health reasons, Vierne took a four-year leave (1916–20) from his post as organist of Notre-Dame, and Dupré assumed Vierne's duties; after such a long period of absence there was naturally some confusion over who was actually the *titulaire*. A lengthy imbroglio ensued between Vierne and Dupré through press notices, advertisements, statements by managers and friends, and their own indiscretions. Widor wrote to Dupré on March 17, 1924, expressing his consternation over the embroilment "between two men whose profession it is to deal with harmony," but to no avail. By that time their relationship had ruptured irreparably. See Smith, *Louis Vierne*, 330–43.

408. Ibid., 273.

409. Ibid.

410. M.S., letter dated April 22, 1928, from Widor to Schweitzer.

411. M.S., letter dated September 12, 1928, from Madame Widor to Schweitzer.

412. Widor, *L'orgue moderne*, 20, 22.

413. Smith, *Louis Vierne*, 269.

414. Vierne wrote, "[Mutin] expressed a fierce hatred of me." Ibid., 274–75.

415. Letter dated February 4, 1931. As a postscript, Widor tacked on: "Do you know that I have not seen you since your return from America, which is not nice! Every morning I receive between 10 and 12 o'clock, quai Conti." Vierne had returned from America in late April 1927—nearly four years earlier! This little reprimand clearly indicates that Widor still felt the master/pupil relationship to be in place. Copy of letter in Family arch.

416. Smith, *Louis Vierne*, 277.

417. Ibid.

418. In the meantime, Charles Mutin, who had blocked Vierne's participation in the discussions, died on May 29.

419. Smith, *Louis Vierne*, 285, 287; *Ménestrel* 94 (1932): 264. Widor played the *Symphonie gothique* on numerous occasions in his later years; when he performed it at Saint-Sulpice on April 29, 1931, for the Société des amis de l'orgue, it was noted, "The clarity of his playing and the vigor of his rhythm remain intact." B.N. Fonds Mont. On October 3, 1932, Widor, Paul Brunold (1875–1948; organist of Saint-Gervais), Charles Tournemire, and Albert Alain (1880–1971; organist of Saint-Germain-en-Laye) formed a commission to judge the Gonzales organ at Saint-Eustache; unlike the Notre-Dame organ, the Saint-Eustache organ was found wanting in many respects. Document in Family arch.

420. Josephson, *Edison*, 333–34.

421. Leray, "Souvenirs d'un maître." Gustave Bret offered a bit more detail about the incident: "In 1889, the famous inventor was in Paris. He got in touch with the great organ builder and acoustician Cavaillé-Coll. On his apparatus, too recently conceived to be beyond the experimental period, Edison wanted to try some musical recordings. They went to Saint-Sulpice and Widor played the organ, but the results were worthless. Edison then wanted to record the voices of some famous contemporaries. Mistral was in Paris, and he happily consented to some experiments, which were more conclusive and which the Pleyel firm facilitated with its traditional kindness. The head of the firm, Gustave Lyon, was a young engineer with a curious and well-informed mind." Bret, "Le grand organist Widor."

422. *Revue Éolienne* 1 (May 1899): 18–19. Using recent experiences, Widor wished for the proof a recording could provide about proper tempos: "Haydn, Beethoven, and Schumann are played every day in ridiculous tempos, either rapidly or with lack of intelligence. About a week ago I heard a brilliant and reputed virtuoso tackle Schumann's *Carnaval*. If I had not had each note of the Finale indelibly ingrained in my brain, I would never have been able to reconstitute the rhythm of it. As for its metronomic speed, it was accelerated by a good third. . . . I would still be able to mention a symphonic Finale by Schumann conducted like a deluxe train going ninety-five kilometers per hour. . . . Ah! if one were able to have a nice little phonograph recording, a sort of distant echo—but faithful to the first performances conducted by the composer or prepared under his direction, if one were able to show the truth forcibly to all these infirm people who don't even take the trouble to think it over, if we had the palpable proof of

the desire of the master, what a benefit for art!" Widor, "Phonographes et programmes," *Piano Soleil* (June 2, 1895): 1.

423. Coppola, *Dix-sept ans de musique*, 145.
424. Family arch., letter dated April 29, 1932, to Marguerite Reynard.
425. Helbig, "La grande pitié," 4:138.
426. Coppola, *Dix-sept ans de musique*, 145–46.
427. Rereleased in 1981 on EMI C 153-16411/5 *Orgues & organistes français en 1930*, and again in 1994 on EMI CDC 5 55037 2 *Composers in Person*.
428. Coppola, *Dix-sept ans de musique*, 147.
429. Ibid.
430. Unidentified news clipping: "À 88 ans, le maître donne à la cathédrale de Salzbourg un magnifique concert d'orgue," B.N. Fonds Mont.
431. Ibid.
432. *Ménestrel* 94 (1932): 335.
433. *Ménestrel* 95 (1933): 457.
434. Philipp, "Charles-Marie Widor," 132.
435. *Ménestrel* 72 (1906): 24.
436. Dupré, *Recollections*, 50.
437. Ramsey, "An Interview," 14–15.
438. Dupré, "Souvenirs sur Ch.-M. Widor," 32.
439. The last notation Widor made in his will indicated her death. Hobbs, "Dernières années," 20.
440. Dupré, "Souvenirs sur Ch.-M. Widor," 33. Already five years earlier, organist Jean Bouvard had thought, "[Widor's] improvisations were somewhat lacking in interest; he seems to have just worn out. But it is surprising to see this elderly man, stooped and with bony hands—he had to possess a tremendous pedal technique. He plays the pedals marvelously well—his legato is impeccable." Bouvard, "My Recollections," 43.
441. Dupré, *Recollections*, 51.
442. Ibid.
443. Valbelle, "Quelques souvenirs," 1; see also Pédron, "Charles Widor."
444. Les Autographes, 45 rue de l'Abbé Grégoire, Paris, sales catalogue 127 "Orgue," January 2009, item 232.
445. Dupré, *Recollections*, 45. Lazare-Auguste Maquaire had been Widor's assistant at Saint-Sulpice since 1900; Dupré succeeded Maquaire upon his untimely death in 1906.
446. Pierre Berlioz, "Les adieux de Widor," *Jour* (April 10, 1934), B.N. Fonds Mont.
447. A.N.(a), AJ37 301 [1908–9]; AJ37 302/1 [1910–11].
448. Family arch.
449. Masterclass with Arthur Poister, Colby College, Waterville, Maine, August 1973.
450. Bouvard, "My Recollections," 43. On the contrary, Widor's grandnephew, Eugène Guibaud, who had lunch on five or six occasions with Widor and Dupré at Chez Foyot, had the distinct impression that Dupré was not entirely sincere in his deference to Widor. Guibaud felt, "Dupré paid great homage to Widor during his lifetime, but not so much afterwards. Dupré was a snob who only thought himself important." Eugène Guibaud, conversation with the author, Persanges, l'Arbresle, July 12, 1990. Ennemond Trillat experienced a taste of Dupré's egotism when he arranged a "Concours Widor" for the centenary of Widor's birth: "I would have liked to include Albert Schweitzer on the jury, presided over by [Widor's] student Marcel Dupré. . . . [I] knew that he [Schwietzer] could not allow the too rapid 'tempi' imposed by Mr. Dupré, who was intoxicated by his own incomparable virtuosity. Dupré judged with

pity this organist-pastor, incapable of playing fast. . . . I couldn't invite Schweitzer without notifying Dupré, and that was an epistolary explosion summed up [by Dupré] with: 'Him or me, but me without him.'" Trillat, "Charles-Marie Widor," 9–10.

451. R. Dumesnil, *Portraits de musiciens français*, 197.

452. M. Dumesnil, "Widor," 143.

453. Dupré, *Recollections*, 52.

454. Dupré, "M. Charles-Marie Widor," 2.

455. *Comœdia*[?] (September 4, 1934), B.N. Fonds Mont.

456. Lehman, "Charles-Marie Widor," 497.

457. Widor, "Souvenirs autobiographiques," 101.

458. A.D., Widor file.

459. Philipp, "Charles-Marie Widor," 131.

460. Although the Invalides organ was the immediate cause of fundraising at this concert, Widor pointed to two instruments in desperate condition:

> There are two organs that are a disgrace in the current state of things and that are found in two incomparable historic monuments, and, therefore, more exposed to the attention and piteous appraisal of the foreigner: the organ of the Chapel of Versailles, and the organ of the Chapel of the Invalides. . . .
>
> As for the Chapel of the Invalides, our shame is still greater than for Versailles: passing through the chapel, the visitor to the palace can today content himself in admiration of the facade . . . without hearing the sonorities of Clicquot. But, at the Invalides, the organ . . . imperfectly cleaned and put in order on two or three different occasions, is today in a state that is really unacceptable for France. In this magnificent chapel, which one can consider the heart of the French Fatherland, and where each week an office, marriage Mass, commemorative ceremony, or Requiem Mass is celebrated, there exhale from the heights sonorities more similar to those of a toothless rattle than those of a musical instrument. And at each ceremony the whole of Europe—the diplomatic body if there is a minister, great politician, or chief of state in attendance—is present at this wreck and is witness to this scandal. Widor, "Souvenirs autobiographiques," 30–31.

461. Of *Da pacem*, Henri Potiron wrote, "[Widor] also corrected his *Da pacem* for choir, organ, and brass . . . that I often directed in the first version in front of him (he would have liked a broader tempo; but how can it be done with such long note values in the upper voice?). This motet was therefore engraved and published anew in another form. It's a magnificent example of artistic conscience." Potiron, "Widor," 84.

462. *Ménestrel* 96 (1934): 161–62.

463. Ibid., 189.

464. M.S., undated letter [likely in June 1934], from Madame Widor to Schweitzer.

465. M.S. [1934], Widor and Madame Widor to Schweitzer.

466. It is unclear to what Madame Widor is referring. A "Société Widor" was created February 6, 1934: A. Barthélemy (Consul général de France), president; Maurice Dumesnil, general secretary; Adolphe Boschot, Marcel Dupré, and Isidor Philipp among the administrative council members. The goal of the society was "to promote all that is of a nature to develop the taste in and knowledge of music in France. It is particularly concerned with the organ, its literature and its conservation, wanting thus to pay homage to the *maître* whose name it has taken." On the back of the program for the Widor Festival held at Saint-Sulpice, April 19, 1934, the society announced the Festival's goal to raise part of the five hundred thousand francs needed to restore the organ at the

Church of Saint-Louis des Invalides; Widor's blunt description of the instrument's condition expressed the urgent need: "the broken-toothed rasping sonority of this instrument causes a scandal in this nave." B.I.(a). Also, Widor, "Souvenirs autobiographiques," 31.

467. According to Dupré, Widor worked on revisions to the *Antique* right up to the end: "About two weeks before his death, he asked me to play on the piano, instrument by instrument, two pages of the orchestra score of his *Symphonie antique*, for he wanted to verify certain changes he was planning to make." Dupré, *Recollections*, 52.

468. While convalescing at the Hotel du Grand Condé, Widor received a phone call from his old friend and equally ailing Edmond de Rothschild (1845–1934). As a last sign of affection, Rothschild said that he wanted to come to Chantilly to see him one more time; but Rothschild's condition was worse than that of Widor: "Knowing his feebleness and wanting to prevent him the sixty kilometer trip, I told him, 'I'm doing much better. I will be in Paris Friday. I will expect you at the Institute.' . . . This was his last visit. Fifteen days later, he was no longer!" Widor, *Edmond de Rothschild*, 15–16. Shortly after Rothschild's death, Widor wrote what must have been one of the most emotionally difficult tributes he ever had to write; Rothschild had been elected a free member of the Academy of Fine Arts in 1906. He was a year younger than Widor and together they had accomplished great projects for the Institute, most notably its London branch.

469. R.B.I. Dupré reported that a stroke had paralyzed Widor's right side and he was able to write only minimally with his left hand. Dupré, *Recollections*, 52.

470. M.S., letter dated December 21, 1934, from Widor to Schweitzer.

471. Widor, *Amateurs honoraires*, 6.

472. M.S., letter dated December 21, 1934, from Widor to Schweitzer. In the same letter, Widor expressed much interest in the work of Donald Francis Tovey (1875–1940) on Bach's "Art of the Fugue"; as "evidence of confraternity," Widor wanted to send to Tovey the score of his Op. 69 Symphony.

473. *Ménestrel* 96 (1934): 256.

474. M.S., letter dated January 11, 1935, from Madame Widor to Schweitzer.

475. *Diapason* 26, no. 6 (1935): 30, col. 2; *Monde Musical* 46 (1935): 109.

476. Family arch., letter from Madame Dupré to Gabrielle Guibaud, dated April 1935, containing snapshots of the occasion.

477. Family arch., letter from Madame Widor to Gabrielle Guibaud, dated March 16, 1935.

478. In his Souvenirs, Widor wrote briefly of this occasion and one nearly fifty-five years earlier when he had inaugurated the organ at the Brussels Conservatory on July 14, 1880. Strangely, *Ménestrel* [46 (1880): 262], and *Revue et Gazette* [47 (1880): 239], report that the inaugural organist was Alphonse Mailly, whose program included Bach, Mendelssohn, Widor, Martini, and Chauvet (*Ménestrel*); Bach, Martini, Mendelssohn, Lefébure, Chauvet and Mailly (*Revue et Gazette*). Nonetheless, Widor recalled the occasion differently: "July 14, 1880: I gave an organ concert at the Conservatory on the Cavaillé-Coll organ that was just built. The Prince of Caraman-Chimay, director of the Beaux-Arts in Brussels and friend of Gevaert, . . . had ordered an organ from Cavaillé and asked me to inaugurate it. It's an excellent instrument. I had the occasion to hear it again last year [1935] when a festival was given there in my honor—a ceremony during which the medal of the royal crown (grand ribbon of the crown) was given to me. At the time of the inauguration of this organ, Gevaert was director of the Brussels Conservatory. I spent three charming days and some dinners at the home of the Minister of Beaux-Arts." Widor, "Souvenirs autobiographiques," 41.

479. Family arch.

480. Boschot, *Charles-Marie Widor*, 10–11; see also Widor, "La Casa Velásquez."

481. Widor, "Madrid et Londres," 349.

482. Widor, "Souvenirs autobiographiques," 76–77. The delegation departed for Seville on May 10.

483. Widor, "Madrid et Londres," 349. The secretary accompanying the mission recorded that the members of the delegation were absolutely enchanted by what they saw as their train traveled toward Seville: "From one side of the car to the other, from one end of the corridor to the other, each academician called to the others, inviting them to see the wonders; above all, Mr. Widor, whose wonderstruck eyes absorbed all the beauty they could, moved about with a rapidity proportional to that of the train." Secretary of the Mission, "Commentaires d'Espagne," 5–6. While in Seville, Widor did not miss the opportunity to try out the organ in the Cathedral; after an improvisation, the Toccata from the Fifth Symphony left the auditors spellbound and not wanting to leave (14–15). The three modern Spanish composers enumerated: Isaac Albéniz (1860–1909); Enrique Granados (1867–1916); Manuel de Falla (1876–1946).

484. A partial list of those who resided in Rome after winning the Rome Prize includes: Berlioz, Bizet, Charpentier, Debussy, Dubois, Henri Dutilleux (b. 1916), Gounod, Halévy, Ferdinand Hérold (1791–1833), Hüe, Jacques Ibert (1890–1962), Massenet, Schmitt, Thomas. See http://www.villamedici.it/home.cfm.

485. Widor, "La distribution des prix au conservatoire," 2.

486. Secretary of the Mission, "Commentaires d'Espagne," 11.

487. Widor, "Madrid et Londres," 349.

488. David, "Quelques souvenirs," 3.

489. Widor, Preface to *J. S. Bach*, ix.

490. Widor, "Souvenirs autobiographiques," 83.

491. Ibid.

492. Widor, "Madrid et Londres," 350.

493. Widor, "Souvenirs autobiographiques," 78.

494. Widor, "Madrid et Londres," 350; also Widor, *Fondations, portraits*, 101. Elsewhere, Widor recounted further details. "I recall that I gathered nearly 200 canvases together in the Caen museum while waiting for the dilapidated vehicles that were to be used for the transport. You can imagine my uneasiness at the idea that a bomb could fall on these canvases; there was the Sarah Bernhard by Bastien Lepage [1848–84], and the Edward VII; the cows by Rosa Bonheur [1822–99] (Consult the catalogue in the Institute cupboard). Imagine my emotions during the nights of bombardment! Happily, we sustained no damage; we came through the bombardments, and we were able to hang the canvases in Madrid, where we had the luck to inaugurate the exhibition with Imbart de la Tour and [Gabriel] Hanotaux [1853–1944]. This exhibition of our great painters of the Romantic period was a complete success, and several canvases exhibited by their painters were purchased by the amateurs of Madrid." Widor, "Souvenirs autobiographiques," 83–84.

495. Widor, "Souvenirs autobiographiques," 84.

496. Widor, "Madrid et Londres," 350. Widor gives the date incorrectly as November 27.

497. Les Autographes, 45 rue de l'Abbé Grégoire, Paris, sales catalogue 127 "Orgue," January 2009, item 275.

498. Widor, "Madrid et Londres," 350.

499. Widor, *Edmond de Rothschild*, 15.

500. *Ménestrel* 82 (1920): 491; Widor, "Madrid et Londres," 350.

501. Widor, "Madrid et Londres," 350.

502. Widor, "Souvenirs autobiographiques," 94.

503. Widor, *Fondations, portraits*, 36–37.

504. Ibid., 33.

505. Author's collection, letter dated August 24, 1920, to Robert Brussel.

506. Widor, "Souvenirs autobiographiques," 91; the Simpson quotation is from Widor, *Fondations, portraits*, 30, which is more complete than that given in "Souvenirs."

507. Widor, *Fondations, portraits*, 31. General Marie-Eugène Debeney (1864–1943); General Ferdinand Foch (1851–1929).

508. Widor, *Charles Girault*, 19.

509. Widor, *Fondations, portraits*, 31.

510. Widor, "Souvenirs autobiographiques," 92.

511. Ibid., 91–92. Admiral David Beatty (1871–1936); Admiral John Jellicoe (1859–1935).

512. Ibid., 92–93.

513. Widor, *Fondations, portraits*, 33.

514. Widor, "Madrid et Londres," 350.

515. Jacque, "Ch.-M. Widor."

516. Widor, *Fondations, portraits*, 25–26; Jacque, "Ch.-M. Widor."

517. Widor, *Fondations, portraits*, 26.

518. *Ménestrel* 88 (1926): 258.

519. *Ménestrel* 90 (1928): 500.

520. *Ménestrel* 91 (1929): 68.

521. Widor, *Charles Girault*, 17.

522. *Ménestrel* 91 (1929): 508.

523. Boschot, *Charles-Marie Widor*, 11–12; *Ménestrel* 97 (1935): 172.

524. "M. Ch. M. Widor à Madrid," *Journal des Débats* (May 20, 1935): 2.

525. Family arch., letter dated May 29, 1935, to Marguerite Reynard. Guite was already manifesting the ill health that would bring on her early death only a few months after that of her uncle Charles. Widor's letters to her were as one convalescent to another; in this letter he reported, "I was accompanied [to Madrid] by the young Lereboulet, a doctor like his father. The abrasions on my two elbows are healing and both Lardenois and Lereboulet senior [Widor's two main doctors] are content with the one on my left hand. . . . How are your maladies?" Three weeks later, he reiterated, "How are you and your maladies? The warm weather that finally seems to have arrived is going to bring us some health. When are you leaving the hospital? I still have not been able to take up my usual work, the two sores on my two elbows are barely healed and the one on my left hand still has a bandage that is soon going to become useless. As for my right arm, it is still weak and you can judge how weak by the difficulty I have in writing! Send me news often. There is not a day when I don't think of you all morning and night." Family arch., letter dated June 21, 1935, to Marguerite Reynard.

526. Widor, *Amateurs honoraires*, 7–8.

527. Dupré, "Souvenirs sur Ch.-M. Widor," 33.

528. Landormy, *Franck à Debussy*, 172.

529. "Widor à Strasbourg," *Comœdia* (July 29, 1935). B.N. Fonds Mont.

530. Feschotte, "Albert Schweitzer," 54.

531. M.S., letter dated April 4, 1918, from Widor to Schweitzer.

532. M.S., letter dated April 22, 1921, from Widor to Schweitzer.

533. M.S., letters dated April 4, 1918; April 22, 1921; August 6, 1936; December 19, 1936.

534. M.S., postcard dated August 20, 1935, from Madame Widor to Schweitzer.

535. M.S., letter dated December 17, 1935, from Widor to Schweitzer.

536. Pédron, "Charles Widor."

537. Dupré, *Recollections*, 52; Jean-Jacques Grunenwald, conversation with the author, Paris, September 19, 1982; Philipp, "Charles-Marie Widor," 131. Mlle Herrenschmidt performed the Op. 62 *Fantaisie* as early as 1920 and recorded it under the direction of Charles Munch between 1935 and 1938.

538. Potiron, "Widor," 83–84.

539. Leray, "Souvenirs d'un maître."

540. Boschot, *Charles-Marie Widor*, 15. Also, David, "Quelques souvenirs."

541. "History of the Casa de Velázquez" http://www.casadevelazquez.org. The fiftieth anniversary celebration took place in 1979 in the presence of Her Majesty Doña Sofia and Madame Anne-Aymone Giscard D'Estaing.

542. M.S., letter dated March 21, 1936, from Widor to Schweitzer.

543. Murray, *Albert Schweitzer*, 128, from a letter dated May 25, 1946, to Archibald T. Davison. In a letter to A. M. Henderson, dated August 24, 1945, Schweitzer described further that last meeting: "Before leaving again for Africa I went to Paris for a few hours to see him once more. He was already very ill (heart and kidneys) and knew that he no longer had much time to live. He was very serene. In his armchair he was at work revising some of his compositions that were to be reprinted. He had a presentiment of the war, and was very grieved by the thought. We talked again of organ building. He disapproved of the departure of French organ building from the traditions of Cavaillé-Coll, and was sad that his voice was not listened to and that some of his pupils wanted to transform the lovely old organs they were in charge of. But he was certain that his works for organ would endure and influence the organists of the future" (129).

544. Dupré, "Souvenirs sur Ch.-M. Widor," 33; also Dupré, *Recollections*, 52.

545. Mairie du 16ème Arrondissement, 71 avenue Henri Martin, Paris.

546. Goodrich, "Charles-Marie Widor Honored," 7.

547. M.S., letter dated January 20, 1939, from Madame Widor to Schweitzer.

548. Maurat, *Souvenirs musicaux et littéraires*, 130.

549. Madame Widor is certainly referring to her husband and her Aunt Hélène Standish.

550. M.S., letter dated June 28. 1937.

551. Family arch., letter dated April 2, 1938. In a 1970 taped interview with Gabrielle Guibaud, she stated that Widor had a profound religious faith and that he very much loved the Holy Virgin. Riemenschneider also felt that Widor expressed "tremendous spiritual values." Riemenschneider, "Tribute to Widor," 26.

552. Family arch., letters dated March 11, 1939, and April 19, 1939, to Gabrielle Guibaud.

553. Family arch., letter dated August 6, 1939, to Gabrielle Guibaud.

554. The bust, signed H. Vernet and dated 1911, is currently in the possession of Widor's grandniece, Marie-Ange Guibaud. Information on the sculptor has not been uncovered; no one by that name was a member of the Academy in that period.

555. Madame Widor and the other heirs were in fact receiving royalties—for instance, in 1943 they were paid a royalty of 3,073 francs from the Librairie Hachette on Widor's *Initiation musicale*. Family arch.

556. Trillat, "Charles-Marie Widor," 11–13.

557. http://guydescars.waika9.com/biographie.htm.

558. des Cars, *Le crime de Mathilde*, 5.

559. Ibid., 13.

560. Ibid., 41.

561. Hobbs, "Madame Widor," 421.

562. This story is related with enough supporting documentation to give it some cre-
dence in Hobbs, "Madame Widor," 420–22. Because the nurse was still living at the time
of Hobbs's article (1990), some sources asked that their identities not be published. The
nurse was reportedly ill natured, obsessed with money, and had contacted several people
regarding last testaments. Hobbs states, "We have carefully verified all the details, and
have been able to ascertain that this 'story' is entirely true" (420).

563. Pelatan et al., *Trois dames*, 94–101.

564. Ibid., 98.

565. Ibid., 99.

566. Ibid., 100. As for the Château d'Hauteville, it was never rebuilt after the disastrous fire of November 13, 1922, and remains a ruin today.

567. M.S.

568. Pelatan et al., *Trois dames*, 100.

569. Ibid., 100–1.

570. Widor's position was such that important foreign ambassadors needed to make
his acquaintance; Widor related one such occasion: "[During World War I], the United
States sent as ambassador to France not a diplomat, but a great merchant named Bacon.
Knowing this, Whitney Warren [1864–1943] rushed from America to France and told
us, 'He knows nothing about the affairs of France, let's help him out!' Making himself
[Bacon's] sightseeing guide in order to introduce him to the greatest number of French
personalities, [Warren] came to my organ gallery at Saint-Sulpice to introduce the new
ambassador to me." Widor, "Souvenirs autobiographiques," 76.

571. R. Dumesnil, *Portraits de musiciens français*, 196. The great dramatic soprano Félia
Litvinne (1860–1936), who often sang Widor's songs, thought of him as the "emperor of
organists." Litvinne, *Ma vie*, 212.

572. Potiron, "Widor," 81–82.

573. "Obsèques de M. Widor," *Journal des Débats* 149 (March 18, 1937): 4.

574. Henderson was likely incorrect when he reported B Minor, Henderson, "Organ
Class," 345; *Figaro* (March 18) reported "E Minor"; Potiron, "Widor," 81, reported "Little
E Minor."

575. Henderson, "Organ Class," 344–45. Potiron, "Widor" describes the music and
the manner in which it was performed in some detail. Though doubtful, another source
claims that Dupré played from the *Symphonie romane* during the procession to the crypt.
R. Dumesnil, *Portraits de musiciens français*, 202.

576. Henderson, "Organ Class," 344–45.

577. Widor had even attended Berlioz' funeral in 1869 at La Trinité. Boschot, *Charles-
Marie Widor*, 4.

578. Widor, *Amateurs honoraires*, 17–18.

579. Widor, *Edmond Paulin*, 4.

580. Curzon, "Charles-Marie Widor," 1.

581. Philipp, "Charles-Marie Widor," 132.

582. Vierne, "Ch.-M. Widor," 76.

583. Widor, *André Messager*, 16.

584. Boschot, *Charles-Marie Widor*, 16–17.

585. *American Organist* 20 (1937): 203.

586. Family arch.

Bibliography

d'Andigné. "Remise à M. Ch.-M. Widor de la grande médaille d'or de la ville de Paris." Address given by Mr. d'Andigné, president of the Municipal Council, Paris, January 18, 1930. Family arch.

Aubry, Pierre. "Les idées de S. S. Pie X sur le chant de l'église." *Correspondant* (July 10, 1904): 35–54.

Austin, William W. *Music in the 20th Century.* New York: W. W. Norton, 1966.

Avery, Stanley R. "Americans at Work at Fontainebleau." *Diapason* 12, no. 10 (1921): 1–2.

Barnes, Edward Shippen. "An Organ Student in France: An Informal Talk." *Diapason* 12, no. 8 (1921): 25; no. 9 (1921): 21.

Barthalay, Raoul. "Notes concernant les orgues et organistes de Saint-François de Sales; Recueilles auprès de M. François Gayet." Received from Louis Robilliard, Lyon. Unpublished typescript in the author's collection.

Bas, Giulio. *Rythme grégorien.* Rome: Desclée, Lefebure, 1906.

Beaumont, Cyril W. *Complete Book of Ballets.* New York: G. P. Putnam's, 1937.

Beechey, Gwilym. "Organ Recitals by French Organists in England." *Organ* 195 (January 1970): 108–17.

Berlioz, Pierre. "Les adieux de Widor." *Jour* (April 10, 1934). B. N. Fonds Mont.

Bernard, Paul. "Un nouvel organiste: M. Alexandre Guilmant." *Ménestrel* 28 (1861): 389.

Bernard, Robert. "Charles-Marie Widor." *Revue Musical* 18 (1937): 310–12.

Bertrand, Paul. "M. Ch.-M. Widor: Conteur d'anecdotes." *Nouvelles Musicales* 1, no. 18 (March 1, 1934): 3.

———. *Le monde de la musique: Souvenirs d'un éditeur.* Genève: La Palatine, 1947.

Bidwell, Marshall. "Organ Music in Paris Cathedrals: 3. Widor and St.-Sulpice." *American Organist* 5 (1922): 419–24.

Blakeman, Edward. *Taffanel: Genius of the Flute.* New York: Oxford University Press, 2005.

Blanche, Jacques-Émile. *La pêche aux souvenirs.* Paris: Flammarion, 1949.

Boschot, Adolphe. "Ch.-M. Widor, organiste et improvisateur." *Ménestrel* 99 (1937): 337–38.

———. *Notice sur la vie et les œuvres de M. Charles-Marie Widor.* Paris: Firmin-Didot, 1937.

Bourligueux, Guy. "Benoist, François." In *Dictionnaire de la musique en France au XIXe siècle,* edited by Joël-Marie Fauquet. Paris: Fayard, 2003.

Bouvard, Jean. "My Recollections of Charles-Marie Widor in Paris." Translated by Rulon Christiansen. *American Organist* 21, no. 11 (1987): 42–43.

Bret, Gustave. "Les *Symphonies pour orgue* de Ch.-M. Widor." *Bulletin Trimestriel des Amis de L'Orgue* 10, no. 35 (1938): 12–16.

——. "Le grand organiste Widor nous parle de théâtre." *Intransigeant* (April 13, 1934).

Brindejoint-Offenbach, Jacques. "Avant *Nerto* une heure avec Charles-Marie Widor." *Gaulois* (October 23, 1924). B. N. Fonds Mont.

Brody, Elaine. *Paris: The Musical Kaleidoscope, 1870–1925.* New York: George Braziller, 1987.

Brogan, D. W. et al. *A Short History of France to the Present Day.* Cambridge: Cambridge University Press, 1961.

Brussel, Robert. "Ch.-M. Widor." *Figaro* (March 14, 1937). B. N. Fonds Mont.

Buhrman, T. Scott. ". . . Beauty in Widor." *American Organist* 20 (1937): 127–28.

——. "Music to Survive." *American Organist* 17 (1934): 228.

——. "Widor Career is Closed." *American Organist* 20 (1937): 128–29.

Burg, Josef. "Charles-Marie Widor, Louis Vierne, et Marcel Dupré sur les bords du Rhin." *L'Orgue* 182 (April–June 1982): 1–12.

Burnand, Robert [Robert-Robert, pseud.]. *Paris Restaurants.* London: Geoffrey Bles, [1924].

Büsser, Henri. "M. Ch.-M. Widor." *Nouvelles Musicales* 1, no. 18 (1934): 3.

——. *De Pelléas aux Indes galantes.* Paris: Arthème Fayard, 1955.

Calvocoressi, Michael D. *Musicians Gallery; Music and Ballet in Paris and London.* London: Faber and Faber, 1933.

Cantagrel, Gilles, and Harry Halbreich. *Le livre d'or de l'orgue français.* Paris: Calliope-Marval, 1976.

Carvalhos, Juan. "Les grandes figures contemporaines: Charles-Marie Widor." *Avenir* (January 22, 1928). B. N. Fonds Mont.

Cavaillé-Coll, Cécile. "Cavaillé-Coll, les orgues et les organistes (1852–1862)." *Ménestrel* 84 (1922): 318.

Cavaillé-Coll, Cécile, and Emmanuel Cavaillé-Coll. *Aristide Cavaillé-Coll: Ses origins, sa vie, ses œuvres.* Paris: Fischbacher, 1929.

Cellier, Alexandre, and Henri Bachelin. *L'orgue: Ses éléments, son histoire, son esthétique.* Paris: Delagrave, 1933.

Chantavoine, Jean. "M. Ch.-M. Widor: L'homme, le bienfaiteur." *Nouvelles Musicales* 1, no. 18 (1934): 3.

Charbonnier, Georges. *Entretiens avec Edgard Varèse.* Paris: Pierre Belfond, 1970.

Cheronnet, Louis. *L'Église Saint-Sulpice.* Paris: Tourelle, 1971.

Chimènes, Myriam. *Mécènes et musiciens: Du salon au concert à Paris sous la IIIe République.* Paris: Fayard, 2004.

——. ed. *Francis Poulenc: Correspondance 1910–1963.* Paris: Fayard, 1994.

Clerc, Maurice. "L'orgue G. et E. Cavaillé-Coll de Charles-Marie Widor et sa récente installation à Selongey (Côte-d'Or)." *Flûte Harmonique* 37 (1986): 11–25.

Conway, Marmaduke P. "Widor's Organ Symphonies." *Musical Opinion* 55 (1931–32): 534, 622–23, 697–98, 780–81, 855–56, 939–40, 1030; 56 (1932–33): 151, 341, 442, 629, 718, 874–75 958, 1047–48; 57 (1933–34): 147, 345–46, 442, 540, 804, 895, 972; 58 (1934–35): 154, 247–48, 534, 790–91, 951–52; 59 (1935–36): 57–58, 343–44, 530–31, 708–9.

Copland, Aaron, and Vivian Perlis. *Copland: 1900 through 1942.* New York: St. Martin's/Marek, 1984.

Coppée, François. "La centième de *La Korrigane.*" *Piano Soleil* (May 3, 1896): 3.

Coppola, Piero. *Dix-sept ans de musique à Paris, 1922–1939.* Lausanne: F. Rouge, 1944.

Craft, Robert, ed. *Stravinsky: Selected Correspondence.* Vol. 2. New York: Alfred A. Knopf, 1984.

Curzon, Henri de. "Charles-Marie Widor." *Journal des Débats* 149 (March 14, 1937): 1.

———. "Reprise de *La Korrigane.*" *Journal des Débats* (December 18, 1933). B. N. Fonds Mont.

Damrosch, Walter. *My Musical Life.* New York: C. Scribner's, 1923.

David, Dom L. "M. Widor, l'édition vaticane et le *Te Deum.*" *Revue du Chant Grégorien* 31, no. 3 (1927): 81–90.

David, Robert. "Quelques souvenirs sur Charles-Marie Widor et la Casa Velásquez." *Journal des Débats* 149 (March 17, 1937): 3.

Delestre, Robert. *L'œuvre de Marcel Dupré.* Paris: Éditions Musique Sacrée, 1952.

des Cars, Guy. *Le crime de Mathilde.* Paris: J'ai lu, 1983.

Dézelan, Loiseau. "Le chant grégorien." *Monde Musical* 38, no. 1 (1927): 4.

Dickinson, Clarence. "Dr. Dickinson Reminisces." *Diapason* 53, no. 4 (1962): 39.

Dieterlen, Michel. "The Harmonium: A Brief History." Booklet in *L'harmonium au salon,* Euromuses CD-2022 (1996).

Doret, Gustave. "Widor: 1845–1937." M.S. Same article as "Widor." *Gazette de Lausanne* (March 16, 1937). B. N. Fonds Mont.

Douglass, Fenner. *Cavaillé-Coll and the Musicians.* 2 vols. Raleigh: Sunbury, 1980.

Doyen, Henri. *Mes leçons d'orgue avec Louis Vierne.* Paris: Musique Sacrée, 1966.

Duchen, Jessica. *Gabriel Fauré.* London: Phaidon Press, 2000.

Dufourcq, Norbert. "À propos du cinquantenaire de la mort de Cavaillé-Coll, (1899–1949): Lemmens et Cavaillé-Coll." *L'Orgue* 53 (1949): 114–17; 54 (1950): 21–22; 55 (1950): 42–44; 57 (1950): 111–12; 58–59 (1951): 58–60; 60 (1951): 85–87; 62 (1952): 22–25; 63 (1952): 57–58; 64 (1952): 87–88; 65 (1952): 111–13; 67 (1953): 59–61; 68 (1953): 84–85.

———. "César Franck et la genèse des premières œuvres d'orgue." *Cahiers et Mémoires de L'Orgue* (special issues of *L'Orgue*) 147 bis (1973).

———. *La musique d'orgue française de Jehan Titelouze à Jehan Alain.* Paris: Floury, 1949.

———. "Panorama de la musique d'orgue française au XXe siècle." *Revue Musicale* 19 (1938): 369–76.

———. *Visites diffusées des églises Saint Sulpice, Saint Eustache, Sainte Clotilde, et Notre Dame de Paris (avec le concours de Marcel Dupré [et al.]).* Paris: Secrétariat Générale des Amis de l'Orgue, 1936.

Dumesnil, Maurice. "Charles-Marie Widor, the Grand Old Man of French Music." *Etude* 53 (1935): 143–44, 192.

Dumesnil, René. *Le monde des musiciens.* Paris: G. Crès, 1924.

———. *Portraits de musiciens français.* Paris: Plon, 1938.

Dunham, Rowland W. "From Yesterday." *American Organist* 37 (1954): 402–3.

———. "Widor Celebrates 60 Years as Organist of Saint Sulpice." *American Organist* 13 (1930): 161.

Dupré, Marcel. "M. Charles-Marie Widor." *Nouvelles Musicales* 1, no. 18 (1934): 1–2.

————. "Marcel Dupré nous conte ses souvenirs sur Ch.-M. Widor." *Paris Soir* (February 24, 1944): 1–2.

————. *Marcel Dupré: Interview and Improvisations.* Interview by M. Murray. Advent 5011 (1974).

————. *Méthode d'orgue.* Paris: Leduc, 1927.

————. "En parlant de Ch.-M. Widor avec Marcel Dupré." *La Liberté* (March 18, 1937). B. N. Fonds Mont.

————. *Recollections.* Translated by R. Kneeream. Melville: Belwin-Mills, 1975.

————. "Souvenirs sur Ch.-M. Widor." *Séance Publique Annuelle des Cinq Académies* 129, no. 17 (1959): 27–34. Paris: Firmin-Didot, 1959.

Eddy, Clarence. "Clarence Eddy on French Organists." *Music* 13 (1898): 589–95.

————. "Great Frenchmen of Organ World in 1897 are Pictured by Eddy." *Diapason* 28, no. 6 (1937): 14.

Erb, Marie-Joseph. "Philippe Bellenot." *L'Orgue* 45 (1947): 100.

Eymieu, Henry. "Biographies musicales: 3. Ch.-M. Widor." *La Libre Critique* 1 [1891]: 132–34; 2 (1892): 2–3.

————. "Ch.-M. Widor." *Piano Soleil* (December 20, 1891): 4.

————. *Études et biographies musicales.* Paris: Fischbacher, 1892.

————. "Nos grands organistes: Ch.-M. Widor." *Revue Pratique de Liturgie et de Musique Sacrée* 5, nos. 59–60 (1922): 415–19; 6, nos. 61–62 (1922): 45–48; 6, nos. 65–66 (1922): 215–21.

Fauquet, Joël-Marie. *César Franck.* Paris: Fayard, 1999.

————, ed. *Édouard Lalo: Correspondance.* Paris: Aux Amateurs de Livres, 1989.

Fauré, Gabriel. "M. Ch.-M. Widor." *Comœdia Illustré* 1, no. 7 (1909): 203.

————. *Hommage à Eugène Gigout (21 Mars 1923).* Paris: Floury, 1923.

Favre, Georges. "Une grande figure d'éducateur, Charles-Marie Widor," *La Petite Maîtrise* 288 (May 1937): 33–35.

————. *Silhouettes du conservatoire.* Paris: Pensée Universelle, 1986.

Ferrard, Jean. "La 'sainte tradition' de Hesse à Dupré." *Flûte Harmonique* 61/62 (1992): 43–61.

Feschotte, Jacques. "Albert Schweitzer et l'orgue: Évocation et souvenir." *L'Orgue* 118 (April–June 1966): 49–55.

Fétis, François-Joseph. *Biographie universelle des musiciens et bibliographie générale de la musique.* 2nd ed. 8 vols. Paris: Firmin Didot, 1860–65. Supplément et complément, edited by Arthur Pougin. 2 vols. Paris: Firmin Didot, 1878–80.

————. "Lemmens, Jacques-Nicolas." In *Biographie universelle des musiciens et bibliographie générale de la musique.* 2nd ed. Vol. 5: 267–68. Paris: Firmin Didot, 1870.

————. "L'orgue mondaine et la musique érotique à l'église." *Revue et Gazette* 23 (1856): 105–6.

Fitz-James, B. de Miramon. "L'orgue français: Hier, aujourd'hui, demain." *Ménestrel* 91 (1929): 21–23.

Frazier, James E. *Maurice Duruflé: The Man and His Music.* Rochester: University of Rochester Press, 2007.

Fromageot, Paul. *Un disciple de Bach: Pierre-François Boëly.* Versailles: L. Bernard, 1909.

Gagnebin, Henry. "Guy Bovet joue Charles-Marie Widor." Jacket notes in *Orgues Historiques de Suisse*, no. 5, Gallo 30–167.

Gaudefroy-Demombynes, Jean. *Histoire de la musique française*. Paris: Payot, 1946.

Gavoty, Bernard. *Louis Vierne: La vie et l'œuvre*. Paris: A. Michel, 1943.

———. *Silhouettes d'organistes*. Nantes: L'Organiste, 1944.

Geer, E. Harold. *Organ Registration in Theory and Practice*. Melville, NY: Belwin-Mills, 1957.

Georges, Alexandre. "Réponse à une préface de M. Ch. Widor." *Maître de Chapelle* 2, no. 6 (1900): 3–5; no. 7 (1900): 4–6.

Gigout, Eugène. "Quelques publications nouvelles d'orgue et de plain-chant." *Ménestrel* 46 (1880): 44–45.

Goodrich, Wallace. "Charles-Marie Widor Honored on 90th Birthday." *Musical America* 55, no. 4 (1935): 7.

———. *The Organ in France*. Boston: Boston Music, 1917.

Goudeket, Willy. "L'institut croule." *L'Intransigeant* (August 29, 1933). B. N. Fonds Mont.

Grace, Harvey. *French Organ Music*. New York: H. W. Gray, 1919.

Grosh, Paul E. "A Widor Reminiscence." *American Organist* 20 (1937): 167.

Guilmant, Alexandre. "La musique d'orgue." In *Encyclopédie de la musique et dictionnaire du conservatoire*, edited by Albert Lavignac and Lionel de La Laurencie. Vol. 2: 1125–80. Paris: Delagrave, 1926.

Halbreich, Harry. *Arthur Honegger*. Translated by Roger Nichols. Portland: Amadeus Press, 1999.

Hambraeus, Bengt. "Aristide Cavaillé-Coll, Charles-Marie Widor: The Organ and the Orchestra." In *L'orgue à notre époque*, edited by D. Mackey. Montreal: McGill University Press, 1981.

Hamel, Charles. *Histoire de l'église Saint-Sulpice*. Paris: Victor Lecoffre, 1900.

Handschin, Jacques, and Hans Oesch. "Charles-Marie Widor." In *Gedenkschrift Jacques Handschin; Aufsätze und Bibliographie*. Bern: P. Haupt, 1957.

Harding, James. *Saint-Saëns and His Circle*. London: Chapman & Hill, 1965.

Harewood, the Earl of, ed. *Kobbé's Complete Opera Book*. London: Bodley Head, 1987.

Havard de la Montagne, Denis. "Les maîtres de chapelle et organistes de chœur de l'église Saint-Sulpice à Paris." *L'Orgue* 260 (2002): 3–26.

———. "Philippe Bellenot." http://www.musimem.com/bellenot.htm.

Hays, William. Review of *The Historic 1892 Johnson Organ of Waterbury, Connecticut*, Susan Armstrong, organist. *Journal of the Organ Historical Society* 31, no. 4 (1988): 4–5.

Heinsheimer, Hans W. "The Saga of Schweitzer's Bach Edition." *Music: The AGO and RCCO Magazine* 9, no. 1 (1975): 30–31.

Helbig, Gustave. "La grande pitié des orgues de France." Personal scrapbooks in 4 vols. B. N. Rés.Vm^c· ms. 15 (1–4).

Henderson, Archibald Martin. "Memories of Widor and His Teaching." *Musical Opinion* 78 (1955): 657–59.

———. "Widor and His Organ Class." *Musical Times* 78 (1937): 341–45.

Henderson, William James. "A Great Organist and His Art." *Mentor* 15, no. 11 (1927): 9–10.

Hensel, Octavia. "Charles-Marie Widor." Review dated 1885, appended to **M.343.31 in Brown Collection. Boston Public Library.

Hilson-Woldu, Gail. "Gabriel Fauré, directeur du conservatoire: Les réformes de 1905." *Revue de Musicologie* 70 (1984): 199–219.

Hobbs, Alain. "Charles-Marie Widor (1844–1937)." *L'Orgue: Cahiers et Mémoires* 40 (1988).

———. "Les dernières années de Charles-Marie Widor." *L'Orgue* 217 (January–March 1991): 6–20.

———. "La triste histoire de Madame Widor et de son château de Hauteville à Charchigné (Mayenne)." *La Province du Maine* 92, 5ᵉ Serie, Tom 4, Fascicule 16 (October–December 1990): 411–23.

Hugounet, Paul. *La musique et la pantomime.* Paris: Ernest, Kolb, [1892].

Huré, Jean. "Eugène Gigout." *L'orgue et les organistes* 2, no. 21 (1925): 2–35.

Imbert, Hugues. "Chez nos compositeurs: Charles-Marie Widor." *Revue d'Art Dramatique* 7 (May 15, 1892): 221–26.

———. *Portraits et études.* Paris: Fischbacher, 1894.

d'Indy, Vincent. *César Franck.* Translated by Rosa Newmarch. London: John Lane, The Bodley Head, 1909.

Jacque, Jean. "Ch.-M. Widor, maître-organiste, compositeur, et 'bâtisseur.'" *Écho de Paris* (April 11, 1934). B. N. Fonds Mont.

Jones, J. Barrie, ed. and trans. *Gabriel Fauré: A Life in Letters.* London: B. T. Batsford, 1989.

Josephson, Matthew. *Edison.* New York: McGraw-Hill, 1959.

Joy, Charles R. *Music in the Life of Albert Schweitzer.* Boston: Beacon, 1951.

Jullian, Philippe. *Robert de Montesquiou, un prince 1900.* Paris: Librairie Académique Perrin, 1965.

Jurine, Michel. *Joseph Merklin, facteur d'orgues européen.* 3 vols. Paris: Aux Amateurs de Livres, 1991.

Klein, Grégor. *Le grand orgue de St. Sulpice.* Paris: Flûte Harmonique, 1981.

Kline, Donna Staley. *Olga Samaroff Stokowski: An American Virtuoso on the World Stage.* College Station: Texas A & M University Press, 1996.

Knauff, Theo. C. *Three Great Organists.* N.p., [1892].

Kooiman, Ewald. "Jacques Lemmens, Charles-Marie Widor, and the French Bach Tradition." Translated by John Brock. *American Organist* 29, no. 3 (1995): 56–64.

Lade, Günther. "A Conversation with Olivier Messiaen." Translated by Timothy Tikker. *American Organist* 34, no. 7 (2000): 80–81.

Lamazou, Abbé Pierre Henri. *Étude sur l'orgue monumentale de Saint-Sulpice et la facture d'orgue moderne.* Paris: E. Repos, 1863.

———. *Grand orgue de l'église métropolitaine Notre-Dame de Paris reconstruit par M. A. Cavaillé-Coll.* Paris: H. Plon, 1868.

Landormy, Paul. *La musique française de Franck à Debussy.* Paris: Gallimard, 1943.

———. "Widor." In *Encyclopédie de la musique et dictionnaire du conservatoire,* edited by Albert Lavignac and Lionel de La Laurencie. Vol. 6: 3564–65. Paris: Delagrave, 1931.

Lang, Paul Henry. *Music in Western Civilization.* New York: W. W. Norton, 1941.

Launay, Paul de. "Charles-Marie Widor." *American Organist* 3 (1920): 275–78.

———. "Louis Vierne." *American Organist* 3 (1920): 14.

———. "Widor as I Knew Him." *American Organist* 20 (1937): 202.

Lavignac, Albert. *Le voyage artistique à Bayreuth*. Paris: Delagrave, 1900.

Le Guillou, C. M. "Inauguration du grand orgue de l'église Saint-François-Xavier." *L'Univers* (March 4, 1879): 3.

Lehman, Evangeline. "Charles-Marie Widor: Teacher of Composition." *Etude* 60 (1942): 450, 494, 497.

Lemesle, Gaston. *L'Église Saint-Sulpice*. Paris: Bloud & Gay, [1931].

Léna, Maurice. "Auditions d'œuvres de Ch.-M. Widor." *Ménestrel* 88 (1926): 222–23.

Leonard, Kendra Preston. *The Conservatoire Américain*. Lanham: Scarecrow Press, 2007.

Leray, Chr. "Souvenirs d'un maître; M. Ch.-M. Widor a tenu pendant soixante-trois ans l'orgue de Saint-Sulpice." *Liberté* (April 16, 1934). B. N. Fonds Mont.

Leroy, Paul. *Panorama* (February 17, 1944). B. N. Fonds Mont.

Lesure, François, and Denis Herlin. *Claude Debussy: Correspondance 1872–1918*. Paris: Gallimard, 2005.

Libert, Henri. "Charles-Marie Widor: La tribune de Saint-Sulpice." *Courrier Musical* 32, no. 4 (1930): 112–13.

Litvinne, Félia. *Ma vie et mon art (souvenirs)*. Paris: Plon, 1933.

Locard, Paul. "Les maîtres contemporains de l'orgue." *Courrier Musical* 4, no. 12 (1901): 133–34.

———. "L'orgue du Conservatoire Américain de Fontainebleau." *Courrier Musical* 27, no. 16 (1925): 462.

Louchart, Jean-Michel. "Charles-Marie Widor (1844–1937): L'heure du facteur d'orgues." *L'Orgue* 201–4 (1987): 102–7.

———. "Les interprètes et leurs instruments." Notes in *Orgue et organistes français en 1930*. EMI C 153–16411/5 (1981).

Lueders, Kurt. "Alexandre Guilmant (1837–1911), organiste et compositeur." Doctorat en musicologie, Université de Paris (Sorbonne), 2002.

———. "A Captivating Repertoire and the Instrument at Its Heart." Notes in *L'harmonium au salon*, Euromuses CD-2022 (1996).

———. "Georges Schmitt." *Le grand-orgue de Saint-Sulpice et ses organistes*. Paris: Flûte Harmonique, 1991.

Malherbe, Henry. "Charles-Marie Widor: Grand-maître pendant soixante-cinq ans des orgues de Saint-Sulpice, secrétaire perpétuel de l'Académie des beaux-arts." [March 1937?]. M.S.

———. "*Nerto* à l'Opéra." *Feuilleton du Temps* (October 29, 1924). B. N. Fonds Mont.

Malo, Pierre. "Ce soir, cinq grands organistes commémoreront à Saint-Sulpice le centenaire de Charles Widor." *Le Matin* (February 24, 1944). B. N. Fonds Mont.

Manouvriez, Abel. "Le testament perdu." *Candide* 764 (November 2, 1938). M.S.

Manuel, Roland. *Maurice Ravel*. Paris: Nouvelle Revue Critique, 1938.

Marhefka, Edmund. "Widors Orgelkompositionen." *Musik und Kirche* 29 (1959): 224–29.

———. "Zum dreissigsten Todesjahr von Charles-Marie Widor." *Ars Organi* 31 (1967): 1102–7.

Massenet, Jules Émile Frederic. *My Recollections*. Translated by H. Villiers Barnett. Freeport: Books for Libraries Press, 1919.

Maurat, Edmond. *Souvenirs musicaux et littéraires.* Edited by Louis Roux. Université de Saint-Étienne: Centre interdisciplinaire d'études et de recherches sur l'expression contemporaine, 1977.

McAmis, Hugh. "Paris Notes." *American Organist* 8 (1925): 121–22.

Messager, André. "Les premières: *Nerto.*" *Figaro* (October 27, 1924). B. N. Fonds Mont.

Meyer-Siat, Pie. *Les Callinet, facteurs d'orgues à Rouffach et leur œuvre en Alsace.* Strasbourg: Istra, 1965.

Milhaud, Darius. *An Autobiography: Notes without Music.* Translated by Donald Evans. Edited by Rollo H. Myers. New York: Alfred A. Knopf, 1953.

Miller, Warren H. "L'école Widor." *Musician* 15 (1910): 488, 556–57.

Monter, Em. Mathieu de. "Lefébure-Wély." *Revue et Gazette* 37 (1870): 11.

Murray, Michael. *Albert Schweitzer, Musician.* Aldershot, England: Scolar Press, 1994.

————. *Marcel Dupré: The Work of a Master Organist.* Boston: Northeastern University Press, 1985.

————. "The Pure Tradition of Bach." *Diapason* 68, no. 11 (1977): 4–6.

Near, John Richard. "Charles-Marie Widor: The Organ Works and Saint-Sulpice." *American Organist* 27, no. 2 (1993): 46–59.

————. "Letters: Charles-Marie Widor (1844–1937)." *American Organist* 21, no. 8 (1987): 10.

————. "The Life and Work of Charles-Marie Widor." DMA diss., Boston University, 1985.

Nectoux, Jean-Michel, ed. *The Correspondence of Camille Saint-Saëns and Gabriel Fauré: Sixty Years of Friendship.* Translated by J. Barrie Jones. Aldershot, England: Ashgate Publishing, 2004.

————. *Gabriel Fauré: A Musical Life.* Translated by Roger Nichols. Cambridge: Cambridge University Press, 1991.

————. *Gabriel Fauré: His Life through His Letters.* Translated by J. A. Underwood. London: Marion Boyars, 1984.

Noisette de Crauzat, Claude. *Cavaillé-Coll.* Paris: Flûte de Pan, 1984.

Ochse, Orpha. *Organists and Organ Playing in Nineteenth-Century France and Belgium.* Bloomington: Indiana University Press, 1994.

Oosten, Ben van. *Charles-Marie Widor: Vater der Orgelsymphonie.* Paderborn, Germany: Verlag Peter Ewers, 1997.

d'Ortigue, Joseph. *La musique à l'église.* Paris: Didier, 1861.

Paderewski, Ignace Jan, and Mary Lawton. *The Paderewski Memoirs.* New York: Scribner's, 1938.

Pearce, William George. "Through Canada with Alex. Guilmant." *Organ* 2 (1893–94): 211–12.

Pearson, Charles A. H. "Organ Study in France." *Diapason* 15, no. 4 (1924): 22.

Pédron, Jean. "Entretien avec M. Charles Widor." *Journal* (April 10, 1934). B. N. Fonds Mont.

Pelatan, Marie-Thérèse, Jean Pelatan, and Odette Tournier. *Trois dames et un château.* Mayenne: Éditions Régionales de l'Ouest, 2007.

Philbert, Charles-Marie. *Causerie sur le grand orgue de la maison A. Cavaille-Coll à Saint-Ouen de Rouen.* Avranches, France: H. Gibert, 1890.

Philipp, Isidor. "Charles-Marie Widor: A Portrait." Translated by G. Reese. *Musical Quarterly* 30 (1944): 125–32.

———. "Paris in the 'Golden Days.'" *Musical Courier* 144, no. 7 (1951): 8–9.

Piccand, Jean. "Trois organistes français." *Schweizerische Musikzeitung* 104 (1964): 297–99.

Pierre, Constant. *Le Conservatoire national de musique et de déclamation: Documents historiques et administratifs.* Paris: Imprimerie Nationale, 1900.

———. *Les facteurs d'instruments de musique.* Paris: Sagot, 1893. Reprint, Geneva: Minkoff, 1976.

Pilling, Julian. "Harmonium and American Organ." In *The New Oxford Companion to Music,* edited by Denis Arnold. Oxford: Oxford University Press, 1983.

Pillois, Jacques. "Ch. M. Widor et l'œuvre de J.-S. Bach." *Courrier Musical* 15, no. 10 (1912): 298–99.

Pirro, André. "L'art des organistes." In *Encyclopédie de la musique et dictionnaire du conservatoire,* edited by Albert Lavignac and Lionel de La Laurencie. Vol. 2: 1181–1374. Paris: Delagrave, 1926.

Pons, Ch. "Charles-Marie Widor, grand officier de la Légion d'honneur." *Ordre* (May 28, 1933). B. N. Fonds Mont.

Potiron, Henri. "Widor." *Revue Liturgique et Musicale* 20, no. 5 (1937): 81–86.

Pougin, Arthur. "Nouvelle académicien." *Ménestrel* 76 (1910): 357.

———. "Les secrétaires perpétuels de l'Académie des beaux-arts" *Ménestrel* 80 (1914): 235.

Prod'homme, Jacques Gabriel. "Charles-Marie Widor." *Rivista Musicale Italiana* 41 (1937): 218–20.

Proust, Marcel. *À la recherche du temps perdu.* Vol. 3, *Le côté de Guermantes.* Paris: Gallimard, 1921.

Puget, Th. "C.-M. Widor et Cavaillé-Coll (1892)." *L'Orgue* 86 (1958): 60–61.

Ramsey, Gordon C. "An Interview." *American Organist* 49, no. 3 (1966): 13–19.

Raugel, Félix. *Les grandes orgues des églises de Paris et du département de la Seine.* Paris: Fischbacher, 1927.

———. *Les organistes.* Paris: Renouard, H. Laurens, 1923.

———. "Widor, Charles-Marie (-Jean-Albert)." In *New Grove Dictionary of Music and Musicians,* edited by S. Sadie. London: Macmillan, 1980.

———, and Andrew Thomson. "Widor, Charles-Marie (-Jean-Albert)." In *New Grove Dictionary of Music and Musicians,* edited by S. Sadie. 2nd ed. London: Macmillan, 2001.

Raynn, J. "Inauguration du grand orgue de l'église Saint-François-Xavier, à Paris." *Musica Sacra* 5 (March 1879): 32.

Reynaud, Hector. *L'œuvre de Ch.-M. Widor.* Lyon: P. Girot, 1900.

Riemenschneider, Albert. "Charles-Marie Widor: An Estimate of His Place in Organ Music." *Diapason* 25, no. 5 (1934): 4.

———. "Charles M. Widor Dies in Paris at Age of 92." *Diapason* 28, no. 5 (1937): 1–2.

———. "Letter." *Diapason* 18, no. 10 (1927): 14.

———. "Program Notes on the Widor 'Symphonies.'" *American Organist* 8 (1925): 262–68.

———. "Tribute to Widor as He Completes Sixty Years at St. Sulpice." *Diapason* 21, no. 7 (1930): 26.

———. "Widor's Organ." *American Organist* 9 (1926): 213.

Robert, Georges. "Les organistes français d'aujourd'hui." *L'Orgue* 114 (1965): 55.

Robilliard, Louis. "Charles-Marie Widor." Notes in *Charles-Marie Widor, œuvres pour orgue*, Louis Robilliard, organist. Arion ARN 38464 (1978).

Rohozinski, Ladislas de, ed. *Cinquante ans de musique française de 1874 à 1925*. 2 vols. Paris: Librairie de France, 1925.

Romain, Louis de. *Essais de critique musicale*. Paris: Lemerre, 1890.

Rosenstiel, Léonie. *The Life and Works of Lili Boulanger*. London: Associated University Presses, 1978.

Rößler, Almut. *Contributions to the Spiritual World of Olivier Messiaen*. Duisburg, Germany: Gilles und Francke, 1986.

Roth, Daniel. *Le grand orgue du Sacré-Cœur de Montmartre à Paris*. Paris: La Flûte Harmonique, 1985.

Rupp, J. F. Emil. *Ch.-M. Widor und sein Werk*. Bremen, Germany: Schweers & Haake, 1912.

Russell, Alexander. "Widor: As Recalled by a Pupil and Friend." *Musical America* 57 (April 25, 1937): 13, 65.

Sabatier, François. "Widor (Charles-Marie)." *Grande Encyclopédie*. Vol. 20: 12788–89. Paris: Larousse, 1976.

Saint-Saëns, Camille. *Harmonie et mélodie*. Paris: C. Lévy, 1885.

———. "Music in the Church." Translated by T. Baker. *Musical Quarterly* 2 (1916): 1–8.

———. "La réforme de la musique religieuse." *Monde Musical* (n.d.): 150–51.

Schweitzer, Albert. *J. S. Bach*. Translated by Ernest Newman. 2 vols. New York: Macmillan, 1911.

———. *J. S. Bach: Le musicien-poète*. Leipzig, Germany: Breitkopf, 1905.

———. Jacket notes for *Albert Schweitzer*. Translated by Nathan Broder. Columbia Masterworks ML 5290 [1958].

———. *Out of My Life and Thought*. Translated by C. T. Campion. New York: H. Holt, 1949.

Schwerké, Irving. "Composers as Human Beings: Reminiscences of a Life in Music." *Stereo Review* 23, no. 5 (1969): 75–78.

Secretary of the Mission of the Institute of France. "Commentaires d'Espagne." [1927]. Family arch.

Shuster, Carolyn. "Autour de l'orgue de Charles-Marie Widor: Notice biographique sur Gabriel et Emmanuel Cavaillé-Coll." *Flûte Harmonique* 37 (1986): 26–36.

Smith, Rollin. *Louis Vierne: Organist of Notre Dame Cathedral*. Hillsdale, NY: Pendragon Press, 1999.

———. "Pipe Organs of the Rich and Famous: Marie Antoinette." *American Organist* 41, no. 6 (2007): 80–81.

———. "Widor's *Symphonie gothique*." *American Organist* 15, no. 12 (1981): 43–45.

Soderlund, Sandra. *How Did They Play? How Did They Teach? A History of Keyboard Technique*. Chapel Hill: Hinshaw Music, 2006.

Sol, Antonio. "Widor et Messager." *Piano Soleil* (December 20, 1891): 5.

Soubies, Albert, and Charles Malherbe. "Histoire de la seconde salle Favart." *Ménestrel* 59 (1893): 65.

Souday, Paul. "*Nerto.*" *Paris-Midi* (October 24, 1924). B. N. Fonds Mont.

Spencer, Louis. "Widor: Le dernier élève de Rossini." *Monde Illustré* (March 20, 1937): 222.

Steed, Graham. "Charles-Marie Widor, 1844–1937: A 150th Anniversary Tribute in Three Parts." *Organists' Review* 80 (February 1994): 11–14; (May 1994): 129–31; (August 1994): 213–16.

Stiven, Frederic Benjamin. *In the Organ Lofts of Paris.* Boston: Stratford, 1923.

Street, Julian. *Where Paris Dines.* Garden City: Doubleday, 1929.

Sumner, William L. "The French Organ School." In *Hinrichsen's Musical Year Book*, edited by M. Hinrichsen. Vol. 6: 281–94. London: Hinrichsen, 1950.

———. "The Organ in the Church of St.-Sulpice, Paris." *Organ* 48, no. 191 (1969): 97–106.

———. "The Organ Class of Charles-Marie Widor." *Musical Opinion* 77 (1954): 427, 429.

———. "Paris Organs and Organists in the 'Twenties': Some Reminiscences." *Organ Yearbook* 2 (1971): 51–57.

Thomas, Fannie Edgar. "Organ Loft Whisperings." *Musical Courier* 27, no. 22 (November 29, 1893): 19–20; no. 24 (December 13, 1893): 11–12; no. 26 (December 27, 1893): 11–12. See also *Organ Loft Whisperings*. Compiled and edited by Agnes Armstrong. Altamont, NY: Sticut tuum, 2003.

Thompson, Owen. "Organ Memories." *Musical Times* 79 (1938): 369–70.

Thomson, Andrew. "C. M. Widor: A Revaluation." *Musical Times* 125 (1984): 169–70.

———. *The Life and Times of Charles-Marie Widor 1844–1937.* Oxford: Oxford University Press, 1987. Reprint, with corrections, 1989.

Tiersot, Julien. "Charles-Marie Widor, *Initiation musicale.*" *Revue de Musicologie* 5 (1924): 85–86.

Tinterow, Gary, and Philip Consibee, eds. *Portraits by Ingres.* New York: Metropolitan Museum of Art, 1999.

Toff, Nancy. *Monarch of the Flute: The Life of Georges Barrère.* New York: Oxford University Press, 2005.

Trillat, Ennemond. "Souvenirs autour de Charles-Marie Widor." February 1968. Private collection; a photocopy is in the author's possession.

Valbelle, Roger. "Quelques souvenirs du maître C.-M. Widor." *Excelsior* (April 4[?], 1934): 1. B. N. Fonds Mont.

Vallas, Léon. *César Franck.* Translated by Hubert Foss. New York: Oxford University Press, 1951.

Van Ausdall, Clair W. Jacket notes for *Marcel Dupré at Saint-Sulpice.* Vol. 3, *Franck.* Mercury SR90228 [1959].

Vanmackelberg, Dom M. "A l'occasion du cinquantenaire de la mort d'Alexandre Guilmant (1837–1911)." *L'Orgue* 100 (1961): 152–80.

Van Wye, Benjamin. "Gregorian Influences in French Organ Music Before the *Moto proprio.*" *Journal of the American Musicological Society* 27, no. 1 (1974): 1–24.

Varèse, Edgar. *Écrits.* Translated by Christiane Léaud. Paris: Bourgois, 1983.

Varèse, Louise. *Varèse: A Looking-Glass Diary.* Vol. 1: 1883–1928. New York: W. W. Norton, 1972.

Véran, Jules. "L'histoire de l'opéra *Nerto.*" *Comœdia* (September 25, 1924). B. N. Fonds Mont.

Vierne, Louis. "Ch.-M. Widor," *Les Amis de l'Orgue* 30/31 (1937): 75–76.

———. "II. Journal (Fragments)." *L'Orgue: Cahiers et Mémoires* 135 bis (1970): 123–85.

———. "Memoirs of Louis Vierne; His Life and Contacts with Famous Men." Translated by E. Jones. *Diapason* 29, no. 10 (September 1938): 6–7; no. 11 (October 1938): 12–13; no. 12 (November 1938): 10–11; 30, no. 1 (December 1938): 6–7; no. 2 (January 1939): 8–9; no. 3 (February 1939): 8–9; no. 4 (March 1939): 8–9; no. 5 (April 1939): 8–9; no. 6 (May 1939): 8; no. 7 (June 1939): 8–9; no. 8 (July 1939): 8–9; no. 9 (August 1939): 8–9; no. 10 (September 1939): 8–9.

———. *In Memoriam Louis Vierne, 1870–1937.* Paris: Desclée de Brouwer, 1939.

———. "Les *Symphonies pour orgue* de Ch.-M. Widor." *Guide Musical* 48 (1902): 319–20. Reprinted in *Revue Musicale de Lyon* 21 (March 5, 1911): 644–47.

Vuillermoz, Émile. "*Nerto* à l'Opéra." *Revue Musicale* 6 (December 1924).

Wallace, Lady, trans. *Letters of Felix Mendelssohn-Bartholdy.* Boston: O. Ditson, [1861].

Waters, Edward N., ed. *The Letters of Franz Liszt to Olga von Meyendorff: 1871–1886.* Washington DC: Dumbarton Oaks, Trustees for Harvard University, 1979; distributed by Harvard University Press.

Whitford, Homer P. "France and Its Student Appeal." *American Organist* 8 (1925): 51–53.

Whitmer, T. Carl. "European Organs and Organists: Bayreuth." *Music* 21 (December 1901): 14–15.

———. *The Way of My Heart and Mind.* Pittsburgh: Pittsburgh Printing, 1920.

———. "Widor's Organ 'Symphonies.'" *American Organist* 17 (1934): 211–15, 259–61, 309–13, 362–64. Reprint from *Music* 15 (March–July 1899).

Williams, Peter. *A New History of the Organ.* Bloomington: Indiana University Press, 1980.

Wilson, John Russell. "The Organ Symphonies of Charles-Marie Widor." PhD diss., Florida State University, 1966.

Index

Widor: A Life beyond the Toccata brings to light the life and work of one of France's most distinguished but overlooked musicians, Charles-Marie Widor. Considered to be among the greatest organists of his time, Widor was a prolific composer in nearly every genre, professor of organ and composition at the Paris Conservatory, academician and administrator at the Institute of France, as well as a journalist, conductor, music editor, scholar, correspondent, and inspired visionary.

Though known mainly as an organist and organ composer, particularly of the famous Toccata, Widor was in fact a man of deep culture who counted among his friends the elite of society and luminaries in nearly every field. He taught an imposing number of students from France and abroad, including the Bach scholar and renowned humanitarian Dr. Albert Schweitzer. This volume, meticulously researched, includes translated press reviews of his work, and correspondence with contemporaries and friends, making it a treasure for historians of the organ and nineteenth century French music.

An appendix to the text constitutes the most complete listing of Widor's oeuvre ever compiled; each work is dated as accurately as possible and includes the publisher, plate number, dedicatee, and relevant commentary. Another appendix lists Widor's published writings. *Widor: A Life beyond the Toccata*—the most complete biography of the composer and organist in any language—illuminates in exceptional detail one of France's great yet neglected artists of the belle époque.

John Near is William Martin and Mina Merrill Prindle Professor of Fine Arts and college organist at Principia College.

"Widor deserves the splendidly full treatment of his life and work that John Near gives us here. At last it is possible to get beyond the narrow perceptions attached for too long to Widor's name and see that he was not only the leading organist of his time but also a prolific composer, a perceptive critic, and the teacher of a whole generation whose influence persists to this day."

—Hugh Macdonald, Avis H. Blewett Professor of Music,
Washington University